W9-DBZ-397

CASES AND MATERIALS

REGULATION AND LITIGATION

OF

INSURANCE

THIRD EDITION

by

ERIC MILLS HOLMES, J.S.D.

International Insurance Consultant/Expert
Former Law Dean, Former Jefferson Smurfit Professor, UCG, Ireland

WILLIAM F. YOUNG

James L. Dohr Professor of Law Emeritus
Columbia University

FOUNDATION PRESS

2007

THOMSON
★
WEST

© 1971, 1985 FOUNDATION PRESS
© 2007 By FOUNDATION PRESS
        395 Hudson Street
        New York, NY 10014
        Phone Toll Free 1–877–888–1330
        Fax (212) 367–6799
        foundation–press.com
Printed in the United States of America

ISBN 978–1–58778–586–3

 TEXT IS PRINTED ON 10% POST CONSUMER RECYCLED PAPER

PREFACE

Studying the law of insurance yields both profit and pleasure. For law students the yield can include proficiency in reading insurance contracts and in litigating about them, and in advising sellers of insurance, and those who buy it or don't. The opportunities for using these skills are magnified in number and importance by the scale of the insurance business, which is mammoth. Even single firms in the business report assets in the hundreds of billions of dollars, and the amount of insurance in force runs into trillions. More than sixty years ago Justice Black found it possible to say this:

> The modern insurance business holds a commanding position in the trade and commerce of our Nation. [I]t has become one of the largest and most important branches of commerce. . . . Perhaps no commercial enterprise directly affects so many persons in all walks of life as does the insurance business. Insurance touches the home, the family, and the occupation or business of almost every person in the U.S.[1]

The intervening years have reinforced those observations.

The business and its products cannot be understood without attention to their history. Both that and their current condition are entangled with powerful social and political attitudes. The law of insurance reflects those attitudes, to be sure, but also presses against them at some points. The behavior of buyers and sellers of insurance has drawn increasing attention from economists, who find it sometimes a challenge to, and sometimes a vindication of, their theories. "Moral hazard" and "risk aversion" are among the counters both in those theories and in insurance law. Studying that law is a broad avenue, then, into various fields of social and economic science. That is one of its pleasures.

That law is not neatly immured from other fields of law. Most notably, much of it is an adaptation of the law of contracts at large, although often with sea changes. The law of torts is also a substratum. Claims made under liability coverages are usually engendered by someone's wrongdoing, or by an allegation of wrongdoing. That is an obvious connection between tort law and insurance-contract law. But there are other major ones; witness the so-called tort of bad-faith conduct by an insurer. Fields of law in

---

1. United States v. South-Eastern Underwriters Association, 322 U.S. 533, 539–44 (1944).

which insurance plays an instrumental part are the law of remedies and the law of corporate governance; and the list goes on.

When Justice Black made the remarks quoted above he was addressing the distribution of constitutional powers. Long before that, and more especially since, the business of insurance has been a proving ground for the problem of allocating those powers as between state and federal authorities. It is a proving ground also for interstate relations and for the powers of administrative agencies, notably state insurance departments.

If this book contributes to the pleasure and profit of studying insurance law, it will have fulfilled the hopes of its editors.

Eric Mills Holmes*

W.F. Young

* Holmes: 507 Graham Road
Danville, Kentucky 40422 [or]
rickholmes2@hotmail.com

Young: 24 Howell Ave.
Larchmont, NY, 10538 [or]
wyoung@law.columbia.edu

SUMMARY OF CONTENTS

TABLE OF CONTENTS

*

TABLE OF APPENDICES

*

TABLE OF CASES

Principal cases are in bold type. Non-principal cases are in roman type. References are to Pages.

*

CASES AND MATERIALS

REGULATION AND LITIGATION
OF
INSURANCE

CHAPTER 1

THE NATURE OF INSURANCE AND OF INSURANCE LAW

This book is designed to train you for competent insurance lawyering, and that should be your goal. You are about to embark on an exciting and edifying journey in one of the largest fields of law. All of us daily face risks of loss or harm, and we are a risk-averse society. Although some persons may be risk neutral or even risk preferring, most are averse to risk and are willing, often, to pay for shifting a significant risk to someone else. Given our risk-averse predilection, insurance arose to transfer and re-distribute (by pooling) a risk of loss among a similarly situated risk group of individuals, of firms, or of both.

During the 20th Century, to satisfy our risk-averse nature, insurance grew to be pervasive and financially critical in our social, commercial, political and personal lives. In 1944, Justice Hugo Black observed:

> The modern insurance business holds a commanding position in the trade and commerce of our Nation. Built upon contracts of indemnity, it has become one of the largest and most important branches of commerce. ... Perhaps no commercial enterprise directly affects so many persons in all walks of life as does the insurance business. Insurance touches the home, the family, and the occupation or business of almost every person in the U.S.[1]

Hardly any momentous mishap or transaction is unaffected by considerations of insurance. Given that fact, together with the scale of the insurance business,[2] one can appreciate the importance to lawyers of knowing the elements of insurance law.

The monies spent on governmental regulation of insurance and the business of insurance have not comparably increased with the mammoth monies spent on insurance. In the main, the states, not the federal government, regulate the business of insurance pursuant to the federal McCarran–Ferguson Insurance Regulation Act of 1945, as discussed later in Chapter 2, see pp. 54 ff below.

---

1. United States v. South–Eastern Underwriters Association, 322 U.S. 533, 539–44 (1944).

2. According to the 2006 annual report of the Metropolitan Life Insurance Company the amount of life insurance in force under policies issued by it and its affiliates was some 2.85 trillions of dollars. The "Met" issues also accident & health policies, and annuity contracts. Its assets were in the billions only.

The recent history of the firm included its acquisition of the Travelers Insurance Company, and its transformation into a capital stock company ("demutualization").

A. "INSURANCE" AND "INSURANCE BUSINESS"

1. Definitions

No one supposes that a single, invariant definition for *insurance*, or for *insurance business*, is serviceable for all occasions of use. For one thing, the word insurance has colloquial uses that are simply metaphors, as in the commonplace observation that bankruptcy is the poor man's insurance against liability. A sociologist has written of religions as a form of insurance.[3] And former Chief Justice Rehnquist came close to metaphor in this observation: "Welfare payments are a form of insurance, giving impoverished individuals and their families the means to meet the demands of daily life while they receive the necessary training, education, and time to look for a job."[4]

Even when a definition is used in applying some legal principle, it may well require modification for use in applying another. This point was definitively made by Jan Hellner, in The Scope of Insurance Regulation: What is Insurance for the Purposes of Regulation?, 12 Am.J.Comp.L. 494 (1963). It is not surprising, therefore, that authorities have provided an array of definitions, not fully consistent. For a criticism of some dictionary definitions, see the dissenting opinion of Judge Wright in Griffin Systems, Inc. v. Ohio Department of Insurance, 575 N.E.2d 803, 811 (Ohio 1991). He quoted Black's Law Dictionary to the effect that insurance is a contract whereby, for a stipulated consideration, one party undertakes to compensate the other for loss on a specified subject by specified perils. Judge Wright objected to the breadth of that definition. It comprehended, he said, a warranty of quality given by the manufacturer of an item, even though no separate charge was made for the warranty. But the sale contract would not be one substantially amounting to insurance, he wrote. And the other judges did not disagree.

Some statutory definitions are objectionable on the same ground. One is a provision of insurance statutes in some western states, based on the Field Code. One of these states is California; the California Insurance Code defines insurance as a "contract whereby one undertakes to indemnify another against loss, damage, or a liability arising from a contingent or unknown event."[5]

We offer below two definitions that are more elaborate. They are not necessarily superior on that ground, for there is sometimes a negative

---

3. See Sumner (William Graham) & Keller, The Science of Society 749 (1927–33). Practitioners of religions, and their observers, have made mixed appraisals of insurance. A proponent compared life insurance with a "provident angel." Another view is that it usurps the divine functions of protection and punishment. See V. Zelizer, Morals and Markets: The Development of Life Insurance in the United States (1979) at 55 and 73.

4. Saenz v. Roe, 526 U.S. 489 (1999), the Chief Justice dissenting at 511, 519.

5. CAL. INS. CODE § 22, which has been extensively copied in the Codes of other states.

return on elaboration. (Learned Hand observed that a universal definition of insurance would be mythically prolix, and fantastically impractical.[6]) As encouragement for you to give these definitions a critical reading, we offer next a set of questions to have in mind.

The Meaning of "Insurance": Questions

(1) Sometimes it is said that insurance entails the pooling of risks. Do you find that element in either of the definitions below? If so, does it indicate what is meant by the pooling of risks?

(2) Sometimes it is said that an insurance contract is an aleatory contract, meaning that the insurance company's liability depends on a chancy event. In other words, a contract of insurance resembles a wager (although gambling generates risk whereas insuring transfers risk). Do you find that element in either definition? If so, does it indicate what is meant by it?

(3) Sometimes it is said that an "insurable interest" is a requisite of an insurance contract. This signifies, loosely speaking, that the chancy event specified in the contract will have an adverse effect on the party insured (or would have that effect but for the insurance). Do you find that element in either definition? If so, does it indicate what is meant by an insurable interest?

A Scholar's Definition

The definition that follows was proposed in 1904 by Professor William R. Vance in his monumental insurance treatise. It is, arguably, the most influential one in American law.

The contract of insurance, made between parties usually called the insured and insurer, is distinguished by the presence of five elements:

(a) The insured possesses an interest of some kind susceptible of pecuniary estimation.

(b) The insured is subject to a risk of loss through the destruction or impairment of that interest by the happening of designated perils.

(c) The insurer assumes that risk of loss.

(d) Such assumption is part of a general scheme to distribute actual losses among a large group of persons bearing somewhat similar risks.

(e) As consideration for the insurer's promise, the insured makes a ratable contribution, called a premium, to a general insurance fund.

A contract possessing only the three elements first named is a risk-shifting device, but not a contract of insurance, which is a risk-distributing device; but, if it possesses the other two as well, it is a contract of insurance, whatever be its name or its form.

6. Sinram v. Pennsylvania RR., 61 F.2d 767, 771 (2d Cir. 1932).

William R. Vance, The Handbook on the Law of Insurance 1–2 (Buise M. Anderson ed. 1951).

A Statutory Definition

The following definition is also, in a sense, a scholar's definition, in that it was designed by a committee chaired by the late Professor Edwin W. Patterson (author of the original edition of this casebook). But it was enacted as part of the New York Insurance Law in 1939. It appears now as section 1101 of that Law—*Definitions. Doing an Insurance Business.*

(a) In this article: (1) "Insurance contract" means any agreement or other transaction whereby one party, the "insurer", is obligated to confer benefit of pecuniary value upon another party, the "insured" or "beneficiary", dependent upon the happening of a fortuitous event in which the insured or beneficiary has, or is expected to have at the time of such happening, a material interest which will be adversely affected by the happening of such event.

(2) "Fortuitous event" means any occurrence or failure to occur which is, or is assumed by the parties to be, to a substantial extent beyond the control of either party.

(3) "Contract of warranty, guaranty or suretyship" means an insurance contract only if made by a warrantor, guarantor or surety who or which, as such, is doing an insurance business.

[Subsection (b), stating what constitutes "doing an insurance business" in New York, is omitted here.]

EXERCISE

In 1987, the Harvard Law School sent to applicants an Application Catalogue describing a program called the "Low Income Protection Plan" as follows:

"We have a long-standing commitment to encourage students to pursue the law-related career of their choice, regardless of salary. Recognizing that our graduates have increasingly high educational debt burdens and that a career choice in public service and some other areas of law will result in relatively low salaries, we established the Low–Income Protection Program (LIPP) in 1978. This program, the first of its type in the country, helps relieve the burden of repayments of educational loans for law school for all graduates in low-paying, law related jobs. LIPP permits participants to apply only a limited percentage of their earnings towards their total annual loan repayment obligations. The Program provides that Harvard Law School will pay any remaining law school payments due that year. For the year July 1, 1987 through June 30, 1988, the Plan provides that a graduate earning less than $20,000 in a law-related position will allocate 0% of his or her salary toward repaying Harvard Law School debts (i.e., Harvard Law School would pay all such debts that year); at the highest eligible income levels, a graduate earning between $26,001 and $29,000 contributes 6% of salary, or $130 to $145 per month, toward Harvard Law School debt repayment."

Questions: (1) Was Harvard doing an insurance business, so as to require a license for doing so from the Commonwealth of Massachusetts? (2) Statutes of the Commonwealth proscribe both unfair or deceptive acts and practices and unfair competition, each in the "business of insurance"[7] Was Harvard doing an insurance business for the purpose of these statutes? See Thornton v. Harvard University, 2 F.Supp.2d 89 (D.Mass. 1998).

Suppose that Harvard were located in New York State, so that the following statutory provision applies:

> In the application of this chapter,[8] the fact that no profit is derived from the making of insurance contracts, agreements or transactions, or that no separate or direct consideration is received therefor, shall not be deemed conclusively to show that the making thereof does not constitute the doing of an insurance business.

Question: Does that provision affect your opinion as to Harvard's "doing an insurance business"?

2. Fortuity

Insurance, as a concept, presupposes that only a small proportion of those exposed to a risk will actually sustain a loss. It is a fundamental principle of insurance law that insurance contracts do not cover harm, injury or financial loss that is not *fortuitous*. One corollary to this principle is that a liability insurance contract affords no coverage for losses intentionally caused by the insured. Insurance insures only fortuitous harm; that is, the insured event which an insurer agrees to underwrite must be a "chance event" substantially beyond the control of the insured and the insurer.

40 Gardenville, LLC v. Travelers Property Casualty of America

United States District Court, W.D.N.Y., 2005.
387 F.Supp.2d 205.

The principals of 40 Gardenville, Gerald Hickson and James Kirchmeyer, purchased a vacant commercial building located at 40 Gardenville Parkway in West Seneca, New York ("the building" or "40 Gardenville"). To cover any loss to the building, Hickson procured an all-risk policy of insurance ("the policy") from Travelers Property Casualty ("Travelers"). The policy provided, in relevant part, "we cover 'loss' commencing during the policy period." Further, the policy set forth the following exclusions:

---

7. See generally § 90.2A "Unfair Competition: Unfair Insurance Practices and Trade Practices," § 90.2B, "Unfair Competition: Unfair Trade Practices and Consumer Protection Acts," and § 90.C "Unfair Competition: Other Regulatory Statutes" in Eric Mills Holmes, 13 Holmes' Appleman on Insurance 2d (2000).

8. N.Y. Ins. § 1101 "Definitions; doing an insurance business" (b)(4) (2005).

We will not pay for "loss" caused by or resulting from any of the following ... (a) Hidden or latent defect, mechanical breakdown or failure ... or any quality in the property that causes it to damage or destroy itself ... (b) Corrosion, rust or dampness.

Travelers' underwriter, David Coad, did not inspect 40 Gardenville or arrange for the building to be inspected prior to issuing the policy.

Before buying the building, however, Hickson and Kirchmeyer had obtained reports from firms they retained about the structural soundness of the building, its fair market value, and environmental considerations. Also, Hickson had inspected the building several times, sometimes accompanied by Kirchmeyer, and once with one Masters, a representative of a firm which been retained to estimate the cost of rehabilitating the building. Hickson was to testify later that he had observed large holes on the exterior walls, water draining into buckets, puddles, wet carpeting throughout, and leaks from the roof and from an open valve on the sprinkler system. Part of his testimony was as follows:

Q: Did you see any mold in the building before closing?

A: We—I saw something at the base which I thought was dirt, now since somebody came in and said it's mold, now I know it is mold.

Hickson was advised by someone, presumably Masters, that the entire roof would have to be replaced.

Repairs on the roof were begun about three months after the sale; before that nothing was done to stop water from infiltrating the building. Soon afterwards, when the rehabilitation firm discovered mold contamination, it ceased all work on the building and advised Hickson and Kirchmeyer that extensive mold remediation would be required. The policyholder, 40 Gardenville, reported mold contamination to Travelers within days of that, and later made a claim for mold loss. Travelers rejected the claim on the ground that the policy did not cover losses commencing before it issued the policy, or for losses caused by dampness.

40 Gardenville brought this action for a declaration that Travelers was obliged to indemnify it for mold-related expenses. Travelers moved for a summary judgment, arguing that the mold loss was not a fortuitous one, and that it was expressly excluded by the terms of the policy.

■ WILLIAM M. SKRETNY, UNITED STATES DISTRICT JUDGE.

. . .

1.   Fortuitous Loss and Known Loss

To establish a prima facie case for recovery in New York State, an all-risk insured must prove: "(1) the existence of an all-risk policy; (2) an insurable interest in the subject of the insurance contract; and (3) the fortuitous loss of the covered property." Int'l Multifoods Corp. v. Commercial Union Ins. Co., 309 F.3d 76, 83 (2d Cir. 2002). In establishing a "fortuitous loss," Plaintiff must show that the damage sustained to the insured property was caused by a "fortuitous" event within the meaning of the policy. ... New York courts have construed the term "fortuitous event" to mean an event "happening by chance or accident." 80 Broad St. Co. v. United States Fire Ins. Co., 389 N.Y.S.2d 214, 215 (N.Y.Sup.Ct. 1975) (internal citations omitted). As such, losses that result from inherent defects, ordinary wear and tear, or intentional misconduct of the insured do not constitute fortuitous losses. *Int'l Multifoods* at 83.

"Broadly stated, the fortuity doctrine holds that insurance is not available for losses that the policyholder knows of, planned, intended, or is aware are substantially certain to occur." Nat'l Union Fire Ins. Co. v. Stroh Cos., 265 F.3d 97, 106 (2d Cir. 2001) (internal quotations and citations omitted). As applied, the fortuity doctrine prevents insurers from having to pay for losses arising from undisclosed events that existed prior to coverage, as well as events caused by the manifestation during the policy period of inherent defects in the insured property that existed prior to coverage. . . . Both federal and state courts in New York recognize the value of preventing recovery for such losses:

> The policy rationale for the fortuity doctrine is simple. When parties enter into an insurance contract, they are, in effect, making a wager as to the likelihood that a specified loss will occur. (internal citations omitted). If the loss has already occurred, or the insured knows that the loss is certain to occur for reasons not disclosed to the insurer, then the insurance contract is not a fair bet. [In other words, the contract lacks the necessary element of fortuity. Thus, fortuity is a concept closely linked to "external cause."]

CPH Intern., Inc. v. Phoenix Assur. Co. of New York, 1994 U.S. Dist. LEXIS 7751, 1994 WL 259810, at *6 (S.D.N.Y. June 9, 1994); Chase Manhattan Bank v. New Hampshire Ins. Co., 749 N.Y.S.2d 632, 639 (N.Y.Sup.Ct. 2002).

. . .

In the instant matter, it is undisputed that the policy is an all-risk policy and that 40 Gardenville, LLC, has an insurable interest in the building. The sole inquiry is whether 40 Gardenville, LLC, has suffered a "fortuitous" loss within the meaning of the policy. This necessarily requires a trier of fact to determine whether Plaintiff's principals knew when they procured the policy from Travelers that the mold contamination existed or was substantially certain to occur. This determination cannot be made on the record before this Court.

Defendant argues that the mold contamination predated the inception of the policy and that Mr. Hickson was aware of the problem based on his inspection of the building prior to its purchase. This argument is unavailing. Mr. Hickson did admit that prior to purchasing the building, he observed a substance on the baseboards of the second floor that he later learned was mold. While this admission certainly supports Defendant's position that mold existed in the building prior to the inception of the policy, it does not compel the conclusion that Mr. Hickson was aware of the mold contamination at that time. Nor does Mr. Hickson's knowledge that water had infiltrated the building establish that he knew that these damp conditions presented a certain risk of mold contamination. Drawing all reasonable inferences in favor of Plaintiff, this Court finds that there is a genuine issue as to whether Plaintiff's principals knew at the time they procured the policy from Travelers that the building was contaminated with mold or was certain to become contaminated with mold. As such, this Court declines to grant summary judgment on the basis that the mold loss or the risk of loss was known to Plaintiff.

2.   Dampness Exclusion

[The court recited some precepts of New York law about construing insurance contracts.]

"Whenever an insurer wishes to exclude certain coverage from its policy obligations, it must do so 'in clear and unmistakable' language." Simplexdiam, Inc. v. Brockbank, 727 N.Y.S.2d 64, 67–68 (App.Div. 2001) (citing Seaboard Surety Co. v. Gillette Co., 476 N.E.2d 272, 275 (N.Y. 1984)). [The court concluded that Travelers had done so. It recited evidence about the origin of the mold.]

Based on the foregoing, this Court finds the water or dampness present in the building was the proximate cause of the mold contamination. As such, the unambiguous language of the policy excluding coverage for losses caused by or resulting from dampness applies to Plaintiff's claim for mold loss, and operates as a bar to Plaintiff's recovery in this matter. For these reasons, Defendant's Motion for Summary Judgment will be granted.

. . .

NOTES

(1) *A Test of Fortuity.* As most of us do, judges find it useful sometimes to express themselves ambiguously. (Insurers do so at their peril.) A reader of the foregoing opinion, laying aside the policy exclusion, might be left with questions. Probably the main question is this: Did the court leave open the possibility of recovery for an expense certain to be required by reason of a condition existing at the inception of coverage? One might think not, on reading that an insurer need not pay for a loss arising from "events that existed prior to coverage". But the issue of fact that led the court to withhold summary judgment appears to have been one about what Hickson and Kirchmeyer *knew* prior to coverage, not one about the condition "mold".

Other cases do not leave the main question open. Under some policies there is a possibility of recovery for a loss already incurred when a policy takes effect. A standard example is a marine policy that insures a vessel "lost or not lost", *e.g.* whether afloat or sunk at the inception of coverage. As to insurance on a life already lost see the Note at p. 577 below, following *National Inspection and Repair v. Valley Forge Life Ins. Co.*. What, in view of those instances, is to be made of the fortuity doctrine?

(2) *Barn-Burning Exclusion.* A reasonable person might expect that an insured who intentionally burns down his or her own barn can not collect payment from insurance on the barn. It has long been understood that a property insurance coverage is subject to a "barn burning" exclusion although it may not be expressed in the contract. See Ritter v. Mutual Life Ins. Co., 169 U.S. 139 (1898); Felsenthal Co. v. Northern Assurance Co., 120 N.E. 268, 1 A.L.R. 602 (Ill. 1918). As a technical

matter it may be said that losses so excluded are not fortuitous ones, and that fortuity figures in the definition of "insurance". As a policy matter, it is thought that property owners ought not to be absolved from loss, and certainly ought not to be rewarded, for damage they inflict deliberately on their own assets. (A possible "reward" is to convert an illiquid asset, such as a barn, into a liquid asset, the proceeds of insurance.)

(3) *Trespass, Intention and Fortuity.* Do you think that a wrongful trespass on another's property can not be fortuitous? For example, if an insured dumps construction debris on another's property without the property owner's permission, do you think that the wrongful trespass constitutes an "occurrence" defined as "an accident" (i.e., a fortuity) in a liability insurance policy? That was the question in Tenn. Standard Constr. Co. v. Maryland Cas. Co., 359 F.3d 846 (6th Cir. 2004) (Tennessee law). A subcontractor, believing it had a valid contract with the landowner, dumped construction debris from a road-widening project on the landowner's property. The dumping was a trespass because, although the subcontractor believed permission was obtained, consent was lacking because the property owner was incompetent and her daughter had no authority to consent on the property owner's behalf. Thus, no contract between the property owner and the contractor existed. The court held that the dumping was an "occurrence" meaning "accident" within the policy because, while the dumping was intentional, the fact that it was done without permission, thus making it wrongful, was not intended by the insured. *Question*: Regarding the court's judgment, do you concur or dissent? Why?

3. Guarantees, Warranties, Service Contracts, and Insurance Contracts

In some of the cases now to be considered promises were made by firms identified as follows, along with some features of their undertakings:

(1) Group Health Association was a nonprofit corporation, its membership being open to dues-paying civilian employees of the United States. For its members, the Association agreed to recruit physicians—not staff members—to attend to certain health needs, both preventive and curative. The undertaking was, the court said, to contract for the rendition of the services by independent contractors, not to supply them. Upon a default by one of those contractors, the Association's only obligation was to "use its best efforts to procure the needed services from another source."[9]

(2) The Transportation Guarantee Corporation (TGC) made truck-maintenance contracts with a trucker, promising him extensive services. These included supplying him with gas, oil, tires, and garaging for the trucks concerned, painting and washing them periodically, and making necessary repairs. (During any considerable period of garaging for repair, TGC agreed to provide the trucker with a substitute vehicle.) Within limitations, TGC agreed also to make good any damage done by collision. But TGC's liability for damage or destruction was "confined to such damage or destruction as is due to a breach by [it] of any of its express

9. Also, Group Health arranged for limited hospitalization, and itself furnished facilities and services in connection with a clinic. The court said that the plan must be taken as a whole, not split up into disconnected parts. But these direct services, the court said, were "merely incidental" to the primary services and must stand or fall with them.

obligations herein contained." TGC undertook also to procure and maintain certain insurance coverages for the trucker, including insurance against liability and property damage.

(3) The Western Auto Supply Company (WASC), a seller of tires, provided its customers with a guarantee against defects in material or workmanship. The guarantee provided also that WASC would either repair or replace a tire it sold that should become unserviceable by reason of various road hazards, including cuts, under-inflation, and faulty brakes (but not fire or theft).

(4) The Ollendorff Watch Company, a retailer, made this promise to buyers of its watches: If the buyer should lose her watch through burglary or robbery within one year of the purchase, Ollendorff would replace it with a new watch of like quality and value. No separate charge was made for this undertaking.

In each of these cases the contention was made that the promisor's agreement amounted to a contract of insurance, or that it was substantially similar to an insurance contract. In some of them that contention prevailed; in others not. The general question presented is how to distinguish between an insurer's commitment on the one side, and on the other a commitment that amounts to a warranty, a guarantee, or a promise to provide service.

A fair starting point is an observation made in Jordan v. Group Health Ass'n, 107 F.2d 239 (D.C.Cir. 1939), concerning agreement #1 above. There the court addressed the question whether the agreement was a contract of insurance or one for the payment of indemnity on account of sickness or accident, in terms of the District-of-Columbia statutes. Believing that the answer was Yes, the District Superintendent of Insurance contended that the Association should have been licensed. But the court answered No. It found some support in the fact that not only the obligations of Group Health, but also those of its dues-paying members, were attenuated. The court said:

> [O]bviously it was not the purpose of the insurance statutes to regulate all arrangements for assumption or distribution of risk. That view would cause them to engulf practically all contracts.... The question turns, not on whether risk is involved or assumed, but on whether that or something else to which it is related in the particular plan is its principal object and purpose.

Id. at 247. This passage was picked up in Transportation Guarantee Company v. Jellins, 174 P.2d 625 (Cal. 1946), and amplified as follows:

> [I]t must be borne in mind that nearly every business venture entails some assumption of risk, some element of gambling. The retail merchant when he purchases his stock assumes the risk of lower prices, of receding demand, of spoilage or deterioration of perishable goods; he gambles on his ability to dispose of the stock before it loses value or, perhaps, to hold it until there is an increment of value. The lawyer who contracts to prosecute a case to final judgment for a fixed or

contingent fee assumes the risk of long litigation, of repeated trials and reversals. The lessee who agrees to hold his lessor harmless for damage to property of, or injury to, third persons occurring on the leased premises; the lessor who agrees to keep the premises in repair; even the surety on a note, assume a risk and indemnify another against loss.... We are satisfied that a sound jurisprudence does not suggest the extension, by judicial construction, of the insurance laws to govern every contract involving an assumption of risk or indemnification of loss; that when the question arises each contract must be tested by its own terms as they are written, as they are understood by the parties, and as they are applied under the particular circumstances involved.

Id. at 629. In this case TGC charged Jellins, the trucker, with breach of the truck-maintenance contracts. Jellins's defense was that the contracts were unenforceable because they were insurance contracts, which TGC was not licensed to make. That was not indubitably so, the court ruled. (Cases are conspicuously wanting in which a promisor, not being licensed as an insurer, contended that its promise constituted part of an insurance contract.)

The Western Auto guarantee described above led to the conclusion that Western Auto had issued, unlawfully, a contract substantially amounting to insurance. The same court was later to say that "a contract 'substantially amounting to insurance' in this context is one that promises to cover losses or damages over and above, or unrelated to, defects within the product itself." Griffin Systems, Inc. v. Ohio Department of Insurance, 575 N.E.2d 803, 806–807 (Ohio 1991). (Further observations in this case are set out in Note 2, p. 15 below.)

The New York Court of Appeals made a comparable ruling about the watch-replacement undertaking by the Ollendorff Watch Company. It said:

[A] warranty would relate in some way to the nature or efficiency of the product sold—in this case, that the watch would work or was of a certain make and fineness. A warranty would not cover a hazard having nothing whatever to do with the make or quality of the watch. A guaranty is an undertaking that the amount contracted to be paid will be paid, or the services guaranteed will be performed. It relates directly to the substance and purpose of the transaction.

This contract goes much further. It has nothing whatever to do with the sale of the watch or the contract of sale. It is an extraneous inducement to procure sales. If the watch is stolen the seller will replace it. In other words, he takes a chance or a risk of theft from his customers; that is, he insures them for a year against such risk.

Ollendorff Watch Co. v. Pink, 17 N.E.2d 676, 677 (N.Y. 1938).

The cases canvassed above are reasonably consistent. The opinion that follows introduces an element of discord. First, however, a few comments and questions about the foregoing cases are in order.

NOTES

(1) *Naming*. What is in substance a contract of insurance cannot be changed into something else by giving it another name. People v. Roschli, 9 N.E.2d 763, 764 (N.Y. 1937).

(2) *Questions*. In determining the principal object and purpose of a plan, as directed in Jordan v. Group Health, where is one to look? To appearances, as an objective theory would suggest? Or to a state of mind? And if the latter, whose mind counts—that of the promisor, or that of one or more promisees? Is any answer suggested by the quotation from *TGC v. Jellins*?

(3) *Problem*. In order to induce a sale, a dealer in lightning rods promises to pay for any damage by lightning to a customer's building after it is equipped with a lightning rod, properly installed. The dealer has made the same promise to other customers. Contract of insurance?

(4) *Competition*. To be regulated as an insurer is burdensome for a firm chiefly engaged in marketing tires, watches, or lightning rods. Better, perhaps, for them to refrain from making insurance-like promises. Very likely, the threat of regulation inhibits the use of a marketing device that might attract many shoppers for these and other goods, and for services, and to that extent inhibits competition. Robust competition among purveyors is a boon to shoppers, who might therefore denounce the threat. On this line of thought, would you favor a narrow definition of insurance contract?

(5) *Duplicate Regulation?* A principal object of insurance regulation is to assure buyers of insurance that the firms they patronize will not suffer such financial distress as to default on their undertakings as insurers. This fact adds a twist to the case about watch-replacements, *Ollendorff Watch Company*. In that case the merchant had bought, from the Travelers Indemnity Company, a policy insuring it against losses it might sustain by reason of the replacement agreements. Connecticut insurance authorities kept watch over the solvency of Travelers, no doubt. Did that make it needless for the New York Superintendent to keep watch over Ollendorff's solvency?

Well, presumably a payout by Travelers would not assure buyers of Ollendorff's watches, in the event of the seller's insolvency, of a greater percentage recovery than other creditors of Ollendorff would get. It would not, that is, unless the Travelers policy was written as a third-party-beneficiary contract, identifying the buyers as beneficiaries. Suppose that it was; does that show up the New York Superintendent as an officious intermeddler?

Griffin Systems, Inc. v. Washburn

Illinois Appellate Court, 1st Dist., 4th Division, 1987.
153 Ill.App.3d 113, 106 Ill.Dec. 330, 505 N.E.2d 1121.

Griffin Systems, Inc. ("Griffin"), brings this appeal seeking reversal of a cease and desist order issued by the Illinois Department of Insurance ("the Department") and affirmed by the trial court, agreeing with the Department's finding that Griffin was engaged in the selling of insurance without a certificate of authority.

■ LINN, JUSTICE.

The Department's cease and desist order prohibits Griffin from distributing its "Vehicle Protection Plan" ["VVP"] (plan). Griffin was marketing the plan to Illinois residents who had recently purchased new automobiles. Under the plan, consumers pay a yearly fee in exchange for Griffin's promise to pay for the repair or replacement of certain automobile parts should those parts break down or fail to operate during a specified coverage period.

The facts of this case are not in dispute. Griffin is an Ohio corporation which began marketing the plan in Illinois in early 1984. Griffin sent a sales brochure and a sales agreement to Illinois residents who had recently purchased new automobiles. The brochure describes the plan as "a mechanical service contract." Under the plan, Griffin agrees to repair or replace any of the specific automobile parts covered by the plan should those parts break down or fail during the coverage period.

The plan provides for a $25 deductible per part. When a customer needs mechanical service, he contacts Griffin, which then forwards the claim request to Great Plains Insurance, Inc. Only upon approval by Great Plains adjusters will a repair be covered by the plan's provisions. A customer can bring his vehicle into any facility the customer selects. Griffin itself, however, does not perform any of the repair services.

The customer is permitted to select one of four different policies. The policies differ in their length of time and with respect to the number of parts covered. The policies also contain certain exclusions, limitations, and conditions.

The Department determined that under Illinois common law the plan indemnified customers against possible future losses and, as a result, the plan constituted an insurance policy. The trial court subsequently agreed with the Department's ruling, prompting Griffin to bring this appeal.

The central issue in this appeal is whether Griffin engages in the business of selling insurance when it offers the plan to Illinois residents.... The Illinois Insurance Code (Ill. Rev. Stat. 1983, ch. 73, par. 733) fails to define the term "insurance." Nevertheless, a definition is provided by the Illinois common law.... [W]e agree with the Department and the trial court that Griffin's plan contains all of the elements contained within the common law definition of insurance. The essence of the plan is to indemnify the customer; to reimburse the customer for a possible future loss to a specified piece of property caused by a specified peril, namely, mechanical failure. Consequently, the plan constitutes insurance and properly falls within the authority of the Department.

The plan is not, as Griffin contends, merely a "service contract," nor does it fall within the purview of a "warranty."

An example of a "service contract" can be found in the case of Rayos v. Chrysler Credit Corp. (Tex. App. 1985), 683 S.W.2d 546. In *Rayos*, the court reviewed a 5–year/50,000–mile owner protection plan issued by Chrysler. Under the Chrysler plan, Chrysler agreed to repair or replace certain parts should those parts fail or break down within the specified period (5 years or

50,000 miles). The court in *Rayos* noted, however, that the Chrysler plan included a requirement that the customer bring his vehicle into a Chrysler Corporation dealer for any of the covered repairs. Because Chrysler built the vehicle to which it was going to make repairs, the *Rayos* court properly determined that the plan issued by Chrysler amounted to a service contract rather than an insurance policy.

A "warranty," on the other hand, was found to exist in GAF Corp. v. County School Board (4th Cir. 1980), 629 F.2d 981. There, a company agreed to repair or replace a roof it had sold to a customer should the roof ever leak in the future. However, the company which agreed to perform the repairs was the same company that had sold the roof. Consequently, because the company promising to make the repairs was the same company that had sold the roof, the *GAF* court found that the agreement to repair or replace constituted a warranty rather than an insurance policy.

An analysis of the cases set forth above reveals that a warranty and a service contract have many of the same features. Nonetheless, the distinguishing feature which sets them apart from an insurance policy is the fact that the respective companies manufacture or sell the products which they agreed to repair or replace. No third parties are involved, nor is there a risk accepted which the company, because of its expertise, is unaware of. Through a warranty or service contract, a company simply guarantees that its own product will perform adequately for a period of time.

Insurance policies, on the other hand, are generally issued by third parties and are based on a theory of distributing a particular risk among many customers. The case of Guaranteed Warranty Corp. v. State ex rel. Humphrey (Ariz.App. 1975), 533 P.2d 87, is a prime example of a company's selling an insurance policy rather than a warranty or a service contract.

In *Guaranteed*, a company was in the business of selling contracts which provided that the company would replace the customer's television picture tube should the tube ever fail as a result of a manufacturing defect. The company, however, did not manufacture, nor did it sell, television sets or television tubes. Instead, the company merely marketed the tube replacement contracts. Because the company did not manufacture or sell the television tubes, the *Guaranteed* court found that the tube replacement contracts were, in reality, promises to indemnify the customer for a potential future loss. The tube replacement contracts were not merely a method to guarantee the performance of the company's product, for the company did not manufacture or sell the tubes in question. That being the case, the *Guaranteed* court found that the tube replacement contracts constituted insurance policies.

Likewise, in the case at bar, it is significant to note that Griffin itself does not perform any of the repairs or replacements covered by the plan. Nor does Griffin manufacture or sell automobiles or automobile parts. Instead, Griffin merely sells a plan which promises to indemnify the customer for any losses he may suffer through the breakdown or failure of certain mechanical parts in his automobile. In this respect, Griffin's plan is analogous to that which was found to constitute an insurance policy by the *Guaranteed* court.

The procedure employed by Griffin also suggests that the plan amounts to an insurance policy rather than a warranty or service contract. The plan requires a customer who needs a repair to first obtain an estimate from an independent automobile service center. The estimate is then reviewed by a claims adjuster with the Great Plains Insurance Company. Upon receiving approval by the adjuster, the customer authorizes the independent service center to perform the work.

Under the plan, the customer is obligated to pay a $25 deductible for each repair performed. Griffin thereafter pays the service center the balance due. Furthermore, like an insurance policy, the plan involves exclusions and limitations as to Griffin's liability.

We believe that based on these facts, the evidence supports the Department's decision that Griffin's plan constitutes an insurance policy. It is clearly not a warranty such as that present in *GAF*, nor is it a service agreement like that existing in *Rayos*. Instead, the plan issued by Griffin is an indemnity agreement whereby Griffin agrees to indemnify its insured for potential losses arising from the mechanical breakdown of the insured's vehicle. That being the case, Griffin is engaged in the business of selling insurance and is therefore subject to the Department's rules and regulations.... Accordingly, for the reasons set forth above, we affirm the decision of the circuit court of Cook County.

NOTES

(1) *Case Comparison*. Compare this opinion with the decision in the watch-replacement case, Ollendorff Watch Co. v. Pink.

(2) *An Opposing View*. This Note contains an excerpt from the court's opinion in Griffin Systems, Inc. v. Ohio Department of Insurance, 575 N.E.2d 803 (Ohio 1991).

. . .

[The Department asserts] that the crucial distinction, as noted by the court of appeals below, is that warranties not sold by either the vendor or manufacturer of the product are not made to induce a purchase of the product, and therefore constitute contracts substantially amounting to insurance. While the foregoing assertion may appear to be facially valid, we find it to be unpersuasive....

In our view, the crucial factor in determining whether a contract is a warranty or something substantially amounting to insurance is not the status of the party offering or selling the warranty, but rather the type of coverage promised within the four corners of the contract itself. [From earlier cases cited] it is clear that warranties that cover only defects within the product itself are properly character-ized as warranties ... whereas warranties promising to cover damages or losses unrelated to defects within the product itself are, by definition, contracts substantially amounting to insurance....

The fact that [Griffin Systems] is not the manufacturer, supplier, or seller of the products it purports to warrant is, in our view, of little or no consequence in determining whether its protection plans are subject to R.C. Title 39 [*Insurance*].

(3) *Three Choices.* The foregoing authorities suggest at least these ways of differentiating between insurance contracts and warranties relating to goods:

(a) A warranty is a quality-related commitment made by a manufacturer or purveyor as such;

(b) A warranty is a quality-related commitment made by anyone; and,

(c) A warranty is a commitment made by a manufacturer or purveyor as such, whether or not it is quality-related.

Questions: Which is the best choice? Is there a connection between any of them and the principal object and purpose of the agreement in question?

(4) *Vocational Guarantors.* In the New York Insurance Law, part of the definition of insurance contract is this (section 1101(a)(3)):

Contract of warranty, guaranty or suretyship means an insurance contract only if made by a warrantor, guarantor or surety who or which, as such, is doing an insurance business.

Question: Which of the three choices in the foregoing Note is most consistent with this provision?

Ollendorff Watch was decided before this provision took effect. Does the provision confirm that decision? Cast any doubt on it?

After reading the opinion that follows, consider whether or not the ruling there would have been the same if the case had been governed by that provision. If so, would the court have had an easier path to its ruling?

(5) *Fortuity.* According to the Ohio opinion quoted in Note 2 above, a "warranty" promises indemnity against defects in the article sold, while "insurance" indemnifies against loss or damage resulting from perils outside of and unrelated to defects in the article itself. Why? Is the distinction based on the fortuity principle? Recall this sentence in § 1101(a)(2) of the New York Insurance Law: " 'Fortuitous event' means any occurrence or failure to occur which is, or is assumed by the parties to be, to a substantial extent beyond the control of either party."

(6) *From Tires to Bicycles.* Assume that your law Student Bicycle Association (SBA) is a corporation, chartered for the purpose of accumulating a fund by assessments for the protection of its members' bicycles. Every member of the Association pays annual dues of $50. Having paid, a member becomes entitled to all the benefits described in a membership card issued to him or her. The card provides: "SBA agrees to (1) clean your bicycle twice during the year; (2) repair any tire punctured by accident; (3) repair bicycle when damaged by accident; (4) replace bicycle when destroyed by accident; (5) replace bicycle when stolen, if not recovered in eight weeks, and provide a bicycle during that time." The Association has no lodge, secret ritual, handshake, sign, or symbol, and does not pay any benefit on an occasion of sickness, disability, or death. *Questions*: Applying the *fortuity* principle, does the SBA arrangement constitute insurance, or doing an insurance business? If it is an insurance business, is it a viable one? See Commonwealth v. Provident Bicycle Ass'n, 36 A. 197 (Pa. 1897).

Riffe v. Home Finders Associates

Supreme Court of Appeals, W.Va., 1999.
205 W.Va. 216, 517 S.E.2d 313.

■ McCRAW, JUSTICE:

. . .

Appellants and plaintiffs below Richard and Brenda Riffe (the "Riffes") appeal a grant of summary judgment against them and in favor of appellee and defendant below, Home Security of America, Inc., in an action the Riffes filed claiming fraud, insurance bad faith, and breach of contract. Because we find that genuine issues of material fact existed as to these issues, we reverse the trial court's grant of summary judgment and remand this case for proceedings consistent with this opinion.

I. Factual Background [Omitted]

II. Standard of Review

Our review of a grant of summary judgment is *de novo*. . . . In the case before us, we must examine the parties' rights and obligations under a contract of insurance. In this arena our review is also *de novo*: "Determination of the proper coverage of an insurance contract when the facts are not in dispute is a question of law." Murray v. State Farm Fire and Cas. Co., 509 S.E.2d 1, 6 (W.Va.1998). . . . The interpretation of an insurance contract, including the question of whether the contract is ambiguous, is a legal determination that, like a lower court's grant of summary judgement, shall be reviewed *de novo* on appeal. . . .

III. Discussion

Chapter Thirty–Three, Article One of our Code states: "Insurance is a contract whereby one undertakes to indemnify another or to pay a specified amount upon determinable contingencies." W. Va. Code § 33–1–1 (1957). . . . The same article provides: "Transacting insurance includes solicitation and inducement, preliminary negotiations, effecting a contract of insurance and transaction of matters subsequent to effecting the contract and arising out of it." W. Va. Code § 33–1–4 (1957).

Specifically, this case concerns what some have called a "service contract," which may be used as a catch-all term for arrangements where a third-party, who is neither the buyer or seller of property, contracts with the buyer to indemnify him or her for repairs made to the property for a certain period of time after a sale.

Home Security maintains that the "service contract" it offers is a warranty and is not insurance, and that the company is not engaged in the business of selling insurance in the State of West Virginia. We do not agree. Under the plan, a homeowner would file a claim, have the repair made, and would be indemnified by Home Security for the cost of a covered repair, minus any deductible. There can be no question that the contract offered by Home Security "is a contract whereby one undertakes to indemnify another or to pay a specified amount upon determinable contingencies." . . . The agreement provided by Home Security, although it claims to offer "warranty coverage" is an insurance policy. . . .

[The court stated the main facts and holding in Griffin Systems, Inc. v. Washburn, above.] We concur with the Illinois Court. A so-called, third party "warranty" contract, in which a third party, who is not the manufacturer or seller of goods or property, agrees to indemnify a buyer for a defect in the goods or property sold, is indeed, "a contract whereby one undertakes to indemnify another or to pay a specified amount upon determinable contingencies," and is therefore an insurance contract under the laws of the State of West Virginia.

Because the policy offered by Home Security is insurance, the Riffes are entitled to all the protections afforded to purchasers of insurance under our law. [At this point the court made reference to several safeguards afforded in West Virginia to buyers of insurance. One is the principle that ambiguous terms in insurance contracts are construed in favor of the insured. Another is protection from conflicts between promotional materials and an insurance policy, a principle applicable to the case at hand.]

. . . Because these considerations of ambiguity, reasonable expectations, exclusionary language, and conflicts with promotional materials may determine the rights of the parties under the contract, genuine issues of material fact exist, and summary judgment is inapposite. . . . Because we find that the "home warranty contract" offered by Home Security is insurance, . . . we reverse the trial court's grant of summary judgment for the defendant and remand this case for additional proceedings consistent with this opinion.

NOTES

(1) *Minor Element.* It can be argued that a "small amount of insurance" ancillary to the principal object of a contract does not require that the contract be classified as one of insurance. How the argument might run is illustrated by the following passage, beginning with a test question.

> Were the elements of risk transference and risk distribution central to and relatively important elements of the transactions (or merely incidental to other elements that gave the transaction their distinctive character)? . . . [I]t seems clear that the insurance regulatory laws are not properly construed as aimed at an absolute prohibition against the inclusion of any risk-transferring-and-distributing provisions in contracts for services. . . . The presence of a minor element of risk transference and risk distribution does not conclusively demonstrate that the transaction should appropriately be classified as within the reach of insurance regulatory laws. The judgment should be based on the predominant characteristic of such transactions, the element that gives the transaction its fundamental nature.

Robert Keeton and Alan Widiss, Insurance Law 951 (Practioner's ed. 1988). See also the Note, "Bits of Insurance Undertaken" at p. 20 below.

(2) *The Home Owner's Warranty.* This Note describes the warranty (HOW); the following one poses some questions about it.

A HOW customarily indemnifies the warranty holder against the cost of repair or replacement of any structural component or "fixture" of a home, necessitated by wear and tear or by an inherent defect of any structural component or appliance, or necessitated by the failure of an inspection to detect the likelihood of any such loss. If a builder of homes wishes to provide buyers with contractual assurance that their homes will not, for a period of years, manifest structural defects, will the builder have to enlist an insurer willing to issue policies to the buyers? What of a bank that, having foreclosed on a housing project, wishes to sell units in it with the same assurance? As to such an assurance, see Vogel v. American Warranty Home Service

Corp., 695 F.2d 877 (5th Cir. 1983) (home builder's contractual assurance to buyers that homes will not, for a period of years, manifest structural defects may be a contract of insurance). See also Home Warranty Corp. v. Elliott, 585 F.Supp. 443 (D.Del. 1984) ("[T]he liabilities arising from the manufacture, design, lease, or sale of a new home may be considered product liabilities under the [Products Liability Risk Retention Act of 1981].)" That Act permits a type of insuring that is partly immune from state regulation. It was intended to make product-liability insurance more efficient. HOW Corporations are now subject to regulation in some respects by every state in which they do business and are fully subject to regulation in the chartering jurisdiction.

(3) *HOW Questions.* (a) Refer to the test of "substantial control" as represented in Note 5, p. 16 above. Apply that test first to the builder/seller and then to the banker/seller. Would you classify either HOW transaction as one of insurance?

(b) Apply the "principal object" test (also known as the "incidental" or "ancillary" test) first to the builder and then to the banker. Would you classify either transaction as one of insurance?

(c) Is either of these tests fully satisfactory, or can a better one be formulated?

Drafting Contract Language for and Against "Insurance"

The drafter of a contract might shape a party's commitments away from "warranty" and in the direction "insurance" by following either of two paths. One is to enumerate the occasions for compensation in terms of notably chancy (fortuitous) events. The other path is to make a sweeping statement of those occasions, or of the risks assumed, and to add exclusions which eliminate all, or virtually all, of the non-chancy events. On pursuing this path, the drafter might go so far as to say that the contract shifts all risks to the promisor (except those enumerated).

To some extent, the second path was followed in writing the contract about home repairs considered in the *Riffe* case. Home Security began by undertaking to pay the purchaser of a home for any repairs that might be required during a specified period. Then it proceeded to qualify that commitment by ruling out various kinds of repair costs that are not associated with casualties, but are entailed by any purchase of a home. Some of these were rot, corrosion, and rust. To judge by these features alone, the contract appears to have been slanted in the direction of insurance: what is left is casualties of the sort for which insurance is commonly bought: fire, accident, acts of God, and the like.

If, instead of shaping a commitment in the direction of insurance, the drafter wishes to shape it in the direction of warranty, there is again a choice between two paths. A drafter intent on that might either limit the repair commitment to defects in the home when sold, or might, on choosing the path of exclusions enlarged, rule out fire, accident, and the like.

Observe that the contract considered in *Riffe* had features indicating warranty as well as others indicating insurance. Not only did the contract rule out rot, rust, and the like, it also enumerated many other kinds of event that might require repairs, and made exceptions for those. Along with some thirty other hazards, they included losses by fire, windstorm, and lightning—the very sorts of loss addressed in ordinary forms of homeowners (HO) insurance.

NOTE

Exclusions Disfavored. In principle, a drafter might expect to reach the same terminus by following either the path of inclusions confined or that of exclusions enlarged. In practice, however, the two may diverge when the contract is one of insurance. Let it be supposed that a loss occurs, the immediate cause of which is the subject of an exception, for instance, "except loss caused by corrosion." Let it be supposed also that the corrosion is traceable to an event the drafter neglected to rule out, discharges of a salt into the drainage system, say, due to the malfunction of a water purifier. On these facts, it may happen that the exception is inoperative. It has been said that when an insured event (one covered in a primary insuring clause) has caused a loss of a type excepted (excluded from coverage), recovery is required. Authorities to that effect are cited in Central International Company v. Kemper Nat'l Insurance Companies, 202 F.3d 372 (1st Cir. 2000) (applying New York law).

But in that case the court called it a dubious move to prefer, in tracing the train of events, the primary, covered risk over the secondary, excluded one. The principle is dubious "even where the covered risk is narrowly defined (*e.g.*, fire)", the court said, "[and] it becomes absurd where the initial coverage is all risk, since every excluded harm has some cause." The court said that the supporting cases are "usually ... better explained as a limiting construction of the exclusion." But: "there is nothing wrong with reading policy language more narrowly (or broadly) than its literal wording might at first suggest where this better captures the reasonable expectation of the parties, the central object of all contract interpretation." Id. at 375.

B.   THE REGULATORY PUBLIC INTEREST

Bits of Insurance Undertaken

The GAF Corporation agreed with a school board to supply materials to be used by builders in erecting schools. GAF agreed, among other things, to pay for damages that might result from leaks if they should occur from slippage in GAF products or from the builder's faulty work. In School Board v. GAF, the trial court concluded that the agreement was an insurance contract. On review, in GAF Corp. v. County School Board, 629 F.2d 981 (4th Cir. 1980), the court conceded that the guarantee contained an "insurance" component. But it reversed, saying:

> We think that the appropriate rule is that a small element of insurance should not be construed to bring a transaction within the reach of the insurance regulatory laws unless the transaction involves one or more of the evils at which the regulatory statutes were aimed and the elements of risk transfer and distribution give the transaction its distinctive character. [(Quoting R. Keeton, Insurance Law (1971)), at 552.]

The law of Virginia applied. The Board had sought to bring GAF into court there by way of the State's Unauthorized Insurers Process Act—a statute favorable to claimants when it applies.

NOTES

(1) *Question*. If the decision had been otherwise, might GAF have suffered worse consequences than the Process Act imposes? (One possible consequence is liability for the claimant's attorney's fee.)

(2) *Non-Professional "Incidental Insurance"—Are Regulatory Concerns Lacking?* GAF's repair undertaking was conditioned (a) on leakage resulting from poor workmanship and (b) on leakage resulting from defects in its products. The court's decision was based on its belief that the former was a "relatively unimportant" transfer of risk and was ancillary to the latter. *Question*: If the undertaking had been to repair roofs damaged (only) by windstorm or by another "natural disaster", would the decision have been different?

(3) *Why Define "Insurance"?* The insurance business is subject to burdensome and expensive regulation. A firm that can offer insurance-like contracts to the public, free of such regulation, will enjoy a competitive advantage. That is a major reason for giving close attention to the legal definitions of "insurance". But there are other reasons. To answer the question, What is insurance?, one must first ask, "Why do you want to know?" The setting for the question may be a tax statute, a statute governing creditors' rights, or a statute regulating the investment business. And the answer may vary according to the context. See Hellner, What is Insurance . . .?, cited at p. 2 above.

Questions: What was the School Board's purpose in contending for a broad definition of "insurance"? What other consequences might have followed for the GAF Corporation if it had been found to be doing an insurance business?

Regulatory Considerations

One of the editors has written that, in determining whether or not a particular transaction constitutes insurance, "courts should examine [it] to determine if [it] ought to be regulated in the public interest as the business of insurance." 1 Eric Mills Holmes, Holmes' Appleman on Insurance 2d 37–38 (1996). In a case described in this Note, public interests were argued to the court on both sides of the question whether an arrangement constituted insuring. First, however, the Note describes an earlier decision by the same court in which the opinion makes no reference to regulatory concerns. This is designated "Case One"; the later is designated "Case Two".

Case One

A firm named Professional Lens Plan, Inc. (Professional) arranged with optometrists a plan to encourage purchases of contact lenses. A patron of an optometrist would become entitled to any number of lenses at a heavy discount—at cost to the optometrist, or little more—upon paying the optometrist an annual fee, set by the optometrist. The firm would charge a subscribing optometrist a small fee, $6 or less, for each subscribing patron, and would in return (aside from handling money transfers) notify patrons of times for annual eye checkups and provide optometrists with materials about the plan.

On an appeal from a ruling by the Florida Department of Insurance, the plan was said not to effect *insurance*, as defined in section 624.02 of the Florida Statutes:

> . . . a contract whereby one undertakes to indemnify another or pay or allow a specified amount or a determinable benefit upon determinable contingencies.

Professional Lens Plan, Inc. v. Department of Insurance, 387 So.2d 548 (Fla.App. 1980).

The court said, drawing on an Arizona opinion, that five elements are normally present in an insurance contract, naming these:

1.   An insurable interest.

2.   A risk of loss.

3.   An assumption of the risk by the insuror.

4.   A general scheme to distribute the loss among the larger group of persons bearing similar risks.

5.   The payment of a premium for the assumption of risk.

Among these, the court said, it might be possible to identify only the first two in the plan. Moreover: "As between Professional and the patient [patron], there is no contractual obligation or duty. This determination alone would, in our opinion, dispose of the contention that Professional is engaging in a business of 'insurance.' " Id. at 550.

Case Two

By paying a substantial annual fee to Liberty Care Plan, a person could become eligible for one or another level of health care, from a designated corporate provider, at a specified daily charge called a "discount". Care could be obtained at home (including cooking) and abroad (including shopping). Subscribers were required to pay to the provider charges in excess of the discount for services it performed. Renewals were permitted indefinitely. The annual fee might increase, but the rate of increase was capped. "THIS IS NOT INSURANCE", according to the Plan agreement. The Florida Department of Insurance (DOI) issued a Declaration to the contrary, and Liberty Care appealed. The court agreed with the Department (DOI), saying:

> The Plan is a contract whereby appellant undertakes to allow a determinable benefit (*i.e.*, home health care services at discount rates) upon a determinable contingency (*i.e.*, the member's exercise of the option to purchase these home health care services at discount rates).

Liberty Care Plan v. Department of Insurance, 710 So.2d 202, 205–06 (Fla.App. 1998).

The Department (DOI) argued that the facts were "not similar to those in *Professional Lens Plan*, in which the appellant merely acted as a 'referral service' on behalf of the providers and had no contract with the members. . . ." It argued also this:

[R]egulation is necessary to protect the elderly in this type of marketing, to make certain that providers have sufficient capital and surplus to stay in business, that reserves are established for early cancellations, that a standardized contract is used to avoid hidden limitations, that annual membership fee (premium) rates are reasonable, and that agents selling memberships are properly trained and licensed.

Id. at 205.

Liberty Care Plan argued that its offering was very similar to that of Professional Lens Plan, and that the Department's decision would "deprive the elderly and needy of low cost home health services."

NOTES

(1) *Questions.* What should the decision have been in Case Two? On what do you base your answer?

(2) *Holmes on Defining "Insurance".* In *Liberty Care Plan*, the Florida court concluded its opinion as follows:

One commentator has observed that three tests may be used in resolving the question of defining "insurance." Eric Mills Holmes, Holmes's Appleman on Insurance § 1.4 (2d ed. 1996). The first test, which conforms to the traditional "indemnity" concept of insurance as an arrangement for transferring and distributing the risk of loss upon the happening of a fortuitous event, is called the "substantial control" test. Holmes notes:

The test derives from Professor William R. Vance's 1904 description of an insurance contract (made between parties customarily called the insurer and the insured) as having the following five elements:

(a) The insured possesses an interest of some kind susceptible to pecuniary estimation, and known as an *insurable interest*;

(b) The insured is subject to a risk of loss through the destruction or impairment of the insurable interest by the happening of certain designated fortuitous perils [today generally called the *insured event*];

(c) The insurer assumes that risk of loss [which today we describe as *risk transference*];

(d) The insurer assumes that risk as part of a general scheme to distribute actual losses among a large group bearing somewhat similar risks; and,

(e) As consideration for the insurer's promise to assume the risk of loss, the insured makes a contribution (called a premium) to the general insurance fund [(d) and (e) constitute *risk distribution*].

Whatever the form it takes or the name it bears, any contract having those five elements is a contract of insurance in the traditional sense ... [W]ithin this classical definition of insurance, the most important element was the insured fortuitous event, that is, an event that is substantially beyond the control of the insured. Id. at 22–29 (emphasis in the original).

Holmes identifies the second test which may be used in resolving the question of defining "insurance" as the "principal object and purpose" test, explaining:

"Rather than exclusively adopting the control test in determining whether a commercial transaction is one of insurance, some courts now ask: Were the elements of risk transference and distribution of a fortuitous insured event a central and relatively significant feature of the commercial transaction *or* simply incidental and ancillary to the other elements that give the transaction its distinctive nature?" Under this test, some courts have asked whether " 'service' or 'indemnity' was the 'principal object and purpose' of the arrangement."

Id. at 31–37.

Holmes suggests that these two tests "should not be the end of the inquiry in determining if a particular commercial transaction constitutes insurance," but that courts "should examine each commercial transaction to determine if the discrete transaction ought to be regulated in the public interest as the business of insurance." Id. at 37–38. He calls this third test the "regulatory value" test and suggests that enterprises which might meet the test include auto clubs, vehicle protection plans, collision damage waivers, homeowner's warranty plans, prepaid service plans, and similar contractual provisions that have a "public interest" insurance element. Id. at 38. He notes the fact that the promise in the "warranty agreement" in Guaranteed Warranty Corp., Inc. v. State ex rel. Humphrey was made by a third party, not the manufacturer or seller, and observes that this fact "was critical to the court's opinion" in that case. He suggests: "Protection of the public from the schemes, deceptions and insolvencies of third parties who make insurance-type promises is another solid reason to justify the application of state insurance regulatory laws." Id. at 38–39.

Liberty Care Plan v. Department of Insurance, 710 So.2d 202, 206–07 (Fla.App. 1998).

Introduction to *In re Feinstein*

New York law as expressed in this case has been modified extensively. Some main features of subsequent legislation and regulation are described in notes following the opinion. The opinion retains its value as a thoughtful discussion of the nature of the insurance business and the reasons for its regulation.

In re Feinstein; In re New York County Lawyers Association

Court of Appeals of New York, 1975.
36 N.Y.2d 199, 366 N.Y.S.2d 613, 326 N.E.2d 288.

[The court considered appeals in two cases. In each case an application was made to the Supreme Court, Appellate Division (First Department) for the approval of a plan for prepaid legal services. The applicants in one case (Feinstein *et al.*) were the trustees of a labor union; in the other the applicant was the New York County Lawyers Association. In each case the lower court had withheld approval. According to § 495 of the N.Y. Judiciary Law, that court was charged with the performance of professional responsibilities by the Bar. "Where there is involved the interposition of an organization or corporation in the rendering of legal services, the Appellate

Division must assure that the link of professional responsibility between lawyers and the clients they serve is not diluted, dissolved, or immunized from judicial oversight."]

■ BREITEL, CHIEF JUDGE. . . .

The first of the two plans was proposed by a union of municipal employees in the City of New York to operate through a welfare fund trust. The plan would provide specified classes of legal service at moderate cost to its members whose salaries range between $4,000 and $15,000. There would be a modest initial charge, the rendition of services by a legal office of lawyers and related personnel supervised by a law firm representing the union, and subsequent reimbursement by the member clients for legal services in excess of those available under the plan. The union's members would have the right to retain their own lawyers but without reimbursement under the plan. . . .

The second plan was promoted by the New York County Lawyers Association and involved a separate corporation to provide reimbursement for legal services at modest cost to middle-income people who subscribed to the plan for an initial subscription fee of $100 per year. The services would be rendered by participating lawyers who would agree to render services to subscribers within limited scheduled fees for rather narrow classes of legal services to be provided. The subscriber clients would be free to choose their lawyers from among the panel of participating lawyers. To this extent the plan would be an "open panel" system as contrasted with the "closed panel" of lawyers provided by the union plan described earlier. . . . [Each of the plans projected operations for only an experimental period.]

[The court discountenanced some grounds on which the lower court had acted. One was "the inadequacy of statutory authority, personnel, and resources to assess and supervise the plans."]

Despite the Appellate Division's proper concern with the possible proliferation of prepaid legal services plans without adequate assessment of their fiscal implications by an agency capable of making that assessment, it lacked the power to withhold approval on that ground. Nor are prepaid legal services plans properly encompassed by the statutes regulating insurance. At least this is true, if one were to consider the essential purpose and scope of those statutes, although to be sure, there are elements of contingency and reimbursement in any such plan which bear a similarity to certain kinds of insurance or indemnity. On this view, the two plans were improperly excluded from approval, and the applications should be remitted to the Appellate Division for reconsideration.

. . . [I]t should be kept in mind that all existing liability insurance is a form of litigation insurance and the attenuation of the relationship between attorney and client is to a degree accepted as reasonable within supervised and supervisable professional bounds. So in this area, as in all other areas of human affairs, there are no easy absolutes to apply.

Proposals for prepaid legal services plans, especially for those of middle income and low income above the level of indigency, have been a matter of widespread interest. The literature is extensive indeed and largely unanimous that new paths must be staked out to make legal services available to persons between those served by poverty-level schemes and those rich enough to purchase legal services without assistance or extraordinary measures. . . . The literature on the subject has of course influenced the very plans before the court at this time. The Bar Association plan reflects in many ways, for example, the difficulties in constructing a broad enough plan which would yet be economically feasible. . . .

And, of course, the Appellate Division expressed the view that the plans submitted may run afoul of the Insurance Law as being in the nature of insurance. In the first place, in a doubtful case it would not necessarily be the province of the Appellate Division but that of the Department of Insurance to seek compliance with its governing law (see Insurance Law, § 35, which provides that the Superintendent of Insurance may maintain and prosecute an action against any person subject to the Insurance Law for the purpose of obtaining an injunction restraining such person from doing any acts in violation of the Insurance Law; if the court finds that a defendant is threatening or is likely to do any acts in violation of the law, and that such acts will cause irreparable injury to the public interests, it may grant an injunction). In a clear case of illegality, of course, approval must be denied. . . . But even assuming that the Insurance Law might determine the validity of the plans, not more than a cursory analysis is merited.

[The court observed that the contestants had not addressed "in depth" the question whether or not the plans were insurance schemes.] Since, it is concluded, that on their face, neither plan involves insurance, the plans should not be rejected out of hand. On any view of the matter if it should now or later appear to the Department of Insurance that either or both plans are prohibited by the Insurance Law, that department should be and is free to pursue the remedies available to it.

Insurance Law is designed to prohibit the business of insurance and related activities, except as licensed and regulated by the Department of Insurance or exempted from such licensure and regulation. . . . The threshold issue arises from the definition of insurance. Section 41 [now Insurance Law § 1101] provides that an insurance contract "[includes] any agreement or other transaction whereby one party, herein called the insurer, is obligated to confer benefit of pecuniary value upon another party, herein called the insured or the beneficiary, dependent upon the happening of a fortuitous event in which the insured or beneficiary has, or is expected to have at the time of such happening, a material interest which will be adversely affected by the happening of such event. A fortuitous event is any occurrence or failure to occur which is, or is assumed by the parties to be, to a substantial extent beyond the control of either party."

A reading of the statute for its sense and purpose does not suggest that the instant plans for prepaid legal services are insurance schemes. A literal reading of the statute, disregarding its sense and purpose, would of course take in some of the prepaid or reimbursable fees for legal services, to the extent that the legal services would not be required until a "fortuitous event" had occurred. As for many of the legal services involved, however, there is no fortuitousness, in any ordinary sense of the word, in the event which precipitates the retention of a lawyer, such as the drafting of a will, a separation agreement, the purchase of a house, and many others of the same kind.

Terms like fortuitousness of event in the law, as with the word accident, have always caused conceptual difficulties (see, *e.g.*, McGroarty v. Great Amer. Ins. Co., 36 N.Y.2d 358). The statute, in circumscribing the term to mean that which is to a substantial extent beyond the control of either party, is useful in relating regulation to insurance schemes as they have been known . . . , but it is not exact in the consideration of agreements to provide services of various kinds. In this area it is easy to slip into metaphysical, even validly metaphysical, distinctions.

But metaphysics is not the concern of section 41 of the Insurance Law; instead the licensure and regulation of insurance activity is. The proposed prepaid legal services plans are not insurance businesses or insurance contracts, although it may be that, in the Appellate Division's judgment and in the future possibly that of the Legislature, they merit the same degree of regulation and supervision from their fiscal aspects and perhaps even from other aspects.

Viewed as a provider of professional services, sought as a matter of choice, at flat fees rather than as reimbursement for material losses or expenses precipitated by fortuitous events, the proposed plans do not pose the dangers that the Insurance Law was designed to obviate. Those dangers embrace inadequate coverage of determinable actuarial risks, excessive premiums on an actuarial basis, and fiscal irresponsibility. . . .

That hospital, medical and dental indemnity contracts have been covered in detailed and close regulation in the Insurance Law is not contradictory of what has been said thus far. As the Bar Association argues: "All that the enactment of (article 1X—C of the Insurance Law) demonstrates is that the legislature believed that such contracts . . . should be regulated by a statute especially tailored to those services and deemed the Insurance Department the most appropriate agency in which to vest the supervision of such corporations." . . .

Both plans are concededly experimental. . . . These obviously are not ventures into the "insurance" business, nor for the moment do they suggest insurmountable difficulties of assessment by the Appellate Division. Most important, plans like these presented and to be operated by benevolent or charitable organizations, the only kind that the Appellate Division has power to approve, provide a natural limitation on those who might present such plans in order to mask an out-and-out insurance or indemnity scheme. This is further evidence that plans like these fall outside the spirit and purpose of the existing provisions of the Insurance Law.

Yet, the discussion should not be closed without agreeing with the Appellate Division that early legislative attention is indicated. . . . The likelihood of significant numbers of such plans being promulgated in this State is quite great.... The kind of broader regulation, especially fiscal regulation, considered necessary by the Appellate Division, may well be appropriate, and may even become urgently needed as prepaid legal services plans become common.

Accordingly, the orders of the Appellate Division should be reversed, without costs, and the matters remitted to that court for reconsideration in the light of this opinion.

NOTES

(1) *Prepaid Legal Services Plans.* To the appeal for legislative attention near the close of the foregoing opinion, the legislature responded in 1984 with a section of the Insurance Laws titled "Experimental projects in prepaid legal services plans." Authorized insurers were permitted to provide legal services insurance only in connection with such a plan. Years later, the legislature dropped the "experimental". A regulation of the Insurance Department, implementing the current provision, gives this definition, in effect:[10]

> *Prepaid legal services plan* means "an arrangement [provided by an authorized insurer] for the providing of legal services on a prepaid fee basis, where such services are not dependent upon the happening of a fortuitous event ...; except that [the] plan may agree to provide such services in the event a separate fee for each such service is charged, and the fee for the service fully covers the cost of rendition, including reasonable overhead." (The phrase omitted here concerns the recipient's interest in averting the fortuitous event.)

A preamble to the regulation speaks further to "fortuitous event", deferring to the definition in Insurance Law § 1101. The preamble gives an example of a legal services arrangement by which services are provided for a prepaid fee, yet the business is not that of insurance within the definition: It provides that the recipient is entitled to have a will drawn upon request, "so long as the arrangement is not conditioned upon the happening of a fortuitous event. [A] prepaid legal services arrangement providing such limited services and being offered by an unlicensed entity would not be subject to the jurisdiction of the Insurance Department." This is offered as guidance, prompted by the fact that "the Department has received many inquiries requesting clarification as to what kinds of prepaid legal services arrangements constitute the doing of an insurance business, thus requiring licensing as an insurer." (*Question*: Are the passages quoted above guidance enough?)

The Superintendent of Insurance is directed to authorize an insurer to provide legal services in connection with a prepaid legal services plan only upon a determination that "the plan attempts to address the problem that desired legal services are unavailable to some citizens of this state because some individuals and families who are not eligible for government subsidized programs cannot afford the cost of those services."

(2) *Legal Services Insurance.* The same legislation provided also that "legal services insurance" may be written "pursuant to a regulation [to be] promulgated by the superintendent [of insurance]". The statute sets these limitations:

---

10. N.Y. Ins. Dep't Regulations, Chapter XI, Section 261.1. The quotation is from subdivision (a), defining "access plan". Subdivision (m) defines "prepaid legal services plan" as "an access plan ..., provided by an authorized insurer...."

(i) The insurance must be "part of a policy of liability insurance covering related risks"; and

(ii) A defense-only coverage for a business entity, applying to business-related proceedings, is to be "not more than an incidental part of such liability insurance."[11]

A limitation comparable to the latter applies to legal services insurance in connection with a prepaid legal services plan. That is, of the plan premium, only an incidental amount is to be attributable to a defense-only coverage of the kind specified in (ii) above.

The Department has said of legal services insurance that it "is often thought of as being 'legal defense insurance', or 'defense-only coverage', particularly in connection with liability insurance. However, legal services insurance is a broader concept.... [For example, it may encompass] an appeal from a license denial by an administrative agency."

The Department has issued a regulation authorizing legal services insurance. One provision is this: "No policy that includes legal services insurance may be issued or delivered except by an insurer authorized to write such insurance." As to the statutory term "related risks", the regulation has this to say:

> This means that the risk exposure under the legal services insurance must relate to the same kind of risk exposure that is covered under the liability provisions of the policy. For example, a medical malpractice policy may include legal services insurance coverage in regard to the medical malpractice exposure, but not for other kinds of liability exposure.

An example given of another kind of liability is motor-vehicle risk.

(3) *Competition.* The New York requirement that makes defense-only coverage a side order only, in relation to legal services insurance, has the appearance of protecting the integrity of commercial liability insurance in its standard form— protecting the turf of its issuers, if you like. The departmental regulation adds to that appearance: "legal services insurance may not provide defense-only coverage for a claim of legal liability that could be covered by a policy of liability insurance [written in New York]."

Like insurance against commercial liability in general, medical-malpractice insurance comprises both payment and defense obligations. Suppose that an association of medical specialists prepares a plan by which subscribers pay into a fund for paying the cost of a defense for any subscriber sued for malpractice, and no other purpose. The defense entitlement is the main course, so to speak. Is that an insuring plan? Whether or not it is, is it open to the objection that it undercuts ordinary malpractice insurance? On any other ground? See Physicians' Defense Co. v. O'Brien, 111 N.W. 396 (Minn. 1907) (contract of insurance), and Vredenburgh v. Physicians Defense Co., 126 Ill.App. 509 (1906) (contract for services only).

Caregiving Contracts

(1) *A Dissenter's Case.* Hansen, a longshoreman, was the claimant in a contract action against his employer. He had been injured in a riot incident to a strike by fellow employees. He was not a striker. The defendant, Dodwell Dock & Warehouse Company, had agreed to provide him with "ample protection" from hurt by the strikers, and "furnish [him with] a safe place in which to work free from assault on the part of any persons

---

11. N.Y. Ins. Law section 1116(a)(2), (3).

whatsoever." Dodwell appealed from a judgment for Hansen. One of its points was that the contract was one of insurance and had not been entered into in conformity with the statutes regulating insurance.

A question was raised about the extent of Dodwell's undertaking. Possibly it extended only to injuries caused by the strikers and their sympathizers. Dodwell contended that it had promised protection against injuries that might be received in other ways. The court thought otherwise. But, it said:

> were the words as broad in meaning as [Dodwell] construes them to be, still, in our opinion, it would not be an insurance contract as that form of contract is defined by the statutes. Assuredly, when a master employs a servant, he may enter into a binding agreement with him to protect him against the hazards of the employment, or the hazards surrounding the employment, without resorting to the forms of contract prescribed by the Insurance Code.

Hansen's judgment was affirmed. Hansen v. Dodwell Dock & Warehouse Co., 170 P. 346 (Wash. 1918).

Questions: If Dodwell had agreed with Hansen to see that strikers did not harm him at home, would that have been to insure him? If it had agreed to see to his safety at home from all hazards, would that have been to insure him? Would it make a difference, in any of the cases supposed, if Dodwell had agreed with Hansen to compensate him for injuries he might suffer?

(2) *Succor for Sick People.* A man of means and prudence, now deceased, contracted for lifetime care, knowing that he was terminally ill. Suppose first that the care giver is a hospice organized to serve people in the sufferer's situation, and that it exacted in exchange a down payment and the promise of a considerable further payment that was never made. Similar agreements were made with other well-to-do patients in the hospice. *Questions*: Is the agreement, being otherwise enforceable, unenforceable by the hospice because it has never been licensed to make a contract of insurance? Suppose that the care giver is a woman, distantly related to the man, who contracted for a promise of a substantial bequest in his will. Does her want of a license as an insurer bar her from enforcing her contract? How would you justify different answers to these questions, if that were your job? See Sisters of Third Order of Saint Francis v. Estate of Guillaume, 222 Ill.App. 543 (1921); cf. Tuckwiller v. Tuckwiller, 413 S.W.2d 274 (Mo. 1967).

(3) *Continuing-Care Contracts.* Persons engaged in institutional projects for housing and caring for senior persons have said that the business is more intensely regulated than are nuclear power facilities. The National Association of Insurance Commissioners has prepared a "Long–Term Care Insurance Model Act." More than forty states have enacted that or similar legislation; and there are related statutes in other states. The Model Act contains an elaborate definition of *long-term care insurance,* and directs that the insurance department issue regulations about it.

In some states, agencies outside their insurance departments have major responsibilities with respect to contracts for long-term care, and to providers of it. In California, for example, the Department of Social Services is charged with approving a *continuing care contract*, as defined. A contract is within that definition if it requires an entrance fee, or the payment of periodic charges, or both, in exchange for a *continuing care promise*. The latter term is also defined: "a promise, expressed or implied, by a provider to provide one or more elements of care to an elderly resident for the duration of his or her life or for a term in excess of one year...."

Question: Consider again the agreements supposed above for the care of a terminally ill man. If they were governed by California law, would either of them require approval by the Department of Social Services?

Concluding Notes

(1) *Insurance as a Disguise*. Investors are wary of firms whose earnings swing widely from year to year. For that reason and others, the managers of such a firm may therefore favor an arrangement that "smooths" its earnings. A possible one is so-called *finite insurance*. "Finite coverages typically are multi-year arrangements, where the present value of the premium payments approximates the aggregate policy limit." The issuer may invest an early payment in a separate account and permit the holder to recover from that account to the extent that it exceeds losses and administrative charges. For the holder, the payment constitutes an item of expense, and the recovery an item of income. Both can be attractive to a firm that has highly variable earnings. Insurers are themselves principal buyers of finite insurance (reinsurance), which has utilities other than the timing of earnings.

The matter can be so arranged that, though the issuer bears some investment risks, it bears little or no risk of a covered loss. When that is done, the Securities & Exchange Commission and other authorities are likely to take a dim view of it. Investigations and charges accumulated during the winter of 2004–05, to and beyond the point when a composer of headlines wrote of "Dark Clouds Settling Over Insurance Industry".

(2) *Shipper vs. Trucker* An agreement for shipping goods by truck in interstate commerce is governed by the Interstate Commerce Act. In 1906 Congress enacted an amendment to the Act—the Carmack Amendment [now 49 U.S.C. § 14706]—"to establish uniformity and consistency among states in the application and resolution of interstate shipping loss and damage cases." In part, Carmack says this:

> A carrier providing transportation or service . . . shall issue a receipt or bill of lading for property it receives for transportation under this part. That carrier [is] liable to the person entitled to recover under the receipt or bill of lading. The liability imposed under this paragraph is for the actual loss or injury to the property. . . .

For commercial shipments, and for shipments of household goods, a carrier may limit its liability to the shipper's declared value. Such limitations are referred to as *released values*. A high declared value commonly entails a high rate (charge for transporting the goods).

Mr. and Mrs. John Nichols engaged Mayflower Transit to carry their household goods from California to Nevada, declaring the value to be $76,000. Later, Mayflower notified them that their goods had been destroyed by a trailer fire while in transit. Being disappointed in their treatment by Mayflower, the Nicholses brought an action against it alleging (among other things) a violation of the California Insurance Code, and a breach of Mayflower's duty to deal with them fairly and in good faith. The court dismissed the action, relying partly on Carmack.

There is a "litany of federal cases", the court said, "holding that Carmack preempts all claims for alleged violations of state insurance codes and/or breach of insurance contracts", citing some. It also said, quoting:

> [T]he contractual limit of liability provided by [the carrier] is a creature of the Carmack Amendment itself and therefore it cannot be, and never has been, considered insurance by the federal courts such that the preemptive effects of the Amendment would give way to state insurance regulations.

Nichols v. Mayflower Transit, LLC, 368 F.Supp.2d 1104, 1108 (D.Nev. 2003).

Question: Suppose that a carrier is accountable to a customer by contract for loss of, damage to, or the destruction of the shipper's goods while in transit, irrespective of the cause. Aside from Carmack, would that contract be one of insurance?

CHAPTER 2

REGULATION OF INSURANCE

A. INSTRUMENTS AND OBJECTIVES: AN INTRODUCTION

The business of insurance is intensely regulated. Every major type of governmental organization is engaged in the regulatory enterprise: legislatures, courts, and administrative agencies. This chapter addresses the work of all three.

In every state there is an insurance code (or law), and a department (bureau, division) of insurance, headed by a commissioner (director, superintendent). Notably, in the United States Code there is no title "Insurance". Laying aside governmentally sponsored insuring plans, the Congress has deferred broadly to state supervision of the business. The degree of deference is, however, a matter of active controversies. Part B–4 of this chapter, on federal-state relations, focuses on some of those.

The methods of regulation almost defy classification. One method is licensing. By and large, one cannot engage in the activity of insuring, or of marketing insurance, without having procured a license to do so from the state where the activity is carried on. Insurers are required, commonly, to file with each appropriate state department the forms of policies they mean to issue and the amounts they propose to charge for their coverages. These filings, especially the latter ("rate filings"), are altered from time to time. Rate filings are subject to objection if they are either excessive or inadequate. The approval and disapproval of proposed rates, and of contract forms, constitute a good part of departmental business.

Legislatures and courts also participate in the formulation of contract ("insurance policy") terms. The courts do so in part by adhering to long-established interpretations of terms in wide use—thereby reinforcing the parties' expectations—and often by fulfilling a "reasonable" expectation. They do so, sometimes, by declaring that a term offends public policy, or is inconsistent with a statutory mandate. All this in addition to the standard procedure of construing an ambiguous term against the interest of the insurer. Some of these measures amount to a form of discipline imposed on insurers. The courts' role in regulating the business is addressed particularly in part C of this chapter.

Legislatures participate dramatically in the formulation of insurance contracts when they outlaw a particular provision, or require that one be included in every policy of a specified type. More artful statutes are not uncommon. One type is to describe a coverage that insurance buyers might want, and to require that insurers doing a cognate line of business make an offer of that coverage to their patrons. At the other extreme, legislatures force the buying of insurance by making it unlawful to engage in an everyday activity (motoring, for example, or engaging employees) unless the actor is provided with a given coverage (auto liability insurance, workers' compensation insurance). Legislatures sometimes engage directly in the setting of premium charges—almost always in the direction of moderating them.

The foregoing description of regulatory measures concerns chiefly the process of "underwriting": preparing and issuing insurance contracts. Governmental organs are active also in regulating two other phases of the business: the marketing of insurance, and the adjusting of claims under insurance policies. Primary targets of regulation of these processes include misleading promotions of a sale, and "bad faith" disregard of a claimant's interest.

Three Objects of Insurance Regulation:
an Introduction

The primary objects of regulation can be grouped under three headings: fairness to consumers (including commercial ones); the financial solidity of insurers; and the availability of essential coverages. Problems of special interest occur when tension arises between two of these objectives. (Can you envisage how tension might arise?)

Solvency

"The prevention of insolvency and the maintenance of 'sound' financial condition in terms of fixed-dollar obligations is precisely what traditional state regulation [of insurance] is aimed at." SEC v. Variable Annuity Life Ins. Co. of Am., 359 U.S. 65, 90–91 (1959). "The primary purpose of state regulation of insurance—at least arguably—is the prevention of insolvency.... Underlying this concern over insolvency is the understanding that, for many reasons, the nature of insurance lends itself to the possibility of substantial abuse.[1] As a result, we have acknowledged the push for special regulation of the insurance industry, with the fundamental goal being 'the protection of solvency of the insurance industry, and the prevention of coercion, which in turn protects all potential, present and future policyholders.' "[2]

---

1. The passage quoted here contains this explanation: "Characteristically, premiums paid by policy holders (along with interest and other earnings derived from those premiums) are used to pay the claims of other policy holders. In essence, the provider pays present claims with proceeds from past and present premiums, while those who pay premiums now will have their future claims satisfied from the proceeds of future premiums. To insure solvency of the system, certain precautions must be taken by providers so that funds will be available to pay all submitted claims in the future. Should a provider redirect the premiums as part of a scheme of embezzlement, or even if the provider merely mismanages the present assets of the company, the future solvency of the system is in jeopardy."

2. Blackfeet National Bank v. Nelson, 171 F.3d 1237, 1242–43 (11th Cir.), cert.denied, 528 U.S. 1004 (1999) (quoting from Barnett Bank of Marion County, N.A. v. Gallagher, 43 F.3d 631, 636 (11th Cir. 1995)), overruled on other grounds sub nom. Barnett

It is natural to ascribe some larger benefit—"the prevention of coercion ...," for example—to measures protecting insurers against insolvency. (What possible connection is there between the insolvency risk and coercion?) Perhaps a better example of a larger benefit is this: If potential buyers of insurance are assured that they need not fear for any underwriter's financial collapse, either because government authorities forestall imprudent risk-taking by insurers or because there is a backstop insurer in place, then buyers will shop for insurance without regard for credit ratings, and will concentrate rather on matches between, on the one hand, coverage, service, and convenience, and on the other hand rates of charge and personal needs and preferences.

In point of fact, careful assessments of financial soundness are readily available, respecting thousands of insurers. One respected source is the A.M. Best Company; another is the Standard & Poor's Company.[3] But a great majority of insurance buyers are indifferent to credit ratings. Insurers who back up their obligations by buying reinsurance, and some other major commercial buyers, who do weigh this factor into their purchasing decisions, are the exception. Indeed, the published assessments are pitched chiefly toward potential *investors* in insurance companies.

Whatever the reasons, heavy public investments are continuously made in forestalling the insolvency of insurers. This is so even for insurers whose commitments are backed up by "guarantee associations" and the like—officially sponsored funds dedicated to honoring the commitments of failing insurers. (The Federal Deposit Insurance Corporation, which protects deposits in failed banks, is an analog.) Costs are incurred, naturally, in providing policyholders with guarantees in this form; and the costs are generally charged to insurers. *Question*: Does that fact make it easier or harder to explain official monitoring of the insurers for solvency?

Capacity

A major concern of insurance regulators is the "capacity" of major segments of the insurance industry. The branch of liability insurance called medical malpractice ("med-mal") insurance has suffered for want of capacity in recent times: premiums have risen, and insurers have withdrawn from some markets. A consequence that has been dreaded, and partly realized, is that practitioners of the healing arts would withdraw their services from the public; and that has led to public protests.

In the belief that immense recoveries in personal-injury suits are a significant cause of constriction in liability-insurance markets, Congress moved to curb them with the Class Action Fairness Act of 2005.[4] In the

Bank of Marion County, N.A. v. Nelson, 517 U.S. 25 (1996).

Much of the opinion in Barnett Bank v. Nelson appears below at p. 60 ff.

3. Detailed information about any number of insurers can be found on the Web. See, for example, LEXIS/Insurance/Company and Financial Information, listing Best's Compa-

ny Reports and Standard & Poor's Company Financials (together with news and corporate descriptions).

4. P.L. 109–2. The statute permits the removal of some state-court actions to federal district courts, including large class actions in which the contestants are citizens of different states. It also directs the district courts to

same belief, President Bush has called for a "cap" on what a patient can recover, in a malpractice action, on account of non-economic damages; *i.e.*, pain and suffering. (Doctors "should be focused on fighting illnesses, not fighting lawsuits.") Caps have been enacted in a number of states.

"The jury is still out on caps," according to one journal article.[5] One study indicated that "median annual premiums increased at a higher rate in states with caps [48%] than in states without caps [36%]." But that study was challenged by the Physicians Insurance Association of America, and other studies differ. Trial lawyers are generally opposed to caps.[6]

When an important coverage is not readily available in the private market, an official reaction may be expected in a form more direct than curtailing demand: it may be to support the supply. This might be done in various ways. One is to provide subventions to buyers, to sellers, or to both. Farmers might be subsidized when buying crop-loss insurance; property insurers offering flood-loss coverage might be subsidized. Even more directly, a legislature might simply demand that some set of insurers make the desired coverage available—with or without a concomitant rate adjustment. Or a legislature might put in place a government-operated issuer of the desired coverage.

In property/casualty lines there is a benchmark measure of an individual insurer's capacity; it is a ratio of net written premiums to the insurer's surplus. Regulators are reasonably comfortable, it is said, if that ratio is not greater than 2:1. Beyond that, the ratio is a red flag: some insurers must be putting their solvency at risk. According to a report for a recent year the overall ratio was less than one. That is a sign of ample capacity, and a red flag for investors.

Fairness

To state "fairness" as a distinct objective of insurance regulation is worrisome not only because the word is vague but also because it comprehends other objectives, such as reasonable access to coverage (capacity). Possibly fairness is best regarded as a residual goal, operative only when a regulatory measure cannot be accounted for otherwise. Even so, countless measures can be ascribed to the goal of fairness to buyers of insurance.

evaluate a proposed settlement with respect to certain payments to class counsel that the settlement may contemplate, and the contemplated benefit to class members.

5. *Statistical Analysis*, in Medical Malpractice Law & Strategy, Jan. 10, 2005 (J.M. Staller). This paper reports on a filing in Texas by the nation's largest med-mal insurer, in which it sought to explain why its premiums were rising sharply although the State had imposed a cap some months earlier.

6. *The New York Times* quoted, early in 2005, a law professor—one licensed as a physician—as follows:

There is a strong consensus among people who have really studied the issue that caps on damages would tend to keep costs down and make liability insurance more affordable for doctors. And there is a universal consensus that caps would do absolutely nothing to reduce medical errors or to compensate injured patients. If anything, caps on damages would make those problems worse.

Professor William Sage, as quoted in *Bush's Next Target: Malpractice Lawyers*, Feb. 27, 2005, Sec. 3, p. 1. (Steve Lohr).

Only one example is offered at this juncture. The Illinois Insurance Code sets out various terms for use in accident-and-sickness policies. One of them, on the subject of liquor, would excuse the insurer from liability for loss sustained "in consequence of the insured's being intoxicated". Now, it happened that an Illinois man bought an accidental-death policy containing a different term on the subject; this would excuse the insurer in the event of death occurring while the buyer's blood-alcohol level was elevated (0.1% or higher). In an action on the policy, the court condemned the policy term. It gave this instance:

> [I]f the insured was sitting on [his] porch drinking beer and was struck by a meteor, [he] would not be covered by the policy.

Not a loss caused by the beer, the court meant to say; yet not a covered loss under the policy as written. The court did not say in so many words that this result would be unfair. It did say that the result was discordant with the statute. That statute has little or no relation to maintaining anyone's solvency, or public access to accident insurance. It may indicate a concern about the use of liquor; but it was evidently written in a spirit of fairness.

Mergers and Acquisitions

In separate parts, this Note concerns two aspects of insurance-department control over the subject. It quotes from a governing statute that embodies at least two of the three objects of regulation indicated above: solvency and fairness, along with others.

i. *Job-related concerns*

This part provides successive bits of information about a proposed takeover by one insurer of another, and asks for views about the transaction. Further issues, about coverage-related concerns, are set out in part ii.

MetLife, a vast concern based in New York City, proposed to acquire from Citigroup Inc. another large concern based in Hartford, the Travelers Life and Annuity Company. (The price was said to be nearly $12 billion.)

The Connecticut Insurance Code confers powers on the State's insurance commissioner with respect to proposed mergers of insurers and acquisitions of one insurer by another. It establishes a procedure including an application, with disclosures, and a hearing. In Section 38a–132 of the General Statutes, subsection (a) describes the transactions concerned. Subsection (b) contains this provision:

> (1) The commissioner shall approve any merger or other acquisition of control referred to in subsection (a) . . . unless, after a public hearing, he finds that:

> (A) After the change of control, the domestic insurance company referred to in subsection (a) of this section would not be able to satisfy the requirements for the issuance of a license to write the line or lines of business for which it is presently licensed;

(B) The effect of the merger or other acquisition of control would be to substantially lessen competition of insurance in this state or tend to create a monopoly herein;

(C) The financial condition of any acquiring party is such as might jeopardize the financial stability of the insurance company or prejudice the interests of its policyholders;

(D) [*Set out below, in part ii.*]

(E) The competence, experience and integrity of those persons who would control the operation of the insurance company are such that it would not be in the interest of policyholders of the insurance company and of the public to permit the merger or other acquisition of control; or

(F) The acquisition is likely to be hazardous or prejudicial to those buying insurance.

(This provision was drawn, almost verbatim, from the Insurance Holding Company System Regulatory Act, as proposed by the National Association of Insurance Commissioners. See III NAIC Model Laws. . . .)

In April of 2005 it appeared that there would be a contested hearing about a proposed takeover of Travelers Life & Annuity by MetLife. The Connecticut Attorney General announced that he "would ask the [Commissioner] to deny approval . . . in light of MetLife's plan to eliminate hundreds of Hartford-based jobs at Travelers. . . ." *The New York Times*, April 14, 2005, C–18. Then the CEO of MetLife negotiated an agreement about jobs with Governor Rell. That did not appease objectors. The Mayor of Hartford weighed in, hoping for commitments by MetLife about jobs in the City, and about "philanthropic giving".

According to the *Times*, the Attorney General had never opposed a comparable application, and—according to someone in the Insurance Department—"to her knowledge [the Department] had never denied a merger application because of concern over job losses."

Question (a): In light of the statute quoted above, should the Connecticut Commissioner have withheld approval of the takeover?

Some years before the MetLife–Travelers problem arose, the Connecticut Department of Insurance had approved the acquisition of two Connecticut insurers—part of a fleet—by another, Aetna, Inc., over the objections of several individuals and groups. The objectors included an employee of Aetna and the "Connecticut Citizens Action Group". They sought to appeal; the Department moved to dismiss the appeal. The court made reference to the statute concerning decisions like that of the Department: "Any person aggrieved (may appeal)." The objectors contended that they were persona aggrieved because the proposed acquisition "may result in the loss of jobs at Aetna."

The court quoted as follows from an earlier case: "The fundamental test for determining aggrievement encompasses a well settled two fold determination: first, the party claiming aggrievement must successfully demonstrate a specific personal and legal interest in the subject matter of the decision, as distinguished from a general interest, such as is the concern of all members of the community as a whole. Second, the party claiming aggrievement must successfully establish that the specific personal and legal interest has been specially and injuriously affected by the decision."[7]

The court dismissed the appeal against Aetna's acquisitions. Citizens for Economic Opportunity v. Department of Insurance, 701 A.2d 340 (Conn. 1997). Relying on earlier authority, it said that the objecting employee had no legal right not to be laid off, and therefore "had no legally protected interest that was adversely affected by the decision." *Question (b)*: How does the decision about Aetna's acquisition bear on the matter of MetLife and Travelers?

From the opinion about Aetna's acquisitions it appears that the departmental decision included a provision by which that firm "committed" that it would not reduce its work force by more than five hundred employees. *Question (c)*: Assuming that the department insisted on this commitment, what ground might the department have had—other than a political one—for insisting?

In June of 2005 MetLife addressed the job-loss problem in communications to the Connecticut Commissioner of Insurance. On the 30th she approved the acquisition. Her order required that her office receive quarterly reports, over several years, about employment levels and other matters.

Question (d). Would the Commissioner have been warranted in requiring, as a condition on her approval, a commitment by MetLife that it maintain or increase the contributions made by Travelers to philanthropies approved in Connecticut?

ii. *Coverage-related concerns*

In the case about Aetna's acquisitions, objections were made by some of its policyholders. By reason of the acquisition, they contended, Aetna would reduce or eliminate their coverage. The fleet to be acquired was headed by U.S. Healthcare, Inc. These objectors presented some evidence that Aetna meant to adjust its coverages of health care, which they held. The ground of their objection was the following subparagraph of § 38a–132(b)(1):

> (D) The plans or proposals which the acquiring party has to liquidate the insurance company, sell its assets or consolidate or merge it with any person, or to make any other material change in its business or corporate structure or management, are unfair and unreasonable to policyholders of the insurance company and not in the public interest.

---

7. Light Rigging Co. v. Department of Public Utility Control, 592 A.2d 386 (Conn. 1991) (citations and internal quotation marks omitted).

The court answered that, though this provision required the commissioner to consider the interests of some policyholders, it did not require attention to the interests of *Aetna* policyholders.

The court went on to consider the possibility that the commissioner had "some generalized ... duty to consider the interests of the Aetna policyholders". Even so, the court said, these objectors had failed to charge Aetna with planning to impair their legally protected interests.

> There is no assertion, for example, that the decision will adversely affect the plaintiffs' existing contractual rights under their policies. Indeed, the evidence ... indicates that Aetna plans to reduce or eliminate insurance coverage only at the end of the coverage term—that is, at renewal time—when the company presumably would be entitled to do so with or without the benefit of the commissioner's decision. The point is that the plaintiffs have not demonstrated that the commissioner's decision adversely affected their rights under their policies. They are thus not aggrieved by it.[8]

Suppose that Aetna's application had disclosed a plan to curtail or withdraw coverages offered by a company it proposed to acquire. *Questions*: (*e*) Would the commissioner be warranted in disapproving if the plan was to alter coverages already written? (*f*) If the plan was to alter only offerings of new and renewed coverages, following the acquisition?

Stimulating Sales: Road–Injury Insurance

Road-injury insurance is something of a special case. In every state legislatures and courts have moved to increase the aggregate level of compensation for road injuries. A principal method is to stimulate demand for various coverages by applying compulsion, or at least persuasion, to motorists. Bismarck's Germany provided a precedent for compulsion, but the leading precedent there and in the United States concerned insurance for workplace injuries that employers were required to procure.

The legislative techniques employed in relation to road injuries are various; some of them seem whimsical, if not bizarre. A straightforward measure is to compel motorists to insure themselves against liability, or another mishap, occasioned by the use of a motor vehicle. That is a commonplace type of measure. The usual mode of compulsion is to withhold a license to drive, or the registration of a vehicle, unless a specified coverage is shown to be in place. A much less intrusive type of measure is to require that insurers doing motor-vehicle business in the state make available to the public this or that coverage.

The statutes exhibit some intermediate types of measure, more or less ingenious. One is to direct that, if a policy insures a particular risk—includes Coverage A, say—it must also insure another—Coverage B. (The typical example of "Coverage A" is motor-vehicle liability insurance.) A

---

8. Also: "[T]he court does not question the genuineness of the plaintiffs' concerns nor doubt their underlying reality. But the court—and the defendant commissioner of insurance—must deal with and enforce the law that exists, not the law that arguably might be."

second type of measure, less demanding, is to direct that when an insurer makes Coverage A available to a particular customer it must also make an offer of Coverage B to that customer.

Still another type of measure lies between the latter two, on the scale of intrusiveness. It is to direct that, when a customer's policy incorporates Coverage A, it also incorporates Coverage B *unless* the customer has executed a rejection of the latter, in writing. (This type is illustrated below in Chapter 9, on automobile insurance.)

B. Legislative and Administrative Regulation

1. The Insurance Department

Departmental Power:
Entrenchment in New York

The New York Department of Insurance occupies a strategic position in the regulation of insurance in the United States. In relation to comparable offices in most other states, it is heavily funded and strongly staffed. It has long experience in its duties; its imprimatur on an insurer ("admitted in New York") carries high prestige; and its rulings are a bellwether for other states.

Excerpts are given below from the opinion in Blue Cross and Blue Shield of Central New York, Inc. v. McCall, 674 N.E.2d 1124 (N.Y.1996). The opinion gives something of the history of the New York Department and describes its responsibilities in general terms. As described, these responsibilities are representative of those entrusted to insurance departments in other U.S. jurisdictions. The ruling in the case indicates, however, that the authority of the New York Department is exceptionally well entrenched—entrenched even against statutory encroachment.

Blue Cross and *Blue Shield* are names applied to major providers of "health insurance," across states and regions of the United States; the latter insures against hospitalization expense, and the former against other medical expenses. The providers are private, not-for-profit corporations, heavily regulated. In New York, they are organized under article 43 of the Insurance Law.

At one time the New York legislature sought to assign to the State Comptroller, as well as the State Superintendent of Insurance, power to conduct audits of firms like "the Blues". The Comptroller and the Superintendent agreed on a plan to coordinate their efforts, under which the Comptroller subpoenaed records of Blue Cross and Blue Shield of Central New York. These firms brought an action against the Comptroller for a determination that the subpoenas were unduly burdensome, and that the underlying statute violated a provision of the State constitution.[1]

---

1. Article V, § 1.

The trial court agreed that the subpoenas were "onerous and overly broad." On a first appeal, the Appellate Division of the Supreme Court ruled that the statute violated a section of the constitution which prohibits the assignment of administrative duties "not incidental to the specified functions" of the Comptroller. On a second appeal, the New York Court of Appeals affirmed, agreeing with the Appellate Division. (It did not rule on the overbreadth objection to the subpoenas.) The court wrote as follows about the regulation of insurance in New York.

. . .

The Superintendent of Insurance, as the head of the Insurance Department of the State of New York, has been given full authority to supervise and regulate the business of insurance in this State (Insurance Law § 201, 301). The responsibility to conduct independent management and financial audits of corporations organized under Insurance Law article 43 was given to the Superintendent of Insurance by legislation enacted in 1992. . . .

. . .

On appeal, defendants contend that the State Constitution expressly permits the assignment of the auditing duties permitted under the Insurance Law to the Comptroller. We disagree.

I

We note at the outset that the State Legislature has long been empowered to regulate the insurance industry through a variety of means (see, *Health Ins. Assn. v. Harnett, 44 N.Y.2d 302, 308*). Such regulation, even down to "the minutest particular in the interest of the public, has never been questioned" (*People v. Formosa, 131 N.Y. 478, 484*). Indeed, the organization of an insurance company and the conduct of the business of writing insurance is not a right but a privilege granted by the State subject to the conditions imposed by it to promote the public welfare (*Health Ins. Assn. at 309*).

Not coincidentally, the administrative agency with regulatory authority for the insurance industry is the Insurance Department of the State of New York (see, *Formosa, 131 N.Y., at 483* [noting that a "department of the state government has been constituted to supervise" and regulate those engaged in the business of insurance]). The head of that Department, the Superintendent of Insurance, has been granted " 'broad power to interpret, clarify, and implement the legislative policy' " underlying the provisions of the Insurance Law (*Matter of New York Pub. Interest Research Group v. New York State Dept. of Ins., 66 N.Y.2d 444, 448,* citing *Ostrer v. Schenck, 41 N.Y.2d 782, 785*).

Article 3 of the Insurance Law outlines the general "Administrative and Procedural Provisions" for the Superintendent. Pursuant to his administrative powers, the Superintendent may make any "order affecting any insurer, insurance agent, insurance broker or other person subject to the provisions of this chapter" (Insurance Law § 302). The Legislature has also decreed that insurance businesses of a certain size must submit to the office of the Superintendent an annual financial statement audited by an independent certified public accountant (Insurance Law § 307). The Superintendent may also make an examination into the affairs of any insurer (Insurance Law § 309; cf., *Schenck v. Executive Life Ins. Co., 74 Misc.2d 12, aff'd 42 A.D.2d 540)* and must be given access "at all reasonable hours to the books, records, files, securities and other documents" of the insurer which are relevant to the examination (Insurance Law § 310[a][2]). [The court took note of evidence that the plaintiffs were audited by the Insurance Department every three years.]

[The court traced the history of the Department, observing that it was created in 1859, and given powers broken out of those of the Comptroller. According to the court, the position of the defendants found support neither in the history nor the plain language of the constitutional provision in question.]

III

Defendants make several arguments based upon practical concerns and public policy. For example, defendants argue that the Comptroller has substantial experience in auditing Medicaid and other State-sponsored insurance programs. Defendants offer no explanation as to why funding suballocated to the Comptroller may not be retained by the Insurance Department to perform the auditing functions it has performed for over a century.

Defendants also argue that this Court should simply defer to the Legislature's law-making power; that there is no longer a "bright line" distinction between the "public" and "private" sectors; and that "the development of New York's health care delivery system and how services are paid for is now a matter of significant governmental concern." Defendants' arguments essentially boil down to a single premise: since the State is empowered to audit plaintiffs, the State auditor should be allowed to do it. Defendants do not explain how or why any of these reasons would overcome a plainly expressed constitutional prohibition. . . . Simply, the Legislature may not delegate administrative duties of the Insurance Department relating to article 43 audits of private insurers when such duties are clearly administrative and not incidental to the primary function of the Comptroller.

Case report: ALLSTATE INS. CO. v. SERIO, 774 N.E.2d 180 (N.Y. 2002). In this case the New York Insurance Department suffered an unusual rebuff from the court. Aside from Allstate, one of the plaintiffs was GEICO Casualty Company. It proposed an arrangement with its policyholders by which their premiums for collision coverage would be reduced by 10%—and premiums for comprehensive coverage by 5%—if they would acquiesce in the following "preferred repairer promotion":

> [Y]ou agree with us that, in the event of a covered loss resulting in damage to your auto, you request that we recommend repair facilities. . . . You agree with us that covered repairs will be completed at a repair shop recommended by us. . . . If you do not have your auto

repaired at a repair facility recommended by us, you will be paid the amount of the estimate prepared by us and/or the preferred repairer.

GEICO submitted this plan to the New York Insurance Department for review and approval. The Department rejected it, relying on § 2610(b) of the N.Y. Insurance Law. With respect to claims for collision or comprehensive loss to a motor vehicle, the statute provides that

> In processing any such claim . . .[2] the insurer shall not, unless expressly requested by the insured, recommend or suggest repairs be made to such vehicle in a particular place or shop or by a particular concern.

In a federal-court action against the Acting Superintendent of Insurance (Sergio), GEICO won an injunction against the enforcement of the statute.

On an appeal, questions were certified to the New York Court of Appeals, including this one: "Under § 2610(b), can the Department of Insurance prohibit the 'preferred repairer' clause proposed by GEICO for its automobile Casualty Manual?" The court answered "no". In *Allstate/GEICO* the court said (Smith, J.): "The Department's rejection of GEICO's proposed preferred repairer promotion was based on restrictions not supported by section 2610(b). The promotion does not require that an insurance company request, recommend or suggest a particular repair shop while an insurer has an active claim, but rather requires a prospective claimant to agree to use a preferred repairer for a reduced contract fee. Thus, the Department's rejection of the proposal on section 2610(b) grounds is not sustainable."

NOTE

Other Matters. Answering other questions, the court disapproved a proceeding by the Department against Allstate. In its offices, Allstate had advertised a program identifying preferred repair shops and recommending them to customers who, on being asked whether or not they had a choice, said they did not. The court declined to answer a further question about § 2610(b): whether or not it amounted to a regulation of commercial speech in violation of the State constitution.

QUESTIONS

(1) In *GEICO* the court declined to consider the Department's suggestion that its action was warranted by subsection (a) of § 2610, partly because the court had not been asked about that. Considering that provision (set out in the footnote[3]), do you see merit in the suggestion?

(2) Why would an insurer in GEICO's position want to steer a policyholder to a particular repair shop?

(3) Is the decision in *Allstate/GEICO* consistent with the broad generalizations in *Blue Cross and Blue Shield*, above?

---

2. The claim being one, that is, other than one solely involving window glass.

3. Whenever a motor vehicle collision or comprehensive loss shall have been suffered by an insured, no insurer providing collision or comprehensive coverage therefor shall require that repairs be made to such vehicle in a particular place or shop or by a particular concern.

2.   Regulation of Contract Terms

Watson v. United Services Automobile Ass'n

Minnesota Supreme Court, 1997.
566 N.W.2d 683.

Elizabeth Watson brought this action for fire loss to a mobile home, of which she was a joint tenant. She sought recovery on a fire policy naming as the insured persons both her and her estranged husband, Keith Watson. (At the time of the fire she did not live in the home; and the Watsons were divorced shortly after the fire.) A jury found that Keith, the other joint tenant, had "participated in, arranged for, or aided or abetted the setting of the fire." According to a policy "exclusion" inserted by the insurer (USAA),

We do not insure for loss caused directly or indirectly by . . .

> Intentional Loss, meaning any loss arising out of any act committed:
>
> (1) by or at the direction of an insured; and
>
> (2) with the intent to cause a loss.

The trial court entered judgment for the insurer. It did so "reluctantly" and urged reversal on appeal.

The court of appeals obliged, and directed the entry of an order allowing Elizabeth to recover her proportionate share of the insured loss. That court believed that the policy as written was at odds with the Minnesota standard fire insurance policy contained in Minn. Stat. § 65A.01. The statutory form excludes losses from acts committed by *"the* insured", and not (as the policy did) by *"an* insured". USAA appealed.

■ Anderson, J.

. . .

A.

[The court agreed with those below that "the 'an insured' language of USAA's policy unambiguously bars coverage for innocent co-insured spouses."]

B.   Statute–Based Theory

But the conclusion that USAA's policy language is unambiguous does not end our inquiry. An emerging theory of recovery for innocent co-insured spouses, a statute-based theory, adds a second step to the contractual analysis. Under the statute-based theory, if an insurance policy provision unambiguously excludes coverage for innocent co-insured spouses, the court must then look to the state's statutory standard fire insurance policy. If the exclusion of coverage contained in the insurance policy conflicts with the level of protection provided in the statutory standard fire insurance policy, the court will hold the insurance policy unenforceable. To date, courts in Michigan, Louisiana, and Georgia have adopted this statute-based theory. See Osbon v. National Union Fire Ins. Co., 632 So.2d 1158, 1161

(La.1994) [and other cases, two of them cited in the footnote that follows]. ... Under the statute-based theory, courts have remedied a conflict between an insurance policy and the statutory standard fire insurance policy by reforming the insurance policy to provide at least the level of coverage provided for in the statute. See, *e.g.,* *Osbon,* 632 So.2d at 1161....[5]

... [W]e consider it an open question whether insurance policy provisions excluding innocent co-insured spouses from recovery are viable under Minnesota law. We conclude that the statute-based theory is the proper approach to follow in resolving this question.

C. Minnesota Standard Fire Insurance Policy

We turn, then, to the question of whether USAA's policy conflicts with the Minnesota standard fire insurance policy. The Minnesota standard fire insurance policy is contained in Minn. Stat. § 65A.01. The statute was enacted to "do away with the evils arising from the insertion in policies of conditions ingeniously worded which restricted the liability of the insurer and gave the insured less protection than he might naturally suppose he was getting under his contract." Heim v. American Alliance Ins. Co. of New York, 180 N.W. 225, 226 (Minn. 1920). Because the statute has a remedial purpose, it must be broadly construed....

Minnesota Statutes section 65A.01 was intended to secure uniformity in fire insurance policies.... Use of the statutory form is mandatory, and its provisions may not be omitted, changed, or waived. This principle is reflected in the statute's "conformity clause," which states:

> No policy or contract of fire insurance shall be made, issued or delivered by any insurer ... on any property in this state, unless it shall provide the specified coverage and conform as to all provisions, stipulations, and conditions, with such form of policy, except as provided in ... statutes containing specific requirements that are inconsistent with the form of this policy.

Minn. Stat. § 65A.01, subd. 1. This court has held that when an insurance policy provision is in direct conflict with a statute regulating the insurance industry, the statute's conformity clause operates to substitute the statutory provisions for the policy provision. Atwater Creamery Co. v. Western Nat. Mut. Ins. Co., 366 N.W.2d 271, 275 (Minn.1985).

---

5. The Michigan courts provide an example of the statute-based theory in operation. In Morgan v. Cincinnati Ins. Co., the Michigan Supreme Court contractually analyzed a provision of the Michigan standard fire insurance policy which stated that the policy shall be void if "the insured" commits fraud, and held that the statutory policy did not bar recovery for insureds who are innocent of fraud. 307 N.W.2d 53, 54–55 (Mich. 1981) (citing M.C.L.A. § 500.2832). Subsequently, in Ponder v. Allstate Ins. Co., [729 F.Supp. 60 (E.D.Mich. 1990), the court] interpreting Michigan law held that an insurance policy's unambiguous concealment or fraud provision barring recovery as to "any insured" committing fraud must be reformed to conform with the fraud clause in the Michigan standard fire insurance policy. Id. at 61–62 (citing M.C.L.A. § 500.2832). Thereafter, in Borman v. State Farm Fire & Cas. Co., [521 N.W.2d 266 (1994)], the Michigan Supreme Court held that a policy's intentional acts and concealment or fraud provisions using the language "you or any person insured" and "you [and/or] any other insured" were both in conflict with Michigan's standard fire insurance policy, and, therefore, were void. Id. at 267 n.4, 269 (citing M.C.L.A. § 500.2832 (repealed 1990)).

We agree with the court of appeals that the Minnesota standard fire insurance policy guarantees a minimum level of coverage that supersedes any attempt to limit coverage to less than the statutory minimum.... Insurance companies may, however, incorporate additional or different terms into their policies that offer more coverage than the statutory minimum. The statute provides conditions under which insurance companies may incorporate additional or different terms into their policies:

> Any policy or contract ... may be issued without incorporating the exact language of the Minnesota standard fire insurance policy, provided: Such policy or contract shall, with respect to the peril of fire, afford the insured all the rights and benefits of the Minnesota standard fire insurance policy and such additional benefits as the policy provides; ... such policy is complete as to its terms of coverage; and, the commissioner is satisfied that such policy or contract complies with the provisions hereof.

Minn. Stat. § 65A.01, subd. 1; see also Fireman's Fund Ins. Co. v. Vermes Credit Jewelry, 185 F.2d 142, 144 (8th Cir.1950)....

USAA argues that Elizabeth Watson cannot recover under the USAA policy because the policy contains an "intentional loss" provision excluding coverage for any loss arising out of any act committed "by or at the direction of an insured," and Keith Watson, an insured, intentionally caused the loss. Because the Minnesota standard fire insurance policy does not contain a parallel "intentional loss" provision, USAA's "intentional loss" provision is an additional term. Therefore, we will uphold USAA's "intentional loss" provision only if it affords the insured all the rights and benefits of the Minnesota standard fire insurance policy or offers additional benefits which provide more coverage to the insured than the statutory minimum.... We conclude that USAA's "intentional loss" provision, insofar as it excludes coverage for innocent co-insured spouses, is at odds with the rights and benefits of the Minnesota standard fire insurance policy.

Even though the Minnesota standard fire insurance policy does not contain a specific "intentional loss" provision, it does contain other provisions dealing with policy exclusions for intentional acts. For example, the "concealment or fraud provision" of the Minnesota standard fire insurance policy states:

> This entire policy shall be void if, whether before a loss, *the insured* has willfully, or after a loss, the insured has willfully and with intent to defraud, concealed or misrepresented any material fact or circumstance concerning this insurance or the subject thereof, or the interests of the insured therein.

Minn. Stat. § 65A.01, subd. 3 (emphasis added). Another provision states that the insurance company shall not be liable for a loss occurring "while the hazard is increased by any means within the control or knowledge of *the insured*...." Id. (emphasis added). We held in Hogs Unlimited [v.Farm Bureau Mut. Ins. Co., 401 N.W.2d 381 (1987)] that a policy containing the "standard fraud provision" using the "the insured" language of Minn.

Stat. § 65A.01, subd. 3, voids the policy only as to "guilty" insureds and not as to innocent co-insureds.... Thus, we conclude that the legislature's use of "the insured" in the Minnesota standard fire insurance policy evinces a general intent to compensate an innocent co-insured spouse despite the intentional acts of the other insured spouse.

Courts in other states have adopted similar reasoning. [The court reviewed the decisions in *Borman* (Michigan) and *Osbon* (Louisiana), above.]

It is settled law in Minnesota that an insurance policy should be construed as a whole, with all doubts concerning the meaning of language to be resolved in favor of the insured.... Given that the Minnesota standard fire insurance policy must be broadly construed, see *Heim*, 180 N.W. at 227–28, it is reasonable to interpret the statute as providing coverage for innocent co-insured spouses generally and prohibiting language which purports to deny coverage to innocent co-insured spouses. Accordingly, we conclude that the "intentional loss" provision in the USAA policy issued to Elizabeth and Keith Watson conflicts with the Minnesota standard fire insurance policy. We hold that, to the extent that USAA's policy purports to exclude innocent co-insured spouses from coverage, it must be reformed to comply with the Minnesota standard fire insurance policy.

III.

USAA additionally argues that its insurance policy must be valid because the Commissioner of Commerce approved it. Minnesota Statutes section 65A.01, subdivision 1 does provide that approval of the commissioner is a prerequisite to the incorporation of additional or different terms into insurance policies. However, a provision in an insurance policy contrary to the Minnesota standard fire insurance policy cannot be permitted to stand even if the commissioner approved it. The commissioner is an administrative official with no power to alter the meaning and intention of the language of the legislature. See *Ponder*, 729 F.Supp. at 62. We conclude that USAA's argument lacks merit.

We remand to the district court for action in conformity with this opinion.

Affirmed.

NOTES

(1) *Question*. USAA did not try to persuade the jury that Elizabeth was complicit with Keith in arranging the fire. Supposing that it had some evidence that she was, did it make a serious tactical error in failing to present that evidence to the jury? (She testified that she was not near the scene when the fire occurred; but Keith testified that he was not.)

(2) *Insurance Departments and Reasonable Expectations*. Part III of the *Watson* opinion throws some light on the roles of legislatures, courts and administrative agencies in protecting the interests of policyholders. In this connection the doctrine of reasonable expectations is of special importance. To speak briefly, it is that the

objectively reasonable expectations of applicants and intended beneficiaries regarding the terms of insurance contracts will be honored, even though painstaking study of the policy provisions would have negated those expectations. (Chapter 3 examines the doctrine in some detail.)

The doctrine is a creature of the courts, according to a general understanding. Might a state insurance department properly develop its own doctrine of reasonable expectations? A reference on this question is an action brought against the Insurance Commissioner for the State of Maine. A proposal of new forms for auto liability insurance, made by the company, had been blocked by various objections in the State's insurance department. As to a form essential to the proposal, the department said: "It is misleading in that the coverage afforded by it is so limited as to be beyond the reasonable comprehension of the average policyholder...."[1] The company brought an action to vindicate its proposal. The action failed, on review of the departmental objections. American Fidelity Co. v. Mahoney, 174 A.2d 446 (1961). But the court sustained only four of the twenty particular findings adverse to the proposal. By inference, it admonished the Commissioner against overstepping the legislative bounds on his authority. "The administrative authority of the defendant as an executive officer is restricted to requisite fact finding and to needful regulation delimited within the policy, standard and rule affirmatively established for his guidance by the Legislature." Id. at 449–50. The opinion suggests that the Commissioner had taken a paternalistic attitude toward buyers of insurance in disregard of that guidance. "The Legislature has not relieved policyholders from the pains and consequences of reading and choosing such policies as are not reprehensibly misleading or amenable to unfair construction. Such policyholders must continue to be presumed by the ordinary rules of law to know the contents of their policies whether the policies are read or not." Id. at 450.

The opinion can be read to support any of these propositions:

(i) The department's authority to raise objections was restricted by legislative directives about the grounds for disapproving proposed forms.

(ii) No objection could be sustained unless it was grounded in an explicit legislative charge to the department.

(iii) The department's objections could be sustained only if the department could support them with empirical evidence of their merit.

None of these constraints operates on the courts, it seems, when they object to policy terms on the ground that they impair the reasonable expectations of policyholders.

PROBLEM

Peter Cruz, Jr. and the State Farm Mutual Automobile Ins. Co. confronted one another over a claim he made for injuries he suffered while driving a car licensed by

---

1. The American Fidelity proposal comprised a basic policy providing liability coverage well short of that almost universally provided in family auto policies, and an endorsement, to be offered separately, that would bring the pair of forms into approximate identity with the broader, familiar form. (Only with the endorsement would an individual's policy insure liabilities incurred by friends and relations while using the individual's car with permission.) The basic policy was to bear, on the cover, a red-letter legend including this caution: "This is not a Standard Automobile Policy.... It protects the individuals, named in the policy, against liability due to their operation of an automobile but in general does not cover operation of the insureds' automobiles by others."

The issues in *American Fidelity* appear to have been superseded by the enactment in Maine of compulsion on motorists to carry liability insurance.

Michigan and insured by State Farm. His claim was, in part, for "PIP" (personal-injury protection) benefits, as provided for in the policy. By applicable law—that of Michigan—cars licensed there must provide for these benefits; the State's No–Fault Insurance Act so requires. State Farm resisted, relying on a policy provision under the heading "REPORTING A CLAIM—INSURED'S DUTIES," as follows:

> The person making the claim also shall answer questions under oath when asked by anyone we name, as often as we reasonably ask, and sign copies of the answers.

This was referred to as an "EUO" provision: "examination under oath." Cruz rejected repeated demands that he submit to an EUO.

In Cruz's action against State Farm he was denied relief in the trial court, but prevailed on a first appeal. On a further appeal, the Michigan Supreme Court had good words to say about EUO provisions.[2] On the other hand, it faced the fact that the State's No–Fault Insurance Act contains various provisions about the processing of PIP claims, and says nothing about EUOs. It provides that the insurers "may require written notice to be given as soon as practicable after an accident involving a motor vehicle...." Further, that "personal protection insurance benefits are payable as loss accrues," that payment is overdue "if not paid within 30 days after an insurer receives reasonable proof of the fact and of the amount of loss sustained," and that overdue payments bear interest at the rate of twelve percent a year. State Farm conceded that Cruz had given it proof of his claim as required by the statute.

The court considered three possible rulings: (a) that the EUO provision was enforceable, (b) that it was not, and (c) that it was a permissible "discovery tool" for State Farm, but could not be invoked to circumvent the payment obligation stated in the statute. The case prompted three opinions, including a partial dissent. Cruz v. State Farm Mutual Auto. Ins. Co., 648 N.W.2d 591 (Mich.2002).

On the facts given, which of the three rulings has most appeal?

3. Regulation of Rates

"Evil" at a low price. Review American Fidelity Company v. Mahoney, as described in Note 2, p. 48 above. There the court spoke in favor of the limited-coverage form proposed by the company, saying that its price would

---

2. "Insurers, ... aware of their fiduciary duty to others in the insurance pool to not dissipate the pool's insurance fund reserves by paying unwarranted benefits, developed systems for processing [claims] that included, as in this case, a contractual right to demand an EUO.

"Examination under oath provisions, which require the insured to answer questions about the accident and damages claimed, existed in many types of insurance policies long before the advent of no-fault automobile insurance. See *Gordon v. St. Paul Fire & Marine Ins. Co.,* 197 Mich. 226, 230, 163 N.W. 956 (1917). Their purpose, in part, was to enable insurers to gather facts so as to discover and eliminate fraudulent insurance claims. *Id.* The general difficulty of determining when a claim was not valid has been described in scholarly writings in the insurance field as being of 'staggering proportions.' [Fn.—Cf. Comment, Property insurance: A call for increased use of examinations under oath for the detection and deterrence of fraudulent insurance claims, 97 Dickinson L.R. 329 (1993).] Given this problem, and the potential ability of EUOs and other discovery vehicles to address it, EUOs in policies have been viewed favorably by courts. *Gordon, supra* at 230. Furthermore, as beneficial as EUOs and similar discovery vehicles have been when employed in policies that may be purchased at the insured's discretion, their potential value is even greater when the coverage is, as in this case, mandated by law." [Some citations and footnotes omitted from this paragraph.—*Eds.*]

make it appealing to persons in the "less endowed financial group," so that offering the form might foster the desirable object of increasing purchases of auto liability insurance. Recall that in Watson v. USAA the court spoke (quoting) of evils that arose from policy terms "ingeniously worded which restricted the liability of the insurer and gave the insured less protection than he might naturally suppose he was getting under his contract." Who is best fitted to decide that, in a given case, the evil outweighs the merit of moderating the cost of insuring? Legislatures, administrative agencies, or courts?

ADJUSTMENTS FOR MOTORISTS

The two items that follow concern rates for automobile insurance. They illustrate a variety of measures designed to promote safe driving practices and to moderate the cost of insurance for motorists who practice them.

. . .

Driver Education

BULLETIN NO.: 99–11

TO: ALL INSURERS WRITING PRIVATE PASSENGER AUTOMOBILE INSURANCE IN NEW JERSEY

FROM: JAYNEE LAVECCHIA, COMMISSIONER, DEPARTMENT OF BANKING AND INSURANCE

RE: DEFENSIVE DRIVING RATE REDUCTIONS N.J.S.A.11:3–24.

N.J.S.A. 17:33B–45.1 (the "Act"), enacted on January 5, 1996, requires every insurer writing private passenger automobile insurance to offer an appropriate rate reduction to their insureds for the successful completion of an approved defensive driving course. The required premium reduction is available to the insured beginning with the next succeeding policy period after the date of completion of the . . . course and is applied for a three-year period or unless the insured accumulates four or more motor vehicle points or the insured's driver's license is suspended. . . . The Department is issuing this bulletin to remind private passenger insurers of the continuing availability of the defensive driving course discount. . . . Administrative rules governing the Defensive Driving Discount can be found at N.J.A.C 11:3–24. . . . The defensive driving discount only applies to defensive driving courses approved by the New Jersey Division of Motor Vehicle Service. . . . A list of entities offering approved defensive driving courses is attached and updates appear on the Department's home page: www.naic. org/nj/filings. . . .

This Bulletin also reminds insurers that the defensive driving course discount should be a minimum of five percent and is to apply to the base premium before expense fees are added for bodily injury liability, property damage liability, personal injury protection and collision coverages. The defensive driving course discount should be applied at new business inception or upon renewal after the successful completion of the course and shall be available for an insured that has taken a defensive driving course for a period of not more than three years per driving course taken. [Two examples are given, one of which appears in the footnote.[1]]

9/27/99

/s/Jaynee LaVecchia, Commissioner

. . .

A Seat-belt Law

By an act effective in 1994,[2] the Massachusetts legislature has required that—with some exceptions—operators of and passengers in private passenger motor vehicles wear safety belts, properly adjusted and fastened. Two further provisions of the act[3] (not codified) are as follows:

> Section 6. The secretary of consumer affairs shall direct the commissioner of insurance to evaluate the effectiveness of this act and frequency of bodily injury claims during the year following the effective date of this act and report its findings and recommendations to the general court.

> Section 7. The commissioner of insurance shall mandate a minimum five percent reduction in bodily injury premiums if the observed safety belt use rate among all occupants equals or exceeds fifty percent one year after this law has been in effect. Annual surveys of belt use shall be conducted by the governor's highway safety bureau. . . .

> Annual safety belt survey results shall be a criterion in all future regulatory actions regarding bodily injury premiums. If at any time the safety belt use rate in the commonwealth exceeds the national average, additional reductions in bodily injury premiums shall take effect.

Action taken by the commissioner to implement this directive was contested by the Massachusetts Automobile Insurers Bureau (AIB) in Automobile Insurers Bureau of Massachusetts v. Commissioner of Insurance, 718 N.E.2d 830 (Mass.1999). An excerpt from the opinion is as follows.

. . .

The Massachusetts Commissioner of Insurance (commissioner) established rates for private passenger automobile insurance for the year 1999. For judicial review of the decision, a justice reported complaints made by

---

1. Example A: An insured's three year discount for successful completion of a defensive driving course ends with the January 10, 1999 policy renewal. Insured successfully completed another approved defensive driving course on July 30, 1999. The insured's policy renews on January 10, 2000. The insured is entitled to a discount when the poli-cy renews on January 10, 2000 and again on January 10, 2001 and January 10, 2002 as long as the insured has not accumulated four or more motor vehicle points or the individual's driver's license is not suspended.

2. Mass. Ann. Laws ch. 90, § 13A.

3. Chapter 387 of St. 1993.

three insurance companies ("Alliance") and by two trade associations, one of these being the Automobile Insurance Bureau of Massachusetts ("AIB").

. . .

. . . The annual safety belt survey relied on by the parties and the commissioner was conducted by the Boston University School of Public Health for the Governor's highway safety bureau (B.U. Survey).

In the main rate case, no party requested an adjustment to the loss pure premiums to reflect the impact of the Act. Based on the B.U. Survey, which was admitted in evidence,[6] the seat belt usage rate in the Commonwealth did not exceed the national average. In her decision, the commissioner determined that the conditions that would require an adjustment based on seat belt usage were not present and made no adjustment.

This decision is consistent with the commissioner's decisions in the prior four years. In 1995, one year after the law took effect, seat belt usage was at fifty-two per cent, and the commissioner made the required downward adjustment in her 1995 and 1996 rate decisions. In both the 1997 and 1998 rate cases, no party requested an adjustment to the rates to reflect the impact of the Act and, after considering the B.U. Survey, the commissioner determined that the conditions that would require an adjustment based on seat belt usage were not present, and she made no adjustment.

The AIB argues that the commissioner's decision was not based on substantial evidence, and that the commissioner failed to make findings on any decrease in seat belt usage. We reject these arguments. It was reasonable for the commissioner to conclude that, based on the B.U. Survey, which only showed a slight decrease in seat belt usage, and the recommendations of the parties, no adjustment should be made. All the commissioner was required to do under the Act was consider the survey results as a "criterion." St. 1993, c. 387, § 7. She did this.[7] The Act does not constrain her judgment in how to use the results, and, on the information presented, it did not obligate her to make an adjustment.

QUESTIONS

Some questions suggested by the foregoing items are these:

(1) Given that the legislatures in Massachusetts and New Jersey had good ideas about differentiating among motorists, why was there a need for legislation? Issuers of insurance are ingenious about varying rates to reflect differences of risk (see Allstate Ins. Co. v. Serio, p. 43 above). And competition drives them to implement these ideas. Would you not expect insurers to offer discounts to motorists exhibiting care and skill without being compelled to do so? Is there a difference

---

6. The AIB made its advisory filing before the B.U. Survey was admitted in evidence. In its advisory filing, the AIB recommended that no adjustment be made to loss pure premiums based on seat belt usage. The B.U. Survey was later admitted in evidence and showed a slight decline in usage from fifty-three per cent to fifty-one per cent.

7. The AIB also contends that the commissioner rejected the seat belt model; violated the Act that requires usage to be a criterion; and deviated from prior rulings without any explanation. These contentions are without merit. The commissioner admitted the B.U. Survey in evidence and specifically referred to it in her decision. . . .

between seat-belt use and safe-driver courses that would deter an insurer from using one of them as a factor in underwriting?

(2) Assuming that the "B.U. Survey" was accurate in finding that the extent of seat-belt use in Massachusetts did not exceed the national average, is it clear that the seat-belt statute failed of its purpose? Presumably it did, if the purpose was simply to make the "buckle up" rate in Massachusetts exceptional across the nation. What other purposes occur to you?

---

4.   Federal–State Interfaces
PREEMPTION AND REVERSE PREEMPTION:
The McCarran Act, and other statutes

When Congress has exercised its constitutionally delegated authority to set aside the laws of a state, the Supremacy Clause of the Constitution requires that courts follow federal law, not state law.[8] Congress may, that is "preempt" any state law by exercising its constitutional powers.

But insurance is a special case. The general and central functions of regulating the business are lodged in the several states and regions of the United States. "The control of all types of insurance companies and contracts has been primarily a state function since the States came into being."[9] Congress has not preempted state regulatory regimes. In 1999 Congress declared that—subject to some qualifications[10]—"[t]he insurance activities of any person . . . shall be functionally regulated by the States."[11]

Naturally, the business is affected by any number of specific provisions in the United States Code. On the other hand, for more than half a century Congress has maintained its freedom to legislate broadly without fear of disrupting the core of state rules regulating the insurance business. Congress declared that freedom in the so-called McCarran–Ferguson Act ("McCarran"—15 U.S.C. § 1011 *et seq*.). The materials in this section concern chiefly that statute and other federal statutes that have been thought to be affected by it.

a.   The McCarran Act

Critical parts of the McCarran text are set out in the footnote.[12] "[T]he Act contains a broad declaration of congressional policy that the continued

---

8.   This is a paraphrase of language in Barnett Bank of Marion County, N.A. v. Nelson, 517 U.S. 25 (1996) (p. 60 below).

9.   Wilburn Boat Co. v. Fireman's Fund Ins. Co., 348 U.S. 310, 315 (1955).

10.   The qualifications appear in § 104 of the Gramm–Leach–Bliley Act of 1999. That section permits affiliations between and associations of insurers and depository institutions, according to the Act. Further particulars of that Act appear at p. 70 ff., below.

11.   Section 301 of the Gramm–Leach–Bliley Act.

12.   *Regulation by State law; Federal law relating specifically to insurance; applicability of certain Federal laws after June 30, 1948* [section 2 of the Act]

(a) State regulation. The business of insurance, and every person engaged therein, shall be subject to the laws of the several States which relate to the regulation or taxation of such business.

regulation of insurance by the States is in the public interest, and that silence on the part of Congress should not be construed to impose any barrier to continued regulation of insurance by the States."[13] A main provision of the Act forbids, it has been said, "construing a federal statute to 'impair any law enacted by any State for the purpose of regulating the business of insurance ... unless such Act specifically relates to the business of insurance.'"[14] The "unless" clause is a natural focus of power struggles. In a case in which the Supreme Court applied the clause, it devoted a separate paragraph to each component: *specifically, relates to,* and *the business of insurance.*[15]

In that case the Court described the circumstances leading to the enactment of McCarran, as follows: "Just prior to the law's enactment, this Court, in *United States* v. *South-Eastern Underwriters Assn.*, 322 U.S. 533 (1944), held that a federal antitrust law, the Sherman Act, applied to the business of insurance. The Sherman Act's highly general language said nothing specifically about insurance. See 15 U.S.C. § 1 (forbidding every 'contract, combination ... or conspiracy, in restraint of trade or commerce among the several States'). The Sherman Act applied only to activities in or affecting interstate commerce. *Hopkins* v. *United States*, 171 U.S. 578, 586 (1898). Many lawyers and insurance professionals had previously thought (relying, in part, on this Court's opinion in *Paul* v. *Virginia*, 75 U.S. 168, 8 Wall. 168, 183 (1869), and other cases) that the issuance of an insurance policy was not a 'transaction of commerce,' and therefore fell outside the Sherman Act's scope. *South-Eastern Underwriters* told those professionals that they were wrong about interstate commerce, and that the Sherman Act did apply. And *South-Eastern Underwriters'* principle meant, consequently, that other generally phrased congressional statutes might also apply to the issuance of insurance policies, thereby interfering with state regulation of insurance in similarly unanticipated ways. In reaction to *South-Eastern Underwriters*, Congress 'moved quickly,' enacting the McCarran–Ferguson Act 'to restore the supremacy of the States in the realm of insurance regulation.' *Department of Treasury* v. *Fabe*, 508 U.S. 491, 500 (1993)."[16]

(b) Federal regulation. No Act of Congress shall be construed to invalidate, impair, or supersede any law enacted by any State for the purpose of regulating the business of insurance, or which imposes a fee or tax upon such business, unless such Act specifically relates to the business of insurance: Provided, That after June 30, 1948, the Act of July 2, 1890, as amended, known as the Sherman Act [15 USCS §§ 1 *et seq.*], and the Act of October 15, 1914, as amended, known as the Clayton Act, and the Act of September 26, 1914, known as the Federal Trade Commission Act, as amended [15 USCS §§ 41 *et seq.*], shall be applicable to the business of insurance to the extent that such business is not regulated by State law.

15 U.S.C. § 1012 (59 Stat. 34, as amended, 61 Stat. 448).

13. Wilburn Boat Co. v. Fireman's Fund Ins. Co., n.9 above, at 319.

14. Doe v. Mutual of Omaha Ins. Co., p. 77 below, quoting from 15 U.S.C. § 1012(b).

15. Barnett Bank of Marion County, N.A. v. Nelson, n.8 above.

16. For other accounts, see both opinions in St. Paul Fire & Marine Ins. Co. v. Barry, 438 U.S. 531 (1978).

Congress has maintained McCarran in force since 1945, notwithstanding repeated urgings to repeal it. Moreover, Congress has supplemented the statute from time to time, when enacting statutes that broadly regulate activities connected with insurance. For example, there is a "saving" clause in the statute known as ERISA—the Employee Retirement Income Security Act of 1974. In § 502 of the statute, subsection (a) is a "preemption" clause: ERISA provisions "shall supersede . . . State laws" to the extent that those laws "relate to any employee benefit plan." Subsection (b) includes the saving clause; it exempts from preemption "any law of any State which regulates insurance." The latter provision has an obvious kinship with McCarran. The Supreme Court has repeatedly remarked on that, although recently it has stepped away from these remarks. Compare UNUM Life Ins. Co. v. Ward (p. 74 below) with Kentucky Association of Health Plans v. Miller (p. 73 below).

Concert among Insurers: "Boycott"?

Some justices of the Supreme Court have described this way the remarkable effect of the McCarran Act on anticompetitive actions by insurers:

> In passing the [] Act, Justice Stewart argued, "Congress plainly wanted to allow the States to authorize anticompetitive practices which they determined to be in the public interest." St. Paul Fire & Marine Ins. Co. v. *Barry*, 438 U.S. 531, 565 (1978) (dissenting opinion). Hence, § 2(b) provides that the federal antitrust laws will generally not be applicable to those insurance business practices "regulated by State law," and presumably state law could, for example, either mandate price fixing, or specifically authorize voluntary price-fixing agreements.

Hartford Fire Ins. Co. v. California, 509 U.S. 764, 784c, 790, n.17 (1993) (concurring opinion). So much for the Sherman Act. So much, except for § 3(b) of McCarran, which provides that nothing there "shall render the . . . Sherman Act inapplicable to any agreement to boycott, coerce, or intimidate, or act of boycott, coercion, or intimidation."

As to the word *boycott* in this context, divergent understandings have their supporters. The divergence surfaced in the *Hartford Fire* case. There the Court recited historic incidents of boycott, including two in the 19th century. The prototype was the shunning by Irish tenant farmers of a property manager (Captain Charles Boycott) because he ordered evictions rather than reducing their rents. Others chargeable with boycotting were members of the American Railway Union, in connection with the "Pullman strike" of 1894. Accepting these as instances of boycott, the Court managed to distinguish the case before it.

In *Hartford Fire* complaints were made by a number of parties (including the State of California and 18 other states) against a number of insurers, some primary insurers and others reinsurance firms. By concerted action, it was charged, the defendants had restricted access to a traditional form of liability insurance, forcing on the market a form of more limited coverage. (Because the petitions had been dismissed by the trial court, the appellate courts assumed the truth of the allegations.) The defendant reinsurers had agreed not to deal with customers—primary insurers—so far as the latter wrote coverage for *their* customers in the broader terms objectionable to all the defendants alike. That was not a "boycott", the Court said. Speaking for a majority of the justices, Justice Scalia called it, instead, a "concerted agreement to seek particular terms in particular transactions". To say "Our terms, or no terms" is not to conduct a boycott. In contrast, it is a boycott to withhold dealing on a matter unrelated to the desired terms. The Pullman strike was, for example, partly a sympathy strike: Eugene Debs had led union members employed by firms other than the Pullman Palace Car Company to support a strike by fellow members, Pullman employees, by refusing to work on any train drawing a Pullman car. Loosely speaking, the distinction has to do with self-regarding action; conduct of that character, though concerted, is not a boycott. On the other hand, four justices saw in this distinction a cramped reading of the word. This difference of opinion did not lead to different conclusions, however. The majority decided to sustain the relevant counts in the petition because they were able to see in these counts charges that would fit their conception of a boycott. It was said, for example, that the defendant reinsurers had threatened to "withdraw entirely from the business of reinsuring primary U.S. insurers" if those insurers should write coverage in an objectionable form.

The primary insurers who were defendants were charged with having instigated the reinsurers to exert themselves in limiting a traditional form of liability coverage because the former objected to its terms. The view of the majority of the justices about "boycott" led them to reflect on the connections between primary insurance and reinsurance. They found an "integral relationship" between the terms of the primary insurance form and the contract of reinsurance.

> [R]einsurance is so closely tied to the terms of the primary insurance contract that one of the two categories of reinsurance (assumption reinsurance) substitutes the reinsurer for the primary or "ceding" insurer and places the reinsurer into contractual privity with the primary insurer's policyholders.... And in the other category of reinsurance (indemnity reinsurance), either the terms of the underlying insurance policy are incorporated by reference (if the reinsurance is written under a facultative agreement) ..., or (if the reinsurance is conducted on a treaty basis) the reinsurer will require full disclosure of the terms of the underlying insurance policies and usually require that the primary insurer not vary those terms without prior approval....

Id. at 806–07. Other justices were inclined to regard the defendant reinsurers as meddlers in the affairs of others (primary insurers and their customers)—somewhat in the way of sympathy strikers. Justice Souter spoke of them as being "outside the primary insurance industry."

The majority expressed an understanding of Justice Souter's view: "Perhaps [he] feels that it is undesirable, as a policy matter, to allow

insurers to 'prompt' reinsurers not to deal with the insurers' competitors—
whether or not that refusal to deal is a boycott. That feeling is certainly
understandable, since under the normal application of the Sherman Act the
reinsurers' concerted refusal to deal would be an unlawful conspiracy, and
the insurers' 'prompting' could make them part of that conspiracy. The
McCarran–Ferguson Act, however, makes that conspiracy lawful (assuming
reinsurance is state regulated), unless the refusal to deal is a 'boycott.' " Id.
at 809–810.

The quotation at the head of this Note is drawn from the Souter
opinion. It continues as follows:

> [On the other hand, Congress intended to delegate regulatory power
> only to the States; nothing in the McCarran–Ferguson Act suggests
> that Congress wanted one insurer, or a group of insurers, to be able to
> formulate and enforce policy for other insurers. Thus, the enforcement
> activities that distinguish § 3(b) "boycotts" from other concerted activ-
> ity include, in this context, *"private enforcement* . . . of industry rules
> and practices, even if those rules and practices are permitted by state
> law." St. Paul Fire & Marine Ins. Co. v. Barry, 438 U.S. 531 (1978),] at
> 565 566 (emphasis in original) (footnote omitted).

Another part of that opinion (this part for the Court) describes a particular
"group of insurers" that Justice Souter had in mind:

> [M]ost primary insurers rely on certain outside support services for the
> type of insurance coverage they wish to sell. Defendant Insurance
> Services Office, Inc. (ISO), an association of approximately 1,400 do-
> mestic property and casualty insurers . . . is the almost exclusive
> source of support services in this country for CGL [Comprehensive
> General Liability] insurance. . . . ISO develops standard policy forms
> and files or lodges them with each State's insurance regulators; most
> CGL insurance written in the United States is written on these
> forms. . . . For each of its standard policy forms, ISO also supplies
> actuarial and rating information: it collects, aggregates, interprets, and
> distributes data on the premiums charged, claims filed and paid, and
> defense costs expended with respect to each form . . . and on the basis
> of these data it predicts future loss trends and calculates advisory
> premium rates. . . . Most ISO members cannot afford to continue to
> use a form if ISO withdraws these support services. . . .

Id. at 772 (citing the parties' pleadings). In large part, the concerted action
charged in *Hartford Fire* against the reinsurers consisted of representations
they were said to have made to the ISO, "encouraging" the filing of new
CGL forms.

NOTES

(1) *Of Triggers and Self-interest.* The opinion in *Hartford Fire* gives this
description of two coverage features favored by the defendant insurers, and resisted
by the plaintiffs: "First, CGL insurance has traditionally been sold in the United
States on an 'occurrence' basis, through a policy obligating the insurer 'to pay or
defend claims, whenever made, resulting from an accident or "injurious exposure to

conditions" that occurred during the [specific time] period the policy was in effect.' App. 22 (Cal. Complaint ¶ 52). In place of this traditional 'occurrence' trigger of coverage, the defendants wanted a 'claims-made' trigger, obligating the insurer to pay or defend only those claims made during the policy period. Such a policy has the distinct advantage for the insurer that when the policy period ends without a claim having been made, the insurer can be certain that the policy will not expose it to any further liability. Second, the defendants wanted the 'claims-made' policy to have a 'retroactive date' provision, which would further restrict coverage to claims based on incidents that occurred after a certain date. Such a provision eliminates the risk that an insurer, by issuing a claims-made policy, would assume liability arising from incidents that occurred before the policy's effective date, but remained undiscovered or caused no immediate harm."

These differences are most germane, of course, to incidents that are not traumatic, and to insults that are slow to manifest themselves. It is therefore not coincidental that the maneuvering recounted by the plaintiffs in *Hartford Fire* were coeval with rapidly escalating liabilities for exposures to toxic and carcinogenic substances (asbestos, for example).

(2) *Boycott: Doctors and Patients.* For a time there was doubt that the "boycott exception" applies to disputes between policyholders and insurers. According to an opinion by Justice Stewart, the exception is limited to "attempts by members of the insurance business to force other members to follow the industry's private rules and practices." St. Paul Fire & Marine Ins. Co. v. Barry, 438 U.S. 531, 565 (1978). (Just what was alleged in *Hartford Fire*, Justice Souter thought.)

But Stewart's opinion was a dissent. In *Hartford Fire* Justice Scalia described the *Barry* decision this way: "[T]he plaintiffs were licensed physicians and their patients, and the defendant (St. Paul) was a malpractice insurer that had refused to renew the physicians' policies on an 'occurrence' basis, but insisted upon a 'claims made' basis. The allegation was that, at the instance of St. Paul, the three other malpractice insurers in the State had collectively refused to write insurance for St. Paul's customers, thus forcing them to accept St. Paul's renewal terms. Unsurprisingly, we held the allegation sufficient to state a cause of action. The insisted upon condition of the boycott (not being a former St. Paul policyholder) ... bore no relationship ... to the proposed contracts of insurance that the physicians wished to conclude with St. Paul's competitors." *Hartford Fire* at 800, 806.

Other allegations in *Barry* were as follows: The St. Paul company had instituted "new ground rules of coverage"; and the other three had refused to sell coverage to the plaintiffs, as a means of compelling them to submit to those rules. Moreover, "it is virtually impossible for a physician, hospital or other medical personnel to engage in the practice of medicine or provide medical services or treatment without medical-malpractice insurance"; and as a result of the conspiracy, the plaintiffs "may be forced to withhold medical services and disengage from the practice of medicine, except on an emergency basis."

(3) *Question.* Some systems of morality observe a distinction between self-regarding behavior and other-regarding behavior (between selfishness and altruism), and place a higher value on the latter. It would seem perverse, according to these systems, to classify a boycott as other-regarding behavior and to hold it in low esteem. Does the Supreme Court classify a boycott that way?

Introduction to *Barnett Bank v. Nelson*

As will be seen (p. 70 below), the outcome of this case was approved by the Congress in the Gramm–Leach–Bliley Act of 1999. The Court's reasoning remains, however, an excellent exemplar of its approach to questions about the McCarran Act, and influential as such. Indeed, the 1999 statute endorsed that reasoning.

Barnett Bank of Marion County, N.A. v. Nelson, Florida Insurance Commissioner

United States Supreme Court, 1996.
517 U.S. 25, 116 S.Ct. 1103, 134 L.Ed.2d 237.

■ JUSTICE BREYER delivered the opinion of the Court.[1]

The question in this case is whether a federal statute that permits national banks to sell insurance in small towns pre-empts a state statute that forbids them to do so. To answer this question, we must consider both ordinary pre-emption principles, and also a special federal anti-pre-emption rule, which provides that a federal statute will *not* pre-empt a state statute enacted "for the purpose of regulating the business of insurance"—*unless* the federal statute "*specifically relates to the business of insurance.*" McCarran–Ferguson Act, 15 U.S.C. § 1012(b) (emphasis added). We decide that the McCarran–Ferguson Act's special anti-pre-emption rule does not govern this case, because the federal statute in question "specifically relates to the business of insurance." We conclude that, under ordinary pre-emption principles, the federal statute pre-empts the state statute, thereby prohibiting application of the state statute to prevent a national bank from selling insurance in a small town.

I

In 1916 Congress enacted a federal statute that says that certain national banks "may" sell insurance in small towns. It provides in relevant part:

> In addition to the powers now vested by law in national [banks] organized under the laws of the United States *any such [bank]* located and doing business in any place [with a population] . . . [of not more than] five thousand . . . *may*, under such rules and regulations as may be prescribed by the Comptroller of the Currency, *act as the agent for any fire, life, or other insurance company* authorized by the authorities of the State . . . to do business [there], . . . by soliciting and selling insurance . . . Provided, however, That no such bank shall . . . guarantee the payment of any premium . . . And provided further, That the

---

1. Briefs amici were filed (i) in favor of reversal, on behalf of the American Bankers Association, the Consumer Bankers Association, the Florida Bankers Association, the New York Clearinghouse Association, and others, and (ii) in favor of affirmance, on behalf of the Council of Insurance Agents and Brokers, the National Association of Insurance Commissioners, the National Conference of State Legislatures, the American Council of Life Insurance, and others.

bank shall not guarantee the truth of any statement made by an assured [when applying] . . . for insurance.

Act of Sept. 7, 1916 (Federal Statute), 39 Stat. 753, as amended, 12 U.S.C. § 92 (emphases changed).

In 1974 Florida enacted a statute that prohibits certain banks from selling most kinds of insurance. It says:

No [Florida licensed] insurance agent . . . who is associated with, . . . owned or controlled by . . . a financial institution shall engage in insurance agency activities. . . .

Fla. Stat. § 626.988(2) (Supp. 1996) (State Statute). The term "financial institution" includes

any bank . . . [except for a] bank which is not a subsidiary or affiliate of a bank holding company and is located in a city having a population of less than 5,000. . . .

§ 626.988(1)(a). Thus, the State Statute says, in essence, that banks cannot sell insurance in Florida—except that an *unaffiliated* small town bank (*i.e.*, a bank that is not affiliated with a bank holding company) may sell insurance in a small town.

In October 1993 petitioner Barnett Bank, an "affiliated" national bank which does business through a branch in a small Florida town, bought a Florida licensed insurance agency. The Florida State Insurance Commissioner, pointing to the State Statute (and noting that the unaffiliated small town bank exception did not apply), ordered Barnett's insurance agency to stop selling the prohibited forms of insurance. Barnett, claiming that the Federal Statute pre-empted the State Statute, then filed this action for declaratory and injunctive relief in federal court.

The District Court held that the Federal Statute did not pre-empt the State Statute, but only because of the special insurance-related federal anti-pre-emption rule. The McCarran–Ferguson Act, which creates that rule, says:

No act of Congress shall be construed to invalidate, impair, or supersede any law enacted by any State for the purpose of regulating the business of insurance, or which imposes a fee or tax upon such business, unless such Act specifically relates to the business of insurance. . . .

McCarran–Ferguson Act, § 2(b).

The District Court decided both (1) that the Federal Statute did not fall within the McCarran–Ferguson Act's exception because it did not "specifically relat[e] to the business of insurance"; and (2) that the State Statute was a "law enacted . . . for the purpose of regulating the business of insurance." *Barnett Banks of Marion County, N. A.* v. *Gallagher*, 839 F.Supp. 835, 840–841, 843 (MD Fla.1993) (internal quotation marks omitted). Consequently, the McCarran–Ferguson Act, in the District Court's view, instructs courts not to "constru[e]" the Federal Statute "to invalidate" the State Statute. 15 U.S.C. § 1012(b). The Eleventh Circuit Court of

Appeals, for similar reasons, agreed that the Federal Statute did not pre-empt the State Statute. *Barnett Bank of Marion County, N. A.* v. *Gallagher*, 43 F.3d 631, 634–637 (1995).

We granted certiorari due to uncertainty among lower courts about the pre-emptive effect of this Federal Statute. . . . We now reverse the Eleventh Circuit.

II

We shall put the McCarran–Ferguson Act's special anti-pre-emption rule to the side for the moment, and begin by asking whether, in the absence of that rule, we should construe the Federal Statute to pre-empt the State Statute. This question is basically one of congressional intent. Did Congress, in enacting the Federal Statute, intend to exercise its constitutionally delegated authority to set aside the laws of a State? If so, the Supremacy Clause requires courts to follow federal, not state, law. U.S. Const., Art. VI, cl. 2; see *California Fed. Sav. & Loan Assn.* v. *Guerra*, 479 U.S. 272, 280–281 (1987) (reviewing pre-emption doctrine).

Sometimes courts, when facing the pre-emption question, find language in the federal statute that reveals an explicit congressional intent to pre-empt state law. . . . More often, explicit pre-emption language does not appear, or does not directly answer the question. In that event, courts must consider whether the federal statute's "structure and purpose," or nonspecific statutory language, nonetheless reveal a clear, but implicit, pre-emptive intent. . . . Alternatively, federal law may be in "irreconcilable conflict" with state law. *Rice* v. *Norman Williams Co.*, 458 U.S. 654, 659 (1982). Compliance with both statutes, for example, may be a "physical impossibility," *Florida Lime & Avocado Growers, Inc.* v. *Paul*, 373 U.S. 132, 142–143 (1963); or, the state law may "stand as an obstacle to the accomplishment and execution of the full purposes and objectives of Congress." *Hines* v. *Davidowitz*, 312 U.S. 52, 67 (1941).

In this case we must ask whether or not the Federal and State Statutes are in "irreconcilable conflict." The two statutes do not impose directly conflicting duties on national banks—as they would, for example, if the federal law said, "you must sell insurance," while the state law said, "you may not." Nonetheless, the Federal Statute authorizes national banks to engage in activities that the State Statute expressly forbids. Thus, the State's prohibition of those activities would seem to "stand as an obstacle to the accomplishment" of one of the Federal Statute's purposes—unless, of course, that federal purpose is to grant the bank only a very *limited* permission, that is, permission to sell insurance *to the extent that state law also grants permission to do so*.

That is what the State of Florida and its supporting *amici* argue. . . . In their view, the Federal Statute removes only federal legal obstacles, not state legal obstacles, to the sale of insurance by national banks. But we do not find this, or the State's related, ordinary pre-emption arguments, convincing.

[The Court referred to several of its prior rulings, including one in a "quite similar" case, *Franklin Nat. Bank of Franklin Square* v. *New York*, 347 U.S. 373 (1954).]

In defining the pre-emptive scope of statutes and regulations granting a power to national banks, these cases take the view that normally Congress would not want States to forbid, or to impair significantly, the exercise of a power that Congress explicitly granted....

. . .

[W]here Congress has not expressly conditioned the grant of "power" upon a grant of state permission, the Court has ordinarily found that no such condition applies....

The Federal Statute before us, as in *Franklin Nat. Bank*, explicitly grants a national bank an authorization, permission, or power. And, as in *Franklin Nat. Bank*, it contains no "indication" that Congress intended to subject that power to local restriction. Thus, the Court's discussion in *Franklin Nat. Bank*, the holding of that case, and the other precedent we have cited above, strongly argue for a similar interpretation here—a broad interpretation of the word "may" that does not condition federal permission upon that of the State.

. . .

In light of these considerations, we conclude that the Federal Statute means to grant small town national banks authority to sell insurance, whether or not a State grants its own state banks or national banks similar approval. Were we to apply ordinary legal principles of pre-emption, the federal law would pre-empt that of the State.

III

We now must decide whether ordinary legal principles of pre-emption, or the special McCarran–Ferguson Act anti-pre-emption rule, governs this case. The lower courts held that the McCarran–Ferguson Act's special anti-pre-emption rule applies, and instructs courts not to "construe" the Federal Statute to "invalidate, impair, or supersede" that of the State. 15 U.S.C. § 1012(b). By its terms, however, the Act does not apply when the conflicting federal statute *"specifically relates to the business of insurance." Ibid.* (emphasis added). In our view, the Federal Statute in this case "specifically relates to the business of insurance"—therefore the McCarran–Ferguson Act's special anti-pre-emption rule does not apply.

Our conclusion rests upon the McCarran–Ferguson Act's language and purpose, taken together. Consider the language—"specifically relates to the business of insurance." In ordinary English, a statute that says that banks may act as insurance agents, and that the Comptroller of the Currency may regulate their insurance-related activities, *"relates"* to the insurance business. The word "relates" is highly general, and this Court has interpreted it broadly in other pre-emption contexts. See, *e.g., Pilot Life Ins. Co.* v. *Dedeaux*, 481 U.S. 41, 47 (1987) (words " 'relate to' " have " 'broad common-sense meaning, such that a state law "relate[s] to" a benefit plan

"... if it has a connection with or reference to such a plan" ' ") (quoting *Metropolitan Life Ins. Co.* v. *Massachusetts*, 471 U.S. 724, 739 (1985), in turn quoting *Shaw* v. *Delta Air Lines, Inc.*, 463 U.S. 85, 97 (1983))....

More importantly, in ordinary English, this statute *"specifically"* relates to the insurance business. "Specifically" can mean "explicitly, particularly, [or] definitely," Black's Law Dictionary 1398 (6th ed.1990), thereby contrasting a *specific* reference with an *implicit* reference made by more general language to a broader topic. The general words "business activity," for example, will sometimes include, and thereby implicitly refer, to insurance; the particular words "finance, banking, and insurance" make that reference explicitly *and specifically*.

Finally, using ordinary English, one would say that this statute specifically relates to the *"business of insurance."* The statute explicitly grants national banks permission to "act as the agent for any fire, life, or other insurance company," to "solici[t] and sel[l] insurance," to "collec[t] premiums," and to "receive for services so rendered ... fees or commissions," subject to Comptroller regulation. 12 U.S.C. § 92. It also sets forth certain specific rules prohibiting banks from guaranteeing the "payment of any premium on insurance policies issued through its agency ..." and the "truth of any statement made by an assured in filing his application for insurance." *Ibid.* The statute thereby not only focuses directly upon industry-specific selling practices, but also affects the relation of insured to insurer and the spreading of risk—matters that this Court, in other contexts, has placed at the core of the McCarran–Ferguson Act's concern. See *Union Labor Life Ins. Co.* v. *Pireno*, 458 U.S. 119, 129 (1982) (citing *Group Life & Health Ins. Co.* v. *Royal Drug Co.*, 440 U.S. 205 (1979); see also *Department of Treasury* v. *Fabe*, 508 U.S. 491, 502–504 (1993).

Consider, too, the McCarran–Ferguson Act's basic purposes. The Act sets forth two mutually reinforcing purposes in its first section, namely, that "continued regulation and taxation by the several States of the business of insurance is in the public interest," and that *"silence* on the part of the Congress shall not be construed to impose any barrier to the regulation or taxation of such business by the several States." 15 U.S.C. § 1011 (emphasis added). The latter phrase, particularly the word "silence," indicates that the Act does not seek to insulate state insurance regulation from the reach of all federal law. Rather, it seeks to protect state regulation primarily against *inadvertent* federal intrusion—say, through enactment of a federal statute that describes an affected activity in broad, general terms, of which the insurance business happens to constitute one part.

[Here the Court gave a description of the "circumstances surrounding enactment" of the McCarran Act, as set out on p. 55 above, concluding with a statement of the congressional object: "to restore the supremacy of the States in the realm of insurance regulation." The opinion continues as follows.]

... But the circumstances we have just described mean that *"restor[ation]"* of "supremacy" basically required setting aside the unanticipated effects of *South-Eastern Underwriters*, and cautiously avoiding similar unanticipated interference with state regulation in the future. It did not require avoiding federal pre-emption by future federal statutes that indicate, through their "specific relat[ion]" to insurance, that Congress had focused upon the insurance industry, and therefore, in all likelihood, consciously intended to exert upon the insurance industry whatever pre-emptive force accompanied its law. See also, *e.g.*, insofar as relevant, 91 Cong. Rec. 483 (1945) (statement of Sen. O'Mahoney, floor manager of the Act, that the Act was intended to be "a sort of catch-all provision to take into consideration other acts of Congress which might affect the insurance industry, but of which we did not have knowledge at the time"); *ibid.* (similar statement of Sen. Ferguson).

The language of the Federal Statute before us is not general. It refers specifically to insurance. Its state regulatory implications are not surprising, nor do we believe them inadvertent. See Part II, *supra*. Consequently, considerations of purpose, as well as of language, indicate that the Federal Statute falls within the scope of the McCarran–Ferguson Act's "specifically relates" exception to its anti-pre-emption rule. Cf. *John Hancock Mut. Life Ins. Co.* v. *Harris Trust and Sav. Bank*, 510 U.S. 86, 98 (1993) (adopting the United States' view that language in the Employee Retirement Income Security Act of 1974 defining a "guaranteed benefit policy" as a certain kind of "insurance" policy "obviously and specifically relates to the business of insurance") (internal quotation marks omitted).

We shall mention briefly why we are not convinced by several of the parties' remaining arguments. [In three further paragraphs the Court rejected various other arguments against its position.]

For these reasons, the judgment of the Court of Appeals is reversed.

NOTES

(1) *Bowing to the Supreme Court.* In order to protect bank-related marketing of insurance, Congress later said that

> [N]o State may . . . prevent or significantly interfere with the ability of a depository institution, or an affiliate thereof, to engage . . . in any insurance sales, solicitation, or cross-marketing activity.[1]

The opening part of this sentence makes a bow in the direction of the Supreme Court. It reads: "In accordance with the legal standards for preemption set forth in . . . Barnett Bank. . . ."

(2) *Pre-and post-McCarran Enactments.* An insurance company was charged with violations of a federal anti-discrimination law, the Fair Housing Act (FHA). It answered, citing the McCarran Act, that the application to it of the FHA was precluded by Wisconsin law. The FHA requires race-blind practices in housing and related services; the alleged violation had to do with how, and at what price, the company wrote (or declined to write) policies of insurance—with "redlining", in other words. " 'Redlining' is charging higher rates or declining to write insurance

---

1. Section 104(d)(2)(A) of the Gramm–Leach–Bliley Act of 1999, described below at p. 70 ff.

for people who live in particular areas (figuratively, sometimes literally, enclosed with red lines on a map)."[2] As for McCarran, the plaintiffs responded that it does not apply to subsequently enacted civil rights statutes. They were supported by an earlier case in the Second Circuit. There the court said:

> Congress, in enacting a statute primarily intended to deal with the conflict between state regulation of insurers and the federal antitrust laws, had no intention of declaring that subsequently enacted civil rights legislation would be inapplicable to any and all of the activities of an insurance company that can be classified as "the business of insurance."[3]

But when the redlining case reached the Court of Appeals for the Seventh Circuit, that court dismissed this view, suggesting that the second circuit take a new look if the opportunity should arise.[4] "Well *of course*," the court said, "Congress had no intention in the 1940s of curtailing the scope of laws yet to be enacted—indeed, inconceivable at the time." But: "What Members of Congress may have 'intended' in 1945, when it enacted a statute limited to the antitrust laws, and 1946, when it extended the McCarran–Ferguson Act to other federal laws, is not [] the question. We must determine what Congress meant *by what it enacted*, not what Senators and Representatives said, thought, wished, or hoped." NAACP v. American Family Mutual Ins. Co., n.2 above, at 294.

(3) *Impairment of State Regulation.* The McCarran Act speaks of the "impairment" of state laws by congressional acts—generally renouncing it. In Humana Inc. v. Forsyth, 525 U.S. 299 (1999), the Court examined the sense of impairment. The plaintiffs (including Mary Forsyth) were beneficiaries of group health insurance policies issued by Humana Health Insurance of Nevada, Inc. They charged Humana with a "scheme" contrary to the Racketeer Influenced and Corrupt Organizations Act (RICO).[5] The scheme appears also to have violated Nevada's Unfair Insurance Practices Act.[6] The State's attorney general investigated it, and won a consent decree under which Humana paid a fine of $50,000.

The trial court granted summary judgment for Humana, believing that RICO impaired the Nevada law. The court of appeals disagreed, and Humana appealed.

Both statutes provided a right of action for persons injured. Nevada law provided for compensatory and punitive damages, as administrative remedies. RICO authorizes treble damages. The Supreme Court stated the question this way: "Does a federal law, which proscribes the same conduct as state law, but provides materially different remedies, 'impair' state law under the McCarran–Ferguson Act?"

The Court professed to follow a middling course. It said: "We reject any suggestion that Congress intended to cede the field of insurance regulation to the States, saving only instances in which Congress expressly orders otherwise."[7] But it

---

2. NAACP v. American Family Mutual Ins. Co., 978 F.2d 287, 290 (7th Cir. 1992).

3. Spirt v. Teachers Insurance and Annuity Ass'n, 691 F.2d 1054, 1065 (2d Cir. 1982), *vacated on other grounds*, 463 U.S. 1223 (1983), *on remand*, 735 F.2d 23 (1984).

4. "No matter how our colleagues on the east coast would approach the subject today, however, we conclude that Congress should be taken at its word."

5. 18 U.S.C. § 1961 *et seq.*

6. Nev.Rev.Stat. § 686A.010 *et seq.* (1996)—a statute "patterned substantially on the National Association of Insurance Commissioners' model Unfair Trade Practices Act."

7. Contrast 29 U.S.C. § 144(a)—the Employee Retirement Income Security Act, addressed below at p. 73 ff.—saying that, subject to exceptions, that Act "supersedes any and all State laws insofar as they may now or hereafter relate to any employee benefit plan."

said also: "While we reject any sort of field preemption, we also reject the polar opposite of that view, *i.e.*, that Congress intended a green light for federal regulation whenever the federal law does not collide head on with state regulation."

Affirming, the Court ruled that McCarran did not block the plaintiffs' action. RICO, it said, "advances the State's interest in combating insurance fraud, and does not frustrate any articulated Nevada policy."

This reasoning suggests the following homely questions: If a horse and an ox are hitched to the same cart, does the ox impair the horse's function? Or the other way about?

(4) *More on Redlining.* As to impairment, Humana v. Forsyth (foregoing Note) was anticipated by the redlining case sketched in Note 2 above. The court was not prepared to apply the Fair Housing Act if it conflicted with state law. But it found nothing at odds with the Act in Wisconsin law, and found two provisions in the Wisconsin statutes that were aligned, roughly, with the Act.[8] "Duplication is not conflict," the court said.

Yet the duplication was inexact. Unlike the federal anti-discrimination statute, the Wisconsin one did not provide for a private right of action—only for administrative enforcement. The state law was, therefore, "less potent" than one enforced by both agencies and private litigants. This was a worry to the court. "One could say," it wrote, "that a federal rule increasing the probability that a state norm will be vindicated (or augmenting the damages assessed in the event of violation) conflicts with a decision by the state that remedies should be limited or rare." The court overcame that worry by finding analogies in somewhat relaxed applications of the general preemption rule. "In the main, federal regulation of a subject—even thoroughgoing federal regulation—does not prevent states from adding remedies to the arsenal established by federal law. The McCarran–Ferguson Act is a form of inverse preemption, so principles defining when state remedies conflict with (and so are preempted by) federal law are pertinent in deciding when federal rules 'invalidate, impair, or supersede' state rules." (In this connection, notice that the Breyer opinion in *Barnett Bank* takes up the general rule and the special anti-preemption rule of McCarran as independent steps.)

(5) *Questions.* Would the ruling in *Barnett Bank* control if Nevada had provided for compensatory damages only (and not punitive damages) against the alleged wrongdoing? If it had provided for nominal damages only? If it had provided for injunctive relief only, pretermitting damages altogether?

McCarran and Civil Rights

The teaching of Humana v. Forsyth has been applied to claims that insurers violated the Civil Rights Act of 1866. An example is Dehoyos v. Allstate Insurance Corporation, 345 F.3d 290 (5th Cir. 2003). In that case some holders of auto and homeowners' policies charged the issuers with violating that Act[9] by engaging in practices that were racially discriminatory (without, so far as appears, having intended wrongful discrimination). According to the suitors, the defendants used "a 'credit-scoring system' to

---

As to a state's power to utilize its authority over the insurance business as a cover for regulating employee-benefit plans that are self-insured, see § 514(b)(2)(B).

8. Quoting: "Wis. Stat. § 101.22(2)(e), which forbids discrimination by casualty insurers on the basis of race, and Wis. Stat. § 628.34(3), which more generally interdicts 'unfair discrimination' in the business of insurance."

9. 42 U.S.C. §§ 1981 and 1982.

target non-Caucasian customers for the sale of more expensive insurance policies than those directed at Caucasian customers.''

The trial court denied a motion by Allstate to dismiss the action, and it appealed. The Court of Appeals described the teaching of *Humana* in a way that can be paraphrased as follows:

A federal statute overrides state law enacted ''for the purpose of regulating the business of insurance'' only

> (a) if it ''specifically relates to the business of insurance'', or

> (b) if, given a ''state law or official policy which is directed at the regulation of insurance'',

>> (i) application of the federal rule would not frustrate it, and

>> (ii) that application would not ''interfere with [the] State's administrative regime''.

The suitors in *Dehoyos* did not contend that the Civil Rights Act specifically relates to the business of insurance. The court therefore turned to the second ''filter''.

In this connection, the court ascribed to Allstate the position that, in *Humana*, the phrase about interfering with an administrative scheme meant that ''if the state has a mechanism in place for performing an insurance-related function and the federal law enters that regulatory arena, then the federal law is 'interfering' with the state's administrative regime.'' The court rejected that position. ''In *Humana* the Court expressly rejected a 'field preemption' approach to [McCarran–Ferguson Act] preemption, holding instead that federal and state law can concurrently affect the same issues and further the same goals as long as the federal law does not *frustrate* the state's *declared* policy. 'Interference,' then, is not synonymous with 'a presence in the regulatory field.' ''

Declared state policy. In *Dehoyos* the court considered the possibility that to apply the Civil Rights Act would frustrate a declared state policy. Not so, it thought. The court relied on a comparable case about Alabama law in which the court was dubious that that State had a declared policy supporting racial discrimination by insurers.[10]

Question. Imagine that a state legislature has ''declared'' such a policy. Suppose also that the statute is unconstitutional. Can it be that the statute would nevertheless preclude the application of federal civil-rights laws?

''... other than sex''

The Civil Rights Act of 1964, Title VII, makes it an unlawful employment practice ''to discriminate against any individual, with respect to his [terms] of employment, because of such individual's ... sex....'' 42 U.S.C. § 20003–2(a)(1). The ''Bennett Amendment'' qualified this prohibition by permitting sex-based differentiations as authorized by the Equal Pay Act.

---

10.   Moore v. Liberty Nat'l Life Ins. Co., 267 F.3d 1209 (11th Cir. 2001).

That Act authorizes differences of pay based on any factor "other than sex".

In considering these provisions, the Supreme Court observed that, as a class, women live longer than men. From that fact, an employer making provision for a lifelong retirement benefit to its employees, and charging them for the benefit, might well conclude that either women should pay more than men for it or men should receive a more generous benefit. In providing for its employees, the State of Arizona drew the latter conclusion. Or if not, at least it made available to its women employees, upon retirement, annuities—privately underwritten—calling for lower periodic payments than those available to men, all else being equal.

When a test of that plan arrived at the Supreme Court, briefs *amici* were filed by groups of several kinds (including the National Association of Insurance Commissioners, the American Academy of Actuaries, and the American Association of University Professors). As the Court framed the question, it was whether or not "Title VII [] prohibits an employer from offering its employees the option of receiving retirement benefits from one of several companies selected by the employer, all of which pay a woman lower monthly benefits than a man who has made the same contributions." Arizona Governing Committee v. Norris, 463 U.S. 1073 (1983).

The Court had earlier ruled that an employer cannot, consistently with Title VII, require women to make larger contributions than men in order to obtain the same monthly benefits. Los Angeles, Dept. of Water & Power v. Manhart, 435 U.S. 702 (1978). Describing that case in *Norris*, the Court said: "we rejected the argument that the exaction of greater contributions from women was based on a 'factor other than sex'—*i.e.*, longevity—and was therefore permissible under the Equal Pay Act." And the Court quoted this from *Manhart*: "[One] cannot 'say that an actuarial distinction based entirely on sex is "based on any other factor than sex." Sex is exactly what it is based on.' "[11]

The basic teaching of *Manhart* is this (according to *Norris*): "Title VII requires employers to treat their employees as *individuals*, not 'as simply components of a racial, religious, sexual, or national class.' " It would be inconsistent with that to say that "that sex may properly be used to predict longevity."

NOTES

(1) *Pregnancy*. At a time prior to *Manhart* a majority of the Court concluded that an employer's disability-benefit plan could exclude pregnancy. General Electric Co. v. Gilbert, 429 U.S. 125 (1976). (Justice Stevens, dissenting, said that the capacity to become pregnant is the primary differentiation between male and female.) Congress overturned that ruling in the Pregnancy Discrimination Act, which amended Title VII so as to say that the term "on the basis of sex" includes "because of or on the basis of pregnancy, childbirth, or related medical conditions." 42 U.S.C. § 2000e(k).

11. *Norris* at 1080, 1081.

(2) *Beyond Employment.* As an individual buying an annuity, a man can get better terms than a woman can, though there is no difference between them other than sex. Is this a distressing social fact? Can it be justified by reference to the further fact that, in buying life insurance, a woman can get better terms than a man can?

(3) *Questions.* Does the McCarran Act cast doubt on the decision in *Norris*? If not, why not?

b. The "Gramm–Leach–Bliley Act" of 1999

In the simplest terms, this Act repealed the "Glass–Steagall Act" of 1933, and replaced it with a host of bank-regulation rules. The 1933 Act was a measure designed to cure problems contributing to the Great Depression. In general, it isolated the banking business from other lines of business—including that of insuring.

Small-town banking was an exception to Glass–Steagall. As indicated in *Barnett Bank*, above, since 1916 banks in small towns had been authorized (subject to rules prescribed by the Comptroller of the Currency) to

> act as the agent for any ... insurance company authorized by the authorities of the State ... to do business [there], ... by soliciting and selling insurance....[12]

This provision remained in general effect after Glass–Steagall. In *Barnett Bank* the federal "small-town" rule trumped an attempt in Florida to stamp out insurance-agency activities by anyone associated with a bank. Congress was gratified by the *Barnett Bank* decision. So much so that, in the Gramm–Leach–Bliley Act, it approved the Court's reasoning and ratified the result. See Note 1, p. 65 above.

Overall, however, that Act (sometimes hereafter, "the Act", or "GLB") changed the landscape fundamentally. It was the product of years of political infighting; it comprises more than a hundred substantive sections. Only some elements of this Act are characterized here.

The Act authorized the creation of a type of bank holding company—called "financial holding company" (FHC)—having exceptional powers. Among these is the power to engage in an activity that has been identified by the Federal Reserve Board as a proper incident to banking. Of special moment here, however, is the authority to engage in "financial activities." These, as specified in the statute, include insuring. More particularly, for this purpose, activities that are "financial in nature" include:

> Insuring, guaranteeing, or indemnifying against loss, harm, damage, illness, disability, or death, or providing and issuing annuities, and acting as principal, agent, or broker for purposes of the foregoing, in any State.[13]

---

12. Cited and more fully quoted at pp. 60–61 above.

13. Inserted in the Bank Holding Company Act of 1956 (12 U.S.C. § 1843 (k)(4)(B).

One of the firstfruits of GLB was an announcement (May 18, 2000) by one of the national's largest insurance companies that it meant to provide banking services, perhaps by buying a bank. The insurer, Metropolitan Life, is a unit of Met Life Inc. No banks, it

The Act specifies in considerable detail the qualifications that a firm must meet in order to qualify as an "FHC".

The Act displays, among others, the following worries that Congress had in making its primary move:

(1) that the move might injure consumer interests;

(2) that it might undercut useful state measures of insurance regulation;

(3) that it might undercut useful federal measures of bank regulation; and

(4) that the general object of the Act—removing barriers to enterprise—might be subverted, either by the deployment of (i) federal law by federal authorities, or (ii) state law by state authorities.

How the Act addresses some of these worries is illustrated in the notes below.

As indicated above, the Act contains this reaffirmation: "The [McCarran–Ferguson Act] remains the law of the United States."[14] On the other hand, as shown by the illustrations below, the Act trenches on state laws in a number of important ways.

NOTES

(1) *Clearing the Field.* According to GLB, a state may not, by law, "prevent or significantly interfere with the ability of any insurer, or any affiliate of an insurer . . ., to become a financial holding company or to acquire control of a depository institution." There are limitations on this prohibition; but two of the limitations are circumscribed as follows:

". . . so long as [the state action concerned] does not have the effect of discriminating, intentionally or unintentionally, against a depository institution or an affiliate thereof, or against any other person based upon an association of such person with a depository institution".

Subparagraphs (A)(ii) and (C) of section 104(c)(2).

(2) *Insurance-customer Protections.* In GLB, Congress directed that, before long, federal authorities publish "customer protection regulations" applicable to the advertising and retail sales practices for insurance products by or on behalf of (among others) a depository institution. According to the Act, the regulations "shall encourage the use of disclosure that is conspicuous, simple, direct, and readily understandable, such as these examples:

NOT GUARANTEED BY THE BANK

NOT INSURED BY ANY GOVERNMENT AGENCY.

Adjustments were expected for purchases "in person, by telephone, or by electronic media".

---

was said, had bought major insurance companies by then. (Source: Ken Reynolds, executive director of the Association of Banks in Insurance.) *The New York Times*, May 19, 2000, C5. A more imposing consequence fol-

lowed: the affiliation of Citibank and the Travelers Insurance Company as units of the FHC Citicorp.

14. Section 104(a).

But the Act shows, in this connection, concern for state sensibilities. The regulations are not to apply in contravention of state "statutes, regulations, orders, or interpretations" having (roughly) the same application.

This deference is, however, qualified in an extraordinary way. If the federal agencies concerned conclude that one of their regulations provides greater customer protection than comparable regulations of a state, they are to notify that state's insurance commissioner,[15] in writing, of that conclusion. Thereafter, having made a "final determination" of the matter, the feds

> shall send a written preemption notice to the [insurance commissioner] to notify the State that the Federal provision will preempt the State provision and will become applicable unless, not later than 3 years after the date of such notice, the State adopts legislation to override such preemption.[16]

Question: Does this mean that a state legislature can say, simply, "We believe that our laws go far enough to protect consumers [in the respect at issue]; and we therefore de-preempt our laws"? Or does it mean that the legislature can "de-preempt" by aligning the state's law with the federal regulation?

The procedure established by GLB with respect to customer protection, when federal authorities determine that one of their regulations goes beyond the comparable provisions of state law, should be compared with the ruling in Humana v. Forsyth, described above in Note 3, p. 66. *Questions*: Does it seem that Congress and the Court have different ideas about the operation of the McCarran Act? If so, whose idea should prevail?

(3) *Direction and Encouragement*. Some provisions of GLB give evidence that Congress felt itself boxed in by three considerations. Two of these were (i) its allegiance to the principle of the McCarran Act, and (ii) its dissatisfaction with insurance marketing practices.

Wishing to reform those practices, Congress established a nonprofit corporation called the National Association of Registered Agents and Brokers (NARAB). Congress meant for state insurance regulators to take an active part in the management and functions of NARAB. Here, however, it faced a third restrictive consideration. The Supreme Court had recently ruled that Congress lacked the constitutional power to coopt state and local officials in the furtherance of its legislative purposes. (The leading case had to do with the services of state law-enforcement officers in controlling the distribution of firearms. Printz v. United States, 521 U.S. 898 (1997).)

In GLB, there is some artful dodging of the latter restriction, notably on the subject of consultation between federal and state officials. The statute mandates that, before making a determination about bank-insurer affiliation, a federal agency "*shall* consult with the appropriate State insurance regulator ... and take the views of [the latter] into account...." (emphasis supplied). It was naturally thought that a federal banking agency should not determine such a matter without the best available information, including information about the insurer in question that might be on file in a state insurance department. But Congress hesitated to impose a reporting obligation on state officials. Hence, on the subject of "state insurance regulator information," it provided only that, upon request by the appropriate federal agency, a state regulator *may* provide "any examination ... or

---

15. What the Act actually says is "appropriate State regulatory authority". In this Note, "insurance commissioner" is used as a fair substitute, for all practical purposes.

16. 12 U.S.C. § 1831x(g)(2)(B)(iii).

other information to which such insurance regulator may have access," with respect to a specified company.

All this is preceded by a hortatory "purpose" subsection, beginning: "It is the intention of the Congress that the Board of Governors of the Federal Reserve System, as the umbrella supervisor for financial holding companies, and the State insurance regulators, as the functional regulators of companies engaged in insurance activities, coordinate efforts to supervise companies that control both a depository institution and a company engaged in insurance activities regulated under State law. . . . The purpose of this section is to encourage [] coordination and confidential sharing of information. . . ."[1]

c. ERISA

The Employee Retirement Income Security Act (ERISA) effects a massive preemption of state laws through section 1144 of U.S.C. Title 29. According to an opening statement in the section, it preempts all state laws "insofar as they may now or hereafter relate to any employee benefit plan". The section continues, however, with a provision that is called, for short, a *saving clause* in some following paragraphs. The clause protects from preemption state laws "which regulate insurance, banking, or securities".

The Supreme Court may have shifted its position somewhat as to what constitute laws which regulate insurance. For a time what seemed to be decisive was a set of three "McCarran factors", so-called. A list of these, appearing in a 1982 case,[2] is this:

first, whether the practice has the effect of transferring or spreading a policyholder's risk; *second*, whether the practice is an integral part of the policy relationship between the insurer and the insured; and *third*, whether the practice is limited to entities within the insurance industry.

In 2003 the Court discounted these factors somewhat; see Kentucky Ass'n of Health Plans, Inc. v. Miller, 538 U.S. 329. Looking back at its earlier opinions, the Court did not see the McCarran factors as having been decisive for the purposes of ERISA.[3] Rather, those opinions spoke of the factors as "considerations", "checking points", and "quideposts".

Miller concerned health-services laws of the type known as *AWP statutes*, in that they sought to open health-maintenance (HMOs) organizations to "any willing provider" of medical services.[4] "While there are variations among them, the basic AWP law allows health care providers (usually physicians but also pharmacies) who have been denied access to a managed care network the opportunity to 'opt in' to the network."[5] The Kentucky statutes compelled HMOs there to admit to their "provider

1. Section 307(a).

2. Union Labor Life Ins. Co. v. Pireno, 458 U.S. 119.

3. In particular, the Court said, it had held that a state law regulating insurance, for the purposes of ERISA, might be one that did *not* have the effect of transferring or spreading a policyholder's risk.

4. As to the character and regulation of HMOs, see B. Furrow *et al.*, Health Law, Cases . . . , 799–802 (3d ed. 1997).

5. Note, *Not Just Old Wine in New Bottles*, 38 Akron L. Rev. 253, 270–72 (2005). (The few lines following the one quoted refer to competing public policies concerned in the "AWP debate".)

networks" persons they might not otherwise admit (chiropractors, for example).[6] The Court ruled that these statutes were protected from ERISA preemption as laws that "regulate insurance", in the sense of the savings clause. The concluding paragraph of the opinion set a new course:

> Today we make a clean break from the McCarran–Ferguson factors and hold that for a state law to be [so protected], it must satisfy two requirements. First, the state law must be specifically directed toward entities engaged in insurance.... Second, ... the state law must substantially affect the risk pooling arrangement between the insurer and the insured. Kentucky's law satisfies each of these requirements.

Id. at 341–42.

QUESTION: **UNUM Life Ins. Co. of America v. Ward**[7]

This was one of the cases preceding *Miller* in which the Court construed the ERISA saving clause. Consider the facts and the law in this case, as drawn from the opinion, in the light of *Miller*.

John E. Ward became disabled and resigned from his job. His employer had arranged, with UNUM Life, a policy of group insurance against long-term disabilities that its employees might suffer; it covered Ward's malady. Ward was late—very late—in presenting proof of his disability to UNUM. Apparently he was unaware of the coverage until, going through his papers, he came upon a booklet that described the insuring plan.

UNUM contended that Ward was too late, by some five months. The policy made it a condition of payment that UNUM receive a proof of claim, at the latest, one year and 180 days after the onset of disability. In pursuing his claim, Ward relied on a feature of California law, the "notice-prejudice rule". To that, UNUM responded that the rule was preempted by ERISA.

In considering that response, the Court relied on a California case for an authoritative statement of the State rule:

---

6. From the *Miller* opinion: "Petitioners include several health maintenance organizations (HMOs) and a Kentucky-based association of HMOs. In order to control the quality and cost of health-care delivery, these HMOs have contracted with selected doctors, hospitals, and other health-care providers to create exclusive 'provider networks.'" Providers in such networks agree to render health-care services to the HMOs' subscribers at discounted rates and to comply with other contractual requirements. In return, they receive the benefit of patient volume higher than that achieved by nonnetwork providers who lack access to petitioners' subscribers.

"Kentucky's AWP statutes impair petitioners' ability to limit the number of providers with access to their networks, and thus their ability to use the assurance of high patient volume as the *quid pro quo* for the discounted rates that network membership entails. Petitioners believe that AWP laws will frustrate their efforts at cost and quality control, and will ultimately deny consumers the benefit of their cost-reducing arrangements with providers."

The Note cited in the foregoing footnote describes some responses to the decision: "State regulators ... viewed the ruling as a victory in their efforts to enforce HMO accountability and consumer access to care...." Id. at 282.

7. 526 U.S. 358 (1999).

[A] defense based on an insured's failure to give timely notice [of a claim] requires the insurer to prove that it suffered actual prejudice. Prejudice is not presumed from delayed notice alone. The insurer must show actual prejudice, not the mere possibility of prejudice.[8]

The Court took notice of points in favor of one party or another. ERISA applied, in that the California rule is one "related to" an employee-benefit plan. Ward conceded that. Also, owing to a broad definition of "State law" in ERISA,[9] this and other judge-made rules were subject to preemption—and to protection.

The Court ruled, unanimously, that ERISA did not preempt the California notice-prejudice rule. Among a number of observations the Court made about the rule, and other features of law, some notable ones—somewhat paraphrased—are these:

1. The rule is, by its very terms, directed specifically at the insurance industry. It is grounded in policy concerns specific to that industry, and is applicable only to insurance contracts.

2. According to the Restatement, Second, of Contracts, in some circumstances a court may excuse the non-occurrence of a condition owing to the threat of a disproportionate forfeiture. Unlike that statement, however, the California notice-prejudice rule is a firm directive to the courts, and not a "principle a court may pliably employ."

3. The maxim that "law abhors a forfeiture" is supported by a variety of California decisions; and the rule is an application of that maxim.

4. In general, the burden of justifying a departure from a contract's written terms rests with the party seeking the departure.

Is any of these particulars significant, in relation to the two requirements for protection announced in *Miller*? If so, which? Given those requirements, the California notice-prejudice rule appears to qualify for protection; in *Miller* the court cited UNUM Life v. Ward with apparent approval.

NOTES

(1) *Changes in Decisional Law.* You should be able, without strain, to imagine an opinion of the California Supreme Court that would retain the notice-prejudice

---

8. Shell Oil Co. v. Winterthur Swiss Ins. Co., 12 Cal.App.4th 715, 760–761, 15 Cal.Rptr.2d 815, 845 (1st Dist.1993) (citations omitted).

The notice-prejudice rule prevails in states other than California, in one version or another. In New Jersey, as in California, it seems that the burden of persuasion—in showing prejudice—lies on the insurer. See Zuckerman v. National Union Fire Ins. Co., 495 A.2d 395 (N.J.1985). In contrast, in Wisconsin a statute provides that "the risk of nonpersuasion is upon the person claiming there was no prejudice". See The Lexington Insurance Company v. Rugg & Knopp, Inc., 165 F.3d 1087 (7th Cir.1999).

9. Defined so as to include "decisions, rules, regulations, or other State action having the effect of law." 29 U.S.C. § 1144(c)(1). The Court has remarked on the "wide variety of state statutory and decisional law arguably affected" by these clauses. Pilot Life Ins. Co. v. Dedeaux, 481 U.S. 41, 47 (1987).

rule and would not change its range of operation, but would alter it in such a way that it looks less like a law regulating insurance.

In another case concerning a decisional rule of a state, and ERISA's saving clause, the rule failed to qualify as one regulating insurance. The case was *Pilot Life*, cited above. According to one expression of the rule, an insurer can be charged with punitive damages for refusing to pay a claim, and having no "reasonably arguable basis" for refusing. The Court was moved by the conviction that this statement was only a corollary of a more general one: The state courts were prepared to charge other contracting parties—not only insurers—with punitive damages on similar grounds. At one time that was the case in California. Since then, however, some retrenchment has occurred there, so that the tort of "bad-faith breach" may now be confined largely to insurer/insured relations.[10] Possibly that development has brought the tort within the protection of the saving clause. If so, the lesson for state law-makers seems to be this: If you wish to control those relationships, even when integrated into employee-benefit plans, it is best to make your controls idiosyncratic. Is that a sensible lesson for federal authorities to teach?

(2) *Another California Rule.* What if Ward's former employer, MAC, knew of his disability within the period allowed by UNUM for reporting his claim to it? That might count as notice to UNUM on the theory that MAC, as administrator of the group policy, acted as UNUM's agent. Ward so contended, hoping to prevail, prejudice or no prejudice. He had some success with this argument in the Court of Appeals, which relied on a California case declaring that "the employer is the agent of the insurer in performing the duties of administering group insurance policies."[11] Does that rule appear to be a law that "regulates insurance," within the meaning of ERISA's saving clause?

Without confronting that question, the Court concluded that the rule did not work in Ward's favor. It reversed the determination below that the rule was not within the preemption clause.

PROBLEM

Rescission. A carrier of liability insurance for X learns, first, that X has been sued on a claim within the coverage, and second, that in issuing the policy the carrier had been misled by a fraudulent and material misrepresentation made by X. Suppose, first, that by an applicable rule of state law, the carrier cannot now rescind the contract. Is that a rule that "regulates insurance"? Suppose next that the converse rule applies: the insurer *can* rescind. Is that a rule that regulates insurance? What else needs to be known, in order to give confident answers?

If you conclude that an anti-rescission rule is one regulating insurance—with respect to a preemption problem—and that a pro-rescission rule is not, does it follow that federal law disfavors rescission?[12]

d. Arbitration

The Federal Arbitration Act provides that arbitration agreements in contracts involving interstate commerce are binding: "shall be valid, irrevocable, and enforceable, save upon such grounds as exist at law or in equity

---

10. See Foley v. Interactive Data Corp., 765 P.2d 373 (Cal.1988).

11. Elfstrom v. New York Life Ins. Co., 432 P.2d 731, 737 (Cal.1967).

12. This problem is derived from the facts in Progressive N. Ins. Co. v. Corder, 15 S.W.3d 381 (Ky. 2000).

for revocation of any contract."[13] A state court must place a contract's arbitration term "on the same footing" as its other terms.[14] As the Supreme Court has construed the Act, a state may not "decide that a contract is fair enough to enforce all its basic terms (price, service, credit), but not fair enough to enforce its arbitration clause."[15]

PROBLEM

Let it be supposed that the laws of two states differ about the enforceability of an arbitration term that appears in a standard-form contract and that governs disputes yet to arise. It is a declared public policy of State Alpha that a term like that should not be enforced against an individual. The law of State Beta is otherwise, except that, by statute, a term like that appearing in an insurance contract is unenforceable against the insured. Suppose further two standard-form policies, one governed by the law of State Alpha and the other by the law of State Beta, each containing an arbitration term, and both issued to individuals.

Develop an argument that the "Alpha" insurer cannot enforce its arbitration term, but that, by force of the Federal Arbitration Act, the "Beta" insurer can. If this distinction holds, does it make sense? See American Bankers Ins. Co. of Florida v. Crawford, 757 So.2d 1125 (Ala. 1999).

e.   The "Americans With Disabilities" Act

Doe v. Mutual of Omaha Ins. Co.

United States Court of Appeals, 7th Cir., 1999.
179 F.3d 557, *cert. denied*, 528 U.S. 1106 (2000).

Mutual of Omaha sold policies of health insurance to "John Doe" and to "Richard Smith", the suitors. Doe and Smith sought to vitiate a provision in each policy, similar in content. These provisions were "caps" on the amounts payable for AIDS or AIDS-related conditions (ARC). For other maladies each policy limit was $1 million. But the limits in question were $25,000 and $100,000, respectively. The basis for contesting these limits was the accommodations provision of the Americans with Disabilities Act (the ADA), § 302(a):[1]

> [N]o individual shall be discriminated against on the basis of disability in the full and equal enjoyment of the goods, services, facilities, privileges, advantages, or accommodations of any place of public accommodation [by the owner, lessee, or operator of such a place].

The district court ruled that the caps violated this provision. Mutual of Omaha appealed. Several points were uncontested. AIDS and ARC are disabilities, it was conceded. The insurer argued only that the ADA does not regulate the content of insurance contracts. Moreover, it stipulated that

---

13.   The Act is at 9 U.S.C. § 1 *et seq.* The quotation is from § 2.

14.   Scherk v. Alberto–Culver Co., 417 U.S. 506, 511 (1974).

15.   Allied-Bruce Terminix Cos. v. Dobson, 513 U.S. 265, 281 (1995).

1.   42 U.S.C. § 12182(a).

it "has not shown and cannot show that its AIDS Caps are or ever have been consistent with sound actuarial principles, actual or reasonably anticipated experience, bona fide risk classification, or state law."

The court's discussion of the statute is abbreviated here. It opened with this statement: "The core meaning ..., plainly enough, is that the owner or operator of a store, hotel, restaurant, dentist's office, travel agency, theater, Web site, or other facility (whether in physical space or in electronic space, ... that is open to the public cannot exclude disabled persons from entering the facility and, once in, from using the facility in the same way that the nondisabled do." The court gave several instances of prohibited refusals to deal; *e.g.*,

> The owner or operator of, say, a camera store can neither bar the door to the disabled nor let them in but then refuse to sell its cameras to them on the same terms as to other customers.... To come closer to home, a dentist cannot refuse to fill a cavity of a person with AIDS unless he demonstrates a direct threat to safety or health, ... and an insurance company cannot (at least without pleading a special defense, discussed below) refuse to sell an insurance policy to a person with AIDS.

But, the court pointed out, Mutual of Omaha had not refused to deal with Doe or Smith: it was "happy" to sell the policies to them.

To be sure, the policies were of less value to AIDS victims than to persons suffering from other disabling maladies, equally expensive to treat. Even to them, however, a capped policy might be worth $1 million: "people with AIDS have medical needs unrelated to AIDS." The court also said: "If all the medical needs of people with AIDS were AIDS-related and thus excluded by the policies, this might support an inference that Mutual of Omaha was trying to exclude such people, and such exclusion, as we shall see, might violate the Act. But that is not argued."

The court pointed out some oddities that would result if the suitors were to prevail. For one thing, an insurer would be permitted to cap benefits for heart disease (not a disabling condition), though not for AIDS. That would be to "discriminate among diseases." Moreover, the suitors did not deny that an insurer can reject an application for health insurance on account of a pre-existing malady. In other words: "If the applicant is already HIV-positive when he applies for a health-insurance policy, the insurer can in effect cap his AIDS-related coverage at $0."

■ POSNER, CHIEF JUDGE.

　　. . .

The common sense of the statute is that the content of the goods or services offered by a place of public accommodation is not regulated. A camera store may not refuse to sell cameras to a disabled person, but it is not required to stock cameras specially designed for such persons. Had Congress purposed to impose so enormous a burden on the retail sector of the economy and so vast a supervisory responsibility on the federal courts, we think it would have made its intention clearer and would at least have imposed some standards. It is hardly a feasible judicial function to decide whether shoestores should sell single shoes to one-legged persons and if so at what price, or how many Braille books the Borders or Barnes and Noble bookstore chains should stock in each of their stores. There are defenses to a prima facie case of public-accommodation discrimination, but they would do little to alleviate the judicial burden of making standardless decisions about the composition of retail inventories. . . .

To summarize the discussion to this point, we cannot find anything in the Americans with Disabilities Act or its background, or the nature of AIDS and AIDS caps, to justify so radically expansive an interpretation as would be required to bring these cases under section 302(a) without making an unprincipled distinction between AIDS caps and other product alterations [other than another provision of the Act, considered below].

We conclude that section 302(a) does not require a seller to alter his product to make it equally valuable to the disabled and to the nondisabled, even if the product is insurance. This conclusion is consistent with all the appellate cases to consider this or cognate issues. [Five court-of-appeals decisions cited]; cf. Modderno v. King, 82 F.3d 1059 (D.C.Cir.1996). And if it is wrong, the suit must fail anyway, because it is barred by the McCarran–Ferguson Act.

That Act, so far as bears on this case, forbids construing a federal statute to "impair any law enacted by any State for the purpose of regulating the business of insurance . . . unless such Act specifically relates to the business of insurance." 15 U.S.C. § 1012(b). Direct conflict with state law is not required to trigger this prohibition; it is enough if the interpretation would "interfere with a State's administrative regime." Humana Inc. v. Forsyth, 525 U.S. 299 (1999); Department of the Treasury v. Fabe, 508 U.S. 491 (1993); Autry v. Northwest Premium Services, Inc., 144 F.3d 1037, 1039–44 (7th Cir.1998). The interpretation of section 302(a) . . . for which the plaintiffs contend would do this. State regulation of insurance is comprehensive and includes rate and coverage issues, see Lee R. Russ & Thomas F. Segalla, Couch on Insurance §§ 2:7, 2:20, 2:26, 2:35 (3d ed.1997), so if federal courts are now to determine whether caps on disabling conditions (by no means limited to AIDS) are actuarially sound and consistent with principles of state law they will be stepping on the toes of state insurance commissioners.

It is one thing to say that an insurance company may not refuse to deal with disabled persons; the prohibition of such refusals can probably be administered with relatively little interference with state insurance regulation, NAACP v. American Family Mutual Ins. Co., 978 F.2d 287 (7th Cir.1992), and anyway this may be a prohibition expressly imposed by federal law because encompassed within the blanket prohibition of section 302(a) . . . , and so outside the scope of the McCarran–Ferguson Act. It is another thing to require federal courts to determine whether limitations on coverage are actuarially sound and consistent with state law. Even if the formal criteria are the same under federal and state law, displacing their administration into federal court—requiring a federal court to decide whether an insurance policy is consistent with state law—obviously would interfere with the administration of the state law. The states are not indifferent to who enforces their laws. . . .

It is true that we are not being asked in this case to decide whether the AIDS caps were actuarially sound and in accordance with state law. But if the McCarran–Ferguson Act does not apply, then we are certain to be called upon to decide such issues in the next case, when the insurer does not stipulate to them. Mutual of Omaha didn't want to get into these messy issues if it could show that the Americans with Disabilities Act did not apply. . . . If the ADA is fully applicable, insurers will have to defend their AIDS caps by reference to section 501(c), and the federal courts will then find themselves regulating the health-insurance industry, which McCarran–Ferguson tells them not to do.

[In the foregoing paragraph the court referred to § 501(c)(1) of the statute. Of that section the court had earlier said: "(It) provides that Title I (employment discrimination against the disabled) and Title III (public accommodations, the title involved in this case) 'shall not be construed to prohibit or restrict an insurer . . . from underwriting risks, classifying risks, or administering such risks that are based on or not inconsistent with State law,' . . . unless the prohibition or restriction is 'a subterfuge to evade the purposes' of either title. (42 U.S.C.) § 12201(c)".]

Section 501(c) itself specifically relates to insurance and thus is not within the scope of McCarran–Ferguson. But the interpretation that the McCarran–Ferguson Act bars is not an interpretation of 501(c); it is an interpretation of section 302(a) that injects the federal courts into the heart of the regulation of the insurance business by the states.

Of course, we can infer from section 501(c)—we have done so earlier in this opinion—and Mutual of Omaha does not deny, that section 302(a) has some application to insurance: it forbids an insurer to turn down an applicant merely because he is disabled. To that extent, as we have already suggested, we can accept (certainly for purposes of argument) that section 302(a) relates specifically to the business of insurance. But thus limited to a simple prohibition of discrimination, section 302(a) does not impair state regulation of insurance; no state wants insurance companies to refuse to insure disabled people. It is only when section 302(a) is interpreted as broadly as it must be for the plaintiffs in this case to prevail that McCarran–Ferguson's reverse preemption comes into play.

Both because section 302(a) of the Americans with Disabilities Act does not regulate the content of the products or services sold in places of public accommodation and because an interpretation of the section as regulating the content of insurance policies is barred by the McCarran–Ferguson Act, the judgment in favor of the plaintiffs must be reversed with directions to enter judgment for the defendant. This does not, however, leave the plaintiffs remediless. If in fact the AIDS caps in the defendant's policies are not consistent with state law and sound actuarial practices (and whether they are or not, the defendant may be bound by its stipulation, though this we needn't decide), the plaintiffs can obtain all the relief to which they are entitled from the state commissioners who regulate the insurance business. Federal law is not the only source of valuable rights. Reversed.

■ Evans, Circuit Judge, dissenting.

. . .

The Americans with Disabilities Act is a broad, sweeping, protective statute requiring the elimination of discrimination against individuals with disabilities.... Because I believe the insurance policies challenged in this case discriminate against people with AIDS in violation of the ADA, I dissent.

The majority believes we are being asked to regulate the content of insurance policies—something we should not do under the ADA. But as I see it we are not being asked to regulate content; we are being asked to decide whether an insurer can discriminate against people with AIDS, refusing to pay for them the same expenses it would pay if they did not have AIDS. The ADA assigns to courts the task of passing judgment on such conduct. And to me, the Mutual of Omaha policies at issue violate the Act.

Chief Judge Posner's opinion likens the insurance company here to a camera store forced to stock cameras specially designed for disabled persons. While I agree that the ADA would not require a store owner to alter its inventory, I think the analogy misses the mark. The better analogy would be that of a store which lets disabled customers in the door, but then refuses to sell them anything but inferior cameras.... Section 501(c)'s "safe harbor" would allow Mutual of Omaha to treat insureds with AIDS differently than those without AIDS if the discrimination were consistent with Illinois law or could be justified by actuarial principles or claims experience. But Mutual of Omaha conceded that its AIDS and ARC caps do not fall under the ADA's safe harbor protection.

The parties stipulated that the very same affliction (e.g., pneumonia) may be both AIDS-related and not AIDS-related and that, in such cases, coverage depends solely on whether the patient has AIDS. In my view that is more than enough to trigger an ADA violation. Chief Judge Posner reasons that, although the policies appear to discriminate solely based on an insured's HIV status, they really don't, when you consider the nature of AIDS. He suggests that the phrase "AIDS related conditions" embodies a unique set of symptoms and afflictions that would make it easy for the insurance company to determine with certainty whether an expense incurred for a particular illness is "AIDS-related" and therefore subject to the cap. His analysis—charitable to Mutual of Omaha to be sure—may very well be medically sound. But it doesn't come from the insurance policies. The policies don't even hint at what illnesses or afflictions might fall within the ARC exclusion. Nor has the medical community embraced an accepted definition for what "conditions" are "AIDS-related." The practical effect of all this, as Mutual of Omaha concedes, is that coverage for certain expenses would be approved or denied based solely on whether the insured had AIDS. Given that the ADA is supposed to signal a "clear and comprehensive national mandate for the elimination of discrimination against individuals with disabilities," see 42 U.S.C. § 12101(b)(1), I would use the statute to right the wrong committed by Mutual of Omaha.

I also part company with the majority on the McCarran–Ferguson Act analysis, and I think the faultiness of its conclusion is evident in the way the issue is framed. The Chief Judge writes: "It is one thing to say that an insurance company may not refuse to deal with disabled persons; the prohibition of such refusals can probably be administered with relatively little interference with state insurance regulation.... It is another thing to require federal courts to determine whether limitations on coverage are actuarially sound and consistent with state law." This is somewhat misleading because, as the majority acknowledges, the question of whether these caps are actuarially sound or consistent with state law has been taken out of the equation by Mutual of Omaha's concession in the parties' stipulation. Consistent with McCarran–Ferguson we can—and we should—decide exactly what the majority seemed to think is permissible: whether an insurer may refuse to deal with disabled persons on the same terms as nondisabled persons. Because any conceivable justification for the caps (under section 501(c)) is not at issue, and because an insurer cannot legally decide to pay or not pay expenses based solely on whether an insured has AIDS and is therefore disabled under the ADA, I dissent from the opinion of the court.

NOTES

(1) *Department-of-Justice View*. As other courts have done, this one disregarded a view of the DOJ, which administers the ADA. According to the Department:

> [The insurer] may not ... limit the amount, extent, or kind of coverage available ... because of a physical or mental impairment, except when the ... limitation ... is based on sound actuarial principles or is related to actual or reasonably anticipated experience.

The Americans with Disabilities Act: Title III Technical Assistance Manual III–3.0000 (1993).

(2) *Reverberations of* Doe. Judge Posner's observations about common sense in relation to camera stores, shoe stores, and bookstores was quoted in an opinion by Justice Scalia. But that was a dissent. PGA Tour, Inc. v. Martin, 532 U.S. 661, 691, 698 (2001). (The case concerned certain golfing tournaments that required a contestant to walk the course.)

The court's observation about Web sites has drawn much attention. Title III of the ADA means, the court said, that the owner or operator of a Web site, open to the public, cannot prevent access to it by disabled persons, or their using it "in the same way that the nondisabled do." Along with other cases, *Doe* has been cited as part of a "thicket of a circuit split" on the issue whether or not Title III applies to Internet Web sites. Access Now, Inc. v. Southwest Airlines Company, 385 F.3d 1324, 1334 (11th Cir. 2004).[1]

---

1. "The case centers around the inaccessibility of Southwest's web site [to persons] who are visually impaired and use the Internet through a special software program called a 'screen reader.' Some features of Southwest.com make it very difficult for the

(3) *More on McCarran*. With respect to the McCarran Act, other federal laws that do not specifically relate to the business of insurance are enforceable to the extent that they do not "invalidate, impair, or supersede" state law. Taking that proposition for granted, is the court's opinion in Doe v. Mutual of Omaha consistent with it?

(4) *Consequences*. The ruling in *Doe* about the ADA is especially momentous for persons having coverage under many group employee-benefit plans, paid for by their employers—"self-funded" plans.[2] Persons otherwise covered may, in many places, get the benefit of state-law anti-discrimination rules. Not so, it is said, for the beneficiaries of self-funded plans: They are governed by ERISA, which preempts the state-law rules.[3] These persons constitute some 40% of Americans having group coverage.[4]

(5) *Adverse Comment*. The ADA ruling in *Doe* and in comparable cases has attracted considerable adverse comment in journals. See, for example, S. Bagenstos, The Future of Disability Law, 114 Yale L. J. 1, at 37–41 (2004): The distinction between access and content "has largely drained the statute of effectiveness in attacking what may be the single most significant employment barrier faced by people with disabilities as a group—the current structure of our health insurance system."

Much adverse comment is cited in Olender, Capping AIDS Benefits ..., 23 Am.J.Law & Medicine 107 (2002). That Note attempts a point-by-point rebuttal of Judge Posner's reasoning, and endorses the views of another observer in this way:

> If courts continue to hold that Title III does not apply to insurance policies' content, several negative consequences will result. First, courts will disregard the ADA's purpose as it relates to discrimination against AIDS patients. Second, AIDS patients will become sicker more quickly and die earlier when unable to access the expensive, early treatment that is accepted as most effective. Third, having exhausted their insurance coverage and their own personal resources, AIDS patients will burden the state that will necessarily assume financial responsibility for their treatment. Finally, by judicially sanctioning insurance companies' discrimination against AIDS patients, courts will reinforce the destructive social stigma that already surrounds these vulnerable members of our society.[5]

Ms. Olender suggested various ways to circumvent the ruling in *Doe*, including increased public funding of health care for persons who suffer from HIV/AIDS. Is that avenue more attractive than overruling *Doe*?

(6) *Mental Health*. So far as the ADA is concerned, the treatment of mental maladies need not be on a par with that of other maladies in medical-expense coverages. This is not discriminatory, it has been said, so far as identical coverage is

---

visually impaired to access using a screen reader." Id. at 1325.

2. See McNeil v. Time Ins. Co., 205 F.3d 179, 190 (5th Cir.2000): "We ... have held that an insurance policy is not governed by ERISA if (1) the employer does not contribute to the plan; (2) participation is voluntary; (3) the employer's role is limited to collecting premiums and remitting them to the insurer; and (4) the employer received no profit from the plan. Meredith [v. Time Ins. Co., 980 F.2d 352 (5th Cir.1993)] at 355."

3. Pursuant to ERISA, the Secretary of Labor has exempted from the statute certain group-insurance programs.

4. B. Furrow et al., Health Law 781 (3d ed.1997).

5. Id. at 108–109. The four footnote citations in this paragraph—omitted here—refer to Joly, Doe ...: The Possible Impact of Insurance Caps on HIV–Infected Individuals, 4 DePaul J. Health Care L. 193, 221 (2000).

extended to persons who enjoy good mental health and to those who do not. Parker v. Metropolitan Life Ins. Co., 121 F.3d 1006 (6th Cir. 1997) (en banc; divided court). For a contrary view see S. Starr, Simple Fairness: Ending Discrimination in the Insurance Coverage of Addictive Treatment, 111 Yale L. J. 2321, 2349–54 (2002) ("[I]t is true but irrelevant that people who do not need mental health benefits are also deprived of them."). The *Parker* opinion describes what Congress has done, and has not done, about disparities.

(7) *Bad deal* vs. *No deal*. Notice the court's surmise, in *Doe*, that an insurer's refusal to deal with disabled persons "may be a prohibition expressly imposed by federal law. . . ." Soon afterward another court of appeals found a strong implication in the ADA that "the Act is intended to reach insurance underwriting practices that are inconsistent with State law." Pallozzi v. Allstate Life Ins. Co., 198 F.3d 28, 32 (2d Cir.1999). According to the plaintiffs, Joseph and Lori Pallozzi, Allstate Life had withheld from them a joint life policy, as applied for, by reason of their disabling psychic disorders (as reported to the defendant by their psychiatrist)[6].

The term "underwriting practice," as used in *Pallozzi*, referred to a risk calculation made when deciding whether or not to provide insurance. This may be called "inquiry underwriting." The term "underwriting" could be stretched to include also the practice of controlling risk through limits on policy benefits, illustrated by the AIDS caps on payouts that Mutual of Omaha deployed. "Contract underwriting," that might be called. The net effect of the two cases seems to be this: Congress has broadly condemned inquiry underwriting—so far as it operates against disabled persons—but has left contract underwriting in place. Is that a wise distinction?

(8) *An Authorization*. Congress declared, in the ADA, that it should not be construed to "prohibit or restrict . . . an insurer [and some other entities] from underwriting risks [or] classifying risks. . . ." 42 U.S.C. § 12201. From this provision it has been argued that the Act *does* prevent an insurer from restricting a benefit available to a disabled person. What possible answer can be made to that argument? See McNeil v. Time Ins. Co., 205 F.3d 179 (5th Cir. 2000).

Review Problem[7]

A decedent's estate is accountable to a hospital, in the amount of $100,000, for care given to the decedent as a victim of AIDS (of which he died). The executor hopes to recoup that amount under a medical-expense policy that the decedent had arranged while he was afflicted but before he suspected his illness. Because the policy was issued to his professional firm, and protected the firm's secretary as well as the decedent, it represented an employee-benefit plan. The policy limit is larger than the hospital's claim.

The executor's claim on the policy faces two impediments. For one thing, the policy excluded coverage of charges for the treatment of any malady existing when the policy took effect. Also, it set a $10,000 ceiling on payable charges incurred—as the hospital's charges were—within two years of that date.

In addition to claiming on the policy, the executor bases claims on the applicable state law of estoppel and common-law discrimination.

---

6. It is safe to suppose that the psychiatrist violated no duty of confidentiality owed to the Pallozzis because, in applying to All-state Life for insurance, they had authorized it to inquire into their medical histories.

7. Based on the facts of *McNeil*.

Questions. What hopes can the executor have of recovering $100,000? Of recovering $10,000? Is ERISA a plausible basis for either claim? Is the ADA? What hope might the executor have of making a claim under a state statute that prohibits, in general, discrimination against handicapped persons?

———

CHAPTER 3

JUDICIAL REGULATION OF INSURANCE CONTRACTS

Judges are given to saying that their way with insurance contracts is to enforce them as written. They qualify this, of course, by saying that they also police contracts for congruence with statutory prescriptions and with public policies otherwise expressed. Like other contracts, insurance contracts are not always plainly written. Hence the courts are called on to construe and interpret them. In doing so they apply some principles that are unique to contracts of insurance, and others that are not. Some of the latter, although applicable to contracts in general, appear to apply with special stringency to insurance contracts.

Some remedies and doctrines of general application also have special force as applied against insurers. These include reformation, waiver, and the "implied duty of good faith". They include also estoppel, whether based on a representation (estoppel *in pais*) or on a promise (promissory estoppel). Insurers are also a target of the so-called "doctrine of reasonable expectations", which, at least in some versions, goes beyond other methods of binding them, and which is largely confined to insurance contracts.

As will be seen, insurance contracts are sometimes construed so as to conform them to a sense of social welfare. That can be characterized fairly as the "judicial regulation" of insurance. Indeed, all the activities mentioned above (other, perhaps, than "enforcing the contract as written") can be so characterized when the matter in hand is about insurance. Some courts and some judges are more inclined than others, naturally, to be freehanded in shaping the obligations of insurers. When grouped into camps, they may be called conservative and liberal, and their methods formal and functional. Readers may discern exemplars of those camps and those methods in this chapter.

Part A of this chapter treats of contract interpretation and construction. Part B collects materials about the remedies and doctrines mentioned in the second paragraph above. Part C is about the explicit policing of insurance contracts with reference to certain public policies.

A. INTERPRETATION AND CONSTRUCTION

This section presents cases ostensibly regulating insurance contracts and policy language by judicial interpretation and construction. But consider the words of Professor Vance: "It must be confessed that many decisions justify the assertion, sometimes made, that a different rule of construction is applied by the courts to insurance contracts from that which applies to contracts of other kinds. But, as a matter of law, an insurance contract should be construed as any other contract, the real purpose of the construction being to give full effect to the expressed intention of the parties so far as that intention is legal. . . . There are countless cases wherein the courts have laid down rules for the construction of insurance policies. With relatively minor exceptions the courts are in substantial agreement in their statements of the rules of construction to be applied, but in the application of these rules to particular cases there is much room for differences of opinion."[1]

This passage indicates one of the difficulties that attend the project of understanding the ways of courts with policy language. Another is that courts often fail to provide principled bases for decisions that effectively regulate insurance contracts. That being so, one is tempted to group these decisions into the political categories *conservative* and *liberal*. Other possible categories, roughly congruent with those, are *formal* and *functional*— words suggestive of the scholastic opposition between positivism and realism.[2]

The following excerpts represent a conservative, traditional attitude toward policy interpretation and construction:

"A contract for insurance is no different than any other contract."[3] "The [insurance] policy is a contract and we cannot rewrite it."[4] "Courts are bound to enforce the contract as written."[5] "Courts must enforce, not write, contracts of insurance and their language must be given its plain, ordinary and popular meaning."[6]

A court so saying may be quick to detect a plain meaning. And a strong commitment to the parol evidence rule, even to the point of excluding extrinsic evidence of the parties' understanding of policy terms, sometimes

1. William R. Vance, Handbook on the Law of Insurance 808–09 (3d Buist M. Anderson ed. 1951).

2. See Peter Nash Swisher, Judicial Rationales in Insurance Law: Dusting Off the Formal for the Function, 52 Ohio St. L. J. 1037 (1991). According to Legal Formalism, correct legal opinions are solely decided by logical deduction based only on pre-existing judicial and legislative precedents. The judge examines the "four corners" of the written insurance-contract document and construes it by applying general contract law and precedent except when the insurance contract or procedure is regulated by statute. The judge remains socially neutral and deductively applies the law to the facts of the particular case. According to Legal Functionalism, courts are concerned with socially desirable consequences and not logical consistency because certainty and predictability are seldom achievable.

3. Drilling v. New York Life Ins. Co., 137 N.E. 314, 316 (N.Y. 1922) (J. Crane).

4. Strickland v. Gulf Life Insurance Co., 237 S.E.2d 530, 531 (Ga.App. 1977).

5. Hebert v. Insurance Center, Inc., 706 So.2d 1007, 1011 (La.App. 3 Cir. 1998).

6. Tobin v. Beneficial Standard Life Insurance Co., 675 F.2d 606, 608 (4th Cir. 1982) (S.C. law). Arizona seems especially keen on plain meaning: Almagro v. Allstate Insurance Co., 629 P.2d 999 (Ariz.App.1981) ("The policy provision must be applied as written, and the court will not pervert or do violence to the language used or extend it beyond its plain and ordinary meaning."); Combined Communications Corp. v. Seaboard Sur. Co., 641 F.2d 743 (9th Cir. 1981) (Ariz. law) ("The courts may not create ambiguities where none exists, even to avoid harsh results.").

reinforces this attitude.[7] Although opinions along these lines appear to disclaim any regulatory function in applying policy language, the appearance may well be deceptive.

Many opinions exhibit a contrary tendency. Thus: "What do they know of the law of insurance who only the law of contract know?"[8] Some courts appear to create phantom bargains recognizing rights in insureds, which contradict reasonably clear and precise insurance policy language. These courts typically adopt a "contract of adhesion" rationale.

> "[A]n insurance policy is not an ordinary contract. It is a complex instrument, unilaterally prepared, and seldom understood by the assured.... The parties are not similarly situated. The [insurer] and its representatives are expert in the field; the [insured] is not. A court should not be unaware of this reality and subordinate its significance to strict legal doctrine."[9]

For that reason, the insurance contract language at issue is held to be ambiguous and is judicially construed against the author, pursuant to the *contra proferentem* rule.[10]

Given a welter of opinions, exhibiting here intemperate views and there irreconcilable ones, an observer may be tempted to dismiss even a justifiable decision as "just another insurance case." That should not be. Competent lawyering presupposes satisfactory guiding patterns, principles, and rules that govern the judicial mode of insurance regulation of policies. Insurance law and litigation is neither entirely a turf battle between conservative (formal) and liberal (functional) approaches nor a struggle between plain meaning and ambiguity. There is no single judicial method and no immutable legal (or equitable) principle of interpretation and construction. There is only the judicial common-law method issuing in an evolutionary body of law. In the common-law tradition, there will always be two large fields of legal uncertainty—the field of the obsolete and dying, and the field of the newborn and evolving.

1.   Plain Meaning

Standard Venetian Blind Co. v. American Empire Insurance

Pennsylvania Supreme Court, 1983.
503 Pa. 300, 469 A.2d 563.

■ ROBERTS, CHIEF JUSTICE.

This appeal presents the question of whether appellee Standard Venetian Blind Company (Venetian), the insured under a policy of liability

---

7. Cases holding that only the written insurance contract may be examined to determine whether it is ambiguous are collected in Comment Note, 40 A.L.R.3d 1384.

8. Satz v. Massachusetts Bonding & Ins. Co., 153 N.E. 844 (N.Y.1926) (J. Pound).

9. Prudential Ins. Co. v. Lamme, 425 P.2d 346, 347 (Nev. 1967).

10. *Contra* means against and *proferentem* means profferor or author of the insurance contract language at issue. Since the profferor/author usually is the insurance company, the rule is often called the "contra insurer" rule.

insurance issued by appellant American Empire Insurance Company (American), may avoid the effect of a clear and unambiguous exclusion clause in the insurance contract by showing that it was neither made aware of nor understood the effect of the exclusion. We conclude that the lack of knowledge or understanding of a clearly drafted exclusion clause in a written contract of insurance executed by both parties does not render the clause unenforceable. Hence we reverse....

I

The present controversy has its origin in an action in assumpsit filed by D. H. Evans against Venetian and one of its partners, appellee Sheldon B. Morris, in which Evans sought to recover for damages to a portico installed by a subcontractor of Venetian pursuant to a contract between Venetian and Evans. The portico had been installed in April of 1974 on property owned by Evans, and was destroyed completely in January of 1978 when it collapsed during a heavy snowstorm. The collapse of the portico also caused damage to property owned by Evans which had been stored underneath the portico. Evans' complaint, which alleged breaches of implied and express warranties, sought damages of $13,826.56, the cost of replacing the portico, and additional damages of $880, the cost of repairing the items stored beneath the portico plus the cost of labor needed to remove the collapsed structure.[a]

At the time of the filing of the action in assumpsit, Venetian was the insured under a liability policy issued by American in May of 1975.... The policy further provided that American had "the right and the duty to defend any suit against the insured seeking damages...." Immediately below the coverage provision was a section captioned "Exclusions." Under this section, conspicuously displayed and sequentially listed, were set forth the types of claims and losses for which American was not obliged to defend or indemnify Venetian. Exclusions (n) and (o) provided:

This insurance does not apply:

. . .

(n) to property damage to the named insured's products arising out of such products;

(o) to property damage to work performed by or on behalf of the named insured arising out of the work or any portion thereof or out of materials, parts or equipment furnished in connection therewith.[b]

a. From the concurring opinion: Venetian and Morris "had agreed to furnish the portico to Evans for a price of $9,200 and that price had apparently been paid. In his action on that contract Evans asserted breach of both express and implied warranties that the portico would not collapse under weights of snow or ice far beyond those seen in the Wilkes–Barre area. In January, 1978, within four years of its installation, the portico collapsed following a heavy snowstorm."

b. Another exclusion (a) concerned "liability assumed by the insured under any contract or agreement except an incidental con-

The policy defined the phrase "named insured's products" as "goods or products manufactured, sold, handled or distributed by the named insured or others trading under his name. . . ."

In a deposition made a part of the record, Sheldon Morris testified that he has a high school education, can read the English language, and has been a self-employed businessman since 1946. He also testified that, although he had received a copy of the policy, he had never read it. He stated that he had not read the policy because he had relied on the judgment of the Block Brothers Insurance Agency and because he had indicated to Block Brothers that "we wanted full coverage on everything we have."[c]

Immediately upon receiving the complaint in assumpsit, Morris filed answers on behalf of himself and Venetian and promptly notified American of the claim. American agreed, on Venetian's behalf, to indemnify Evans for the cost of the damaged property which had been stored beneath the portico as well as the cost of labor, but refused to defend the assumpsit action or tender payment for the cost of the portico itself. American's refusal was based on its assertion that, while the policy provided coverage for damage caused by products of Venetian, the policy expressly excluded coverage for damage to Venetian's products themselves. Trial then commenced on the breach of warranty action, at the conclusion of which a jury returned a verdict against Venetian and Morris in the amount of $13,094.64.

While trial on the action in assumpsit was still pending, Venetian commenced the present proceedings by filing a petition for a declaratory judgment. The court of common pleas found that exclusions (n) and (o) set forth in the policy were "plain and free of ambiguity," and that these provisions expressly excluded coverage for damage to the portico. Nonetheless, the court of common pleas, relying on language in the Superior Court's decision in Hionis v. Northern Mutual Insurance Co., 327 A.2d 363 (Pa.Super. 1974), held that because Venetian had neither been made aware of the exclusions nor had their meaning been explained to it, coverage existed under the policy for the full amount of the judgment entered against Venetian. A panel of the Superior Court affirmed, also on the authority of *Hionis*, and this appeal followed.

II

The principles governing our interpretation of a contract of insurance are familiar and well settled. The task of interpreting a contract is generally performed by a court rather than by a jury. (citations omitted) Where a provision of a policy is ambiguous, the policy provision is to be

---

tract; but this exclusion does not apply to a warranty of fitness or quality of the named insured's products or a warranty that the work performed by or on behalf of the named insured will be done in a workmanlike manner."

c. From the concurring opinion: "He explained complete and full coverage to mean 'that we would be free of any involvement in the thing in the event anything should happen, our fire insurance, our products liability, our contingent liability and all of the items that go into making up these policies.' "

construed in favor of the insured and against the insurer, the drafter of the agreement. See Mohn v. American Casualty Co. of Reading, supra. Where, however, the language of the contract is clear and unambiguous, a court is required to give effect to that language. (citation omitted) "[I]n the absence of proof of fraud, 'failure to read [the contract] is an unavailing excuse or defense and cannot justify an avoidance, modification or nullification of the contract or any provision thereof.'" Olson Estate, 447 Pa. 483, 488, 291 A.2d 95, 98 (1972), quoting Orner v. T.W. Phillips Gas & Oil Co., 401 Pa. 195, 199, 163 A.2d 880, 883 (1960).*

Application of these precepts to the insurance contract in this case requires the conclusion that Venetian is bound by the agreement it signed. As found by the court of common pleas, the exclusions at issue are "plain and free of ambiguity," and could have been readily comprehended by Mr. Morris had he chosen to read them. Those provisions expressly excluded coverage for "property damage to the named insured's products arising out of such products," and for "property damage to work performed by or on behalf of the named insured arising out of such work ... or out of materials, parts or equipment furnished in connection therewith," the very types of losses sustained here. It has not been suggested, much less shown, that either exclusion is contrary to law or to regulations of the Insurance Department. Manifestly, to allow Venetian to avoid application of the clear and unambiguous policy limitations in these circumstances would require us to rewrite the parties' written contract.

In *Hionis* upon which both the court of common pleas and the Superior Court relied, the Superior Court stated:

[W]here a policy is written in unambiguous terms, the burden of establishing the applicability of the exclusion or limitation involves proof that the insured was aware of the exclusion or limitation and that the effect thereof was explained to him.

327 A.2d at 365. Venetian maintains that this Court should adopt this language as a rule of insurance law, as the Superior Court has done here and in other cases decided since *Hionis*. ...

We believe that the burden imposed by *Hionis* fails to accord proper significance to the written contract, which has historically been the true test of parties' intentions. By focusing on what was and was not said at the time of contract formation rather than on the parties' writing, *Hionis* makes the question of the scope of insurance coverage in any given case depend upon how a factfinder resolves questions of credibility. Such a process, apart from the obvious uncertainty of its results, unnecessarily delays the resolution of controversy, adding only unwanted costs to the cost of procuring insurance. Thus, *Hionis*, which would permit an insured to

---

* [Court's opinion has no footnotes except this footnote identified by *] As Chief Justice John Bannister Gibson observed, "[i]f a party, who can read ... will not read a deed put before him for execution; or if, being unable to read, will not demand to have it read or explained to him, he is guilty of supine negligence, which ... is not the subject of protection, either in equity or at law." *Greenfield Estate*, 14 Pa. 489, 496 (1850).

avoid the application of a clear and unambiguous limitation clause in an insurance contract, is not to be followed.

Although on this record we reject *Hionis*, we note that in light of the manifest inequality of bargaining power between an insurance company and a purchaser of insurance, a court may on occasion be justified in deviating from the plain language of a contract of insurance. See 13 Pa.C.S. § 2302 [UCC 2–302 as enacted in Pennsylvania] (court may refuse to enforce contract or any clause of contract if court as a matter of law deems the contract or any clause of the contract to have been "unconscionable at the time it was made"). This record does not present such an occasion. We hold only that where, as here, the policy limitation relied upon by the insurer to deny coverage is clearly worded and conspicuously displayed, the insured may not avoid the consequences of that limitation by proof that he failed to read the limitation or that he did not understand it.

The order of the Superior Court is reversed and the record is remanded to the Court of Common Pleas of Luzerne County with the direction that judgment be entered in favor of appellant.

■ HUTCHINSON, JUSTICE, concurring.[d]

I concur in the result. I write separately because I believe a general liability policy protects the policyholder by covering him against claims made by third parties for injuries to their person or property resulting from the policyholder's negligence. A liability policy does not provide a guarantee of the policyholder's workmanship.[1] Such a guarantee is not within its coverage. I do not believe a businessman of ordinary intelligence could reasonably expect[2] to obtain a defense against and indemnity for the cost of properly performing his contract or replacing his failed product under a liability policy. Of course, such a holding would not negate general liability coverage for damage to third persons, their property, or the insured's other property, where that damage to others or other property is caused by the insured's improper performance of his contract or his delivery of a defective product. In short, this case involves an absence of coverage itself, not an exclusion negating coverage which would otherwise exist. The majority by interpreting the issue in terms of exclusions misses the point.

. . .

Having carefully examined the entire policy appellant issued in the context of the whole record, I would not here disturb the lower courts' conclusion that the exclusions, in and of themselves, are plain and free of ambiguity. Nevertheless, I note that the time and concentration an ordinarily intelligent businessman would have had to spend to review the whole policy to gain an appreciation of the effect of those exclusions, is such that analysis in terms of ambiguity is not truly meaningful. Moreover, such

---

d. Joined by Flaherty, J.

1. [Concurring opinion has numbered footnotes. Some footnotes are omitted.] Henderson, Insurance Protection for Products Liability and Completed Operations— What Every Lawyer Should Know, 50 Nebraska L.Rev. 415, 441 (1971).

2. Selected Risks Insurance Company v. Bruno, 718 F.2d 67 (3rd Cir. 1983).

analysis does not explain the variations in result, in this or other jurisdictions, in cases addressing the scope of coverage a general liability policy affords to a contractor. Those authorities do reach different results on coverage, depending on whether the occurrence causes damage to third parties, to property other than that which is the subject of the insured's contractual obligation, or damage to the subject of the insured's contractual obligation itself. Generally the cases find liability coverage in the first two instances and deny it in the third. (citation omitted)

II

... Whatever its merits, I do not believe the *Hionis* dictum is the appropriate principle for analysis of this particular case in which this court is called upon to interpret a comprehensive general liability policy purchased by a businessman to protect himself from unexpected and unintended "occurrences" which cause injury to the person or property of another.

Analysis of such policies generally, and this policy particularly, in terms of their clarity to ordinary businessmen has little relevance to the conduct of affairs in the real world. Such policies are ordinarily "clear" and "unambiguous," if at all, only to underwriters, statisticians or actuaries who have expert knowledge in the evaluation and classification of risks. Thus, it strikes me as inappropriate to analyze this case in terms of antedated objective notions of late nineteenth and early twentieth century contract law expressed in terms of meeting of the minds. Moreover, such analysis fails to explain the cases in this or other jurisdictions. Recognizing this discrepancy, some courts have analyzed coverage issues involving exclusions of the kind here present in the following terms: Such a "policy contemplates payment generally in situations where the ordinary degree of care is the measure of liability. The premium is determined on that basis." Royal Indemnity Company v. T. B. Smith, 173 S.E.2d 738, 740 (Ga.App. 1970) quoting F. D. Cooke, Jr., *Care, Custody or Control Exclusions*, [1959] Ins. L. J. 7 at p. 10.

Other courts have over the years expended whole forests analyzing the clarity or ambiguity of these exclusions. *See, e.g.* 8 A.L.R. 4th 563, Annotation on Scope of Clause Excluding from Contractor's or Similar Liability Policy Damage to Property in Care, Custody, or Control of Insured. I agree in part with Presiding Judge Hall of the Court of Appeals of Georgia, Division No. 3, who said:

> We believe the better approach is to examine the purposes of the exclusion in the policy and determine whether this is the type of risk against which the insurance company had not calculated its premiums.
>
> ... There are several different reasons for such an exclusion in the policy. Fundamentally, were it not for the exclusion there would be a greater moral hazard as far as the insurance company is concerned. It also eliminates the possibility of the insured making the insurance company a guarantor of its workmanship.

Royal Indemnity Company v. T. B. Smith, *supra* [173 S.E.2d 738 (Ga.App. 1970)] at 740.

On the other hand, I do not believe these cases can be decided solely on the basis of the insurer's unilateral analysis and pricing of the risk. Consideration must also be given to the insured's reasonable expectations in purchasing the policy, whether created by the policy language itself or the seller's representations concerning its coverage. This is the conclusion our sister state of New Jersey has reached in construing automobile liability policies. DiOrio v. New Jersey Manufacturers Insurance Company, 398 A.2d 1274 (N.J. 1979).[8] So viewed it is possible to rationalize the otherwise bewildering results justified by ambiguity, possessory versus proprietary control, presumptions *"contra proferentem"* and other devices which display a certain amount of internal semantic logic but leave the law governing contractor's liability insurance without coherence.

A businessman purchases a liability insurance policy to transfer the risk and cost of unexpected and unintended happenings (occurrences) to his insurance company. The company agrees to assume that risk for a calculated premium. The company does not, however, provide a guarantee of the businessman's workmanship or his products for that premium and typically protects itself against such claims by excluding coverage for property in the care, custody or control of the insured or property as to which the insured for any purpose is exercising control or by language such as we find in Exclusions (n) and (o) of the policy before us. "There is usually some form of insurance available to cover injury to or destruction of the excluded property at a higher premium which is commensurate with the risk. The exclusion is to eliminate securing the same coverage under a liability policy at cheaper rates." F. D. Cooke, Jr., *Care, Custody or Control Exclusions, supra.*

In the seventy-one pages summarizing cases on this subject at 8 A.L.R. 4th 563, the insurance carrier has generally had to provide coverage for unanticipated damage to property belonging to a third party but the purchaser of the insurance policy has generally been denied coverage for damage caused by defects in his own workmanship and to his own product.[10] The various rationalizations given for these results are conflicting, sometimes unhelpful and occasionally misleading.

[Justice Hutchinson reviewed Pennsylvania decisions about coverage.]

... Both the trial court and Superior Court have reasoned from the dictum in *Hionis* that the insurance company must provide coverage for the insured's completed operations or defective performance of his contract because it failed to prove that the insured was aware of the exclusions in his policy and failed to explain their effect. I think it more appropriate to focus on whether an insured who is asked to replace or return the price of his own failed product could reasonably expect coverage from his liability carrier. The cases I have examined indicate he cannot. For the foregoing

---

8. *Accord.*, Garber v. Travelers Insurance Companies, 280 Pa. Superior Ct. 323, 421 A.2d 744 (1980).

10. Similar differences in result can be traced in other types of liability policies such as errors and omissions policies.

reasons, I agree that the order of Superior Court and the judgment of the Court of Common Pleas of Luzerne County should be reversed. . . .

■ Nix, Justice, dissenting.

I dissent. The issue in this appeal is whether an exclusion in a liability insurance policy is enforceable. The majority, relying upon standard principles of contract law, focuses upon the question of ambiguity in the policy's language. Mr. Justice Hutchinson in his concurrence suggests the use of a "reasonable expectation" test. In my view both tests are equally nebulous and neither is appropriate in the area of insurance contract interpretation.

An insurance contract is essentially a contract of adhesion. Its terms are not bargained for but rather dictated by the insurer. Thus the insured's awareness and understanding of exclusions set forth in an insurance policy should not be presumed from the mere presence of such exclusions among the policy's terms. The very fact that the insurer prescribes particular exclusions indicates an assumption that the purchaser could otherwise reasonably expect to be covered against the risk so excluded.

It is therefore crucial that the insurer explain and the insured understand the precise nature of the policy's limitations. For this reason I would apply the test adopted by the Superior Court in *Hionis* employed by both that court and the trial court in this matter, and hold the insured to a standard of proving the insured was aware of and fully appreciated the effect of exclusions in the insurance policy before permitting the insurer to escape its duty to defend the insured. Because the insurer in the instant case failed to sustain that burden, I would affirm the order of the Superior Court.

NOTES

(1) *The E–Z Reader Car Policy.* Haynes v. Farmers Insurance Exchange, 89 P.3d 381 (Cal. 2004), concerned an automobile collision, personal injury, and an automobile liability coverage. Aside from the insurer, the parties chiefly concerned were a passenger in one of the cars ("Rider"), the owner of that car ("Owner"), and the person driving the car ("Driver"). Rider was injured in the collision. He sued Owner and Driver for damages. If Driver was liable to him for negligence, Owner was also liable, it seems, by statute, but not for more than $15,000.

Owner was required by statute to maintain liability coverage in that amount. (All sums mentioned in this Note are "per person per injury".) He held a Farmers Exchange policy providing him with coverage in a much larger amount: $250,000. As required by statute, the policy provided liability coverage for Driver as well as for Owner, Driver's use of the car having been permitted by Owner. By endorsement, however, the policy provided that Driver's coverage was limited to $15,000. That seemed too little to Rider, although the limitation was authorized by statute.[1]

Rider brought another action against the insurer, seeking a declaration of his rights; he contended that the ceiling on Driver's coverage was invalid. The trial court entered summary judgment for the insurer. That was reversed on a first

---

1. The statutes concerned are cited, and were applied, in Mid–Century Ins. Co. v. Haynes [a different Haynes], 267 Cal.Rptr. 248 (Cal.App. 1990).

appeal. The case arrived in the California Supreme Court on a further appeal by the insurer.

That court emphasized the complexity of the policy. Though called an " 'E–Z Reader' policy", it was 39 pages long, and was intricately structured. The endorsement in question was on page 24, under a heading of which the court said: "There is nothing [in it] to alert a reader that it limits permissive user coverage, nor anything ... to attract a reader's attention to the limiting language." The declarations page, which presumably followed the cover, stated the amount of "COVERAGES" in dollar numbers relating to Owner (*e.g.*, $250,000). That page did refer cryptically to the provision in question, but only under the unilluminating heading "ENDORSEMENTS". Only the endorsement number (S9064) was given there; it was the eighth of eleven numbers in the list.

"Conspicuous placement of exclusionary language", the court said, "is [] one of two rigid drafting rules required of insurers to exclude or limit coverage. [Also:] The language itself must be plain and clear."[2] The court concluded that neither requirement was met. Going further, it said: "Coverage may be limited by a valid endorsement and, if a conflict exists between the main body of the policy and an endorsement, the endorsement prevails. [But a limitation of coverage] must be placed and printed so that it will attract the reader's attention. Such a provision also must be stated precisely and understandably, in words that are part of the working vocabulary of the average layperson."

The court affirmed, one justice dissenting. The opinion runs to 23 pages in the official reports. It contains a conspectus of scholarship about construing insurance contracts.

Question a: Compare *Haynes* with the opinion in *Hionis*, described in the main case. How far do they differ with regard to construing policy language?

In *Wagner v. Erie Insurance Co.*, 847 A.2d 1274 (Pa. 2004), the court affirmed a holding that a pollution exclusion applied to preclude coverage for clean-up costs incurred when the rupture of an underground pipe at a service station released gasoline into the soil and under neighboring properties. Justice Nigro, with Justice Newman joining, wrote this brief dissent:

> I simply cannot accept the Superior Court's position that an insurance company providing general liability coverage for an insured's operation of a gasoline station can deny coverage for damages from a gasoline leak based on a general pollution exclusion, when that exclusion is buried on page twenty-five of the policy and the policy's definition of "pollutant" does not specifically reference gasoline.

Id. at 1275.

Question b: When the *Haynes* court spoke of requiring plain language, it added: "This means more than the traditional requirement that contract terms be 'unambiguous'. Precision is not enough. Understandability is also required." Does it follow that, under California law, an insurer must explain its coverage terms to a customer?

(2) *Precedents and Ambiguity*. In New Castle County v. National Union Fire Ins. Co., 243 F.3d 744 (3d Cir. 2001), the court sought to determine whether or not, under Delaware law, there was ambiguity in the phrase, "invasion of the right of

---

2. Quoted from Jauregui v. Mid–Century Ins. Co., 3 Cal.Rptr.2d 21, 24 (Cal.App. 1991).

private occupancy". Some courts had found the phrase ambiguous, the court said, "simply because of the wide variance among judicial decisions. See Travelers Indem. Co. v. Summit Corp. of America, 715 N.E.2d 926, 937–38 (Ind.App. 1999) ('This disagreement among the courts further indicates the ambiguity of the personal injury provisions.')." In *New Castle County*, the court cited an opinion of its own[3] where it had said: "That different courts have arrived at conflicting interpretations of the policy is strongly indicative of the policy's essential ambiguity."

But judges are at odds about that. See, for example, Peace v. Northwestern Nat'l Ins. Co., 596 N.W.2d 429 (Wis. 1999), a case concerning the pollution exclusion in a commercial general liability (CGL) policy. In that case, Chief Justice Abrahamson thought the conflicting understandings of courts in other cases signified ambiguity. She wrote:

> When numerous courts disagree about the meaning of language, the language cannot be characterized as having a plain meaning. Rather, the language is ambiguous; it is capable of being understood in two or more different senses by reasonably well-informed persons even though one interpretation might on careful analysis seem more suitable to this court. (Id. at 449).

But she said that in a dissent. The majority opinion took issue with her, saying, "The pollution exclusion clause does not become ambiguous merely because the parties . . . can point to conflicting interpretations of the clause by different courts. If the existence of differing court interpretations inevitably meant ambiguity, then only the first interpretation by a court would count." Id. at 442.

On an intermediate view, the fact of discordant judicial interpretations does not lead inexorably to a finding of ambiguity, but is rather some evidence of it. *Question*: Who has the better view about the effect of discordant precedents on the issue of ambiguity?

(3) *Disputes and Ambiguity*. Should ambiguity be found in a policy term because the litigants are in dispute about the right way to understand it? Courts have said both Yes and No. For "yes", see Northwest Airlines, Inc. v. Globe Indemnity Co., 225 N.W.2d 831, 837 (Minn. 1975) ("The very fact that [the parties'] positions as to what this policy says are contrary compels one to conclude that the agreement is indeed ambiguous."). For "no", see Farm Bureau Mutual Ins. Co. v. Sandbulte, 302 N.W.2d 104, 108 (Iowa 1981) ("The mere fact that parties disagree on the meaning of a phrase does not establish ambiguity. . . . The test is an objective one: Is the language *fairly* susceptible of two interpretations? We conclude it is not.").

Question: If you and your instructor disagree about the assignment for today's class, does it follow that the assignment was stated ambiguously?

---

2. Ambiguity and *Contra Proferentem*

One style of interpreting and construing insurance contracts is that employed for contracts at large when the parties have engaged in arms'-length bargaining on a relatively equal footing. The terms they have agreed upon can be assumed to express their common intent, each having pursued its own advantage. A court may well take a neutral attitude about contest-

---

3. Little v. MGIC Indem. Corp., 836 F.2d 789, 796 (3d Cir.1987).

ed language in an agreement, not wishing to "make a contract for the parties." A court may, that is, subscribe to the ideal of freedom to contract.

To ascribe meaning to a contract in that style is often at odds with reality. Whether the contract is one of insurance or not, it may appear that, for one reason or another, one of the parties was dominant in the bargaining. Market dominance is one reason; or that party may have made common cause with its competitors. A deeper pocket is one possible reason. Deeper and broader experience in transactions of the kind concerned is another. On finding or assuming bargaining inequality between the parties, a court may well take a partisan stance when called on to interpret or construe their agreement.

All the foregoing observations relate to contracts in general. They have issued in a doctrine known by the Latinate tag *contra proferentem*:[4] Ambiguous language is to be understood contrary to the interest of the one who prepared it. The Restatement of Contracts puts the matter this way:

§ 206. Interpretation Against the Draftsman

In choosing among the reasonable meanings of a promise or agreement or a term thereof, that meaning is generally preferred which operates against the party who supplies the words or from whom a writing otherwise proceeds.

That party is sometimes called the "profferor".

The doctrine has special force in litigation about insurance contracts. The underlying reasons commonly apply, in that the popular contracts are standardized, insurers are usually the profferors, and often they can insist on their terms. It is not always so of course; many policy buyers are themselves insurers, and others are represented by experienced and influential brokers and risk managers. When *contra proferentem is* applied against an insurer the effect is sometimes dramatic, almost as if the court were condemning the insurer's position as unconscionable.

World Trade Center Properties, L.L.C. v. Hartford Fire Ins. Co.

United States Court of Appeals, Second Circuit, 2003.
345 F.3d 154.

■ JOHN M. WALKER, CHIEF JUDGE

This case arises out of the devastating tragedy that occurred at the World Trade Center ("WTC") in lower Manhattan, New York, on the morning of September 11, 2001. At issue in this case is the amount of insurance that is recoverable for the total destruction of the WTC that occurred after the buildings were struck by two fuel-laden aircraft that had been hijacked by terrorists. The appellants are numerous entities that have

---

4. Short for *Ambigua responsio contra proferentem est accipienda.*

varying property interests in the WTC, including the Port Authority of New York and New Jersey (the "Port Authority"), which owns the property in fee simple, and Silverstein Properties, Inc. and several related entities ("Silverstein Properties"). In the spring of 2001, Silverstein Properties was the successful bidder on a 99–year lease for the property from the Port Authority. In July 2001, Silverstein Properties obtained primary and excess insurance coverage for the WTC complex from about two dozen insurers (most of which constitute the appellees and other counter-defendants in this case) in the total amount of approximately $3.5 billion "per occurrence." Because Silverstein Properties is the party that actually obtained the insurance coverage at issue in this case and was the primary insured, for ease of reference all appellants will hereafter be referred to collectively as the "Silverstein Parties."

The parties do not dispute that the destruction of the WTC resulted in a loss that greatly exceeded $3.5 billion. The broad question presented in this case is whether the events of September 11, 2001 constituted one or two "occurrences." The answer will determine whether the Silverstein Parties can recover once, up to $3.5 billion, or twice, up to $7 billion, under the insurance coverage. Complicating the resolution of this question is the fact that as of September 11, 2001, only one of the many insurers that bound coverage on the WTC had issued a final policy, necessitating an individualized inquiry to determine the terms of the insurance binders issued by each insurer.

BACKGROUND

As a condition of its 99–year lease of the WTC, Silverstein Properties was required to obtain first-party property insurance on the property. Silverstein Properties engaged Willis of New York ("Willis"), an insurance broker, to set up a multi-layered insurance program, which consisted of a primary insurance layer and 11 excess insurance layers providing a total of approximately $3.5 billion insurance on a "per occurrence" basis. In soliciting insurers for the program, Willis circulated a Property Underwriting Submission (the "Underwriting Submission") containing information regarding the proposed placement, including descriptions of the property and the insureds, desired coverage terms and conditions, estimated property values, engineering information, and a property loss history. With respect to at least the four insurers involved in these appeals, the Underwriting Submission also included a specimen copy of Willis's own "broker" form (the "WilProp form"). Section VIII of the Underwriting Submission states:

> Policy Form and Contract between Silverstein and the [Port Authority] are attached. DRAFT WilProp for Real Estate Risks is attached. We anticipate that this form will ultimately require amendment to comply with the Contract between Silverstein Properties, Inc. and the [Port Authority]. In the meantime, we provide this document as a starting point.

Of the four insurers in these appeals, Travelers was the only insurer to submit its own specimen policy form (the "Travelers form") during the course of negotiating the terms of coverage. Whereas the Travelers form did not define the term "occurrence," the WilProp form defined occurrence as follows:

> "Occurrence" shall mean all losses or damages that are attributable directly or indirectly to one cause or to one series of similar causes. All such losses will be added together and the total amount of such losses will be treated as one occurrence irrespective of the period of time or area over which such losses occur.

SR Int'l Bus. Ins. Co. v. World Trade Ctr. Props. LLC, 222 F.Supp.2d 385, 398 (S.D.N.Y. 2002).

As we will explain in greater detail, each of the appellees negotiated separately with Willis concerning its participation in the insurance program and all had bound coverage on various layers as of July 20, 2001. During the course of the next several weeks, Willis negotiated with Travelers over the terms of its final policy, but the Silverstein Parties have presented no evidence to indicate that any of the other appellees participated in or were aware of the details of those negotiations. As of September 11, 2001, none of the appellee-insurers had issued a final policy form, nor had Willis issued the WilProp form as a final policy form, although at least one other participating insurer, Allianz Insurance Company ("Allianz"), had issued a final policy. SR Int'l Bus. Ins. Co. v. World Trade Ctr. Props. LLC, 2002 U.S. Dist. LEXIS 9966, 2002 WL 1163577, at *2 & n.3 (S.D.N.Y. June 3, 2002); see also SR Int'l Bus. Ins. Co. v. World Trade Ctr. Props. LLC, 2003 U.S. Dist. LEXIS 1103, 2003 WL 192487, at *4 (S.D.N.Y. Jan. 29, 2003). On September 14, 2001, three days after the WTC was destroyed, following discussions between Willis and Travelers, Travelers issued its final policy form.

DISCUSSION

I.   JURISDICTION [The court concluded that it had jurisdiction.]

II.   RULE 54(B) APPEAL—HARTFORD, ROYAL, AND ST. PAUL

... The district court granted the motions by Hartford, Royal, and St. Paul seeking partial summary judgment on the grounds that each of the insurers had issued a binder that incorporated the terms of the WilProp form and that under the WilProp form's definition of "occurrence" there was only one occurrence on September 11, 2001. See SR Int'l Bus. Ins. Co. v. World Trade Ctr. Props. LLC, 222 F.Supp.2d 385, 393–95, 398–99 (S.D.N.Y. 2002) ("*Hartford Dec.*"). The district court found that the only relevant question was what were the terms to which the parties had agreed to be bound pending issuance of a final policy, and thus deemed irrelevant evidence indicating that the parties might have agreed to ultimately issue policies tracking the Travelers policy. Id. at 389. The district court then reviewed each of the negotiating histories between Willis and Hartford, Royal, and St. Paul and analyzed the language of their binders. In part because the only policy form before the parties during these negotiations was the WilProp form furnished by Willis, the district court concluded that as a matter of law each of the three insurers had bound coverage on the basis of the WilProp form, rather than, as the Silverstein Parties contended, the Travelers form. Id. at 393–95, 398. The district court further held that, as a matter of law, under the WilProp form's definition of "occurrence" the damage caused on September 11th was the result of one occurrence, entitling the Silverstein Parties to no more than a single policy limit on each of the insurers' policies. Id. at 399.

As noted by the district court, an insurance binder is a "unique type of contract." Id. at 388.

> It is a common and necessary practice in the world of insurance, where speed often is of the essence, for the agent to use this quick and informal device to record the giving of protection pending the execution and delivery of a more conventionally detailed policy of insurance. Courts, recognizing that the cryptic nature of binders is born of necessity and that many policy clauses are either stereotypes or mandated by public regulation, are not loath to infer that conditions and limitations usual to the contemplated coverage were intended to be part of the parties' contract during the binder period.

Employers Commercial Union Ins. Co. v. Firemen's Fund Ins. Co., 384 N.E.2d 668, 670 (N.Y. 1978) ... Thus, a binder is "a short method of issuing a temporary policy for the convenience of all parties, to continue until the execution of the formal one." Lipman v. Niagara Fire Ins. Co., 24 N.E. 699, 700 (N.Y. 1890).... As the New York Court of Appeals has explained,

> it has long been settled in this State that an insurance binder is a temporary or interim policy until a formal policy is issued. A binder provides interim insurance, usually effective as of the date of application, which terminates when a policy is either issued or refused.

Springer v. Allstate Life Ins. Co., 731 N.E.2d 1106, 1108 (N.Y. 2000). While not all of the terms of the insurance contract will be set forth in the binder, a binder is nevertheless a fully enforceable "present contract of insurance." Ell Dee Clothing Co. v. Marsh, 160 N.E. 651, 652 (N.Y. 1928).

[The Silverstein Parties argued that in construing the binders issued by the insurers Hartford, Royal and St. Paul, the district court erred in rejecting evidence of the insurers' agreement to "follow the [Travelers'] form" which created material factual issues in dispute about whether the WilProp definition of "occurrence" applies to these insurers. The court found otherwise as explained further in the last sentence of the following paragraph.]

The only question we must decide is what the term "occurrence" means under the specific binders that appellees issued and that were in force when the planes destroyed the WTC on September 11, 2001. Should we infer that the parties to the binder intended to: (1) incorporate the specific definition of "occurrence" contained in the WilProp policy; (2) forgo a specific definition (as is the case in the customary Travelers form);

or (3) treat "occurrence" in some other fashion? The evidence offered by the Silverstein Parties to demonstrate that the appellees agreed that they would "follow the [Travelers] form" at such time as it might issue is relevant only if, and to the extent that, the facts of the parties' pre-binder negotiations can support a finding that the parties intended the insurer's binder, the policy that was to be in effect until the Travelers form was issued, to incorporate the terms, not of the September 14 Travelers policy ultimately issued, but of Travelers' customary or specimen form (the "Travelers form").

. . . [W]e agree with the district court that there can be no genuine dispute here that the binders issued by Hartford, Royal, and St. Paul were issued on the basis of negotiations involving the WilProp form, a copy of which had been provided to each insurer by Silverstein Properties' insurance broker, Willis, and that the parties intended and understood the binders to incorporate the terms of the WilProp form except as expressly modified.

. . .

B.   Application of the WilProp Definition

Our conclusion that each of the three [insurers Hartford, Royal, and St. Paul] bound coverage on the basis of the WilProp form leaves only the Silverstein Parties' claim that there are issues of fact as to whether there were one or two occurrences on September 11th under the WilProp form's definition. As noted earlier, the WilProp form contains the following definition:

> "Occurrence" shall mean all losses or damages that are attributable directly or indirectly to one cause or to one series of similar causes. All such losses will be added together and the total amount of such losses will be treated as one occurrence irrespective of the period of time or area over which such losses occur.

Hartford Dec., 222 F.Supp.2d at 398. Although the Silverstein Parties attempt to argue that this definition is ambiguous, we agree with the district court that no finder of fact could reasonably fail to find that the intentional crashes into the WTC of two hijacked airplanes sixteen minutes apart as a result of a single, coordinated plan of attack was, at the least, a "series of similar causes." Accordingly, we agree with the district court that under the WilProp definition, the events of September 11th constitute a single occurrence as a matter of law.

III.   SECTION 1292(B) APPEAL–TRAVELERS

The Silverstein Parties' appeal from the denial of their motion for summary judgment against Travelers raises a different set of issues from those just discussed. This motion was based chiefly on the argument that where an insurance policy uses the term "occurrence" without defining the term, then, as a matter of law, the term's meaning is not ambiguous and must be decided by reference to well established New York legal precedent. The Silverstein Parties further argue that under the definition of "occurrence" established by New York law, the events of September 11th constituted two occurrences as a matter of law.

. . .

[A]s we held in connection with the Rule 54(b) appeal [of the insurers Hartford, Royal, and St. Paul], it is the Travelers binder, not the September 14 Travelers policy that applies to determine Travelers' obligations.

D. Is the Binder Ambiguous?

The Silverstein Parties argue that the meaning of "occurrence" as used in the Travelers insurance coverage is not ambiguous and, therefore, that resort to extrinsic evidence to construe it is both unnecessary and improper. Because nothing in the documents that constitute the Travelers binder defined "occurrence," we must decide whether the undefined term "occurrence" when used in a first-party property damage contract is ambiguous.

Applying New York law, we have held that

the cardinal principle for the construction and interpretation of insurance contracts—as with all contracts—is that the intentions of the parties should control. Unless otherwise indicated, words should be given the meanings ordinarily ascribed to them and absurd results should be avoided. As we have stated before, the meaning of particular language found in insurance policies should be examined "in light of the business purposes sought to be achieved by the parties and the plain meaning of the words chosen by them to effect those purposes."

Newmont Mines Ltd. v. Hanover Ins. Co., 784 F.2d 127, 135 (2d Cir. 1986).

. . .

1. Applicability of Extrinsic Evidence

The first argument made by the Silverstein Parties invokes the doctrine that "whether an ambiguity exists must be ascertained from the face of an agreement without regard to extrinsic evidence," Reiss v. Fin. Performance Corp., 764 N.E.2d 958, 961 (N.Y. 2001); see also Md. Cas. Co. v. W.R. Grace & Co., 23 F.3d 617, 625 (2d Cir. 1993) ("Interpretation of unambiguous contract language does not bring extrinsic evidence into play."). This argument fails because it is based on the faulty premise that the September 14 Travelers policy rather than the Travelers binder governs the parties' obligations. New York law is clear that extrinsic evidence may not be used to contradict clearly unambiguous language contained in an insurance binder. . . . [The court recognized this proposition as an application of the parol evidence rule, which protects the documentation of an agreement. The court recognized also a limitation on that rule: it allows for proof of unwritten terms to *supplement* those in a document that appears to be incomplete—i.e., not fully "integrated". The court referred to this limitation as an "exception", although it expressed agreement with the following excerpt from a brief of the Silverstein Parties.] "[T]he parol evidence rule does not come into play at all when dealing with unintegrated contracts, such as appellees' binders. Rather, extrinsic evidence is 'admissible to supply the terms that the parties intended to incorporate into their agreement.' . . . And, in such circumstances, 'summary judgment does not lie' unless the extrinsic evidence itself is so one-sided as to negate the existence of a triable issue of fact. Lowell v. Twin Disc, 527 F.2d 767, 770 (2d Cir. 1975). . . ." We agree with this statement of the law, which fully applies to the Travelers binder.

2. Custom and Usage

The Silverstein Parties' next contention, that the undefined term "occurrence" is not ambiguous because it is typical for insurance policies not to define "occurrence" and, further, that the WilProp definition is "atypically broad," is undercut by the policy forms of the two other WTC insurers who provided their own forms for coverage, each of which defined occurrence. [Industrial Risk Insurers] issued a binder expressly incorporating its own policy form, which defines "loss arising out of one Occurrence" as "the sum total of all loss or damage insured against arising out of or caused by one event." Allianz, in the only final policy to issue before September 11, 2001, defined occurrence in language similar to the WilProp definition: "any one loss, disaster or casualty, or series of losses, disasters or casualties arising out of one event."

In addition, in order to demonstrate the ambiguity of the undefined term "occurrence," Travelers has proffered evidence of industry custom and usage concerning the meaning of occurrence that differs from the definition asserted by the Silverstein Parties. For example, a Willis forms specialist testified that she did not believe that the WilProp form definition of an occurrence as, *inter alia*, losses attributable to "one series of similar causes" deviated from the commonly understood meaning of "occurrence." Similarly, Daniel McCrudden, an underwriter at Travelers, testified that "it's recognized that multiple causes of loss can be involved in a single occurrence, and it's recognized that all loss arising out of an overriding cause or group of causes is considered a single occurrence. It's never been a question."

Although the Silverstein Parties argue that it was improper for the district court to consider such evidence of custom and usage in deciding whether the policy is ambiguous, we have specifically instructed courts to consider the "customs, practices, usages and terminology as generally understood in the particular trade or business" in identifying ambiguity within a contract. Int'l Multifoods Corp. v. Commercial Union Ins. Co., 309 F.3d 76, 83 (2d Cir. 2002). . . . And New York courts have long held that such evidence is admissible for purposes of construing an insurance binder. See, e.g., Underwood, 55 N.E. at 937 (holding that binder "was open to explanation by parol proof as to . . . the established custom of the business").

3. Meaning of Occurrence under New York Law

Finally, the Silverstein Parties assert that the mere fact that the word "occurrence" was not defined in the binder is not enough to render it ambiguous. They contend that in the absence of a definition in the binder, a court seeking to construe the meaning of "occurrence" must first turn to well established New York precedent. If there is a clear and uniform meaning of the term under the law, they argue, then a court must reject a claim of ambiguity and apply that definition. This argument fails because its underlying premise—that there is a uniform meaning of "occurrence" under New York law—is erroneous.

The Silverstein Parties maintain that under New York law, there is but one meaning of "occurrence," which is the direct, physical cause of a loss and not more remote causes. This definition is so accepted and well settled, they contend, that it must be implied into the Travelers binder as a matter of law. Applying this definition to the facts of this case, it follows that because the destruction of the WTC was the result of two physical impacts from two separate planes, there were two occurrences as a matter of law.

To support their argument, the Silverstein Parties rely on a string of authorities beginning with Arthur A. Johnson Corp. v. Indem. Ins. Co., 164 N.E.2d 704 (N.Y. 1959). In Arthur A. Johnson, the court considered whether there was one or two accidents within the meaning of a third-party liability insurance policy where two separate walls constructed by the same insured contractors in two adjacent buildings collapsed 50 minutes apart during the course of an unusually heavy rainfall and caused flooding within the buildings. The insurer argued that there was only one occurrence because all the damage was ultimately caused by the heavy rainfall. In rejecting this argument, the court started from the premise that in determining the number of accidents, it must consider "the 'reasonable expectation and purpose of the ordinary business man when making an ordinary business contract.'" Id. at 706.... The court then held that "the term [accident] is to be used in its common sense of an event of an unfortunate character that takes place without one's foresight or expectation ... that is, an unexpected, unfortunate occurrence." Id. at 707. Reviewing the facts before it, the court concluded that there had been two separate accidents on the rationale that the walls that collapsed belonged to separate buildings, there was no indication that the flooding in the first building would have caused the flooding in the second building in the absence of a second defective wall, and the two walls collapsed almost an hour apart. Id. at 708.

Because *Arthur A. Johnson* and nearly all of the other cases relied on by the Silverstein Parties to provide the definition of "occurrence" are third-party liability insurance cases, however, they involve different interests, both public and private, than first-party property insurance cases such as the instant case. (citations omitted) For example, for third-party liability policies, there is no reason to look any further back in the chain of causation than to the insured's acts of negligence, because it is the insured's negligence that triggers liability. See, e.g., In re Prudential Lines Inc., 158 F.3d 65, 80–81 (2d Cir. 1998) (holding, in third-party liability context, that "courts should look to the event for which the insured is held liable," regardless of whether it is the physical impact closest in time) (internal quotation marks and emphasis omitted); Stonewall Ins. Co. v.

Asbestos Claims Mgmt. Corp., 73 F.3d 1178, 1213–14 (2d Cir. 1995) (same), modified on other grounds, 85 F.3d 49 (2d Cir. 1996). Thus, the approach taken by courts reviewing the number of occurrences in the context of third-party liability—such as the court's focus in *Arthur A. Johnson* on the separate wall collapses rather than the rain—makes sense for such policies because the insured is held liable only for its own negligence and not for the act of nature that may have been the initiating cause. See *Arthur A. Johnson*, 164 N.E.2d at 708 ("Here the proximate cause cannot be said to be the heavy rainfall but separate negligent acts of preparing and constructing separate walls which, for all we know, may have been built at separate times by separate groups of workmen.").

In addition, construction of the term "occurrence" in a liability insurance context is influenced by the public policy concern of ensuring adequate compensation for injured third-parties who are not parties to the insurance contract, and, perforce, played no role in negotiating its terms. See Affiliated FM Ins. Co., 311 F.3d at 233. It is no surprise, therefore, that a salient characteristic of the third-party liability cases relied on by the Silverstein Parties is that each one involved multiple liability claims filed against the insured by multiple parties. See, e.g., *In re Prudential Lines*, 158 F.3d at 68 (liability on multiple asbestos claims); *Stonewall Ins.*, 73 F.3d at 1187 (liability on thousands of asbestos claims); Travelers Cas. & Sur. Co. v. Certain Underwriters at Lloyd's of London, 760 N.E.2d 319, 322 (N.Y. 2001) (liability claims involving decades of commercial activities at numerous industrial and waste disposal sites); Hartford Accident & Indem. Co. v. Wesolowski, 305 N.E.2d 907, 908 (N.Y. 1973) (car liability insurance where insured struck two different cars); *Arthur A. Johnson*, 164 N.E.2d at 704 (liability for destruction of retaining walls of two buildings owned by different owners). And the "test" that the Silverstein Parties argues is universally applicable in all insurance contexts was described by the *Arthur A. Johnson* court as applying "in a given set of circumstances when the damage is to several persons." *Arthur A. Johnson*, 164 N.E.2d at 706. In such cases, of course, a finding of a separate occurrence as to each claimant ensures compensation for the injured third parties. See Affiliated FM Ins. Co., 311 F.3d at 233.

In a first-party property case, by contrast, the insured's negligence is not at issue; rather, the policy insures against external perils such as fires, floods, and intentional acts that cause damage to the insured's property, and against which a property interest holder can take adequate measures to protect his investment in advance of any loss. See *Newmont Mines*, 784 F.2d at 136 ("The goal of such a [first-party] policy, simply stated, is to provide financial protection against damage to property."). As a result of these differences, a court's construction of the undefined term "occurrence," or the synonymous term "accident," as intended by the parties for use in the third-party context is not necessarily applicable in the context of first-party property insurance.

We also find it noteworthy that while the Silverstein Parties assert that *Arthur A. Johnson* "provides the applicable legal test for determining number of occurrences," they do not try to apply that case's definition to the facts of this case. Instead, they assert that "the governing test under 'well-established precedent' under New York law is to look to the immediate, efficient, physical cause of the loss, and not to some indirect or remote cause of causes." . . . But no New York case of which we are aware has set forth such a test for purposes of determining the number of occurrences that comprise a loss.

. . .

In any event, we are not called upon here to decide whether there was one occurrence or two in this case, only whether the district court properly concluded that because there is no well settled definition of the term "occurrence" under New York law, the Travelers binder was sufficiently ambiguous to preclude summary judgment and to permit the factfinder to consider extrinsic evidence of the parties' intent.

We think the case most directly on point is our decision in *Newmont Mines*, the only first-party property insurance case cited by the Silverstein Parties that addresses the meaning of "occurrence." 784 F.2d at 135–37. In that case, we were "not persuaded . . . [by defendants] that the term 'occurrence' has obtained any . . . specialized or singular meaning in the context of property insurance," and we interpreted both *Arthur A. Johnson* and *Wesolowski* as "rejecting any single definition of occurrence." Id. at 136. Our conclusion, at bottom, was that "the meaning of 'occurrence' must be interpreted in the context of the specific policy and facts of the case." Id. at 136 n.9.

In *Newmont Mines*, a heavy accumulation of snow caused two separate parts of a roof to collapse several days apart, requiring two independent repairs. Id. at 129–31. We held that there was sufficient evidence to support the jury's verdict that the two partial losses constituted two occurrences under the policies. Id. at 137. We also upheld the instruction given to the jury on the meaning of occurrence:

> it is for you to decide whether or not the losses which are alleged to have occurred or the loss that's alleged to have occurred in this case was the result of a single, continuous event or incident, or whether or not it was the result of two separate incidents. If you find that the collapse of the two sections of the roof was a single, continuous event or incident, then the collapse constituted a single occurrence—and there would be only one loss. If, on the other hand, you find that the collapse of the two sections of the roof constituted separate events or incidents that were not causally related, then of course you would have two separate losses.

Id. at 134. We held that the instruction was proper on the rationale that given the goals of first-party property insurance, "the parties . . . must have intended to provide coverage for property damage each time it occurred unexpectedly and without design, unless the damage occurring at one point in time was merely part of a single, continuous event that already had caused other damage." Id. at 136.

Notwithstanding the express statements to the contrary in our decision, see id. at 135–36 & n.8. (rejecting any one definition of "occurrence" and stating that "the meaning of 'occurrence' must be interpreted in the context of the specific policy and facts of the case"), the Silverstein Parties contend that *Newmont Mines* sets forth "the rule of law" with respect to the meaning of "occurrence" in the context of first-party property insurance, and that this rule favors them. However, even if we were to agree with the Silverstein Parties that the approved jury instruction and our separate definition of "occurrence" are applicable to this case (a question we need not and do not reach), the one thing *Newmont Mines* makes certain is that the question of how many occurrences the events of September 11th constituted is a question properly left to the fact-finder. To be sure, a jury could find two occurrences in this case, as it did in *Newmont Mines*, or it could find that the terrorist attack, although manifested in two separate airplane crashes, was a single, continuous, planned event causing a continuum of damage that resulted in the total destruction of the WTC, and, thus, was a single occurrence. Instead of supporting the Silverstein Parties' argument that New York law mandates a finding of two occurrences under the Travelers binder as a matter of law, *Newmont Mines* confirms our belief that in a first-party property insurance case, the meaning of the undefined term "occurrence" is an open question as to which reasonable finders of fact could reach different conclusions.

Accordingly, we conclude that given the significant distinction between first-party and third-party insurance policies, the fact-specific nature of the inquiry, and the fact that it is the parties' intent that controls, the district court properly concluded that the meaning of "occurrence" in the Travelers binder is sufficiently ambiguous under New York law to preclude summary judgment and to warrant consideration by the fact finder of extrinsic evidence to determine the parties' intentions. We therefore affirm the denial of summary judgment against Travelers.

CONCLUSION

For the foregoing reasons, we affirm the judgments of the district court.

NOTES

(1) *Travelers*, Contra Proferentem *Quandary*. The insureds made a summary judgment motion against Travelers, asserting that since the meaning of "occurrence" in Travelers' binder was not defined, then, as a matter of law, the meaning of occurrence is not ambiguous. *Questions*: Is that role reversal?[1] If so, why did the insureds not assert *contra proferentem*, claiming that occurrence, not being defined, is ambiguous and should be construed in favor of coverage? Does the judge or jury make that determination?

What is Travelers' role in this motion? Assume that you represent Travelers in opposition to summary judgment. Then: Would you argue that the occurrence-is-unambiguous argument is incorrect? Why or why not?

---

1. Insureds typically argue: Language in the policy (here binder) is ambiguous, the court should apply *contra proferentem* and construe the ambiguity against the insurer. Insurers typically argue the language has a plain meaning and is not ambiguous.

(2) *9/11 and Liability Insurance Litigation*. Actions were brought against the owner (the Port Authority of New York and New Jersey) and the lessees of the World Trade Center properties by victims of the attack, persons injured and the survivors of those killed. *See* In re September 11th Liability Insurance Coverage Cases, 333 F.Supp.2d 111 (S.D.N.Y. 2004). The claimants alleged breach of duties of care. The defendants demanded that certain liability insurers provide them with defenses. On 9/11 the only written commitments by a liability insurer were two "binders" of the Zurich American Insurance Company. Some months after 9/11, pursuant to the binders, Zurich issued two policies superseding the binders—a commercial general liability (CGL) policy—and other insurance carriers issued policies for amounts of liability coverage in excess of Zurich's coverage. Zurich disclaimed any obligation to defend the actions against the owner and the lessees. In its initial opinion, the court concluded:

> At this stage of the proceedings, and before discovery, it is unclear if the parties intended the [Owner] to be an Additional Insured under Zurich's Binder, nor what scope any such coverage might have. I hold also that [New York Insurance Law] does not require rewriting the CGL Binder and Policies to include defense costs.

Id. at 129. When this casebook was written in early 2007, liability insurance coverage was not judicially determined.

(3) *More on Binders*. Most property and casualty binders are based on standard contract forms. However, large corporate insureds often negotiate specific terms with the insurer, which results a manuscript policy. Originally, a manuscript policy was written by hand (*mano scriptum*–later typed) especially for the policyholder. In modern times, a manuscript policy is defined as an insurance policy containing nonstandard provisions that have been negotiated between the insurer and the insured. See manuscript policy under "insurance policy" in Black's Law Dictionary (8th ed. 2004). Professor Peter Swisher has explored the distinction between a standard form policy and a manuscript policy. He concluded that where parties contract through a manuscript form binder, the binder is invalid and unenforceable unless the parties agree upon some draft or model terms and conditions that may be inferred to be part of the policy. Peter Nash Swisher, "Insurance Binders Revisited," 39 Tort Trial & Ins. Prac. L.J. 1011 (2004). *Question*: Were there some draft or model terms in the above case to validate the Hartford, Royal, and St. Paul binders?

(4) *Practical Construction*. Although policy (or binder) language may be ambiguous, a course of conduct between the insured and insurer may indicate that they understood the language to have a particular meaning. Where a course of conduct removes an ambiguity in the written policy terms, the rule of practical construction usually takes precedence over the *contra proferentem* rule. Once an ambiguity is removed by the parties' conduct, there is no longer a need to apply a rule of construction. See, e.g., William C. Roney & Co. v. Federal Insurance Co., 674 F.2d 587, 590 (6th Cir. 1982) (Mich.law).

Morgan Stanley Group Inc. v. New England Ins. Co.
United States Court of Appeals, 2d Cir., 2000.
225 F.3d 270.

Morgan Stanley Group, Inc. and Morgan Stanley & Co., Inc. (collectively "Morgan Stanley") were sued on account of their role in promoting a transaction in which the plaintiffs were interested, a real-estate loan that had failed. The plaintiffs (hereafter "Investors") were a borrower and two purchasers of participation interests. Morgan Stanley settled with the plaintiffs and demanded indemnification from New England Insurance Company and the ITT New England Management Company (collectively "New England"). The present action was brought after the demand was rejected.

New England had issued to Morgan Stanley a policy covering errors and omissions ("E & O" coverage[1]) in the role of "investment counselor". The trial judge was presented with two understandings of investment counseling. One was limited to instances in which a customer agrees to pay a fee for investment advice. The Investors had made no such agreement with Morgan Stanley. The other understanding was a broader one, comprising the giving of investment advice, without regard to the relation between the giver and the recipient. After hearing evidence, the trial judge ruled against Morgan Stanley who appealed.

■ JACOBS, J.

A.   Applicable Law

Under New York law, "an insurance contract is interpreted to give effect to the intent of the parties as expressed in the clear language of the contract." Village of Sylvan Beach v. Travelers Indem. Co., 55 F.3d 114, 115 (2d Cir. 1995). "The initial interpretation of a contract 'is a matter of law for the court to decide.' " K. Bell & Assocs. v. Lloyd's Underwriters, 97 F.3d 632, 637 (2d Cir. 1996) (quoting Readco, Inc. v. Marine Midland Bank, 81 F.3d 295, 299 (2d Cir. 1996)). Part of this threshold interpretation is the question of whether the terms of the insurance contract are ambiguous. See Alexander & Alexander Servs., Inc. v. These Certain Underwriters at Lloyd's, 136 F.3d 82, 86 (2d Cir. 1998). An ambiguity exists where the terms of an insurance contract could suggest "more than one meaning when viewed objectively by a reasonably intelligent person who has examined the context of the entire integrated agreement and who is cognizant of the customs, practices, usages and terminology as generally understood in the particular trade or business." Lightfoot v. Union Carbide Corp., 110 F.3d 898, 906 (2d Cir. 1997) (citation and internal quotation marks omitted). Once a court concludes that an insurance provision is ambiguous, "the court may accept any available extrinsic evidence to ascertain the meaning intended by the parties during the formation of the contract." *Alexander & Alexander*, 136 F.3d at 86.... "If the extrinsic evidence does not yield a conclusive answer as to the parties' intent," a court may apply other rules of contract construction, including the rule of *contra proferentem*, which

---

1. [Editor's footnote] New England's errors and omissions ("E & O") policy indemnifies for "loss which the Insured shall become legally obligated to pay, from any claim made against the Insured during the Policy Period, by reason of any actual or alleged negligent act, error or omission committed in the scope of the Insured's duties as investment counselors." The term "investment counselors" is undefined. An Errors and Omissions (E & O) insurance policy has no provision requiring the insurer to defend the insured. An E & O Insurer's primary obligation is to reimburse "costs and expenses incurred in the defense of any claim for which coverage is provided hereunder."

generally provides that where an insurer drafts a policy "any ambiguity in [the] ... policy should be resolved in favor of the insured." McCostis v. Home Ins. Co., 31 F.3d 110, 113 (2d Cir. 1994).

B. The Meaning of "Investment Counselor"

Applying these principles, the district court concluded that the parties' different interpretations of "investment counselor" raised an ambiguity that ... required consideration of any extrinsic evidence. The evidence adduced at trial convinced the court that New England's interpretation— based on whether or not a fee was paid for the service—was unsound and too narrow, and (at the same time) that Morgan Stanley's interpretation was too broad. Instead, the court found that the hallmark of investment counseling is independent analysis and, because Morgan Stanley proffered no evidence of having conducted independent analysis, the district court entered judgment in favor of New England.

We take a slightly different approach, but arrive at the same result. It is well established under New York law that a policyholder bears the burden of showing that the insurance contract covers the loss. See, e.g. [four cases cited]. If the court concludes that an insurance policy is ambiguous, then the burden shifts to the insurer to prove that its interpretation is correct: if extrinsic evidence is available but inconclusive, the burden shifts at the trial stage, see Union Ins. Soc'y v. William Gluckin & Co., 353 F.2d 946, 951–52 (2d Cir. 1965) (remanding for trial in order to allow district court to consider extrinsic evidence before applying *contra proferentem*); in the absence of extrinsic evidence, the burden shifts at the summary judgment stage, see Twombly v. AIG Life Ins. Co., 199 F.3d 20, 25–26 (1st Cir. 1999).

"The fact ... that terms of a policy of insurance may be construed as ambiguous where applied to one set of facts does not make them ambiguous as to other facts which come directly within the purview of such terms." 2 Lee R. Russ & Thomas F. Segalla, Couch on Insurance 3d § 21:14 (1997). If the insurance contract cannot reasonably be construed to cover the claim, regardless of which interpretation may have been intended, then the policyholder has not met its burden of proving that it suffered a covered loss.... As a matter of law, an ambiguity is insufficient to shift the burden to an insurer if the possible range of meanings does not extend far enough to cover the particular loss.

Morgan Stanley failed to carry its burden. The term "investment counselors" is vague within certain parameters, but it does not render this policy ambiguous for purposes of this suit because no interpretation of "investment counselors" within the range of reasonable meanings would extend coverage for the particular conduct underlying [Morgan Stanley's] settlements." Even a vague clause may be ambiguous only at its edges." United Nat'l Ins. Co. v. Waterfront N.Y. Realty Corp., 994 F.2d 105, 108 (2d Cir. 1993)....

The district court found that: "Morgan Stanley was acting as an agent for [the Investors] in the underlying transactions [Morgan Stanley Group,

Inc. v. New England Ins. Co.,] 36 F. Supp. 2d at 611; after [the Investors] purchased participation interests in the Fourth & Broadway loan, [the Investors] paid Morgan Stanley an 'agency fee,' id.; Morgan Stanley had no contractual relationship with [the Investors], . . . and Morgan Stanley's purpose was to 'facilitate sales' of the participation interests, id. at 613. In short, Morgan Stanley was pitching to potential buyers as an agent for a seller. No reasonable person would believe that errors or omissions in this marketing activity were 'committed in the scope of the Insured's duties as investment counselors.' "

A "counselor" is one who gives advice, regardless of whether a fee is paid; thus legal counsel usually involves a retainer, while pastoral counseling does not. In most instances, counseling can be distinguished conceptually and functionally from the recommendations of one who is a seller or the disclosed agent of a seller. A car salesman may offer a potential customer an opinion on the car's reliability, but no one could deem the dealer sufficiently disinterested to be a "counselor," and the advice, which cannot reliably be assumed to have been offered for the good of the buyer, is no counsel. . . . To hold that Morgan Stanley acted as an investment counselor in this case would transform every effective salesman into an investment counselor.

C.

. . .

D. Considerations on Remand

The district court articulated the principles of New York law applicable to resolving ambiguities in insurance contracts:

> Once a court determines that, as a matter of law, a term of an insurance policy is ambiguous, "it may accept any available extrinsic evidence to ascertain the meaning intended by the parties during the formation of the contract." Where extrinsic evidence is conclusory or does not shed light upon the intent of the parties, a court may resort to the *contra proferentem* rule of contract construction and construe any ambiguities in the contract against the insurer as a matter of law. However, where the relevant extrinsic evidence offered "raises a question of credibility or presents a choice among reasonable inferences" the construction of the ambiguous terms of the contract is a question of fact which precludes the application of the *contra proferentem* rule.

[Morgan Stanley Group, Inc. v. New England Ins. Co.,] 36 F. Supp. 2d at 609 (citations omitted). In applying these principles, the district court did not apply *contra proferentem* in Morgan Stanley's favor, partly because "both parties are sophisticated financial entities." Id. However, there is no general rule in New York denying sophisticated businesses the benefit of *contra proferentem*. See, e.g., [two cases cited]; see also 2 Couch on Insurance 3d § 22:24 ("Avoidance of the rule . . . is not required merely because an insured party is a business rather than an individual."). This is not a case between two insurance companies . . . , nor a case where the policyholder is "akin to . . . an insurance company" because of its sophistication in matters of insurance coverage, Loblaw, Inc. v. Employers' Liab. Assurance Corp., 446 N.Y.S.2d 743, 745 (App.Div. 4th Dep't 1981).

It is unsettled in New York whether *contra proferentem* applies if the policyholder is a sophisticated entity that negotiated contract terms. See Schering Corp. v. Home Ins. Co., 712 F.2d 4, 10 n.2 (2d Cir. 1983) (noting that the issue remains unresolved); see also Pittston Co. Ultramar Am. Ltd. v. Allianz Ins. Co., 124 F.3d 508, 521 (3d Cir. 1997) (refusing, under New Jersey law, to apply *contra proferentem* on behalf of a sophisticated insured who negotiated the insurance contact); 2 Couch on Insurance 3d § 22:24 (noting that the rule might not apply if a sophisticated insured "fully negotiated the insurance contract"). But we need not decide this issue because Morgan Stanley (although sophisticated) did not negotiate its coverage terms. A New England insurance agent who participated in the insurance transaction testified that it was a "standard policy" that New England "didn't amend for anybody."

Therefore, if on remand the extrinsic evidence sheds no light on the ["investment counselor"] ambiguity or "does not yield a conclusive answer," the district court should apply *contra proferentem* . . . .

NOTES

(1) *The "Sophisticated Insured" Exception to* Contra Proferentem. The foregoing case explains that New York law is unsettled vis-à-vis the "sophisticated insured" exception (or, more accurately, the "legal equals" exception). However, some courts have adopted this exception. Missouri was one of the first jurisdictions in which this was done. See Koch Engineering Co. v. Gibraltar Casualty Co., 878 F.Supp. 1286 (1995). The court stated:

[T]he Court finds that the doctrine of *contra proferentem,* which construes the policy against the insurance company as the drafter of the contract, does not apply. In addition to the lack of ambiguity in the policy which would preclude the application of the doctrine, [*contra proferentem*] does not apply to sophisticated contractors. In analyzing a dispute involving Missouri law, Judge Wisdom warned against the automatic adoption of the *contra proferentem* doctrine: "We do not feel compelled to apply, or, indeed, justified in applying the general rule . . . in the commercial insurance field when the insured is not an innocent but a corporation of immense size, carrying insurance with annual premiums in six figures, managed by sophisticated business men and represented by counsel on the same professional level as the counsel for insurers." Eagle Leasing Corp. v. Hartford Fire Ins. Co., 540 F.2d 1257, 1261 (5th Cir. 1976). That analysis applies to the situation in this case. [The insured] negotiated a complex, twenty million dollar policy with the Defendants. In fact, the parties negotiated what they called a manuscript policy, the mere title of which indicates that it was not an adhesion, preprinted contract but a policy negotiated by two equal parties on a level playing field; therefore, [the insured] is not entitled to any special protection.

Koch Engineering at 1288.

Similarly, the Seventh Circuit Court of Appeals, in interpreting Ohio law, held that *contra proferentem* is inapplicable when "its underlying rationale is inapplicable." Northbrook Excess & Surplus Ins. Co. v. Procter & Gamble Co., 924 F.2d 633 (7th Cir. 1991). The court found that Ohio applies *contra proferentem* only to protect the insured from an insurer with *exclusive* control of the drafting process. The Supreme Court of New Jersey has said: "An exception to [the *contra proferentem*] rule exists for sophisticated commercial entities that do not suffer from the same inadequacies as the ordinary unschooled policyholder and that have participated in the drafting of the insurance contract." Benjamin Moore & Co. v. Aetna Cas. & Sur. Co., 843 A.2d 1094, 1103 (2004). Moreover, a Massachusetts court refused to apply *contra proferentem* where the insured's insurance agent negotiated the insurance policy with the insurer, implicitly equating the sophistication and expertise of the insurance agent with that of the insurer. Simon v. National Union Fire Ins. Co., 782 N.E.2d 1125 (Mass.App. 2003); *accord*, Puerto Rico Electric Power Authority (PREPA) v. Philipps, 645 F.Supp. 770 (D.P.R. 1986).

A Wisconsin court recognized the exception regarding a fidelity bond issued by an insurer; the rule was justified by unequal bargaining power, but the insured was a bank, and therefore the insurer and insured had relatively equal bargaining power and had negotiated the terms of the bond. Tri City Nat. Bank v. Federal Ins. Co., 674 N.W.2d 617 (Wis. Ct. App. 2003).[2] Some courts refuse to recognize this exception or limit its application. See, *e.g.*, Boeing Co. v. Aetna Cas. and Sur. Co., 784 P.2d 507 (Wash. 1990), where the court did not apply a different rule of construction to an insurance policy based on the fact that policy was issued to a corporate giant rather than an individual. Once the court construes a standard-form coverage clause as matter of law, the court's construction will bind any policyholders regardless of the size of its business.

Regrettably, courts, recognizing this exception, have failed to provided any consistent definition for the term "sophisticated insured" and to elucidate the factors characterizing a sophisticated insured. Nevertheless, a case-law review demonstrates at least these six characteristics that courts employ, in varying degrees of importance, to describe a sophisticated insured: (1) The insured completely or partially drafted or prepared the policy; (2) The insured was a large, sophisticated, commercial corporation; (3) The insured had at least equal bargaining power to the insurer; (4) The insured used a broker or an agent; (5) The insured employed lawyers; and (6) The insured had in-house risk managers. Arguably, the most significant factor in assessing the insured's sophistication is the amount of the insured's participation in the drafting of the insurance policy. However, courts differ about what amount of participation is necessary to characterize an entity as sufficiently sophisticated to rebut the presumption underlying the *contra proferentem* rule. For example, regarding disparity in bargaining power between insurer and purchaser of insurance, a Pennsylvania court held that a businessman who owned and operated a gasoline service station for nearly 30 years did not warrant deviating from the plain language of his liability insurance policy; given his experience, it was incumbent upon him to read the policy and, if necessary, ask questions or obtain advice before purchasing them. Wagner v. Erie Ins. Co., 801 A.2d 1226 (Pa.Super. 2002).[3]

2. See also AIU Ins. Co. v. Superior Court, 799 P.2d 1253 (Cal. 1990), Courts need not "go far" in protecting insured from ambiguous or highly technical drafting of policy where the insured does not suffer from lack of legal sophistication or relative lack of bargaining power, and where it is clear that the insurance policy was actually negotiated and jointly drafted.); Garcia v. Truck Ins. Exchange, 682 P.2d 1100 (Cal. 1984), Principle that ambiguities in insurance policies must be strictly construed against insurer was irrelevant, where terms of policy were negotiated between malpractice carrier and hospital association, and language in contention was product of joint drafting).

3. For a further explanation and analysis of the sophisticated insured exception, see Eric Mills Holmes, 14 Holmes' Appleman on Insurance 2d § 105.3[B][3] "Legal Equals:

(2) Contra Proferentem *in California.* As in other jurisdictions, the doctrine *contra proferentem* yields to the plain-meaning rule in California: it applies only when an ambiguity has been detected. But there its application does not follow directly upon a finding of ambiguity. Rather, a court is first to apply the "doctrine of reasonable expectations". That doctrine is examined later in this chapter commencing at page 144. A form of the "doctrine of reasonable expectations" is stated in Cal. Civil Code § 1649: "If the terms of a promise are in any respect ambiguous or uncertain, it must be interpreted in the sense in which the promisor believed, at the time of making it, that the promisee understood it." This provision applies to contracts in general, including those of insurance. ("While insurance contracts have special features, they are still contracts to which the ordinary rules of contractual interpretation apply." Montrose Chem. Corp. v. Admiral Ins. Co., 897 P.2d 1 (Cal. 1995).) The statutory provision protects, it has been said, "the objectively reasonable expectations of the insured." Bank of the West v. Superior Court, 833 P.2d 545, 551–52 (Cal. 1992).

In *Bank of the West,* speaking of *contra proferentem,* the court admonished the insured claimant that it had "invoked this rule of construction too early in the interpretive process.... Only if [the rule protecting the insured's reasonable expectations] does not resolve the ambiguity do we then resolve it against the insurer." Id. at 551–52. In short, an application of *contra proferentem* occurs only as a third step, following two others: (a) a finding of ambiguity in the policy, and (b) a finding that the ambiguity persists after allowing for the reasonable expectations of the insured. For a thorough analysis of the California cases and the sequenced steps, see Eric Mills Holmes, 16 Holmes' Appleman on Insurance 2d § 116.1[C][3], at 13–33 (2000). Note also that some lower California opinions further restrict *contra proferentem* by applying the sophisticated insured exception.[4]

———

EXERCISES

Except for the first and last, each of these exercises is based on a reported case. (The first is based on a dispute that was settled.) The cases are cited in the footnote, in sequence.[5] You should work on the exercises without consulting them. In each case cited the claimant presented an argument for finding ambiguity. What arguments occur to you? What counter-arguments? In each case cited the claimant's argument prevailed— with one exception. Try to identify the exceptional case.

The so-called 'Sophisticated Insured' Exception to the 'Contra Proferentem' Rule," 283–89 (2000).

4. In Vons Companies, Inc. v. United States Fire Ins. Co., 92 Cal.Rptr.2d 597 (Cal. App.2.Dist. 2000), the court held the sophisticated insured exception to *contra proferentem* controls when policy was negotiated by parties with equal bargaining positions; however, the exception does not control unless there is evidence that actual insurance policy provision in dispute was jointly drafted. Evidence that policy was negotiated and that insured had legal sophistication and substantial relative bargaining power is not enough. *Accord*: Shell Oil Co. v. Winterthur Swiss Ins. Co., 15 Cal.Rptr.2d 815 (Cal.App.1.Dist. 1993).

5. (2) Nedrow v. Unigard Security Ins. Co., 974 P.2d 67 (Idaho 1998); (3) Steil v. Humana Kansas City, Inc., 124 F.Supp.2d 660 (D.Kan.2000); (4) Tobin v. Beneficial Standard Life Ins. Co., 675 F.2d 606 (4th Cir. 1982)(applying South Carolina law); (5) Vargas v. Ins. Co. of North America, 651 F.2d 838 (2d Cir. 1981)(applying New York law).

(1) Your client has received treatment for alcohol addiction. Your client was insured under a health-insurance policy. The policy has this exclusion: "Services in conjunction with abuse of or addiction to alcohol and drugs (including detoxification services, long-term rehabilitation services for treatment of alcoholism and drug addiction, and including prolonged rehabilitation in a specialized inpatient or residential facility)." On behalf of your client, explain how the exclusion is ambiguous.

(2) Ty Nedrow (Ty) was a partner in a partnership, engaged in farming, known as Nedrow Brothers. The other members are Ty's brother Tuk and their father. Ty was not paid a salary or wages by the partnership, but made a monthly draw as a partner. The partners divided any profits of the partnership among themselves. The partnership employed seasonal workers. While Ty was at work on the partnership farm, he was injured.

The partnership and its members were among those insured by a policy including medical-payment insurance:

> We will pay, to or for each "farm employee" who sustains "bodily injury" caused by an accident, all reasonable medical expenses to which this insurance applies. The "bodily injury" must arise out of and in the course of the injured employee's employment by the insured.

The policy defines "farm employee" as

> "any insured's employee whose duties are principally in connection with the maintenance or use of the 'insured location' as a farm. These duties include the maintenance or use of the insured's farm equipment."

Ty's injury occurred one morning when Tuk directed him to cut a barrel in two with a torch. The barrel exploded, causing the injury. Is it reasonably possible to understand the policy to provide medical-payment coverage for Ty's injury?

(3) The issuer of a policy of medical-expense insurance declined to pay for treatment of a malady as desired by the sufferer. "No services will be provided," the policy stated, "for procedures and treatment methods which are experimental and investigational." The policy specified in considerable detail what would count as an "experimental and investigational procedures and treatment methods". For example: "Reliable evidence shows the . . . treatment, or procedure when applied to the circumstances of a particular patient is the subject of ongoing . . . clinical trials."

Are there situations in which payment might be required for the desired treatment even though, as to be applied, it is the subject of ongoing clinical trials?

(4) Cheryl was named as the beneficiary of accidental-death insurance on the life of her husband, Thomas, maintained by his employer. The policy provided also for compensation in the event of his hospital confinement. Thomas, a taxi driver, was killed on the job by an armed robber. The insurer resisted paying the death benefit, relying on this provision: "No benefits are payable under this policy because of injury for which compen-

sation is payable under any Workmen's Compensation Law...." Cheryl was entitled, by statute, to a workers' compensation benefit. A part of the policy about exclusions stated that they extended to losses whether fatal or not. Elsewhere the policy spoke of injury that might result in death. Might a reader suppose that the policy entitled Cheryl to a death benefit?

(5) A policy of "aviation insurance" provided life insurance, but only to death occurring "within the United States of America, its territories or possessions...." The policy was endorsed, however, with an Extension of Territorial Limits: The "limits set forth in the conditions of this policy are extended to include" various places, including the Bahama Islands.

The pilot of a small aircraft, holding that coverage, has died in a crash at sea, midway between Haiti and Puerto Rico. For him, Haiti was a rest stop on a flight from New York to Puerto Rico (a U.S. territory).

Is there an ambiguity that might make the insurer accountable for the death benefit?

(6) *Questions*: Would the ordinary person understand that a hot air balloon fitted with a passenger gondola is an "aircraft"? Aetna Insurance Co. v. Apollo Sleep Products, 296 S.E.2d 781 (Ga.App. 1982). According to its plain, ordinary and popular meaning, is a raccear a "motor vehicle"? Is a farm tractor a "motor vehicle"? Nicholson v. First Preferred Insurance Co., 618 S.W.2d 560 (Tex.Civ.App. 1981). Is a brand-new Rolls Royce loaned by a car dealership to the insured for display in the insured's hotel an "automobile"? Heshion Motors v. Western International Hotels, 600 S.W.2d 526 (Mo.App. 1980) (The policy provided that the word "automobile" does not include "any vehicle maintained for use exclusively on premises owned by or rented to the named insured.").

NOTE

The word *suit* was once a short form of *lawsuit*, a proceeding at law for damages. According to an edition of Webster's New Collegiate Dictionary (9th, 1987), the term *suit* "has generally been replaced by [the] term 'action'; which includes both actions at law and in equity." And includes, it may be added, actions for declaratory judgments. The word *proceeding*, now common, has a still wider sense. The development of the more inclusive diction was loosely parallel to the 20th-century evolution of the regulatory state, in which persons and firms are often thrown on the defensive by moves by and before administrative agencies.

Whether or not by design, the development of policy language providing liability coverage did not keep pace: the defense of "suits" has remained a common undertaking of insurers. Hence disputes have arisen about the scope of that undertaking in relation to actions and proceedings that are not traditional civil actions in courts, between private parties.

An instance is Foster–Gardner, Inc. v. National Union Fire Ins. Co. of Pittsburgh, 959 P.2d 265 (Cal. 1998). A trigger of the dispute there was an order issued to a firm wholesaling pesticide and fertilizer by a unit of the California Environmental Protection Agency. In the upshot, the court was divided about the firm's entitlement under its comprehensive general liability (CGL) policy. In the words of the dissent, the agency action was a "notice identifying the [firm] as a party potentially responsible for environmental pollution, and directing [it] to assume responsibility for remediation of the pollution". If that action initiated a "suit", the insurer owed the firm a defense; otherwise, not.

The court ruled, 4–3, that the agency action was sufficiently coercive and threatening to constitute a *suit*. The court rejected the so-called literal approach of some courts. It withheld a decision whether or not a less minatory move by the agency would also amount to a suit. The court relied on the statement, in another case, that

> [The] origins and purpose of the duty to defend seem best accommodated ... by focusing ... [on the] coerciveness, adversariness, the seriousness of the effort with which the government hounds an insured, and the gravity of imminent consequences.

Ryan v. Royal Ins. Co. of America, 916 F.2d 731, 741–742 (1st Cir. 1990). The court relied also on cases avowing a public interest in hazardous-waste management. According to one of these,

> if the receipt of a [potentially responsible party (PRP)] notice is held not to trigger the duty to defend under CGL policies, then insureds might be inhibited from cooperation with the [United States Environmental Protection Agency] in order to invite the filing of a formal complaint. It is in the nation's best interests to have hazardous waste cleaned up effectively and efficiently.

Aetna Cas. & Sur. Co., Inc. v. Pintlar Corp., 948 F.2d 1507, 1517 (9th Cir. 1991).[6]

Questions: (a) If prompt compliance with a clean-up order is in the public interest, what of compliance with a demand for unpaid taxes? Equally strong public interest? Stronger or weaker? Or might that depend on the reason for nonpayment? (b) Imagine that a word used in a policy acquires an additional widely understood meaning during the life of a policy (*e.g.*, "virus", as in "computer virus"). Might that introduce ambiguity into a policy otherwise unambiguous?

---

6. The Connecticut Supreme Court summarized the law as of 2005 as follows:

> Although the issue of whether a PRP letter constitutes a suit within the meaning of a comprehensive general liability insurance policy is one of first impression in Connecticut, various state and federal courts have addressed the question and have arrived at differing results. See generally 1 B. Ostrager & T. Newman, Insurance Coverage Disputes (12th Ed. 2004) § 10.04 [c], pp. 700–15; 20 Eric Mills Holmes, Holmes' Appleman on Insurance 2d (2002) § 129.2 H, pp. 91–103. The courts of Colorado, Iowa, Massachusetts, Michigan, Minnesota, New Hampshire, North Carolina and Wisconsin have all held that a PRP letter, or its state equivalent, constitutes a suit triggering an insurer's duty to defend. These courts have reasoned that the term suit is ambiguous and that, because "CERCLA has given the EPA and governmental agencies statutory power to hold PRPs liable for substantial and significant cleanup costs", 20 Eric Mills Holmes, supra, § 129.2, p. 97, a PRP letter constitutes a suit. The courts of California, Illinois and Maine, however, have held that a PRP letter, or its state equivalent, is not a suit and does not trigger an insurer's duty to defend. These courts have reasoned that "the term suit unambiguously refers to an actual court proceeding initiated by the filing of a complaint." (Internal quotation marks omitted.) 20 Eric Mills Holmes, Id., p. 93. Thus, although "neither side of the issue appears to enjoy a clear majority ... state adjudicators evidently tend towards granting coverage." ... We agree with the majority of the states that a PRP letter is a suit and triggers an insurer's duty to defend. R.T. Vanderbilt Co. v. Cont'l Cas. Co., 870 A.2d 1048, 1058 (Conn. 2005).

B.   Fairness As an Objective

1.   Reformation, Waiver, Estoppel, and Election

a.   Reformation

Like the documentation of other kinds of agreement, an insurance policy may be reformed if, by reason of mistake, its language deviates from the parties' agreement. "If the language of a written instrument does not reflect the true intent of both parties, the mutual mistake is reformable. The mistake must either be mutual or unilateral, made by one party and known to the other party. To be entitled to reformation, a party must present full, clear, and decisive proof of mistake. The parol evidence rule does not bar extrinsic proof of intent in these circumstances. Insurance policies may be reformed on the same principles." Polaroid Corp. v. Travelers Indemnity Co., 610 N.E.2d 912, 917 (Mass. 1993) (citations omitted). Fraud in preparing the documentation is another ground of reformation.

Reformation of insurance policies is not commonplace, perhaps because most buyers of insurance don't comprehend in depth the terms offered by their insurers.

NOTES

(1) *Equity*. Reformation is an "equitable" remedy in the sense that it was developed initially by English courts of equity. Waiver, estoppel, and election are not doctrines of equity in that sense. They are equitable in the looser sense that they represent the ideal of fairness. In particular, "equitable estoppel" is a familiar expression. It is helpful as a way to distinguish the doctrine of promissory estoppel, featured in courses on contract law. "Estoppel *in pais*" is an alternate name.

(2) *Facts* vs. *Hopes*. When terrorists took down the World Trade Towers, one of the losses was earnings, over a very long term, at a nearby hotel. The owner held business-interruption insurance in several layers. One of its excess insurers was a firm named, fittingly, Travelers. Seeking to limit its liability, Travelers contended that its coverage extended for less than two years. But its policy said, in effect, that its coverage mimicked that of the primary policy, which was for period as long as four years. That is, the Travelers policy contained a "follow the fortunes" clause as excess policies usually do. Travelers sought to sustain its position through an action against the owner in which it sought either rescission or reformation of its policy.

While the policies were being arranged, the brokerage firm representing the owners, Willis of New York, showed Travelers drafts of the primary coverage. Travelers objected to the duration they expressed and repeatedly proposed the shorter duration. The final exchange between the broker and Travelers on this topic occurred in the winter before 9/11, but only days before Travelers issued its policy. At that time the conversation ran this way:

> Travelers agreed to leave the issue of lengths of time . . . to the primary policy language, but [it] nevertheless expected Willis to seek to incorporate Travelers' changes to the business interruption coverage into the primary policy. Willis again requested an enlargement of the extended period of indemnity . . . and

was again rebuffed by Travelers. Travelers again requested a copy of the primary policy reflecting the changes [it] had proposed relating to the business interruption coverage.

In the spring, Willis was still negotiating with the primary insurer over duration. But Travelers did not know this. Willis provided it with a copy of the "long term" primary policy only after the tragedy.

The "facts" stated above are those stated in the insurer's complaint, and related documents. The court dismissed the action, so far as relevant here, with leave to amend. Travelers Indemnity Co. v. CDL Hotels USA, Inc., 322 F.Supp.2d 482 (S.D.N.Y. 2004).

As for an alleged mutual mistake, the court said: "New York law permits reformation or rescission of a contract for mutual mistake.... Allen v. Westpoint–Pepperell, Inc., 945 F.2d 40 (2d Cir. 1991). [But neither] is permitted if the parties entered an agreement based upon uncertain or contingent events and the claim is based upon mistake as to the outcome of such an event." The content of the primary policy was yet uncertain when Travelers contracted with the owner.

So far as the action was based on a unilateral mistake by Travelers, the court said, "New York law does not permit reformation or rescission of a contract for [that] alone. A unilateral mistake must be 'coupled with some fraud.' *Allen* at 44." And Travelers had not alleged the elements of fraud.

New York law as stated by the court does not stand alone.[1]

b. Waiver, Estoppel, and Election

These doctrines are far from singular to contract law, much less to the law of insurance. But they are applied with special frequency and stringency against insurers; or so at least it is of waiver and estoppel. The three doctrines are related intricately to one another. The illustration that follows is drawn from a case about burglary.

The Phoenix Insurance Company resisted a claim made by Ross Jewelers, Inc. on a policy of burglary insurance it had issued. The policy insured Ross against losses to merchandise at its retail store. Burglars had taken merchandise from counters, from a display window, and from a vault in the store. Conditions in the policy required that Ross maintain (A) an operating alarm on the vault, and (B) a detailed and itemized inventory of the merchandise. When the loss occurred, the store had received a shipment of merchandise worth about $40,000 which had not been entered in the stock record or upon the inventory. As for the vault, the store manager had activated the alarm when he closed for the day but, as was his wont, had left the key in the lock.

The General Adjustment Bureau (GAB) reported to Phoenix a loss of more than $60,000. In doing so, for want of a current inventory, it had recourse to the "gross profit percentage method, rather than to actual book figures." V.J. Rogers, the supervisor of Phoenix's inland-marine claim department wrote to GAB that Phoenix would pay only $10,328.07, the value of goods taken from outside the vault. He referred to condition (A) in

---

1. See generally Eric Mills Holmes, 9   Insurance Law of Reformation (1999).
Holmes' Appleman on Insurance 2d § 53.15

the policy, and did not mention condition (B). Ross declined an offer of that amount. These were the facts assumed in Phoenix Ins. Co. v. Ross Jewelers, Inc., 362 F.2d 985 (5th Cir. 1966). Let it be assumed also that, after the events so far recounted, but before the action was brought, Phoenix had refused to make any payment to Ross.

On these facts a judgment in favor of Ross for the amount of the loss outside the vault might conceivably be supported on any of three grounds, as follows:

1) *Election*. On behalf of Phoenix, Rogers faced a choice between two courses: offering to pay for part of the loss, and denying liability altogether. By acting as he did he committed Phoenix to paying for the loss outside the vault.

2) *Waiver*. Through Rogers, Phoenix knew that the inventory condition (B) might well excuse it from liability altogether, but made a knowing decision not to resist Ross's claim on that ground. (One can imagine that Phoenix perceived an advantage in that, possibly saving the cost of mounting that defense, possibly sparing it a loss of reputation.)

3) *Estoppel*. Possibly Ross would have accepted Phoenix's offer if Phoenix had announced earlier that condition (B) was still in play, and would not have incurred the expense of suing. That being so, it might be said that Ross relied to its detriment, and justifiably so, on an indication by Phoenix that it would not invoke that condition.

Efforts to disentangle these three doctrines have not fully succeeded. One scholar, examining a host of "waiver" cases, concluded that each of them could be ascribed to some other doctrine. J.S. Ewart, Waiver Distributed Among the Departments ... (1917). It has been said that waiver and estoppel should be recognized as distinct doctrines, though they are often confused. Employers Commercial Union Ins. Co. of America v. Great American Ins. Co., 200 S.E.2d 560, 562 (Va. 1973).

In the opinion that follows the court sought to distinguish between waiver and estoppel, but concluded that the insurer was bound by both. One difference is that a waiver can be retracted and an estoppel cannot. That is, a waiver can be retracted until the beneficiary has relied upon it in a sympathetic way. Rephrasing that, one can say that little waivers sometimes grow up to be great estoppels.

NOTE

The Burglary Case. In Phoenix Ins. Co. v. Ross Jewelers, Inc., the trial court entered a summary judgment in favor of Ross for much more than the out-of-vault loss. On appeal, Phoenix won a reversal and remand. The court rejected reasons given by the trial court for passing over the alarm-system condition. As to the inventory condition, the court said it had been waived. (Other issues remained for consideration by the trial court.)

.   .   .

McCollum v. Continental Casualty Co.

Arizona Court of Appeals, 1986.
151 Ariz. 492, 728 P.2d 1242.

Dr. Daun Battersby applied to the Continental Casualty Company for a professional malpractice liability insurance policy. Some weeks before the policy was issued, but after paying the premium, Dr. Battersby learned of a malpractice lawsuit filed by a patient, McCollum. In settling that suit, McCollum acquired the doctor's rights on the policy. He brought this action. Continental contended that the doctor had a duty to disclose the lawsuit once he learned of it. The Court of Appeals held otherwise: Continental assumed the risk of like incidents occurring after it received the application.

■ CORCORAN, JUDGE.

. . .

Even if we were to hold that Battersby had a legal duty to disclose the McCollum suit to Continental once he learned of its existence, the doctrines of waiver and estoppel would prevent Continental from prevailing in this action.

> Waiver, either express or implied, has been defined as the voluntary and intentional relinquishment or abandonment of a known right. It is unilateral in that it arises out of either action or nonaction on the part of the insurer or its duly authorized agents and rests upon circumstances indicating or inferring that the relinquishment of the right was voluntarily intended by the insurer with full knowledge of all of the facts pertaining thereto.

> Estoppel, on the other hand, refers to a preclusion from asserting a right by an insurer where it would be inequitable to permit the assertion. It arises by operation of law, and rests upon acts, statements or conduct on the part of the insurer or its agents which lead or induce the insured, in justifiable reliance thereupon, to act or forbear to act to his prejudice. Abatement of the right or privilege involved by way of estoppel need not be intentionally, voluntarily or purposely effected by or on the part of the insurer.

Buchanan v. Switzerland Gen. Ins. Co., 455 P.2d 344, 349 (Wash. 1969). Despite these generally recognizable distinctions between waiver and estoppel, the two terms are often employed in insurance law as synonyms and used indiscriminately. American Nat'l Ins. Co. v. Cooper, 458 P.2d 257, 260 (Colo. 1969).

Continental learned of the McCollum suit in June 1981, and yet it retained and continued to accept premiums from Battersby. When an insurer has knowledge of facts allegedly justifying a denial of coverage or the forfeiture of a policy previously issued, an unequivocal act that recognizes the continued existence of the policy or an act wholly inconsistent with a prior denial of coverage constitutes a waiver thereof. ... Continental's retention of Battersby's premiums was such an act....

An insurer cannot treat a policy as void for the purpose of denying coverage, and at the same time treat it as valid for the purpose of retaining premiums collected thereon. See Collier v. General Exch. Ins. Corp., 118 P.2d 74 (Ariz. 1941); Glens Falls Indem. Co., 279 N.W. 845, 847 (Minn. 1938) (the insurer is "not privileged 'to run with the hare and hold with the hounds' until such time as it should become plain on which side its advantage lay"). Continental is barred by both waiver and estoppel from avoiding its obligations under the policy. . . .

NOTES

(1) *Question.* In *McCollum*, could Continental's conduct be called, fairly, an election?

(2) *Non-Waiver Agreements.* Early in the morning of March 25, 1964, a fire did serious damages to a motel—the Firebird Motor Hotel. On June 6 the owners filed a proof of loss. Their delay was a ground for the rejection of a claim by the owners for payment under their fire-insurance policy. The policy provided that, "within sixty days after the loss, unless such time is extended in writing by this Company, the insured shall render to this Company a proof of loss". In an action by the owners, they contended that the insurer had waived that ground.

The owners had signed a non-waiver agreement on the day after the fire. It provided that various actions by the insurer would not waive any rights of a party: "any action taken by the [insurer] in ascertaining the amount of the actual cash value; and the amount of the loss and damage . . . and in investigating the cause thereof".

The owners prevailed in the trial court and the insurer appealed. The court affirmed. It said:

> [T]here can be no doubt of the validity of insurance non-waiver agreements, which, despite investigation into a claim by an insurer, nevertheless maintains the status quo of the policy and its conditions precedent to recovery. Had the insurer here through its adjusters done no more than investigate the fire loss, we would be loathe to say in light of the non-waiver agreement that this effectively waived the proof of loss requirement. But more was done than a mere investigation.

Connecticut Fire Ins. Co. v. Fox, 361 F.2d 1, 13–14 (9th Cir. 1966) (Wyo.law). What more there was is indicated in the footnote.[2]

(3) Ex post *Waiver.* In the case just described the insurer faced another obstacle. On June 3 an adjuster deputized by the insurer had handed the owners a letter, signed by the adjuster for the insurer, that if proof of loss were to be filed within a month the insurer would not object on the ground of delay. As for that the insurer contended that a waiver of timely filing cannot be effectuated once the time for filing has expired. The court said: "While there is some authority to that effect

---

2. The court described the activity of one Foster, an adjuster for the General Adjustment Bureau: "In taking complete charge of the loss, he instructed the [owners] to secure the property, to winterize the motel and to have the area cleaned and the remaining undamaged units made available for busi- ness, all of which was done. According to [one owner], Foster told them to keep a file on all these expenses and it would be included in settlement. Clearly by all these acts, Foster went beyond a mere investigation of the fire." Id. at 7.

[citing some], we believe the other rule should prevail under the facts here. . . ." Id. at 8.

(4) *Intent.* The definition of waiver given in *McCollum* is standard: "intentional relinquishment . . . of a known right". It is, however, somewhat infirm if understood to require an intention to effect a waiver. See the ruling described in Note 2 above. See also the burglary case described at pp. 120–21 above: *Ross Jewelers.* There, it may be recalled, Phoenix's claims man, Rogers, wrote a letter omitting reference to the "inventory defense." In the trial he gave affidavit testimony that when he wrote the letter he had not intended to waive that defense. (Saying: "he had hastily prepared and mailed the letter and did not think of or consider the inventory question.") The court made light of that. "While it may be said that waiver depends upon intention, the intention may be inferred from acts and conduct." Id. at 988.

No one supposes that an estoppel arises only when there is an intent to lay the ground for one.

(5) *The Curve of History.* Professor Clarence Morris ascribed the multiplication of waivers and estoppels to changes in the practices of insuring. In early days "marine insurance contracts were handwritten; hull and cargo owners and their brokers knew insurance as thoroughly as the underwriters. When a marine policy buyer entertained a proposal of a warranty, he bargained for important premium concessions and knew the courts would construe the warranty strictly against him." Much later, "American draftsmen-lawyers, sometimes in the hire of fly-by-night companies, proliferated fine print in . . . fire and life insurance policies. Companies, spurred by competition, debased their product. . . ." Morris drew this conclusion: "[W]aiver and estoppel are two of several guises that cloak the courts' part in changing insurance from a service safely bought only by sophisticated businessmen to a commodity bought with confidence by untrained consumers. Judges, at the urging of policyholders' advocates, have used waiver and estoppel to convert insurance from a custom-made document designed in part by knowing buyers to a brand-name staple sold over the counter by mine-run salesmen to the trusting public." Waiver and Estoppel in Insurance Policy Litigation, 105 U.Pa.L.Rev. 925 (1957).

PROBLEM

A.T. Dickson died on November 23, 1987. He had bought insurance for $2 million on his life, payable to a trust bearing his name. When he died, a monthly premium payment of $1,904.50, for October, was unpaid. The policy provided for a 31–day "grace period" for paying premiums. That period ended on November 3. The policy provided that it could be reinstated within a further period of 20 days. Within that period, and before Dickson died, the insurer received a check from the trust, which it treated as payment of the October premium. But two days after Dickson's death that check bounced.

On the same day the insurer received a similar check from the trust. This was marked "November premium", and the insurer treated it accordingly. In December, this check also bounced. (The insurer was trying to collect the former check even after that.)

The insurer brought an action for a declaratory judgment that it did not owe payment. The court granted a summary judgment in its favor. According to the court, the record indicated conclusively that "the policy lapsed as a result of non-payment of the [October] premium. The policy lapsed . . . on November 3, and no valid payment was made during the 20–day reinstatement period. . . . The only payment received prior to [Dickson's death] . . . was returned for insufficient funds. The policy specifically provided that a dishonored check would not constitute payment of a premium." American Crown Life Ins. Co. v. Dickson, 748 F.Supp. 184, 187 (S.D.N.Y. 1990).

Why did not the insurer waive the defense of lapse by depositing and re-depositing checks after Dickson died? Can the case be distinguished from *McCollum*?

Waiver by Insurance Agent's Conduct

An insurer may lose the benefit of a protective term in a policy by the very act of issuing the policy. If the insurer then knows that the applicant is not in compliance with that term, it may well find that it has waived compliance with it. The example now to be given concerned a certificate of credit life insurance bought by E.A. Caves. The function of "credit life", or of "credit accident & health", is to discharge a debt if the customer should suffer (as the case may be) death or disability before paying it. On buying a car, Caves used the proceeds of a bank loan.

The loan and insurance were arranged through Sue Tanner, an officer of the bank and licensed agent for the insurance company. Tanner knew Caves and had done business with him for many years. She knew that Caves had had a serious heart attack. She knew also that he had since done heavy physical work. Tanner was under no duty or direction from the insurer to inquire about the health of potential insureds, but was to use her discretion in issuing insurance to those applying.

On granting credit life coverage to Caves, the insurer gambled and lost. Before committing itself the insurer inquired only about his character and mode of living, according to its standard underwriting method. Caves died within a month. Only then did the insurer learn that for years he had taken medication, and had received medical care, for a progressive disease of the heart. Also, he received disability benefits from the social-security system.

The insurer resisted paying, relying on a condition in the contract that Caves be in insurable health. In an action on the contract by his administratrix, the trial court granted summary judgment in her favor. The insurer's agent knew, when she took the first premium from Caves, that he had suffered a severe heart attack.

On appeal, *held*: Affirmed. Southern United Life Ins. Co. v. Caves, 481 So.2d 764, 55 A.L.R.4th 233 (Miss. 1985). The court said that the question of liability was not a difficult one. "The condition of insurability was effectively waived. . . ." Id. at 767.

NOTES

(1) *Some Quantities.* In *Caves* the court was aggrieved, it seems, by a combination of facts: the insurer had investigated too little, and—through its agent—it knew too much.[3] Might the court have pitched the waiver on the first point alone?

---

3. See Chapter 70 "Agent's Duty To Inform Insurer and Disclose Information to Insurer" in 11 Eric Mills Holmes, Holmes' Appleman on Insurance 2d at 417 ff. (1999).

Consider how much can wisely be spent on investigation with reference to consumer credit life insurance. The amount of a single policy is commonly modest, and diminishes over time as installments of debt are paid.[4]

(2) *Alternatives*. If the insurer's home office had learned the full extent of Caves's health problems after committing itself, but before he died, perhaps it could have terminated the coverage. And perhaps not. If not, the case is one of a waiver that cannot be withdrawn.

Might the court have used estoppel or election to reach its conclusion?

(3) *A Temporal Distinction*. Dr. D.K. Goel and an insurer ("Provident") had a serious standoff over successive applications he made for disability insurance. Provident wanted him to cancel similar coverage he had with another insurer; he wanted coverage from both. At length Providence accepted an application, given Goel's assurance that he would cancel the other policy. When he became disabled, it emerged that he had not complied. That led to litigation in which Goel contended that Providence was bound by waiver or estoppel. He cited *Caves* as authority that if an insurer makes a contract with knowledge that circumstances are not as required by the contract, it cannot resist payment on account of the discrepancy. He contended that Providence was bound by that rule, for Providence's soliciting agent knew that Goel intended to retain coverage with the other insurer. Dr. Goel's contention failed. What the agent was alleged to know was not an "existing fact", but a "future intention" on Goel's part. Provident Life & Accident Ins. Co. v. Goel, 274 F.3d 984 (5th Cir. 2001).

For some purposes the law regards a party's intention as a fact. The state of a man's digestion, it has been said, "is as much a fact as the state of his digestion." Bowen, L.J., in Edgington v. Fitzmaurice, LR 29 Ch.Div. 459, 483. Why not in *Goel*'s case? The court gave a clue in saying that the doctrines of waiver and estoppel do not permit a policyholder to benefit from his own dereliction.

Harr v. Allstate Ins. Co.

New Jersey Supreme Court, 1969.
54 N.J. 287, 255 A.2d 208.

Together with his wife, Herman Harr brought this action on a policy of "fire insurance" that he had arranged in January of 1963. The loss in question was water damage to equipment that Harr had stored in the basement of his home: valves, tanks, and the like, related to his business of selling and servicing dispensers for drinks. In the opinion that follows, a sentence omitted here is this: "The heading 'Fire Insurance Policy' is itself something of a misnomer these days, when almost all such contracts, including this one, insure against, and are generally known to cover, some additional perils." On the day after contracting for the policy, Harr left for an extended vacation in Florida. During his absence a pipe burst, cascaded

---

See also Chapter 65 "Agent's Knowledge or Conduct as Estoppel or Waiver of Applicant/Insured's Health/Medical Misrepresentations" in 10 Eric Mills Holmes, Holmes' Appleman on Insurance 2d at 395 ff. (1999).

4. In *Caves* the court said: "The total payment for the loan was $11,902.80, less $1,041.50 for credit life and disability insurance. The cost of credit life alone was $416.60."

some 90,000 gallons of water through the area, and so caused damage to the equipment (along with other damage).

The evidence for Harr was inconclusive about what coverage he expected. He testified, however, that he had arranged for it through a person—Meinsohn—who was, the court assumed, employed by the insurer.[5] According to Harr's testimony, he had telephoned Meinsohn and asked whether Meinsohn could "cover" the merchandise in the basement, which Harr described, in the amount of $15,000. Meinsohn said: "Mr. Harr, we can cover you for $7,500 and you are fully covered. Go to Florida ... and have a good time." Harr sent a check for the premium, but did not receive the policy, before leaving. Harr also testified that he took Meinsohn's word that he was "fully covered". When the Supreme Court considered the case it made a study of the policy and concluded, as the trial court had done, that the policy provided no coverage for the damage described above. (It said, however, that the policy would be "confusing and abstruse to the average person.")

The trial court dismissed the action, believing that in a suit at law, as distinct from an action in equity to reform a policy, statements made by the insurer's agent at the inception of the contract could not be considered to broaden the coverage of the policy because of the parol evidence rule. On a first appeal the court affirmed, though on a different ground. As an exercise of fact-finding jurisdiction it found that there was insufficient proof both of representation of coverage by Meinsohn and of reliance by the plaintiffs.

The Supreme Court granted petitions for certification. It said: "We agree with the Appellate Division that New Jersey should adopt the view that equitable estoppel is available, under appropriate circumstances, to bring within insurance coverage risks or perils which are not provided for in the policy or which are expressly excluded." The part of the opinion supporting this conclusion is as follows (some omissions not indicated).

■ HALL, JUSTICE.

. . .

II.

We turn to the principal legal question in the case—whether, in an action at law on an insurance policy, equitable estoppel may operate to bring within its coverage risks or perils which are not provided for, or which are expressly excluded.

The courts of this state early held that estoppel was not available at law if the estopping conduct occurred before or at the inception of the contract. While the complete separation between law and equity, which

---

5. The Supreme Court's footnote 1 is as follows: "Meinsohn countersigned [the policy] for defendant as 'authorized agent'. It is our understanding that defendant does not write insurance through so-called 'independent' agents but rather does business only by its own employees. Consequently we assume that Meinsohn was defendant's employee. This probably accounts for the fact that suit was not also brought against him individually, as is quite customary where the agent is an 'independent' one and thus can be said to have the dual capacity of a broker for the prospective insured at the same time. Here plaintiffs had no broker."

remained in this state until 1948, undoubtedly contributed to this view, the main thesis of the cases was that an insurance policy was no different from any other integrated written contract between knowledgeable and sophisticated parties, and the parol evidence rule was thus held a bar to proofs which would vary the terms of the instrument. [The court cited two "leading cases", including Dewees v. Manhattan Ins. Co., 35 N.J.L. 366 (N.J. 1872).] In each there was a misdescription in the policy of the use to which the insured premises were put that was held to be a warranty; and in each the actual use was fully known to the insurer's agent at the time the policy was written, but that evidence was held inadmissible and recovery on the contract denied. The idea of estoppel *in pais* was cast aside as nothing more than a mere evasion of the parol evidence rule.

The holding of *Dewees* has persisted, despite the soundly established rule elsewhere that "any words or acts raising an equitable estoppel may be shown by parol testimony, and it is immaterial whether they occurred before or after the making of the formal contract." Vance on Insurance § 90(c), p. 541 (3rd ed. 1951).

New Jersey insureds have therefore been largely remitted to the rather strict remedy of reformation where the estopping conduct arose before or at the inception of the contract.... But reformation, with its rigid requirements, including among other things that the proofs be clear, convincing and free from doubt, is frequently of no help, even though parol evidence is admissible in such cases. Again *Vance* ... succinctly summarized the difficulty:

> The equitable remedy of reformation is not sufficiently broad to be available in securing the results arrived at under the rule of equitable estoppel. It frequently happens that evidence, that is sufficient to show clearly such inequitable conduct on the part of the insurer as to estop him from setting up a breach of condition, falls short of that certainty that is required to prove the terms of a contract which a court of equity is asked to substitute, by reformation, in place of the one actually executed.... It is not at all impossible that the insurer intended to make the contract exactly as written, though knowing that as so written it imposed no enforceable duty upon him and that he was taking the insured's premium money without rendering any consideration therefor. Upon proof of such a state of facts, there is no intended agreement which the court can substitute for that executed. But there is an estoppel which will preclude the insurer from profiting by his fraud.... (at p. 471, n.3).

[Here the court set out several paragraphs from Morris, *Waiver and Estoppel* ..., the "penetrating" article cited above on p. 124, including the quotation there.]

It is clear that this court's approach to defenses to claims on insurance contracts has changed very substantially in recent years. Our expressions have come in a variety of issues and contexts, but all have indicated as their keystone the goal of greater protection to the ordinary policyholder untutored in the intricacies of insurance. We have realistically faced up to the fact that insurance policies are complex contracts of adhesion, prepared by the insurer, not subject to negotiation, in the case of the average person, as to terms and provisions and quite unintelligible to the insured even were he to attempt to read and understand their unfamiliar and technical language and awkward and unclear arrangement. Recognition is given to the usual and justifiable reliance by the purchaser on the agent, because of his special knowledge, to obtain the protection he desires and needs, and on the agent's representations, whether that agent be a so-called "independent" but authorized representative of the insurer, or only an employee. We have stressed, among other things, the aim that average purchasers of insurance are entitled to the broad measure of protection necessary to fulfill their reasonable expectations; that it is the insurer's burden to obtain, through its representatives, all information pertinent to the risk and the desired coverage before the contract is issued; and that it is likewise its obligation to make policy provisions, especially those relating to coverage, exclusions and vital conditions, plain, clear and prominent to the layman.

Although we have not previously passed upon the question here involved, we have no hesitation in deciding, in line with the rationale just outlined, that, speaking broadly, equitable estoppel is available to bar a defense in an action on a policy even where the estopping conduct arose before or at the inception of the contract, and that the parol evidence rule does not apply in such situations. The contrary holding of *Dewees* ... can no longer be considered to be the law of this state.

However, many jurisdictions which have long followed this view nevertheless hold that equitable estoppel is not available to broaden the *coverage* of a policy so as to protect the insured against risks not included therein or expressly excluded therefrom, as distinct from alleviation of other limitations or conditions of the contract. [The court reviewed New Jersey cases.]

The cases outside New Jersey are collected and discussed in an extensive annotation [at] 1 A.L.R. 3d 1139 (1965). While there is a clear split of authority, with the decisions holding estoppel not available to broaden coverage presently representing the majority view, many of the cases so stating are confusing and not clear cut. Estoppel and waiver are often interchangeably and improperly used, and in many cases where estoppel is held unavailable the necessary elements have not been made out anyway, or the insured by reason of his own conduct is clearly not entitled to relief. The reasons generally advanced in support of the majority view are that a court cannot create a new contract for the parties, that an insurer should not be required by estoppel to pay a loss for which it charged no premium, and perhaps that a risk or peril should not be imposed upon an insurer which it might have declined.

We are more impressed with the decisions in those jurisdictions which hold that equitable estoppel is utilizable to bar a defense of non-coverage of the loss claimed, *i.e.*, the minority rule. [The court cited eleven illustrative cases, including Golden Gate Motor Transport Co. v. Great American Indemnity Co., 58 P.2d 374 (Cal. 1936).]

These decisions all proceed on the thesis that where an insurer or its agent misrepresents, even though innocently, the coverage of an insurance contract, or the exclusions therefrom, to an insured before or at the inception of the contract, and the insured reasonably relies thereupon to his ultimate detriment, the insurer is estopped to deny coverage after a loss on a risk or from a peril actually not covered by the terms of the policy. The proposition is one of elementary and simple justice. By justifiably relying on the insurer's superior knowledge, the insured has been prevented from procuring the desired coverage elsewhere. To reject this approach because a new contract is thereby made for the parties would be an unfortunate triumph of form over substance. The fact that the insurer has received no premium for the risk or peril as to which the loss ensued is no obstacle. Any additional premium due can be deducted from the amount of the loss. See ... *Golden Gate Motor Transport*.... If the insurer is saddled with coverage it may not have intended or desired, it is of its own making, because of its responsibility for the acts and representations of its employees and agents. It alone has the capacity to guard against such a result by the proper selection, training and supervision of its representatives.[6] Of course, the burden of proof of equitable estoppel rests on the insured and, since evidence of representations is almost always oral, a trial court must be convinced that the requisite elements have been established by reliable proof and that the insured has met his burden by a fair preponderance of the evidence.

III

In the light of what has just been said, we shall now consider the precise issue before us: Whether plaintiffs made out a sufficient case of equitable estoppel to withstand the motion for involuntary dismissal and to require defendant to go forward with its proofs.

As to the element of misrepresentation, we have fully set forth earlier in this opinion plaintiffs' proofs and the legitimate inferences to be drawn therefrom. We need now only summarize.

[Given the information that Meinsohn had] it may be inferred that he should have realized that Harr, when he used the word "cover", had in mind and would reasonably expect [coverage of water damage from bursting pipes] in the policy to be written on the merchandise and that, in the absence of an express statement to the contrary, Meinsohn's use of the phrase "fully covered" would be understood by Harr to encompass that peril, and that Harr could and would reasonably rely thereon. This would be true even if Meinsohn were innocently mistaken and believed at the time that the fire policy to be issued would insure against this peril. Therefore there was enough to make out *prima facie* the element of misrepresentation.

---

6. In any event, the defendant here has not contended that water damage from bursting pipes in a dwelling is a peril, which it would not insure against. It is expressly included in the homeowner's policy covering household goods and effects and, as we have indicated, is also included in the provisions of the broad form of fire policy extended coverage.

With respect to the element of reliance, it will be recalled that the policy was not issued until 15 days after Mr. Meinsohn told Mr. Harr he was "fully covered" and, by reason of his absence in Florida known to Meinsohn, was not actually received until some undisclosed date thereafter. Mr. Harr expressly testified that he had confidence in Meinsohn and relied on his representation of full coverage, which certainly demonstrates sufficient reliance at least until the written contract reached him and he had a reasonable opportunity to examine it.... [If, on reading the policy in Florida, Harr] thoroughly understood the policy provisions, and if there was sufficient time to act, but he did nothing, reliance could not be found.

... While we have said that, in general, an insured is chargeable, for reasons of business utility, with knowledge of the contents of a policy in the absence of fraud or inequitable conduct on the part of the insurer, ... where such fraud or inequitable conduct does appear, as here in the light of Harr's testimony with respect to the agent's representations as to coverage, the insured is bound only to make such examination as would be reasonable for the average person under the particular circumstances, and he will only be held to that to which he would be thereby alerted.... Indeed, even absent such representations by the agent, where the language of the policy is such that the layman would not understand its full import were he to attempt to plow through it, such provisions will be deemed to give the maximum protection consistent with its language and the reasonable expectation of the insured.... And we have also held that where the insured was entitled to and did rely upon the representations of an agent as to coverage, the insured can assume that the policy conforms to the representations and he is not barred from an action against the agent for negligence (or presumably against the agent's principal, the insurer) because he failed to read it at all. Rider v. Lynch, 42 N.J. 465, 482 (1964).

Therefore, under the proofs and inferences as they exist at this posture of the case, we conclude plaintiffs made a sufficient showing of reliance to defeat the dismissal motion. That such reliance was to their detriment is obvious. All the elements of equitable estoppel were consequently *prima facie* established.

[Reversed and remanded for a new trial.]

NOTES

(1) *Premium Adjustments.* Reflect on this point made by the court: "The fact that the insurer has received no premium for the risk or peril as to which the loss ensued is no obstacle. Any additional premium due can be deducted from the amount of the loss." Suppose that an insurer has misled a number of its customers about their coverages, overstating some and understating others. Would you expect the premiums paid by all of these customers to be adjusted? Or only those paid in cases of overstatement? Or not even all those, for some of them would not have suffered from justifiable reliance on the overstatement?

Some additional premiums might be "collected", presumably, from customers who are successful in fabricating evidence of overstatements, of reliance, or of both.

On the whole, it seems that premium adjustments would be most valuable to insurers of two sorts, those whose agents are given to loose talk and those most susceptible to faked estoppels. Is this a satisfying set of beneficiaries?

(2) *Opposing Authority*. The split of authority referred to in *Harr* continues. A 21st-century ruling opposed to *Harr* is Royal Maccabees Life Ins. Co. v. James, 146 S.W.3d 340 (Tex.App. 2004). There the court said:

> Under Texas law, it has long been established that waiver and estoppel cannot be used to create insurance coverage: "Whereas waiver and estoppel may operate to avoid forfeiture of a policy and may prevent an insurance company from avoiding payment because of the failure on the part of the insured to comply with some requirement of the policy, waiver and estoppel cannot enlarge the risks covered by a policy and cannot be used to create a new and different contract with respect to the risk covered and the insurance extended." Minn. Mut. Life Ins. Co. v. Morse, 487 S.W.2d 317, 320 (Tex. 1972).

Id. at 350.

(3) *To Defend or Not to Defend*. Liability insurers have to contend, sometimes, with charges of waiver or estoppel when they have undertaken the defense of actions against their insureds, and wish thereafter to disclaim responsibility. A refusal to provide a defense may threaten an insurer with several serious disadvantages. It may, for example, believe that a defense mounted by the insured on its own behalf would be of inferior quality. Insurers habitually seek to thread their way through the minefield, when a defense is demanded, by providing it under an express "reservation of rights", or under a "non-waiver agreement", so as not to concede the entitlement claimed.

For a discussion of relevant New York law, see Steadfast Ins. Co. v. Stroock & Stroock & Lavan LLP, 277 F.Supp.2d 245, 254–55 (S.D.N.Y. 2003). These matters are further pursued in Chapter 6, Liability Insurance: Duty to Defend.

----

2.   Promissory Estoppel

The doctrines of waiver and estoppel have multiple uses.[1] By invoking one or another, a claimant may be able to circumvent a condition limiting a promise; witness waiver of the "inventory condition" in the burglary case, p. 120 above. By invoking waiver or estoppel, a claimant may be able to circumvent a term in a written contract forbidding an oral modification.[2]

1. See generally Chapter 54 "Waiver and Estoppel Explained" in 9 Eric Mills Holmes, Appleman on Insurance 2d at 195 ff. (1999). Waiver and estoppel are not interchangeable synonyms. Professor Kimball explained:

"Waiver is consensual, based on the insurer's voluntary, intentional relinquishment or abandonment of a known right, with a root basis in contract. In contrast, estoppel is delictual, based on detrimental reliance by the insured, with a root basis in tort. Waiver enforces the insurer's intent in relinquishing a right arising out of its insurance contract.

An estoppel rectifies the insured's detrimental reliance on the insurer's conduct. These different focuses require separate analysis. The focus of waiver is on the insurer's intent and the focus of estoppel is on the insured's justifiable reliance."

Spencer L. Kimball, Cases and Materials on Insurance Law 80–81 (1992).

2. Section 1698 of the California Civil Code makes a term like that enforceable. But subsection (d) states that "nothing in this section precludes in an appropriate case the application of rules of law concerning estop-

Promissory estoppel has those uses also,[3] and more.[4] It is a ground for enforcing a promise that is not part of a bargained-for exchange. A doctrine very like it is also a surrogate for a writing required by the Statute of Frauds; see Restatement of Contracts, Second, § 139. These matters are subjects of instruction in every law-school course initiating the study of contract law. The doctrine is not about regretted assertions of fact, as estoppel *in pais* is, but is, as the name indicates, about regretted promises. In general outline, it is not now controversial. The Restatement, Second, of Contracts provides a statement of the doctrine as authoritative as any:

Section 90. *Promise Reasonably Inducing Action or Forbearance*

(1) A promise, which the promisor should reasonably expect to induce action or forbearance on the part of the promisee or a third person and which does induce such action or forbearance is binding if injustice can be avoided only by enforcement of the promise. The remedy granted for breach may be limited as justice requires.

The doctrine has been praised as one that was "born out of conscience", aims to right wrongs, and achieves justice and fair dealing. Roseth v. St. Paul Property & Liability Ins. Co., 374 N.W.2d 105, 110–11 (S.D. 1985).

The materials that follow concern the application of promissory estoppel when an insurer or its agent is the promisor. Curiously, an early manifestation is about an agent's promise to procure insurance for the principal's customer: Siegel v. Spear & Co., 138 N.E. 414 (N.Y. 1923). The agent was not an insurance agent. Should it make any difference?[5]

---

pel, oral novation and substitution of a new agreement, rescission of a written contract by an oral agreement, waiver of a provision of a written contract, or oral independent collateral contracts."

3. As for an oral modification, see Blanton v. State Farm Mutual Automobile Ins. Co., 2005 WL 1231634 (2005). See generally "Primer on Promissory Estoppel" in 11 Eric Mills Holmes, Holmes' Appleman on Insurance 2d § 67.1 (1999).

4. Unlike waiver or estoppel, promissory estoppel may create insurance coverage. The Fifth Circuit, applying Texas promissory estoppel law, for example, explained:

The case ends as, for all purposes, it began. The Travelers agent wrote: "My question is, is Mr. Holman properly covered under the Comprehensive Personal Liability policy or should he have an OL & T policy on this duplex and include with it the vacant property surrounding it?" The underwriter likewise speaking for Travelers answered: "Coverage exists." We agree.

Travelers Indem. Co. v. Holman, 330 F.2d 142, 151 (5th Cir. 1964). *See also* Midamar Corp. v. National–Ben Franklin Ins. Co. of Ill., 898 F.2d 1333 (8th Cir. 1990) (quoting

section 90 from the Second Restatement and applying Iowa promissory estoppel law to an agent's assurances of insurance coverage for a specified loss); Green v. Helmcamp Ins. Agency, 499 S.W.2d 730 (Tex. Civ. App. 1973) (applying the first Restatement of Contracts § 90).

5. In Thorne et al. v. Deas, 4 Johns. 84, 1809 WL 1151 (N.Y. 1809), Thorne and Deas were joint owners of a ship that was wrecked. Deas (not a commercial insurance agent) had promised Thorne that he would provide insurance for the ship before its voyage. When Deas did not procure insurance, Thorne inquired while the ship was at sea, and Deas "replied that 'he (Thorne) might make himself easy, for he (Deas) would that day apply to the insurance offices, and have it done.'" Deas again did not and Thorne sued. The following opinion "headnote" summarizes the court's opinion.

Where A and B were joint owners of a vessel, and A [Deas] voluntarily undertook to get the vessel insured, but neglected to do so, and the vessel was lost, it was held that no action would lie against A [Deas] for the nonperformance of his promise, though B [Thorne] sustained a damage by the nonfeasance,

An estoppel *in pais* can provide or augment coverage based on an agent's statements. It is equally plausible that a promissory estoppel provides or augments coverage based on an insurer's promise or an insurer's agent's promise. Visit "Insurance Promissory Estoppel Law: Some Insurance Promissory Estoppel Cases" in Eric Mills Holmes, 11 Holmes' Appleman on Insurance 2d § 67.5 (1999).

Prudential Insurance Company of America v. Clark

United States Court of Appeals, 5th Cir., 1972.
456 F.2d 932.

The Prudential Insurance Company (sometimes hereafter "the Pru") paid $10,000 to the parents of Steve Clark, a serviceman who had been killed in a helicopter crash in Viet Nam. His parents were the beneficiaries of a life-insurance policy issued to him by the Pru. The payment was made on the authority of Raymond Thomas, the Pru's chief claims consultant, after an appeal for payment was made by its agent, Robert Brumell, who had sold the policy to Steve. The appeal referred to the standing of Steve's parents in their community and to the possible impairment of the Pru's "image". It referred also to the circumstances leading to Steve's purchase of the policy. On further consideration at the Pru's home office, it was thought that the payment should not have been made. This action was brought against the parents for restitution. The policy contained exclusions relating to aviation and war risks.

On these facts some courts might well withhold restitution on the ground that the Pru suffered from no mistake in making the payment, but acted as a "volunteer". Indeed, Thomas testified that he knew a war death was involved when he reviewed the claim, and a jury found that the Pru had intentionally waived the exclusionary clauses. (The jury must not have believed Thomas when he said that he paid the claim through oversight and mistake.) But Florida law, which governed, is exceptional; a statute

there being no consideration for the promise; but a factor or commercial agent, who is entitled to a commission, will be answerable for not executing an order to insure.

Other early cases cited and applied *Thorne* in holding the non-insurance agent's promise to procure insurance gratuitous and unenforceable. See *Brawn v. Lyford, 69 A. 544 (Me. 1907), citing and applying* Thorne.

But in Spiegel v. Metropolitan Life Ins. Co., 160 N.E.2d 40 (App.Div. 1959), the New York court held a commercial insurance agent liable for failure to keep a policy of insurance in force after promising to do so. And the Second Circuit Court of Appeals, in a subsequent case, explained:

Liability on the facts of this case is also supported by the principles of Section 90 of the Restatement (Second) of Contracts (Tent. Draft No. 2, 1965). The elements of a promise which should reasonably induce action, justifiable reliance and damages are present. Although the defendant claims that gratuitous promises inducing detrimental reliance have not been enforced in New York except in charitable subscription cases, this is not strictly true in the light of the New York cases imposing liability on those who promise that there will be insurance and fail to fulfill that promise, Siegel v. Spear & Co., 138 N.E. 414 (1923) . . . or who let insurance lapse, Spiegel v. Metropolitan Life Ins. Co., 160 N.E.2d 40 (App. Div. 1959).

Bethlehem Fabricators, Inc. v. British Overseas Airways, 434 F.2d 840, 844 (2d Cir. 1970) (New York law).

there qualifies the usual rule about voluntary payments.[5] Hence the trial court entered judgment for the Pru, which was appealed.

The Court of Appeals described at length the circumstances attending Steve's purchase of the policy. He had earlier bought a similar policy from World Service Life. After Steve enlisted in the Marine Corps, Brumell advised him to replace that with a Prudential policy, which would not exclude aviation or war risks. On applying to the Pru, Steve dropped the existing policy. Owing to complications that ensued, he served a tour of duty and came home to his parents without having received a substitute policy. At Brumell's instigation, Steve applied again to the Pru. Brumell explained that in the circumstances he thought it would be possible to obtain a policy without the two critical exclusions. Steve returned to Viet Nam in May of 1968. In June 1968, the Prudential policy took effect. It contained those exclusions. The court said: "Steve never had a chance to protest. The policy was not delivered to him, and no one told him that it contained war risk and aviation exclusion clauses. Brumell either had no chance to communicate this information, or remained silent in the hope that these exclusions would not become material; but this was not to be." Steve was killed in July. His parents' claim for payment was accompanied by a letter of appeal by Brumell, mentioned above, and payment followed.

■ CLARK, CIRCUIT JUDGE:

[After reciting the facts, the court referred to a supposed "waiver" defense, and referred to the Florida statute about "the defense of voluntary payment".] This statute negates the common law defense of voluntary payment. The district court believed that the defenses of intentional waiver and voluntary payment were one and the same, and thus that the statute proscribed the waiver defense as well. Apparently, the judge applied the rationale that the defendant's position was based upon nothing more than a waiver of an unenforceable obligation. This action is understandable, in light of the fact that courts have long been reluctant to utilize waiver and estoppel doctrines in cases involving claims on insurance policies, lest it create a coverage neither the insurer nor the insured ever agreed would apply. Contracts should not be court evolved from action or non-action that is not expressive of a desire to be contractually bound.

[The court then turned to the doctrine of promissory estoppel as expressed in the first Restatement of Contracts, § 90.] Promissory estoppel, as a contractual precept, has added a new reflection to the kaleidoscope of contract law. Its stated purpose is to bridge the lack of consideration gap by using the detriment of the promisee to supply the consideration necessary to enforce the promise.... Promissory estoppel does not depend upon conduct which may be contractually equivocal, as do the waiver and other estoppel doctrines above discussed. It requires affirmative action indicative

---

5. "When a suit is instituted by a party to a contract to recover a payment made pursuant to the contract and by the terms of the contract there was no enforceable obligation to make the payment or the making of the payment was excused, the defense of voluntary payment may not be interposed by the person receiving payment to defeat recovery of the payment." Fla.Stat.Ann. § 725.04.

of a desire to be contractually bound. In the case at bar, that affirmative action manifested itself when the agent, Brumell, promised to obtain a policy without the exclusion clauses and thereby induced Steve to drop his other policy in reliance upon that promise. *See* 16A J. Appleman, Insurance Law and Practice §§ 8766–67 (1968)] at 329–30.

.   .   .

Prudential argues that under no theory may this Court take cognizance of the agent's promise and its inequitable conduct because of the Florida rule that any matters transpiring prior to or contemporaneous with the signing of an application for insurance are waived or merged into the application. . . . The rule is nothing more than an embodiment of the parol evidence rule. . . . This argument highlights the basic error of Prudential's position in the court below and here. The jury's verdict found that Prudential did not part with its monies because of a mistaken supposition that they were owed on the policy of insurance it issued to Steve. Rather, this verdict recognized a duty of Prudential, *dehors* the writing, to act in an honorable and upright way in accordance with its agent's promise. Thus, application of promissory estoppel in no way trammels upon the parol evidence rule. Involved here is a separate enforceable promise and not a variance or modification of the terms of the policy. Additionally, Prudential's act of payment, which ratified its agent's commitment, and thereby recognized its duty to honor this action which had enriched the company and misled Steve to drop the World Life policy to the detriment of his beneficiaries, could not have been merged into the document since it did not occur until after the instrument was in being. The Florida "merger" rule is wholly inapplicable to either legalism which would support the jury's verdict.

The judgment of the court below is reversed and the cause is remanded with directions to enter judgment on the jury verdict for the defendants. . . .

NOTES

(1) *Detrimental Reliance?* Say that when Steve dropped the World Life policy he relied justifiably on a promise, made on the Pru's authority, to provide him with insurance against the kind of death that came to him. How was that detrimental to him? Is it apparent that he relied in any other way?

(2) *More on Florida Estoppels.* Years after the foregoing decision, a federal court certified this question to the Florida Supreme Court: "May the theory of equitable estoppel be utilized to prevent an insurance company from denying coverage?" The response was, in part, as follows:

> Equitable estoppel may generally be used defensively to prevent a forfeiture of insurance coverage, but not affirmatively to create or extend coverage. An exception to the general rule is the doctrine of promissory estoppel, a qualified form of equitable estoppel which applies to representations relating to a future act of the promisor rather than to an existing fact. It applies where to refuse to enforce a promise, even without consideration, would sanction fraud or injustice. Such injustice may be found where the promisor reasonably should have expected that his affirmative representations would induce the promisee into

action or forbearance substantial in nature, and where the promisee shows reliance to his detriment. The form of equitable estoppel known as promissory estoppel may create insurance coverage where to refuse to do so would sanction fraud or other injustice.

Crown Life Ins. Co. v. McBride, 517 So.2d 660, 661–62 (1987).

What may have led the Florida court to speak of a promise as a "representation relating to a future act"? And to characterize promissory estoppel as "a qualified form of equitable estoppel"?

Justice Grimes, concurring in *McBride*, said that "the application of promissory estoppel to create coverage facilitates the possibility of fraudulent claims." Nevertheless: "Because of my confidence in our adversary system of justice, I am compelled to come down on the side which authorizes a just result when the true facts are developed." The Justice seems to have thought that the evidence supporting a promissory estoppel must be clear and convincing, at least in cases of coverage disputes.

PROBLEM

Bill Brown ("Bill") is one of the owners of Brown Trucking, Inc. (BTI), which specializes in hauling oversized items. While one of its trucks was carrying heavy equipment on I–40, the equipment struck an overhead bridge, to its damage. BTI was insured against damage to the equipment by reason of, among other things, "Collision of the conveyance with any other vehicle or object."

Earlier, when arranging the insurance, Bill had asked an agent of the insurer for a "full coverage policy" on the cargo transported in his business. He had shown the agent photographs of BTI's tractor-trailer units loaded with typical cargos. The agent had told Bill "That's no problem, you've got full coverage."

After the loss, the insurer rejected a claim by BTI on the ground that the truck had not struck the bridge, and was not damaged. Should BTI prevail in an action brought on the policy? See Bill Brown Construction Co. v. Glens Falls Ins. Co., 818 S.W.2d 1 (Tenn. 1991).

NOTE

Employee Retirement Income Security Act (ERISA) and Promissory Estoppel. ERISA may bar promissory estoppel against an ERISA plan. The Second Circuit Court of Appeals set forth a framework for a successful **promissory estoppel** claim under ERISA as follows:

> "Principles of estoppel can apply in ERISA cases under extraordinary circumstances." Schonholz v. Long Island Jewish Medical Ctr., 87 F.3d 72, 78 (2d Cir. 1996). A plaintiff must satisfy four elements to succeed on a claim of promissory estoppel: " '(1) a promise, (2) reliance on the promise, (3) injury caused by the reliance, and (4) an injustice if the promise is not enforced.' " Aramony v. United Way Replacement Benefit Plan, 191 F.3d 140, 151 (2d Cir. 1999).... Additionally, "an ERISA plaintiff must 'adduce [] not only facts sufficient to support the four basic elements of promissory estoppel but facts sufficient to [satisfy an] "extraordinary circumstances" requirement as well.' " *Aramony*, 191 F.3d at 151.... *Schonholz* provides an example of such extraordinary circumstances, where the employer used promised severance benefits to induce the plaintiff to retire. *Schonholz*, 87 F.3d at 79–80.... We agree with appellants and therefore remand this claim to the district court. These appel-

lants have sufficiently demonstrated the four basic elements of promissory estoppel plus "extraordinary circumstances" to avoid summary judgment.

Calogera Abbruscato v. Empire Blue Cross & Blue Shield, 274 F.3d 90, 100–02 (2d Cir. 2001).

---

3.   Good and Bad Faith

This section provides an introduction to the insurance law doctrines of "good faith" and "bad faith" which are thoroughly examined later in Chapter 7. The doctrines have roots in contract law. "Every contract imposes upon each party a duty of good faith and fair dealing in its performance and its enforcement." Restatement, Second, of Contracts § 205. A representative application of this principle to insurance contracts is this:

> Insurance policies are contracts of utmost good faith and must be administered and performed as such by the insurer. Good faith "demands that the insurer deal with laymen as laymen and not as experts in the subtleties of law and underwriting." ... In all insurance contracts, particularly where the language expressing the extent of the coverage may be deceptive to the ordinary layman, there is an implied covenant of good faith and fair dealing that the insurer will not do anything to injure the right of its policyholder to receive the benefits of his contract.

Bowler v. Fidelity and Casualty Company of New York, 250 A.2d 580, 587–88 (N.J. 1969).[1]

To say that a covenant is implied in a contract is to say that the terms agreed upon are supplemented by an undertaking that the parties did not express. The duty of good faith is "implied by law" and serves to prevent an inequitable result. There is no generally accepted definition or meaning of "good faith" and "bad faith". However, as a policing principle to achieve fairness in insurance contract performance, "good faith" provides a standard for evaluating the conduct of the insurer in performing its insurance contract duties, such as defending the insured under a third-party liability policy or indemnifying an insured under a first-party property insurance policy. If the standard is not met, "bad faith" conduct is typically found.

An action taken in good faith is one that is reasonable, having regard to both the law and the facts. It is quite possible for an insurer to act in

---

1. The court continued: "In situations where a layman might give the controlling language of the policy a more restrictive interpretation than the insurer knows the courts have given it and as a result the uninformed insured might be inclined to be quiescent about the disregard or nonpayment of his claim and not to press it in timely fashion, the company cannot ignore its obligation. It cannot hide behind the insured's ignorance of the law; it cannot conceal its liability. In these circumstances it has the duty to speak and disclose, and to act in accordance with its contractual undertaking. The slightest evidence of deception or overreaching will bar reliance upon time limitations for prosecution of the claim." Ibid.

good faith when rejecting a valid property insurance claim on its policy. The usual case of first-party insurance bad-faith action is, however, to withhold from a customer a benefit that the policy calls for, and to do so without any plausible basis in law or on the facts or both. Bad faith may inhere in an insurer's failure to investigate the facts underlying a claim against it. Insurers are expected to exercise good faith at every stage of dealing with customers.

The bad faith doctrine in insurance historically developed first in third-party liability insurance cases[2] and emerged fully developed in Hilker v. Western Auto. Ins. Co., 235 N.W. 413 (Wis. 1931), *aff'd on rehg.*, 235 N.W. 413. Regarding the third-party liability insurer's duty to defend, the Wisconsin Supreme Court explained the good faith obligation.

> Generally speaking, good faith means being faithful to one's duty or obligation; bad faith means being recreant thereto. In order to understand what is meant by bad faith a comprehension of one's duty is generally necessary.... By the terms of this contract the absolute control of the defense of such actions is turned over to the insurer, and the insured is excluded from any interference in any negotiations for settlement or legal procedure.... So long as the recovery does not exceed the limits of the insurance, the question of whether the claim be compromised or settled, or the manner in which it shall be defended, is a matter of no concern to the insured. However, where an injury occurs for which a recovery may be had in a sum exceeding the amount of the insurance, the interest of the insured becomes one of concern to him. At this point a duty on the part of the insurer to the insured arises. It arises because the insured has bartered to the insurance company all of the rights possessed by him to enable him to discover the extent of the injury and to protect himself as best he can from the consequences of the injury. He has contracted with the insurer that it shall have the exclusive right to settle or compromise the claim, to conduct the defense, and that he will not interfere except at his own cost and expense....
>
> It is the right of the insurer to exercise its own judgment upon the question of whether the claim should be settled or contested. But because it has taken over this duty, and because the contract prohibits the insured from settling, or negotiating for a settlement, or interfering in any manner except upon the request of the insurer, ... its exercise of this right should be accompanied by considerations of good faith. Its decision not to settle should be an honest decision.

---

2.   Scholarly literature on "bad faith" is a mountainous mass. A collection of 19 articles and essays citing other scholarly writings is in "Symposium on the law of Bad Faith in Contract and Insurance," 72 Tex.L.Rev. 1203 (1994). For a more detailed historical discussion, see Robert H. Jerry, "The Wrong Side of the Mountain: A Comment on Bad Faith's Unnatural History," 72 Tex.L.Rev. 1317 (1994). See also Stephen S. Ashley, "One Hundred Years of Bad Faith," 15 Bad Faith L. Rpt. 207 (1999), where the noted bad-faith commentator claims that Industrial & Gen. Trust v. Tod, 73 N.E. 7 (N.Y. 1905), is the earliest example of a court invoking an implied covenant of good faith and fair dealing.

Hilker, supra at 235 N.W. 414. Although *Hilker* speaks strongly of "bad faith", it did not answer this crucial question: Does the bad faith cause of action establish some new damage rules in contract or does it sound in tort as a bad faith tort or as a negligence "due care" tort or does it matter? Years passed as courts wrestled with this question.[3] The following landmark California *Comunale* opinion (which relied, in part, on *Hilker*) provided this response to the question.

Comunale v. Traders & General Ins. Co.

Supreme Court of California, 1958.
50 Cal.2d 654, 328 P.2d 198.

■ GIBSON, CHIEF JUSTICE.

Mr. and Mrs. Comunale were struck in a marked pedestrian crosswalk by a truck driven by Percy Sloan. Mr. Comunale was seriously injured, and his wife suffered minor injuries. Sloan was insured [against liability] by defendant Traders and General Insurance Company under a policy that contained limits of liability in the sum of $10,000 for each person injured and $20,000 for each accident. He notified Traders of the accident and was told that the policy did not provide coverage because he was driving a truck that did not belong to him. When the Comunales filed suit against Sloan, Traders refused to defend the action, and Sloan employed competent counsel to represent him. On the second day of the trial Sloan informed Traders that the Comunales would compromise the case for $4,000, that he did not have enough money to effect the settlement, and that it was highly probable the jury would return a verdict in excess of the policy limits. Traders was obligated to defend any personal injury suit covered by the policy, but it was given the right to make such settlement as it might deem expedient. Sloan demanded that Traders assume the defense and settlement of the case. Traders refused, and the trial proceeded to judgment in favor of Mr. Comunale for $25,000 and Mrs. Comunale for $1,250.

Sloan did not pay the judgment, and the Comunales sued Traders under a provision in the policy that permitted an injured party to maintain an action after obtaining judgment against the insured. (See Ins. Code, § 11580, subd. (b)(2).) In that suit judgment was rendered in favor of Mr. Comunale for $10,000 and in favor of Mrs. Comunale for $1,250. This judgment was satisfied by Traders after it was affirmed in Comunale v. Traders & General Ins. Co., 253 P.2d 495.

Comunale obtained an assignment of all of Sloan's rights against Traders and then commenced the present action to recover from Traders the portion of his judgment against Sloan which was in excess of the policy limits. The jury returned a verdict in Comunale's favor, but the trial court entered a judgment for Traders notwithstanding the verdict.

---

3. Compare Southern Farm Bureau Cas. Ins. Co. v. Parker, 341 S.W.2d 36 (Ark. 1960) with Home Indem. Co. v. Snowden, 264 S.W.2d 642 (1954).

The following questions are presented on Comunale's appeal from the judgment: (1) Did Sloan have a cause of action against Traders for the amount of the judgment in excess of the policy limits? (2) Was Sloan's cause of action against Traders assignable? (3) Was the cause of action barred by the statute of limitations?

Liability in Excess of the Policy Limits

In determining whether Traders is liable for the portion of the judgment against Sloan in excess of the policy limits, we must take into consideration the fact that Traders not only wrongfully refused to defend the action against Sloan but also refused to accept an offer of settlement within the policy limits. It is not claimed the settlement offer was unreasonable in view of the extent of the injuries and the probability that Sloan would be found liable, and Traders' only reason for refusing to settle was its claim that the accident was not covered by the policy. Because of its wrongful denial of coverage, Traders failed to consider Sloan's interest in having the suit against him compromised by a settlement within the policy limits.

There is an implied covenant of good faith and fair dealing in every contract that neither party will do anything which will injure the right of the other to receive the benefits of the agreement. Brown v. Superior Court, 212 P.2d 878, 880–81 (Cal. 1949). This principle is applicable to policies of insurance. Hilker v. Western Automobile Ins. Co., 231 N.W. 257, 258 (1931) *aff'd on rehg.*, 235 N.W. 413. In the *Hilker* case it is pointed out that the rights of the insured "go deeper than the mere surface of the contract written for him by defendant" and that implied obligations are imposed "based upon those principles of fair dealing which enter into every contract." 231 N.W. at p. 258. It is common knowledge that a large percentage of the claims covered by insurance are settled without litigation and that this is one of the usual methods by which the insured receives protection. (See Douglas v. United States Fidelity & Guaranty Co., 127 A. 708, 712 (N.H. 1924); *Hilker, supra*). Under these circumstances the implied obligation of good faith and fair dealing requires the insurer to settle in an appropriate case although the express terms of the policy do not impose such a duty.

The insurer, in deciding whether a claim should be compromised, must take into account the interest of the insured and give it at least as much consideration as it does to its own interest. See Ivy v. Pacific Automobile Ins. Co., 320 P.2d 140, 145–46 (Cal.App. 1958). When there is great risk of a recovery beyond the policy limits so that the most reasonable manner of disposing of the claim is a settlement which can be made within those limits, a consideration in good faith of the insured's interest requires the insurer to settle the claim. Its unwarranted refusal to do so constitutes a breach of the implied covenant of good faith and fair dealing.

There is an important difference between the liability of an insurer who performs its obligations and that of an insurer who breaches its contract. The policy limits restrict only the amount the insurer may have to pay in the performance of the contract as compensation to a third person for personal injuries caused by the insured; they do not restrict the damages recoverable by the insured for a breach of contract by the insurer.

The decisive factor in fixing the extent of Traders' liability is not the refusal to defend; it is the refusal to accept an offer of settlement within the policy limits. Where there is no opportunity to compromise the claim and the only wrongful act of the insurer is the refusal to defend, the liability of the insurer is ordinarily limited to the amount of the policy plus attorneys' fees and costs. Mannheimer Bros. v. Kansas Casualty & Surety Co., 184 N.W. 189, 191 (Minn. 1921). In such a case it is reasoned that, if the insured has employed competent counsel to represent him, there is no ground for concluding that the judgment would have been for a lesser sum had the defense been conducted by insurer's counsel, and therefore it cannot be said that the detriment suffered by the insured as the result of a judgment in excess of the policy limits was proximately caused by the insurer's refusal to defend. *Cf.* Lane v. Storke, 101 P. 937, 938 (Cal.App. 1909). This reasoning, however, does not apply where the insurer wrongfully refuses to accept a reasonable settlement within the policy limits.

Most of the cases dealing with the insurer's failure to settle involve an insurer who had assumed the defense of the action against the insured. It is generally held that since the insurer has reserved control over the litigation and settlement it is liable for the entire amount of a judgment against the insured, including any portion in excess of the policy limits, if in the exercise of such control it is guilty of bad faith in refusing a settlement.... We do not agree with the cases that hold there is no liability in excess of the policy limits where the insurer, believing there is no coverage, wrongfully refuses to defend and without justification refuses to settle the claim. See State Farm Mut. Auto. Ins. Co. v. Skaggs, 251 F.2d 356, 359, and Fidelity & Casualty of New York v. Gault, 196 F.2d 329, 330. An insurer who denies coverage does so at its own risk, and, although its position may not have been entirely groundless, if the denial is found to be wrongful it is liable for the full amount which will compensate the insured for all the detriment caused by the insurer's breach of the express and implied obligations of the contract. Certainly an insurer who not only rejected a reasonable offer of settlement but also wrongfully refused to defend should be in no better position than if it had assumed the defense and then declined to settle. The insurer should not be permitted to profit by its own wrong....

... Section 3358 [of the Civil Code] provides that a person cannot recover a greater amount in damages for the breach of an obligation than he could have gained by full performance. The question is what would Sloan have gained from the full performance of the policy contract with Traders.... If Traders had performed its contract, it would have settled the action against Sloan, thereby protecting him from all liability. The allowance of a recovery in excess of the policy limits will not give the insured any additional advantage but merely place him in the same position as if the contract had been performed.

It follows from what we have said that an insurer, who wrongfully declines to defend and who refuses to accept a reasonable settlement within the policy limits in violation of its duty to consider in good faith the interest of the insured in the settlement, is liable for the entire judgment against the insured even if it exceeds the policy limits.... An action for damages in excess of the policy limits based on an insurer's wrongful failure to settle is assignable whether the action is considered as sounding in tort or in contract. See Civ. Code, § 954.... Accordingly, Sloan could assign his cause of action to Comunale.

. . .

Although a wrongful refusal to settle has generally been treated as a tort, see Keeton, Liability Insurance and Responsibility for Settlement, 67 Harv. L. Rev. 1136, 1138; Anno., 131 A.L.R. 1499, 1500, it is the rule that where a case sounds both in contract and tort the plaintiff will ordinarily have freedom of election between an action of tort and one of contract. Eads v. Marks, 249 P.2d 257....

The judgment is reversed with directions to the superior court to enter judgment on the verdict.

NOTES

(1) *Issues Not Resolved*. In *Comunale*, the court said that a claim like Sloan's is assignable whether the action is considered as sounding in tort or in contract. What does the quoted phrase "action is considered as sounding in tort or in contract" mean? Is the cause of action ("claim for relief" in modern pleading) a tort claim or a contract claim? What standard does the court adopt to evaluate the insurer's settlement conduct? A tort standard of negligence? A good faith/bad faith standard? Regarding damages for an insurer's wrongful failure to settle, the court stated that it must compensate the insured for "all the detriment caused". Did the court mean tort damages or contract "expectation" damages[1] Are emotional stress damages recoverable? Punitive damages?

(2) *The Rest of the Story*. This section provides only an introduction to an insurer's liability in excess of the policy limits—often called "excess liability". Chapter 7, Excess Liability of Insurers: Good and Bad Faith, Negligence and Depravity, provides the rest of the story. It begins with the next landmark California case, Crisci v. Security Ins. Co., 426 P.2d 173 (Cal. 1967), which clarifies and resolves many of the issues addressed and not addressed in *Comunale*.

---

1. "**Recovery measured by expectation interest.** In general, the amount of the award is measured by the promisee's *expectation interest* or, as it is sometimes said, 'the benefit of the bargain.' The court attempts to put the *promisee in the position in which the promisee would have been had the promise been performed* (i.e., had there been no breach)." E. Allan Fornsworth, Contracts 44 (3d ed. 1999). But note:

The traditional measure of recovery for failure to pay money due under contract is the amount agreed to be paid. Clark v. Life & Casualty Ins. Co., 53 S.W.2d 968, 84 A.L.R. 1420 (Ky. 1932); 22 Am.Jur.2d 97 (Damages, § 64); 29A Am.Jur. 776 (Insurance, § 1696).

General Accident Fire & Life Assurance Corp. v. Judd, 400 S.W.2d 685, 687 (Ky. 1966).

4. The Doctrine of Reasonable Expectations

The doctrine of reasonable expectations (sometimes "DRE") began to flourish in a handful of opinions issued in the 1960s, although it has older roots.[1] The doctrine was foreshadowed in Kievit v. Loyal Protective Life Ins. Co., 170 A.2d 22, 26 (N.J. 1961). Its most distinctive mark is that it applies to expectations that are objectively reasonable notwithstanding that those expectations would have been negated by a meticulous reading of the policy provisions. See, e.g., Riffe v. Home Finders Assocs., p. 16 above. This doctrine is now recognized in at least ten states in a form explicitly going beyond resolving ambiguities against insurers (*contra proferentem*).

A principle of honoring reasonable expectations not perceived as a distinctive doctrine no doubt had earlier influence and continues to influence decisions. Whether or not formally recognized, the principle of honoring reasonable expectations is, of course, no guarantee of victory for a plaintiff against an insurer. Davenport Peters Company v. Royal Globe Ins. Co., 490 F.Supp. 286, 291 (D.Mass. 1980) is an apt illustration. As this introduction suggests, much more than a capsule statement is wanted for a fair understanding and appraisal of the doctrine.

The opinion that follows refers to some sources of the doctrine of reasonable expectations, notably including the conception *contract of adhesion*, including some sources that do not relate to insurance. In various courts accepting the doctrine, it seems, it applies only to contracts of insurance. This appears to be the view taken in the *Riffe* case. There the court said: "Because the [home warranty contract] offered by Home Security is insurance, the Riffes are entitled to all the protections afforded to purchasers of insurance under our law [including] *[w]ith respect to insurance contracts, the doctrine of reasonable expectations. . . .*" *Riffe*, supra, 517 S.E.2d at 318. On reading further about the doctrine, look for indications from other courts that they apply the DRE more expansively or not at all.

Gray v. Zurich Insurance Company

Supreme Court of California, 1966.
54 Cal.Rptr. 104, 419 P.2d 168.

■ TOBRINER, J.

This is an action by an insured against his insurer for failure to defend an action filed against him which stemmed from a complaint alleging that he had committed an assault. The main issue turns on the argument of the insurer that an exclusionary clause of the policy excuses its defense of an action in which a plaintiff alleges that the insured intentionally caused the bodily injury. Yet the language of the policy does not clearly define the application of the exclusionary clause to the duty to defend. Since in that event we test the meaning of the policy according to the insured's reason-

---

1. In 1918 Cardozo took the "reasonable expectation" of a hypothetical business buyer of insurance as his guide in the well-known case of the "Black Tom" explosion: Bird v. St. Paul Fire & Marine Ins. Co., p. 434 below.

able expectation of coverage and since the language of the policy would lead the insured here to expect defense of the third party suit, we cannot exonerate the carrier from the rendition of such protection.

Plaintiff, Dr. Vernon D. Gray, is the named insured under an insurance policy issued by defendant. A "Comprehensive Personal Liability Endorsement" in the policy states, under a paragraph designated "Coverage L," that the insurer agrees "[To] pay on behalf of the insured all sums which the insured shall become legally obligated to pay as damages because of bodily injury or property damage, and the company shall defend any suit against the insured alleging such bodily injury or property damage and seeking damages which are payable under the terms of this endorsement, even if any of the allegations are groundless, false or fraudulent; but the company may make such investigation and settlement of any claim or suit as it deems expedient." The policy contains a provision that "[This] endorsement does not apply" to a series of specified exclusions set forth under separate headings, including a paragraph (c) which reads, "under coverages L and M, to bodily injury or property damages caused intentionally by or at the direction of the insured."

The suit which Dr. Gray contends Zurich should have defended arose out of an altercation between him and a Mr. John R. Jones.[1] Jones filed a complaint in Missouri alleging that Dr. Gray "wilfully, maliciously, brutally and intentionally assaulted" him; he prayed for actual damages of $50,000 and punitive damages of $50,000. Dr. Gray notified defendant of the suit, stating that he had acted in self defense, and requested that the company defend. Defendant refused on the ground that the complaint alleged an intentional tort which fell outside the coverage of the policy. Dr. Gray thereafter unsuccessfully defended on the theory of self defense; he suffered a judgment of $6,000 actual damages although the jury refused to award punitive damages.

Dr. Gray then filed the instant action charging defendant with breach of its duty to defend. Defendant answered, admitting the execution of the policy but denying any such obligation. . . . [T]he court rendered judgment in favor of defendant. We must decide whether or not defendant bore the obligation to defend plaintiff in the Missouri action.

Defendant argues that it need not defend an action in which the complaint reveals on its face that the claimed bodily injury does not fall within the indemnification coverage; that here the Jones complaint alleged that the insured committed an assault, which fell outside such coverage. [Other contentions made by the defendant are described below.]

We shall explain our reasons for concluding that defendant was obligated to defend the Jones suit, and our grounds for rejecting defendant's remaining propositions.

---

1. Immediately preceding the altercation Dr. Gray had been driving an automobile on a residential street when another automobile narrowly missed colliding with his car. Jones, the driver of the other car, left his vehicle, approached Dr. Gray's car in a menacing manner and jerked open the door. At that point Dr. Gray, fearing physical harm to himself and his passengers, rose from his seat and struck Jones.

Since the policy sets forth the duty to defend as a primary one and since the insurer attempts to avoid it only by an unclear exclusionary clause, the insured would reasonably expect, and is legally entitled to, such protection. As an alternative but secondary ground for our ruling we accept, for purposes of argument, defendant's contention that the duty to defend arises only if the third party suit involves a liability for which the insurer would be required to indemnify the insured, and, even upon this basis, we find a duty to defend.

In interpreting an insurance policy we apply the general principle that doubts as to meaning must be resolved against the insurer and that any exception to the performance of the basic underlying obligation must be so stated as clearly to apprise the insured of its effect.

These principles of interpretation of insurance contracts have found new and vivid restatement in the doctrine of the adhesion contract. As this court has held, a contract entered into between two parties of unequal bargaining strength, expressed in the language of a standardized contract, written by the more powerful bargainer to meet its own needs, and offered to the weaker party on a "take it or leave it" basis carries some consequences that extend beyond orthodox implications. Obligations arising from such a contract inure not alone from the consensual transaction but from the relationship of the parties.

Although courts have long followed the basic precept that they would look to the words of the contract to find the meaning which the parties expected from them,[5] they have also applied the doctrine of the adhesion contract to insurance policies, holding that in view of the disparate bargaining status of the parties[6] we must ascertain that meaning of the contract which the insured would reasonably expect.[7] Thus as Kessler stated in his

---

5. The traditional rules of construction for contracts require the courts to take cognizance of the expectations of the parties. "If the court is convinced that it knows the purposes of the parties, the intended legal result, however vaguely expressed and poorly analyzed, it should be loath to adopt any interpretation of their language that would produce a different result." (3 Corbin on Contracts, p. 164.)

6. Isaacs, *The Standardizing of Contracts* (1917) 27 Yale L.J. 34, in an early analysis, suggests the basis for the adhesion contract, pointing out that standardized contracts create "status" relationships as opposed to individualized relationships. The article states: "The movement toward status law clashes, of course, with the ideal of individual freedom in the negative sense of 'absence of restraint' or *laissez faire*. Yet, freedom in the positive sense of presence of opportunity is being served by social interference with contract. There is still much to be gained by the further standardizing of the relations in which society has an inter-

est, in order to remove them from the control of the accident of power in individual bargaining. The new school of jurisprudence has a great work before it in educating the courts. It must, indeed, dispel the fear of status as an archaic legal institution which we have outgrown." (At p. 47.) Pound, The Spirit of Common Law (1921) states: "Taking no account of legislative [i.e., non-common law] limitations upon freedom of contract, in the purely judicial development of our law we have taken the law of insurance practically out of the category of contract, and we have established that the duties of public service companies are not contractual, as the nineteenth century sought to make them, but are instead relational; they do not flow from agreements which the public servant may make as he chooses, they flow from the calling in which he has engaged and his consequent relation to the public." (At p. 29.)

7. Courts have long applied the doctrine of reasonable expectation to the interpretation of insurance contracts. Thus in

classic article on adhesion contracts: "In dealing with standardized contracts courts have to determine what the weaker contracting party could legitimately expect by way of services according to the enterpriser's 'calling', and to what extent the stronger party disappointed reasonable expectations based on the typical life situation." (Kessler, *Contracts of Adhesion* (1943) 43 Colum.L.Rev. 629, 637.)

Professor Patterson, in describing one characteristic consequence of "the conception of adhesion, whether that term is used or not," writes: "The court interprets the form contract to mean what a reasonable buyer would expect it to mean, and thus protects the weaker party's expectation at the expense of the stronger's. This process of interpretation was used many years ago in interpreting (or construing) insurance contracts...." (Fn. omitted; Patterson, *The Interpretation and Construction of Contracts* (1964) 64 Colum.L.Rev. 833, 858.)

Thus we held in *Steven* v. *Fidelity & Casualty Co.,* [377 P.2d 284 (Cal. 1982)], that we would not enforce an exclusionary clause in an insurance contract which was unclear, saying: "If [the insurer] deals with the public upon a mass basis, the notice of noncoverage of the policy, in a situation in which the public may reasonably expect coverage, must be conspicuous, plain and clear." [P.194][8]

When we test the instant policy by these principles we find that its provisions as to the obligation to defend are uncertain and undefined; in the light of the reasonable expectation of the insured, they require the performance of that duty. At the threshold we note that the nature of the obligation to defend is itself necessarily uncertain. Although insurers have often insisted that the duty arises only if the insurer is bound to indemnify the insured, this very contention creates a dilemma. No one can determine

Coast Mutual B.-L. Assn. v. *Security T. I. & G. Co.* (1936) 14 Cal.App.2d 225, 229 [57 P.2d 1392], the court said: "In the decision of this question we are to be guided by well-established rules relating to the construction of insurance policies. Not only the provisions of the policy as a whole, but also the exceptions to the liability of the insurer, *must be construed so as to give the insured the protection which he reasonably had a right to expect,* and to that end doubts, ambiguities, and uncertainties arising out of the language used in the policy must be resolved in his favor." (Italics added.) *Atlantic Nat. Ins. Co.* v. *Armstrong* (1966) [52 Cal.Rptr. 569, 416 P.2d 801] is a recent example of the application of the doctrine. We there recognized that the insured would not have reasonably expected a policy provision requiring him to indemnify his insurer for a risk not covered by the policy but which was required by law to be contained in all such policies. In holding the provision therefore unenforceable we said: "In interpreting an insurance contract we must consider the intent and reasonable expectations of the parties in entering into the

agreement. Hence, we must evaluate not only [the insurer's] contract form, but also [the insured's] knowledge and understanding as a layman and *his normal expectation of the extent of coverage of the policy.*" (Italics added.) (*Id.* at p. 112.)

8. In *Steven* we relied upon the early California case of *Raulet* v. *Northwestern etc. Ins. Co.* (1910) 157 Cal. 213 [107 P. 292], which aptly said: "It is a matter almost of common knowledge that a very small percentage of policyholders are actually cognizant of the provisions of their policies and many of them are ignorant of the names of the companies issuing the said policies. The policies are prepared by the experts of the companies, they are highly technical in their phraseology, they are complicated and voluminous—the one before us covering thirteen pages of the transcript—and in their numerous conditions and stipulations furnishing what sometimes may be veritable traps for the unwary." (At p. 230.)

whether the third party suit does or does not fall within the indemnification coverage of the policy until that suit is resolved; in the instant case, the determination of whether the insured engaged in intentional, negligent or even wrongful conduct depended upon the judgment in the Jones suit, and, indeed, even after that judgment, no one could be positive whether it rested upon a finding of plaintiff's negligent or his intentional conduct. The carrier's obligation to indemnify inevitably will not be defined until the adjudication of the very action which it should have defended. Hence the policy contains its own seeds of uncertainty; the insurer has held out a promise that by its very nature is ambiguous.

Although this uncertainty in the performance of the duty to defend could have been clarified by the language of the policy we find no such specificity here. An examination of the policy discloses that the broadly stated promise to defend is not conspicuously or clearly conditioned solely on a nonintentional bodily injury; instead, the insured could reasonably expect such protection.

The policy is a "comprehensive personal liability" contract; the designation in itself connotes general protection for alleged bodily injury caused by the insured. The insurer makes two wide promises: "[1.] To pay on behalf of the insured all sums which the insured shall become legally obligated to pay as damages because of bodily injury or property damage, and [2.] the company shall defend any suit against the insured alleging such bodily injury or property damage and seeking damages which are payable under the terms of this endorsement, even if any of the allegations of the suit are groundless, false, or fraudulent": clearly these promises, without further clarification, would lead the insured reasonably to expect the insurer to defend him against suits seeking damages for bodily injury, whatever the alleged cause of the injury, whether intentional or inadvertent.

But the insurer argues that the third party suit must seek "damages which are *payable* under the terms of this endorsement"; it contends that this limitation *modifies* the general duty to defend by confining the duty only to actions seeking damages within the primary coverage of the policy. Under "Exclusions" the policy provides that it "does not apply ... under coverage L and M to bodily injury ... caused intentionally by ... the insured."

The very first paragraph as to coverage, however, provides that "the company shall defend any such suit against the insured alleging such bodily injury" although the allegations of the suit are groundless, false or fraudulent. This language, in its broad sweep, would lead the insured reasonably to expect defense of *any* suit regardless of merit or cause. The relation of the exclusionary clause to this basic promise is anything but clear. The basic promise would support the insured's reasonable expectation that he had bought the rendition of legal services to defend against a suit for bodily injury which alleged he had caused it, negligently, nonintentionally, intentionally or in any other manner. The doctrines and cases we have set forth tell us that the exclusionary clause must be "conspicuous, plain and clear."

(*Steven* v. *Fidelity & Casualty Co., supra*, 58 Cal.2d 862, 878.) This clause is not "conspicuous" since it appears only after a long and complicated page of fine print, and is itself in fine print; its relation to the remaining clauses of the policy and its effect are surely not "plain and clear."

A further uncertainty lurks in the exclusionary clause itself. It alludes to damage caused "intentionally by or at the direction of the insured." Yet an act of the insured may carry out his "intention" and also cause unintended harm. When set next to the words "at the direction of the insured" the word "intentionally" might mean to the layman collusive, wilful or planned action beyond the classical notion of intentional tort.[11] This built-in ambiguity has caused debate and refined definition in many courts; in any event, the word surely cannot be "plain and clear" to the layman.

The insured is unhappily surrounded by concentric circles of uncertainty: the first, the unascertainable nature of the insurer's duty to defend; the second, the unknown effect of the provision that the insurer must defend even a groundless, false or fraudulent claim; the third, the uncertain extent of the indemnification coverage. Since we must resolve uncertainties in favor of the insured and interpret the policy provisions according to the layman's reasonable expectations,[13] and since the effect of the exclusionary clause is neither conspicuous, plain, nor clear, we hold that in the present case the policy provides for an obligation to defend and that such obligation is independent of the indemnification coverage.

The insurer counters with the contention that this position would compel an insurer "issuing a policy covering liability of the insured for maintenance, use or operation of an automobile . . . to defend the insured in an action for damages for negligently maintaining a stairway and thereby allegedly causing injury to another—because the insured claims that the suit for damages was false or groundless." The "groundless, false, or fraudulent" clause, however, does not extend the obligation to defend without limits; it includes only defense to those actions of the nature and kind covered by the policy. Here the policy insures against "damages

---

11. Thus Prosser points out: "The defendant who acts in the belief or consciousness that he is causing an appreciable risk of harm to another may be negligent and if the risk is great his conduct may be characterized as reckless or wanton, but it is not classed as an intentional wrong. In such cases the distinction between intent and negligence obviously is a matter of degree." (Prosser, Law of Torts (3d ed. 1965) p. 32.)

13. Courts have recognized the application of the reasonable expectation doctrine to a policy of insurance, which sought to distinguish between intentional and accidental conduct. In *Meyer* v. *Pacific Employers Ins. Co.,* 233 Cal.App.2d 321, [43 Cal. Rptr. 542 (1965)], a policy covered "injury to or destruction of property . . . unless caused by accident." (P. 324.) In a third party suit the

plaintiff claimed that the insured's well drilling operations resulted in property damage; the trial court there found that the insured " 'intentionally caused an indirect trespass. . . .' " (P. 323.) Reasoning that the consequent damages were not "intentional" and were "not expected," the appellate court held the damages "accidental in character" (p. 327) and covered by the policy. The court said, "A policy of insurance should not be so interpreted as to remove from the coverage of the policy a risk against which the circumstances under which and the purposes for which the policy was written indicate the insured *intended* to protect himself, unless such an interpretation is compelled by the express and unambiguous language of the policy." (Pp. 327–328; italics added.)

because of bodily injury." As we have pointed out, in view of the language of the policy, the insured would reasonably expect protection in an action involving alleged bodily injury. On the other hand the insured could not reasonably expect protection under an automobile insurance policy for injury which occurs from defect in a stairway. Similarly an insured would not expect a defense for an injury involving an automobile under a general comprehensive policy which excluded automobile coverage. We look to the nature and kind of risk covered by the policy as a limitation upon the duty to defend; we cannot absolve the carrier from the duty to defend an insured for loss of the nature and kind against which it insured.[14]

Our holding that the insurer bore the obligation to defend because the policy led plaintiff reasonably to expect such defense, and because the insurer's exclusionary clause did not exonerate it, cuts across defendant's answering contention that the duty arises only if the pleadings disclose a cause of action for which the insurer must indemnify the insured. Defendant would equate the duty to defend with the complaint that pleaded a liability for which the insurer was bound to indemnify the insured. Yet even if we accept defendant's premises, and define the duty to defend by measuring the allegations in the Jones case against the carrier's liability to indemnify, defendant's position still fails. We proceed to discuss this alternative ground of liability of the insurer, accepting for such purpose the insurer's argument that we must test the third party suit against the indemnification coverage of the policy. We point out that the carrier must defend a suit which *potentially* seeks damages within the coverage of the policy; the Jones action was such a suit.

Defendant cannot construct a formal fortress of the third party's pleadings and retreat behind its walls. The pleadings are malleable, change-able and amendable. Although an earlier decision reads: "In determining whether or not the appellant was bound to defend ... the language of its contract must first be looked to, and next, the allegations of the complaints ..." (*Lamb* v. *Belt Casualty Co.,* [40 P.2d 311, 313 (Cal.App. 1935)], courts do not examine only the pleaded word but the potential liability created by the suit. Since the instant action presented the potentiality of a judgment

---

14. "As to the insured's expectations, it is safe to assume that if the ordinary insurance consumer had thought about them, his expectations would be that the insurer would defend him whenever there was a threat of liability to him and the threat was based on facts within the policy. The insured probably would be surprised at the suggestion that defense coverage might turn on the pleading rules of the court that a third party chose or on how the third party's attorney decided to write the complaint. In some cases the insured might think in terms of his own conduct. The bar owner, for example, might well think that he is insulated from any legal expense arising from injuries to patrons so long as he personally does not intentionally injure someone or tell an employee to do so.

To him the possibility of an ambitious claimant who would begin a lawsuit with a charge of an intentional injury for the sake of a favorable bargaining position and later be willing to abandon that charge for one of simple negligence might not occur; or if the possibility did occur the insured might not pause to consider whether it would be fatal to part of his insurance coverage. In short, the limits of the phrase 'suits alleging such injury,' prepared by lawyers, defended by lawyers and authoritatively interpreted by lawyers, are probably not appreciated by the lay insured. And even the more sophisticated insured has no choice in the matter, since the provision is standard." (Comment, *supra*, 114 U.Pa.L.Rev. 734, 748 [fn. omitted].)

based upon nonintentional conduct, and since liability for such conduct would fall within the indemnification coverage, the duty to defend became manifest at the outset.

To restrict the defense obligation of the insurer to the precise language of the pleading would not only ignore the thrust of the cases but would create an anomaly for the insured. Obviously, ... the complainant in the third party action drafts his complaint in the broadest terms; he may very well stretch the action which lies in only nonintentional conduct to the dramatic complaint that alleges intentional misconduct. In light of the likely overstatement of the complaint and of the plasticity of modern pleading, we should hardly designate the third party as the arbiter of the policy's coverage.

Since modern procedural rules focus on the facts of a case rather than the theory of recovery in the complaint, the duty to defend should be fixed by the facts which the insurer learns from the complaint, the insured, or other sources. An insurer, therefore, bears a duty to defend its insured whenever it ascertains facts which give rise to the potential of liability under the policy. In the instant case the complaint itself, as well as the facts known to the insurer, sufficiently apprised the insurer of these possibilities; hence we need not set out when and upon what other occasions the duty of the insurer to ascertain such possibilities otherwise arises.

Jones' complaint clearly presented the possibility that he might obtain damages that were covered by the indemnity provisions of the policy. Even conduct that is traditionally classified as "intentional" or "willful" has been held to fall within indemnification coverage. Moreover, despite Jones' pleading of intentional and willful conduct, he could have amended his complaint to allege merely negligent conduct. Further, plaintiff might have been able to show that in physically defending himself, even if he exceeded the reasonable bounds of self-defense, he did not commit wilful and intended injury, but engaged only in nonintentional tortious conduct. Thus, even accepting the insurer's premise that it had no obligation to defend actions seeking damages not within the indemnification coverage, we find, upon proper measurement of the third party action against the insurer's liability to indemnify, it should have defended because the loss could have fallen within that liability.

. . .

[The following four paragraphs describe, in summary fashion, other contentions made by the insurer, and the court's responses to them.

1. To read the contract so as to require the insurer to defend a charge of intentional wrongdoing would violate public policy.

Answer (in part): A contract to defend against a mere accusation of a wilful tort does not encourage such wilful conduct.

2. The duty to defend "dissolves" upon a recovery by the injured party by reason of a finding of the assured's wilful conduct.

Answer: "If [the insured] is to be required to finance his own defense and then, only if successful, hold the insurer to its promise by means of a second suit for reimbursement, we defeat the basic reason for the purchase of the insurance.... 'The courts will not sanction a construction of the insurer's language that will defeat the very purpose or object of the insurance.'...'"

3.   A ruling against the insurer would embroil it in a conflict of interests.

Answer: "Since the court in the [injured party's] suit does not adjudicate the issue of coverage, the insurer's argument collapses. The only question there litigated is the insured's *liability*. The alleged victim does not concern himself with the theory of liability; he desires only the largest possible judgment. Similarly, the insured and insurer seek only to avoid, or at least to minimize, the judgment.... Thus the question of whether or not the insured engaged in intentional conduct does not normally formulate an "issue which is resolved in that litigation. In any event, if the insurer adequately reserves its right to assert the noncoverage defense later, it will not be bound by the judgment."

4.   The court should require only the reimbursement of the insured's expenses in defending the third party action, and not the payment of the judgment.

Answer: Prior authority, including this statement: "Sustaining such a theory ... would tend ... to encourage insurance companies to similar disavowals of responsibility with everything to gain and nothing to lose." Arenson v. National Auto. & Cas. Ins. Co., 310 P.2d 961, 968 (Cal. 1957).]

. . .

In summary, the individual consumer in the highly organized and integrated society of today must necessarily rely upon institutions devoted to the public service to perform the basic functions which they undertake. At the same time the consumer does not occupy a sufficiently strong economic position to bargain with such institutions as to specific clauses of their contracts of performance, and, in any event, piecemeal negotiation would sacrifice the advantage of uniformity. Hence the courts in the field of insurance contracts have tended to require that the insurer render the basic insurance protection which it has held out to the insured. This obligation becomes especially manifest in the case in which the insurer has attempted to limit the principal coverage by an unclear exclusionary clause. We test the alleged limitation in the light of the insured's reasonable expectation of coverage; that test compels the indicated outcome of the present litigation.

The judgment is reversed and the trial court instructed to take evidence solely on the issue of damages alleged in plaintiff's complaint including the amount of the judgment in the Jones suit, and the costs, expenses and attorney's fees incurred in defending such suit.

NOTE

The DRE and Equity. Judicial opinions recognize the equitable roots of the doctrine of reasonable expectations. For instance, one court stated:

> We ascertain justice by natural reason or ethical insight, independent of the formulated body of law. We call it "equity," and we say that "Equity delights to do justice and that not by halves," or "Equity looks upon that as done which ought to have been done," or "Equity suffers not a right without a remedy." I simply call all of these maxims a search for "fair play" in the social and business relationships of our society.

> The doctrine of "reasonable expectations" is an equitable approach to a solution of this controversy. By this doctrine we mean that the insured is the "Rock of Gibraltar;" that the insurance policy will yield the maximum of protection to, and the reasonable expectation of, the insured; that the insurer will not be permitted to take an unconscionable advantage. Thus far, we have related the doctrine to ambiguities in the language of the policy.... This doctrine has been extended beyond the ambiguity problem.

> The basis for this extended version of the doctrine is to fulfill the insured's objectively reasonable expectation even though the policy excludes coverage for the particular loss sustained.... Public policy and "fair play" dictate that we read into the policy in bold face type:

> **The objectively reasonable expectations that you have regarding the terms of this policy will be honored.**

Thompson v. Occidental Life Ins. Co., 567 P.2d 62, 68–70 (N.M.App. 1977). (wanting a statement of the evidence, this opinion is not otherwise instructive)

Another court observed: "[W]e note that the reasonable expectations doctrine has been urged because of the supposed inadequacy of the existing equitable doctrines available to courts confronted with overreaching insurers.... It is not clear why estoppel, waiver, unconscionability, breach of the implied duty of good faith and fair dealing, and the rule that ambiguous language is to be resolved against the drafter, for example, are insufficient to protect against overreaching insurers when applied on a case-by-case basis. We also recognize that the reasonable expectations doctrine was developed in part because established equitable doctrines were found to be inadequate theoretically." Allen v. Prudential Property & Casualty Ins. Co., 839 P.2d 798, 805–06 (Utah 1992).

Sources of Expectations at Variance with Policy Terms

A. *Ambiguity*

If a policy term has two or more plausible senses, one leading to coverage of the claim in question, the insured may have a reasonable expectation that the claim is covered.[1]

---

1. See Max True Plastering Co. v. United States Fidelity & Guaranty Co., 912 P.2d 861 (Okla. 1996) [presented at p. 155 below.]

B. *Complexity*

If a limitation on coverage is expressed in a way difficult to discern, the insured may have a reasonable expectation that it is inapplicable to the claim in question.[2]

C. *Misstatements by or on behalf of insurers*

If a representative of the insurer has made an authorized statement of the coverage provided, describing it so as to comprehend the claim in question, and the insured has relied justifiably on that statement, the insured has a justifiable expectation that the claim is covered.[3]

D. *Prevalence of opposing terms*

If the policy in question is, in the relevant market, the only one, or nearly the only one, to disclaim coverage of the claim in question, the insured may be warranted in disregarding that disclaimer.[4]

E. *Course of dealing and usage of trade*

If it is either (i) customary in the relevant line of insurance for claims to be honored if they are similar to the one in question, or (ii) common, in the experience of the insurer and the insured, for a like claim to be honored, the insured may have a reasonable expectation that the claim in question will be honored.[5]

F. *Skimpiness of the risk transferred*

If the extent of coverage, as propounded by the insurer, is so meager, in relation to the charge for it, as to occasion wonderment, the insured has a reasonable expectation that the coverage is broader than that.[6]

G. *Unconscionable conduct by insurer*

If the insurer knew when issuing the policy, that the coverage as written is not of appreciable benefit to the insured, the insured may reasonably expect that it would be.

H. *Public policy*

In instances in which the insurance contract is inconsistent with public expectations and commercially accepted standards, judicial regulation of insurance contracts is essential in order to prevent overreaching and injustice.[7]

Questions: (i) Is any one of the foregoing circumstances indispensable? (ii) If not, which is the most compelling? (iii) Which of the ones listed, standing alone, is the weakest support for a reasonable expectation? (iv)

2. See Gerhardt v. Continental Insurance Companies, 225 A.2d 328 (N.J. 1966).

3. See Dilworth v. Metropolitan Life Ins. Co., 418 F.3d 345 (3d Cir. 2005).

4. See Rodman v. State Farm Mutual Automobile Ins. Co., 208 N.W.2d 903 (Iowa 1973) ("An insurance agent testified for plaintiff that to the best of his knowledge defendant is the only automobile insurer in Iowa whose policies exclude the insured from bodily injury liability recovery." Id. at 905.)

5. See Glassalum International Corp. v. Albany Ins. Co., 2005 WL 1214333 (S.D.N.Y. 2005) ("industry custom and practice, and course of dealing"); International Ins. Co. v. RSR Corp., 426 F.3d 281 (5th Cir. 2005) (course of dealing).

6. See Riffe v. Home Finders Assocs., 517 S.E.2d 313, 318 (W.Va. 1999).

7. See Sparks v. St. Paul Ins. Co., 495 A.2d 406 (N.J. 1985).

Would some other doctrine serve? That is, given one or more of the circumstances listed, would it be possible to honor the insured's expectations without resort to the doctrine of reasonable expectations?

NOTES

(1) *Objective* vs. *Subjective Expectations?* Should the test of reasonableness in an insured's expectations be *objective*: what a hypothetical reasonable person would expect? In Sparks v. St. Paul Ins. Co., n.7 above, the court said that a policy will be enforced "only to the extent that the policy language conforms to public expectations and commercially reasonable standards." According to another case the DRE applies if a lay person would misunderstand the policy. Vos v. Farm Bureau Life Ins. Co., 667 N.W.2d 36 (Iowa 2003).

Possibly the test of reasonableness should be *subjective*: what the actual person buying a policy believed that he or she was purchasing. Should the expectations of an attorney, or of an insurance agent or broker, when purchasing professional liability insurance, be subject to a more stringent test than those of mine-run purchasers?

(2) *Whose Expectations Count?* In Wilkie v. Auto–Owners Ins. Co., 664 N.W.2d 776 (Mich. 2003), an automobile policy issued to a mother provided liability coverage for her son Stephen, while driving her car (with her permission). Stephen's negligent driving of his mother's car caused a two-car collision in which Janna, the other driver, was injured, and Paul, a passenger in Janna's, car was killed.

Suppose that a question arose about the expectations generated by the mother's policy. Are the mother's expectations the ones that count, in that she had bought the insurance? Do Stephen's count? Janna's? Surely Paul's don't count, do they? A possible answer is "none of the above", but the expectations of a hypothetical person, as suggested in the foregoing Note. If so, however, the main question recurs in this form: In whose position does that person stand? Materials below throw some light on the questions above.

It may be that an answer depends on the source of the expectation in question. For example, an expectation on Stephen's part might have no weight if based on the amount of premium paid by his mother, but might be critical if based on an overstatement of the coverage made to him by the insurer's agent. *Question*: Supposing a misstatement to Stephen about the coverage, what doctrine other than the DRE might vindicate his expectations?

Max True Plastering Co. v. U.S. Fid. & Guar. Co.

Supreme Court of Oklahoma, 1996.
1996 OK 28, 912 P.2d 861.

The federal District Court for the Northern District of Oklahoma certified questions to this court.

■ Kauger, Vice Chief Judge.

Two issues are presented by the questions certified: 1) whether the doctrine of reasonable expectations applies to the construction of insurance contracts in Oklahoma; and 2) what circumstances give rise to the doctrine's operation. . . .

FACTS

Jeff R. Johnson (Johnson/agent), sold a fidelity bond to the plaintiff, Max True Plastering Company (True/insured), insuring True for some losses arising from employee dishonesty. The bond was purchased from the defendant, United States Fidelity and Guaranty Company (USF&G/insurer). In the summer of 1991, True discovered that employees in his Dallas office had formed a corporation, LCR, Inc. (LCR), and that they were diverting True business to it. True filed suit against LCR and the employees in October of 1991. The following June, True wrote the agent notifying him of losses from employee dishonesty; and he claimed coverage under the USF&G policy. USF&G denied coverage asserting that True had not complied with the policy's notice and proof of loss requirements and that losses of intellectual property, such as the diversion of job opportunities and lost profits, were not covered by the policy.

[The editors have recast the statement of facts slightly, omitting references to dates of no apparent significance and to a related claim, USF&G vs. Johnson. No published record indicates much more about the issues between True and USF&G. Presumably the bond called for timely notification to USF & G of any loss, and USF&G considered excessive the period summer-to-summer. As for coverage, we are given this definition in the bond: Covered Property: "Money", "securities", and "property other than money and securities . . ."]

True filed suit against USF&G to recover under the policy. True contended that coverage existed either under the express terms of the policy or that he was insured because of his reasonable expectations that the losses were covered. USF&G filed a motion for summary judgment. True filed an objection to USF&G's motion claiming coverage either under the plain reading of the policy or pursuant to his reasonable expectations. Finding no Oklahoma precedent to resolve the questions of law, the trial court certified two questions to this Court. . . .

I. UNDER OKLAHOMA LAW, THE REASONABLE EXPECTATIONS DOCTRINE MAY BE APPLICABLE TO CONSTRUE INSURANCE CONTRACTS.

True argues that although this Court has not expressly adopted the reasonable expectations doctrine, many of the principles applied in Oklahoma to the construction of insurance contracts conform to the spirit of the doctrine. It urges us to join the majority of jurisdictions which have considered the doctrine by recognizing it as part of Oklahoma law. USF&G and Johnson insist that insureds are adequately protected by existing principles applied to the construction of insurance contracts and they contend that those courts which have rejected the doctrine offer the better reasoned opinions. . . .

Under the doctrine, if the insurer or its agent creates a reasonable expectation of coverage in the insured which is not supported by policy language, the expectation will prevail over the language of the policy. The doctrine does not negate the importance of policy language. Rather, it is justified by the underlying principle that generally the language of the policy will provide the best indication of the parties' reasonable expectations. The standard under the doctrine is a "reasonable expectation"; and courts must examine the policy language objectively to determine whether an insured could reasonably have expected coverage. Courts adopting the reasonable expectations doctrine have found its rationale for interpretation of the usual insurance contract to be sensible. They also recognize that insurance law is the basis of the doctrine. These courts acknowledge that different rules of construction have traditionally been applied to insurance contracts because of their adhesive nature. Tribunals embracing the doctrine recognize that it is consistent with numerous other interpretive rules pertaining to adhesion contracts. Many of these rules are a part of Oklahoma law. For instance: 1) ambiguities are construed most strongly against the insurer; 2) in cases of doubt, words of inclusion are liberally applied in favor of the insured and words of exclusion are strictly construed against the insurer; 3) an interpretation which makes a contract fair and reasonable is selected over that which yields a harsh or unreasonable result; 4) insurance contracts are construed to give effect to the parties' intentions; 5) the scope of an agreement is not determined in a vacuum, but instead with reference to extrinsic circumstances; and 6) words are given effect according to their ordinary or popular meaning. Nevertheless, these rules of construction are often inadequate because they may fail to recognize the realities of the insurance business and the methods used in modern insurance practice.

Of the thirty-six jurisdictions which have addressed the reasonable expectations doctrine, our research reveals only four courts which have rejected the rule. Although the Utah court recognized its duty to invalidate insurance provisions contrary to public policy, it refused to adopt the [DRE] doctrine on the basis that its operation is not well-defined, and its deference to the occupation of the insurance field by the legislative and the executive branches. [Allen v. Prudential Property & Casualty Ins. Co., 839 P.2d 798, 803–04 (Utah 1992).] The three other courts rejected the doctrine in favor of traditional construction guidelines relating to insurance contracts. [Here the court cited decisions in Idaho, Illinois, and Ohio.]

Although the reasonable expectations doctrine has not been adopted per se in Oklahoma, several cases indicate that the reasonable expectations of an insured will be considered in the construction of insurance contracts. In Homestead Fire Ins. Co. v. De Witt, 245 P.2d 92, 94 (Okla. 1952), this Court quoted from Bird v. St. Paul Fire & Marine Ins. Co., 120 N.E. 86–87, 13 A.L.R. 875 (N.Y. 1918) referring to the construction of an insurance policy: "Our guide is the *reasonable expectation* and purpose of the ordinary business man making an ordinary business contract. It is his intention, expressed or fairly to be inferred, that counts." (Emphasis supplied.) ...

... Generally, absent an ambiguity, insurance contracts are subject to the same rules of construction as other contracts. However, because of their adhesive nature, these contracts are liberally construed to give reasonable effect to all their provisions. Our case law and the interpretive rules applied to insurance contracts demonstrate that Oklahoma law is consistent with the spirit and the policy of the reasonable expectations doctrine. The same case law coincides with the reasoning of the majority of jurisdictions adopting the doctrine....

II.   THE REASONABLE EXPECTATIONS DOCTRINE MAY APPLY TO THE CONSTRUCTION OF AMBIGUOUS INSURANCE CONTRACTS OR TO CONTRACTS CONTAINING EXCLUSIONS MASKED BY TECHNICAL OR OBSCURE LANGUAGE OR HIDDEN POLICY PROVISIONS.

True urges us to adopt a version of the reasonable expectations doctrine which does not require a finding of ambiguity in policy language before the doctrine is applied. Although they urge us not to adopt the doctrine, USF&G and Johnson argue that if the doctrine is to apply in Oklahoma, it should be limited to situations in which the policy contains an ambiguity or to contracts containing unexpected exclusions arising from technical or obscure language or which are hidden in policy provisions. We agree with this limitation.

If the doctrine is not put in the proper perspective, insureds could develop a "reasonable expectation" that every loss will be covered by their policy and courts would find themselves engaging in wholesale rewriting of insurance policies. Therefore, the jurisdictions which have adopted the doctrine apply it to cases where an ambiguity is found in the policy language or where the exclusions are obscure or technical or are hidden in complex policy language. In these cases, the doctrine is utilized to resolve ambiguities in insurance policies and considers the language of the policies in a manner which conforms the policies with the parties' "reasonable expectations."

A policy term is ambiguous under the reasonable expectations doctrine if it is reasonably susceptible to more than one meaning. When defining a term found in an insurance contract, the language is given the meaning understood by a person of ordinary intelligence. The doctrine does not mandate either a pro-insurer or pro-insured result because only *reasonable* expectations of coverage are warranted....

The reasonable expectations doctrine comports with our case law and with the rules of construction applied to insurance contracts. Oklahoma law mandates that we join the majority of jurisdictions which have considered application of the doctrine and apply it to cases in which policy language is ambiguous and to situations where, although clear, the policy contains exclusions masked by technical or obscure language or hidden exclusions.

CONCLUSION

The reasonable expectations doctrine recognizes the true origin of standardized contract provisions, frees the courts from having to write a contract for the parties, and removes the temptation to create ambiguity or invent intent to reach a result. The underlying principle of the reasonable expectations doctrine—that reasonable expectations of insurance coverage should be honored—has been recognized by the majority of jurisdictions which have considered the issue and by a steady progression of Oklahoma law beginning in 1952.... By adopting the reasonable expectations doctrine, we recognize that it is important that ambiguous clauses or carefully drafted exclusions should not be permitted to serve as traps for policy holders. Nevertheless, it is equally imperative that the provisions of insurance policies which are clearly and definitely set forth in appropriate language, and upon which the calculations of the company are based, should be maintained unimpaired by loose and ill-considered judicial interpretation....

QUESTIONS ANSWERED

We find that under Oklahoma law, the reasonable expectations doctrine may be applied in the construction of insurance contracts and that the doctrine may apply to ambiguous contract language or to exclusions which are masked by technical or obscure language or which are hidden in a policy's provisions.

NOTES

(1) *Ambiguity and Expectations.* Ambiguity has been referred to as a source of expectations (p. 153 above). Is an expectation founded on an ambiguity necessarily reasonable?

(2) *Gradations of the DRE.* The doctrine of reasonable expectations has different gradations of form for different jurisdictions. One commentator would withhold the name "DRE" from those decisions. For clarity's sake, he wrote, the name should be reserved for versions of the doctrine which "openly disregard policy language instead of purporting to interpret it." Ware, "A Critique of the Reasonable Expectations Doctrine," 56 U.Chi.L.Rev. 1461, 1469 (1989). *Question*: Does this comment convey a strong grade of the DRE?

Another commentator observes two possible gradations: DRE as a broad, substantive doctrine "granting substantive rights" and DRE as a weaker rule of construction that does "not embrace its broader, substantive application". See Henderson, The Doctrine of Reasonable Expectations ..., 51 Ohio St.L.J. 823, 832 (1990). *Question*: Does this observation, based on case opinions, suggest both a *strong grade* of DRE and a *limited grade* of the doctrine?

Does the opinion in *Max True Plastering* express the strong grade of the doctrine? A limited grade? Is the judicial ambiguity version of the DRE identical to the judicial practice of construction of ambiguities against the insurer except that the ambiguity version of the DRE adds a new step in following the insured's reasonable expectations?

(3) *DRE's Future.* As of this writing (early 2007), one may say that (i) a majority of jurisdictions adopt some form of the DRE (a strong form or a limited form or an inconsistent[8] form), and (ii) a minority of jurisdictions reject the DRE

---

8. Pennsylvania has taken an inconsistent judicial approach to the doctrine of reasonableness (DRE). *Compare* Standard Venetian Blind Co. v. American Empire Ins. Co., 503 Pa. 300, 469 A.2d 563 (1983) (rejects the DRE) *with* Tonkovic v. State Farm Mut. Automobile Ins. Co., 513 Pa. 445, 521 A.2d 920 (1987) (accepts the DRE). Regarding the inconsistent approaches to the DRE by Pennsylvania courts, *see* Thomas J. Rueter and Joshua H. Roberts, "Pennsylvania's Reasonable Expectations Doctrine: The Third Cir-

(no form DRE). A few jurisdictions have no opinion accepting or rejecting the DRE. The Supreme Court of Ohio, for instance, stated that the claimants

> ask this court to apply the reasonable-expectations doctrine. This doctrine is explained in Restatement of Law 2d, Contracts (1981), Section 211(3), which provides: "Where the other party has reason to believe that the party manifesting such assent would not do so if he knew that the writing contained a particular term, the term is not part of the agreement." While the [claimants] raise compelling arguments, there is not yet a majority on this court willing to accept the reasonable-expectations doctrine.

Wallace v. Balint, 761 N.E.2d 598, 606 (Ohio 2002). South Dakota has not accepted the doctrine of reasonable expectations. See American Family Mut. Ins. Group v. Kostaneski, 688 N.W.2d 410, 414 (S.D. 2004)

The future of the doctrine of reasonable expectations appears to be full of twists and turns.[9] Acceptance of the doctrine of reasonable expectations has, perhaps, lost momentum in the 21st Century. Professor Peter Swisher made a forecast in 2000, saying:

> "The vast majority of American courts today likewise remain unwilling or unable to reject ... contractually based interpretive rules and remedies in order to ascertain the reasonable expectations of the parties in insurance contract disputes. Instead of adopting Professor Keeton's 'strong' 'rights at variance' doctrine of reasonable expectations, the vast majority of contemporary American courts instead have rediscovered—and have more fully utilized—a growing number of contractually based reasonable expectations rights and remedies, including: (1) the doctrine of ambiguities, (2) contract unconscionability and public policy issues, (3) equitable remedies such as waiver, equitable estoppel, promissory estoppel, election, and contract reformation, and (4) a number of additional interpretive rules applied to standardized insurance contracts as contracts of adhesion.

> "A realistic consensus approach to the insurance law doctrine of reasonable expectations therefore provides a number of well-established contractual parameters for allowing judicial discretion, when justice and equity requires it, to recognize and honor the reasonable expectations of the parties to coverage in insurance contract disputes that are supplemental to—rather than at variance with—the terms of the parties' insurance contract. A contractually based doctrine of reasonable expectations also serves as an interpretive shield as well

cuit's Perspective," 45 Vill. L. Rev. 581 (2000), stating "We are unable to draw any categorical distinction between the types of cases in which Pennsylvania courts will allow the reasonable expectations of the insured to defeat the unambiguous language of an insurance policy and those in which the courts will follow the general rule of adhering to the precise terms of the policy."

9. At the 1998 Annual Meeting of the Association of American Law Schools, for instance, the AALS Insurance Law Section presented a program entitled "The Insurance Law Doctrine of Reasonable Expectations after Three Decades." The presentations resulted in ten notable articles discussing the status and stature of the DRE as of 1998, which appear as a law review symposium in volume 5 of the Connecticut Insurance Law Journal (1998). After summarizing the ten DRE articles, Professor Swisher provided a Selected Bibliography of forty-two articles and treatises analyzing the insurance law doctrine of reasonable expectations. See Peter Nash Swisher, "Symposium Introduction," 5 Conn. Ins. L.J. 1, 17 (1998). For a discussion of this scholarship and its relation to the evolution of a reasonable expectations doctrine (DRE), see Robert H. Jerry, II, "Insurance, Contract, and the Doctrine of Reasonable Expectations," 5 Conn. Ins. L.J. 22, 42–50 (1998).

as a sword to the insured policyholder since, as Professor Eric Mills Holmes aptly observes:

> Finally, any rule of law can be used offensively as well as defensively. Although [few] opinions have addressed this issue, an insurance carrier (in an appropriate set of objective circumstances) could assert the [insurance law doctrine of reasonable expectations] defensively by alleging that no reasonable person would objectively expect insurance coverage. 2 Holmes' Appleman on Insurance 2d, § 8.6 at 421...."

A Realistic Consensus Approach to the Insurance Law Doctrine of Reasonable Expectations, 35 Tort & Ins. L.J. 729, 779 (2000). For an opinion eschewing the DRE in favor of the four "expectations rights and remedies" named by Professor Swisher, and referring compendiously to the secondary literature, see Allen v. Prudential Property & Casualty Ins. Co., 839 P.2d 798 (Utah 1992).

Even Professor (now Judge) Keeton, who coined the term doctrine of reasonable expectation, concedes that it is "[t]oo general to serve as a guide from which particularized decisions can be derived through an exercise of logic and too broad to be universally true." Keeton, "Insurance Law Rights at Variance with Policy Provisions," 83 Harv.L.Rev. 961, 967 (1970).

C. Misconduct By Persons Insured

1. Liability Insurance for Malefactors

Misconduct—including criminal behavior—commonly gives rise to claims for damages against the malefactor. And, if the malefactor is provided with insurance against liabilities, these claims often generate disputes about the accountability of the insurer. Liability insurers deploy provisions in their policies with a view to avoiding the duty to provide a defense for entities charged with misconduct, and the duty to pay if liability is established. The materials that follow concern two matters. Provisions of that kind are one. The other is a principle more or less firmly established by statutes and judicial decisions: Insurance against civil liability for serious and knowing misconduct ought not to be tolerated.

As will be seen, insurers and courts are especially averse to granting indemnification to criminals against the consequences of their crimes. But of course the depravity of criminals occurs in differing degrees. Near one extreme is the sexual molestation of a child by an adult. (As to that see Note 2, p. 174 below.) Near the other extreme is speeding on a public road. Speedsters who carry liability insurance and incur liability for deaths, injuries, and collision damage are routinely indemnified. What their victims complain of is not criminal conduct, but negligence, even though that may be imputed to the criminal. Even an extreme of negligence does not suspend coverage. That point was nicely made in a brief filed in New York, New Haven & Hartford R. Co. v. Gray, 240 F.2d 460 (2d Cir. 1957), and quoted there with approval. "A serious want of care did not render the loss non-fortuitous nor bar a recovery from the underwriters.... The law of insurance is not like the law of torts to be used as an instrument of coercion upon assureds to improve operating practices. Assureds do not go into the insurance market to buy themselves an overseer." Id. at 465, n.7 (concerning property coverage, not a liability coverage).

In many cases cited below misconduct was alleged but not established. Given a suit against the insured, for example, the insurance company may bring an action for a declaratory judgment that its coverage does not extend to the alleged liability. Cases of that sort are described below as if the alleged misconduct had been established as fact—an assumption made by the courts in rulings on coverage issues.

Road rage. Gross misconduct by motorists inflicts some quantity of bodily injuries, sometimes fatal, and of property damage. Often it is claimed that one of these harms, or an ensuing liability, is covered by a policy of automobile insurance, and the claimant meets resistance of a kind illustrated in this section. The issues these cases present are dealt with in Chapter 9—Automobile Insurance—rather than in this section, because they are heavily influenced by the network of statutes that encourage or compel the purchase of insurance against road injuries and liabilities for them.

EXERCISES

Consider the tragic facts of two cases about liability coverages, each concerning the misconduct of a juvenile in using a weapon:

Case A. In a Michigan case an action for damages was brought against Robert, a 16–year-old, and his grandparents, with whom he lived. After some horseplay with a young friend, in which the friend refused to hand over some crackers, Robert had pulled a .410 shotgun from under his grandfather's bed. It was usually kept there, unloaded. Robert's father had given him the gun some time earlier. Robert pointed the gun at his friend's face, about a foot away. He pretended to pull the trigger once or twice, and then did so. Apparently Robert had forgotten that he had earlier put the gun away hastily, after some target practice. He thought it was unloaded. It was not; the friend was killed. Later, Robert pleaded *nolo contendere* to a charge of manslaughter. Robert and his grandparents were insured against certain liabilities under a homeowner's policy. The insurer brought an action for a determination that the civil liability asserted was not covered.

Case B. In a New Jersey case an action was brought against Tim, a 14–year-old, and his parents. Late on a sleety, moonless night, Tim and two teen-aged friends had climbed onto a platform in a tree 25 yards from a road. Two of the boys took turns firing BBs at passing cars. The third, a bit younger than the other two, remembered later saying to them, "I don't think we should be doing this." Tim appears to have been the better marksman. Judging by sounds, he and his friends thought he had hit several cars, whereas the 15–year-old hit none. One car struck was a "soft-cover" Jeep. The pellet penetrated the windshield and blinded the driver in one eye.

According to a later account by Tim, he had shot at cars intentionally, knowing that to be wrong, but never thought of a pellet's going inside a car. He was just "having fun with friends." Consequences for him included a fine, probation, and requirements that he take a gun-safety course and engage in community service. Another consequence was a damage action against Tim and his parents, brought by the motorist and her husband. The defendants were insured against certain liabilities under a home-owner's policy. The insurer brought an action against the claimants and the defendants for a determination that the civil liability asserted was not covered.

NOTES

(1) *Results.* In both Case **A** and Case **B** the insurance litigation was somewhat inconclusive. In Case **A**, the Michigan Supreme Court was so divided on a critical issue (3–3, one justice concurring in the result) that the ruling has no precedential value. In Case **B**, one justice of the New Jersey Supreme Court did not participate. The others being equally divided, the decision below was affirmed.

(2) *Statutes.* Representative statutes on the subject of insurance and willful or intentional misconduct in general are these:

Cal.Ins.Code § 533. *Wilful act of insured*

An insurer is not liable for a loss caused by the wilful act of the insured; but he is not exonerated by the negligence of the insured, or of the insured's agents or others.

Mass. Gen. L. ch. 175, § 47, Sixth (b).

[N]o company may insure any person against legal liability for causing injury, other than bodily injury, by his deliberate or intentional crime or wrongdoing, nor insure his employer or principal if such acts are committed under the direction of his employer or principal. . . .

What impact might these statutes have on Case A? On Case B?

(3) *Exclusions.* Policy language appearing in Cases **A** and **B**, and in some other recent and comparable cases, is set out next. Each excerpt states an exception to the coverage otherwise provided for an insured person. You are asked to consider the facts given above with reference to these excerpts.

Misconduct Exclusions—a Selection

The Criminal Acts Exclusion[1]

1.   "We will not cover bodily injury or property damage arising out of: a. violation of any criminal law for which any insured is convicted . . . or c.

---

1.   Among the diverse liability insurance policies in the liability insurance industry, the language of this exclusion varies, as does the name of the exclusion. For examples of the different exclusions with accompanying explanation and cases, see Eric Mills Holmes, 21 Holmes' Appleman on Insurance 2d, Chapter 134 Criminal Acts or Illegal Acts Exclusion, Willful Criminal Violation Exclusion, Law Enforcement Exclusion, and Willful Harm or Knowing Endangerment Exclusion (2002). If a liability insurer seeks to invoke a criminal acts exclusion, but the action alleged does not meet the elements of the crime, the exclusion will not apply.

violation of any criminal law for which any insured is not convicted due to mental incapacity."[2]

2. "We do not cover any bodily injury or property damage intended by, or which may reasonably be expected to result from the intentional or criminal acts or omissions of, any insured person. This exclusion applies even if:

a) such insured person lacks the mental capacity to govern his or her conduct;

b) such bodily injury or property damage is of a different kind or degree than intended or reasonably expected; or

c) such bodily injury or property damage is sustained by a different person than intended or reasonably expected.

This exclusion applies regardless of whether or not such insured person is actually charged with, or convicted of a crime."[3]

3. "We do not cover bodily injury or property damage, whether or not expected or intended by the insured, which is a consequence of an insured's willful harm or knowing endangerment. We provide no insurance for any sort of damages, expenses, liability, or loss directly or indirectly, wholly or partially, aggravated by, consisting of, or resulting from ... knowing violation of penal law or ordinance committed by, or with the consent of, an insured...."

The Intentional Injury Exclusion

4. "This insurance does not apply to ... 'Bodily injury' or 'property damage' expected or intended from the standpoint of the insured. This exclusion does not apply to 'bodily injury' or 'property damage' resulting from the use of reasonable force to protect persons or property."

The intentional injury exclusion was designed by the Insurance Services Office in 1986, and has been adopted generally for liability coverages. Opinions presented below, in Beckwith v. State Farm Fire & Cas. Co. (p. 167), illustrate the struggles of courts with the expression "expected or intended from the standpoint of the insured." Dean Holmes has marshaled

---

2. The quoted language, from American Family Mut. Ins. Group v. Kostaneski, 688 N.W.2d 410, 413 (S.D. 2004), is a criminal acts exclusion, which bars liability insurance recovery for criminal acts. If allegations in a civil complaint are limited to conduct based on which a criminal conviction was obtained, the conviction would be dispositive of the duty to defend, but where a complaint included allegations of separate bodily injury, a court found the insurer did have a duty to defend. Teachers Ins. Co. v. Schofield, 284 F. Supp. 2d 161 (D. Me. 2003). The following cases held that the criminal acts exclusion did not violate their state's public policy.

Allstate Ins. Co. v. Lewis, 918 F.Supp. 168, 171–173 (S.D. Miss. 1995). Allstate Ins. Co. v. Peasley, 80 Wash.App. 565, 910 P.2d 483, 484–485 (1996), *aff'd*, 932 P.2d 1244 (Wash. 1997) (Homeowner's policy exclusion for unintentional criminal acts, such as reckless endangerment, did not violate Washington public policy).

3. Some liability insurance policies have added a penal act exclusion, which excludes liability arising from criminal acts of "any" insured. As to that see Bagley v. Monticello Ins. Co., 720 N.E.2d 813, 815 (Mass. 1999), and All American Ins. Co. v. Burns, 971 F.2d 438, 442–443 (10th Cir. 1992).

the many cases state by state, and according to events insured: Eric Mills Holmes, 17 Holmes' Appleman on Insurance 405–653 (2001).

Apply the intentional injury exclusion to Case **A** and then to Case **B**. *Questions*: (i) What results? (ii) Regarding "expected or intended," can a mentally incapacitated insured "intend" or "expect'" injury?[4] Should an insured's criminal conviction by jury verdict or by guilty plea for harmful conduct trigger the exclusion?[5]

NOTE

Minimizing Misconduct. Exclusions of the kind illustrated above have been attacked for ambiguity, for defeating the reasonable expectations of the insured, and for violating public policy. The attacks have sometimes succeeded, but not often. For an instance of success see Tower Ins. Co. v. Judge, 840 F.Supp. 679 (D.Minn. 1993), concerning a criminal-acts exclusion. The court was influenced by Allstate Ins. Co. v. Zuk, 574 N.E.2d 1035 (N.Y. 1991), "a case which also involved the accidental killing of a friend." It said: "Although the policy language in *Zuk* specifically provided that the injury must be a reasonably expected result of a criminal act, [this] Court will imply such a requirement in the case at bar as within the reasonable expectations of the insureds." Id. at 693.

The record in Washington State is mixed. Long ago the high court considered a criminal-acts exclusion in an insurance-like contract carrying a death benefit, the holder of which had died because of his reckless driving. His driving violated numerous traffic laws, and constituted criminal misdemeanor. Yet the exclusion did not apply, the court ruled, saying that *criminal* meant, in context, "an act done with malicious intent, from evil nature, or with a wrongful disposition to harm or injure other persons or property." Van Riper v. Constitutional Gov't League, 96 P.2d 588, 591 (Wash. 1939).

More recently the court dealt with a comparable exclusion as to the liability coverage in a homeowner's policy: Allstate Ins. Co. v. Peasley, 932 P.2d 1244 (Wash. 1997).[6] Peasley argued that his policy's reference to criminal acts could reasonably be understood to signify only *intentional* crimes. He had shot a guest in his home and, as part of a plea bargain, received a suspended sentence for reckless endangerment. Both he and the guest maintained that the shooting was accidental. Peasley also argued that allowing an insurer to exclude coverage for injuries resulting from "non-intent" criminal acts of the insured violates a public policy. As to that, he relied on indications that public policy favors assured compensation for victims of road injuries. The court was divided. A majority ruled that the exclusion was applicable and enforceable. "[W]e do not perceive the same level of concern for financial compensation by negligent homeowners as exists for negligent automobile owners and users." Id. at 1250. As to the court's reading, in the *Van Riper* case above, of the exclusion there, it said that it did not disregard conduct that is, as

---

4. See Eric Mills Holmes, 18 Holmes' Appleman on Insurance 2d, Chapter 122 Effect of Insured's Mental Incapacity or Intoxication on the Intentional Injury Exclusion (2001).

5. See Eric Mills Holmes, 18 Holmes' Appleman on Insurance 2d, Chapter 124 Effect of Insured's Criminal Conviction on the Intentional Injury Exclusion (2001).

6. The exclusion in question was: "We do not cover any bodily injury which may reasonably be expected to result from the intentional or criminal acts of an insured person or which are in fact intended by an insured person."

Peasley said, *unintentional*, but rather conduct not *seriously* criminal. While "serious crime" may not encompass a traffic violation, Peasley had admitted to one. "A reckless act creating a substantial risk of death or serious injury is undeniably a serious act and a serious crime." Id. at 1248.[7]

PROBLEMS

(1) A firm has sent, by fax, unsolicited ads to prospective customers. It is a defendant in an action by some recipients, charging it with having violated a state statute proscribing that practice. The firm holds insurance against liability for wrongful advertising practices, and obligating the insurer to defend the firm when it is charged with one. But the policy excludes a liability arising from the violation of a penal statute. The statute would attach a penalty to the firm for sending the faxes if the recipients were to be charged for the sending. No one has said that they were. Is the insurer obligated to provide the firm with a defense? See Western Rim Inv. Advisors, Inc. v. Gulf Ins. Co., 269 F.Supp.2d 836 (N.D.Tex. 2003).

(2) The facts are those stated in the first problem, with an alteration and a supplement: (a) In suing the firm, the recipients alleged that it had charged them with the cost of sending the faxes; and (b) They supported their claim by reference to a federal statute, non-penal. Is the insurer obligated to provide the firm with a defense? See Teachers Ins. Co. v. Schofield, 284 F.Supp.2d 161 (D.Me. 2003) (exclusion for violation of criminal statute; conviction of manslaughter; allegations against the insured both of abuse leading to conviction and of other abuse).

"Occurrence" = "Accident"

Commonly the limitations quoted above do not come into question until a prior issue has been resolved in favor of coverage. That issue concerns the policy terms *occurrence* and *accident*. (These terms are considered also in Chapter 5 on liability insurance, at p. 249 ff.) If a claim against an insured is not one "arising from an occurrence", the liability coverage does not extend to it.

So it was in the Michigan case described above as Case **A**. The operative policy term is set out in the footnote.[8] The policy included also a definition of *occurrence*: "an accident ... resulting in bodily injury or property damage." The court had to decide, therefore, whether or not the shotgun death of Robert's friend was the result of an accident. The case came twice before the Michigan Supreme Court, first in Allstate Ins. Co. v. McCarn, 645 N.W.2d 20 (2002) (*McCarn I*). There it ruled that the friend's death resulted from an accident, and remanded for a determination whether or not the exclusion for intentional or criminal acts applied.

On the second appeal of the case the court addressed that question. *McCarn II*, 683 N.W.2d 656 (2004). The court had encountered similar problems before. It had put the question this way in one case: "whether the consequences of the insured's intentional act either were intended by the

7. "[O]ur reading of the phrase 'criminal acts' is supported by nearly every jurisdiction in our country which has examined that phrase." Id. at 1249.

8. "Subject to the terms, conditions and limitations of this policy, Allstate will pay damages which an insured person becomes legally obligated to pay because of bodily injury or property damage arising from an occurrence to which this policy applies, and is covered by this part of the policy."

insured or reasonably should have been expected because of the direct risk of harm intentionally created by the insured's actions."[9] In *McCarn II* the court put to itself the question whether or not a reasonable person, thinking the shotgun to be unloaded as Robert did, would have expected bodily harm to result when it was "fired". And the court answered No, "because, obviously, an unloaded gun will not fire a shot." Id. at 660.

In *McCarn I* the justices discussed at length the choice between objective and subjective tests of intent and expectation. The majority, favoring coverage, preferred a subjective test: It is the standpoint of the insured that counts. In contrast, the minority preferred an objective test of Robert's expectation in pulling the trigger: Was it reasonable? In this connection, a point of grammar arose. Take the phrase "by the insured" in the passage quoted in the foregoing paragraph, posing a subjective inquiry. *Question*: Does it modify "should have been expected", as well as "were intended"? The minority opinion charges the majority with misreading the passage—referred to as the "*Masters* standard—so as to avoid an objective inquiry:

> [G]rammatically speaking, the phrases "intended by the insured" and "reasonably should have expected" modify "consequences." Therefore, the *Masters* standard unqualifiedly and grammatically requires an inquiry into the reasonableness of the insured's expectations concerning the consequences of his intentional acts.

Id. at 30.

Introduction to *Beckwith v. State Farm*

Unruly behavior by children has been depicted above. What of unruly behavior by deranged adults? A deranged adult is sometimes regarded as childlike (and sometimes a child is regarded as a deranged adult). With respect to liability coverages, should unruly behavior by that adult be treated with the same indulgence shown (sometimes) to that of a child? More indulgence? The opinions in this case suggest some answers.[10]

Beckwith v. State Farm Fire & Cas. Co.

Supreme Court of Nevada, 2004.
83 P.3d 275.

■ By the Court [*en banc*], MAUPIN, J.

In this appeal, we consider whether the intentional misconduct of an intoxicated insured is covered under a homeowner's personal third-party liability policy. We conclude that, regardless of the insured's intoxicated state, the act of striking another is intentional, that such an act is not a

---

9. On both occasions the court was closely divided. The several opinions contain a large array of arguments for and against coverage (and exhibit some vitriol).

10. See also Eric Mills Holmes, 18 Holmes' Appleman on Insurance 2d, Ch. 122 Effect of Insured's Mental Incapacity or Intoxication on the Intentional Injury Exclusion (2001).

covered occurrence under the policy in question here, and that such incidents are subject to a properly drafted "intentional acts" exclusion clause. Consequently, we hold that the liability insurer in this instance is under no duty to defend or indemnify its insured in connection with an action seeking damages stemming from the insured's intentional infliction of bodily injury, even when the insured was intoxicated or believed he acted in self-defense.

FACTS

On July 7, 2000, appellant Joshua L. Beckwith ingested alcohol, LSD, and marijuana during a party at a friend's residence. While walking home, he experienced hallucinations, disrobed, and entered a trailer park near the Truckee River in downtown Reno. Shortly thereafter, appellant William Martin Reccelle confronted Beckwith because children were playing in the area. In response, Beckwith began screaming and writhing on the ground, asking Reccelle if he was God. Apparently, Beckwith also believed that he was a dog and Reccelle was his "evil master." Although Reccelle attempted to reassure Beckwith, Beckwith struck Reccelle in the face, rupturing Reccelle's eye.

Beckwith pleaded nolo contendere to criminal charges stemming from the assault. Subsequently, Reccelle filed a civil complaint against Beckwith, alleging assault and battery, and negligence. Beckwith requested that respondent State Farm Fire and Casualty Company defend and indemnify him with respect to the civil action, pursuant to his homeowner's insurance policy. State Farm initially agreed, but then filed a declaratory judgment action seeking a judicial declaration of non-coverage in connection with the incident.

State Farm ultimately moved for summary judgment on the coverage issues, arguing that the incident was not a covered "occurrence" as defined in the policy, and that the policy's intentional-acts exclusionary clause precluded coverage. Beckwith and Reccelle filed separate cross-motions for summary judgment, arguing that due to his intoxication, Beckwith could not have acted intentionally when he struck Reccelle. Beckwith also argued that, at the time he struck Reccelle, he believed he was acting in self-defense and, thus, his actions were not intentional.

The district court granted State Farm's motion for summary judgment, concluding that the insurance policy did not cover Beckwith's intentional act of striking Reccelle. Beckwith and Reccelle appeal jointly.

DISCUSSION

We review orders granting summary judgment de novo. Summary judgment is appropriate when, after a review of the record viewed in a light most favorable to the non-moving party, there remain no genuine issues of material fact, and the moving party is entitled to judgment as a matter of law.

The insurance agreement in this case obligates State Farm to defend and indemnify Beckwith in connection with actions brought against him for damages caused by an "occurrence." The policy defines the term "occurrence" as an accident resulting in bodily injury. Although the policy does not define the term "accident," a common definition of the term is "a happening that is not expected, foreseen, or intended."[4] In addition, the policy contains exclusionary language precluding coverage for bodily injury or property damage "(1) which is either expected or intended by the insured; or (2) which is the result of willful and malicious acts of the insured."

This court dealt with a similarly worded insurance policy in Mallin v. Farmers Insurance Exchange [839 P.2d 105 (1992)]. In *Mallin*, this court observed that " 'intent' or 'intention' denotes a design or desire to cause the consequences of one's acts and a belief that given consequences are substantially certain to result from the acts." Applying this definition of intent, we concluded that a homeowner's liability insurance policy did not cover the insured's actions of fatally shooting his wife and two of her friends, despite a claim that the insured did not intend his actions because he acted in a psychotic fit of rage. We also noted that the insured's "supposed inability to control his acts [was] not the same as an inability to intend his acts."[8]

We take this opportunity to extend our holding in *Mallin* and reject appellants' argument that Beckwith was unable to act intentionally as a result of his voluntary intoxication.[9] Whether Beckwith thought Reccelle was God or his evil master is of no matter because he admittedly struck Reccelle in the eye with the desire of getting away from him. This is a non-accidental intentional act even if Beckwith did not intend to harm Reccelle. Thus, we conclude that Beckwith's act of striking Reccelle is not an occurrence under the insurance policy[10] and is excluded from coverage under the policy language concerning intentional misconduct. In this, we recognize Beckwith's claims that the intentional-acts exclusion does not apply because, given his advanced state of intoxication, he did not intend to injure Reccelle and that, because he believed he acted in self-defense, his conduct was not malicious. We reject this line of argument because the exclusion properly dovetails with the reasonable construction of the policy that an occurrence requires an accidental event. Accordingly, State Farm is not obligated to defend or indemnify Beckwith with respect to any judgment obtained against him by Reccelle.

4. Webster's New World Dictionary 8 (3d ed. 1988).

8. Id. at 107.

9. See, e.g., Wessinger v. Fire Ins. Exchange, 949 S.W.2d 834, 840 (Tex.App. 1997), concluding that "voluntary intoxication cannot be used to defeat the intent requirement in an insurance policy".

10. See Hooper v. State Farm Mut. Auto. Ins. Co., 782 So. 2d 1029, 1033 (La. App. 2001), observing that summary judgment was properly granted in favor of the insurance company because an insured acts intentionally when he strikes another in the face with a closed fist, despite a claim that the act was not intentional); Royal Indem. Co. v. Love, 630 N.Y.S.2d 652, 654 (Sup.Ct. 1995), concluding that intentional assault is an intentional act, and thus, cannot constitute an accident); *Wessinger*, 949 S.W.2d at 841, holding that the act of striking another is not an occurrence because such an act is voluntary and intentional, not accidental).

CONCLUSION

Applying this court's holding in *Mallin*, we conclude that Beckwith's act of striking Reccelle was intentional; and thus, the act was not an occurrence under the insurance policy. Likewise, notwithstanding Beckwith's claim that he was too intoxicated to intend the acts and resulting injuries to Reccelle, the intentional-act exclusionary clause applies to negate coverage.

We therefore affirm the district court's order granting summary judgment in favor of State Farm.

■ AGOSTI, J., concurring.

I concur with the majority because under the circumstances presented here, the insured's intoxication was voluntary. I do not believe that one who voluntarily intoxicates or drugs oneself and then relinquishes all responsibility for one's acts, claiming them to be negligent or accidental, ought to obtain the protection from personal liability that a policy of insurance affords. I believe, however, that if one's intoxication or drugged state is imposed upon him or her, the coverage result would be far different. In that case, I would agree with the dissent that public policy considerations ought to favor coverage.

■ ROSE, J., with whom, SHEARING, C.J., agrees, dissenting.

I disagree with the majority's conclusion that an insured's intoxication should not be considered in determining whether he acted intentionally. Additionally, I do not believe that this court's holding in Mallin v. Farmers Insurance Exchange[1] requires us now to dismiss the possibility that intoxication may vitiate intent. Indeed, in *Mallin*, this court observed that "there is certainly a possibility that some kinds of circumstances could, in certain cases lead to the conclusion that a person was suffering from such a mental disorder as to be incapable of forming the intent to kill."[2] I believe that intoxication may present such a circumstance.

Several courts have held that intoxication may negate an insured's intent.[3] These courts have based their decisions on public policy considerations, namely:

> With respect to voluntary intoxication, the public policy considerations applicable to a criminal prosecution are not decisive as to liability insurance coverage. In criminal matters there is reason to deal cautiously with a plea of intoxication, and this [sic] to protect the innocent from attack by drunken men. . . .

---

1. 839 P.2d 105 (Nev. 1992).

2. Id. at 108.

3. See, e.g., Republic Ins. Co. v. Feidler, 875 P.2d 187, 192 (Ariz.App. 1993), observing that a voluntarily intoxicated insured may lack the mental capacity to form the intent required to invoke a policy exclusion for intentional acts of the insured); State Farm Fire & Cas. Co. v. Morgan, 364 S.E.2d 62, 64 (Ga.App. 1987) (same); Allstate Ins. Co. v. Carioto, 551 N.E.2d 382, 389 (Ill.App. 1990) (same); Hanover Ins. Co. v. Talhouni, 604 N.E.2d 689, 692 (Mass. 1992) (same); Safeco Ins. Co. v. McGrath, 817 P.2d 861, 864 (Wash.App. 1991) (same); Morris v. Farmers Ins. Exchange, 771 P.2d 1206, 1215 (Wyo. 1989) (same).

But other values are involved in the insurance controversy. The exclusion of intentional injury from coverage stems from a fear that an individual might be encouraged to inflict injury intentionally if he was assured against the dollar consequences. Pulling the other way is the public interest that the victim be compensated, and the victim's rights being derivative from the insured's, the victim is aided by the narrowest view of the policy exclusion consistent with the purpose of not encouraging an intentional attack. And the insured, in his own right, is also entitled to the maximum protection consistent with the public purpose the exclusion is intended to serve.[4]

I agree with the policy behind allowing an insured to argue that intoxication vitiated his intent. Based on the facts presented in this case, the question of whether Beckwith's intoxication vitiated his intent should be a factor for the trier of fact to consider when determining whether State Farm has a duty to defend and indemnify Beckwith.[5] Accordingly, I would reverse the district court's order granting summary judgment in State Farm's favor.

NOTES

(1) *The Hypnotized Killer.* Consider the quotation from *Mallin* appearing in Justice Rose's dissent at fn.2: "possibility that some kinds of circumstances could, in certain cases lead to the conclusion that a person was suffering from such a mental disorder as to be incapable of forming the intent to kill." Are there states of trance that might convert what would otherwise be a murder into an accident?

(2) *Damages as a Deterrent.* Maybe the prospect of an uninsured liability is more likely to deter an adult from dangerous misbehavior, no matter how he or she is tempted by drugs and alcohol, than it is likely to deter a thoughtless youngster. If that is so, does it explain how a shotgun death at the hands of a teenager is the result of an accident, but a bodily injury born of a grownup's hallucination is not?[6]

(3) *Imagine This.* Suppose that, by an innovative statute, State Farm were required to provide a defense for Beckwith against Reccelle's claim and, if the claim were to prevail, to pay it. Suppose further that the statute entitled State Farm, in that event, to reimbursement from Beckwith. Would that statute resolve the tension that Justice Rose described, in her *Beckwith* dissent, between the public interest in deterrence and that ("pulling the other way") of compensating the victim?

---

4. Burd v. Sussex Mutual Insurance Company, 267 A.2d 7, 15 (N.J. 1970) (citations omitted).

5. See *McGrath*, 817 P.2d at 864 (concluding that whether an insured may be so intoxicated as to be unable to form an intent to commit an act is a question for the trier of fact).

6. See Eric Mills Holmes, 18 Holmes' Appleman on Insurance 2d, Ch. 122 Effect of Insured's Mental Incapacity or Intoxication on the Intentional Injury Exclusion (2001). See also J.C. Penney Casualty Ins. Co. v. M.K., 804 P.2d 689 (Cal. 1991). The court addressed the statute set out at p. 163 above, and applied the first part of it. Experts testified that the felony was a misconceived display of affection. As to that the court said: "testimony, psychiatric or otherwise, that no harm was intended flies 'in the face of all reason, common sense, and experience.' " Id. at 700, quoting from CNA Ins. Co. v. McGinnis, 666 S.W.2d 689 (Ark. 1984) at 691. Justice Broussard, dissenting, called this a "shocking attack on the science of psychiatry." Id. at 701, 704.

Do you see any major objection to reform of that kind? (It would be more appealing, of course, for a case in which the insured assailant set out, sober, to injure the victim.) Conceivably the reform would lead insurers to provide stubborn defenses for impecunious defendants, and perfunctory defenses for wealthy ones.

(4) *The Force of Convictions*. People who have been sentenced for crimes sometimes seek recompense for losses occasioned by the conduct underlying their convictions. That was the situation in Frankenmuth Mutual Ins. Co. v. Masters, 595 N.W.2d 832 (Mich. 1999). If held liable for fire damage to the buildings of neighbors, the claimants, father and son, expected to be compensated through their coverage as shopkeepers. The fire had started in their clothing store, "by accident" they said. The insurer contended that its coverage did not apply because there was no accident. It pointed out that the claimants had been convicted of arson in setting the fire. The court applied the doctrine of issue preclusion. It agreed with the insurer that the fire was no accident, saying that for purposes of the insurance case "it is a settled question."

The claimants would have been in a better position, vis-á-vis their insurer, if they had pleaded *nolo contendere* to the criminal charge. See Tower Ins. Co. v. Judge, 840 F.Supp. 679 (D.Minn. 1993), at 692: "[A] no contest plea 'cannot be used against the defendant as an admission in any civil suit for the same act.' Bell v. C.I.R., 320 F.2d 953, 956 (8th Cir. 1963)."

To plead guilty is less promising. In Allstate Ins. Co. v. Peasley, p. 165 above, the court was divided about whether or not a guilty plea was conclusive, in relation to a criminal acts exclusion. The justices who thought not, concurring, reviewed authorities; see p. 1253. But they also quoted from the Restatement of Judgments, Second, as follows:

> A defendant who pleads guilty may be held to be estopped in subsequent civil litigation from contesting facts representing the elements of the offense.

Section 85, Comment *b*.

No conviction is conclusive as to issues not relevant to the definition of the crime. As to this, again, the judges in Peasley's case were divided. Considering whether or not he should have expected his crime, reckless endangerment, to entail the injuries it did, four judges said that, "by definition" of the crime, the injuries were reasonably to be expected. The concurring justices disagreed.

PROBLEM

In the case of arson referred to in the foregoing Note, a further question arose about the difference between minor and major fires. The shopkeepers had planned to set a "small smokey fire" in their store and to collect insurance on the inventory. The fire they set got out of hand, causing damage to the building and to adjacent stores. Owners of those stores, and their insurers, sought to charge the arsonists with liability. The arsonists held a commercial liability coverage, and asked the insurer to defend them. The insurer sought a declaratory judgment that it was not accountable. The trial court entered summary judgment for the insurer. It ruled that the questions of whose property and how much property the arsonists intended to burn were "wholly irrelevant." On appeal, should that ruling be approved?

Misconduct Exclusions (Reprise)

For some courts the exclusions quoted under this heading, p. 163 above, are needless, at least in part: they do no more than exclude liabilities that would anyway be excluded by force of law. Representative expressions are these:

> -[T]he general rule is that it is against public policy for insurance to indemnify an insured against his own criminal acts.[1]

> - [A]s a matter of public policy, people and businesses cannot purchase insurance coverage for illegal activities. For we do not allow corporations or persons "to insure themselves against acts prohibited by law."[2]

A comparable view, though more restrained, appears in a Pennsylvania case. The insured pleaded guilty to various criminal charges, including manslaughter for the death of a young woman. For years, the two had traded drugs with one another. She came to Greenfield's home on the night of her death, and got a dose. Considering Greenfield's liability coverage, the court said:

> The public policy in our Commonwealth, as articulated by the legislature, is clear: possession, sale, and use of heroin are illegal. Public policy does not allow recovery under an insurance contract where a willing and frequent participant in this type of criminalized activity dies as a result. This is true regardless of whether the victim intended to die or whether the criminal intended the death, for we will not countenance the turning of illegal activities regarding Schedule I controlled substances into money-making occasions.

Minnesota Fire & Cas. Co. v. Greenfield, 855 A.2d 854, 869 (2004) (opinion by fewer than a majority).

Sometimes, however, even a very powerful public policy gives leeway to a coverage term. So it was in Town of Cumberland v. Rhode Island Interlocal Risk Management Trust, 860 A.2d 1210 (R.I. 2004). In a "dark chapter" of the Town's history, it managed to incur liability by amending its zoning laws without according due process to some of its landowners. The Town had procured insurance against several kinds of wrongdoing, including false imprisonment, malicious prosecution, libel, and—as in this case—violation of civil rights. The Town's insurers were held to be accountable; the court said: "Rhode Island public policy does not bar an insured from indemnification for intentional torts when the insurance policy explicitly provides such coverage." Id. at 1219.

NOTES

(1) *Policy Construction.* Suppose that an exclusionary policy term might be read in two ways, one of them withholding coverage of liability for a lawless act, and the other not. In that situation, a court might be inclined to construe the coverage narrowly out of respect for public policy about flouting the law. Or it might be

---

1. Landry v. Leonard, 720 A.2d 907, 909 (Me. 1998).

2. Farmland Mutual Ins. Co. v. Scruggs, 886 So.2d 714, 720 (Miss. 2004) [quoting from Delta Pride Catfish, Inc. v. Home Ins. Co., 697 So.2d 400, 405 (Miss. 1997), quoting in turn from Graham Resources, Inc. v. Lexington Ins. Co., 625 So.2d 716, 721 (La.App. 1993)].

inclined to construe the coverage broadly, on the principle of taking ambiguities in favor of the insured. *Question*: Given these conflicting inclinations, which should control?

A policy concerned in the case last cited, *Town of Cumberland*, contained an exclusion that the court might have applied. The court declined to apply it, relying on the usual rule about ambiguities. But some judges do not believe that "accident" comprises a mishap attendant on deliberate conduct known to be lawless and seriously dangerous. See the concurring opinion of Justice Castille in *Greenfield* (the "heroin case") at 869.

(2) *Inferred Intent*. Given a policy that excludes coverage for personal injuries expected or intended by the insured, an insurer is not required to defend an insured in a suit seeking damages for alleged sexual molestation of a child because an intent to cause harm is inferred in cases of sexual molestation of a minor. Where a taxicab driver sexually molested a minor, the court stated:

> We agree with the majority rule that in liability insurance cases involving sexual abuse of children, the intent to cause injury can be inferred as a matter of law. The majority of courts agree with this rule because "the harm to the victimized child is no less serious when the abusive adult's subjective intentions are purportedly 'benign.' "[3]

Kim v. National Indem. Co., 6 P.3d 264, 267–68 (Alaska 2000).

All too often the question has arisen whether or not an intent to harm should be inferred when the molestation of a minor is committed *by* a minor. See West Virginia Fire & Cas. Co. v. Stanley, 602 S.E.2d 483 (W.Va. 2004), collecting cases and saying that they are about evenly divided. "Because our adoption of the inferred-intent rule in sexual abuse cases is based on the *inherently* injurious nature of the wrongful sexual act, the age of the actor is irrelevant." Id. at 494. The doctrine of inferred intent might be applied in cases far afield from those of sexual molestation of a minor. But there is resistance to that. See, again, *Greenfield*, the herion case ("Jurisprudence in Pennsylvania does not support the extension of inferred intent to cases other than exceptional ones involving child sexual abuse." 855 A.2d at 863.)

----

3. In a footnote the court cites many cases including the following: Whitt v. De-Leu, 707 F.Supp. 1011 (W.D. Wis. 1989).

> [Courts following the majority view find that] the alleged sexual contact is so substantially certain to result in some injury, or so inherently injurious, that the act is considered a criminal offense for which public policy precludes a claim of unintended consequences, that is, a claim that no harm was intended to result from the act.

Id. at 1014–15. Other citations include: J.C. Penney Cas. Ins. Co. v. M.K., 804 P.2d 689, 695 (Cal. 1991) ("the intent to molest [a child] is, by itself, the same as the intent to harm"); Allstate Ins. Co. v. Mugavero, 589 N.E.2d 365, 369 (N.Y. 1992) (the majority rule "finds support in logic and in the generally accepted conception of harm as being inherent in the act of sexually abusing a child"); Horace Mann Ins. Co. v. Leeber, 376 S.E.2d 581, 584 n.7, 585 (W.Va. 1988) (citing states following majority approach at n.7); 2 Eric Mills Holmes, Holmes's Appleman on Insurance 2d § 9.4, at 539 (1996), For claims arising out of sexual molestation perpetrated by insureds, "no coverage should be provided regardless of the insured's protestation that no injury was intended. An intent to injure should be presumed from the nature of the act."; 4 Holmes, Holmes' Appleman on Insurance 2d § 23.4, at 513 (1998), "In certain situations, such as child sexual molestation, intent to harm may be inferred as a matter of law."

2.   Civil Rights and Liability Coverages

Violations of civil rights commonly give rise to liabilities established by judgments in private actions. Allegations of violations commonly give rise to liabilities established by settlements of private actions. Whether settled or not, these actions often impose on the defendants substantial expenses in the way of preparing and presenting defenses and of negotiating toward a settlement. If an entity—person or firm—charged with a violation of civil rights holds a liability coverage, it is likely to try to pass on to the insurer any liability or expense relating to the charge. Those efforts are the subject of the materials that follow.

Several policy forms provide coverages that may apply. The one featured in these materials is the commercial general liability (CGL) form. Another is the "errors & omissions" (E & O) form, sometimes designated "professional liability".

But a claimant may well be disappointed by one or another limitation on the coverage provided. An example concerns a charge of sexual harassment against the insured, an operator of a residential treatment facility. The complainants, employees of the insured, alleged that it had failed to protect them from assaults by an autistic youngster in residence. The insured held a CGL policy. It did not cover harms expected or intended by the insured. But the harms alleged were expected or intended, if at all, only by the youngster. More to the point, the policy contained an exclusion of liability arising from

> *bodily injury* to . . . an *employee* of the Insured arising out of and in the course of . . . employment by the Insured [or] performing duties related to the conduct of the Insured's business. . . . [Defined terms in italics.]

The insured held also a professional liability policy. But it too contained an "employee exclusion". Moreover, its coverage of liabilities for damages extended only to those incurred

> because of a professional error or mistake [by you] arising out of the performance or failure to perform any professional services for others in your capacity as a residential care facility.

The employees did not allege an error or mistake of that sort. Neither of the policies required the insurer to provide a defense against the harassment charge. Agricultural Ins. Co. v. Focus Homes, Inc., 212 F.3d 407 (8th Cir. 2000).

(As to any liability coverage that might have applied to the youngster, note the exceptional supposition of molestation by a minor of persons presumably adult. Compare Note 2, p. 174 above.)

Aside from explicit coverage limitations, insurers take refuge in what may be called an "implied exclusion": Public policy precludes coverage of loss attendant on misconduct of certain kinds. Most of the materials that follow concern that proposition, earlier introduced.

Workplace Discrimination and Public Policy

By a large body of legislation, both federal and state, persons deprived of employment, or of benefits associated with it, by reason of discrimination can get redress through private civil actions. Among the statutes a bellwether is the federal Civil Rights Act of 1964,[1] in which Title VII is a main avenue for relief. The types of discrimination it condemns are those based on race, color, religion, sex, and national origin. Other like statutes condemn discrimination by reason of age and disability.[2] The Civil Rights Act of 1991[3] condemns sexual harassment in workplaces as well as certain discriminatory conduct by employers in making decisions about hiring, firing, and promotion. Insurance against a liability for violating one of the statutes is sometimes problematic, as indicated above, in part because often a violation is in some sense intentional.

The following materials concern chiefly coverage provided by the standard CGL policy in relation to actions for the redress of unlawful discrimination in the workplace. First, however, two cases not fitting that description are presented: one about social discrimination; and after that, one about workplace discrimination that did not, apparently, concern a CGL policy. Case 1 concerns a Florida club and its liability, under Florida anti-discrimination law, for excluding applicants from membership. Case 2 is about a violation of the Age Discrimination in Employment Act (ADEA) of 1967.[4]

i.   *Religious Discrimination*

Phil and Rona Skolnick charged the Bal Harbour Club with covert antisemitism in rejecting their application for membership, a rejection that cost them an opportunity to purchase a homesite. The Club, having settled the claim, then litigated with its insurer, Ranger Insurance, over coverage of its liability. From this litigation emerged a question certified to the Florida Supreme Court about the State's public policy: Does it preclude indemnity for a loss "resulting from an intentional act of religious discrimination?"

The court found little authority in point about the coverage of *intentional* discrimination. The Club argued that the coverage it claimed would not tempt others to practice unlawful discrimination. But this supposition, the court said, "defies human experience." The court wanted to know whether the primary purpose of liability like that of the Club was to deter wrongdoing or to compensate its victims. As to compensation, the court indicated that the Skolnicks' case was exceptional: "The bulk of discrimination cases are brought against commercial enterprises [which] have far greater resources than do individuals...." As to deterrence, the court

---

1. 42 U.S.C. § 2000e.

2. As to disabilities, see the Americans with Disabilities Act (ADA) of 1990, 42 U.S.C. § 12101.

3. Pub.L. No. 102–166, 105 Stat. 1071 (codified in titles 2 and 42 of the United States Code).

4. 29 U.S.C. § 626.

reflected on punitive damages, but concluded that they do not make punishment by any means certain because they are not awarded with sufficient frequency, in statutory discrimination cases, for that.

"[W]e hold", the court said, "that the public policy of Florida prohibits an insured from being indemnified for a loss resulting from an intentional act of religious discrimination." Ranger Insurance Company v. Bal Harbour Club, Inc., 549 So.2d 1005 (1989).

ii. *The Case of the Senior Professor*

In an action for violation of the ADEA, brought against a school by a professor it had discharged, a jury found that there was a willful violation of the Act. The school sought to pass on to its insurer its liability and its cost of defending the action.

Two questions and their answers were helpful to the school. First, the jurors may have been uncomfortable in finding a willful violation on the part of a theological school. During deliberations they had asked the judge, in effect, "Can a violation be willful without being intentional?" And the judge said that a defendant acts willfully "if it knows its conduct was prohibited by federal law *or if it acts in reckless disregard as to whether its conduct is prohibited by federal law*." Second, when the dispute about coverage arrived before the First Circuit Court of Appeals, the court inquired of the Massachusetts Supreme Judicial Court (SJC) about the Massachusetts statute set out at p. 163 above. "Does a finding of willfulness under the ADEA, if based on a finding of 'reckless disregard ...,' constitute 'deliberate or intentional ... wrongdoing' ...?" And the SJC answered, No: A wrongful act bars coverage only if "done deliberately or intentionally, in the sense that the actor knew that the act was wrongful."

As to the school's litigation expenses the Court of Appeals concluded that, even if the school could not pass on its liability, neither the state statute nor the contract excluded defense costs associated with uninsurable claims. As to the liability, the court reversed a summary judgment that the district court had entered for the insurer. Andover Newton Theological School, Inc. v. Continental Casualty Co., 930 F.2d 89 (1st Cir.1991).

Commercial General Liability (CGL) Insurance Coverages

Commercial General Liability (CGL) Insurance is the subject of Chapter 5. CGL coverages are an awkward fit, often, with charges of workplace wrongdoing. One coverage concerns bodily injury, and another property damage. Complainants do not frequently charge employers with having inflicted bodily injury, or damage to assets in hand. They do often complain of loss of pay and other financial harm; but these do not count as damage, as required by the policy form, to *tangible* property.

A third coverage offers better hope to employers in mine-run cases, that concerning "personal injury" which the CGL policy covers. Defined in the CGL as libel, slander and an oral or written publication violating a person's right to privacy, personal injury provides no other coverage for charges of workplace wrongdoing. Some policies expand the conception of personal injury to include, in addition to bodily injury, humiliation, mental anguish, and "discrimination". This definition is not, however, standard in primary CGL policies, but appears in excess policies. Indeed, even a limited personal-injury coverage is usually the subject of a CGL endorsement.

Absent the expansive definition, the term "bodily injury" has been held to embrace psychic injury, owing to a supposed ambiguity. Evans v. Farmers Ins. Exch., 34 P.3d 284 (Wyo. 2001). But that is a minority position. A decision to the contrary is Trinity Universal Ins. Co. v. Cowan, 945 S.W.2d 819 (Tex. 1997) (collecting cases).

Assuming that a policy purports to provide coverage of an employer's liability for an unlawful discriminatory practice, the question arises whether or not public policy condones that coverage. The two opinions that follow address that question.

Foxon Packaging Corp. v. Aetna Cas. and Surety Co.

United States District Court, D.R.I., 1995.
905 F.Supp. 1139.

Hugo Hernandez suffered indignities while working for Foxon Packaging. Soon after he began working there, other employees posted a sign containing the initials "KKK" at his work station. When Hernandez complained of that to his foreman, the foreman made light of it ("old joke", the foreman said, with a smile), and took no action to address the complaint.

A statute of Rhode Island, the Fair Labor Practices Act, declares that "the right of all individuals in this state to equal employment opportunities, regardless of race or color, religion, sex, handicap, age or country of ancestral origin, is ... a civil right." Another, the Fair Employment Practices Act, declares a public policy "to foster the employment of all individuals in this state in accordance with their fullest capacities, regardless of their race or color ... and to safeguard their right to obtain and hold employment without such discrimination." R.I.G.L. § 28–5–3. That Act also provides that it is an unlawful practice for an employer to discriminate against an employee because of (among other things) race or color with respect to (among other things) "terms, conditions or privileges of employment, or any other matter directly or indirectly related to employment[.]" R.I.G.L. § 28–5–7 (A), (B). The State's Commission for Human Rights took action on Hernandez's behalf and won a judgment against Foxon, payable to him, for nearly $90,000. Some of this was for attorney's fees; most was for back pay.

Foxon was insured by Aetna under a "Broad Form Comprehensive General Liability" policy. It had asked that Aetna defend and indemnify it against Hernandez's claim pursuant to the policy. Aetna had denied coverage. This action was brought by Foxon, based on breach of the insurance contract, among other things. Aetna moved for a summary judgment.

■ Mary M. Lisi, Judge.

. . .

Duty to Defend and Indemnify

The crux of Foxon's claims involves whether Aetna breached its insurance contract with Foxon by refusing to defend and indemnify Foxon against Hernandez's intentional discrimination lawsuit. . . .

[The court made reference to the statutes partly described above.]

The Complaint

[The complaint by the Commission against Foxon included allegations made by Hernandez, which the court quoted.] The heart of the complaint is Hernandez's claim of intentional racial discrimination in the workplace. The complaint clearly states that Hernandez left his position at Foxon due to a discriminatory work environment. Hernandez alleges no other injuries except financial losses resulting from his loss of employment.

[The court referred to the terms of Foxon's policy and concluded that it did not cover "acts of intentional discrimination".]

Aetna argues, and this court agrees, that the public policy of the State of Rhode Island as articulated in the Fair Labor Practices Act, militates against judicial creation of a safe harbor within which Foxon may presumably violate the law at will with impunity. Such a result would do violence to the public policy of the state and eviscerate the statute's intended guarantee of a workplace free of discrimination. . . .

The Rhode Island Supreme Court has consistently held that insurance policies cannot insure for actions which are contrary to public policy. See Allen v. Simmons, 533 A.2d 541, 543–44 (R.I. 1987). A contract or agreement is contrary to public policy when it "is injurious to the interests of the public, interferes with the public welfare or safety, is unconscionable, or tends to injustice or oppression." City of Warwick v. Boeng Corp., 472 A.2d 1214, 1218 (R.I. 1984). Furthermore, when a state's legislature has enacted legislation that forbids certain conduct, that conduct is against public policy. Lucas v. Brown & Root Inc., 736 F.2d 1202, 1205 (8th Cir. 1984).

Foxon comes before this court to seek, in essence, insulation from its own wrongdoing. When notified of the Ku Klux Klan sign, Foxon's superiors not only failed to take disciplinary action against the employees, but actively encouraged the continuation of a racially hostile work environment. It would be a clear violation of public policy if businesses and individuals could insure themselves against liability for committing intentional acts of discrimination. This result would promote, rather than deter discriminatory behavior. "If an insurance policy were to cover [Foxon's] wilful racial discrimination ... [Foxon] could indulge [its] own preference for racial discrimination at little risk to" itself. Western Casualty and Surety Co. v. Western World Insurance Co., 769 F.2d 381, 385 (7th Cir. 1985). Foxon's knowing failure to address the blatantly discriminatory acts of its employees should not be condoned by shifting the burden of satisfying Hernandez's damage awards to Aetna.

For the foregoing reasons, Aetna's motion for summary judgment is granted.

Introduction to *Union Camp*

Two types of actionable discrimination have been recognized ever since the decision in Griggs v. Duke Power Co., 401 U.S. 424 (1971). One is "disparate treatment", the other "disparate impact". The action against Duke Power proceeded not because it discriminated purposefully against African Americans, but because it screened persons for employment and promotion by reference to a factor, "neutral on its face", that tended to their disadvantage.[5] That is the essence of a disparate-impact claim. It can be countered by proof that the factor in question does not have an acceptable substitute in light of the employer's needs. In a later case the Supreme Court said:

> Claims of disparate treatment may be distinguished from claims that stress "disparate impact." The latter involve employment practices that are facially neutral in their treatment of different groups but that in fact fall more harshly on one group than another and cannot be justified by business necessity. Proof of discriminatory motive, we have held, is not required under a disparate-impact theory.... Either theory may, of course, be applied to a particular set of facts.[6]

Writing about disparate-impact claims that succeed, the New York Department of Insurance has said in a circular letter that "specific discriminatory acts ... are not an element of the wrong.... Rather, such results are normally grounded upon statistical or other numerical profiles that reflect disparities between or among groups sufficient to support a finding of discrimination...."[7]

---

5. At one time Duke Power had discriminated overtly against African Americans in its employment practices. Having reversed course, it gave preference to persons holding high-school diplomas or scoring well on a test of general intelligence. These standards were applied fairly to whites and others, with no "invidious intent". These were among the findings of the trial court. Reversing a ruling of that court, the Court of Appeals "rejected the claim that because these two requirements operated to render ineligible a markedly disproportionate number of Negroes, they were unlawful under Title VII unless shown to be job related." *Griggs* at 429. The Supreme Court reversed. It said: "Nothing in the Act precludes the use of testing or measuring procedures; obviously they are useful. What Congress has forbidden is giving these devices and mechanisms controlling force unless they are demonstrably a reasonable measure of job performance." Id. at 436.

6. International Brotherhood of Teamsters v. United States, 431 U.S. 324, 335 (1977).

7. This and other Departmental views appear in American Management Ass'n v. Atlantic Mutual Ins. Co., 641 N.Y.S.2d 802 (Sup.Ct. 1996).

Once these two types of wrongful discrimination were established, questions arose about insurance coverages. Policy language might be construed to embrace a liability for wrongdoing indicated by disparate impact and not for that indicated by disparate treatment. In School District No. 1 v. Mission Ins. Co., 650 P.2d 929 (Ore.App.), *petition for review denied*, 662 P.2d 725 (1983), the court ruled that the latter was outside a coverage of claims made "by reason of any negligent act, error or omission of the insured". That case was distinguished in Independent School District No. 697 v. St. Paul Fire & Marine Ins. Co., 515 N.W.2d 576 (Minn. 1994), owing to differences in the policy language.

Moreover, it became a question whether or not insurance against liability of either type is consistent with public policy. The question about disparate treatment was finessed in Solo Cup Company v. Federal Ins. Co., 619 F.2d 1178 (7th Cir.), *cert. denied*, 449 U.S. 1033 (1980). "[W]e do not consider whether the degree of motive which must be proved in that type of action would be equivalent to a knowledgeable and intentional wrong such as would void policy provisions purporting to cover those claims." Id. at 1187. Assuming voidness, a case in which disparate impact is charged can be differentiated.

The New York Department finessed the question about disparate treatment in the letter quoted above. But it pronounced in favor of coverage, as written, in disparate-impact cases. Indeed, it argued that the coverage *furthers* the public policy against discrimination:

> By bringing to employers' attention practices that can potentially result in unlawful discrimination, insurers' loss prevention programs and underwriting standards should discourage such practices. Any employer who does not diligently attempt to modify employment procedures accordingly may well be denied insurance coverage.

In *Solo Cup* the court echoed that hope, adding the thought that "disparate impact" may have a disparate impact on disparate employers: Careful analyses of employment standards, the court said, "may well become ... beyond the financial capabilities of all but the largest employers. The involvement of insurance [might] ease the burden on smaller employers by making claim prevention services available on a cost effective basis to help employers evaluate their employment standards." Id. at 1188.

Question: It would be interesting to know whether or not monitoring by insurers of the employment practices of their customers has helped to suppress unlawful discrimination. Your editors do not know. What is your surmise?

What is at stake in a case of disparate impact may be not so much the cost to an employer to satisfy a successful claim of discrimination as the cost of resisting the claim. As the New York Department has indicated, a defense may require the rebuttal, or the preparation, of "statistical or other numerical profiles". Often, as in the following case, the employer is faced with a class action. There the employer, Union Camp, engaged in four years of discovery and negotiation before settling the claim against it. The aspect of public policy in relation to insuring against defense costs is complicated by the fact that complainants often charge both disparate treatment and disparate impact.

The opinion in *Union Camp* illustrates the complexities. We are told that the suit against the employer charged it with acting "with the 'purpose and design' of discriminating against its black employees." But in suing its insurer, we are told, Union Camp argued that the earlier suit "was not based on the theory of intentional discrimination." We are told that Union Camp sought to recover from its insurer $800,000 that it had paid to the class-action claimants. But we are told also that, according to Union Camp, all it sought was a remedy for the insurer's refusal to provide it with a defense. In view of these curiosities, it is a challenge to know what the decision stands for.

Union Camp Corp. v. Continental Casualty Co.

United States District Court, Southern District of Georgia, 1978.
452 F.Supp. 565.

■ LAWRENCE, DISTRICT JUDGE.

Is an insurance policy that insures an employer against losses resulting from racially discriminatory practices under Title VII and 42 U.S.C. § 1981 violative of public policy? Contending that the insuring of employers against the consequences of violations of the Civil Rights Acts serves to encourage acts of discrimination, defendant moves to dismiss Union Camp's action. Both sides agree that this is a pioneer case.

Between 1969 and 1972, plaintiff carried, at separate periods, two insurance policies with Continental Casualty Corporation (CNA). Both were "umbrella excess coverage" policies. They provided protection against losses exceeding the coverage afforded by underlying policies. They also covered certain claims not covered by them. Claims not covered by other policies (discrimination) arc the basis of this suit.

CNA's 1966 policy provided coverage for certain "occurrences." "The term 'Occurrence' means an event or continuous or repeated exposure to conditions which unexpectedly causes Personal Injury...." "The term 'Personal Injuries' whenever used herein, shall mean: ... Discrimination...." The 1969 policy covered "discrimination except that committed by, at the direction of, or with the consent of the insured." Assuming coverage, CNA was required to defend suits covered by the insurance policies.

In 1971 a class action under Title VII and 42 U.S.C. § 1981 was brought against Union Camp. (Boles et al. v. Union Camp Corporation et al.). The suit alleged that Union Camp's alleged actions were done with the "purpose and design" of discriminating against its black employees.[1] CNA

---

1. Two months before the *Boles* action was filed against Union Camp the Supreme Court had ruled in Griggs v. Duke Power Co., 401 U.S. 424, that discriminatory intent was

denied coverage and declined to provide a defense. Union Camp retained other counsel and defended the suit. More than four years of discovery and negotiation followed.

Plaintiff reached a voluntary settlement with the affected members of the class in 1975. The settlement included back pay to the class members amounting to $800,000. A final decree was entered in September, 1975 in which this Court approved the settlement agreement following a hearing.

Thereafter, Union Camp filed the present suit against CNA seeking to recover the amount of back pay and the attorneys' fees expended in defending the action. As stated, CNA has moved to dismiss the complaint on the theory that the relevant provisions in the contract violate public policy.

II

Defendant contends that insuring against discrimination would encourage violation of the Civil Rights Acts of 1866 and 1964. It argues that to permit the writing of such insurance "would undermine enforcement of the strong public policy of equal treatment of all persons expressed in the Fourteenth Amendment to the Constitution and in federal anti-discrimination statutes. . . ."

Defendant's basic argument is that an insurance contract is unenforceable if "it is injurious to the public or contravenes some established interest of society." L'Orange v. Medical Protective Company, 394 F.2d 57, 60 (6th Cir.). CNA argues that there is a strong public interest in equal employment opportunity. See Franks v. Bowman Transportation Co., Inc., 424 U.S. 747, 763. The "reasonably certain prospect of a backpay award" provides incentive for employers to comply with Title VII. Albemarle Paper Co. v. Moody, 422 U.S. 405, 417–18. Back pay liability under Title VII is aimed at providing an "economic incentive for an employer to obviate discrimination voluntarily, rather than by court decree. . . ." United Transportation Union Local 974 v. Norfolk and Western Railway Company, 532 F.2d 336, 342 (4th Cir.). Consequently, back pay awards compensate injured employees while serving the public goal of equal employment opportunity. If, CNA contends, back pay awards were covered by insurance, such deterrent effect would be mitigated.

III

Union Camp responds that the motion to dismiss fails on four grounds. First, it contends that the Fifth Circuit has specifically approved insurance for civil rights liability. Caplan v. Johnson, 414 F.2d 615 (5th Cir.). In that case the Court of Appeals held that coverage for a § 1983 claim existed under a policy covering false arrests. Public policy was not discussed by the Court in its decision.

Second, plaintiff argues that public policy prohibits insuring against intentional injury and not against intentional acts which unintentionally

not required under the Act which was directed to the consequences of employment practices and not simply the employer's motivation.

result in injury. See Travelers Indemnity Company v. Hood, 140 S.E.2d 68 (Ga.App.). Furthermore, says Union Camp, the suit against it was not based on the theory of intentional discrimination.

Third, Union Camp asserts that its action against CNA is not to recover for the assessed damages but is one for the breach of the insurer's duty to defend under the policy.

Finally, Union Camp contends that the cases cited by CNA, particularly the securities cases, *e.g.*, Globus v. Law Research Service, 287 F.Supp. 188 (S.D.N.Y.), modified 418 F.2d 1276 (2nd Cir.), cert. denied 397 U.S. 913, are all distinguishable or inapposite.

IV

An insurance policy that is clear and unambiguous and is neither illegal nor against public policy should be enforced by the courts. American Empire Insurance Company of South Dakota v. Fidelity and Deposit Company of Maryland, 408 F.2d 72 (5th Cir.), cert. denied, 396 U.S. 818. "A contract can not be said to be contrary to public policy unless the General Assembly has declared it to be so, ... or unless the contract is entered into for the purpose of effecting an illegal or immoral agreement or doing something which is in violation of law." Camp v. Aetna Insurance Company, 152 S.E. 41, 43 (Ga.).

The proposition that insurance taken out by an employer to protect against liability under Title VII will encourage violations of the Act is based on an assumption that is speculative and erroneous. Defendant's conclusion is but an *a priori* response to the relation between violations of statutes forbidding discriminatory practices and the existence of insurance protecting against same. The argument assumes that employers would deliberately violate the law because their actions are protected by insurance. Here the policy would not cover intentional or consensual acts of discrimination by the insured. The fact that coverage would be excluded in these circumstances would in itself be a deterrent to incentive to violate the Civil Rights Act.

The payment of a large award of back pay to a class and imposition of attorney's fees in a discrimination case conceivably could cripple the employer financially or even put the offending company out of business. Conversely, insurance against liability for discriminatory practices in employment could benefit discriminatees. Where a class of employees is entitled to back pay under a court order and the employer is financially unable to comply with the same, insurance would provide the mandated compensation.[2]

Continental and other insurers which have issued policies containing such clauses have not up to now conceived that they were violating public policy by writing insurance policies insuring against losses resulting from discriminatory employment practices. Neither Congress nor EEOC has

---

2. Defendant characterizes as "slim" the "likelihood that particular employees may not receive back pay because their em-ployer is insolvent." See Reply Brief of CNA, p. 8.

interdicted such contracts. Only the issuer of the policy sued on makes such a claim. Exercise of the freedom of contract is not lightly to be interfered with. It is only in clear cases that contracts will be held void as against public policy. Steele v. Drummond, 275 U.S. 199, 205; Greenwood Cemetery, Inc. v. Travelers Indemnity Company, 232 S.E.2d 910 (Ga.). This is not one.

ORDER Defendant's motion to dismiss is denied.

NOTES

(1) *Burdens of Producing Evidence and of Persuasion.* When disparate impact does not figure in a Title VII case about employment, the complainant bears both of these burdens with respect to the issue of an intent to discriminate. Texas Dep't of Cmty. Affairs v. Burdine, 450 U.S. 248, 253 (1981). It is otherwise when the claim is one of disparate impact. First, a claimant can throw a burden on an employer by showing its use of a discriminatory standard in employment practices. The burden then shifts to the defendant employer to rebut the presumption of discrimination by producing evidence that the plaintiff was rejected, or someone else was preferred, for a legitimate, nondiscriminatory reason. For instance, the employer can throw a burden back on the claimant by demonstrating that the standard is job-related. The claimant can then proceed by showing that the employer can satisfy its needs by using a non-discriminatory standard. Does this alternation of burdens have a bearing on the question how far disparate impact embodies conscious wrongdoing?

(2) *An* Ad-hominem *Rule.* A ruling similar to that in *Union Camp*, but more limited, was made in Independent School District No. 697 v. St. Paul Fire & Marine Ins. Co., 515 N.W.2d 576 (Minn. 1994). The court said, "We do not believe that a school district will discriminate against its employees simply because it carries wrongful act insurance coverage." Id. at 580. Possibly public policy tolerates, for entities whose e-mail addresses end in ".edu" ".org" or ".gov", a coverage that would not be permitted to a Dot com. Is that an attractive rule?

See BLaST Intermediate Unit 17 v. CNA Insurance Companies, 674 A.2d 687 (Pa. 1996). BLaST was a public entity providing special education services for children. It had to pay some female employees for having, through negligence, violated the Equal Pay Act. The court approved a judgment against its insurers, saying that "the purchase of insurance by a public entity for losses resulting from its negligent actions should be encouraged." Id. at 691.

(3) *The Artful Dodger.* The suggestion has been made that a public-policy objection to coverage should prevail against a coverage only if the insured committed a wrong either (a) with the "design of producing loss", or (b) on a calculation of self-interest—formal or informal—in which the coverage figured as a plus. Willborn et al., *Employment Law* (2d ed. 1998). The author considered the case for a broader objection, but would have settled for this owing to the proclivity of insurers to protect themselves through policy drafting and to the general advantages of coverage (monitoring by insurers, and assuring payouts to victims) when they do not.

PROBLEM

When a school board bought an Educators Legal Liability policy, it obtained coverage against liability for "wrongful acts", explicitly including discrimination based upon race, "actual or alleged". But the policy excluded liability "brought about … by any Wrongful Act committed with actual knowledge of its wrongful nature.…'' The board was charged with a wrongful act, firing an employee by reason of her race. When it sought a defense by the insurer, it met resistance based on the exclusion.

The board contended that the coverage and the exclusion were at war with one another: "the policy offers coverage that is illusory and meaningless, giving rise to ambiguity which must be resolved in favor of the insured."

(A) As counsel to the insurer, develop an answer to that argument. (B) In order to say whether or not the insurer should provide a defense for the board, what more would you like to know about the allegations against the board? See Coleman v. School Board of Richland Parish, 418 F.3d 511 (5th Cir. 2005).

———

CHAPTER 4

THE SELECTION AND CONTROL OF RISKS

A. MISREPRESENTATION AND CONCEALMENT

An applicant for an individual automobile policy is asked, commonly, to provide information about her experience as a motorist. An applicant for individual life-insurance policy is asked, commonly, to provide information about his age, sex, health, and medical history. And so on. In a case to follow, for example, an application read:

> Have you ever been treated for, or ever been told that you had any one or more of the following: . . . Heart Disease? . . .

Given a policy issued in reliance on a false answer, the insurer may be permitted to rescind the contract or, in response to a claim, to withhold performance. The materials that follow address questions about misrepresentation as a basis for avoiding an insurance contract.

Take "fraud" to signify an instance of knowing deception practiced on an insurer in procuring a policy. The representation "No indication of heart disease" may well be false but not fraudulent. That is, an applicant may suffer from that malady, and may have been treated for it, yet believe otherwise. That being the case, the applicant's misstatement is a commonplace instance of "innocent misrepresentation."

Not having investigated the matter, one would suppose that an insurer can avoid a policy procured by the applicant's fraud. Some formulations of U.S. law express that proposition. It appears, for example, in a Florida statute about insurance:

> A misrepresentation, omission, concealment of fact, or incorrect statement may prevent recovery under the contract or policy [] if any of the following apply [sic]:
>
> (a) The misrepresentation, omission, concealment, or statement is fraudulent. . . .

But that bare proposition is not fully consistent with contract law in general, and is not trustworthy. Most formulations put the insurer to proof of some other element of fraud. Consider, for example, the several requirements of the Ohio "False answer" statute:

> No answer to any interrogatory made by an applicant in his application for a policy shall bar the right to recover upon any policy issued thereon . . . unless it is clearly proved that such answer is willfully false, that it was fraudulently made, that it is material, and that it induced the company to issue the policy, that but for such answer the policy would not have been issued, and that the agent or

company had no knowledge of the falsity or fraud of such answer. Rev.Stat. § 3911.06.

In the Restatement, Second, of Contracts, a fraudulent misrepresentation is said to entail voidability only if it is one "upon which the recipient is justified in relying".[1]

The full catalog of fraud effects contains still other entries. By Missouri law, for example, the cover-up of a malady in applying for a life policy, although done in writing, and fraudulent, and efficacious, does not entail loss of the death benefit unless the malady was a contributing cause of death. And Wisconsin law addresses the curious case in which an applicant has made a misrepresentation with intent to deceive, and "should have known" that it was false.

The law of concealment is modeled closely on the law of misrepresentation. In the law of contracts at large, a person's failure to speak about a matter sometimes counts as a misrepresentation. The Restatement, Second, of Contracts describes situations in which a person's "non-disclosure of a fact known to him is equivalent to an assertion that the fact does not exist". One of those is the case

> where he knows that disclosure of the fact would correct a mistake of the other party as to a basic assumption on which that party is making the contract and if non-disclosure of the fact amounts to a failure to act in good faith and in accordance with reasonable standards of fair dealing.[2]

The offense of silence may be called, in a word, concealment.

The word *concealment* indicates wrongdoing more strongly than *misrepresentation* does. "Innocent concealment" is not a recognized category in the law. An applicant for insurance cannot, for example, conceal a fact not known to the applicant. (One might conceal a suspicion of having heart disease; but the suspicion is not an unknown fact.) On the other hand, there is an implication of innocent concealment in the portion of the Florida statute quoted above. It declares that the concealment of a fact is a reason for denying recovery, but only if the concealment is fraudulent.

Relatively few recent cases are reported in which concealment was the ground for avoiding an insurance contract. As to individual policies of life insurance, one of the reasons is that an applicant may fairly suppose that everything needful has been said, once he or she has answered a long list of questions about medical history. Even so, a case of vitiating fraud can be imagined. This hypothetical case has been put:

> [W]here the undisclosed fact is palpably material to the risk the mere nondisclosure is itself strong evidence of a fraudulent intent. Thus, if a man, about to fight a duel, should obtain life insurance without disclosing his intention, it would seem that no argument or

---

1. Section 164; but cf. § 163.   **2.** Section 161(b).

additional evidence would been needed to show the fraudulent character of the nondisclosure.

Penn Mut. Life Ins. Co. v. Mechanics' Savings Bank & Trust Co., 72 F. 413, 435 (6th Cir. 1896) (Taft, J.). *Caution*: This passage might be taken to signify that an applicant's fraud is a necessary and sufficient basis for avoidance. But it is not always so, as will be seen.

NOTES

(1) *The Wages of Crime*. The *Penn Mutual* case concerned a policy insuring the life of John Schardt, a teller and cashier at a bank. A fact he failed to mention in applying for the policy was his career as an embezzler. One might suppose Schardt's life would not be cut short on that account. But it may have been. Shortly after his crime was discovered, the bank closed its doors and on the same day Schardt "departed this life". Let it be supposed that the cause of death was apoplexy, brought on by being found out. By the law of Missouri, as indicated above, that chain of causation would be momentous. But it was not under the applicable law. (A decision for the claimant was reversed for error in excluding evidence.)

The court made this observation in support of the claim: A person applying for insurance cannot be expected to speak evil of himself.[3] Suppose a contrasting case: Schardt is the bank's chief financial officer. Knowing of his embezzlement, but saying nothing about it, the bank procures insurance on his life. Let it be supposed that this policy is voidable; the "speak no evil" principle does not apply. Would it seem odd to charge the bank with bad faith in its dealings with the insurer, and to ascribe good faith to similar conduct by the malefactor himself?

(2) *A Challenge*. To construct a case in which a court would deny the enforcement of a policy because, in applying for the policy, the claimant had withheld information in all innocence is something of a challenge. If that case exists, it is likely to have these elements: (i) If disclosed, the information would have deterred the insurer from issuing the policy as it stands; (ii) The applicant was unaware of the importance of the information to the insurer; and (iii) The insurer could fairly expect the applicant to know that the information was critical to it. What undisclosed facts might be supposed, figuring in a plausible case of innocent, but operative, concealment?

Johnson v. Metropolitan Life Ins. Co., 251 A.2d 257 (N.J. 1969).[4] James Johnson bought health insurance in 1961. His application contained this question and this answer:

> 13. Have you consulted a physician or other practitioner within the past five years or to the best of your knowledge and belief have you had any illness or disease not mentioned in the answers above? Yes [X] No [ ]

The application called for "full details" concerning the answer Yes. Johnson's response was that a Dr. Gove had removed a hydrocele.

---

3. For this point the court relied on Sun Mut. Ins. Co. v. Ocean Ins. Co., 107 U.S. 485 (1882), and on New York Bowery Fire Ins. Co. v. New York Fire Ins. Co., 17 Wind. 359 (N.Y. 1837).

4. The claim considered was actually one against the Progressive Life Insurance Company. A related claim against the Metropolitan Life Insurance Company had been "disposed of by the parties."

In fact, Johnson had consulted Gove in 1957 about chest pains, and another physician in 1959 about tiredness. Both took electrocardiograms, though neither was a cardiologist. Dr. Gove was to testify, later, that he supposed Johnson to suffer from a coronary insufficiency, that he would have told Johnson so, that he gave Johnson a medication used primarily for cardiac distress, and that he advised Johnson, a builder, not to work so hard. He testified also, however, that he did not regard coronary insufficiency as a "disease" or "illness" in itself, but understood it as "more of a symptom, really." The other physician found no coronary artery disease, told Johnson that, and said that Johnson should go about his work.

In 1963 Johnson became disabled with Alzheimer's disease, a disease of the brain, and ultimately died of it. The insurer resisted a claim that he (and later the representative of his estate) made on the policy.

What follows is a fragment of a lengthy opinion on the case. Much of it concerns another question in the application (#10): "Have you ever been treated for, or ever been told that you had any one or more of the following: . . . Heart Disease? No . . . ."

■ WEINTRAUB, CHIEF JUSTICE. . . . Question 13 deals with two subjects, (1) consultation with physicians during a five-year period and (2) the existence, to the applicant's knowledge, of any illness or disease not mentioned in prior answers. Although the two subjects are separated by the word "or," it would be a strained reading to say Question 13 called for a disclosure of all medical consultations even though there was no "illness or disease." An applicant could readily believe the subjects were meant to be related and were dealt with in a single question for that reason. We should therefore take that view of the question.

What then is an "illness or disease"? Surely it is not every passing indisposition. . . . An applicant would assume the reference is to illnesses and disease entities as they are commonly understood. Upon that view, the supposed coronary insufficiency, if deemed a distinct disease entity separate from "heart disease," could come within Question 13, but the question is addressed to the understanding of the applicant, and there is no evidence that he understood coronary insufficiency to be itself an "illness" or "disease." . . . We do not understand [the insurer] to maintain that coronary insufficiency is a disease within Question 13 rather than a symptom of a "heart disease" within Question 10. Surely it could not be held as a matter of law on this record that the insured had some other "illness" or "disease."

[The court reinstated a judgment of the trial court for the claimant, which had been reversed by the Appellate Division.]

PROBLEM

State one or more additional facts about Johnson, not threatening to his health or changing his application, on which the insurer could have based a successful defense in the nature of concealment.

Gatlin, Administrator v. World Service Life Ins. Co.

Tennessee Supreme Court, 1981.
616 S.W.2d 606.

■ FONES, J.

Several related issues have been raised in this case involving an assertion of "good health" by decedent when she applied for group credit life insurance. We view the controlling issue to be whether such an assertion constituted a "misrepresentation" as a matter of law, thereby mandating a directed verdict in favor of defendant because the falsity of this assertion "increased the risk of loss" to the insurance company as a matter of law. The trial court and the Court of Appeals held that there was a misrepresentation that increased the risk of loss and the Court of Appeals affirmed the trial court's decision to direct a verdict in favor of defendant. For the reasons set forth below, we hold that the trial court and Court of Appeals were in error and the issue should have been submitted to the jury for a determination of whether decedent reasonably and in good faith asserted her opinion of good health.

I.

The facts in this case are not controverted. On May 21, 1976, Freida Gatlin, decedent, went to Truex Chevrolet in Jackson to purchase a car. The testimony of her aunt who accompanied her, and of the salesman revealed that when she filled out the paper work the salesman told her he would like to sell her group term credit life insurance. She did not ask for this insurance but accepted his offer. He gave her the application form and she signed it.

Next to the line where she was instructed to sign was the following sentence: "I hereby certify that I am in good health as of the effective date above." The application also stated that, "In consideration of the premium shown above and the representation of good health, the company certifies that the above named Debtor is afforded the coverage or coverages for which a premium or premiums are specified ... subject to the terms and conditions of the above numbered Group Life Policy." The application form contained specified conditions and limitations of coverage, but none referred to the applicant's health.

The application was accepted by defendant, World Service Life Insurance Company, and decedent was issued a policy. One of the conditions for acceptance of the policy was as follows:

6. INSURABILITY OF INSURED DEBTORS. No certificate of Insurance shall be delivered to any Debtor of the Creditor unless the Creditor or Creditor's agent ascertains and believes that the Debtor is in good health on the effective Date Specified in said Certificate of Insurance.

The record reveals that the salesman who sold decedent this policy accepted her assertion of "good health" without reservation and asked her no questions whatsoever concerning her health. The application form contained no space or specific questions whereby the applicant could elaborate on, qualify, or explain his or her assertion of "good health."

On August 4, 1976, less than three months from these transactions, decedent died of a cerebral hemorrhage. The record reveals that decedent suffered from hypertension, or high blood pressure, but was taking medication to control this condition under the medical care of Dr. Kendall. Dr. Kendall admitted the condition of decedent, but also made the following comments:

Q. Did you examine Mrs. Gatlin on April 1st, 1976?

A. Yes.

Q. Was this the last time that you examined or treated Mrs. Gatlin prior to May 21, 1976?

A. Yes.

Q. How would you describe her condition at that time, on April 1, 1976?

A. The only thing I could note would be from my records because of the length of time since that date, but on that occasion her blood pressure was probably the lowest it had been or as low as it had been since I had been seeing her since 1975. Her blood pressure on this occasion was down to 150 over 100, and she was going quite well at that time. She had no problems that she admitted to. She said she felt fine, and we felt like her blood pressure was probably under as good a control as it had been since we had started seeing her.

Q. Did you tell her that she was doing very well on that occasion?

A. I'm not sure, but I would imagine, based on what is written here, that I probably did.

Q. May I see your chart?

A. Yes, sure.

Q. Could you just read the first three sentences of the entry on April 1, 1976.

A. "Mrs. Gatlin comes in today. Her blood pressure is 150 over 100. I think she is doing quite well."

Dr. Kendall further testified that although hypertension was "more serious than a temporary thing," a person could be considered in "fairly good health" if his or her blood pressure was kept under control. Addressing the question of control with Mrs. Gatlin, he testified that he first saw her on November 21, 1975, at which time her blood pressure was 190 over 130. By December 29, 1975, her blood pressure had been reduced to 150 over 100 and was the same on April 1, 1976. Dr. Kendall answered the question as to whether this was "normal" or not as follows:

A. In her age category a blood pressure of 140 over 90 is considered to be the standard as a normal cutoff. Most authorities feel that you want to get the blood pressure down to 90, but most people feel if you can get it below 100 you are doing very well in most cases.

Mrs. Gatlin had no other complaints other than those related to hypertension.

II.

The issues presented involve the proper interpretation and application of T.C.A. § 56–7–103, which states:

Misrepresentations or warranty will not avoid policy—Exceptions.—No written or oral misrepresentations or warranty therein made in the negotiations of a contract or policy of insurance, or in the application therefor, by the assured or in his behalf, shall be deemed material or defeat or void the policy or prevent its attaching, unless such misrepresentation or warranty is made with actual intent to deceive, or unless the matter represented increases the risk of loss.

In this Court's recent opinion of Womack v. Blue Cross and Blue Shield of Tennessee, 593 S.W.2d 294 (Tenn.1980), we noted that application of this statute involved two steps:

To avoid coverage the insuror must first prove that the answers in the application were false; then it must prove either that the false answers were given with intent to deceive the insuror or that the false answers materially increased the risk of loss. Id. at 295.

The Court further stated that normally, "unless the minds of reasonable men could reach only one conclusion," the question as to whether the answers in the application were true or not was a jury decision; once it was determined that the answers were false, however, it was a question of law for the court to decide whether the false answers materially increased the risk.

It is clear, therefore, and must be kept in mind, that the concept of "misrepresentation" is totally distinct and separate from the concepts of "intent to deceive" or "increase in the risk of loss." The latter elements are not analyzed at all until and unless a matter has been "misrepresented." The trial court and the Court of Appeals were of the opinion that here there had been a misrepresentation as a matter of law because decedent was not *in fact* in "good health" when she had represented that she was. This conclusion, we hold, was error.

In order to determine whether a matter has been misrepresented it must first be determined what the insurer asked, required, or expected the applicant to represent.

In the present case, even if decedent was representing that she was *in fact* in "good health" on the day of these negotiations, the facts are sufficiently close so that reasonable minds might differ on this issue, and it should have been submitted to the jury. We do not decide this case on that point alone, however, for we hold that under the facts of this case decedent did not intend, nor was she asked, to *warrant* that she was *in fact* in "good health."

In 26 A.L.R.3d 1061 (1969) the compiler makes an exhaustive study of decisions dealing with representations of "sound" or "good" health. [Here the court quoted at some length from the Annotation, in which it was said that courts have taken the position, generally, that "a statement as to the condition of one's health, or the health of another, being as to a matter about which one may be honestly mistaken, is not, in the absence of some express directive, the absolute assertion of a fact."]

In Knights of Honor v. Dickson, 52 S.W. 862 (Tenn. 1899), it was alleged by the insurer that the insured had made certain misstatements in his application as to the exact disease of which his brother died; that the statements were untrue and material to the risk involved, and thus he could not recover under his insurance policy. The Court disagreed:

> We are of opinion the criticisms made upon the charge are not well made. It is true that any statement made of a material fact which forms the basis of the contract must be considered as a warranty, and if false will vitiate the contract whether made in good faith though ignorantly, or willfully and with knowledge of the falsity. But there is a difference between statements of fact as such and statements of opinion on matters where only opinion can be expressed. Falsehood may be predicated of a misstatement of fact but not of a mistaken opinion as to whether a man has a disease when it is latent and it can only be a matter of opinion. As to what a person may have died of may be largely, if not altogether, a matter of opinion, about which attending physicians often disagree, and as to such matters their statement made can only be treated as representations and not as warranties, and if made in good faith and on the best information had or obtainable, they will not vitiate a policy if incorrect and not willfully untrue.

Id. at 863.

We find the above quoted language most applicable to situations where a layman is asked to state whether he is in "good health." Such a broad and general question can only be categorized as an opinion and not a warranty of fact.

In the case of Metropolitan Life Ins. Co. v. Chappell, 269 S.W. 21 (Tenn. 1924), the Court was faced with a situation where one of the *conditions* of the insurance contract were that the insured be in "sound health" *in fact* before any obligations were assumed. The evidence revealed that the insured was not *in fact* in "good health" and the Court ruled that this evidence relieved the insurer from its obligations under the contract. The Court noted:

> "It is clear *from the language of the policy* that defendant's promise of insurance was not absolute, but conditional, and that *the existence of* life and *sound health* in the insured on the date of the policy *is the condition* on which the promise is made. *It is the fact of sound health* of the insured which determines the liability of the defendant *in this character of policies*, not apparent health, or his or any one's opinion or belief that he was in sound health." (Emphasis added.) Id. at 25.

This language clearly indicates that the result may well have been different had the insured's mere *opinion* of "good health" been the only basis of the contract. In the present case the *fact* of "good health" was not a condition to the acceptance of coverage.

In other jurisdictions the distinction between warranties and representations of "good health" has been emphasized. We note the state of Massachusetts has a statutory provision for all practical purposes identical to T.C.A. § 56–7–103. *See* M.G.L.A. c. 175, § 186. . . .

In a trilogy of cases the Massachusetts Supreme Court has held that vague and broad questions regarding whether the insured is in "good health" or has ever had an "illness" or "disease," would be construed as mere representations of opinions and *not* warranties; that such questions would be construed against the insurance company and would not avoid the policy if not answered fraudulently; and that the issue of good faith and reasonableness of the insured's responses were a question for the jury. [Three cases cited.]

The analysis used by the Massachusetts Court has also been followed in several other jurisdictions. *See* 26 A.L.R.3d 1061, § 10 (1969).

In the case of Ford Life Insurance Company v. Jones, 563 S.W.2d 399 (Ark. 1978), the facts were quite similar to those of the present case. The Court, in the admittedly close two-to-two decision affirming the decision of the trial court, concluded that the statement of "good health" should not be used as a defense by the insurance company when there was no evidence of misrepresentation or fraud. We find Chief Justice Harris' concurring opinion, however, to be most persuasive. Quoting from his own concurring opinion in National Old Line Insurance Co. v. People, 506 S.W.2d 128 (Ark. 1974), he states:

> " 'I have noticed from time to time, in these cases involving credit life insurance that the affirmative statement called for from the applicant is rather general in nature, (I am now in good health) and can, in many instances, be honestly answered by the applicant by "Yes," though actually he or she may not be in good health. For instance, perhaps one had open heart surgery a few months ago, or an operation on one of his carotid arteries which was partially blocked, endangering the flow of blood to the brain. He is told by his doctor that the operation was successful, and he genuinely feels that he has no further problems and is in good health. In fact, I know of an individual who underwent open heart surgery, and who is using a pacemaker. He constantly plays tennis and engages in other sports and considers himself as getting along fine, but I doubt seriously that an insurance company would consider him an acceptable risk. This man probably could honestly answer the question by stating that he is in good health, though the prospective insurer would disagree.
>
> It would appear to me that the company selling credit life insurance, in its application form, could follow the practice generally followed by insurance companies selling regular life insurance policies,

and propound more specific questions ... I refer to such questions as whether one has been in the hospital any time during the last three years, consulted a physician within the last three years, ever been told he had high blood pressure, heart disease, diabetes, cancer, etc. On the basis of such answers, the company can intelligently determine whether to consider the man a good insurance risk. If answers are in the negative and are false, this fact should not be difficult to establish. . . .

I can only say if the insurance company selling credit life insurance is willing to take the risk of asking only general questions, it will just have to also take the chance of perhaps paying benefits to the designee of an applicant who was not in good health when he applied for the policy.' "

Jones at 402–03.

In this Court's recent decision of Broyles v. Ford Life Insurance Co., 594 S.W.2d 691 (1980), the Court was faced with a situation involving a term life insurance policy in which the insured had stated that he was in "good health." In that case the insured had been under treatment for leukemia; the treatment caused him to experience blurred vision, headaches, stomach disorders, and rendered him unable to take some medication. He was undergoing frequent tests and although the treating physician would not say that he specifically told Broyles that he had "leukemia," he testified that Broyles positively knew he had a medical problem. There was a concurrent finding by the trial court and the intermediate appellate court that Broyles did not know he had leukemia, but this Court found, as a matter of law, that he had misrepresented the state of his health, based upon the overwhelming evidence that he knew he had a serious medical problem. Another important distinction between the *Broyles* case and the present one is that in *Broyles* the application form contained a place for exceptions or limitations on the general statements of health where it was indicated that applicants should qualify the assertion of "good health," if appropriate. Thus, it was much more evident in that case that the insurance carrier was relying on the *fact* of "good health" rather than the mere representation or opinion of such status.

In the present case decedent went to purchase a car, not insurance. When the salesman told her that he wanted her to buy credit term life insurance, she accepted. The document she signed contained only the simple request that she certify that she was in "good health" without any explanation as to what constituted "good health" or any space or follow-up questions indicating that she was to qualify this assertion. The application clearly stated that she would be insured "in consideration of the premium ... and the *representation* of good health." (Emphasis added.) The salesman accepted her assertion of "good health" and asked her no questions. The *fact* of her "good health," an elusive term at best, was never indicated to be a condition upon which the policy was based. Based on the testimony of her doctor, she may have reasonably and in good faith thought that she was in "good health."

Under these facts we hold that the good faith and reasonableness of decedent's assertion of "good health" were the determining factors as to whether there was any "misrepresentation" involved in this case. These are matters upon which reasonable minds may differ under the facts of this case, and thus should have been submitted to the jury to consider along with all the surrounding circumstances.

Should the jury, in the new trial, conclude that decedent asserted her opinion as to her "good health" reasonably and in good faith, then there would be no "misrepresentation" and the jury should find for the plaintiff. If the jury finds that decedent did not give her opinion reasonably or in good faith, then they should conclude that there was a "misrepresentation." Only then will it be left to the trial court to determine, as a matter of law, that this misrepresentation increased the risk to the insurer. If upon retrial the proof presents the issue of whether the decedent misrepresented her opinion of her health with "actual intent to deceive" this issue should also be presented to the jury. Of course, the issue or issues to be submitted to the jury on retrial must be governed by the proof offered. . . .

. . . The decision of the Court of Appeals is reversed and the case remanded for a new trial. . . .

PROBLEM

The facts of a Tennessee jury case are digested here (many being omitted). The claim was based on a $50,000 policy on the life of Tony Ginn. His widow, Pamela Ginn, won a verdict and judgment in the trial court. On appeal, the insurer assailed an instruction given to the jury, in that it relied on language in *Gatlin*. The insurer thought that the facts were more nearly analogous to those in Broyles v. Ford Life, a case described in the *Gatlin* opinion. Whether *Broyles* or *Gatlin* was more like the situation presented here is submitted to your judgment. [For the court's conclusion, see Ginn v. American Heritage Life Ins. Co., 173 S.W.3d 433 (Tenn.App. 2004).]

Mrs. Ginn had bought the policy when solicited at her place of work as a seamstress. She then told the salesman that her husband was in "basic good health". That statement was the basis for the insurer's rejection of her claim. Mr. Ginn had died of a myocardial infarction the day after Mrs. Ginn received the policy. At the time of the purchase, he was taking medication every day for stomach spasms. According to Mrs. Ginn's testimony, her husband was going to a doctor on a regular basis during the last year of his life, although he would do so only when the pain was so bad that he "couldn't take it no longer." On one occasion, apparently not long before Mrs. Ginn bought the insurance, he had made the following entries on a "Patient Information Sheet":

Diverticulitis; High Blood Pressure; Adrenal Nodule 2.3 x 1.7 cm, Hidal Hernia (sic); and Hemerode Disease (sic).

The diverticulitis had been treated with antibiotics some eight years before Mrs. Ginn applied for the policy, and again the year before. On the second occasion he had lost 60 pounds (of 190), though he was able to regain 20 of that. Despite his medical problems, Mr. Ginn continued working at a paint and body shop, and took part in recreation with his children.

What differentiates these facts from those of *Gatlin*? From those of *Broyles*?

NOTES

(1) *The Law of New York.* The following provision appears in the New York Insurance Code:

> A misrepresentation that an applicant for life or accident and health insurance has not had previous medical treatment, consultation or observation, or has not had previous treatment or care in a hospital or other like institution, shall be deemed, for the purpose of determining its materiality, a misrepresentation that the applicant has not had the disease, ailment or other medical impairment for which such treatment or care was given or which was discovered by any licensed medical practitioner as a result of such consultation or observation. If in any action to rescind any such contract or to recover thereon, any such misrepresentation is proved by the insurer, and the insured or any other person having or claiming a right under such contract shall prevent full disclosure and proof of the nature of such medical impairment, such misrepresentation shall be presumed to have been material.[5]

If the law of New York is otherwise like that applied in *Johnson*, what result in the case under the law of New York?

(2) *Fact* vs. *Opinion.* When Viola Turner applied for insurance on her life, she answered "no" to the question whether or not she had "been diagnosed with . . . congestive heart failure" within the previous 24 months. In fact she had, although she did not know it. The policy applied for was issued. After Ms. Turner's death the insurer, learning of the error, brought an action to rescind the contract. The trial court declined to enter a summary judgment for the insurer. On appeal, *held*: Reversed. Alfa Life Ins. Corp. v. Lewis, 910 So.2d 757 (Ala. 2005). "[W]e hold that Turner's incorrect answer . . ., although innocently given, is a sufficient basis for Alfa's rescission of the policy, if that answer was material to Alfa's issuance of the policy [as, the court said, it was]."

The case was governed by an Alabama statute similar to a good many others on the subject. It reads, in part: "All statements and descriptions in any application for an insurance policy or annuity contract, or in negotiations therefor, by, or in behalf of, the insured or annuitant shall be deemed to be representations and not warranties. . . . Misrepresentations . . . and incorrect statements shall not prevent a recovery under the policy or contract unless . . . (2) Material either to the acceptance of the risk or to the hazard assumed by the insurer. . . . "

Would it be plausible to say that Ms. Turner made no misrepresentation, in that the question asked for her opinion about diagnoses, and she gave her honest opinion? The court did not say that.

Introductory Note to *Massachusetts Mutual v. Manzo*

"Equitable fraud" is a term used frequently in the opinion in this case. The term was discussed in part II of the *Johnson* opinion, not included above. There the court used the term to indicate an "innocent" misrepresentation—one made without an intent to do wrong. But the court introduced another consideration. Given the general principle that a transaction can be "undone" upon a finding of innocent misrepresentation, an objec-

---

5. Section 3105(d).

tion arises when it is no longer possible to restore the parties to their pre-transaction position. Equitable fraud, the court said "is a debatable doctrine after the loss." How the court dealt with that objection in *Manzo* is an interesting feature of the opinion.

What it means to say that a misrepresentation is "material" was a principal concern of the court. By the law of New Jersey, an insurance claim may fail by reason of a pre-loss misrepresentation even though the matter misrepresented had nothing to do with the cause of the loss. That was the situation in this case it seems. In applying for insurance on his life, Manzo made misrepresentations about symptoms of, and treatment for, diabetes. Presumably that malady was not a cause contributing to his death; his body was found, shot, in the trunk of his car. By hindsight, one might say that Manzo's misrepresentations were not material. But the critical perspective is that of foresight, by the prevailing view.

In support of its conception of materiality the court cited its earlier decision in Longobardi v. Chubb Ins. Co., 582 A.2d 1257 (N.J.1990). There the court said: "The right rule of law, we believe, is one that provides insureds with an incentive to tell the truth...." This is a telling point. But it does not persuade everyone; as will be seen, the law is otherwise in some states.

Massachusetts Mutual Life Ins. Co. v. Manzo

Supreme Court of New Jersey, 1991.
122 N.J. 104, 584 A.2d 190.

On August 31, 1983, an insurer ("Mass. Mutual") issued a policy of insurance for $500,000 on the life of Albert Manzo, Jr., effective on the previous June 13. On the issue date, Manzo was dead, his body having been found on August 22. The insurer brought an action for rescission of the policy against the primary beneficiary, Anna Marie Manzo, and against the Manzo estate. The ground was misrepresentations by Manzo concerning, in the main, diabetes. The New Jersey Chancery Division granted rescission. On a first appeal, the Appellate Division reversed. That court said that Mass. Mutual had failed to prove that Manzo's diabetes either rendered him uninsurable or had caused his death. It ordered reformation of the policy, thereby entitling defendants to the death benefit, less the premiums that Manzo would have paid had Mass. Mutual known of his disease.

On a second review, the Supreme Court reinstated the judgment of rescission. As to the facts, it said: "the application asked Manzo whether he had been 'advised of, treated for, or had any other known indication of' diabetes or sugar in his urine. The application also inquired whether Manzo had consulted a physician within the preceding five years. Manzo answered these questions falsely. He also falsely answered the question whether he had suffered any 'mental or physical disorder' within the preceding five years. The trial court found that Manzo knew and believed that he had diabetes at the time that he answered those questions."

■ POLLOCK, J.

... In sum, we hold that equitable fraud should be available as a grounds for post-loss rescission and that within the period of contestability an insurer may rescind a policy if the insured knowingly misrepresented facts that would have affected the estimate of the risk and the premium charged.

-II-

Initially, the Appellate Division questioned the fairness of allowing a life insurer to invoke equitable fraud after the death of the insured. The principle that equitable fraud, like legal fraud, is available to rescind a life insurance policy even after the death of the insured is, however, "firmly embedded in the jurisprudence of this State." *Formosa v. Equitable Life Assurance Soc'y*, 166 *N.J.Super.* 8, 13, 398 A.2d 1301 (App.Div.), *certif. denied*, 81 *N.J.* 53, 404 A.2d 1153 (1979) (citations omitted). Purporting to rely on *Johnson v. Metropolitan Life Insurance Co.....*, the Appellate Division concluded that rescission based on equitable fraud would be unduly harsh because the parties could not be restored to their position before Manzo's death. The *Johnson* opinion, however, did not undermine the fundamental principle that equitable fraud is available to rescind a life insurance contract after the insured's death.... *Johnson* held only that equitable fraud was not available to the insurer as a grounds for rescission after the expiration of the period of contestability.... In *Johnson*, we did not address whether equitable fraud would be available to rescind an insurance policy after a loss, but within that contestability period.

[*Formosa* and another case cited] held that a life insurance policy may be rescinded because of equitable fraud, even after the death of the insured, if the insurer files suit within the period of contestability.... Viewed in isolation, this rule may sometimes yield a seemingly harsh result. The rule must be considered, however, in light of *N.J.S.A.* 17B:25–4, which renders a life insurance policy incontestable, except for non-payment of premiums, two years after issuance. So viewed, the rule reflects a fair balancing of the interests of the insurer and the insured.

The statute provides:

> There shall be a provision that the policy (exclusive of provisions of the policy or any contract supplemental thereto relating to disability benefits or to additional benefits in event of death by accident or accidental means or in event of dismemberment or loss of sight) shall be incontestable, except for nonpayment of premiums, after it has been in force during the lifetime of the insured for a period of 2 years from its date of issue.

[*N.J.S.A.* 17B:25–4.]

Through limiting the time period in which insurance companies could contest life insurance contracts, the Legislature balanced the interests of the insurer in rescinding a fraudulently-obtained policy with those of the insured in security of coverage. By its terms, the statute does not limit contestability to the lifetime of the insured. We would contravene the words and policy of the statute if we were to impose such a limitation. A court may not disregard the plain words of a statute merely because they occasionally lead to an unhappy result. Within the period of contestability, an insurer may contest a policy for equitable fraud whether the insured is dead or alive. . . .

-III-

It remains to consider whether Mass. Mutual has established that Manzo committed equitable fraud. To warrant rescission, Manzo's misrepresentations must be material within the meaning of *N.J.S.A.* 17B:24–3(d), which provides:

> The falsity of any statement in the application for any policy or contract covered by this section may not bar the right to recovery thereunder unless such false statement materially affected either the acceptance of the risk or the hazard assumed by the insurer.[a]

In its construction of the statute, the Appellate Division concluded that the insurer must prove that the insured lied with the intent to defraud, and that the misrepresented disability either rendered the insured uninsurable or was causally related to his or her death. We disagree with both conclusions.

-A-

We first discuss the Appellate Division's conclusion that *N.J.S.A.* 17B:24–3(d) allows rescission only if the applicant had an "intent to defraud" the insurance company. . . . The imposition of that requirement was error.

N.J.S.A. 17B:24–3(d) addresses only the effect of the false statement on the actions of the insurer. It says nothing about the intent of the insured. . . .

The Appellate Division was concerned about the seeming unfairness of permitting an insurer to rescind after the death of the insured on the basis of an unintentional misrepresentation. New Jersey courts have traditionally attempted to alleviate this apparent unfairness by distinguishing between "subjective" and "objective" questions. . . . The line between the terms is sometimes indistinct. For example, courts have characterized the questions "do you have diabetes," and "have you any physical defect," as subjective. [*Formosa*; *Russ v. Metropolitan Life Ins. Co.*, 112 *N.J.Super.* 265, 278–79, 270 A.2d 759 (Law Div.1970).] In the present case, however, the parties have not questioned the distinction in the lower courts or before us. Furthermore, we are confronted with an insured who knowingly misrepresented that he did not have diabetes. Hence, we need not consider the extent to which an innocent misrepresentation may justify the rescission of a life insurance policy.

a. The following subsection is "e. This section shall not apply to group life insurance, group health insurance, or blanket insurance policies or to group annuity contracts."

-B-

We now turn to the interpretation of the "materiality" requirements of *N.J.S.A.* 17B:24–3(d). The language of the statute is in the disjunctive. A false statement bars "the right of recovery" if it "materially affected *either* the acceptance of the risk *or* the hazard assumed by the insurer." *N.J.S.A.* 17B:24–3(d) (emphasis added). The Appellate Division determined that Manzo's misrepresentations did not affect either alternative. In making that determination, the Appellate Division concluded that only those misrepresentations that render an applicant uninsurable are material to the acceptance of the risk. We believe that conclusion is too restrictive. So stringent a test would be an incentive for dishonesty; it puts the dishonest applicant in a better position than the honest one. Under such a test, an insurer would be bound unless the misrepresented disability would have precluded the issuance of the policy. Thus, the dishonest applicant would stand to gain if the lie goes undetected and would risk nothing by lying.

We believe that a better test of materiality is one that encourages applicants to be honest. See *Longobardi v. Chubb*, 121 *N.J.* 530, 541–42, 582 *A.*2d 1257. That belief is supported by established law.

In 1922, the Court of Errors and Appeals found that false concealment of medical history on a life insurance application was material to the insurer's risk if it "naturally and reasonably influence[d] the judgment of the underwriter in making the contract at all, or in estimating the degree or character of the risk, or in fixing the rate of premium." *Kerpchak v. John Hancock Mut. Ins. Co.*, 97 *N.J.L.* 196, 198, 117 *A.* 836 (1922). Here, the Appellate Division concluded that the Legislature had overruled *Kerpchak* by enacting *N.J.S.A.* 17B:24–3(d), which permits rescission only if a false statement "materially affected either the acceptance of the risk or the hazard assumed." 234 *N.J.Super.* at 287, 560 *A.*2d 1215. We find no support for that conclusion. Contrary to the Appellate Division, we conclude that *N.J.S.A.* 17B:24–3(d) was not intended to alter the *Kerpchak* definition of materiality.

New Jersey courts have uniformly relied on *Kerpchak* to determine the materiality of false statements in life insurance applications. . . . By denying coverage to insureds who lie, the test encourages applicants to tell the truth.

. . .

Leading commentators on insurance law similarly have embraced a definition based on whether the misrepresentation reasonably related to the estimation of the risk or the assessment of the premium. *See* Appleman, *supra*, § 7294 at 368; 7 Couch, *Insurance 2d* § 35:79 at 127 (1965) (Couch). Additionally, the test has been widely accepted by courts in other jurisdictions when interpreting language similar to that of *N.J.S.A.* 17B:24–3(d). . . . In sum, we conclude that such a reasonable-relationship test correctly defines the circumstances under which misrepresented facts "materially affect" an insurer's "acceptance of the risk."

In this case, Manzo misrepresented his health and medical history on his application for insurance. If Mass. Mutual had known the facts, it would have requested more information and issued a policy at a premium two and one-half times the standard rate that Manzo was charged. Thus, Manzo's misrepresentations "naturally and reasonably" affected Mass. Mutual's estimation of the degree of the risk and its calculation of the premium. It follows that the misrepresentations "materially affected ... the acceptance of the risk" and that Mass. Mutual is entitled to rescind the policy. As regrettable as the loss of coverage may be to his beneficiary, that loss is compelled by Manzo's misrepresentations.

[On the reasoning below] "the hazard assumed ... includes the requirement that there be a causal connection between the insured's false statements and the ultimate cause of death." ...

By requiring a causal connection between the disability misrepresented and the insured's death, the decision below conflicts not only with *Formosa*, but also with the general rule that "in the absence of a statute establishing a different rule, there need be no causal connection between the cause of death and the misrepresentation." Couch, *supra*, § 37:110 at 632. This rule is accepted by a majority of jurisdictions. Couch, *supra*, §§ 37:87 at 102 and 37:110 at 632; Appleman, *supra*, § 245 at 125; R. Keeton and A. Widiss, *Insurance Law, A Guide to Fundamental Principles, Legal Doctrines and Commercial Practices* 572 n. 20 (West 1988) (the "clear majority rule" is that no causal connection is required); *see, e.g., Shafer v. John Hancock Mut. Life Ins. Co.*, 410 *Pa.* 394, 399, 189 A.2d 234, 237 (1963) ("It is of no consequence that the death ensued from a cause unconnected with the false representations."). We are persuaded that the majority rule is the correct one. An insurer is entitled to relief when it relies on incorrect information provided by an insured in an insurance application if the information was material either to the insurer's decision to insure or to the terms of the contract. As the Legislature perceived in *N.J.S.A.* 17B:24–3(d), the law should encourage insureds to tell the truth, not to conceal information from the insurer and gamble that they will not die of a concealed disease.

The judgment of the Appellate Division is reversed and the judgment of the Chancery Division is reinstated.

B. Insurance Warranties

A breach of an insurance warranty affords a defense for the insurer, subject to various qualifications. This proposition entails three questions at the forefront of this Section: What constitutes a *warranty*, in the lingo of insurance? How is the fact of a breach determined? (Commonly, of course, this question calls for construing the language of the warranty in question.) And third: In what circumstances can a breach be disregarded?

The New York Standard Fire Insurance Policy

The New York Standard Fire Policy, now set out at § 3404 of the State's Insurance Code, is widely accepted as a template form. It is prescribed by statute in most states, in the sense that an insurer providing fire insurance on other terms must not make those terms less favorable than those enacted. The policy form includes two terms generally regarded as creating warranties, as follows:

> *Conditions suspending or restricting insurance.* Unless otherwise provided in writing added thereto this Company shall not be liable for loss occurring (a) while the hazard is increased by any means within the control or knowledge of the insured, or (b) while a described building, whether intended for occupancy by owner or tenant, is vacant or unoccupied beyond a period of 60 consecutive days....

Clause (a) is called the "increase-of-hazard" (IOH) warranty. It was echoed in the policy under litigation in the case that follows. There the trial court found that the insurer had failed to demonstrate any increase of hazard, so that there was no breach of the IOH warranty.

The appellate court did not actually call the IOH provision a warranty. But it set out a definition of "warranty" which seems clearly to embrace clause (a), and to embrace clause (b) as well.

The fact that a provision of a fire policy is mandated by statute sometimes has major significance. See, for example, Pappas Ent. v. Commerce & Ind. Ins. Co., 661 N.E.2d 81 (Mass. 1996), a case construing the warranty against long-term vacancy. There the court acknowledged the general principle that an ambiguity in a policy should be construed against the interest of the insurer. But it said: "That principle has no proper place in construing policy language that is, as in this case, dictated by statute." In the opinion that follows the court had to construe the term "owner occupied". It did so in a way favoring the interest of the claimant, noticing a tendency not to project language of that sort into the future. That tendency might be at odds with the remark just quoted if the term "owner occupied" were included in the standard fire policy. But it is not.

Another provision of the standard fire policy is also mentioned in the following opinion. The standard provision is:

> This entire policy shall be void if, whether before or after a loss, the insured has wilfully concealed or misrepresented any material fact or circumstance concerning this insurance or the subject thereof, or the interest of the insured therein, or in case of any fraud or false swearing by the insured relating thereto.

This provision is not generally regarded as a warranty. On reading the opinion you should have in mind the question, Why not?

For the moment, no attention need be paid to the question how it matters whether or not a given policy provision is a warranty. Materials on that question begin four pages after this one.

Reid v. Hardware Mutual Ins. Co. of The Carolinas, Inc.

Supreme Court of South Carolina, 1969.
252 S.C. 339, 166 S.E.2d 317.

Zelphia Reid brought this action on a policy issued to her by the Hardware Mutual Insurance Company ("Hardware"), insuring her against fire damage to a property described as a "one story frame constructed, approved roof, owner occupied, one family dwelling." The property had been destroyed by fire. More than a year before that, Ms. Reid had conveyed the property to M.E. Tollison. Sitting without a jury, the trial court entered a judgment in favor of Reid. On appeal, Hardware sought reversal on several grounds, each related in one way or another to the transfer. As presented here, the opinion deals with only two of those grounds.

■ Moss, CHIEF JUSTICE.

Among the conditions attached, and under the title "Conditions suspending or restricting insurance" there was stated: "Unless otherwise provided in writing added thereto this Company shall not be liable for loss occurring (a) while the hazard is increased by any means within the control or knowledge of the insured; . . . ."

The appellant contends that it is not liable for the fire loss that occurred because there was an increase in the hazard insured against by reason of the respondent's conveyance of the insured property to a third party who made certain improvements and repairs thereto and converted the premises to rental property.

The record shows that following the conveyance of the insured premises by the respondent to Milford E. Tollison that he placed a new roof on the dwelling and installed a hot water heater, water piping, new windows, bath fixtures and new water pump and tank. It also appears that after such repairs and improvements had been made that the dwelling was occupied by a tenant. The trial judge held that the record is devoid of any basis for a finding or conclusion that the hazard insured against was increased by the conveyance of the insured premises to Tollison or the improvements and repairs made thereto by him and its conversion to rental property. This finding of fact by the trial judge has the same force and effect as the verdict of a jury unless the evidence is reasonably susceptible of the opposite conclusion only . . . . . We have carefully examined the record in this case and find that there is ample evidence to support the conclusion of the trial judge.

The policy with which we are concerned provided that the same would be void if the insured willfully concealed or misrepresented any material fact or circumstance concerning this insurance or the subject thereof or the interest of the insured therein. The trial judge has found that the appellant did not contend that the insured willfully concealed or misrepresented any material fact but asserted that under the foregoing provision it was entitled to notice of the change in ownership. The policy does not so provide but only makes such policy void in the event the insured willfully concealed or misrepresented any material fact. The record is devoid of proof that the respondent willfully concealed or misrepresented any material fact.

The final question for determination is whether the designation, at the time the policy was issued, that the insured dwelling was "owner occupied" was a continuing warranty.

A warranty, in the law of insurance, is a statement, description, or undertaking on the part of the insured, appearing in the policy of insurance or in another instrument properly incorporated in the policy, relating contractually to the risk insured against. Generically, warranties are either affirmative or promissory. An affirmative warranty is one which asserts the existence of a fact at the time the policy is entered into, and appears on the face of said policy, or is attached thereto and made a part thereof. A promissory warranty may be defined to be an absolute undertaking by the insured, contained in a policy or in a paper properly incorporated by reference, that certain facts or conditions pertaining to the risk shall continue, or that certain things with reference thereto shall be done or omitted. 29 Am. Jur., Insurance, Sections 708 and 709. While it is generally recognized that a warranty may be "promissory" or "continuing", the tendency is to construe a statement in the past or present tense as constituting an affirmative rather than a continuing warranty. Thus, a description of a house in a policy of insurance, as "occupied by" the insured, is a description merely and is not an agreement that the insured should continue in the occupation of it. *Joyce v. Maine Ins. Co.*, 45 Me. 168. *O'Niel v. Buffalo Fire Ins. Co.*, 3 N.Y. 122. A statement in an insurance policy that the property is occupied by the insured as a dwelling for himself and family, is not a warranty that it shall continue to be so occupied but is only a warranty of the situation at the time the insurance is effected. *German Ins. Co. v. Russell*, 65 Kan. 373, 69 P. 345, 58 L.R.A. 234.

There is no provision in the policy contract that the dwelling would be "owner occupied" during the term of the insurance contract nor any requirement that if the premises are otherwise occupied than by the owner, notice of such change of occupancy or use would be given to the insurer.

The insurance contract here involved contained a description of the dwelling insured as being "owner occupied". This was an affirmative warranty, not a continuing warranty, by the respondent that the dwelling was so occupied by him at the time the contract of insurance was made. The appellant argues that a breach of the warranty as to occupancy at the time the contract of insurance was made would defeat a recovery by the respondent. Even though this question is argued in the brief it is not supported by an exception and raises no issue for determination by us. . . . It is our conclusion that the representation by the respondent that the insured dwelling was owner occupied at the effective date of the insurance contract was not a continuing warranty but an affirmative one.

. . . Affirmed.

NOTES

(1) *Alternate Reasoning.* An alternate way to arrive at the same conclusion would be to say that, although "owner occupied" was a promissory warranty, so that there was a breach, the breach should be disregarded because the insurer failed to show that it was a material breach. Other entries in this Section concern the standing of the proposition that an immaterial breach of warranty affords no defense to an insurer.

(2) *Heniser's Case.* The *Reid* case was discussed at some length in Heniser v. Frankenmuth Mutual Insurance, 534 N.W.2d 502 (Mich. 1995). Heniser brought the action on a homeowner's policy to recover for the destruction of a home by fire. One defense made by the insurer was that he had sold the home before the loss (retaining title only to secure the unpaid part of the purchase price). Heniser's claim depended on a showing that the home was within the policy definition of "residence premises", which included the phrase "where you reside". Read as a whole, the court said, the policy was unambiguous; it "does not cover the loss because the property was not a 'residence premises' at the time of the loss." Also, the policy was clear: "if Mr. Heniser did not 'reside' at the insured property at the time of the loss, the property is not a 'residence premises,' as defined by the policy, and the policy does not cover the loss."

In *Reid*, the court said, the *owner occupied* language was "in a list of statements describing the building covered by the policy. Read in context, it is clear that 'owner occupied' was simply a description of the dwelling in the same way that stating the building had an 'approved roof' merely commented on the structure at the time the policy was created." Yet the court said also that, in *Reid*, the critical language was viewed as an affirmative warranty. On that basis, the court said, the cases were distinguishable: unlike the language in *Reid*, "the phrase 'where you reside' in the policy before us is not a warranty but a statement of coverage." If it were construed as an affirmative warranty, "we would freeze coverage at the time the policy is entered into and render subsequent events irrelevant."

Justice Levin dissented from the *Heniser* decision, relying in part on the decision in *Reid*.

(3) *"Affirmative"* vs. *"Promissory"*. In a policy insuring a fishing vessel this term appeared:

> It is understood and agreed that the Captain of the vessel is Gregory P. Walker.... If [he] is not aboard the vessel while it is navigating, and if Underwriters have not previously agreed to a suitable replacement, coverage under this policy shall be suspended until [he] returns to the vessel.[1]

Possibly this term comprised two warranties, an affirmative one in the first sentence and a promissory one in the second. Otherwise, the term constituted a warranty of *both* types. Cf. the court's observation in *Reid*: "Generically, warranties are either affirmative or promissory."

The promissory aspect of some warranties marks a clear differentiation between warranty and representation, for a representation can relate only to the present. To be sure, as pointed out above, one can make an assertion about one's present intention: *e.g.*, "We mean to retain Walker as captain." And that might be a falsehood. But if it were truthful, it would not become a misrepresentation if Walker were to be replaced.

---

1. Yu v. Albany Ins. Co., 281 F.3d 803 (9th Cir. 2002).

The Massachusetts "Condition Precedent"

Martin Fraidowitz bought disability insurance from the Massachusetts Mutual Insurance Company. The policy had an "increased-benefits option", by which Fraidowitz could add to the benefits during an annual option period. That privilege was made subject, however, to the qualification that *"if [he were to be] disabled during any option period [then the] option to buy additional benefits [would be] postponed until the option period following [his] recovery."* After suffering from depression, for which he was treated, Fraidowitz applied for additional benefits. In doing so, he answered a question put by the insurer, saying that he was not then disabled. His tender of an additional premium for the additional coverage was accepted. Later, however, the insurer brought an action for a declaratory judgment that it was not bound to afford the additional coverage.

Fraidowitz was in an awkward situation when making the application. He had already submitted a disability claim, and was pursuing it. Mass Mutual was in an awkward situation also: it had contested the claim (relying on advice of the sort "Fraidowitz is a faker, who does not want to work"). Why, then, take his money for the additional coverage?

Fraidowitz appealed from a summary judgment against him. He persuaded the court to say that it was "not obvious" that he had made a misrepresentation, in view of all he had said when applying. But the court affirmed. It relied on the provision italicized above, calling it a condition precedent, and on these propositions of Massachusetts law:

- A statement required by an insured in applying for insurance may either be a warranty, or it may establish a condition precedent.

- If an insured fails to satisfy a condition precedent, the coverage is void regardless of whether there was proof of an intent to deceive or an increased risk of loss.

- [A] statement required of the insured is a condition precedent to obtaining coverage only if (1) the statement relates "essentially to the insurer's intelligent decision to issue" the coverage, and (2) the statement is "made a condition precedent to recovery under the policy, either by using the precise words 'condition precedent' or their equivalent[.]" Charles, Henry & Crowley Co. v. Homes Ins. Co., 212 N.E.2d 240, 242 (Mass. 1965).

Massachusetts Mut. Life Ins. Co. v. Fraidowitz, 443 F.3d 128, 132 (1st Cir. 2006).

The New York "Warranty"

What follows is a provision of the New York Insurance Law which defines *warranty*, and makes a statement about the effect of a breach. According to the definition, a warranty is either of two specified types of conditions precedent. The two types are identified below by numerical insertions. Naturally, the word *warranty* is sometimes used in ways less precise, and less circumscribed, than this provision indicates.

Section 3106. *Warranty defined; effect of breach*

(a) In this section "warranty" means any provision of an insurance contract which has the effect of requiring, [i] as a condition precedent of the taking effect of such contract or [ii] as a condition precedent of the insurer's liability thereunder, the existence of a fact which tends to diminish, or the non-existence of a fact which tends to increase, the risk of the occurrence of any loss, damage, or injury within the coverage of the contract. The term "occurrence of loss, damage, or injury" includes the occurrence of death, disability, injury, or any other contingency insured against, and the term "risk" includes both physical and moral hazards.

(b) A breach of warranty shall not avoid an insurance contract or defeat recovery thereunder unless such breach materially increases the risk of loss, damage or injury within the coverage of the contract. If the insurance contract specified two or more distinct kinds of loss, damage or injury which are within its coverage, a breach of warranty shall not avoid such contract or defeat recovery thereunder with respect to any kind or kinds of loss, damage or injury other than the kind or kinds to which such warranty relates and the risk of which is materially increased by the breach of such warranty.

(c) [The foregoing provisions do not affect certain major warranties under marine-insurance contracts, nor certain post-loss conditions. See Note 1, p. 228 below.]

QUESTION

In how many and what ways does the New York "warranty" differ from the Massachusetts "condition precedent"?

Minimizing by a Maxim

This Note describes a technique for limiting the scope of a warranty ("minimizing" it) by using a precept ("maxim") for construing a contract. Several precepts about the meaning of a particular term call on one or more other terms for assistance. Examples are *ejusdem generis* and *noscitur a sociis* ("a word is known by the company it keeps," Gustafson v. Alloyd Co., 513 U.S. 561, 575 (1995)). These are readily applied to elucidate the significance of terms in insurance contracts. The one noticed here is the maxim that a specific term controls a general term.

An illustration can be made of the facts in Reid v. Hardware Mutual. There the policy contained an "increase-of-hazard" term, and an "owner occupied" term. Let it be supposed that the former constituted a *general* warranty, and the latter a *specific* warranty requiring continuous occupation by the owner. The maxim suggests that a change of occupancy could not have been a breach of the increase-of-hazard (IOH) warranty, even if the new occupant was a more risky one than Reid was. The argument is, in other words, that the policy said everything it had to say about occupancy in the words "owner occupied", and that some other change of circumstances was required to establish a breach of the IOH warranty (storing large quantities of fireworks on the premises, say). On that reasoning, it would not have mattered how the property was treated by the transferee,

Tollison, or by his tenant. If the policy contained also a warranty against overlong unoccupancy, the argument would have to be adjusted a bit, but would not lose its force.

In Heniser's case ("where you reside") Justice Levin, dissenting, used similar reasoning. He sought to show, by reference to another policy term, that Heniser's claim was not defeated by the sale of Heniser's home. The other term stated, as conditions, "Your duties after loss". One of these was to provide, on request, a proof of loss indicating "changes in title or occupancy of the property during the term of the policy...." Drawing an inference from this term, Justice Levin said: "because the policy does not oblige the insured to notify the insurer of a change of occupancy until after a fire loss, it is at least ambiguous whether 'where you reside' speaks as of an indefinite future date after issuance requiring the insured to actually reside in the dwelling when a fire loss may occur."

As indicated above, the standard fire policy contains, side by side, an IOH warranty and a warranty that the property insured is not to remain vacant for a period longer than 60 days. The maxim, Specific > General, might be apt in a case of vacancy for a shorter period. Perhaps an insurer should not be heard to say, in that case, that the vacancy increased the fire hazard; for the specific 60–day warranty preempts the more general IOH warranty on the subject of vacancy. Compare this thought with Justice Levin's reasoning about the proof-of-loss condition. Which is more apt, as an application of the maxim?

Recalling that the standard fire policy is installed by statute in most states, one might question the reasoning in the foregoing paragraph; a given precept about construing contracts may not work in construing statutes. But this one does. On the other hand, the Supreme Court has said, in relation to a statute, that the precept applies only when there is conflict between the specific and the general.[2] Consider a one-month period of vacancy in relation to the increase-of-hazard warranty. Is there conflict between that warranty and the 60–day warranty?

———

Dynasty, Inc. v. Princeton Ins. Co.

Supreme Court of New Jersey, 2000.
165 N.J. 1, 754 A.2d 1137.

Hollywood Lights was a "virtual nightclub" in Bloomfield, N.J., owned by Dynasty, Inc. In June of 1994 it was destroyed by fire. Dynasty made a claim on a fire policy issued by Princeton Insurance, and when the claim was resisted brought this action on the policy. There was uncontradicted evidence that arson was the cause of the fire. Princeton's theory at trial was that the owner of Dynasty, Donald Esposito, had set the fire, or had facilitated it, in order to alleviate financial burdens associated with the

---

2. Also: "The specific controls but only within its self-described scope." See National Cable & Telecommunications Ass'n, Inc. v. Gulf Power Co., 534 U.S. 327, 335–36 (2002).

business. Esposito denied any complicity or knowledge in the setting of the fire and specifically denied under oath that he had turned off the sprinkler system. He suggested that a former investor in Dynasty may have set the fire as an act of vengeance.

The trial judge instructed a jury that there was no coverage if the fire was brought about by, or at the direction of or with the knowledge, consent, or acquiescence of, Dynasty through its officer, Esposito. The jury returned a verdict in favor of Dynasty.

There was evidence that Esposito had disabled a sprinkler system at the premises, and so (Princeton contended) had "facilitated" the arson. The sprinkler system was found chain-locked in the "off" position at the time of the fire. About two months before, when the system was installed and inspected by the local fire department, its control valve had been locked in the "on" position. Esposito testified that the key for the valve was kept nearby in the event that someone, presumably a patron, intentionally activated the sprinkler with a cigarette lighter.

Princeton had asked the judge to instruct the jury as follows: "if you find that the sprinkler system had been turned off, without justifiable reason by means within the control or knowledge of [Dynasty] through its officers or principals, . . . you must find for the defendant." The basis for the requested instruction was this term in the policy:

> Unless otherwise provided in writing added hereto this Company shall not be liable for loss occurring. . . . while the hazard is increased by any means within the control or knowledge of the insured. . . .

The term is standard language required by a New Jersey statute. The judge had refused to give the requested instruction, calling it "in essence duplicative" of the one about arson. ("If [Esposito] interfered with the sprinkler system, knowing that there was going to be a fire, it's the same as if he lit it as far as I'm concerned.")

A first appeal by Princeton was unsuccessful. Further review ensued.

■ VERNIERO, J. . . .

II.

. . .

To resolve this dispute, we must answer four related questions: Does an intentionally-disabled sprinkler system constitute an increase of hazard? Was the charge given by the trial court duplicative of Princeton's proposed charge? Was there a basis in the evidence to sustain a separate increase-of-hazard charge? If that charge should have been given, did the court's failure to deliver the charge constitute reversible error?

A.

We first consider whether an intentionally-disabled sprinkler system constitutes an increase of hazard within the meaning of the statute. The Appellate Division in Industrial Development Associates v. Commercial Union Surplus Lines Insurance Co., 222 N.J.Super. 281, 291–92, 536 A.2d

787 (App.Div.), *certif. denied*, 546 A.2d 546 (1988), succinctly summarized the law in this area:

> "An increase in hazard takes place when a new use is made of the insured property, or when its physical condition is changed from that which existed when the policy was written, and the new use or changed condition increases the risk assumed by the insurer." [8 George J. Couch, Cyclopedia of Insurance Law § 37A:291, at 329 (Mark S. Rhodes ed., 2d ed. rev. vol. 1985)]. An increase of hazard will generally not be found if there has been merely " ... a casual change of a temporary character." Id. at 330. Thus, the negligence of the insured does not constitute an increase in the hazard, unless that negligence results in a change of some duration of the structure, use or occupancy of the premises. Orient Ins. Co. v. Cox, [218 Ark. 804, 238 S.W.2d 757, 761–62 (Ark. 1951)]; Couch, *supra*, § 37A:280 at 316. Whether there has been an increase of hazard suspending coverage under a policy is a question of fact which should be determined by a jury unless the evidence is so conclusive that reasonable minds could not differ. Orient Ins. Co. v. Cox, *supra*, 238 S.W.2d at 762; Couch, supra, § 37A:302 at 346. Moreover, the insurer bears the burden of proving that the insured has increased the hazard. Couch, *supra* at § 37A:305 at 352.

In applying those tenets, we must decide whether a sprinkler system locked in the off position represents a "new use" of the insured's property or a "changed condition" that has increased the risk assumed by the insurer....

[The court reviewed precedents in and out of New Jersey. It found very little assistance in them, and none in legislative history.]

... That said, we can discern no reason to exclude from the purview of an increase-of-hazard clause an insured who unjustifiably disables a sprinkler system using any method directly within the insured's knowledge or control. In our view, an insured who acts in such a manner has forfeited or suspended the underlying insurance policy as contemplated by the statute.

That Dynasty's policy fails to denominate specifically a disabled sprinkler as an increase of hazard is not dispositive. By design, increase-of-hazard clauses are stated in general terms because parties to an insurance contract cannot with certainty spell out every possible scenario that may lead to an increase of hazard. In that regard, one legal commentator has observed:

> The standard fire insurance policy and many other kinds of property insurance policies state that the insurer shall not be liable for loss occurring "while the hazard is increased by any means within the control or knowledge of the insured." This clause can be viewed as a modern-day warranty. Instead of including a laundry-list of situations in which insureds would forfeit coverage if they failed to take certain risk-reducing measures, insurers now state that insureds lose coverage in the event the hazard is increased. Such a condition is eminently reasonable; even if this provision were not set forth in an insurance

policy in express terms, it would be an implied term in the policy that the insured could not do anything to materially increase the risk during the policy's term without forfeiting the coverage.

[Robert H. Jerry, II, Understanding Insurance Law § 62B, at 375 (2d ed. 1996) (footnote omitted).]

Consistent with those observations, we are persuaded that an insured's unjustified disabling of a sprinkler system falls within the realm of an increase-of-hazard clause. Accordingly, coverage will be suspended pursuant to that clause provided the insurer proves the insured's conduct to the satisfaction of the jury.

[On considering the other issues before it, the court concluded that the trial court "erred in instructing the jury solely on arson", and so "unjustly denied the insurer an alternative basis on which to defend this action."]

III.

We emphasize that this is an idiosyncratic case. The more typical application of an increase-of-hazard clause involves some change in the physical condition of the property or some new use that is alleged to have increased a hazard that did not exist prior to the issuance of the policy. *Industrial, supra*, 222 N.J. Super. at 291–92. We also reiterate that casual, temporary changes generally do not amount to an increase of hazard, nor does the negligence of the insured constitute an increase of hazard "unless that negligence results in a change of some duration of the structure, use or occupancy of the premises." Ibid.

Our holding today is dictated as much by common sense as by a straightforward reading of the statute. . . . By plain logic, an insured who is alleged to have disabled a sprinkler system may be found on sufficient proofs to have increased the hazard by changing the condition of the premises using means within his or her control or knowledge. We cannot fathom that the Legislature would have intended a contrary conclusion in mandating the increase-of-hazard clause in policies like the one issued to Dynasty. In other words, we are persuaded that Princeton did not assume the risk that a sprinkler system required by the local fire code would be chain-locked in the off position at the time of this fire. Accordingly, the insurer was entitled to have the jury consider whether the increase-of-hazard clause in Dynasty's policy operated to suspend coverage on the record presented.

IV.

The judgment of the Appellate Division is reversed and the matter is remanded to the trial court for further proceedings.

[Justice Long dissented. "I am in complete agreement," he said, "with the majority's crystalline clarification of the previously murky law of increase-of-hazard." He disagreed, however, with the court's finding evidence requiring an increase-of-hazard instruction. Princeton had made a "thin circumstantial case" that Esposito had locked the sprinkler system "off" so as to set or facilitate the fire, and so to alleviate his financial burdens. "There was, however, no evidence, circumstantial or otherwise, that Esposito (or anyone in his control or with his knowledge) locked the system in the off-position for a reason other than to facilitate the arson. That missing proof is what would have been necessary to justify an increase-of-hazard instruction."]

NOTE

A Letter to the Editors. Mr. Allan Maitlin, who represented Princeton, has reported to the editors that a subsequent trial produced the decision, "no cause for action". Mr. Maitlin's letter reports also his opinion, based on long experience, that juries in comparable cases are reluctant to base their verdicts on findings of arson, fearing that "the result will cause the prosecutor's office to either open the case or reopen the case and have the insured go to jail." In the first trial, according to the letter, the judge took the view that the issues of arson and of increase-of-hazard were identical. "As [that judge] succinctly stated [with reference to Esposito], 'Either he set the fire or he didn't.' "

PROBLEMS

(1) In *Dynasty, Inc.*, Princeton's policy contained a specific provision about sprinklers: the coverage did not extend to a loss caused by sprinkler leakage if the property had been vacant for sixty days before the loss and the insured had failed to protect the sprinkler system against freezing. Consider the argument that, because the policy dealt specifically with failure in the system, the IOH warranty could not be broken by disabling the system. If that is a weak argument, what is its weakness?

(2) Suppose, to change the facts in *Dynasty, Inc.*, that Esposito had noticed a leak in the sprinkler system ten days before the fire, had shut the system down, and had neglected to call for repair service. On those facts, should Princeton get a jury instruction about increase of hazard?

Kansas Mill Owners, and Manufacturers, Mutual Fire Ins. Co. v. Metcalf

Kansas Supreme Court, 1898.
59 Kan. 383, 53 P. 68.

■ DOSTER, C. J.

Mrs. S.E.F. Arter was the owner of a mill building, fixtures and machinery, and miller's stock. It was insured by the plaintiff in error. The amount of the policy was payable in the event of loss to the defendant in error [Metcalf]. The mill building, with other insured property, was destroyed by fire about 12 o'clock at night. In the application for the insurance the question was asked: "Do you agree to keep a watchman on the premises at all times when (the mill is) not in operation?" This question was answered, "yes." This question and its answer, of course, formed a part of the insurance contract. Suit was brought upon the policy by [Metcalf], the assignee under the contingency of the loss which occurred.

Verdict was returned and judgment rendered for him, and the defendant, the Insurance Company, prosecuted error to this court.

The testimony in behalf of the plaintiff tended to show that, in the evening preceding the fire, the mill was shut down for the night; that Mrs. Arter engaged one Randolph as watchman during the time it was shut down; that he in turn engaged one Aldrich, the engineer of the mill, to act in his place; that Aldrich was in and about the mill until 10 o'clock P. M., and then went to a tent about two hundred feet distant, which was used by him and his family for household purposes; that he sat in the tent until he heard the alarm of fire; and, going out, he discovered the mill in flames. The special findings of the jury were in accordance with this testimony. Two questions arise. First. Was the suspension of the work of the mill over night a cessation of its operation, within the meaning of the agreement contained in the application for insurance?[2] Second. If so, was a watchman kept upon the premises during such non-operation of the mill? In relation to these two questions the court below instructed the jury as follows:

> "The language used in this agreement is to be taken in its ordinary sense and significance, and the agreement should be construed in the light of common observation and experience. Still some suggestions may be helpful. Thus, when a contract requires a thing to be done, but is silent as to the particular manner of performance, the law holds that it must be reasonable in this respect, having regard to the object and purpose of the stipulation, which, in this case, is the safety of the property. If it is done in the manner in which men of ordinary care and skill in similar business manage their own affairs of like kind, it is ordinarily sufficient. A mere temporary absence of the watchman from the premises in circumstances where a man of reasonable prudence would do the like, would not constitute a breach of the agreement. It does not require that the sole duty of the watchman shall be to watch, and that he shall always be present. He may perform other duties if they do not materially impair his usefulness as a watchman, and he may be temporarily or casually absent, whenever a man of reasonable skill and prudence exercising reasonable and ordinary diligence, would do the same. The functions and duties of a watchman vary in different places and circumstances, according to the danger to which the property is exposed, and the nature and value of the property. The court cannot, in the nature of things, precisely define what particular care a watchman should exercise. The jury must determine that in the particular case. The insured, however, was bound by her contract to have a watchman on the premises when the mill was not in operation and that watchman was bound to exercise reasonable care and diligence in attending to his duties, considering the situation, nature and value of the property, and the dangers that might reasonably be apprehended.

2. As to what constitute "business hours" and "non-business hours", see Raino v. Navigators Ins. Co., 702 N.Y.S.2d 94 (App. Div., 2d Dept., 2000).

"It is proper, also, for me to say, that I do not regard the stoppage of the mill at night, while business is ordinarily and generally suspended, as ceasing to operate it, where it is regularly operated during the usual working hours each day. The words, 'not in operation,' refer to times when work in the mill is not carried on; when it is lying idle, or shut down, and not in the usual nightly suspension of business. With these observations you must find as a question of fact whether the owner, Mrs. Arter, complied with her agreement respecting a watchman, you being the sole judges of the facts."

We approve this instruction so far as it relates to the character and degree of watchfulness to be exercised under the agreement before quoted. Admitting that the shutting down of the mill for the night was a suspension of its operation within the meaning of the insurance contract, yet a watchman was kept on the premises within the terms of the agreement as defined by the court. The jury so found, and the rules laid down by [to?] them by which their conclusion was reached were correct. What we regard as a leading case, and one quite closely in point, is *Hanover Fire Insurance Company v. Gustin*, 40 Neb. 828, 59 N.W. 375. It was there held that "the statement in the application for the issuance of a policy of insurance on a planing mill, that 'a watchman is kept on the premises during the night and at all other times when the works are not in operation or the workmen present,' should receive a reasonable construction, and therefore the mere temporary absence of such watchman within the time contemplated did not necessarily relieve the insurer from liability for loss caused by a fire which originated during such absence."

The opinion following is cogent in reasoning, is replete with citations of authorities, and fully sustains the instruction of the court so far as the one question is concerned. Whether the court erred in that part of the instruction which defined the meaning of the words "not in operation," we need not inquire. If it did, the error was not prejudicial, because the keeping of a watchman on the premises as though the mill "were not in operation," fulfilled all the requirements of the definition of those words as proposed by plaintiff in error.

. . .

The judgment of the court below is affirmed.

NOTE

Warranty? Assuming that a warranty was in question, the foregoing opinion is instructive about how to construe a warranty. It appears that neither the court nor the parties applied the name "warranty" to Mrs. Arter's answer "Yes". But naming is not dispositive.

Consult the New York statutory definition at p. 209 above. How well does it fit the question and answer (Q & A) about watchmen? Watching tends to forestall fire losses, no doubt. Before that, however, one wants to know whether or not watching was any kind of condition on the insurer's accountability.

And before that: Was the Q & A even a "provision of an insurance contract"? On this question the court said two important things: The Q & A "of course" formed a part of the insurance contract; and Mrs. Arter "was bound by her contract to have a watchman on the premises when the mill was not in operation." Taking the court at its word, one can readily believe that the policy contained a reference to the application. But it is hard to shake the contrary impression; perhaps the court meant only that a contract can sometimes be avoided for the misrepresentation of a party's intent.

Warranty vs. Representation

A breach of warranty is at least as momentous as a misrepresentation, as a rule, and is considerably more so in some jurisdictions. A difference is apparent from the argument in a case in which the court applied Hawaii law to a claim on a marine policy. The claim encountered a defense based on a "Captain's warranty". (The case is cited, and the policy quoted from in Note 3, p. 207 above.) According to a Hawaii statute, "A misrepresentation shall not prevent a recovery on the policy unless made with actual intent to deceive or unless it materially affects either the acceptance of the risk or the hazard assumed by the insurer." The claim was based on the sinking of the claimants' fishing vessel, the *Liberty*. She was commanded by one Perez at the time; the person designated as captain in the policy was not aboard then. "If [Walker] is not aboard the vessel while it is navigating," the policy said, "coverage under this policy shall be suspended...."

The claimants invoked the statute as a way to override this provision. The term was a misrepresentation, they said, and did not impair their claim because the insurer had failed to establish fraud or materiality. The court disagreed. The statute, it said, "applies only to statements or descriptions in an application for an insurance policy or in negotiations therefor." The term in question, the court said, "was neither of these, but rather part of the insurance contract itself. Indeed, [the statute] clearly distinguishes between warranties and representations, and imposes limitations only on the latter."[1]

In some bodies of insurance law even an immaterial breach of warranty is fatal to a policy claim. "For nearly a century," it was said recently, "California courts have held that the breach of even an immaterial warranty will void a policy 'where the policy expressly declares that it shall avoid it.'" Certain Underwriters at Lloyd's v. Montford, 52 F.3d 219, 223 (9th Cir. 1995) [citing to and quoting from Fountain v. Connecticut Fire Ins. Co. (The *Fountain* opinion appears next.)] That rule is more stringent than many versions of the law of misrepresentation.

NOTE

Strategy. Representations and warranties may be considered as techniques competing for the favor of insurers as means of evaluating and controlling the risks they assume. For example, when providing insurance against the theft of a truck used to transport valuables, a firm might consider either

- eliciting from the insured a representation that an attendant is habitually present in the truck when it stores valuables, or

---

1.   Yu v. Albany Ins. Co., 281 F.3d 803, 810 (9th Cir. 2002).

- inserting in the policy a warranty that the truck will not be left unattended when it stores valuables.

The comparative merits of these techniques can be considered helpfully from the standpoint of an insurer.

In principle, a misrepresentation on the subject need not be embodied in the policy. The parol evidence rule does not preclude the avoidance of a documented agreement by reason of an oral misrepresentation. In contrast, because a warranty is a contract term highly germane to other terms, the rule would be violated by giving effect to an oral warranty, if made at or before the time of an agreement documented in a policy even moderately complete in itself. Even a recorded warranty would be barred by the rule if the record were not part of the "integrated" contract.

Second, so far as materiality is a requisite of an actionable misrepresentation, and is not a requisite of an operative warranty, an insurer would naturally prefer using a warranty to control the risk assumed, over using a representation to help evaluate the risk.

Third, an insurer has reason to put a warranty in place, rather than to ask for a representation, so far as it is concerned about a change of circumstances that might exacerbate the risk. See Note 3, p. 207 above.

Envisage an acquiescent applicant for insurance—a supplicant—dealing with a canny insurer. If the insurer wishes to avert a particular type of risk by deploying either a representation or a warranty, it can be expected to select the one better fitted to that purpose. What of utilizing a warranty that is neither embodied in the policy nor referred to in it, as compared with a like representation? As indicated above, the parol evidence rule counsels against the former but not the latter. But in this respect any supposed advantage for a representation is illusory. Simple prudence counsels against both. Moreover, statutes in some states extend to representations what may be called a version of the rule. An example is given in the footnote.[2]

What of selecting a warranty, with a view to avoiding an issue of materiality? Again, legislation makes this an illusory basis for choice, in many states, in connection with popular lines of insurance. See, for example, the Alabama statute quoted in Note 2, p. 198 above.

What, then, of dealing with changing circumstances? As to this, to deploy a promissory warranty has a clear advantage over a representation. An affirmative warranty may and may not, depending on applicable law. According to a Louisiana statute, what may be called a "warranty", appearing in an application for life insurance, is to be "deemed" a representation.

2. *Wisconsin Insurance Code* § 631.11. Representations, warranties and conditions. (1) EFFECT OF NEGOTIATIONS FOR CONTRACT.

a) Statement or warranty. No statement, representation or warranty made by a person other than the insurer or an agent of the insurer in the negotiation for an insurance contract affects the insurers obligations under the policy unless it is stated in any of the following:

1. The policy.

2. A written application signed by the person, provided that a copy of the written application is made a part of the policy by attachment or endorsement.

3. A written communication provided by the insurer to the insured within 60 days after the effective date of the policy.

QUESTION

Consider the foregoing case, Insurance Company v. Metcalf. There the insurer was concerned, evidently, about having a watchman on the premises. What advantage might the insurer have seen in insisting on a warranty on the subject, as opposed to a representation?

Reprise: Affirmative and Promissory Warranties

Somewhat discordant attitudes prevail about future-regarding terms in insurance contracts. What may be called a centrist position is illustrated by hypothetical expressions in an auto policy insuring against theft and collision, as follows.

(i) *"The vehicle insured is garaged in Grovers Corners."* This is an affirmative warranty only; it gives no assurance that the car will continue to be garaged there.

(ii) *"... and will remain garaged there."*

This adds a promissory warranty.

(iii) *"The insured intends to keep the vehicle garaged in Grovers Corners."*

If this is a warranty at all, it is an affirmative one only.

"The insured intends ..." may be false, the insured intending soon to move the car to Gotham. And if so, that intention may well be a ground for rejecting a claim. (Moreover, if the place of garaging has changed shortly after the policy took effect, a finder of fact might infer falsity.) But a change in the place of garaging is not itself a breach of the warranty.

A breach of a promissory warranty may be innocuous because immaterial. So also a breach of an affirmative warranty about intention.

The foregoing points represent the law in a number of states, including the law of New York. In other states, flanking views have been expressed—in California and Pennsylvania, for examples. On the one side are some remarkable statutory rules in the California Insurance Code:

A warranty may relate to the past, the present, the future, or to any or all of these.

A statement in a policy, which imports that there is an intention to do or not to do a thing which materially affects the risk, is a warranty that such act or omission will take place.[3]

These rules, taken, literally, leave little or no space between the garaging terms (ii) and (iii) above.

Case law in Pennsylvania has been erratic. In Karp v. Fidelity–Phenix Fire Ins. Co., 4 A.2d 529 (Pa.Super. 1939), the court considered this entry in an auto policy insuring against fire, theft, and collision, under the title "WARRANTED BY THE ASSURED":

---

3. Sections 404 and 405 respectively.

> The automobile described is usually kept in *public and/or private* garage, located [in] *Camden, N.J.*

The court said that this was not a "warranty proper". The opinion gives the impression that, in the court's view, a term is not a true warranty unless a breach defeats recovery whether the breach is material or not. The court was aware, it said, of terms that would be called "promissory warranties" in some jurisdictions. But to speak strictly, it said, these are "agreements, covenants or conditions . . . rather than warranties."

> A warranty proper, carrying with it the avoidance of the policy in case the fact is not as warranted, is limited to the warranty of an existing fact and will not be extended so as to include promises or agreements as to future acts. Breach of the latter will not be held to avoid the policy unless they are material to the risk insured against.[4]

How well the *Karp* opinion reflects Pennsylvania law today is questionable, however.[5] So far as it does, it places great weight on the distinction between present-related and future-related terms: The latter, and not the former, call for inquiries into materiality.

NOTE

Variable Materiality. Barnett Karp's claim was one for collision damage occurring on a highway. The court said that it was not material to the collision risk whether his car was usually garaged in Camden, N.J., or in Philadelphia. (He lived in Philadelphia, had his office in Camden, and traveled about on his job.) Perhaps the difference was material to some other risk insured against; and perhaps the court was wrong. In any event, Karp's case was referred to in a case appearing below, *Diesinger*, at p. 234.

Notwithstanding the reference in *Karp* to covenants, what a promissory warranty distinctly is *not* is an undertaking, or promise, by the insured. A California statute squares with this conception: "A breach of warranty without fraud merely exonerates an insurer from the time that it occurs, or where the warranty is broken in its inception, prevents the policy from attaching to the risk." Insurance Code § 449.

Fountain v. Connecticut Fire Ins. Co.

Supreme Court of California, 1910.
158 Cal. 760, 112 P. 546.

■ SHAW, J.

This is an action to recover upon a policy of insurance issued by the defendant, covering goods of the plaintiff contained in a two-story brick

---

4. Id. at 518.

5. The analysis in *Karp* was applied in Pugh v. Commonwealth Mut. Fire Ins. Co., 195 F.2d 83 (3d Cir. 1952). The court ruled that the term in question was not a "warranty proper". Hence it did not call for application of the rule that "warranties in insurance policies must be literally fulfilled without regard to their materiality to the risk, or else. . . ." The term was not a warranty prop-er because it referred to the future: circumstances prevailing "at the time of any loss".

Two years later, however, the Pennsylvania Supreme Court spoke of a future-regarding term as a promissory warranty. Dale v. Mutual Fire Ins. Co. of Hummelstown, 103 A.2d 414, 44 A.L.R.2d 1044. The court had no occasion to consider the materiality of the breach; there was no breach at the time of the loss.

building situated in the city of Santa Rosa, known as the Shea Building. It had two store rooms on the ground floor, one of which was occupied by Fountain. The second floor was divided into rooms used and occupied for offices and one room which was occupied by the society of "Eagles" as a lodge room. The defendant appeals from an order denying its motion for a new trial, after a verdict for the plaintiff.

The policy contained the following clause:—

"If a building, or any part thereof, fall, except as a result of fire, all insurance by this policy on such building or its contents shall immediately cease." The building referred to was the Shea Building aforesaid.

Upon the trial it was admitted by the defendant that it was liable to the plaintiffs for the loss to the full amount of the policy ($1,000), "unless it could make good its defense based upon" the above-quoted clause thereof. The fire was on April 18, 1906, and it immediately followed the earthquake which occurred at fifteen minutes after five o'clock in the morning of that day. [The court reviewed testimony offered by several witnesses who had been near the scene about that time. Some testimony offered by the plaintiff was said to be "clear, direct, positive, and satisfactory". The court seems to have been satisfied that when fire reached the Shea Building "great chunks" of the front wall already lay in the street.[1] Some testimony to the contrary was "vague and uncertain," the court said, and failed to rebut that of other witnesses. According to the court, these other witnesses had "testified either directly that the Shea Building was not on fire at the time they reached it, or saw it, after the earthquake, or to circumstances about which they could not well be mistaken and which if true would render it extremely improbable, if not impossible, that the building could have begun to burn until at least fifteen minutes after the earthquake and then only from fire communicated from the adjoining buildings. It thus being established that the building was not on fire immediately after the quake there is no basis for the supposed inference that the fire therein may have begun before the wall fell."] . . . The defense was established, the verdict was contrary to the evidence, and the new trial should have been granted for that reason.

One of the instructions was as follows:—

"It is not sufficient for defendant, in order to avoid its policy, to establish the fact that the building described in the policy in suit had, before it began to burn, suffered some injury, or that any part of the walls

---

1. The court said: "The evidence introduced by the defendant . . . showed that before the fire started the front wall of the Shea Building, from the roof down to the second floor, had fallen down, leaving the roof unsupported in front so that the front part of it dropped and rested upon the second floor at the top of the first story. . . . That this front wall was a substantial and important part of the building and that the falling thereof would immediately terminate the policy by force of this clause, cannot be seriously disputed. The defense was therefore established, and the order must therefore be reversed, unless other evidence raised a substantial conflict on the subject." The other evidence failed to do so.

of said building had fallen before the contents of the building were destroyed by fire, to avoid its policy herein; but the defendant must establish by a preponderance of evidence that such a material portion of the building had fallen before the fire started as would have increased the fire risk which defendant assumed by its policy on such building and its contents. That if the evidence does not establish the falling of such a material portion of the building, then I instruct you to find for the plaintiff.''

In anticipation of a new trial it is proper to determine whether or not this instruction is correct.

Section 2611 of the Civil Code declares that "A policy may declare that a violation of specified provisions thereof shall avoid it, otherwise the breach of an immaterial provision does not avoid the policy."

[*In the current California Insurance Code, this provision appears, having been derived from former § 2611:*

§ 448.   *Breach of immaterial provision*

Unless the policy declares that a violation of specified provisions thereof shall avoid it, the breach of an immaterial provision does not avoid the policy.[2]]

We are bound by this statutory declaration of the law, whether it accords with justice or not. The clause of the policy on this subject is in substance the same as this provision of the code. To declare that, upon the happening of a given event, "all insurance shall immediately cease," is but another way of saying that, if the event happens, the obligation created by the policy shall become void. The effect of this section of the code, in connection with the fallen-building provision of the policy, is that the question whether the falling of a part of the building increased the fire risk or not, is wholly immaterial, provided the part of the building which had fallen at the time the fire started was a material or important part of it. The instruction was erroneous in so far as it directed the jury that the effect of the falling of the part of the building must have been to increase the fire risk and that, if it did not, the defendant would be liable. The parties had the legal right to make the contract that in such an event there should be no necessity for any inquiry as to the increase of risk therefrom and that the mere event should at once terminate the insurance, and having done so, the defendant is lawfully entitled to the advantage thereof. The instruction was imperative in its direction to the jury, and although other instructions given omitted the element of increase of risk they merely caused a conflict and did not cure the error. It is impossible to say which instruction the jury obeyed.

---

2. The former provision was taken from the Field Code, prepared for New York but never enacted there. Much of it was enacted in California in the 19th century. See Patterson, Some Contract Provisions of the California Insurance Code, 32 So.Cal.L.Rev. 227 (1959) at pp. 228. Patterson ascribed good intentions to the drafter, but said, of the successor statute, "not adequate to protect the insured against the overreaching insurer in those branches of insurance where warranties are not standardized." Id. at 242–43.

The decision of the court in *Bastian* v. *British A. A. Co.*, 143 Cal. 287, [77 Pac. 63], was in substance based upon the principles above stated. The doctrine that the breach of an immaterial provision of the policy does not avoid it, is not applicable, under the code, where the policy expressly declares that it shall avoid it. . . .

The question involved in this instruction is of no practical importance upon a new trial, unless the evidence should be more favorable to the plaintiff than that given upon the trial under consideration. For there can be no doubt that the falling of even so much of the building as Burris testified had fallen, would increase the risk of fire. It is proper to remark further that the evidence does not present the question whether or not the defendant would be liable if the fire had started in the building before any part of it fell, and before it reached plaintiff's goods a material part of the building had fallen as a result of the earthquake and not as a result of the fire.

. . .

The order denying a new trial is reversed.

NOTES

(1) *The Connection: Falls to Flames*. As is well known, the City of San Francisco was also visited by a severe earthquake shock early on April 18, 1906, and by aftershocks. The destruction of a five-story building there gave rise to a case comparable to *Fountain*: Clayburgh v. Agricultural Ins. Co. of Watertown, N.Y., 102 P. 812 (Cal.). The court filed its opinion there in 1909, more than a year before filing the opinion in *Fountain*.

The trial court had entered a judgment for the claimant, based on a jury verdict. The defense was based on this policy provision: "If a building or any part thereof fall, except as the result of fire, all insurance on such building or its contents shall immediately cease." The jury had been instructed, "I charge you that the meaning of the language is that the building must have fallen in whole or part to such an extent that its integrity as a building was destroyed or substantially impaired." A photograph taken after the earthquake, but before fire reached the property, showed the upper part of the walls to have been "shaken down to such an extent as to expose to sight the uprights supporting what appeared to be the roof of the building." But the appellate court affirmed. It minimized the damage. What appeared to be the roof was in fact a tin deck, installed four or five feet above the roof so as to moderate temperatures within the building. So, at least, the jury could find. Of the fallen-building clause, the court said: "The reason for its insertion in a policy is to be found in the knowledge of the fact that a building which has fallen or has suffered the loss of so material a part as to afford a more ready means of access to flames, is more likely to burn than one which is intact. The fall of a trivial or minute part of a building may, however, occur without increasing the hazard in the slightest degree. It is not to be supposed that the parties intended to contract that such fall should avoid the policy." Id. at 813–14.

Recall this statement in the *Fountain* opinion: "the question whether the falling of a part of the building increased the fire risk or not, is wholly immaterial, provided the part of the building which had fallen at the time the fire started was a material or important part of it." Does it seem that the court changed its mind between 1909 and 1910?

(2) *Condition Precedent.* Was the fallen-building provision a warranty? With reference to the New York definition above (p. 209), hardly any serious doubt arises. A possible doubt concerns the expression "condition precedent". The sound of the policy term is that of a condition *subsequent*: "insurance ... shall immediately cease." But this is not a serious doubt. *Condition subsequent* is a sharply limited conception of contract law, now largely faded away. In the Restatement, First, of Contracts, the conception signified the termination of a claim immediately actionable. (The expression "condition subsequent" was dropped in the Restatement Second.[1]) The "building fall" provision did not have that effect. Rather, it can fairly be rephrased in the form of a patent condition precedent; *e.g.*, "Insurer's liability for fire loss conditioned on the integrity of the building at the time of the fire."

In an action on a policy of insurance against theft, the insurer relied on the claimant's failure to comply with a term about using an alarm system. The claimant contended that the term "did not create a condition precedent to liability, but only a warranty". This argument rested on the assumption, evidently, that noncompliance with a condition is more damaging to a claimant than a mere breach of warranty. The court did not accept that assumption, it seems. (The case is the next one below: Fidelity–Phenix Fire Ins. Co. v. Pilot Freight Carriers.) Moreover, the court said, "the term 'warranty' in an insurance contract ordinarily imports an assurance on the part of the policy holder that a certain situation exists or will continue, which diminishes the likelihood that the event insured against will not[?] occur; and hence 'warranty' and 'condition precedent' are often used interchangeably to create a condition of the insured's promise. See Patterson, Cases on Insurance, p. 452; Couch on Insurance, Sec. 870; 29 Am.Jur.,Insurance, Sections 529, 530; 59 A.L.R. 611."

(3) *Excepted Cause.* Would the outcome in *Fountain* have been different if (a) the break of the building were the cause of the fire, (b) the policy had made an exception for earthquake-caused fires, and (c) the fire would have been quenched before reaching the Shea Building, except that the earthquake broke the City's water mains?

Following the quake in San Francisco fires broke out and spread, destroying the building of the Pacific Union Club. The Club brought an action on its policy insuring "against all direct loss or damage by fire except as hereinafter provided." One exception was this: "This company shall not be liable for loss caused directly or indirectly by invasion, earthquake, riot, civil war or commotion." The insurer answered that, before the quake, the City was provided with a functioning fire department and mains providing ample water to fire hydrants, that one or more shocks broke the mains so that "the said fire department was without water to play upon said fires ... by reason whereof ... fire spread throughout said city," reaching the Club's property, and that "said loss would not have resulted if said water supply had not been cut off as [herein] set forth."

The trial court entered a judgment for the Club, on its demurrer to the answer. On appeal, the court put the question before it this way: "Was the loss in legal contemplation caused either directly or indirectly by the excepted peril, earthquake?" Pacific Union Club v. Commercial Union Assurance Co., 107 P. 728, 729 (Cal.App. 1910).

The court affirmed. It did so in reliance on the rule about consequential damages for the breach of a contract. " 'It is the well-settled rule ... that the damages that can be recovered ... are only such as may reasonably be supposed to

---

1.   See the Reporter's Notes to § 224.

have been within the contemplation of the parties at the time of the making of the contract, as the probable result of a breach. Other damages are too remote.'[2] . . . We see no reason why the rule should not equally apply where the plaintiff seeks to recover under a covenant in the contract and where the defendant seeks to evade liability under the contract.'' Id. at 731–32.

THE COMMON–LAW RULE, AND SOME VARIANTS

The California rule declared in *Fountain* resembles what has been called "the old common-law doctrine of forfeiting all right of recovery in the absence of strict and literal performance of warranties". Wilburn Boat Co. v. Fireman's Fund Ins. Co., 348 U.S. 310, 373–74 (1955). In *Wilburn Boat* the Court called that a harsh rule, and said: "Most States, deeming the old rule a breeder of wrong and injustice, have abandoned it in whole or in part." In a number of states legislatures have enacted variant rules. Some of those enactments are represented here.

. . .

Massachusetts:

See the statute cited at p. 195 above: ". . . made with actual intent to deceive, or [] the matter . . . made a warranty increased the risk of loss."

Wisconsin:

See the statute set out at p. 218 n.2 above: "Representations, warranties and conditions."

As to an affirmative warranty, "either material or made with intent to deceive [or] The fact . . . falsely warranted contributes to the loss."

As to a promissory warranty (or a failure of condition), "either increases the risk at the time of the loss or contributes to the loss."

New York Insurance Law:

See the statute set out at p. 209 above: "Warranty defined; effect of breach".

. . .

Neb. Rev. Statutes:

§ 44–358. Policies; misrepresentations; warranties; conditions; effect

No oral or written . . . warranty made in the negotiation for a contract or policy of insurance by the insured, or in his behalf, shall be deemed material or defeat or avoid the policy, or prevent its attaching, unless such . . . warranty deceived the company to its injury. The breach of a warranty or condition in any contract or policy of insurance shall not avoid the policy nor avail the insurer to avoid liability, unless such breach shall exist at the time of the loss and contribute to the loss, anything in the policy or contract of insurance to the contrary notwithstanding.

---

2. Quoting from Hunt Bros. Co. v. San Lorenzo Water Co., 87 Pac. 1093, 1095 (Cal. 1906).

The Nebraska statute will be recognized as an example of a "contribute to loss" rule. It embraces misrepresentations as well as warranties. For a comparable statute that does not embrace misrepresentations, see Iowa Code § 515.101.

Two Test Cases

(1) *"Where you Reside"*. Recall Heniser v. Frankenmuth Mutual, p. 207, Note 2 above, and the policy term in issue there: " 'residence premises' means [dwelling] where you reside". The court treated the phrase *where you reside* as a restriction on the property insured. Might the court have characterized it as a warranty?

If the phrase had been a warranty, making Heniser out of compliance because he had sold his vacation home, would the breach have provided the insurer with a defense? Consider the statutes quoted above. Which of them gives the clearest answer?

(2) *The Case of the Student Pilot*. A corporate aircraft crashed while being piloted by the owner's president, McDowell. He was experienced as a pilot, but was certified only as a student pilot. The issuer of a hull and liability policy on the aircraft disclaimed liability, relying on this provision in the "Exclusions" section of its policy:

This policy does not apply: . . .

6.   Under coverages [provided by the policy] while the aircraft is in flight and . . .

(d) operated by a Student Pilot unless such flight or attempted flight is with the specific advance approval of and under the supervision and control of an F.A.A. Certificated Commercial Instructor Pilot.

The owner brought an action against the insurer for a declaration of insurance coverages and liabilities.

The trial court ruled that the insurer was liable for the loss of the aircraft. It relied, in part, on the ground that no causal connection had been shown between McDowell's certification as a student pilot and the crash. On appeal, *held*: Reversed. "It is our opinion that no proof of causal connection is necessary." Macalco, Inc. v. Gulf Ins. Co., 550 S.W.2d 883, 892 (Mo.App. 1977).

The court did not characterize the quoted provision as a warranty. Was it a warranty as defined in the New York statute at p. __ above? If so, would the breach have prevented recovery? Would the decision have been different if the case had been governed by the Nebraska statute set out above?

The Law of the Sea

It is widely supposed that an established federal rule of admiralty law overrides any contrary state rule about the effect of a breach of warranty in

a marine-insurance contract. But the principal case on the subject—
Wilburn Boat—may be said to waffle about that.

The houseboat "Wanderer" burned while moored on Lake Texoma.
That lake was created by damming the Red River, at a point where the
river forms the boundary between Texas and Oklahoma. The vessel had
been insured against "all perils", including fire, in favor of three men
named Wilburn. A claim was made by the men, and by the Wilburn Boat
Company, to which they had transferred the vessel. The insurer resisted
the claim on the ground of the transfer, and because the *Wanderer* was
used commercially. The policy provided that it would be void in case the
vessel should transferred, and included a warranty that the vessel would be
used for private pleasure purposes only, and would not be hired or chartered—unless, in either event, written assent were to be given by the
insurer. In litigation, it was not shown that the fire was caused by any
violation of the contract.

When the case reached the Court of Appeals, that court ruled against
the claim, saying:

> Under general maritime law, contracts of insurance must be enforced
> as written and this court in common with other courts, so holds.... In
> Home Ins. Co. v. Ciconett [179 F.2d 892 (6th Cir. 1950)], the court, in
> language which we approve, declared: "It is settled that a warranty in
> a contract of insurance must be literally complied with; that the only
> question in such cases is whether the thing warranted to be performed
> was or was not performed; and that a breach of the warranty releases
> the company from liability regardless of the fact that a compliance with
> the warranty would not have avoided the loss."

Wilburn Boat Co. v. Fireman's Fund Ins. Co., 201 F.2d 833, 836 (5th Cir.
1953). The court accepted that rule as being federal law and used it to
override a Texas contribute-to-loss statute. (The current version of the
statute is set out in the footnote.[3]) The Supreme Court reversed, directing
that the Texas statute be applied. It expressed doubt that the lower court
was right about federal law. Wilburn Boat Co. v. Fireman's Fund Ins. Co.,
348 U.S. 310 (1955). Justice Frankfurter, concurring, emphasized the
particulars of the case: Lake Texoma, though navigable, is not the high
seas; and the *Wanderer* was not (say) a Carnival Lines cruise ship.[4]

Recent lower-court cases have paid scant attention to the issues left
open by *Wilburn Boat*. An exception is the case of the "Captain's warran-

---

3. Section 862.054 of the Texas Insurance Code: *Fire Insurance: Breach by Insured; Personal Property Coverage*

  Unless the breach or violation contributed to cause the destruction of the
property, a breach or violation by the
insured of a warranty, condition, or provision of a fire insurance policy or contract of insurance on personal property,
or of an application for the policy or
contract:

  (1) does not render the policy or
contract void; and

  (2) is not a defense to a suit for loss.

Compare the Nebraska statute at p. 225
above.

4. The Justice described the subject of
the insurance as a "small houseboat yacht,
inappropriately named *The Wanderer*, plying
the waters of Lake Texoma, an artificial in-
land lake between Texas and Oklahoma."

ty'', described at p. 207 above, where the court said that Hawaii law applied "because there is no general federal rule governing how the language in marine insurance contracts is to be construed."[5] "Disputes arising under marine insurance contracts are governed by state law," the court said, "unless an established federal rule addresses the issues raised, or there is a need for uniformity in admiralty practice." 281 F.3d 803 at 806 and 807 n.3. Another court relied on federal marine-insurance precedents, without explanation. Underwriters at Lloyd's v. Labarca, 260 F.3d 3 (1st Cir. 2001). And another applied California law, by agreement between the parties. Certain Underwriters at Lloyd's v. Montford, 52 F.3d 219, 222 n.1 (9th Cir. 1995). There the court said that the federal admiralty law was "materially the same on the issues raised." *Ibid.*[6]

Montford concerned the disappearance of a vessel from her berth in Costa Rica. The vessel had voyaged in Colombian waters not long before the loss. The policy forbad that, and stated that a breach of the "cruising warranty" would render the policy null and void. The court referred to section 448 of the California Insurance Code, set out at p. 222 above, and disregarded the fact that the vessel was berthed in Costa Rica when the loss occurred.

NOTES

(1) *Deference in New York.* In the New York statute quoted at p. 209 above, the final subdivision is as follows:

> (c) This section shall not affect the express or implied warranties under a contract of marine insurance in respect to, appertaining to or in connection with any and all risks or perils of navigation, transit, or transportation, including war risks, on, over or under any seas or inland waters, nor shall it affect any provision in an insurance contract requiring notice, proof or other conduct of the insured after the occurrence of loss, damage or injury.

Assuming that the New York legislature thought the rule stated elsewhere in the section to be the best, what legislative judgment does this qualification indicate? That New York is powerless to alter a rule about marine insurance? That New York courts should be free to follow a federal rule—even an inferior one—in a matter of national concern, or in the interest of uniformity? That New York courts should be free to follow the rule of some other state, even if that rule is inferior?

(2) *Misrepresentation and Concealment at Sea.* In 1896 the Court of Appeals for the Sixth Circuit (Taft, J.) was confident that misrepresentation and concealment were defenses broadly available to marine-insurance claims. As to concealment, an applicant is expected to disclose any material circumstance and it is no excuse that the applicant did not know it to be material. "The great and leading case on the subject is that of Carter v. Boehm, 3 Burrows, 1905 [Mansfield, L.J.].... That it states the rule enforced by the courts of this country in cases of marine insurance is

5. Here the court cited Morrow Crane Co. v. Affiliated FM Ins. Co., 885 F.2d 612 (9th Cir. 1989), where the court said: "Marine insurance contracts are governed by federal admiralty law when an established federal rule exists, and by state law when one does not. *Wilburn Boat Co.* [at] 313–14 (1955);

Ahmed v. American S.S. Mutual Protection & Indemnity Ass'n, 640 F.2d 993, 996 (9th Cir. 1981)." Id. at 614.

6. The "Captain's warranty" case concerned the sinking of a fishing vessel off Hawaii; *Labarca* concerned the sinking of a motor vessel in San Juan Bay.

established by many decisions." As to misrepresentation, the court quoted Lord Blackburn as follows:

> In policies of marine insurance, I think it is settled by authority that any statement of a fact bearing upon the risk introduced into the written policy, is 189 to be construed as a warranty, and prima facie, at least, that the compliance with that warranty is a condition precedent to the attaching of the risk.

By those rules "the utmost good faith (*uberrima fides*) is required" of an applicant for insurance.[7] That was a concession made to the precedents in Penn Mut. Life Ins. Co. v. Mechanic's Savings Bank & Trust Co., referred to on p. 189 above. The opinion consists largely of an effort to ward off the application of "the harsh and rigorous rule of marine insurance" to life and fire policies—"a class of insurance contracts differing so materially from marine policies in the circumstances under which the contracting parties agree that the reason for the rule ceases." Id. at 434–37.

A hundred and ten years later, the Court of Appeals for the First Circuit was not so sure about the state of marine-insurance law. See *Pesante*, quoted in n.7 above. The insurer argued that the doctrine *uberrimae fides* is an "established rule of maritime law". Pesante argued that it is not. The court skirted that issue, deciding that the policy was voidable under the law of Rhode Island.[8] While at sea, Pesante had suffered a collision that engendered claims against him. The liability coverage in his policy was in issue. The district court had declined to grant a summary judgment for the insurer, relying on the fact that, at the time of the collision, Pesante was not fishing but was returning to port from a fishing expedition.

Compare the statement in the case of the Captain's warranty (p. 207 above), "Disputes arising under marine insurance contracts are governed by state law unless...."

Fidelity–Phenix Fire Ins. Co. of New York v. Pilot Freight Carriers, Inc.

United States Court of Appeals, 4th Cir., 1952.
193 F.2d 812, 31 A.L.R.2d 839.

The driver of a tractor-trailer rig, Salvatore Sinno, was kidnaped at gunpoint in Hoboken. On approaching a warehouse where his cargo was to be delivered, he had left the rig for 15 minutes for coffee and cake, and to visit the warehouse for instructions. On returning, he found a gunman in

7. " 'Uberrimae fidei' roughly means 'of the utmost good faith.' Grande v. St. Paul Fire & Marine Ins. Co., 436 F.3d 277, 282 (1st Cir. 2006). Under this doctrine, the insured is required 'to disclose to the insurer all known circumstances that materially affect the insurer's risk, the default of which ... renders the insurance contract voidable by the insurer.' [Windsor Mount Joy Mut. Ins. Co. v. Giragosian, 57 F.3d 50, 54 (1st Cir. 1995)]." Commercial Union Ins. Co. v. Pesante, 459 F.3d 34 (1st Cir. 2006).

8. In applying for insurance Pesante had described the subject as a lobster boat. In fact, he used it for gill-net fishing, had never engaged in lobstering—something radically different—and did not mean to. Warranted, the policy said, that "the only commercial use of the insured vessel(s) shall be for lobstering." The court skirted also the question whether or not the insurer was excused by breach of that provision.

the cab, and was abducted by the gunman and a confederate. That evening the rig was found in New York City. The trailer was then empty of its cargo, hundreds of cases of cigarettes which had been loaded in North Carolina.

The owner of the cargo, the R. J. Reynolds Tobacco Company, was paid for its loss by Pilot Freight Carriers, the owner of the rig and Sinno's employer. Then Pilot Freight made claim on a cargo insurance policy, protecting Pilot Freight from liability for a loss of goods by theft and other perils. The insurer resisted, relying on part of a policy rider referred to as the "Babaco warranty". In several paragraphs the rider concerned the maintenance and use of two anti-theft devices. Each device was designed to set off a siren unless turned "off" with a key: one when the rig was moved, and the other when the trailer doors were opened. The rider included this provision:

> "5.   It is further warranted by the Assured that ... the 'Parker' device on each trailer will be in the 'on' position when such vehicles arc parked unattended, when loaded with commodities...."

Sinno had not been supplied with a key for the former device; Pilot Freight had "somehow ... dropped off the 'Parker' key business."

In an action by Pilot Freight on the policy, the trial court awarded judgment for the policy limit, nearly $50,000. The insurer appealed.

■ SOPER, J.

[The insurer] contended that the theft ("larceny") occurred only after Sinno had returned to the rig: "We are told that ... the crime of larceny is not committed by the mere seizure or taking control of an article, but there must also be an asportation or carrying away...." [The court brushed aside the law of larceny.] [T]he question for our determination is whether the facts justify the restoration to full vigor of a policy which had been suspended during a breach of the contract. Manifestly such a revival should not and cannot take place unless nothing has happened in the meanwhile to increase the insurer's risk of loss. Since the property had passed out of the control of the agent of the company during the interval in which he left the vehicle unattended, it would be nearer the truth to say that the loss had become well nigh an assured fact before the driver's return, and consequently no revival of the policy took place.[3]

[Pilot Freight contended that ¶ 5, above, did not create a condition precedent to liability but only a warranty and that mere breach of the warranty does not bar recovery for the loss. The district judge had thought that a failure to comply with the provision would avoid the policy. The court of appeals agreed.] It is well established in North Carolina decisions, which control us in this case, that if a policy of insurance contains a stipulation material to the risk, on breach of which the policy is to be avoided, there can be no recovery if the stipulation is not fulfilled.... [The

---

3. We have considered the cases cited by the plaintiff in this respect but none of them seem [sic] to us to be in conflict with this conclusion. See [four cases cited].

court rejected Pilot Freight's contention, doing an analysis of ¶ 5 in light of ¶ ¶ 1 and 2. (See the footnote for excerpts.[2])]

. . .

The insured makes the additional contention that even though the driver left the vehicle unattended for a period during which the insurance became inoperative, the policy was revived when the driver returned and resumed attendance, and since this happened before the theft was complete, the loss was covered by the policy. This construction rests upon the rule which prevails in North Carolina and elsewhere that the violation of a continuing condition which works the forfeiture of a policy of insurance merely suspends the insurance during the violation, and if it is discontinued during the life of the policy and does not exist at the time of the loss, the policy revives and the insurer is liable. Cottingham v. Maryland Motor Car Ins. Co., 84 S.E. 274, L.R.A. 1915D, 344 (N.C.); Crowell v. Maryland Motor Car Ins. Co., 85 S.E. 37 (N.C.).

To obtain the benefit of this rule in the pending case the insured must show that the evidence justified the finding of the jury that the driver was in attendance when the theft occurred. On this point the judge instructed the jury that for attendance upon a motor vehicle something more is required than the mere physical presence of the operator; he must be in a position free to perform his duty; and one wholly deprived of liberty of action cannot be said to be in attendance within the meaning of the policy

2.   1. In consideration of the rate at which this policy is written, it is a condition precedent to the liability of the Insurer hereunder and to the effectiveness of this policy as respects theft coverage for vehicles, that trucks and trailers owned, hired or used by the Assured will be equipped with a Senior Babaco Alarm including Parker when more than 50% of the load consists of manufactured tobacco products, textiles, alcoholic beverages or any or all combined; that such Babaco Alarm System and Parker will be maintained in working order at all times, inspected and approved once each month by the Babaco Alarm Systems, Inc. and proper inspection certificates issued.

2.   It is also a condition precedent to the liability of the insurer hereunder and to the effectiveness of this Policy as respects theft coverage for vehicles, that all the Babaco equipment protecting the cargo compartment of each vehicle equipped as aforesaid shall be in the 'on' position while aforementioned merchandise is contained in said compartment, except with respect to any trailer which is actually being loaded, and/or unloaded and that while any trailer is being loaded and/or unloaded, at least one man shall be in actual attendance on the cargo compartment.

3.   It is further warranted by the Assured that the Babaco Alarm System on the

cargo compartment of each and every truck or trailer transporting a load 50% or more of which consists of manufactured tobacco products, textiles, alcoholic beverages or any or all combined and covered hereunder shall be sealed by the Terminal Dispatcher or agents as designated below immediately after loading is completed and prior to the trailers leaving the loading terminal or shipping point, and unsealed by only the Terminal Dispatcher at Assured's regular terminals or by agents as designated below upon the arrival of said vehicles-the Babaco Alarm System to be sealed by means of the 'Sealed Load' key provided by the Babaco Alarm Systems, Inc.

5.   It is further warranted by the Assured that the Babaco Alarm System on the Cargo compartment of each trailer and the 'Parker' device on each trailer will be in the 'on' position when such vehicles are parked unattended, when loaded with commodities and in amounts stated above.

6.   The assured agrees, by acceptance of this policy, that the foregoing conditions precedent relate to matters material to the acceptance of the risk by the Insurer. Failure of the insured to comply with any of the foregoing conditions precedent in any instance shall render policy null and void as respects theft coverage for vehicles.

in suit. Up to this point in the charge of the court the matter was left to the determination of the jury; but the judge went on to say that if in the course of his duty the truck driver came back to the truck and started to get into it, with the intention of driving it into his employer's warehouse, and if he was then acting voluntarily in order to carry out his employer's orders, then he was in attendance upon the truck within the meaning of the policy. Since the facts in regard to the driver's leaving and returning to the truck were not controverted, these instructions amounted in effect to a direction to find the issue for the plaintiff. In our opinion the undisputed facts preclude such action. The meaning of attendance upon the tractor trailer was correctly stated to involve not merely physical presence but freedom to perform the duties of an attendant. In this instance, however, it was proved that the driver was deprived of all freedom of action the moment he entered the cab of the trailer since the armed bandit had already taken forcible possession of the vehicle. In our opinion there should have been a directed verdict for the defendant on this point.

. . .

It is said that the breach of warranty in the pending case had no causal connection with the loss. The reason given is that even if the Parker device had been placed in the 'on' position when the driver left the vehicle, he would have turned it off before he entered the cab of the truck to drive to the warehouse. There may be room for a difference of opinion on this point, since it seems clear that the thieves had the stolen vehicle under close observation and were probably well aware of the driver's actions throughout. But it is not necessary to pursue this inquiry because under the law of North Carolina no causal connection need be shown between the breach and the loss if the loss occurs while the breach continues. Ritchie v. Travelers' Protective Ass'n, 166 S.E. 893 (N.C.). See also, Flannagan v. Provident Life & Accident Co., 4 Cir., 22 F.2d 136; Home Ins. Co. v. Ciconett, 6 Cir., 179 F.2d 892.

The decision in Smith v. Fire Ins. Co., 175 N.C. 314 (1918), is not at variance with this rule for in that case the condition of the fire insurance policy that a space of 200 feet be maintained between the insured property and any woodworking establishment was not actually violated, the court being of the opinion that the terms of the policy did not cover a woodworking establishment within the prohibited area which was not in operation.

The judgment of the District Court is reversed and the case is remanded with directions to grant defendant's motion to set aside the verdict and enter judgment n.o.v. for the defendant.[b]

EXERCISE

Sinno was the assigned driver only for the final leg of the rig's trip, within Hoboken only. Another driver had brought it there from Winston–

----

b. Portions of the opinion have been rearranged.

Salem, N.C. Suppose that Sinno had been provided with a key to the "Parker" device, and that the device was turned on all the while he was out of the driver's seat. Now, it can be imagined easily that the loss would have occurred anyway (*e.g.*, the malefactors took the key from him, and used it, before moving the rig). Would the loss have been recoverable in that event? Develop an argument for the answer Yes. Develop an argument for the answer No, building on the circumstance that Pilot Freight had "dropped off" using the device for long hauls.

Does either of these arguments depend on a fact not given?

NOTE

Theft from Vehicle: an Exclusion. Traveling salesmen of jewelry are tempting targets for thieves, it seems. And some thieves have the effrontery to make off with the merchandise when the salesman has stepped out of it briefly, as when pumping gas. Incidents like this were reviewed in E.M.M.I., Inc. v. Zurich American Ins. Co., 84 P.3d 385 (Cal. 2004). There the salesman, troubled by a clanking, had crouched at the rear of his car to examine its exhaust pipes, and had looked up to see it driven away. E.M.M.I, an owner of jewelry in the car, having lost it, make a claim on its jeweler's block policy. (Jeweler's block insurance is described briefly in the footnote.[1])

Resisting the claim, the insurer relied on an exclusion often invoked in comparable cases: A theft of jewelry is not covered unless the insured or its representative was "actually in or upon such vehicle at the time of the theft." In *E.M.M.I.* the court found ambiguity in the quoted phrase and disapproved a summary judgment in favor of the insurer. "Construing the exception in the insured's favor, we hold that E.M.M.I.'s salesman, who was approximately two feet from and actually attending to his vehicle when the theft occurred, came within the scope of the exception to the vehicle theft exclusion." Id. at 397–98. (4–3 decision) "[I]t appears most reasonable", the court said, "to read the exclusion as applying when the vehicle and the insured jewelry were left unattended and, hence, more vulnerable to thievery."

In part, the court relied on a dictionary definition of "on" (interchangeable with "upon") which included "in close proximity." The phrase "on a motorcycle" may signify physical contact, but "there is no indication that motorcycles are widely used by jewelry salespeople as a means of transporting jewelry". Id. at 390–91. Also, a reasonable buyer of the insurance might well infer from the word "or" that proximity in space satisfies the requirement, "actually in or upon. . . ."

Compare the warranty in the main case: "when . . . parked unattended". In *E.M.M.I.* the majority opinion seeks to distinguish some cases on the ground that in

---

1. "Jeweler's block insurance, conceived at the turn of the [20th] century [by Lloyd's of London], provides coverage under a single policy for the 'various risks inherent' in the jewelry business. (Annot., Construction and Effect of 'Jeweler's Block' Policies or Provisions Contained Therein (1994) 22 A.L.R.5th 579; 1 Couch on Insurance (3d ed. 1997) § 1:57.) It 'is different from most other traditional forms of property insurance which are considered "named-peril" insurance policies. Under named-peril policies, an insurer agrees to indemnify its insured for losses resulting from certain risks of loss or damage which are specifically enumerated within the provisions of the policy. In contrast, under a jewelers' block policy all risks of loss or damage to jewelry may be insured, subject to certain exceptions.' (*Star Diamond, Inc. v. Underwriters at Lloyd's, London* (E.D.Va. 1997) 965 F.Supp. 763, 765.) Thus, the coverage language in this type of insurance policy is quite broad, generally insuring against all losses not expressly excluded." Id. at 388–89.

those cases the salesman had "abandoned" his car temporarily and was returning to it when the theft occurred. Does the reasoning in *Pilot Freight Carriers* help in understanding those cases?

—————

Diesinger v. American & Foreign Ins. Co.

United States Court of Appeals, 3d Cir., 1943.
138 F.2d 91.

■ KIRKPATRICK, DISTRICT JUDGE.

These appeals are from a judgment entered upon the verdict of a jury in an action upon a policy of insurance described as a Jeweler's Block Policy, covering loss from any cause, with certain exceptions not relevant to this case.

The claim arose from the robbery of a small jewelry store which the plaintiff conducted at Ardmore, Pennsylvania. On December 21, 1940, at about noon, two armed men entered the store by the street door, and looted it of practically the entire stock, part of which was in the show window and part in the vault. The total value of the articles stolen was $10,700, of which $7,891 represented jewelry displayed in the show window and $2,809 jewelry in the vault. The robbers did not smash or cut the plate glass window. The facts relating to the robbery were undisputed and evidence of the value and location of the jewelry taken was supplied by the defendant.

The verdict was for the plaintiff in the full amount of his claim less $2,891 (the amount by which the value of the jewelry taken from the show window exceeded $5,000), the Court having instructed the jury to make the deduction. Both sides have appealed, the defendant from the Court's refusal to set aside the verdict and the plaintiff from the Court's refusal to enter judgment for him in the full amount of his claim.

The Defendant's Appeal (No. 8343)

The defendant's contention is that the plaintiff by displaying more than $5,000 of jewelry in the window breached a warranty and so avoided the policy.

The policy was issued upon a "Proposal" which consists of four pages of questions, with answers supplied by the insured. One of its provisions is "... it is agreed that this proposal shall constitute a Warranty should a Policy be issued." A recital in the policy is "whereas, the assured hereby warrants the truth of each and every statement and particular contained therein" (referring to the Proposal).

The Proposal contained the following:

"3. Show Windows

"(c) What will be the maximum value displayed?

"(1) when premises are open for business ... (in any one window) ... $5,000."

It is not disputed that the amount actually displayed in the show window was in excess of $5,000.

The law of Pennsylvania governs. "A warranty proper, carrying with it the avoidance of the policy in case the fact is not as warranted, is limited to the warranty of an existing fact and will not be extended so as to include promises or agreements as to future acts. Breach of the latter will not be held to avoid the policy unless they are material to the risk insured against." Karp v. Fidelity–Phoenix Fire Ins. Co., 4 A.2d 529, 531 (Pa.Super.).

The promise here is "as to future acts"—the value of jewelry to be kept in the window during business hours. It is perfectly clear that the answer which set $5,000 as the maximum was elicited in connection with the risk of loss through window smashing or cutting—a form of robbery so common that the parties made it the subject of a clause in the policy and two endorsements. The promise is obviously material to that risk, but any fancied relation between the proportion of the merchandise kept in the store window and the risk that the store would be robbed in a hold-up by armed bandits during business hours is too tenuous and speculative to support a finding that the promise is material to the risk of that kind of robbery.

The decision in Price v. Century Indemnity Co., 5 A.2d 130 (Pa.), is not in conflict with the *Karp* case, *supra*. It has no bearing on a case involving breach of a promise, such as the one in this case, not material to the risk. The promise in the *Price* case was that a guard would always accompany the person who carried the jewelry insured—a promise clearly material to the risk of hold-up, which was the way in which the loss was incurred.

We therefore hold that the fact that the insured had some 50 percent more jewelry in the window than he had agreed to keep there did not avoid the policy in so far as it insured against loss by armed robbery.

The Plaintiff's Appeal (No. 8348)

The trial judge held that the contract of insurance set a limit of $5,000 upon the Company's liability for loss of jewelry in the show window.

[Color to that ruling was provided by a question and answer in the proposal about the value of merchandise to be exhibited in one or all windows "to be covered when premises are open for business". But the appellate court rejected the ruling upon examining the structure of the policy. The court concluded that the Q & A limited the insurer's liability with respect to that merchandise only in the case of a loss by window smashing—not in the case at hand.]

In No. 8343, the appeal is dismissed for want of merit. In No. 8348 the judgment is reversed and the cause remanded with directions to enter judgment in favor of the plaintiff for the full amount of the claim with interest.

QUESTIONS

(1) A key point in the opinion has to do with the breach (overstocking the store window) in relation to the risk of an armed robbery; the court said there was no relation it could take cognizance of. How might an argument to the contrary be framed?

(2) Compare with the *Diesinger* doctrine of unrelated risks a statutory provision in New York: the second sentence of Insurance Code § 3106(b), at p. 209 above. How different are they?

———

Rodriguez v. Northwestern National Ins. Co.

Court of Appeal of Louisiana, First Circuit, 1977.
347 So.2d 1238.

■ LANDRY, J.

Defendants, Northwestern National Insurance Company and Interstate Surplus Underwriters, Inc. (Insurers), appeal from judgment awarding plaintiff, Robert Rodriguez (Insured), recovery of $25,000, pursuant to a fire insurance policy covering a 1972 Model Case Log Skidder (a log rolling and loading machine used in timber cutting operations), which machine burned while being used in Insured's logging business.

[The insurers had been held liable also to an intervening party, a firm from which Rodriquez had bought the machine. In connection with the sale Rodriquez had given that firm a mortgage on the machine, on which a balance remained unpaid at the time of the fire. The policy named the holder of the mortgage as an additional insured. The insurers appealed also from the judgment for the intervenor.[1] Officers of the intervenor, William Flores and William J. Busbee, gave evidence in the trial.]

. . .

Insurers urge that the trial court erred in: (1) Holding that the Insured's breach of certain warranty provisions of the policy did not bar recovery for the loss; and (2) Awarding Insured the face value of the policy instead of a lesser sum for which the skidder could have been repaired.

. . .

On January 8, 1973, Northwestern's agent, Interstate Surplus Underwriters, Inc., insured the skidder against loss by fire "(among others)" in the sum of $25,000, for a period of one year. . . .

Insurers declined payment of the loss because of Insured's alleged breach of the following policy warranty condition:

_____

1. Actually, the policy named as the additional insured a second firm to which the first one had transferred the mortgage. The opinion does not explain why the first firm, and not the second, intervened and won a judgment. Possibly the mortgage had been reassigned after the fire.

It is understood and agreed by the assured that as respects the peril of Fire this insurance is NULL and VOID if any condition of this warranty is violated as respects equipment insured hereunder while operating or located in woods or forest or while land clearing.

. . .

2. It is warranted that an underwriters laboratory approved all purpose fire extinguisher with a rating of at least 1A or 10BC will be provided on each piece of equipment insured at all times such equipment is being operated and such extinguisher will be maintained in good working condition and recharged when necessary. The assured may remove the extinguisher when the equipment is not in operation to prevent theft.

3. It is warranted that all equipment operated in the woods or forest or while land clearing shall be shut down and inspected at frequent intervals during the working day to remove any accumulation of leaves, trash or fuel from the engine compartment and specifically from the exhaust manifold and protection belly pan. It is specifically a condition that such trash and accumulation shall be removed before discontinuing work for the day.

The skidder is best described as a ponderous machine equipped with a front end bulldozer type blade designed to roll and move logs. [The court described the machine in some detail, from blade and engine in front to a "crane type unit in the back." Between these was an operator's cab, with a driver's seat. "The cab floor is covered by a metal plate referred to as the 'floor boards' and which is held in place by a number of nuts and bolts." The transmission was beneath the driver's seat.] Subject skidder came factory equipped with a 5BC fire extinguisher mounted on a metal bracket welded to the right side of the driver's cab. Prior to the fire, the fire extinguisher on Insured's skidder was placed in a tool box at the rear of the unit because the bracket in which it was kept had been broken off by a tree or limb.

On November 29, 1973, the skidder was being operated by Insured's employee, Jack Lanier, an experienced operator.... About noon ... Lanier noted fire coming from beneath the driver's seat and floorboards of the cab. He jumped from the machine, obtained the fire extinguisher from the tool box, and attempted to put out the fire, but the extinguisher would not work. After several unsuccessful attempts to use the extinguisher, Lanier got into his truck, drove [to] a telephone, and summoned the Springfield Fire Department. A fire truck arrived on the scene approximately 20 to 30 minutes later, at which time the fire was raging up the sides of the skidder. The fire was eventually extinguished but the skidder was virtually a total loss. Neither the precise cause nor the origin of the fire could be determined.

Insured concedes he never checked the fire extinguisher after purchasing the skidder. He trained Lanier as an operator but never instructed Lanier to clean the machine daily at frequent intervals. He did suggest that the machine be cleaned in the evening before Lanier left the jobsite. To Insured's knowledge, Lanier never cleaned the skidder during the day unless some unexpected event, such as brush or limbs becoming lodged in the blade, made it necessary to shut the skidder down temporarily. Insured readily acknowledged that a skidder is highly susceptible to fire damage if trash and other combustibles are allowed to accumulate in the engine compartment and protection belly pan.... Insured explained that he did not check the extinguisher or comply with the warranty regarding cleaning, because he had little formal education and did not read the insurance policy.

Lanier testified he cleaned the skidder each morning before beginning work and rarely cleaned it during the day. On the day of the fire he cleaned the machine before starting work and did not clean it thereafter. He stated he would occasionally clean the skidder during operation time but only when he felt he had some spare time. He testified that when he noticed the fire it was not coming from the engine compartment but from the transmission area beneath the driver's seat.

[Flores and Busbee] testified in effect that their examinations disclosed the fire probably started in the transmission because that area of the machine appeared most heavily damaged. They both attested to extreme vulnerability of a skidder to fire, for which reason such equipment was difficult to insure. Busbee added that fire in the transmission would be difficult to combat without removing the floorboards which requires removal of several nuts and bolts which hold it in place. He explained that the only openings in the floorboards were intended to accommodate control devices and that these openings were small. He would not say that a fire in the transmission could not be controlled with a hand operated fire extinguisher, but he had serious doubts about the matter. He was of the opinion that to combat such a fire effectively, the floorboards would have to be removed. Busbee conceded that the collection of leaves, straw and oil in a skidder are the main causes of fire in such equipment. He expressed the opinion that there is no really effective way to combat fire on skidders but that frequent cleaning during daily operation would materially reduce the hazard. He added, however, that such frequent shutdowns for cleaning would render skidders almost useless. He personally felt that, all things considered, a daily cleaning is a reasonable safety precaution.

Insured concedes the warranty conditions were not fulfilled. He reasons, however, that the breaches did not increase the physical hazard involved because the record shows an operable fire extinguisher of the type called for would not have extinguished the fire and also because the cleaning process was reasonable.

Insurers argue that the policy is subject to the general insurance law governing warranty as set forth by LSA–R.S. 22:641 because the policy warranty is in the nature of an executory or promissory warranty which is part of a "floater policy" providing multiple coverage. Section 641, above, provides:

If any breach of a warranty or condition in any insurance contract occurs prior to a loss under the contract, such breach shall not avoid the contract nor avail the insurer to avoid liability, unless the breach exists at the time of the loss.

Insurers urge that since the breaches existed prior to and at the time of the fire, the policy was voided pursuant to Section 641, above. On this premise, it is argued that to avoid liability for the loss, Insurers are not required to establish that the moral or physical risk was increased by the derelictions shown.

We disagree with Insurers' contention because we are here concerned with fire coverage to which LSA–R.S. 22:692 applies, which said section provides:

No policy of fire insurance issued by any insurer on property in this state shall hereafter be declared void by the insurer for the breach of any representation, warranty or condition contained in the said policy or in the application therefor. Such breach shall not avail the insurer to avoid liability unless such breach (1) shall exist at the time of the loss, and be either such a breach as would increase either the moral or physical hazard under the policy, or (2) shall be such a breach as would be a violation of a warranty or condition requiring the insurer to take and keep inventories and books showing a record of his business. . . .

We note that Insurers' argument was expressly rejected by the Supreme Court in *Lee v. Travelers Fire Insurance Company,* 53 So.2d 692 (La. 1951). In *Lee,* above, it was held that Section 692, above, applied to a policy which provided "fire coverage (among others)", on an insured truck. On authority of *Lee,* above, we hold Section 692 applicable to subject policy.

Citing Keeton, Insurance Law § 5.6 p. 320 (1971), Insured points out that the warranty concept in matters of this nature has been attributed to the opinions of Lord Mansfield during the 18th century. From his opinions, the rule evolved that if a policy condition is classified as a warranty, the policy is void if the warranty is breached. The rule applies irrespective of whether the breach contributed to the loss or damage. It would appear the rationale of the rule is that breach terminates all coverage because the insurer declines to continue the policy thereafter. As originally conceived, the rule voids the policy irrespective of whether the breach was material to the loss and even though it did not contribute to the loss or damage.

Keeton, above, p. 321, notes that the harshness of this rule resulted in policies containing numerous warranties, many of trivial character and nature which, in effect, constituted a trap for unsuspecting policy holders whose coverage was voided for insignificant warranty violations, regardless of how honest, sincere and careful the insured might be.

At page 382, Keeton observes that American legislatures have statutorily alleviated the harshness of the rule by enactment of laws falling into two general categories. The first type of such laws provides that to void coverage, the insurer must show an increase in risk resulted from the breach. The second type of such laws provides that coverage is not voided by warranty breach unless the breach contributes to the loss.

In interpreting LSA–R.S. 22:692, and its predecessor statutes, our jurisprudence has established the rule that an insurer is not required to show causal relation between warranty breach and loss to avail himself of warranty provisions in a fire policy. The insurer must, however, establish that the breach increased either the moral or physical hazard.

Apparently the earliest case dealing with the subject is *Dittmer & Pelle v. Germania Ins. Co. of New Orleans*, 23 La.Ann. 458 (1871). In this case, an insured's claim under a fire policy was resisted for breach of warranty against storage of the insured goods in a building containing hay pressed in bales. The merchandise was kept in a structure containing loose unbaled hay. The court held that a policy provision, prohibiting an increase in the risk by act of the insured, is an independent condition in itself and is not controlled or limited by a prior specification of risks or hazards which the insured agrees to guarantee against. The court also held that because the act of the insured increased the physical hazard, it voided the policy even though the particular hazardous condition brought about by the insured was not included in a specified list of hazards included in the policy. The court found that loose, unbaled hay increased the physical risk to the insured goods and thus voided coverage.

[The court's review of several other Louisiana cases is omitted here, except to say that in one of them it was found that the insured had not increased the risk to his property by "keeping four or five sticks of old dynamite" there.]

It thus appears that our courts have repeatedly applied the rule that breach of warranty will void a policy of fire insurance, provided the insurer bears the burden of establishing a resultant increase in either the moral or physical hazard.... No case in our jurisprudence has held that the breach must bear a causal relationship to the damage or loss.

It is well settled that insurers may, by unambiguous and clearly noticeable provisions, limit their liability by imposing such reasonable conditions as they desire upon the obligations they assume. *Breaux v. St. Paul Fire & Marine Insurance Co.*, 326 So.2d 891 (La.App.3rd Cir. 1976).

When the terms of an insurance contract are clear and unambiguous, they form the law between the parties and are entitled to enforcement according to their terms. LSA–C.C. Article 1901; *Mauterer v. Associated Indemnity Company*, 332 So.2d 570 (La.App.4th Cir. 1976).

In this instance, the record establishes beyond question that failure to have an operable fire extinguisher of the type required by the policy, or an equivalent thereof, on the machine while it was operating in the woods, is a patent breach of the insured's warranty. So, too, is the insured's failure to substantially comply with the warranty provision of cleaning the machine during daily operation and at the end of each day's work.

The record is clear that breach of these warranties resulted in a significant increase in the physical hazard to the machine. The record shows clearly that a skidder is highly vulnerable to fire which may result from the accumulation of tinder like materials in its engine compartment incident to its operation in the woods. To reduce this known and recognized hazard, the insurer reasonably required periodic cleaning during daily use, and also at the end of each day's work. The latter requirement was obviously intended to reduce the hazard of fire occurring after workmen retired from the scene upon completing their day's work, leaving the machine unattended.

We find no merit in Insured's contention that the presence of an operable fire extinguisher would not have reduced the risk of this particular fire because the fire was beneath the floorboards and therefore inaccessible. Assuming this to be true, it is a matter of no consequence. The absence of an operable fire extinguisher increased the risk of damage by fire which is all that is required to void the policy for breach of warranty.

We also find no merit in Insured's contention that the fire did not start in the engine compartment but under the operator's seat. In this regard, the evidence does not show where the fire began; it is shown merely that the operator first detected the fire coming from beneath the floorboards of the cab. Moreover, it is immaterial where the fire began. Since Insured's breach of warranty increased the physical risk, the policy is voided.

The judgment of the trial court is reversed and judgment rendered herein in favor of defendants Northwestern National Insurance Company and Interstate Surplus Underwriters, Inc., and against plaintiff, Robert Rodriguez and Intervenor, Crawler Supply Company, Inc., rejecting Insured's demands with prejudice, all costs of these proceedings to be paid by Insured and Intervenor.

Reversed and rendered.

■ CLAIBORNE, JUDGE (concurring).

I concur with the result and with the legal conclusions of the majority....

I do not agree with some of the factual conclusions reached by the majority concerning the origin of the fire.... As I read the evidence the preponderance establishes that the fire began in the concealed transmission and its controls where the fire was first noticed rather than the more visible engine compartment, exhaust manifold and protection belly pan all of which are situated to the front of the operator, and where no flames were noticed. It was an oil or fuel fire; not a trash fire. These facts are relevant to the position of the dissent, although immaterial to the majority holding. If I agreed with the view of the law held by the dissent, the facts would compel me to join the dissent.

The majority points out that insurers, by unambiguous and clearly noticeable provisions, may limit their liability by imposing reasonable conditions on the obligations they assume. Whether the conditions imposed by the insurer are "reasonable" deserves consideration in the instant case. In my opinion the requirement that the machine be equipped with a fire extinguisher other than standard factory equipment without a showing that the standard equipment was smaller, less effective or in any way inferior to the specified model, and particularly when the matter is not discussed with the insured, is unreasonable.

A warranty which would require an industrial machine to be stopped and cleaned so often that the machine becomes economically useless is an unreasonable condition. The warranty provision in this case does not, however, necessarily require such frequent stoppage. Since the number of times per day is not specified, the clause is subject to judicial interpretation, and a reasonable number of times would satisfy the warranty. This condition was not fulfilled. The warranty provision requiring removal of trash and accumulations of fuel and leaves from the specified areas before discontinuing work for the day is reasonable. It was shown that this practice would reduce the physical hazard of fire, although no causal relationship to the fire loss in the present case was shown.

The violation of these warranty conditions void the policy.

I concur.

■ COLE, J., dissenting.

The opinion of the majority holds, in part, that "our jurisprudence has established the rule that an insurer is not required to show causal relation between warranty breach and loss to avail himself of warranty provisions in a fire policy." An examination of the authorities cited in support of this conclusion does not convince me that in those instances where a physical hazard is at issue it is a well-founded statement of law. Several of the cases relied upon were decided prior to the 1928 enactment of R.S. 22:692 which is applicable to the subject insurance policy. Other cited cases dealt with a *moral* hazard and not a *physical* hazard as is found herein. Still other cited cases deal with "vacant" premises and, therefore, present a vastly differing factual context. Based upon the authorities cited, I am not prepared to agree that there is no necessity for the breach to bear a causal relationship to the damage or loss.

It is understandable that where a moral hazard is at issue, *i.e.*, the risk of intentional destruction by fire for monetary gain, it is virtually impossible to establish causation and the insurer should not bear the burden of proving same.... Causation is implied in such an instance. However, it is an entirely different situation in regard to a physical hazard. The very nature of physical hazards denotes causation factors and it is not an unreasonable burden for the insurer to bear to show that the breach of a warranty probably brought about the loss.

If we relieve insurers from the burden of proof of causation with respect to physical fire hazards, recovery for loss could be denied under the facts of this case even if a total stranger to the appellee had poured gasoline over the log skidder at midnight and then applied a torch causing its destruction. I cannot agree that such a result is envisioned by the language of LSA–R.S. 22:692. When Section 692 speaks of "such a breach as would increase the ... physical hazard", one must look to the nature of the hazard to determine if the risk thereof was increased by the breach of the stated warranty. The hazard with which we are concerned is a fire within the enclosed area of the log skidder and which could not have been prevented or reasonably diminished by the requisite fire extinguisher or frequent cleaning of the exposed parts of the equipment. In effect, the breach of the two warranties by the appellee did not increase the hazard of such a fire and is not related to the loss.

The record does bear out that the physical hazard at issue in this case is that of a fire originating in the inaccessible transmission area of the log skidder. This risk or hazard resulted in the loss. The record further establishes that a breach of the policy warranties did not increase this physical hazard and did not contribute to or cause the loss. The majority is correct in its holding that the burden of proof is on the insurer to show that an increase in risk resulted from the breaches. The trial court, in holding for the insured, had to find that the insurer failed to bear its burden. I find no error whatever and certainly no manifest error in this factual finding by the trial court. The majority result is to reverse the trial court on a factual finding contra to the rule enunciated in *Canter v. Koehring Company*, 283 So.2d 716 (La. 1973).

Finally, it cannot be overlooked that the insured did not personally arrange for or purchase the policy, has a fourth-grade education, did not read the policy, and was without knowledge of warranty violations. Even the fire extinguisher had been supplied by the manufacturer as standard equipment. These facts become significant when we consider the language of *Lee, supra*, to the effect:

> . . . No inquiry was made of plaintiff by anyone respecting encumbrances affecting the truck. It is fair to assume that he was without knowledge that such information was a prerequisite for the insurance's effectiveness." (53 So.2d at 697)

I respectfully dissent.

NOTES

(1) *Points of Opposition.* Taken together, the concurring and dissenting opinions make four distinct points, it seems, in favor of Rodriquez's claim. They might be expanded fairly into these propositions:

[From the concurring opinion:]

a.   Only a "reasonable" prescription can count as a warranty (and it was unreasonable to specify a fire extinguisher as the policy did).

[From Judge Cole's dissent:]

b.   Given Rodriguez's level of acumen, and the offhand way he gave assent to the policy terms, he should not be charged with prescriptions so detailed as the warranties in question.

c.   A breach of warranty about a physical hazard usually provides no defense if the loss was not attributable to it (and the breaches in question did not cause Rodriquez's loss).

d.   The operation of a warranty should be restricted to losses of a kind that might be prevented or moderated by compliance (and compliance with the warranties in question could not have prevented or moderated a fire originating within the skidder's transmission).

Which of these propositions is the most plausible? Which the least?

As to the latter one (d), reconsider Diesinger v. American & Foreign Ins. Co., above. *Diesinger* concerned a loss caused by a holdup by armed bandits during business hours. The court distinguished between that kind of risk, as addressed in a jeweler's block policy, and the risk of "window smashing or cutting", also covered. The court confined the warranty in question to the latter kind of risk. Should similar reasoning have been applied to Rodriguez's case? If not, is that because the jeweler's block policy is more highly structured than the one in Rodriguez's case?

(2) *Moral Hazard.* An instance of a moral-hazard warranty would be a term suspending coverage while Rodriguez's skidder was the sole collateral under a security agreement (*e.g.*, chattel mortgage) and the amount owed exceeded any reasonable valuation of the skidder. For the thought that these circumstances might well violate an increase-of-hazard warranty, see Nemojeski v. Bubolz Mutual Town Fire Ins. Co., 74 N.W.2d 196, 56 A.L.R.2d 419 (Wis. 1956). If so, it is not because the circumstances enhance the *physical* hazard, but because they weaken the owner's incentive to care for the property.

That, or any other "moral hazard warranty", might be thought operative even if, under an applicable statute, a breach of warranty is innocuous if it does not contribute to the loss. A court might confine the statutory rule to physical-hazard warranties, that is, reasoning that the breach of a moral-hazard warranty cannot be a cause of an otherwise compensable loss. So, for example, it has been said of the Texas contribute-to-loss statute that it does not affect policy provisions "the breach of which could not in any event bring about the loss". McPherson v. Camden Fire Ins. Co., 222 S.W. 211, 215 (Tex.Comm.App. 1920). But see Security State Bank v. Aetna Ins. Co., 183 N.W. 92 (Neb. 1921); and see Hawkins v. New York Life Ins. Co., 269 P.2d 389 (Kan. 1954) (misrepresentation case).

Notice that, in advocating a contribute-to-loss rule, Judge Cole suggested a fictive application to moral-hazard warranties: "Causation is implied in such an instance." The function he ascribed to moral-hazard warranties is to suppress the risk of intentional destruction. That is not their sole function. The owner of a skidder heavily mortgaged may be less careful of its safety than an "outright" owner would be. That is, a moral-hazard warranty may provide some assurance that the insured will take precautions against loss.

(3) *General and Specific Terms (reprise).* Some text at p. 209 above calls attention to the maxim that a specific term in a contract controls a general one, and shows how it might be used to minimize the effect of a general warranty. With that, compare the court's statement of *Dittmer & Pelle*, the case about the risk of fire and the storage of unbaled hay. The decision there was that a warranty against increase of hazard was not "controlled or limited by" the insured's acceptance of the risk entailed by the storage of *baled* hay. Is that decision at odds with the maxim?

One might think that the answer to this question depends on whether baled hay was the subject of a warranty or of an excepted cause of loss (*e.g.*, "Excluded:

fire to which the presence of baled hay contributes"). How would an argument to that effect run? How would the contrary argument run?[1]

---

1. According to the opinion, the claimant contended that " 'hay pressed in bales' [was] expressly named and classed as hazardous and excepted in the conditions annexed to the policy".

Chapter 5

COMMERCIAL GENERAL LIABILITY INSURANCE

Policies going by this name provide, as the name indicates, liability coverage for business firms. The name is regularly abbreviated to "CGL".[1] CGL policies stand in contrast with the "personal" lines of insurance, which provide liability coverages for individuals, firms, or both. Examples of those are homeowners policies, for individuals, and automobile insurance. CGL policies stand in contrast also with various specialized policies designed to insure against the liabilities of, among others, physicians, directors and officers, and retail liquor dispensers.

General liability insurance came into prominence in the United States around 1880. Automobile insurance was introduced in 1898. The first liability insurance was commercial liability insurance created to protect employers from liability claims of their employees. Soon thereafter products liability insurance followed. But there was no uniform or standard liability insurance policy prior to 1940, because each liability insurer drafted its own CGL policy. Liability insurers came to recognize the problem and the insurance industry voluntarily standardized CGL insurance policy language. Most GCL policies have taken forms prepared by the Insurance Services Office (ISO), which represents and serves property-casualty insurers. Predecessor organizations introduced a standard form in 1940. Unlike the current one, that form spoke of liabilities "caused by accident". In a successor form that expression was replaced with "caused by an occurrence". Still later, the ISO revised that form and introduced an alternate one providing what is known as "claims made" coverage. Differences between the two are considered at pp. 302 ff.

Following the "Declarations", the CGL policy consists of five numbered sections. Section I describes three coverages:

A. Bodily injury and property damage liability,

B. Personal injury and advertising injury liability, and

C. Medical payments.

---

1. The CGL insurance form is and has been the cornerstone of liability protection for most businesses. The CGL insurance policy originated to provide insurance coverage to defend and to indemnify an insured against liability to third parties for harm caused by the insured. The original CGL insurance policy was the Comprehensive General Liability Insurance Policy, used from the 1940s until the 1986 ISO commercial general liability revision. The 1986 ISO revision of the standard policy eliminated the word "comprehensive" and substituted "commercial" in its place. Hence, the modern Commercial General Liability (CGL) Insurance Policy is the successor to the original Comprehensive General Liability Insurance Policy.

246

Coverage C is not about liabilities. Rather, it provides first-party benefits akin to those provided by accident and health insurance, payable regardless of fault.

This chapter deals with the limitations "caused by an occurrence" and "claim made", and with further limitations expressed in Parts A and B of Section I. Coverage A begins with this sentence, under the heading "Insuring Agreement":

> We will pay those sums that the insured becomes legally obligated to pay as damages because of "bodily injury" or "property damage" to which this insurance applies.

Close readers will understand that they must read farther to understand what, exactly, is being promised. Indeed, they must read *much* farther, for the terms in quotation marks are among the subjects of definitions in Section V. Moreover, a reader may find further restrictions on coverage in one or more endorsements to the policy.

On reading farther in a CGL policy, one finds that the insurer undertakes to provide an insured with a defense to certain suits. The defense obligation is considered squarely hereafter, in Chapter 6. It is the subject also, however, of a number of cases presented in this chapter. The reason is that they throw light on the obligation to indemnify ("We will pay...."). They do so because the defense obligation is limited by reference to the policy coverages. In short, an insurer has no obligation to defend unless the charges made against the insured can be understood to include a covered liability. This matter is illustrated by a case below, Everson v. Lorenz; see p. 252.

A.   CGL COVERAGE A: LIABILITIES FOR BODILY INJURY AND PROPERTY DAMAGE

Elements. A few words from COVERAGE A. BODILY INJURY AND PROPERTY DAMAGE LIABILITY are quoted above. This and other passages in the CGL policy are set out next as a further indication of the structure and sense of the policy.

SECTION I—COVERAGES

COVERAGE A. BODILY INJURY AND PROPERTY DAMAGE LIABILITY

1. Insuring Agreement.

    a. We will pay those sums that the insured becomes legally obligated to pay as damages because of "bodily injury" or "property damage" to which this insurance applies. We will have the right and duty to defend the insured against any "suit" seeking those damages....

    b. This insurance applies to "bodily injury" and "property damage" only if:

   (1) The "bodily injury" and "property damage" is caused by an "occurrence" that takes place in the "coverage territory";

   (2) The "bodily injury" or "property damage" occurs during the policy period. . . .

[The "coverage territory" is specified in Section V—Definition 4. and the "policy period" is specified on page 1 of the Declarations at the beginning of the policy.]

   . . .

SECTION V—DEFINITIONS . . .

3. "Bodily injury" means bodily injury, sickness or disease sustained by a person, including death resulting from any of these at any time.

   . . .

13. "Occurrence" means an accident, including continuous or repeated exposure to substantially the same general harmful conditions.

   . . .

17. "Property damage" means:

   a. Physical injury to tangible property, including all resulting loss of use of that property. All such loss of use shall be deemed to occur at the time of the physical injury that caused it; or

   b. Loss of use of tangible property that is not physically injured. All such loss of use shall be deemed to occur at the time of the "occurrence" that caused it.

PROBLEM

Vincent and Janice DiMare were disappointed in the home they had bought from Lamar Homes, Inc., its builder. In a suit against Lamar they alleged that it had failed to design and to construct the foundation as warranted in the purchase contract. Lamar held insurance coverage in the terms set out above. It brought an action against the insurer, hoping for a declaratory judgment that the DiMare claim was within that coverage. After losing in the federal district court, Lamar appealed.

Being uncertain about the applicable law, that of Texas, the court of appeals certified questions to the State's Supreme Court. Two of these were parallel, except for words drawn from the policy statement of coverage. Those words are represented by blanks in the following quotation of the questions. On a careful reading of the policy terms above, one ought to gather what words are represented by blanks.

"When a homebuyer sues his general contractor for construction defects and alleges only damage to or loss of use of the home itself, do such allegations allege (1 ___) (2 ___) sufficient to trigger the duty to defend or indemnify under a CGL policy?"

The questions appear in full in Lamar Homes, Inc. v. Mid–Continent Cas. Co., 428 F.3d 193 (5th Cir. 2005). What should the answers be? (They are awaited at this writing.)

———

Sub–Part 1 next concerns the definition of *occurrence*, for that is—apart from the matters of place and time—the outermost limit of Coverage A. In particular, Sub–Part 1 concerns the requirement of an "accident", disregarding the included element "exposure to ... harmful conditions". That element is treated at p. 293 ff. Then Part 2 concerns restrictions imposed by the definitions of *bodily injury* and *property damage*.

1. "Occurrence" > "Accident"

One might expect the CGL policy to contain a fuller definition of "accident". It does not, but relies largely on the courts to ascribe meaning to the word. One would expect the courts, given as they are to expanding uncertain terms in policies, to understand the word in a broad sense, and they do. One of the broadest possible conceptions of *accident* treats it as embracing every act of negligence. Some opinions come close to that. Others are more restrained.

The Wisconsin Supreme Court appears to have wavered somewhat in recent years. Three of its opinions are represented next. The first is reported under the heading *Employer's Negligence*. There the court suggested that "accidents" embrace acts of negligence, at least if they are harmful. The court adhered to that thought in *American Family Mutual Ins. Co. v. American Girl*, which follows. Then, however, the court decided *Everson v. Lorenz*, p. 252 below, which can be understood to say that a typographical error is not an accident.

The following Wisconsin employer's-negligence case concerned a charge against an employer that it was negligent in the hiring, training, and supervision of its employees. Cases of this sort have evoked varying responses, as will be seen.

Employer's Negligence

An employer is accountable for bodily injury and physical damage inflicted by an employee acting in the scope of his or her employment. That doctrine is an instance of vicarious liability known as *respondeat superior*. It applies no matter how prudent the employer has been in hiring, training, and supervising employees. Quite apart from that, and whatever the scope of an employment, an employer is accountable for similar injuries if they are the result of substandard conduct in hiring and the like. Often a claim is made against an employer on both counts.

Sometimes a claimant charges an employer with harm that is *accidental*; sometimes not. A road injury caused by the carelessness of a company driver on company business is the result of an "accident" from every point of view. In contrast, if a sales person exhibits a long-standing grievance by punching a customer the harm is not accidental—not, at least, from the employee's point of view. The difference is of some importance when the employer, having provided itself with comprehensive general liability insurance, expects the insurer to provide a defense to the claim.

The word "accident" figured prominently in a policy issued by the St. Paul Fire & Marine Insurance Company to a firm referred to as "WVCY" (Wisconsin Voice of Christian Young, Inc.). WVCY expected St. Paul to defend it when an action was brought against it by one Doyle. Doyle alleged that employees of WVCY had injured her tortiously by filing in a State office a false security agreement, appearing to encumber her assets. (Earlier, she said, she had been kicked in the face while praying outside an abortion clinic.) St. Paul contended that whatever harm the filing had done was not accidental, and so was not within the coverage of its policy.

Anyone might agree that a filing made under Article 9 of the Uniform Commercial Code, concerning secured transactions, was not an accident from the filer's point of view if made with the intent of doing harm. But Doyle charged WVCY with negligence in supervising its employees. When her case reached the Wisconsin Supreme Court, that court had "little trouble" concluding that she had alleged harm stemming from an accident. In default of a definition of the word in the policy, the court consulted dictionary definitions. It was significant, the court thought, that the definitions centered on "an unintentional occurrence leading to undesirable results." CGL policies are designed, the court said, (quoting) "to protect an insured against liability for negligent acts resulting in damage to third-parties." A reasonable insured would expect the word *accident* to include a negligent act. Doyle v. Engelke, 580 N.W.2d 245, 250 (Wis. 1998).

American Family Mutual Ins. Co. v. American Girl, Inc.

Wisconsin Supreme Court, 2004.
673 N.W.2d 65.

This case concerned a "construction project gone awry". The Renschler Company received poor advice from a soils engineer, one Lawson, when preparing to build a warehouse known as the "94DC" for American Girl, Inc., in Middleton, Wisconsin. Hence Renschler failed to do a proper job of compacting soft soil at the site. After completion of the building the foundation sank, the structure buckled and cracked, and the warehouse was declared unsafe and torn down. Renschler was potentially liable to the owner under certain contractual warranties. It held insurance under several CGL policies. A dispute arose over coverage and the issue was submitted in a declaratory-judgment action by one of the insurers, American Family. Along with Renschler, American Girl was a defendant, and later an appellant. The trial court found coverage under some of the policies and not under others. On a first appeal it was decided that none of the policies provided coverage.

On a further appeal American Girl was faced with objections based on a number of exclusions in the CGL policy. Before addressing those the court considered whether or not the claim of loss was covered by the initial statement of the insuring agreement. That statement referred, as usual, to "property damage" resulting from an "occurrence".

[In construing "occurrence", the court referred to the so-called *business-risk* exclusions. Other parts of the opinion deal specifically with those and with other exclusions. The following part of the opinion deals only with the basic insuring agreement. The portions of the opinion dealing specifically with exclusions are presented below in Part C, "EXCLUSIONS (COVERAGE A)", at p. 279 ff.]

The court sometimes referred to the builder by the name it used while doing the work—The Pleasant Company—and before changing it to "American Girl".

■ Diane S. Sykes, Justice.

The CGL's insuring agreement

. . .

i. "Property damage" and the economic loss doctrine

The policy defines "property damage" as "physical injury to tangible property, including all resulting loss of use of that property." The sinking, buckling, and cracking of the 94DC as a result of the soil settlement qualifies as "physical injury to tangible property."

American Family characterizes Pleasant's claim against Renschler as one for economic loss rather than property damage, and argues that the economic loss doctrine bars coverage. The economic loss doctrine generally precludes recovery in tort for economic losses resulting from the failure of a product to live up to contractual expectations. . . . The economic loss doctrine is "based on an understanding that contract law and the law of warranty, in particular, is better suited than tort law for dealing with purely economic loss in the commercial arena." Daanen & Janssen, Inc. v. Cedarapids, Inc., 573 N.W.2d 842, 846 (Wis. 1998).

The economic loss doctrine operates to restrict contracting parties to contract rather than tort remedies for recovery of economic losses associated with the contract relationship. Vogel v. Russo, 613 N.W.2d 177 (Wis. 2000). The economic loss doctrine is a remedies principle. It determines how a loss can be recovered—in tort or in contract/warranty law. It does not determine whether an insurance policy covers a claim, which depends instead upon the policy language.

The economic loss doctrine may indeed preclude tort recovery here (the underlying claim is in arbitration and not before us); regardless, everyone agrees that the loss remains actionable in contract, pursuant to specific warranties in the construction agreement between Pleasant and Renschler. To the extent that American Family is arguing categorically that a loss giving rise to a breach of contract or warranty claim can *never* constitute "property damage" within the meaning of the CGL's coverage grant, we disagree. "The language of the CGL policy and the purpose of the CGL insuring agreement will provide coverage for claims sounding in part in breach-of-contract/breach-of-warranty under some circumstances." 2 Stempel, [Law of Insurance Contract Disputes (2d ed. 1999)] § 14A.02[d], 14A–10. This is such a circumstance. Pleasant's claim against Renschler for the damage to the 94DC is a claim for "property damage" within the meaning of the CGL's coverage grant.

ii. "Occurrence"

Liability for "property damage" is covered by the CGL policy if it resulted from an "occurrence." "Occurrence" is defined as "an accident, including continuous or repeated exposure to substantially the same general harmful conditions." The term "accident" is not defined in the policy.... No one seriously contends that the property damage to the 94DC was anything but accidental (it was clearly not intentional), nor does anyone argue that it was anticipated by the parties. The damage to the 94DC occurred as a result of the continuous, substantial, and harmful settlement of the soil underneath the building. Lawson's inadequate site-preparation advice was a cause of this exposure to harm. Neither the cause nor the harm was intended, anticipated, or expected. We conclude that the circumstances of this claim fall within the policy's definition of "occurrence."

. . . .

The court of appeals has previously recognized that the faulty workmanship of a subcontractor can give rise to property damage caused by an "occurrence" within the meaning of a CGL policy. In Kalchthaler v. Keller Construction Co., 591 N.W.2d 169, 172 (Ct.App. 1999), a general contractor subcontracted out all the work on a construction project; the completed building subsequently leaked, causing over $500,000 in water damage. The court of appeals concluded that the leakage was an accident and therefore an occurrence for purposes of the CGL's coverage grant. Id.

The same is true here. We conclude that the property damage to the 94DC was the result of an "occurrence" within the meaning of the insuring agreement. This brings us to the policy exclusions....

[Reversed and remanded.]

Everson v. Lorenz (and Lorenz Land Development, Inc.)

Wisconsin Supreme Court, 2005.
280 Wis.2d 1, 695 N.W.2d 298.

■ N. Patrick Crooks, J.

This case comes before us on certification from the court of appeals.... Richard Lorenz and Lorenz Land Development, Inc. (Lorenz) seek review of an order ... granting Intervenor Pekin Insurance Company's (Pekin) motion for summary judgment. This case presents the issue of whether Pekin's insurance policy provides coverage to its insured, Lorenz, for strict responsibility misrepresentation and/or negligent misrepresentation claims filed against it by Paul and Michelle Everson (Everson).

The court of appeals certified three questions to this court: (1) Does an alleged strict responsibility misrepresentation and/or negligent misrepresentation in a real estate transaction constitute an "occurrence" for the purpose of a commercial general liability insurance policy such that the insurer's duty to defend the insured is triggered?; (2) What allegations must a complaint contain to plead sufficiently "loss of use" within the meaning of a commercial general liability insurance policy?; and (3) Under what circumstances does a misrepresentation, negligent or strict responsibility, cause the "loss of use" of property such that a "causation nexus" is established?

We conclude that since there is no coverage based on Everson's complaint and the language of the Pekin insurance policy, Pekin has no duty to defend and no duty to indemnify Lorenz against Everson's claims for strict responsibility and/or negligent misrepresentation. The alleged misrepresentation was not an "occurrence" within the meaning of the policy. We hold that Everson must plead more than "damages" in relation to the misrepresentation claims to plead sufficiently a "loss of use" under the policy. We further conclude that since the complaint fails to allege "property damage," in that there is no allegation of an "occurrence," and no allegation of "loss of use," there clearly is not a sufficient allegation of "causation nexus." The "property damage" was caused by defects in the property, not by any misrepresentations of Lorenz.

I. FACTS

For the purposes of this review, the facts of this case are undisputed. [For the purpose of building a home, Everson bought from Lorenz, a real-estate developer, Lot 31 in a subdivision in Brillion, Wisconsin. In this action Everson alleged that Lorenz had represented that no part of Lot 31 lay within a 100-year flood plain, and that part of it did.] The claims alleged in the complaint were as follows: (1) negligent misrepresentation; (2) strict responsibility misrepresentation; (3) intentional misrepresentation; and (4) breach of contract. . . .

At the time of the purchase, Pekin insured Lorenz under a commercial general liability policy. Following the initiation of suit by Everson, Lorenz tendered its defense to Pekin. Pekin has since moved to intervene, bifurcate the insurance coverage issues from the liability and damage issues, and stay all liability and damage issues until the insurance coverage issues have been decided. The circuit court granted this motion. . . .

[The circuit court also granted a motion by Pekin for a summary judgment, ruling that Pekin's policy afforded no coverage with respect to Everson's claims and that, therefore, Pekin owed to Lorenz no duty to defend or to indemnify Lorenz. In an appeal to the court of appeals, the case was certified to this court.]

II. STANDARD OF REVIEW

We review a circuit court's grant of summary judgment de novo. . . . According to Wis. Stat. § 802.08(2), summary judgment will be granted "if the pleadings, depositions, answers to interrogatories, and admissions on file, together with the affidavits, if any, show that there is no genuine issue as to any material fact and that the moving party is entitled to a judgment as a matter of law."

We also address issues regarding the interpretation of an insurance contract. Such interpretation, we have held, presents a question of law which we review de novo. . . .

III. ANALYSIS

The determinative issue presented in this case is whether Pekin's insurance policy provides coverage to Lorenz for the strict responsibility and/or negligent misrepresentation claims filed by Everson. We have held that an insurer's duty to defend its insured is triggered by comparing the allegations of the complaint to the terms of the insurance policy. . . .

Since Pekin's duty to defend is determined by the language in both the policy provisions and the complaint, we set forth the relevant portions of each. The insurance policy states in part:

> [The court's quotation is identical to the parts of the CGL policy set out above (p. 247), except that it omits references to bodily injury, and includes a sentence set out here in the footnote.[2] The court stressed the reference to property damage "during the policy period".]

. . . The relevant allegation of the complaint is as follows:

7. Subsequently, the Plaintiffs discovered that a substantial portion of Lot 31 lay within the 100 year flood plain making the construction of the home which they wished to construct on the property impossible in the location in which the Plaintiffs wished to build based upon the pre-sale representations of Lorenz, rendering the property unbuildable for the Plaintiffs and causing the Plaintiffs to incur damages as a result in excess of $37,000.

In looking at the four corners of the complaint and the insurance policy, we recognize that "[o]ur objective is to further the insured's reasonable expectations of coverage while meeting the intent of both parties to the contract." *Benjamin v. Dohm*, 189 Wis.2d 352, 359, 525 N.W.2d 371 (Ct.App. 1994) (citation omitted). Accordingly, we must not rewrite the insurance policy to bind an insurer to a risk which the insurer did not contemplate and for which it has not been paid. *Id.* at 365.

A. "OCCURRENCE"

Pekin's insurance policy would cover liability for "property damage" if it resulted from an "occurrence." In the policy, "occurrence" is defined as "an accident, including continuous or repeated exposure to substantially the same general harmful conditions." Although the term "accident" was not defined by the policy, this court has often relied on dictionary definitions for assistance. . . . *Black's Law Dictionary* defines "accident" as "[a]n unintended and unforeseen injurious occurrence; something that does not

---

2. We may at our discretion investigate any "occurrence" and settle any claim or suit that may result.

occur in the usual course of events or that could not be reasonably anticipated." *Black's Law Dictionary* 15 (7th ed. 1999). Additionally, we have defined accident to mean " '[a]n unexpected, undesirable event' " or " 'an unforeseen incident' " which is characterized by a " 'lack of intention.' " *Doyle [v. Engelke]*, 219 Wis.2d at 289 (quoting *The American Heritage Dictionary of the English Language* 11 (3d ed. 1992)).

Lorenz, in relying on these definitions, argues that the misrepresentation was an "accident." It contends that a reasonable insured would expect that the Pekin policy definition of "occurrence" as an "accident" would cover the typographical error relied upon by Everson in the pre-sale representation. In support of this claim, Lorenz cites a Maryland Court of Appeals case, *Sheets v. Brethren Mutual Insurance Co.*, 679 A.2d 540 (Md. 1996), where the court held that negligent misrepresentation can be considered an "accident." In *Sheets*, the insureds sold their farmhouse. After the transaction, the buyers claimed that the insureds intentionally and negligently misrepresented that the septic system at their farmhouse was in "good working condition." *Id*. at 541. The buyers alleged that the septic system began leaking and flooding, which required it to be replaced. The court acknowledged that "negligent misrepresentation is a form of negligence," and that "an act of negligence constitutes an 'accident' under a liability insurance policy when the resulting damage was 'an event that takes place without [the insured's] foresight or expectation.' "[6] *Id*. at 548 (quoting *Harleysville v. Harris & Brooks*, 235 A.2d 556, 559 (Md. 1967)).

Lorenz insists that our negligence analysis in *Doyle*, a case involving allegations of negligent supervision of employees, is "strikingly similar" to the analysis in *Sheets*. [For a description of *Doyle* see p. 250 above.] In *Doyle*, we held that an insurance policy using the term "event" covered negligent acts. The policy defined "event" the same as this policy defines "occurrence," as " 'an accident, including continuous or repeated exposure to substantially the same general harmful conditions.' " *Doyle*, 219 Wis.2d at 289. The court then held that both the definition for "negligence" and "accident" "center on an unintentional occurrence leading to undesirable results." *Id*. at 290. As a result, the court found that a reasonable person would expect the policy provision using the term "event" to cover negligent acts. Lorenz asks this court to extend that holding to acts involving negligent misrepresentation.

This court has never specifically held that strict responsibility and/or negligent misrepresentation are similar to other kinds of negligence so as to categorize them as "accidents." *See Smith [v. Katz*, 226 Wis.2d 798, 806 (1999)] at 822. We specifically left the question open in *Smith*, to determine if "these torts are sufficiently different from other kinds of negligence to

---

6. The court in *Sheets v. Brethren Mutual Insurance Co.*, 679 A.2d 540, 551 (Md. 1996), recognized that jurisdictions split on whether a negligent misrepresentation can constitute an "occurrence." The court stated: "We prefer to follow those cases that treat negligent misrepresentation like other forms of negligence, which are covered as accidents if the insured did not expect or foresee the resulting damage. In accordance with our own precedent outlined above, the ultimate inquiry is whether the resulting damage is 'an event that takes place without one's foresight or expectation.' " *Id*. (citation omitted).

preclude their categorization as 'accidents' " in insurance liability policies. *Id*. We now conclude that Lorenz's misrepresentation cannot be considered an "accident" for the purpose of Pekin's liability insurance coverage.

Lorenz's misrepresentation can be defined as an "act of making a false or misleading statement about something. . . ." *Black's Law Dictionary* 1016 (7th ed. 1999). To be liable, Lorenz must have asserted a false statement, and such an assertion requires a degree of volition inconsistent with the term accident. *See Sheets*, 679 A.2d at 552–53 (Karwacki, J., dissenting). Although this assertion may be prompted by negligence, it is nevertheless devoid of any suggestion of accident. *See C.Y. Thomason Co. v. Lumbermens Mut. Cas. Co.*, 183 F.2d 729 (4th Cir. 1950). More specifically: "Injury that is caused by negligence must be distinguished from injury that is caused by a deliberate and contemplated act initiated at least in part by the actor's negligence at some earlier point." *GATX Leasing Corp. v. Nat'l Union Fire Ins. Co.*, 64 F.3d 1112, 1118 (7th Cir. 1995).

This interpretation is distinguishable from our previous discussion of the terms "event," "negligence," and "accident" which, in *Doyle*, centered on an unintentional, rather than volitional, act. *See Doyle*, 219 Wis.2d at 289. Accordingly, in this case, we do not determine that injury or damage prompted from a negligent misrepresentation is ipso facto caused by "accident," within the meaning of commercial general liability policies. *See* J.P. Ludington, Annotation, *Liability Insurance: Accident or "Accidental" as Including Loss Resulting from Ordinary Negligence of Insured or His Agent*, 7 A.L.R.3d 1262, § 4 (1966). We conclude instead that where there is a volitional act involved in such a misrepresentation, that act removes it from coverage as an "occurrence" under the liability insurance policy.

This holding is similar to a case decided by the Seventh Circuit, *Red Ball Leasing, Inc. v. Hartford Accident & Indemnity Co.*, 915 F.2d 306 (7th Cir. 1990). There, the insured financed the sale of four trucks to a lessee. The insured later repossessed the trucks based on the mistaken belief that the lessee had defaulted on his payments. The insured was sued and claimed that it should be defended and reimbursed under the terms of its insurance policy. The insurance company refused to defend, arguing that the conversion was not an "accident" triggering such a duty. The court held that coverage was not required for the conversion because it was an intentional act, and intentional acts are not "accidents" under the terms of the policy. *See Mindis Metals, Inc. v. Transp. Ins. Co.*, 209 F.3d 1296 (11th Cir. 2000). Specifically, the court held:

> A volitional act does not become an accident simply because the insured prompted the act. Injury that is caused directly by negligence must be distinguished from injury that is caused by a deliberate and contemplated act initiated at least in part by the actor's negligence at some earlier point. The former injury may be an accident. . . . However, the latter injury, because it is intended and the negligence is attenuated from the volitional act, is not an accident.

Red Ball Leasing, 915 F.2d at 310l (citations and footnote omitted). Since this determination in *Red Ball*, several courts have cited this holding positively. *See* [four cases cited].

Likewise, Lorenz may have made a mistake of fact and/or error in judgment, but it later acted with volition. It is clear that Lorenz intended to give Everson information as to whether the property was within the 100–year flood plain. *See Red Ball*, 915 F.2d at 311. What happened here, stripped to its essentials, is that an "action," not an "accident," of Lorenz gave Everson the misleading information.... Even if there was a mistake made in filling out the Real Estate Condition Report, and that mistake induced reliance, the decision to give Everson the report is not an "accident" within the meaning of the policy. *See Red Ball*, 915 F.2d at 311.

. . .

The judgment of the circuit court is affirmed.

■ Ann Walsh Bradley, J. (*dissenting*).

. . .

I

The majority concludes that "where there is a volitional act involved in such a misrepresentation, that act removes it from coverage as an 'occurrence' under the liability insurance policy." The problem with the majority opinion lies not with this conclusion. Rather, the problem arises when in identifying the relevant act, the majority shifts focus from a specific non-volitional act to a more general volitional act. Of course, if the level of generality is extended far enough, a volitional act can always be found somewhere down the line.

As in many cases, the relevant facts here drive the analysis. Lorenz gave the Eversons a Real Estate Condition Report that contained a typographical error, mistaking Lot 21 for Lot 31. The parties agree that the Eversons' Lot 31 has a portion of the property in the flood plain, but the Real Estate Condition Report failed to disclose that fact. Instead, the report erroneously listed Lot 21 as part of the flood plain.

The Eversons attached to the complaint the Real Estate Condition Report which stated, "[s]ome lots as shown on Exhibit A attached have as part of their back lots land that lies within the approximate 100[-]year flood plain. On lots 14–22 this area falls in the wooded ravine area and for lots 23–27, *21* & 32 it falls within the grassland area on the back of the lots." (Emphasis added.)

According to the complaint, the Eversons received the Real Estate Condition Report, which provided that "no portion of Lot 31 lay within the 100[-]year flood plain." When they purchased Lot 31, the Eversons received a Warranty Deed, incorporating by reference the representations contained in the report. After the transaction was completed, the Eversons discovered that a substantial portion of Lot 31 was located within a 100-year flood plain. They alleged that the flood plain made "the construction of the home which they wished to construct on the property impossible in the location in which the Plaintiffs wished to build based upon the pre-sale representations of Lorenz." As a result, they sustained damages having already paid for items that they could no longer use.

The majority, however, tucks away in a footnote the relevant facts of the negligent misrepresentation claim. [The footnote quoted, as above, from the Real Estate Condition Report.] In doing so, it shifts the focus away from the accidental typographical error contained in the report and instead focuses in the text on the general action that Lorenz gave the report to Everson [citing the paragraph preceding this opinion]. Consequently, the majority then opines that there is no accident here at all because the decision to give Everson the report is not an "accident." *Id.* Accordingly, the majority concludes that because there is no accident, there is no coverage under the policy.

No one asserts that the "act" of giving the report was an accident. Of course it was volitional or intentional. As part of the real estate transaction, Lorenz needed to provide the Real Estate Condition Report.

Stripped to its essentials, the majority here determines that an accidental act (a typographical error) is not an accident. How can it arrive at such an anomalous conclusion? Only by skewing the focus as described above and ignoring the "negligent" component of a negligent misrepresentation claim.

II

[Justice Bradley referred to the two dictionary definitions quoted in the majority opinion.] Both of the definitions . . . center on an unintentional and unforeseeable event leading to undesirable results. In this case, the alleged negligent misrepresentation of Lorenz meets these criteria. However, in its efforts to convince the reader that there was no accident, the majority emphasizes only "misrepresentation" and ignores the "negligent" component of the negligent misrepresentation claim. It defines Lorenz's misrepresentation as an " 'act of making a false or misleading statement about something. . . .' " (citing *Black's Law Dictionary* 1016 (7th ed. 1999)). This characterization in itself is a "false and misleading statement," for the conduct at issue is Lorenz's alleged *negligent* misrepresentation.

Negligent misrepresentation is defined as "[a] careless or inadvertent false statement in circumstances where care should have been taken." *Black's Law Dictionary* 1016 (7th ed. 1999). Unlike the majority, I have little trouble concluding that a reasonable insured would expect the term "accident" to include a "careless or inadvertent false statement." On this matter, I find the case of *Sheets v. Brethren Mut. Ins. Co.*, 679 A.2d 540 (Md. 1996), instructive.

. . .

As this court stated in *Smith*, 226 Wis.2d at 822, the decision in *Sheets* is "strikingly similar" to our negligence analysis in *Doyle v. Engelke*, 580 N.W.2d 245 (1998). . . . Because the conduct in this case also involves a negligent act, *Doyle* cannot be meaningfully distinguished.

Accordingly, I would conclude that a negligent misrepresentation can constitute an "occurrence" or "accident" for purposes of general liability insurance. After all, language in an insurance policy must be construed as understood by a reasonable person in the position of an insured.... In this case, a reasonable person would not split the legal hair advanced by the majority.... Rather, a reasonable person would expect that the policy would cover the typological error relied upon by Everson in the pre-sale representation.[1]

[Justice Bradley concluded also that the Eversons' complaint sufficiently alleged "loss of use" and "causation", the "remaining elements necessary to trigger a duty to defend".

[Chief Justice Shirley S. Abrahamson joined in the dissent. Justice Louis B. Butler, Jr., agreed with Part II of the dissent. But he concurred in the result, saying: "I agree with the majority that the misrepresentation alleged in the complaint is insufficient to establish a 'causation nexus' within the terms of that insurance policy. The preexisting 100-year flood plain in this case caused any 'property damage,' not Lorenz's presale misrepresentation."]

NOTES

(1) *Reconciliation.* Are the two foregoing decisions easy to reconcile?

In *American Girl* the court made an interesting argument, omitted above, in support of its broad understanding of "occurrence", based on some exclusions in the CGL policy form. Some of these are called "business-risk exclusions"; they work primarily against mishaps in construction work and the production of goods. The court said:

> If, as American Family contends, losses actionable in contract are never CGL "occurrences" for purposes of the initial coverage grant, then the business risk exclusions are entirely unnecessary.... Why would the insurance industry exclude damage to the insured's own work or product if the damage could never be considered to have arisen from a covered "occurrence" in the first place?

This argument might lead one to think that *occurrence* has a broader meaning in relation to insureds who are builders and manufacturers than it does in relation to one whose business, like that of Lorenz, is subdividing real estate and selling lots. How plausible is that?

(2) *Judge and Jury.* Juries are consulted routinely about accidents. When there is conflicting evidence about, say, why a car fell off a bridge, or why Humpty Dumpty fell off a wall, a jury may well decide. That is, a jury may write the history of a loss. It is another matter, however, to ascribe meaning to the word *accident* in a policy. If a jury has anything to say about that, one would not know it from the foregoing cases.

On the other hand, the New York Court of Appeals approved these questions, submitted to a jury in Consolidated Edison Company v. Allstate Ins. Co., 774 N.E.2d 687 (N.Y. 2002): "Was the property damage the result of an accident?", and "Was the property damage the result of an occurrence?" ("a clear and simple statement of the issue, importing the language of the policies" Id. at 692). The judge had given

---

1. Alternatively, I note that to the extent the term "accident" is ambiguous, it must be construed against an insurer and in favor of coverage....

the jury some assistance in understanding the policy language, but only with respect to the intention of the actor, Con Ed. The case concerned the pollution of a site formerly owned by Con Ed. When the jury asked for the "legal definition" of accident/occurrence, they were told that unintended damage caused by intentional conduct can qualify.

(3) *Burden of Persuasion.* In *Consolidated Edison* the claimant (Con Ed) objected that the trial court had placed on it the burden of persuading the jury that the damage concerned was a consequence of an accident. It should not have been required, it thought, to establish the contrary. "Con Edison argues that compelling it to prove that property damage is a result of an accident or occurrence forces it to prove a negative—that it did not intend to cause the property damage." Id. at 691.

That argument was at least ingenious. It rested on the propositions that the words "occurrence" and "accident" operated, in effect, as an exclusion of intended harm, and that insurers bear the burden of persuasion as to exclusions. The court rejected the first of these propositions. "*Any* language," it said, "providing coverage for certain events of necessity implicitly excludes other events."

The court buttressed its ruling with policy considerations. "Especially in the environmental pollution context [the ruling] 'provides the insured with an incentive to strive for early detection that it is releasing pollutants into the environment' (*Northville Indus.* [*Corp. v. Nat'l Union Fire Ins. Co.,* 679 N.E.2d 1044, 1049 (N.Y. 1997)]). In addition, it 'appropriately places the burden of proof on the party having the better and earlier access to the actual facts and circumstances surrounding the discharge,' including information about its own intentions and expectations (*id.*)."

(4) *Second Thoughts.* Reconsider the two parallel questions about Texas law indicated in the Problem at p. 248 above. If Texas law is like Wisconsin law, what will the answers be?

---

2.   Harms

Consult the terms of the CGL Coverage A, set out on pp. 247–48 above, noticing especially the definitions of *bodily injury* and *property damage.* Obviously these expressions are vital to an understanding of the coverage. They are frequently litigated. The phrase "to which this insurance applies", which concludes the first sentence of the Insuring Agreement, restricts the coverage to instances within the definitions.[1] Although the definitions provide a degree of certitude about coverage, they leave some questions open. Does "bodily injury" include mental disturbance? Does "property damage" include a firm's financial reverse? These and other questions are pursued in the Exercises that follow.

A. BODILY INJURY

EXERCISE

This exercise analyzes this CGL Section V definition: "Bodily injury" means bodily injury, sickness or disease sustained by a person, including death resulting from any of these at any time.[2]

---

1. Friar v. Statutory Trustees of Kirkwood Sports Ass'n, 959 S.W.2d 808 (Mo.App. 1997).

(1) *The Physical Inquiry.* **Question #1**. Does the CGL "bodily injury" definition mean only physical injuries and not nonphysical harm such as an emotional, mental or psychological injury? Why or Why not?

Most courts hold that "bodily injury" refers *only to physical injuries* and not to nonphysical or emotional harm standing alone.[3] In Tackett v. American Motorists Ins. Co., 584 S.E.2d 158 (W.Va. 2003), "Miss L.," a fifteen year old customer, alleged sexual harassment by an assistant store manager in front of another individual. The West Virginia Supreme Court explained:

> There are no averments that bodily injury resulted from Mr. Tackett's alleged sexual misconduct. Instead, the complaint alleges that Miss L. has sustained "great embarrassment, consternation, mental pain and anguish, and emotional upset." We have held, though, that such injuries, standing alone, do not constitute "bodily injury": In an insurance liability policy, purely mental or emotional harm that arises from a claim of sexual harassment and lacks physical manifestation does not fall within a definition of "bodily injury" which is limited to "bodily injury, sickness, or disease".

Id. at 166.

But the cases are split. Some courts hold that a purely nonphysical or emotional harm standing alone is a bodily injury.[4] Cf. Aetna Cas. & Sur. Co. v. O'Rourke Brothers, Inc., 776 N.E.2d 588 (Ill.App. 2002), in which one of the policies concerned defined "bodily injury" so as to include mental injury.

Question #2. Regarding an "emotional injury" standing alone as a defined bodily injury, can you construe the entire bodily-injury definition as ambiguous so that the *contra proferentem* rule (ambiguity construed against the insurer) applies? Why or Why not?

In Lavanant v. General Acc. Ins. Co., 595 N.E.2d 819 (N.Y. 1992), the New York Court of Appeal stated:

---

2. See generally Eric Mills Holmes, Vol. 20 Holmes' Appleman on Insurance 2d § 129.2 [C] "Meaning of 'Bodily Injury' " in Coverage A *and* [D] "Emotional Distress May Constitute a 'Bodily Injury' " (2002).

3. See, e.g., E–Z Loader Boat Trailers, Inc. v. Travelers Indem. Co., 726 P.2d 439, 443 (Wash. 1986); Nationwide Mut. Fire Ins. Co. v. Somers, 591 S.E.2d 430 (Ga.App. 2003), holding "bodily injury" pertains to physical injury to body and does not include non-physical, emotional or mental harm; United Servs. Auto. Ass'n v. Doe, 792 N.E.2d 708 (Mass.App.Ct. 2003) (bodily injury does not embrace emotional distress).

4. *See* Nelson v. Want Ads of Shreveport, Inc., 720 So.2d 1280, 1283 (La. Ct. App.

1998), holding bodily injury includes emotional harm without any physical trauma.; NPS Corp. v. Insurance Co. of N. Am., 517 A.2d 1211 (N.J.App.Div. 1986)(Sexual harassment claim for emotional distress and mental anguish was within the definition of "bodily injury"); State Farm Mut. Auto Ins. Co. v. Ramsey, 368 S.E.2d 477 (S.C. Ct. App. 1988), holding negligent infliction of emotional trauma is a bodily injury. Cf. Gehan Homes, Ltd. v. Employers Mut. Cas. Co., 146 S.W.3d 833 (Tex.Ct.App. 2004) (insurers did not establish as a matter of law that there was no allegation of bodily injury). *See also* Annot, "Homeowner's Liability Insurance Coverage of Emotional Distress Allegedly Inflicted on Third Party by Insured," 88 A.L.R.5th 254.

Unambiguous provisions of a policy are given their plain and ordinary meaning. But where there is ambiguity as to the existence of coverage, doubt must be resolved in favor of the insured and against the insurer. . . . We conclude that the key term "bodily injury," as used in the policy before us, is ambiguous. . . . The ambiguity is heightened, not eliminated, by the policy's explicit definition of "bodily injury" as "bodily injury, sickness or disease." The categories "sickness" and "disease" in the insurer's definition not only enlarge the term "bodily injury" but also, to the average reader, may include mental as well as physical sickness and disease. We decline General Accident's invitation to rewrite the contract to add *"bodily* sickness" and *"bodily* disease," and a requirement of prior physical contact for compensable mental injury. General Accident could itself have specified such limitations in drafting its policy, but it did not do so.

We note that the definition proposed by plaintiffs—one that includes coverage for purely emotional distress—is consistent with recent case law in this State allowing recovery for such injuries in a variety of contexts. In upholding such claims, we have recognized that emotional trauma may be as disabling as physical injury, and that whether a person suffers one form of injury or the other may be a fortuity determined solely by the particular vulnerability of an individual. In a given situation "one person may be susceptible to a heart attack while another may suffer a depressive reaction."

Id. at 822. In sum, purely mental injuries incurred in the absence of any physical injury are within the policy's definition of "bodily injury".[5]

Question #3. Should "sickness or disease" in the bodily injury definition include emotional or psychological injury?[6]

Question #4. Should it make any difference if the emotional injury produces physical manifestations?[7]

---

5. *Accord* Evans v. Farmers Ins. Exch., 34 P.3d 284, 287 (Wyo. 2001). Regarding an insured's pure emotional distress, the court stated: "The New York Court of Appeals thus held that the term bodily injury, as defined in the policy before it, was ambiguous. We make the same conclusion and resolve the ambiguity in favor of coverage."). *Cf.* Workers' Compensation: As a matter of first impression in Guess v. Sharp Manufacturing Co. of America, 114 S.W.3d 480, 487 (Tenn. 2003), the Tennessee Supreme Court held that a worker must demonstrate actual HIV exposure to collect workers' compensation benefits for mental injury due to potential HIV exposure. A Tennessee assembly worker alleged mental injuries after she was exposed to blood of a co-worker who she believed was HIV positive. The court, concerned with furthering AIDS-related prejudices and stereotypes, denied her workers' compensation claim because she offered no credible evidence of actual HIV exposure.

6. *See* American Economy Ins. Co. v. Fort Deposit Bank, 890 F.Supp. 1011 (M.D. Ala. 1995) (Under Alabama law, mental anguish is "bodily injury." The terms "sickness" or "disease" necessarily encompasses mental anguish.).

7. Most courts hold that emotional distress itself causing physical manifestations is within the "bodily injury" definition. In Garvis v. Employers Mut. Cas. Co., 497 N.W.2d 254 (Minn. 1993), the court explained:

Emotional distress with appreciable physical manifestations can qualify as a "bodily injury" within the meaning of an insurance policy. The term "bodily injury," as ordinarily understood, would not draw a nice distinction between emotional distress and its harmful physical consequences, if any; rather, "bodily injury" would be thought of as encompassing both because they are so closely interrelated.

Question #5. Does emotional distress with accompanying physical manifestations produced by a noncovered economic loss constitute "bodily injury"?[8]

(2) *Other "Bodily Injury" Definitional Questions.*

a. Motorola, a manufacturer of cellular wireless handheld telephones ("cell phones"), was sued in a number of class action lawsuits seeking recovery of sums of money allegedly owed by Motorola to alleviate customers' allegedly harmful exposure to radio frequency radiation. Cellular telephone users' claims against the insured manufacturer were for the cost of "headsets" to alleviate exposure to radio frequency radiation and to prevent damage to the users' cells and nerves.

Question #6. Were the cellular telephone users' claims within the following CGL language: "We will pay those sums that the insured becomes legally obligated to pay as damages because of 'bodily injury'?" See Motorola, Inc. v. Associated Indem. Corp., 878 So.2d 838, 841–42 (La. App. 2004).[9]

b. Prior to undergoing chemotherapy treatment, Harry Kurchner and his wife, Suzanne Kurchner, decided to cryopreserve Harry's sperm with South Florida Institute for Reproductive Medicine ("SFIRM"). Cryopreservation offered the Kurchners an opportunity to have children in the future should Harry's chemotherapy treatment make him sterile. Harry subsequently deposited five sperm samples with SFIRM. SFIRM was to store the sperm samples separately in tanks maintained with alarms that were to set off when the cooling apparatuses of the tanks failed. SFIRM instead stored all of the samples together and the samples were destroyed when the storage tank's cooling apparatus failed. Harry eventually became sterile as a result of his chemotherapy treatment.

Question #7. If the Kurchners sued SFIRM for damages because of the destroyed sperm, would SFIRM's CGL provide coverage for "bodily injury" damages? See Kurchner v. State Farm Fire & Cas. Co., 858 So.2d 1220 (Fla.App. 2003).

Id. at 257. Moreover, the New Jersey Supreme Court added:

> The term "bodily injury" is ambiguous as it relates to emotional distress accompanied by physical manifestations. That ambiguity should be resolved in favor of the insured.... That emotional distress can and often does have a direct effect on other bodily functions is well recognized. An insured who is sued on account of an injury involving physical symptoms could reasonably expect an insurance policy for liability for bodily injuries to provide coverage.

Voorhees v. Preferred Mut. Ins. Co., 607 A.2d 1255, 1261 (N.J. 1992).

8. Under California law, the policy did not required defendant to defend plaintiff on the claims of emotional and physical distress, as the claims arose from economic loss, which was not covered by the policy. See Keating v. National Union Fire Ins. Co., 995 F.2d 154 (9th Cir. 1993) (Cal. law); Waller v. Truck Ins. Exchange, Inc., 900 P.2d 619 (Cal. 1995).

9. *Cf.* Associated Aviation Underwriters v. Wood, 98 P.3d 572, 600–02 (Ariz. App. 2004). Bodily injury included cellular damage caused by exposure to chemical trichloroethylene (TCE) even after exposure ceased; exposure and exposure-in-residence occurring during policy period triggered coverage as well as manifestation of "disease" during policy period.

B. PROPERTY DAMAGE

EXERCISE

Review the definition of "property damage" quoted above in Section V Definitions.[10] Beginning with the 1966 ISO revision, CGL policies consistently limit property damage to "tangible property" that can be physically handled or touched.[11] Since the CGL policy confines property damage to tangible property, injury to or destruction of property refers only to physical or tangible property. In Capitol Indem. Corp. v. Wright, 341 F. Supp.2d 1152 (D.Nev. 2004), for example, nursing-home employee's conversion or loss of funds in "nursing-home" patient's bank account involved property damage as defined within nursing home's liability insurance policy, as it amounted to a loss of "tangible property," particularly where money was converted in its physical form.

Question #1. Would any of the following "a., b., or c." be "property damage" under a CGL policy?

a. Contractors and homebuilders knew hazardous materials were present on residential property, which diminished the value of the residential property. See Auto–Owners Ins. Co. v. Carl Brazell Builders, Inc., 588 S.E.2d 112 (S.C. 2003).[12]

b. Diminution in value of homes caused by installation of allegedly defective polybutylene plumbing system. See Travelers Ins. Co. v. Eljer Mfg., Inc., 757 N.E.2d 481 (Ill. 2001), overruling Marathon Plastics, Inc. v. International Insurance Co., 514 N.E.2d 479 (Ill.App. 1987).[13]

c. America Online's Version 5.0 access software altered customers' existing software, disrupted their network connections, caused them loss of stored data, and caused their operating systems to crash—in other words, damage to computer's circuits, switches, drives, data and instructions

---

10. See generally Eric Mills Holmes, Vol. 20 Holmes' Appleman on Insurance 2d § 129[D] Meaning of "Property Damage" in Coverage A (2002).

11. See, e.g.: Nautilus Ins. Co. v. John Gannon, Inc., 103 Fed. Appx. 534 (5th Cir. 2004) (Tex. law). Any damage which billboard company may have against insured, in connection with agreement to jointly build and sell sign, was purely economic damage and not CGL "property damage". Amerisure Mut. Ins. Co. v. Paric Corp., 2005 WL 2708873 (E.D. Mo. 2005). Allegations of damage to hotels arising from defective synthetic stucco and windows qualify as an "occurrence" and "property damage," triggering a CGL insurer's duty to defend. Jares v. Ullrich, 667 N.W.2d 843 (Wis.App. 2003). Buyers' complaint alleged (1) insured misrepresented animal infestation in home sold to buyers, and (2) buyers were unable to occupy home for two months and incurred repair and restoration costs. Complaint stated claim of physical injury to tangible property or loss of use of property within homeowners insurance policy's definition of property damage.

12. The property was used as a training site for aerial bombing during World War II. The complaint in underlying action did not allege any physical injury that would meet CGL definition of "property damage".

13. Diminution in value constitutes an intangible economic loss rather than "property damage" under CGL insurance policies defining "property damage" as physical injury to tangible property that occurs during the policy period. See also Generali–U.S. Branch v. Alexander, 87 P.3d 1000 (Mont. 2004). Motel owners' complaint alleging contractor's liability for full refund due to failure of heating and plumbing system for building addition sought compensation for lost payments not for physical injury to their property or loss of use of that property.

caused by defective software. See America Online, Inc. v. St. Paul Mercury Ins. Co., 347 F.3d 89 (4th Cir. 2003), applying Virginia law.[14]

The California Supreme Court explained that the "the focus of coverage for property damage is ... the property itself, and does not include intangible economic losses, violation of antitrust law or nonperformance of contractual obligations.... The occurrence or act leading to coverage must be an injury to tangible property, not one's economic interest." Id. at 626, 633. As a consequence, damage to "intangible" property such lost profits, investments, copyrights, good will, and other commercial economic losses, are generally held not to constitute property damage. Waller v. Truck Ins. Exch., 900 P.2d 619 (Cal. 1995).[15] See generally Jay M. Zitter, Annotation, "Liability Policy Coverage for Insured's Injury to Third Party's Investments, Anticipated Profits, Goodwill, or the Like, Unaccompanied by Physical Property Damage," 18 A.L.R.5th 187.

In contrast, damage from "loss of use" of property is property damage. In the CGL definition (quoted above) "loss of use" as property damage is defined alternatively: "**a.** Physical injury to tangible property, including all resulting loss of use of that property. ... or **b.** Loss of use of tangible property that is not physically injured."

Consequently, loss-of-use of "tangible" property is recoverable when tangible property is or is not physically injured. *See* Lyons v. State Farm Fire & Cas. Co., 811 N.E.2d 718 (Ill.App. 2004). Lyons, an insured, allegedly built levees that protruded onto Rendleman's property. Rendleman sued for a permanent injunction for their removal. The complaint alleged that Lyons's actions interfered with the Rendlemans' "actual possessory rights" in their property. The court said: "A more clear statement of a 'loss of use' could not be made without using the exact policy language."

Question #2. Assume a manufacturer of construction cranes, insured under a CGL policy, sells a defective crane that collapses in front of a restaurant thereby impairing the restaurant's income. If the restaurant sues the manufacturer and recovers lost income, would the manufacturer be covered by the "loss of use" under the CGL policy? *See Waller* at 628.[16]

---

14. A series of class actions were filed against America Online, alleging that its Version 5.0 access software had "bugs" in it. While any damage to circuits, switches, drives, or any other physical components of a computer caused by defective software are covered, there would be no coverage for the loss of instructions to configure the switches or of data stored magnetically. Instructions, data, and information are abstract and intangible. Damage to them would not be physical damage to tangible property. The litigation was settled, with AOL establishing a $15.5 million fund to compensate the plaintiffs.

15. *See also*: Cunningham v. Universal Underwriters, 120 Cal.Rptr.2d 162 (Cal.App. 2002). Landlord's alleged failure to timely deliver real property to the tenant for use as an automobile dealership did not cause "property damage"; the landlord at most caused intangible economic damage. United National Ins. Co. v. Frontier Ins. Co., Inc., 99 P.3d 1153 (Nev. 2004). Subcontractor's allegedly negligent welding of support structure for sign and modifications of bolts (sign fell later) were not "property damage". Auto-Owners Ins. Co. v. Carl Brazell Builders, Inc., 588 S.E.2d 112 (S.C. 2003). Great American Lloyds Ins. Co. v. Mittlestadt, 109 S.W.3d 784 (Tex.App. 2003). Economic losses do not constitute "property damage".

16. *See also*: Hartzell Industries, Inc. v. Federal Ins. Co., 168 F.Supp.2d 789 (S.D. Ohio 2001). Power company's partial loss of use of boiler house because house became hot due to company's inability to use insured's

Finally, consequential economic losses due to physical damage to commercial property are insured. The CGL insuring agreement, quoted above, states: "We will pay those sums that the insured becomes legally obligated to pay as damages *because of . . . 'property damage' . . . .*" (emphasis supplied) Accordingly, if tangible property is physically injured, then consequential economic loss "because of . . . property damage" is insured.[17] In Cyprus Amax Minerals Co. v. Lexington Ins. Co., 74 P.3d 294 (Colo. 2003), for instance, two years after the insured sold a mine, the mine experienced substantial damage stemming from a landslide deep below the ground. After years of litigation, the insured and the purchaser settled their claims and the insured sought indemnification from its insurers. The Colorado Supreme Court held that "property damage" was at issue because "property damage" under the language of the policies could have included the costs of repairing the mine and the costs incurred by the purchaser after the landslide.

Question #3. Assume an insured's defective synthetic oil caused property damage to a customer's gear boxes, resulting in financial harm incurred by the customer from repairing and replacing the gear boxes and recalling gear boxes containing the insured's oil. Would the customer's economic losses be covered "because of . . . property damage"? See St. Paul Fire & Marine Ins. Co. v. Amsoil, Inc., 51 Fed. Appx. 602 (8th Cir. 2002) (Wis. law).[18]

---

roof fans constituted "property damage" under the CGL policy definition as "loss of use of tangible property that is not physically injured," even though loss constituted purely economic damages. Liberty Mut. Ins. Co. v. Wheelwright Trucking Co., Inc., 851 So.2d 466 (Ala. 2002). Trailer buyer's inability to use truck tractors for its most profitable loads due to failure of trailers to carry heavy loads was "property damage" even though the tractors were not useless. CGL policy defined "property damage" to include the loss of use of tangible property that was not physically injured and did not specify any particular degree or extent of the loss of use.

17. *See* Viking Constr. Mgmt. v. Liberty Mut. Ins. Co., 831 N.E.2d 1 (Ill. App. 2005). Where underlying complaint alleges no physical damages but only damages for repair and replacement of defective product or construction, damages constitute economic losses, not "property damage".

18. The court first held that coverage under the CGL policies was limited to actual physical harm to property caused by the insured's negligence, and thus did not extend to the diminution in the value of the customer's business caused by the damaged machines. Nonetheless, because the repair and replacement costs of the gear boxes were caused by property damage, they were not exempt economic losses and must be reimbursed by the insurers under the policies. *See also* Unionamerica Ins. Co., Ltd. v. Nufab Corp., 30 Fed.Appx. 30 (3d Cir. 2002). Under Pennsylvania law, "loss of use" provision in insured nightclub's CGL policy covered loss of use of another nightclub's property, which occurred when patrons of insured's nightclub allegedly formed large and unruly crowds that denied the other nightclub's employees and patrons the use of their business premises, which, in turn, undermined the other nightclub's ability to sell food, beverages, and entertainment to its patrons.

B.   GCL Coverage B: Personal and Advertising Injury Liability

This title is that of Coverage B in Section I of the CGL. The term *personal and advertising injury* is defined in Section V of the CGL. The definition lists seven offenses liability for which may be covered. The materials that follow concern chiefly the first two of these four:

> The wrongful eviction from, wrongful entry into, or invasion of the right of private occupancy of a room, dwelling or premises that a person occupies, committed by or on behalf of its owner, landlord or lessor;

> Oral or written publication of material that violates a person's right of privacy;

> The use of another's advertising idea in your "advertisement"; or

> Infringing upon another's copyright, trade dress or slogan in your "advertisement".

The other three (of the seven offenses) are set out in the footnote.[1] The list is preceded by this statement:

> "Personal and advertising injury" means injury, including consequential "bodily injury", arising out of one or more of the following offenses: . . .

Section V contains also this definition:

> "Advertisement" means a notice that is broadcast or published to the general public or specific market segments about your goods, products or services for the purpose of attracting customers or supporters.

The definition continues with refinements concerning the Internet, set out on p. 271 below. Complaints asserting advertising injury usually concern, aside from publications, the infringement of a copyright or trademark, or the misappropriation of an idea.

Turning back now to Coverage B in Section I of the CGL, one finds this insuring agreement:

> a.   We will pay those sums that the insured becomes legally obligated to pay as damages because of "personal and advertising injury" to which this insurance applies. . . .

---

1.   a. False arrest, detention or imprisonment; b. Malicious prosecution; c. [Wrongful eviction, as above]; d.   Oral or written publication of material that slanders or libels a person or organization or disparages a person's or organization's goods, products or services; e. [Violations of a right of privacy, as above]; f. [Misuse of another's advertising idea, as above]; or g. [Infringement, as above.]

All the language quoted hereabout is from ISO Form CG 00 01 10 01, copyrighted by ISO Properties, Inc. 2000.

b.   This insurance applies to "personal and advertising injury" caused by an offense arising out of your business but only if the offense was committed in the "coverage territory" during the policy period.

[Material omitted here concerns the insurer's duty to defend and rights to investigate and to settle suits.]

Coverage B differs from Coverage A in notable respects. It is not confined to liability for *occurrences*. It is not confined to liabilities for *bodily injuries* or *physical damage*. There is no question that it extends to liabilities for *economic harm*. Indeed, the principal liabilities it covers are for economic harm, for psychic harm, and for harm to reputation. On the other hand, aside from "personal injury", it is confined, as Coverage A is not, to liabilities for a set of nominate torts (*e.g.*, libel, slander, and copyright infringement).

1.   Advertising Injuries

The conception of advertising injury embraces, by definition, a publication that violates a person's right of privacy. The general shape of this right is almost always traced to the 1890 article *The Right of Privacy*, by Warren and Brandeis, at 4 Harv.L.Rev. 193. For further references see Resources Bankshares Corp. v. St. Paul Mercy Ins. Co., 407 F.3d 631 (4th Cir. 2005). The conception took a new turn in the Telephone Consumer Protection Act of 1991, 47 U.S.C. § 227—"the Act". One offense described in the Act is sending unsolicited ads by fax. The offense is known as a "blast fax" when the same ad is sent at one time to many addresses. Some courts have been persuaded that an offender's liability to a recipient, created by the Act, is within the CGL definition of *advertising injury*. But not all, as the following opinion shows.

American States Ins. Co. v. Capital Associates
United States Court of Appeals, 7th Cir., 2004.
392 F.3d 939.

Capital Associates of Jackson County was the target of a class action brought on the JC Hauling Company alleging a violation of the Act. The premise was subsection (b)(1)(C) of the Act. American States, which had issued a CGL policy to the defendant, undertook a defense of the action, but only upon reserving its right to disclaim coverage. It then brought this action for a declaratory judgment that coverage did not exist. The district court ruled that American States was required to defend the action, believing that an unsolicited ad by fax violates the recipient's right of privacy. It therefore dismissed the declaratory-judgment action. It made no ruling about the claimants' right to indemnity, and none about expected or intended injury, the subject of an exclusion. American States appealed.

■ EASTERBROOK, CIRCUIT JUDGE.

[The court decided to address the "duty-to-defend" question, despite a complication about its jurisdiction. It turned then to consider what counts as a violation of "a person's right of privacy".]

"Privacy" is a word with many connotations. The two principal meanings are secrecy and seclusion, each of which has multiple shadings. See *Restatement (Second) of Torts* § 652 (1977); Richard S. Murphy, *Property Rights as Personal Information*, 84 Geo. L.J. 2381 (1996). A person who wants to conceal a criminal conviction, bankruptcy, or love affair from friends or business relations asserts a claim to privacy in the sense of secrecy. A person who wants to stop solicitors from ringing his doorbell and peddling vacuum cleaners at 9 p.m. asserts a claim to privacy in the sense of seclusion. Some other uses of the word "privacy" combine these senses: for example, a claim of a right to engage in consensual sexual relations with a person of the same sex, or to abort an unwanted pregnancy, has both informational (secrecy) and locational (seclusion) components, with an overlay of substance (the objection to governmental regulation).

American States contends that its advertising-injury coverage deals with secrecy rather than seclusion. The language reads like coverage of the tort of "invasion of privacy," where an oral or written statement reveals an embarrassing fact [or] brings public attention to a private figure, or casts someone in a false light through publication of true but misleading facts.... Perhaps the language reasonably could be understood to cover improper disclosures of Social Security numbers, credit records, email addresses, and other details that could facilitate identity theft or spamming....

JC Hauling does not allege that Capital Associates published any information about it, and the district judge did not directly address whether the policy is limited to publication of secret information. Indeed the judge did not remark the difference between secrecy and seclusion. Instead the judge stated that § 227(b)(1)(C) has been understood to protect privacy—see *International Science & Technology Institute, Inc. v. Inacom Communications, Inc.*, 106 F.3d 1146, 1150 (4th Cir. 1997)(dictum) (quoting from legislative history)—and deemed that observation conclusive. *International Science & Technology Institute* used the word in the sense of seclusion: an unexpected fax, like a jangling telephone or a knock on the door, can disrupt a householder's peace and quiet, even though it is easy to throw a junk fax, like a piece of junk mail, in the trash without any risk that someone will observe activities that occur inside one's home. Section 227(b)(1)(C) doubtless promotes this (slight) interest in seclusion, as it also keeps telephone lines from being tied up and avoids consumption of the recipients' ink and paper.... But the question is not how the word "privacy" was used in the debates that led to § 227(b)(1)(C), or in its implementing regulations, but what the word means in this insurance policy. To say, as the district court did, that § 227(b)(1)(C) protects privacy, and then stop the analysis, is to avoid the central question in the case: whether the policy covers the sort of seclusion interest affected by faxed ads.

One reason to doubt that the policy covers the claim is the identity of the plaintiff. JC Hauling is a corporation, and businesses lack interests in seclusion. It is not just that they are "open for business" and thus welcome phone calls and other means to alert them to profitable opportunities. It is that corporations are not alive. Where does a corporation go when it just wants to be left alone? Most states hold that business entities lack privacy interests. See *Restatement (Second) of Torts* § 652I Comment c. Cf. *United States v. Morton Salt Co.*, 338 U.S. 632, 652 (1950). Our point is not that business entities lack interests protected by § 227(b)(1)(C), but that it does not help to call them "privacy" interests. Corporate managers have interests in seclusion, but the state suit was filed by the corporation rather than by any natural person. A fax is less disturbing than a phone call, and a business-related call at work does not invade the managers' interest in seclusion.

The class of junk-fax recipients may include real rather than artificial people, however, so we cannot stop yet. The structure of the policy strongly implies that coverage is limited to secrecy interests. It covers a "publication" that violates a right of privacy. In a secrecy situation, publication matters; otherwise secrecy is maintained. In a seclusion situation, publication is irrelevant. A late-night knock on the door or other interruption can impinge on seclusion without any need for publication. Contacting one customer at a time may not be "publication" at all for purposes of advertising-injury coverage. ... Perhaps automated faxes to hundreds of recipients could be deemed a form of publication, but this would be irrelevant to the seclusion interest. To put this differently, § 227(b)(1)(C) condemns a particular means of communicating an advertisement, rather than the contents of that advertisement—while an advertising-injury coverage deals with informational content.

[The court observed that the scope of the "privacy" coverage under the advertising-injury clause had not been adjudicated previously by the highest court of any state, or by any Illinois court, or by any appellate federal court. "We hold," the court said, "that an advertising-injury clause of the kind in American States' policy does not cover the normal consequences of junk advertising faxes."]

For completeness we add that the property-damage clause in the policy is no more useful to Capital Associates; junk faxes use up the recipients' ink and paper, but senders anticipate that consequence. Senders may be uncertain whether particular faxes violate § 227(b)(1)(C) but all senders know exactly how faxes deplete recipients' consumables. That activates the policy's intentional-tort exception (which applies to the property-damage coverage though not the advertising-injury coverage): it forecloses coverage when the recipient's loss is "expected or intended from the standpoint of the insured." Because *every* junk fax invades the recipient's property interest in consumables, this normal outcome is not covered.

So clear is this that American States need not provide a defense to the suit, even though Illinois (whose law applies) requires insurers to defend when coverage is a close issue, whether or not the policy would provide indemnity.... This issue is not close.

Reversed

NOTES

(1) *More on Faxes and Privacy.* The Court of Appeals for the Fourth Circuit has approved the analysis in the main case ("adept"), ruling that the policies before it did not cover the sorts of privacy invasions envisaged by the Act. Resource Bankshares Corp. v. St. Paul Mercury Ins. Co., 407 F.3d 631 (4th Cir. 2005).

The Court of Appeals for the Eighth Circuit found ways to distinguish *American States* in another case in which a violation of the Act was charged. The insured, an auto dealer, held a "Garage coverage" which combined features of Coverages A and B of the CGL. The coverage insured against liability for damages "because of injury to which the insurance applies caused by an occurrence arising out of garage operations". *Injury* was defined so as to include "invasion of rights of privacy". *American States* was different, the court said, in that the policy it concerned addressed invasion of privacy only as a form of "advertising injury", and not as a component of injury at large. Also, in *American States*, "the intentional nature of the violations appeared undisputed". Not so in the car dealer's case. Universal Underwriters Ins. Co. v. Lou Fusz Auto. Network, Inc., 401 F.3d 876 (8th Cir. 2005).

Are both of these distinctions solid? (In *American States* Judge Easterbrook disapproved the district-court decision, which was affirmed in *Lou Fusz Auto.*)

(2) *The Internet.* The definition of *advertisement,* quoted above (p. 267), continues by saying that, for purposes of the definition, "Notices that are published include material placed on the Internet or on similar electronic means of communication;" and "Regarding websites, only that part of a website that is about your goods, products or services for the purposes of attracting customers or supporters is considered an advertisement."

————

Amazon.com International, Inc. v. American Dynasty Surplus Lines Ins. Co.

Washington Court of Appeals, 2004.
85 P.3d 974, *review denied*, 103 P.3d 200 (Wn.2004).

A suit against Amazon charged it with patent infringement. The claimant was Intouch Group. Amazon tendered its defense to two insurers, one of which was American Dynasty, which insured Amazon against patent infringement, but only as excess coverage. The other was the Atlantic Mutual Insurance Company, which had issued a CGL policy to Amazon.

Both insurers refused to undertake the defense. Amazon settled with American Dynasty and in that connection assigned to American Dynasty its rights against Atlantic Mutual. This action was brought by American Dynasty against Atlantic Mutual, charging that Atlantic Mutual should have provided a defense because the Intouch suit had alleged an advertising injury. The CGL policy defined "advertising injury" so as to include "Misappropriation of advertising ideas or style of doing business".

■ ELLINGTON, J.

. . .

According to Intouch's complaint, Intouch holds patents for technology that "provides a method by which consumers can download and listen to portions of pre-selected music over the Internet." The samples are compressed or otherwise digitally altered. Intouch alleged Amazon [and others had] used Intouch's technology to enable consumers to preview music available for purchase: "Each of the Defendants has at least one network web site, which allows consumers to preview pre-selected portions of pre-recorded music over the internet.... Intouch contends that each of the Defendants' web sites ... infringe upon the Patents."[a]

Advertising Injury

. . .

Misappropriation of an advertising idea may be accomplished by the "wrongful taking of another's manner of advertising,"[9] by "the wrongful taking of an idea concerning the solicitation of business and customers,"[10] or by "the wrongful taking of the manner by which another advertises its goods or services."[11] The misappropriation must occur "in the elements of the advertisement itself—in its text, form, logo, or pictures—rather than in the product being advertised."[12]

Patent infringement arising from the manufacture of an infringing product is not an advertising injury even if the infringing product is used in advertising.[13] But patent infringement may constitute an advertising injury *"where an entity uses an advertising technique that is itself patented."*[14] That was the essence of Intouch's allegation against Amazon.[15] Giving the

a. The quotations in this paragraph and elsewhere, not otherwise attributed, are from "Clerk's Papers".

9. *Am. States Ins. Co. v. Vortherms*, 5 S.W.3d 538, 543 (Mo.Ct.App. 1999); *Fluoroware, Inc. v. Chubb Group of Ins. Cos.*, 545 N.W.2d 678, 682 (Minn.Ct.App. 1996).

10. *Green Mach. Corp. v. Zurich–Am. Ins. Group*, 313 F.3d 837, 839 (3rd Cir. 2002); *Frog, Switch & Mfg. Co. v. Travelers Ins. Co.*, 193 F.3d 742, 748 (3rd Cir. 1999).

11. *Applied Bolting Tech. Prods., Inc. v. United States Fid. & Guar. Co.*, 942 F.Supp. 1029, 1034 (E.D.Pa. 1996).

12. *Iolab Corp. v. Seaboard Sur. Co.*, 15 F.3d 1500, 1506 (9th Cir. 1994).

13. *Id.* ("While patent infringement can be piracy of the advertised product, generally it is not piracy of the elements of the advertisement itself.").

14. *Id.* at 1507 n.5 (emphasis added) (citing *Bank of the W. v. Superior Court*, 2 Cal.4th 1254, 1275, 833 P.2d 545 (1992)); *see also State Auto Prop. & Cas. Ins. Co. v. Travelers Indem. Co. of Am.*, 343 F.3d 249, 258 & n.12 (4th Cir. 2003) (trademark that serves to promote a company's products to the public is an advertising idea, and not merely a label or identifier).

15. In the event this was not clear from the complaint, Intouch filed a claim chart in support of its complaint pursuant to the requests of federal patent local rule 3.6 (N.D.Cal. 2001) in which it detailed this allegation:

> After entering the AMAZON.COM web site, users can navigate through the AMAZON.COM music area and view various music products, such as CD's, that are available for purchase on-line. The AMAZON.COM music web site also provides the user the ability to choose pre-selected

required liberal construction to the pleadings, Intouch alleged that its patented music preview technology was an element of Amazon's advertisement. The Intouch complaint thus conceivably alleged misappropriation of an idea concerning the solicitation of business and customers.

Course of Advertising

An advertising injury must occur in the course of advertising goods for sale. "Advertising" normally refers to " 'any oral, written, or graphic statement made by the seller in any manner in connection with the solicitation of business.' "[16] It may also involve the "widespread distribution of promotional material to the public at large."[17] Amazon's website exists for the purpose of promoting products for sale to the public. This is advertising. Intouch's complaint thus implicitly alleged that Amazon used its product in its course of advertising.

Causal Connection Between Advertising and Injury

An advertising injury must also have a causal connection with the insured's advertising activities.[18] That is, the advertising activities must cause the injury, not merely expose it; an injury that could have occurred independent and irrespective of any advertising is not an advertising injury.[19]

This causal requirement is the reason most patent infringement claims do not constitute advertising injuries. The basis of such claims is typically the sale of infringing products, not their advertisement.[20] Nor does an advertising injury occur where the injury is caused by the subsequent advertising of an already infringing product.[21]

Atlantic Mutual contends that a software program embedded in a website cannot satisfy the causation requirement for an advertising injury. Atlantic relies particularly upon *Microtec Research, Inc. v. Nationwide*

---

portions of pre-recorded music products by clicking on an icon that identifies a music product available for preview.

16. *State Auto Prop. and Cas. Ins. Co.*, 343 F.3d at 259 (quoting *Elan Pharm. Research Corp. v. Employers Ins. of Wausau*, 144 F.3d 1372, 1377 (11th Cir. 1998)).

17. *Vortherms*, 5 S.W.2d at 542, 544.

18. *Simply Fresh Fruit, Inc. v. Cont'l Ins. Co.*, 94 F.3d 1219, 1221 (9th Cir. 1996) (citing *Bank of the W.*, 2 Cal. 4th at 1277).

19. *Id.* at 1222–23.

20. *Id.* (quoting *Iolab*, 15 F.3d at 1506) ("a patent is infringed by making, *using*, or selling a patented invention, not by advertising it") (emphasis added). As American Dynasty points out, the 1994 amendment to the patent law allowing an infringement claim to be based on an offer to sell has removed any suggestion that patent infringement cannot occur in the course of an insured's advertising activities as a matter of law. *See Homedics*, 315 F.3d at 1139 (recognizing the basis

for such holdings as invalidated by recent changes in patent law). But because Intouch's complaint alleges an infringement based on Amazon's *use* of its patented product, the 1994 amendments do not affect the outcome here.

21. *See, e.g., Simply Fresh Fruit*, 94 F.3d at 1222–23 (allegation that defendant infringed on patent for automated fruit slicer and then advertised improved product did not meet causation requirement for advertising injury); *Microtec Research, Inc. v. Nationwide Mut. Ins. Co.*, 40 F.3d 968, 971 (9th Cir. 1994) (harm caused by misappropriation of competitor company's software code, not by subsequent advertising that might have misled customers); *Gitano Group, Inc. v. Kemper Group*, 26 Cal.App.4th 49, 60, 31 Cal.Rptr.2d 271 (1994) (infringement of patented method for acid washing jeans, where the jeans were later advertised, did not constitute advertising injury).

Mutual Insurance Co.[22] But the facts and issues there were different. In *Microtec,* a software company allegedly passed off a competitor's software as its own, misleading customers "into thinking [it] was capable of writing leading edge compiler code as good as [the competitor's]."[23] As the circuit court noted, however, there was no allegation that Microtec used the stolen code in its advertising. Injury resulted from Microtec's misappropriation of the code, not from any advertising, and there was thus no advertising injury under the policy.[24]

By contrast here, the alleged injury derived not merely from misappropriation of the code, but from *its use as the means to market goods for sale.* In other words, the infringement occurred in the advertising itself. Intouch's allegations therefore satisfied the causation requirement for a potential advertising injury.[25]

Atlantic Mutual had a duty to defend Amazon unless the injuries alleged by Intouch were clearly not covered by the policy. Because the injuries were conceivably covered, Intouch's complaint triggered Atlantic Mutual's duty to defend. As Amazon's assignee, American Dynasty was entitled to summary judgment in its favor.

. . .

Reversed and remanded for entry of summary judgment in favor of American Dynasty, and for a fees award.

NOTES

(1) *Advertising Idea* vs. *Advertising Product Idea.* Another division of the Washington Court of Appeals had occasion to distinguish *Amazon.com* in Auto Sox USA v. Zurich North America, 88 P.3d 1008 (Wash.App.2004). Auto Sox, the insured, makes and sells advertising signs for attachment to the roofs of vehicles. One Elmer invented and patented an improved way of displaying rooftop advertising. Suing Auto Sox, he charged it with having infringed his patent. The CGL policy concerned did not cover the infringement claim, but Auto Sox claimed the right to a defense under its coverage of liability for "misappropriation of an advertising idea".

The appellate court reversed a ruling in favor of Auto Sox. It cited a number of judicial definitions of "advertising idea", and said: "Generally, these definitions focus on what the insured has taken. If the insured took an idea for soliciting business or an idea about advertising, then the claim is covered. But if the allegation is that the insured wrongfully took a patented product and tried to sell that product, then coverage is not triggered."

Auto Sox had argued that the Elmer patent was an advertising idea because it pertained to displays designed to advertise. Not so, the court said: "this argument ignores the distinction between an advertising idea and an advertised product. Auto Sox did not take Mr. Elmer's ideas about how to solicit customers with his patented design for a rooftop sign. Auto Sox took his idea for the manner in which a rooftop

---

22.   40 F.3d 968, 971 (9th Cir. 1994).

23.   *Id.*

24.   *Id.*

25.   Atlantic Mutual also argues in passing that Intouch's injury cannot have been caused by Amazon's advertising because customers would not have been aware that they were using an infringing product. Whether the customer knows about the infringement is irrelevant.

sign is attached to a vehicle. In other words, Auto Sox's alleged infringement occurred not in advertising but in the manufacture and sale of an infringing product." Id. at 1011.

(2) *Mom & Pop Stores*. "Advertising" has been understood often to mean "widespread promotional activities directed to the public at large." See Hayward v. Centennial Ins. Co., 430 F.3d 989, 990 (9th Cir. 2005) (Cal.law); Bank of the West v. Superior Court, 833 P.2d 545, 553 n.9 (Cal. 1992). It might follow that the CGL "advertising" coverage is of little value to a small-business firm having a limited clientele. To that objection the California Supreme Court has responded that firms like that should buy broader coverages. Hameid v. National Fire Ins. of Hartford, 71 P.3d 761 (Cal.2003). A critic has objected, believing that the court overlooked market realities; various coverages are unavailable to a small firm privately held, especially if it is a sole proprietorship.[1]

(3) *". . . as damages"*. Coverage B in the CGL policy form requires the insurer to account for sums that the insured becomes obligated to pay "as damages".[2] If the insured is charged with disgorging unlawfully acquired gains, and no more, the insurer is not required to provide a defense. So it was held in *Bank of the West*, cited in Note 2 above. Coverage A is limited in the same way; but disgorgement alone is less likely to be sought in a claim otherwise within that coverage.

Cases about Coverage A are divided about whether or not the word *damages* comprises cleanup costs that are charged, by legislative authority, against firms found to have caused environmental degradation. For a ruling that it does, see Morton International v. General Accident Ins. Co. of America, 629 A.2d 831 (N.J. 1993).

(4) *"Unfair Competition" Confined*. The claim asserted against the insured in *Bank of the West* was one based on a statute prohibiting unfair business practices. The court joined others in ruling that "the term 'unfair competition' as used in policy language defining 'advertising injury' refers to the common law of unfair competition. . . . [T]his conclusion substantially limits the scope of coverage." Id. at 551.

The court justified the limitation by reference to the "deterrent goal" of the statute. One having violated the statute ought not to be permitted simply to "shift the loss to his insurer and, in effect, retain the proceeds of his unlawful conduct." Id. at 553.

PROBLEM

The HAL Corporation is a provider of computing services known globally by the logo "HAL". HAL Inc. is a provider of local catering. HAL Inc. has registered on the

---

1. See D. Gauntlett, The Proper Definition of "Advertising" . . ., Mealey's Emerging Insurance Disputes, Oct. 21, 2003.

2. See SECTION IV—COMMERCIAL GENERAL LIABILITY CONDITIONS

. . .

5. Premium Audit

a. We will compute all premiums for this Coverage Part in accordance with our rules and rates.

b. Premium shown in this Coverage Part as advance premium is a deposit premium only. At the close of each audit period we will compute the earned premium for that period and send notice to the first Named Insured. The due date for audit and retrospective premiums is the date shown as the due date on the bill. If the sum of the advance and audit premiums paid for the policy period is greater than the earned premium, we will return the excess to the first Named Insured.

c. The first Named Insured must keep records of the information we need for premium computation, and send us copies at such times as we may request.

Internet under the name www.hal.com. Searchers for computing services have hit that web site hundreds of thousands of times. "Big HAL" has sued "little HAL" for, among other things, "domain name piracy". Little HAL holds coverage of liability for the "misappropriation of advertising ideas or style of doing business". Must the insurer provide little HAL with a defense? See State Auto Property & Casualty Ins. Co. v. Travelers Indemnity Co. of America, 343 F.3d 249 (4th Cir. 2003).

If so, can it be said that Coverage B of the CGL policy form is of little value to small business firms?

2.   Personal Injuries

As used in the CGL policy form the term *personal injury* does not signify a broken bone or other bodily injury, as it does in ordinary speech. Rather, it signifies the harms, chiefly psychic and financial, arising from specified offenses. The coverage extends to liabilities for harms inflicted on disembodied beings, such as business firms.

The standard list of offenses appears above at p. 267 and n.1 there. A complaint that does not charge one of the specified offenses does not require that the insurer defend or indemnify the insured defendant. So ALPA, the pilots' union, found when a member charged it with a violation of its duty to represent him competently in a grievance proceeding, and with the intentional infliction of emotional distress. ALPA's "broad form" policy included coverage for "humiliation that results in injury to the feelings . . . of a natural person. . . ." The plaintiff had been humiliated, he charged. But, on parsing his complaint, the court found that it mentioned humiliation as a kind of injury suffered, and not as a recognized tort claim. "The gist of the complaint concerns the inadequate representation. . . . We conclude that Virginia law does not require coverage in these circumstances." Air Line Pilots Ass'n v. Twin City Fire Ins. Co., 803 A.2d 1001, 1004, 1006 (D.C.App. 2002).

Even a liability based on an offense specified in the policy may not be covered, owing to one or another exclusion. ALPA's policy did not cover "humiliation" inflicted by its intention. The standard policy does not cover damages arising out of the willful violation of a penal statute, or those arising from a false and defamatory statement made with knowledge of its falsity.

Litigation is common in which liability for an advertising injury is charged, along with liability for a "personal injury". The two are not coupled in the cases that follow.

Westfield Insurance Group v. J.P.'s Wharf, Ltd.
Delaware Supreme Court, 2004.
859 A.2d 74.

In 2001, the State Human Relations Commission found that J.P.'s Wharf Restaurant, and its owner, Peter Russo (collectively "Wharf"), engaged in racial discrimination when Wharf refused to serve certain patrons and ordered them to leave. The Commission ordered Wharf, *inter alia*, to pay damages totaling $6,000 to the complaining patrons, and to pay a $5,000 civil penalty. Wharf was insured by Westfield Insurance Group, under a commercial policy covering "personal injury," defined as: injury, other than "bodily injury," arising out of. . . .

> c. The wrongful eviction from, wrongful entry into, or invasion of the right of private occupancy of a room, dwelling or premises that a person occupies by or on behalf of its owner, landlord or lessor.

After Wharf filed an insurance claim for expenses related to the discrimination complaint, Westfield sought a declaratory judgment that its policy did not cover those expenses. The Superior Court held that the "wrongful eviction" clause provided coverage for Wharf's discriminatory conduct. This appeal followed.

■ Berger, Justice.

The sole issue is the scope of the coverage provided under the Westfield insurance policy. . . . Several other jurisdictions have considered similar policy language, reaching different conclusions. In *Insurance Company of North America v. Forrest City Country Club*, 819 S.W.2d 296 (Ark.Ct.App. 1991), for example, the policy language defined "personal injury" to include "wrongful entry into, or eviction of a person from a room, dwelling or premises that the person occupies. . . ." The Arkansas appellate court found the language ambiguous, as "eviction" could mean interference with a possessory property interest or, if used in its popular sense, simply the process of being forcefully removed or ejected from a particular location. Giving the insured the benefit of a liberal construction, the Arkansas court held that the insurer had a duty to defend a claim of racial discrimination brought by a woman who was barred from playing tennis at the insured's country club.

In *STK Enterprises, Inc. v. Crusader Insurance Company*, 14 P.3d 638 (Ore.Ct.App. 2000), the insured sought coverage for the costs of defending and settling three racial discrimination claims brought by patrons who were refused entry into the insured's restaurant and bar. An Oregon appellate court held that the same "wrongful eviction" clause as that considered in *Forrest City* covers only claims arising from a possessory interest in the property. Similarly, in *Zelda v. Northland Insurance Company*, 66 Cal.Rptr.2d 356 (Cal.Ct.App. 1997), a California appellate court concluded that the same "wrongful eviction" language covers tort claims involving interference with an interest in real property, not claims made by business patrons.

We are satisfied that Westfield's "wrongful eviction" clause plainly requires that the claim involve a possessory interest in property, and adopt the reasoning of the *Zelda* court:

> An insurance policy, like any other contract, must be construed in its entirety, with each clause lending meaning to the other. The proposal that the policy definition covers any wrongful "eviction," understood

in the popular sense, fails to give the phrase "from, a room, dwelling or premises that the person occupies" a function in the definition. Because an eviction, popularly understood, is necessarily from *somewhere* the phrase in question is redundant unless it means something other than merely "from somewhere." In this regard, we observe that the term "to occupy," in one of its popular senses, means "to reside in as an owner or tenant." Thus, the only reasonable explanation for the additional phrase is to clarify that the wrongfulness of the ejection must consist in, or attach to, an invasion of the right of occupation.[9]

Since the patrons who filed their racial discrimination complaints against Wharf had no possessory interest in the restaurant premises, the "wrongful eviction" provision in Wharf's insurance policy does not cover expenses it incurred in resolving those complaints.

Based on the foregoing, the Superior Court judgment is reversed.

NOTES

(1) *Occupancy and Right to Occupy*. This Note puts together two rulings about the CGL-policy phrase "invasion of the right of private occupancy of a room, dwelling or premises that a person occupies". One question about it is whether or not *occupancy*, as distinguished from a right to occupy, is required by the phrase. The answer given in Hobbs Realty & Constr. Co. v. Scottsdale Ins. Co., 593 S.E.2d 103 (N.C.App. 2004), was No. The court said that the phrase "includes situations wherein a party suffers injury after he has entered into a contract for possession of realty and thus has gained a 'right of' private occupancy, even if he has not yet assumed physical possession of the property." Id. at 108. Hence the court reversed a summary judgment against a firm which had leased a beach property to a family and had refused to provide a key to a member of the family. The action was brought by that firm to establish coverage under its policy. (According to the tenants, in an action against that firm, the refusal was based on racial prejudice.) The court relied on a supposed ambiguity in the phrase in contention. *Question*: Where is the ambiguity?

Neither occupancy nor a right to occupy was alleged when a Bronx realty firm was sued for having violated fair-housing laws. One claimant was an association for "Reform Now". Its employees had presented themselves to the firm as prospective tenants, it alleged, and, owing to their skin color, were either referred to a rental agency or "steered" to the South Bronx. In an action by the firm against its CGL insurer, the court considered the same phrase construed in *Hobbs Realty*, and ruled that it did not encompass the fair-housing claim. The allegations against Hobbs Realty stood in sharp contrast to those against the Bronx firm, the court said. Rosenberg Diamond Dev. Corp. v. Wausau Ins. Co., 326 F.Supp.2d 472 (S.D.N.Y. 2004).

(2) *Questions*. If a lawn-care firm were to repudiate a contract to mow a homeowner's lawn, would the phrase quoted in the foregoing Note be applicable? If not, would the phrase apply if the firm were to scatter filth on the lawn? An astonishing answer to the latter question is suggested by Nationwide Mut. Fire Ins. Co. v. Somers, 591 S.E.2d 430 (Ga.App. 2003). There, however, the insured was charged by a woman with having desecrated her son's grave site, contrary to its

---

9.   66 Cal.Rptr.2d at 364 (Emphasis in original. Citations omitted.).

agreement, causing her emotional distress. If that charge amounts to charging invasion of a right of occupancy, as the court saw it, who is the occupant? (The insurer was excused from indemnifying the insured by reason of an exclusion of "personal injury.... For which the insured has assumed liability in a contract or agreement".)

(3) *Pollution Liability: Personal Injury?* The New York Court of Appeals has concluded that, unless pollution is a purposeful act, liability for it is not among those for personal injuries. It did so upon consulting the other offenses listed in the CGL policy as sources of personal injury, and finding them to require purposeful conduct. County of Columbia v. Continental Ins. Co., 634 N.E.2d 946 (N.Y.1994). Even if that is wrong, it seems, a liability for pollution may be excluded unless it is sudden and accidental. That view was taken both in *County of Columbia* and in Buell Indus., Inc. v. Greater N.Y. Mut. Ins. Co., 791 A.2d 489 (Conn. 2002), each court reasoning from a pollution exclusion. In *Buell Industries* the insured objected that the exclusion in one of its policies was not made applicable to the personal-injury coverage. To that the court answered, quoting, "The fact that coverage ... for 'personal injury' does not contain its own pollution exclusion clause merely points out that the insurance company never contemplated (justifiably) that [personal injury coverage] might be interpreted to cover pollution damages to land, given the context of the whole policy." Id. at 510, n.28. The New York court reasoned somewhat more technically: the exclusion would be surplusage if it could be circumvented via the personal-injury coverage.

C. Exclusions (Coverage A)

American Family Mutual Ins. Co. v. American Girl, Inc.

Wisconsin Supreme Court, 2004.
673 N.W.2d 65.

The portions of this opinion dealing specifically with the "basic insuring agreement" and the meaning of "occurrence" commence above at p. 250. A refreshing review of those portions might be helpful. The part of the opinion adjudicating "exclusions" appears here.

The parties disputed the applicability of several exclusions: "expected or intended" losses; "contractually-assumed liability"; and certain "business risks" (a/k/a "your work" or "your product" exclusions). There was also a question about the applicability of the "professional services liability" exclusion in certain excess policies.

Among the exclusions dealt with, the first was the " 'expected or intended' exclusion". As to that the court noticed that Renschler had engaged Lawson, the soils engineer, to analyze conditions at the site before beginning work, and on his advice had engaged in "rolling surcharging" to prepare the site for construction. (" 'Surcharging' is a process by which soils are compressed to achieve the density required to support the weight of a building or other structure.'') The insurer argued that the "expected or intended" exclusion applied because of Renschler's expectation that some settlement would occur. The court disagreed. It said: "American Family does not argue that 'property damage' was expected or intended by the insured (which is what the exclusion requires), only that some degree of settlement must have been expected under the circumstances. This is insufficient to trigger the exclusion.''

■ DIANE S. SYKES, JUSTICE

D.   The "contractually-assumed liability" exclusion

The court of appeals held that exclusion (b), for contractually-assumed liabilities, applied to preclude coverage under all the policies at issue in this case. Exclusion (b) states:

This insurance does not apply to: . . .

b.   "Bodily injury" or "property damage" for which the insured is obligated to pay damages by reason of the assumption of liability in a contract or agreement. This exclusion does not apply to liability for damages:

(1) Assumed in a contract or agreement that is an "insured contract," provided the "bodily injury" or "property damage" occurs subsequent to the execution of the contract or agreement; or

(2) That the insured would have in the absence of the contract or agreement.

. . . "The key to understanding this exclusion . . . is the concept of liability assumed." 2 Rowland H. Long, The Law of Liability Insurance § 10.05[2], 10–56, 10–57 (2002). As one important commentator has noted,

Although, arguably, a person or entity assumes liability (that is, a duty of performance, the breach of which will give rise to liability) whenever one enters into a binding contract, in the CGL policy and other liability policies an "assumed" liability is generally understood and interpreted by the courts to mean the liability of a third party, which liability one "assumes" in the sense that one agrees to indemnify or hold the other person harmless.

16 Eric Mills Holmes, Holmes' Appleman on Insurance 2d (2d ed. 2000), § 132.3, 36–37.

The term "assumption" must be interpreted to add something to the phrase "assumption of liability in a contract or agreement." Reading the phrase to apply to all liabilities sounding in contract renders the term "assumption" superfluous. We conclude that the contractually-assumed liability exclusion applies where the insured has contractually assumed the liability of a third party, as in an indemnification or hold harmless agreement; it does not operate to exclude coverage for any and all liabilities to which the insured is exposed under the terms of the contracts it makes generally.

This reading is consistent with the general purposes of liability insurance because it enables insurers to enforce the fortuity concept by excluding from coverage any policyholder agreements to become liable after the insurance is in force and the liability is a certainty. See 2 Stempel, supra, § 14.14, 14–141. Limiting the exclusion to indemnification and hold-harmless agreements furthers the goal of protecting the insurer from exposure to risks whose scope and nature it cannot control or even reasonably foresee. The relevant distinction "is between incurring liability as a result of a breach of contract and specifically contracting to assume liability for another's negligence." Olympic, Inc. v. Providence Washington Ins. Co., 648 P.2d 1008, 1011 (Ala. 1982).

Courts in other jurisdictions have held that the contractually-assumed liability exclusion "refers to a specific contractual assumption of liability by the insured as exemplified by an indemnity agreement." 21 Eric Mills Holmes, supra § 132.3, 40 (2002) (case citations omitted).

This interpretation of exclusion (b) is consistent with the evolution of the CGL policy over time. Prior to the 1986 revision, the exclusion for contractually-assumed liabilities was achieved through language in the insuring agreement that granted coverage for "contractual liabilities." Coverage was extended to certain types of contractual obligations but not others. With the 1986 revision, however, this language was moved into the exclusions section, and the basic coverage for certain contractual obligations was retained by inserting an exception to the exclusion for "insured contracts."

... This case does not involve a claim for "contractually-assumed liability," properly understood. The breach of contract/warranty liability at issue here is Renschler's direct liability to its contract partner, Pleasant, pursuant to warranties in the construction contract. Renschler is not claiming coverage for a claim made against it pursuant to a third-party indemnification or hold harmless agreement.

E. The "business risk" exclusions

The business risk exclusions (j) through (n) preclude coverage generally for property damage to the work of the insured. Several of these are implicated here. The first, exclusion (j), contains the following language:

This insurance does not apply to:

> j. "Property damage" to: ... (6) That particular part of any property that must be restored, repaired or replaced because "your work" was incorrectly performed on it....

The policy defines "your work" as: a. Work or operations performed by you or on your behalf;....

Renschler's work on the [large distribution center warehouse], as well as Lawson's engineering work under subcontract to Renschler, both fall within the definition of "your work." Exclusion (j) comes into play because Pleasant's claim against Renschler involves the repair and replacement of the [large distribution center warehouse].

However, if the property damage that occurred falls within the "products-completed operations hazard," exclusion (j) does not apply. The "products-completed operations hazard" includes:

All "bodily injury" and "property damage" occurring away from premises you own or rent and arising out of "your product" or "your work" except: (1) Products that are still in your physical possession; or (2) Work that has not yet been completed or abandoned.

The damage to the [large distribution center warehouse] occurred away from premises that Renschler owns or rents, and it arose out of Renschler's "own work" because, as we have indicated, Renschler's work on the [large distribution center warehouse] falls within the policy definition of "your work." Work ... was substantially completed in August 1994, and Pleasant occupied the premises at that time. The settlement was noticed in March 1995. Damage to the property therefore occurred after the work had been completed, so exception (2) does not apply. Thus the property damage at issue in this case falls within the "products-completed operations hazard" and exclusion (j) does not apply.

This brings into play exclusion (*l*), for "property damage to your work" inside the "products-completed operations hazard": This insurance does not apply to:

l.   "Property damage" to "your work" arising out of it or any part of it and included in the "products-completed operations hazard."

This exclusion does not apply if the damaged work or the work out of which the damage arises was performed on your behalf by a subcontractor.

By its terms, exclusion (*l*) would operate to exclude coverage under the circumstances of this case but for the exception that specifically restores coverage when the property damage arises out of work performed by a subcontractor. It is undisputed that Lawson's negligent soils engineering work was a cause of the soil settlement and resultant property damage to the [large distribution center warehouse].

This subcontractor exception dates to the 1986 revision of the standard CGL policy form. Prior to 1986 the CGL business risk exclusions operated collectively to preclude coverage for damage to construction projects caused by subcontractors. Many contractors were unhappy with this state of affairs, since more and more projects were being completed with the help of subcontractors. In response to this changing reality, insurers began to offer coverage for damage caused by subcontractors through an endorsement to the CGL known as the Broad Form Property Damage Endorsement, or BFPD. Introduced in 1976, the BFPD deleted several portions from the business risk exclusions and replaced them with more specific exclusions that effectively broadened coverage. Among other changes, the BFPD extended coverage to property damage caused by the work of subcontractors. In 1986 the insurance industry incorporated this aspect of the BFPD directly into the CGL itself by inserting the subcontractor exception to the "your work" exclusion. See generally 21 Eric Mills Holmes, Holmes' Appleman on Insurance 2d, supra, § 132.9, 152–53.

Cases in Wisconsin and in other jurisdictions have consistently recognized that the 1986 CGL revisions restored otherwise excluded coverage for damage caused to construction projects by subcontractor negligence. In *Kalchthaler*, the court of appeals concluded that "the only reasonable reading of [the 1986 exception] is that it restores coverage for damage to completed work caused by the work of a subcontractor." *Kalchthaler*, 591 N.W.2d at 171.

The court of appeals' straightforward reading of the subcontractor exception to the business risk exclusion in *Kalchthaler* was buttressed by a similar holding in a case from Minnesota, O'Shaughnessy v. Smuckler Corp., 543 N.W.2d 99 (Minn.Ct.App. 1996), in which the Minnesota Court of Appeals found coverage for improper subcontractor performance that caused damage to a residential home project.

Like the *O'Shaughnessy* court, the court in *Kalchthaler* recognized that the effect of the 1986 revision of the CGL could not be defeated by reliance upon broad judicial holdings interpreting pre–1986 policies that did not contain the subcontractor exception. "For whatever reason, the industry chose to add the new exception to the business risk exclusion in 1986. We may not ignore that language when interpreting case law decided before and after the addition. To do so would render the new language superfluous." *Kalchthaler*, 591 N.W.2d at 174

Courts in other jurisdictions have reached the same conclusion when interpreting the post–1986 subcontractor exception or policy endorsements containing identical language. (citations omitted) . . . Noting the apparent conflict between *O'Shaughnessy*, *Kalchthaler*, and similar cases on the one hand, and contrary cases on the other, one commentator has pointed out that "those cases [finding no coverage] involved the older policy language while the current policy specifically provides that the 'own work' exclusion does not apply 'if the damaged work or the work out of which the damage arises was performed on your behalf by a subcontractor.'" 2 Stempel, supra, § 14.13[a], 14–132.

This interpretation of the subcontractor exception to the business risk exclusion does not "create coverage" where none existed before, as American Family contends. There is coverage under the insuring agreement's initial coverage grant. Coverage would be excluded by the business risk exclusionary language, except that the subcontractor exception to the business risk exclusion applies, which operates to restore the otherwise excluded coverage.

Accordingly, Renschler's CGL base policies with American Family cover Pleasant's claim. . . .

. . .

[The court rebuffed the claimants in only one respect. It found a "Professional liability exclusion" in an excess-liability policy issued to Renschler:

Insurance under this policy does not apply to any liability arising out of the rendering of or failure to render professional services in the conduct of your business or profession.

According to the court, this exclusion applied because Lawson's bad professional advice was a substantial factor in causing the loss of the warehouse, and Renschler was responsible to American Girl for it under a warranty in the construction contract.]

. . .

The decision of the court of appeals is reversed and the cause remanded for proceedings consistent with this opinion.

NOTES

(1) *Business-risk Exclusions and American Girl.* Business-risk exclusions refer to five exclusions.[1] The *American Girl* opinion examines the interplay among two policy definitions and two exclusions (exclusions l. Damage To Your Work and j. Damage To Property). One of the definitions was that of "Your work".

The claimant escaped both of these exclusions owing to exceptions within them having to do with what may be called the "P-cOH"—the "products-completed operations hazard". In part, this is the definition of that term:

All "bodily injury" and "property damage" occurring away from premises you own or rent and arising out of "your product" or "your work" except:

(1) Products that are still in your physical possession; or

(2) Work that has not yet been completed or abandoned.

It was fortunate for the claimant that the damage to American Girl's warehouse occurred after Renschler had completed work on it. That fact brought the damage within the definition, even though it occurred away from premises owned or rented by Renschler.

The two exclusions concerned (One) some property damage to "your work", and (Two) damage to some property requiring attention because "your work" was incorrectly performed on it. The claimant escaped the exclusion designated here as "One" because that exclusion does not affect damage included in the P-cOH.

Exclusion "Two", more fully stated, applies to property damage to a "particular part of any property that must be restored, repaired or replaced" because of the incorrect performance—property that obviously included the whole of the destroyed warehouse. This exclusion would have applied, except that it also contains an exception for property damages included in the P-cOH.

(2) *A "Stucco" Case and the "Your work" Exclusion.* In French v. Assurance Company of America, 448 F.3d 693 (4th Cir. 2006), faulty work in the construction of a home for James and Kathleen French required them to spend more than $500,000 on repairs. They brought an action on CGL policies issued to the general contractor, Jeffco Development Corporation. As part of a settlement with Jeffco, it had assigned its rights under the policy to them.

---

1. The phrase "business risk exclusions" customarily refers to these five "Coverage A" exclusions in the standard ISO CGL policy: **j.** Damage To Property, **k.** Damage To Your Product, **l.** Damage To Your Work, **m.** Damage To Impaired Property Or Property Not Physically Injured, and **n.** Recall Of Products, Work Or Impaired Property.

The fault was that of a subcontractor, in cladding the exterior of the home with "synthetic stucco". In part the repairs were required by damage to the structure and walls that were properly erected but suffered damage from water and moisture admitted by the defective cladding. In part, repairs were required to the cladded exterior walls. According to the policy:

This insurance does not apply to: . . .

Damage to Your Work

"Property damage" to "your work" arising out of it or any part of it and included in the "products-completed operations hazard." This exclusion does not apply if the damaged work or the work out of which the damage arises was performed on your behalf by a subcontractor.

"Your work" is defined, in part, this way:

Work or operations performed by you or on your behalf; . . . "Your work" includes: a. Warranties or representations made at any time with respect to the fitness, qualify, durability, performance or use of "your work".

The trial court entered a summary judgment in favor of the insurers. It applied an exclusion of property damage expected by Jeffco, the insured.

On appeal, the court concluded that the trial court was partly right. As to the exterior walls the court said (quoting): "The obligation to repair the facade itself is not unexpected or unforeseen under the terms of the sales contract. Therefore, the repair or replacement damages represent economic loss and consequently would not trigger a duty to indemnify under a CGL policy."

As to the other damage, however, the trial court was wrong. The insurers virtually conceded that: "At oral argument, counsel for Insurance Defendants candidly and correctly acknowledged that had a portion of the defective [] exterior on the Frenches' home fallen outwardly onto an automobile or inwardly onto a painting hanging on an interior wall or on furniture in the home, the 1986 ISO CGL Policies would have provided Jeffco liability coverage for damages to the automobile, the painting, and the furniture."

No distinction could be drawn, the court said, between damage of that kind and the damage within the Frenches' home. Also: "The 1986 ISO CGL Policies . . . are structured such that express exclusions . . . limit an initial grant of coverage. Then exceptions to exclusions . . . restore otherwise excluded coverage." The court ruled that the subcontractor exception to the "Your Work" exclusion has this effect.

The opinion in *French* relies heavily on that in *American Girl*, where the insurers also invoked the "Your work" exclusion. In *American Girl* the court observed that Lawson, the soils engineer, was a subcontractor, and said: "Coverage would be excluded . . . except that the subcontractor exception . . . applies, which operates to restore . . . coverage." What would the decision have been if Lawson had been an employee of Renschler, the warehouse builder? If different, is there a good reason to extend the coverage of a general contractor who relies largely on subcontractors, over that of one who does not?

(3) *A Case for Comparison.* The general contractor on a home-construction project faced losses when the project was destroyed by fire, and brought an action for a declaration that the losses were covered by a CGL policy issued to the contractor. One claim against the contractor had been made by the owner of the project for the repayment of advances made to cover expenses of the work. Others were made by unpaid vendors and subcontractors. These were the losses in question.

The policy excluded from coverage property damage for which "the insured is obligated to pay damages by reason of the assumption of liability in a contract or agreement". The court entered a summary judgment against the contractor, saying: "Under the law of Florida, general liability policies ... clearly do not cover damages that are purely economic in nature.... It is equally clear that breach of contract claims for the recovery of money are not covered by general liability insurance policies." Key Custom Homes, Inc. v. Mid–Continent Cas. Co., 450 F. Supp.2d 1311 (M.D.Fla. 2006).

Is this decision completely at odds with *American Girl*? Partially? If so, which is the better decision?

(4) *The Sistership Exclusion.* The cost of recalling products is the subject of exclusion "**n.** Recall Of Products, Work Or Impaired Property" going by the name "sistership exclusion". In origin the name had to do with the malfunction of an aircraft which leads to the grounding of aircraft like it ("sister airships") suspected of sharing the same flaw. See Menasha Corp. v. Lumbermens Mut. Cas. Co., 361 F.Supp.2d 887 (E.D.Wis. 2005).

(5) *Why the Business–Risk Exclusions?* A possible answer to this question is that losses entailed by substandard products and services are less than fully fortuitous, being largely within the control of the insured. Another is that the exclusions preserve the incentive of the insured to maintain high quality in its products and services. A third is that prices charged by an insured to its customers should include the cost to the insured of substandard performance. If these answers are distinguishable at all, certainly they are closely interrelated. The first, "controllable losses", is a premise of the other two. And the obvious reason for the third ("should include the cost") is that enterprises should have a disincentive to doing shoddy work.

(6) *Intended Injury and Damage.* Exclusions of liability for "intended" injury and damage commonly evoke from courts a distinction between an intended *act* and intended *harm*. An instance is a case about unseemly conduct of youngsters at a riverbank, which ended when one pushed another toward the water, into which she fell and in which she drowned. Coverage of the other youngster, available to him under a homeowners policy, came into question. His pushing was intended, he said, but not her death. The insurer contended that (i) there was no "accident" (= "occurrence"), and (ii) any wrongful-death liability was excluded because the injury was intended. The court ruled that a summary judgment in favor of the insurer was not warranted. Auto–Owners Ins. Co. v. Harvey, 842 N.E.2d 1279 (Ind. 2006).

The court ruled that the term "occurrence" applied to the slip, fall, and drowning, and not to the push. The court took note of some cases to the contrary. One of those was *Red Ball Leasing*, relied on in Everson v. Lorenz (see p. 256 above). This line of cases, the court said, "does not accurately state Indiana law." What of *Everson* itself?

The court also worked its way around this sentence in the intended-injury exclusion: "This exclusion applies even if the bodily injury ... is of a different kind or degree ... than that reasonably expected or intended." To what kind of case does that sentence apply?

———

D. Notifications as Conditions of an Insurer's Obligations

Igo Maidenek was a tenant in a New York City apartment building (Kew Gardens, Queens County). He slipped and fell on a sidewalk adjacent to the building, and brought an action for personal injuries against a firm, Argo Corporation, that managed the building. Some time after Argo received the summons and complaint, it received notice of a proposed default judgment against it and, a week later, a notice of readiness for trial. These incidents began in January of 1997. Maidenek brought his suit in February of 2000. The notice of trial readiness was served almost a year later.

Argo held commercial liability insurance provided by the Greater New York Mutual Insurance Company (GNY). Argo notified GNY of the occurrence and suit on May 2, 2001.

Liability insurers are not content with delays in advising them of events, and of suits, that may generate covered liabilities. Hence almost all their policies impose "duties" of early notification on insured entities. An example taken from a CGL policy form is quoted in the footnote.[1] Argo's policy contained such a term. GNY disclaimed responsibility to Argo, characterizing the term as a "condition precedent" to coverage. Argo brought an action against GNY for a declaratory judgment that the disclaimer was wrongful. An opinion of the New York Court of Appeals in that action is presented below.

Left to their own devices, the courts have exhibited various attitudes toward notification terms like that in Argo's case. On one view, GNY was right, and "a condition precedent . . . must be performed before any obligation on the part of the assurer commences." *Watson v. U.S.F. & G. Co.*, 189 A.2d 625, 627 (Md. 1963). A contrasting one is this:

---

1. From the 2004 ISO CGL policy form (used by permission). Italics identify defined words.

Section IV—Commercial General Liability Conditions . . .

. . .

2. Duties in The Event of Occurrence, Offense, Claim Or Suit

    a. You must see to it that we are notified as soon as practicable of an *occurrence* or an offense which may result in a claim. To the extent possible, notice should include:

        (1) How, when and where the *occurrence* or offense took place;

        (2) The names and addresses of any injured person and witnesses; and

        (3) The nature and location of any injury or damage arising out of the *occurrence* or offense.

    b. If a claim is made or *suit* is brought against any insured, you must:

        (1) Immediately record the specifics of the claim or *suit* and the date received; and

        (2) Notify us as soon as practicable.

You must see to it that we receive written notice of the claim or *suit* as soon as practicable.

    c. You and any other involved insured must:

        (1) Immediately send us copies of any demands, notices, summonses or legal papers received in connection with the claim or *suit*; . . .

> [T]he harsh results of denying coverage necessitate an exception to the strict interpretation of contract provisions. Enforcement of the notice provision would constitute a forfeiture because the insured would lose insurance coverage despite paying premiums to the insurer.

Prince George's County v. Local Gov't Ins. Trust, 879 A.2d 81, 95 (Md. 2005) (reporting the view of some courts).

Some courts, resisting the notion of *forfeiture*, have recited numerous benefits that an insurer may enjoy by reason of early notifications. These include, as to notification of suits, the opportunity to engage in discovery, and otherwise participate in the defense. As to other events (slipping and falling, for examples), the benefits include an opportunity to investigate the facts before they are stale.

A riposte to that is the observation that, in a particular case, a delay in notification may not occasion any prejudice to the insurer. Over this point a major fault line has developed in the cases. Some courts subscribe to a "prejudice rule", which permits an inquiry, case by case, into the impact of delay on the insurer. Others subscribe to the "no prejudice rule", which assumes in effect that an undue delay was damaging to the insurer. As will be seen, some variations on these rules have emerged.

(In Chapter 3 reference was made to a rule of California law: "A defense based on an insured's failure to give timely notice of a claim requires the insurer to prove that it suffered actual prejudice." The issue described there was whether or not federal law preempts that rule, as it applies to disability insurance, not liability insurance. The materials in this section concern *liability* insurance. It will be seen, however, on consulting pp. 74–75 above, that somewhat parallel reasoning has been employed with respect to first- and third-party coverages.)

The courts have not been left entirely to their own devices. Concern about the matter among insurance buyers has led to a number of legislative moves which, in general, counteract the no-prejudice rule. An example is Section 19–110 of the Maryland Insurance Code, as follows (emphasis supplied):

Disclaimers of coverage on liability policies

> An insurer may disclaim coverage on a liability insurance policy on the ground that the insured or a person claiming the benefits of the policy through the insured has breached the policy by failing to cooperate with the insurer or by not giving the insurer required notice *only if the insurer establishes by a preponderance of the evidence that the lack of* cooperation or *notice has resulted in actual prejudice to the insurer.*

Comparable provisions appear in the statutes of Utah and Wisconsin. The no-prejudice rule that once obtained in Texas was overturned by an order of the State Board of Insurance; see Booking v. General Star Mgmt. Co., 254 F.3d 414, 420 (2d Cir. 2001) (Tex. law).

Argo Corporation v. Greater New York Mutual Ins. Co.

New York Court of Appeals, 2005.
4 N.Y.3d 332, 827 N.E.2d 762.

Some of the essential facts of this case, including a slip-and-fall accident, are stated in the first two paragraphs of the text above. The court used "Argo" to refer to two insured firms, both managers of the building and both plaintiffs.

In Section IV, "Commercial General Liability Conditions", Argo's policy contained these provisions among others:

Duties in The Event of Occurrence, Offense, Claim Or Suit

a. You must see to it that we are notified as soon as practicable of an 'occurrence' or an offense which may result in a claim....

b. If a claim is made or 'suit' is brought against any insured, you must:

(1) Immediately record the specifics of the claim or 'suit' and the date received; and

(2) Notify us as soon as practicable.

You must see to it that we receive written notice of the claim or 'suit' as soon as practicable.

The trial court granted a motion to dismiss Argo's action, for Argo's failure to give timely notice to GNY. The Appellate Division affirmed, saying, "[T]he insureds are unable to provide an excuse for their failure to comply with the policy's notice provisions." That court distinguished the Court of Appeals' earlier decision in Matter of Brandon (Nationwide Mut. Ins. Co.), 769 N.E.2d 810 (2002).

■ G.B. Smith, J.

The issue in this case is whether a primary insurer can disclaim coverage based solely upon a late notice of lawsuit or must show prejudice. We hold that, under the circumstances of this case, plaintiffs' late notice was unreasonable as a matter of law, that the Appellate Division correctly applied *Matter of Brandon,* and that the insurer need not show prejudice.

. . .

For years the rule in New York has been that where a contract of primary insurance requires notice "as soon as practicable" after an occurrence, the absence of timely notice of an occurrence is a failure to comply with a condition precedent which, as a matter of law, vitiates the contract (see Security Mutual Ins. Co. of N.Y. v. Acker–Fitzsimons Corp., 31 N.Y.2d 436, 440–443, 293 N.E.2d 76 (1972)). No showing of prejudice is required. Strict compliance with the contract protects the carrier against fraud or collusion; gives the carrier an opportunity to investigate claims while evidence is fresh; allows the carrier to make an early estimate of potential exposure and establish adequate reserves and gives the carrier an opportunity to exercise early control of claims, which aids settlement. . . .

We have applied the no-prejudice rule in various contexts in recent years: supplementary underinsured motorist (SUM) insurance . . . *Matter of Brandon* and Rekemeyer v. State Farm Mut. Auto. Ins. Co., 828 N.E.2d 970 (2005) and excess insurance. . . . We have held, however, that the rule enunciated in *Security Mutual* does not apply to reinsurance and a reinsurer must show prejudice before it can be relieved of its obligations to perform under a contract (Unigard Sec. Ins. Co. v. North Riv. Ins. Co., 79 N.Y.2d 576, 582–584, 594 N.E.2d 571 (1992)).

In *Matter of Brandon*, we again departed from the general no-prejudice rule and held that the carrier must show prejudice before disclaiming based on late notice of a lawsuit in the SUM context. Under the facts of *Brandon*, the carrier received timely notice of claim but late notice of a lawsuit. We were unwilling to extend the no-prejudice exception in regard to late notice of a lawsuit because "unlike most notices of claim—which must be submitted promptly after the accident, while an insurer's investigation has the greatest potential to curb fraud—notices of legal action become due at a moment that cannot be fixed relative to any other key event, such as the injury, the discovery of the tortfeasor's insurance limits or the resolution of the underlying tort claim" (*see id.* at 814).

Brandon did not abrogate the no-prejudice rule and should not be extended to cases where the carrier received unreasonably late notice of a claim. The facts here, where no notice of claim was filed and the first notice filed was a notice of lawsuit, are distinguishable from *Brandon* where a timely notice of claim was filed, followed by a late notice of lawsuit, and distinguishable from *Rekemeyer*, where an insured gave timely notice of the accident, but late notice of a SUM claim. Argo was notified of the lawsuit against it in February 2000 but did not notify GNY until May 2001. The burden of establishing that the delay was not unreasonable falls on the insured (see U.S. Underwriters Ins. Co. v. A & D Maja Constr. Inc., 160 F.Supp.2d 565, 569 (S.D.N.Y. 2001)).

. . .

The rationale of the no-prejudice rule is clearly applicable to a late notice of lawsuit under a liability insurance policy. A liability insurer, which has a duty to indemnify and often also to defend, requires timely notice of lawsuit in order to be able to take an active, early role in the litigation process and in any settlement discussions and to set adequate reserves. Late notice of lawsuit in the liability insurance context is so likely to be prejudicial to these concerns as to justify the application of the no-prejudice rule. Argo's delay was unreasonable as a matter of law and thus, its failure to timely notify GNY vitiates the contract. GNY was not required to show prejudice before declining coverage for late notice of lawsuit.

[Affirmed (Chief Judge Kaye taking no part).]

NOTES

(1) *Evidence and Presumptions about Prejudice.* Evidence of prejudice to an insurer, due to a late notice, may be difficult for it to come by. Evidence of *no* prejudice may be even more difficult for an insured to come by. Either party may find it useful to look into the availability of witnesses to an incident and of any official report of it, and the ability of experts to reconstruct it. The fact of "no prejudice" is strongly indicated if the insurer had early knowledge of the incident, or suit, from a source other than the insured. Cf. Brandon & Nationwide Mut. Ins. Co., 769 N.E.2d 810 (N.Y. 2002) (reported in the following Note).

An estimate of the comparative difficulty of adducing evidence, one way or the other, might lead one to prefer either the *prejudice rule* or the *no-prejudice rule*. On that ground or another, which is preferable?

The difficulty of proving prejudice has been ratcheted up by a requirement that the insurer show *appreciable* or *substantial* prejudice. See Transportes Ferreos de Venez. II CA v. NKK Corp., 239 F.3d 555 (3d Cir. 2001) (New Jersey law). In contrast, some courts have alleviated the difficulty by developing a rebuttable presumption in favor of the insurer.

> [W]hen an insured has failed to provide timely notice of a claim against it in accordance with the liability insurance policy, it is presumed that the insurer has been prejudiced by the breach. The insured may rebut this presumption by proffering competent evidence establishing that the insurer was not prejudice by the insured's delay.

American Justice Ins. Reciprocal v. Hutchison, 15 S.W.3d 811, 818 (Tenn. 2000).

(2) *A Self-inflicted Injury.* According to William, he was injured when the car he was in was struck by Griselda's, through her negligence. Soon after that, he notified his insurer that he intended to make a claim under his policy's "uninsured automobile endorsement". Much later he notified the insurer of a claim under another coverage in the policy, "no-fault". Meanwhile, the insurer awaited developments. After the second notice, it objected that that notice had come too late. The objection met with little favor. Brandon v. Nationwide Mut. Ins. Co., cited in Note 1 above.

Although *Brandon* did not concern a third-party coverage, it is instructive about liability insurance; it was a focus of the opinion in *Argo Corporation*.

(3) *Taxis and Surrogates.* Two statutes in New York, concerning notifications to liability insurers, were noticed in American Transit Ins. Co. v. Sartor, 814 N.E.2d 1189 (N.Y. 2004). One of these speaks of insurers and sureties bound, as required, to protect persons injured by operators of taxis. The operator of a taxi, or other vehicle for hire, "in any manner involved in an accident" is expected to give a written notice to the insurer or surety within five days. Veh. & Traffic Law, § 370(4). The failure to do so is not, however, to affect the liability of the insurer or surety; it constitutes a misdemeanor.

More germane to this chapter is a provision of the Insurance Law—Section 3420(a)(3)—requiring that all liability policies include a provision that "written notice by or on behalf of the injured person or any other claimant ... shall be deemed notice to the insurer."

Question: Might it be that a passenger, being injured in a taxi through the negligence of the driver, gives notice within four days of the incident to the driver's insurer, and nevertheless fails to get compensation because (a) the driver is impecunious, (b) no other notice was given, and (c) that notice was not given as soon as practicable?

Surprise

Many people profess surprise when visited with severe legal sanctions for supposed misconduct—surprise because they were not aware of wrong-doing or of the degree of harm flowing from it. It is hard to know how much of their "surprise" is genuine; but some of it surely is. It is no wonder, then, that a person insured against liability sometimes offers surprise as an excuse for not having advised the insurer that a claim against it is in prospect. The insured may have expected that he would be exonerated of liability, or may have supposed that any loss charged to him would be well within a policy deductible, or—if the policy in question is one of excess insurance—that any loss would be covered by the primary policy. If one of these opinions was truly and reasonably held, it goes far to explain why the insured did not trouble the insurer with a notice that a covered loss was possible.

A case that is hypothetical, but only in an incidental way, will put the problem. The insured is a trucking company, "Schneider". Suit is brought against it by Roderick Zachery, charging Schneider with liability for the death of his wife and permanent injuries to a daughter, the consequences of a truck-car collision. Schneider holds liability coverages amounting, in total, to $7.5 million. Of this, a minor part is primary coverage; most is provided by three excess carriers. The residual coverage is for $2.5 million, provided by Evanston Insurance.

Schneider gives prompt notice of the collision, claim, and suit, to almost everyone in sight. But not to Evanston. The reason for that omission is that Schneider and its advisers make a spectacular misjudg-ment about the prospect of Zachery's claims. Their highest projections of his recovery were about $3.5 million. (That statement, the following ones, and the parties' identities, are drawn from an actual case: Evanston Ins. Co. v. Stonewall Surplus Lines Ins. Co., 111 F.3d 852 (1997).) The jury returned a verdict of $23.2 million. The trial judge was shocked by that number, and refused to accept it. A second trial was concluded by a settlement of $7.5 million, exactly the aggregate limits of Schneider's coverages. Evanston had been notified of the matter only days before the $23.2–million verdict.

Litigation followed between Schneider and Evanston in which the issue of Evanston's liability was raised. Evanston appealed from a ruling against it.

The Court of Appeals for the Eleventh Circuit did not have occasion to say what the result would have been if Evanston's policy had required that it be given notices "as soon as practicable". But the court did make a suggestive statement about the prescience that could be expected of Schneider: "The contract does not, *indeed could not*, require that Schneider be right 100% of the time." The phrase put in italics here might be understood to say that surprise at some level would be an excuse for a failure to give timely notice, no matter what the policy required. At most, however, the phrase is an offhand dictum in a lengthy opinion.

What Evanston's policy actually required was that it be given immediate notice of an occurrence, claim, or suit, "reasonably likely to involve [it] under this policy." That is a usual requirement in excess policies. The trial court had denied a motion for summary judgment favoring Schneider. It was not prepared to say, as a matter of law, that notice to Evanston was not required before the jury gave its verdict. The appellate court, reversing, was prepared to say that. "Whether notice is timely is ordinarily a question of fact for the jury to determine."[1] But not when the likelihood of the insurer's involvement falls short of being reasonable.

The court used a familiar phrase to express the issue before it: "what Schneider knew, and when...." To that extent the test of reasonableness was subjective. But the court declined to decide whether "reasonably" was an objective or subjective measure of "likely". On either measure, it said, Schneider was not required, before the verdict, "to conclude that it was reasonably likely that Evanston's coverage would become 'involved'...."[2]

There was expert testimony that it would have been reasonable, and "good insurance practice", for Schneider to give notice to Evanston before it did. But that was beside the point, the court said. Evidence that did impress the court was assessments made by competent and knowledgeable lawyers, before the verdict, of the value of Zachery's claims. (These included Zachery's own lawyer.) None estimated a recovery of more than $5 million. Surprise!

NOTE

Defenders and Notices. Unlike policies of primary liability insurance, an excess policy does not confer on the insurer either the right to control the defense of an action or the duty to provide one. What bearing does that fact have on the responsibility of an insured to give early notice to an excess insurer of occurrences, claims, and suits?

E.   LATENT AND ONGOING HARMS: TOXINS IN THE BODY AND THE ENVIRONMENT

The harms chiefly addressed in this section are those that develop over substantial periods of time, those inflicted by long antecedent causes, and those detected long after their onset. Asbestosis is an instance, both in that the harm accumulates gradually and in that symptoms are slow to emerge.

---

1. Id. at 860.

2. The plaintiff in *Evanston Insurance* was Evanston. It had paid $2.5 million to Zachery as its part of the settlement, and sought to recover that amount. Schneider National Carriers, Inc. was one defendant. Others were Schneider's primary insurer and two excess insurers whose layers of coverage were antecedent to that of Evanston. The liabilities of these defendants to Evanston, if any, rested on their liabilities to Schneider and on Evanston's position as subrogee of Schneider; so the court ruled.

Degradation of the environment is another. This section deals with two features of CGL policy forms related especially to harms of this type.

Pollution Liabilities

Those who draft and use CGL policies have labored repeatedly for more than three decades to express the coverage of liabilities for the discharge of pollutants. With respect to that the standard policy form has developed through several phases. One phase was marked by a broad exclusion. It was designed to counteract broad interpretations of "accident" in the policy, and (later) similar interpretations of "occurrence", defined as "an accident, including injurious exposure to conditions, which results ... in bodily injury and property damage that was neither expected nor intended from the standpoint of the insured." A description of this development is as follows:

> [F]oreseeing an impending increase in claims for environmentally-related losses, ... the insurance industry drafting organizations began in 1970 the process of drafting and securing regulatory approval for the standard pollution-exclusion clause.[3]

The upshot has been called the "original general pollution exclusion". It excluded coverage for "Bodily injury or property damage arising out of the discharge, dispersal, release or escape of [among other things] pollutants...."

Thereafter the exclusion was modified. "Over time, many policies began to include a 'sudden and accidental' exception to this pollution exclusion: 'This exclusion does not apply if such discharge, dispersal, release or escape is sudden or accidental.' ... According to the Supreme Court of New Jersey, the purpose of the 'sudden and accidental' exception to the pollution exclusion was to deny coverage only to intentional polluters." Richardson v. Nationwide Mutual Ins. Co., 826 A.2d 310, 317 (D.C.App. 2003).[4]

Industry dissatisfaction persisted. It was intensified by diverse judicial rulings about the word "sudden". Some courts took the word to mean *abrupt*, but others expanded the coverage provided by the exception beyond that.[5] Moreover, in 1980 Congress passed the Act known as CERCLA: the Comprehensive Environmental Response, Compensation, and Liability Act. "CERCLA was enacted in order to allow the government and private individuals or entities to act as quasi-regulators over environmental pollution by allowing them to carry out the cleanup of hazardous waste sites and then recover the expenses of the cleanup from the responsible parties.... [B]etween 1970 and 1985, 'insurers [were] held liable for many billions of

---

3. Morton International Inc. v. General Accident Ins. Co. of America, 629 A.2d 831, 849–50 (N.J. 1993).

4. Opinions, both majority and dissenting, ultimately vacated owing to a settlement.

5. The word has an "elastic temporal connotation", one court has said, as in "Suddenly it's spring." Claussen v. Aetna Casualty & Sur. Co., 380 S.E.2d 686, 688 (Ga. 1989).

dollars in defense and response costs incurred pursuant to laws that did not even exist at the time the exclusion, with its exception was written.' "[6]

There followed, with "lightning speed", the current exclusion, commonly known as the *absolute* pollution exclusion.[7] It superseded what may be called the *qualified* exclusion (which in turn succeeded the *original, general* exclusion). It appears in Coverage A, under the head "Exclusions", and is set out in the footnote.[8] For further particulars of its development see the opinion in *Richardson* and the full opinion in the following case.

NOTES

(1) *Hoodwinking the Regulators?* At a time when the industry was moving away from the original exclusion, and seeking official approval of a new form, a supporting memo was submitted to insurance departments. Three sentences in the memo were later to evoke scathing judicial rebukes. Quotations from those sentences are as follows, each followed by comment on it—in italics—drawn from the opinion in Morton International Inc. v. General Accident Ins. Co. of America, n.3 above.

"Coverage for pollution or contamination is not provided in most cases under present policies because the damages can be said to be expected or intended...." *Simply untrue.*

"Coverage is continued for pollution or contamination caused injuries when the pollution or contamination results from an accident...." *Camouflage: does not alert regulators to [a] critical change* (accidental damage to be excluded, unless the result of an accidental *discharge*).

"The [proposed] exclusion clarifies [the] situation so as to avoid any question of intent." *Even more misleading than the first sentence; a paradigm of understatement; indefensible.*

---

6. *Richardson* (quoting from a brief *amicus* filed on behalf of the District of Columbia Commissioner, Department of Insurance and Securities Regulation).

7. Essex Ins. Co. v. Tri–Town Corp., 863 F.Supp. 38, 39–40 (D.Mass. 1994).

8. *Copyright 2004 Insurance Services Office, Inc.*

This insurance does not apply to:

. . .

f.(1). "Bodily injury" or "property damage" arising out of the actual, alleged or threatened discharge, dispersal, release or escape of pollutants:

(a) At or from premises you own, rent or occupy;

(b) At or from any site or location used by or for you or others for the handling, storage, disposal, processing or treatment of waste;

(c) Which are at any time transported, handled, stored, treated, disposed of, or processed as waste by or for you or any person or organization for whom you may be legally responsible; or

(d) At or from any site or location on which you or any contractors or subcontractors working directly or indirectly on your behalf are performing operations:

(i) if the pollutants are brought on or to the site or location in connection with such operations; or

(ii) if the operations are to test for, monitor, clean up, remove, contain, treat, detoxify or neutralize the pollutants.

(2) Any loss, cost, or expense arising out of any governmental direction or request that you test for, monitor, clean up, remove, contain, treat, detoxify or neutralize pollutants.

Pollutants means any solid, liquid, gaseous or thermal irritant or contaminant, including smoke, vapor, soot, fumes, acids, alkalis, chemicals and waste. Waste includes materials to be recycled, reconditioned or reclaimed.

The court discerned in the proposed revision a "monumental" reduction of coverage of unintended pollution-caused damage, confining it to "the unusual 'boom-event' type case". To describe a reduction in coverage of that magnitude as a "clarification", the court said, came perilously close to deception. "[T]he conclusion is virtually inescapable that the memorandum's lack of clarity was deliberate.... Moreover, had the industry acknowledged the true scope of the proposed reduction in coverage, regulators would have been obligated to consider imposing a correlative reduction in rates."[9] (The proponents of the revision were not quite "the industry", but were organizations of insurers, now superseded: the Insurance Rating Board and the Mutual Insurance Rating Bureau.)

Assuming that major players in the insurance business set out to hoodwink supervisors of the business, what does that fact suggest about the expectations of the miscreants? Assuming also that they succeeded across the country, what does that fact suggest about the quality of supervision?

(2) *Mercury in Berry's Creek.* In *Morton International*, the case last cited, it was found that the concentration of mercury in a stretch of Berry's Creek was the highest found in fresh-water sediments in the world. Several firms faced the prospect of paying for "remediation", at the instance of New Jersey's Department of Environmental Protection. They were faced also with a pollution exclusion in their liability coverages: The contamination was not *sudden and accidental*, the insurers contended.

The court invoked the State's public policy about the rates and terms of insurance contracts, saying, "we decline to enforce the standard pollution-exclusion clause as written." To do so, the court said, "would condone the industry's misrepresentation to regulators in New Jersey and other states concerning the effect of the clause.... [R]egulators would reasonably have understood the effect of the clause to have denied coverage [only] for the intentional discharge [etc.] of known pollutants...." Id. at 848.

This passage suggests that sometimes, in applying the doctrine of reasonable expectations, a court will take the expectations of regulators as a surrogate for those of insureds. Would it be better to say that, when representatives of the insurance business have hoodwinked regulators about the purport of a forms revision, the appropriate sanction is to disregard the revision altogether? If the court had taken that line, what difference would it have made in the entitlements of policyholders?

Compare Sunbeam Corp. v. Liberty Mutual Ins. Co., 781 A.2d 1189 (Pa. 2001), lending color to a claim of "regulatory estoppel" based on a submission to the Pennsylvania Insurance Department identical to that denounced in *Morton International*.[10]

---

9. Id. at 852–53.

10. The court directed the trial court to consider a claim by Sunbeam and others of "regulatory estoppel, a form of judicial estoppel". But the Pennsylvania court said that the part of the memo in issue was not as clear as the claimants argued. And two justices, dissenting, observed that the Department had not altered its approval practices over the decades since approving the revision, although it "must have become aware of the interpretation that the insurance industry subsequently accorded to the 'sudden and accidental' clause". Id. at 1195, 1196. The dissenters observed also that the Department had not intervened on behalf of the claimants. (A dozen other entities had filed *amicus* briefs.)

American States Ins. Co. v. Koloms

Illinois Supreme Court, 1997.
177 Ill.2d 473, 687 N.E.2d 72, 227 Ill.Dec. 149.

■ Justice McMorrow delivered the opinion of the court.

We granted leave to appeal in this case in order to examine the scope of the absolute pollution exclusion provision contained in a commercial general liability (CGL) policy. The dispositive issue for our review is whether that exclusion bars coverage for claims of carbon monoxide poisoning caused by an allegedly defective furnace. For the reasons that follow, we hold it does not.

Background

The facts of this case, as taken from the pleadings, are relatively straightforward. [Suits were filed against the owners of a commercial building, Harvey and Nina Koloms—"Koloms"—by workers in the building who alleged that they had become ill when a furnace in the building malfunctioned, emitting carbon monoxide and other noxious fumes. Koloms were charged with negligence in maintaining the furnace. The suits were defended, on behalf of Koloms, by American States Insurance—"ASI"— which had issued to Koloms a standard-form CGL policy. But ASI reserved the right to contest coverage by reason of an "absolute" pollution exclusion in the policy. ASI brought this action for a declaration that it did not have a duty to defend or indemnify Koloms.]

In response, Koloms denied the material allegations of the complaint and filed two separate affirmative defenses. In one of the affirmative defenses, Koloms alleged that the pollution exclusion did not apply to injuries caused by a leaking furnace, but rather was limited to injuries resulting from industrial, commercial or large scale pollution. They claimed that the CGL policy exclusion was ambiguous to that extent, and that an insured person in their position would not reasonably expect carbon monoxide, a commonly occurring chemical compound, to be considered a pollutant.[1]

[The trial court entered a summary judgment in favor of Koloms. On a first appeal the judgment was affirmed as to ASI's duty to defend. (The court ruled, however, that a decision about the duty to indemnify should be deferred.) The court said that, as the trial court had done, "we too find that the clause is ambiguous, as it can reasonably be interpreted as applying only to environmental pollution." 666 N.E.2d 699, 731 (1996).]

The matter is currently before this court on ASI's petition for leave to appeal.[2] . . .

---

1. In their second affirmative defense, which is not relevant to the disposition of this appeal, Koloms asserted that ASI was estopped from denying coverage on the basis of certain representations made by Richard McClure, a purported sales agent acting on behalf of ASI. According to Koloms, McClure had informed them that they would be covered for all commercial risks associated with the property in question.

2. The court granted various entities leave to file briefs *amici curiae*, including the Environmental Litigation Association and the Lead Elimination Action Drive.

[The court set out as follows language of the policy which may be recognized as a virtual excerpt from that in footnote 8 above.]

This insurance does not apply to:

f.(1) "Bodily injury" or "property damage" arising out of actual, alleged or threatened discharge, dispersal, release or escape of pollutants:

(a) At or from premises you own, rent or occupy. . . .

The exclusion further defined "pollutants" as "any solid, liquid, gaseous or thermal irritant or contaminant, including smoke, vapor, soot, fumes, acids, alkalis, chemicals and waste."

Analysis

[The court dealt warily with Koloms' contention that the exclusion was ambiguous. Against that contention, ASI relied on Bernhardt v. Hartford Fire Insurance Co., 648 A.2d 1047 (Md.App. 1994), *cert. allowed*, 655 A.2d 400 (1995).]

In affirming [a decision for the insurer there], the Maryland Court of Special Appeals observed that an insurance policy can be viewed as ambiguous in one of two ways. First, the language itself " 'may be intrinsically unclear, in the sense that a person reading it without the benefit of some extrinsic knowledge simply [could] not determine what it means.' " *Bernhardt*, 648 A.2d at 1051, quoting Town & Country Management Corp. v. Comcast Cablevision, 520 A.2d 1129, 1132 (Md.App. 1987). Second, the language, although clear on its face, may become uncertain when applied to a particular object or circumstance. As to this latter type of ambiguity, the court noted that it is well settled " 'that a term may be free from ambiguity when used in one context but of doubtful application in another context.' " *Bernhardt*, 648 A.2d at 1051, quoting Tucker v. Fireman's Fund Insurance Co., 517 A.2d 730, 732 (1986). . . . After reviewing the language of the exclusion, the court of appeals determined that neither type of ambiguity was present. The court explained that, although the title "pollution exclusion" could, standing alone, be viewed as ambiguous, the actual language contained in the exclusion was "quite specific." *Bernhardt*, 648 A.2d at 1051. The court also found that "a person of ordinary intelligence reading the language" would conclude that the exclusion applied to carbon monoxide poisoning. *Bernhardt*, 648 A.2d at 1051.

[The court spoke of a "vast divergence of the jurisprudence from across the country which have already struggled with the question now facing this court."]

The source of the disagreement within the jurisprudence seems to lie in the fact that the language of the clause is, as the *Bernhardt* court observed, "quite specific" on its face, and yet a literal interpretation of that language results in an application of the clause which is "quite broad." We note that when the definition of the term "pollutant" is inserted into the body of the exclusion, the clause eliminates coverage for " 'bodily injury' or 'property damage' arising out of actual, alleged or threatened discharge, dispersal, release or escape of ... any solid, liquid, gaseous or thermal irritant or contaminant, including smoke, vapor, soot, fumes, acids, alkalis, chemicals and waste." A close examination of this language reveals that the exclusion (i) identifies the types of injury-producing materials which constitute a pollutant, *i.e.,* smoke, vapor, soot, *etc.,* (ii) sets forth the physical or elemental states in which the materials may be said to exist, *i.e.,* solid, liquid, gaseous or thermal, and (iii) specifies the various means by which the materials can be disseminated, *i.e.,* discharge, dispersal, release or escape. To that extent, therefore, the exclusion is indeed "quite specific," and those courts wishing to focus exclusively on the bare language of the exclusion will have no difficulty in concluding that it is also unambiguous. *See, e.g.,* Reliance Insurance Co. v. Moessner, 121 F.3d 895, No. 95–1899 (3d Cir. August 5, 1997).

Not all courts, however, find the bare language of the exclusion dispositive. A number of courts, while acknowledging the lack of any facial ambiguity, have nevertheless questioned whether the breadth of the language renders application of the exclusion uncertain, if not absurd. For instance, in addition to the cases discussed above, the Ohio Court of Appeals has observed that "the extremely broad language of the 1987 exclusion, in conjunction with the definition of a pollutant, raises an issue as to whether the exclusion is so general as to be meaningless." Ekleberry. Inc. v. Motorists Mutual Insurance Co., No. 3–91–39, 1992 Ohio App. LEXIS 3778 at *7 (July 17, 1992); see also American States Insurance Co. v. Kiger, 662 N.E.2d 945, 948 (Ind. 1996) ("Clearly, this clause cannot be read literally as it would negate virtually all coverage") [and two other cases cited]. These courts, troubled by the results which obtain when the terms of the clause are applied in the context of an actual claim, often decline to apply the pollution exclusion to injuries other than those caused by traditional environmental contamination. See, *e.g.,* Weaver v. Royal Insurance Co. of America, 674 A.2d 975, 977 (N.H. 1996) ("While courts freely apply the pollution exclusion to environmental contamination, they are generally unwilling to hold that its scope reaches other pollution-related injuries").

... Like many courts, we are troubled by what we perceive to be an overbreadth in the language of the exclusion as well as the manifestation of an ambiguity which results when the exclusion is applied to cases which have nothing to do with "pollution" in the conventional, or ordinary, sense of the word.... Accordingly, we agree with those courts which have restricted the exclusion's otherwise potentially limitless application to only those hazards traditionally associated with environmental pollution. We find support for our decision in the drafting history of the exclusion, which reveals an intent on the part of the insurance industry to so limit the clause.

The events leading up to the insurance industry's adoption of the pollution exclusion are "well-documented and relatively uncontroverted." Morton International, Inc. v. General Accident Insurance Co., 629 A.2d

831, 848 (N.J. 1993). [At this point the court recited the history of the pollution exclusions, as partly set out above at pp. 294–96 above.]

Our review of the history of the pollution exclusion amply demonstrates that the predominate [sic] motivation in drafting an exclusion for pollution-related injuries was the avoidance of the "enormous expense and exposure resulting from the 'explosion' of *environmental* litigation." (Emphasis added.) *Weaver*, 674 A.2d at 977, quoting Vantage Development Corp. v. American Environmental Technologies Corp., 598 A.2d 948, 953 (N.J. Super. 1991). Similarly, the 1986 amendment to the exclusion was wrought, not to broaden the provision's scope beyond its original purpose of excluding coverage for environmental pollution, but rather to remove the "sudden and accidental" exception to coverage which, as noted above, resulted in a costly onslaught of litigation. We would be remiss, therefore, if we were to simply look to the bare words of the exclusion, ignore its *raison d' etre,* and apply it to situations which do not remotely resemble traditional environmental contamination. The pollution exclusion has been, and should continue to be, the appropriate means of avoiding " 'the yawning extent of potential liability arising from the gradual or repeated discharge of hazardous substances *into the environment.' "* (Emphasis in original.) [West American Ins. Co. v. Tufco Flooring East, Inc., 409 S.E.2d 692, 699 (N.C.App. 1991)], quoting Waste Management of Carolinas, Inc. v. Peerless Insurance Co., 340 S.E.2d 374, 381 (N.C. 1986). We think it improper to extend the exclusion beyond that arena.

Notwithstanding the above, ASI submits that the deletion of the requirement that the pollution be "[discharged] into or upon land, the atmosphere or any watercourse or body of water" should be viewed by this court as a clear signal of the industry's intent to broaden the exclusion beyond traditional environmental contamination. [For the full exclusion, as revised, see n. 8, p. 295 above.] We disagree. This same argument was rejected in West American Insurance Co. v. Tufco Flooring East, Inc., 409 S.E.2d 692 (N.C.App. 1991), a case which involved the application of the pollution exclusion to damages caused by the release of fumes from a flooring sealant. In *Tufco,* the court noted that, even after its amendment in 1986, the absolute pollution exclusion continued to employ terms of art which bespeak of environmental contamination. The court reasoned:

> "Because the operative policy terms 'discharge,' 'dispersal,' 're-lease,' and 'escape' are environmental terms of art, the omission of the language 'into or upon land, the atmosphere or any watercourse or body of water' in the new pollution exclusion is insignificant. The omission of the phrase only removes a redundancy in the language of the exclusion that was present in the earlier pollution exclusion clause. Consequently, we find that any 'discharge, dispersal, release, or escape' of a pollutant must be into the environment in order to trigger the pollution exclusion clause and deny coverage to the insured." *Tufco,* 409 S.E.2d at 700.

See also Center for Creative Studies [v. Aetna Life & Casualty Co., 871 F.Supp. 941 (E.D.Mich. 1994)] at 946 ("the fact that the [former version] contained language relating to discharge 'into or upon land, the atmosphere ...' is not significant"). We agree with this analysis. In our view, the deletion of the aforementioned language does not portend an expansion of the pollution exclusion beyond the context of traditional environmental contamination.

Conclusion

Given the historical background of the absolute pollution exclusion and the drafters' continued use of environmental terms of art, we hold that the exclusion applies only to those injuries caused by traditional environmental pollution. The accidental release of carbon monoxide in this case, due to a broken furnace, does not constitute the type of environmental pollution contemplated by the clause. Accordingly, the judgment of the appellate court is affirmed.

■ JUSTICE HEIPLE, dissenting:

This case turns on the interpretation of an exclusion clause in a policy of insurance. The facts are simple. Plaintiffs alleged injury from carbon monoxide fumes escaping from a malfunctioning furnace. The insurance company denied coverage on the basis of policy language which excluded coverage for injury from the escape of pollutants. The language further defined pollutants as any gaseous irritant or contaminant including fumes.

Choosing to override the clear language of the insurance contract, however, the majority purports to divine the unstated intent of the parties. With this analysis, coverage is found to be provided. What we have here is not a case of contract construction. It is, rather, a case of contract reconstruction. As such, it is thimblerigging pure and simple. It also indicates the depths to which a court will go to achieve a desired result. If any principle can be derived from this ruling, it is that words have no meaning.

Accordingly, I respectfully dissent.

NOTES

(1) *More History.* Another carbon-monoxide case was *Richardson*, quoted on p. 294 above. There the court said that the exclusion in question "cannot be construed ... without an understanding of the business and regulatory context in which the policy of which it is a part was written." Id. at 315. Part of that context was the history of the pollution exclusions, summarized above. A similar conclusion was reached in Andersen v. Highland House Co., 757 N.E.2d 329 (Ohio 2001). There the court said: "Based on the history and original purpose of the pollution exclusion, it was reasonable for [the insureds] to believe that the policies purchased for their multiunit complex would not exclude claims for injuries due to carbon monoxide leaks." Id. at 333. Oddly, however, a version of that history has been used also to support a broad and literal application of a pollution exclusion. Peace v. Northwestern Nat'l Ins. Co., 596 N.W.2d 429 (Wis. 1999).

In *Andersen*, Justice Cook, dissenting said: "the majority apparently credits [the insureds] as having had knowledge of the historical development of absolute pollution exclusions at the time they purchased the relevant policies and accepts this as informing the relevant policy language." This, Justice Cook thought, was without basis.

(2) *Third-party Interests.* A passionate view of the problem was expressed by Justice Crooks, dissenting from the decision in *Peace*, above. The insured, a landlord, had been charged with liability on behalf of a child who, it was said, was injured by having ingested paint chips and flakes and dust, all contaminated with lead in paint at the child's home. The court ruled that a pollution exclusion applied. Justice Crooks said: "I cannot join the majority's apparent assault on child victims of lead poisoning." Id. at 449, 455.

The assumption seems to be that compensation could not be had from the insured landlord. Would it be well to construe the policy one way for an impoverished insured and another for a well-heeled one?

PROBLEM

Walter the welder was injured when a canister of compressed oxygen that he was using broke open with explosive force. He brought a bodily injury action against the firm that had made the item and had sold it to him. He charged that firm with negligence both in molding the metal canister and in overcharging it with oxygen. The firm, Welding Supply Inc., has held insurance against liabilities at all relevant times, written in the form of the current CGL policy. The insurer has refused to provide Welding Supply with a defense, referring to the pollution exclusion in its policy, as set out at p. 295, n.8 above. Was that wrongful?

F.   CLAIMS–MADE POLICIES

In 1986 the ISO introduced a CGL policy form as an alternative to the existing "occurrence-based" form: the "claims-made" form. The most important distinction between the "occurrence" policy and the "claims made" policy is the difference between the "peril insured" and the "trigger" activating coverage. In the occurrence policy, the peril insured is the occurrence. When the occurrence occurs *during the policy period*,[1] coverage is triggered (activated) even though the claim may not be made for some time thereafter.

In contrast, in the "claims made" policy, the making of the claim against the insured *during the policy period* is the peril being insured regardless of when the occurrence occurs. But to trigger claims-made coverage, the claim must be reported, typically by giving notice or making a demand to the insurer during the policy period. In other words, the trigger of coverage in a claims-made policy is a claim made against the insured during the policy period *and* reported by the insured to the insurer during the policy period.[2]

---

1. The "Policy Period" is the specific time period in which the policy is in effect. For example, 12:01 A.M. EST FROM 01–01–07 TO 01–01–08. The "policy period "is customarily stated on the Declarations page of the policy.

2. For a detailed explanation and analyzes, see Bob Works, "Excusing Nonoccurrence of Insurance Policy Conditions in Order to Avoid Disproportionate Forfeiture: Claims Made Formats as a Test Case," 5 Conn. Ins. L.J. 505 (1998).

Distinguishing "Occurrence" and "Claims Made" Coverages

The occurrence CGL policy insures "harm" (bodily injury, property damage, advertising injury and personal injury) to third parties that "occurs" during the policy period even when the claim is made or a lawsuit is filed subsequent to the policy period. Moreover, significant insurer coverage risks are pre-policy-period, retroactive risks. In addition, the occurrence CGL policy does not define (or explain) how to determine "when" the occurrence (notably bodily injury or property damage) occurs. To resolve these problems, the ISO created the CGL claims made policy.

The claims-made policy requires that both the claim be made during the policy period and the claim be reported to the insurer during the policy period to *trigger* coverage.[3] Consequently, the claims-made policy resolves the occurrence policy's failure to state how to determine "when" the occurrence occurs (takes place) to trigger coverage. Unlike the occurrence policy,[4] pre-policy-period latent, ongoing harms caused by toxins in the body or environment resulting in bodily injury or property damage cannot trigger claims made coverage. A typical "claims-made" policy covers acts and omissions happening before the policy-period term provided the claim is first discovered and reported to the insurer during the same policy term.[5]

The insurer and insured are said to benefit. The insurer is able significantly to decrease its exposure by limiting its liability to claims reported in the fixed "policy period" of time.[6] The claims-made insurer can "close its books" on a claims-made policy at the expiration of the "policy period" thereby permitting a level of predictability unattainable under the standard occurrence policy.[7] In return for this limited exposure, the insured benefits from lower insurance premiums.[8] But the insured also suffers detriment from the added exposures of no coverage which differs from the standard occurrence policy.

---

3. An insured may negotiate for simple claims-made coverage at a higher premium rather than claims made and reported coverage. A simple claims-made policy eliminates the mandatory reporting requirement that the claim be reported by the insured in the "policy period". The simple claims-made policy is rare today.

4. Occurrence policies typically provide coverage for any act or omission by an insured occurring during the period in which the insured maintained the policy, even if the claim ultimately made against the insurance company was neither discovered nor reported to the insurance company until after the expiration of the policy period.

5. Because it is often difficult to ascertain the precise date of insured's conduct, for example malpractice, the pivotal event for claims-made insurance coverage is the date the claim is made against the insured rather than the date of the insured's conduct form-

ing the basis for the claim. As the risks assumed under an "occurrence" policy often entail delays of unpredictable duration between the occurrence of the covered bodily injury or property damage and any ultimate payout by the insurer (the "tail" exposure), premium rates tend to be significantly higher than those charged for comparable "claims-made" policies.

6. See United States v. Strip, 868 F.2d 181, 187 (6th Cir. 1989).

7. As the risks assumed under an "occurrence" policy often entail delays of unpredictable duration between the occurrence of the covered act or omission and any ultimate payout by the insurer (the "tail" exposure), premium rates tend to be significantly higher than those charged for comparable "claims-made" policies.

8. *See, e.g.,* Sigma Fin. Corp. v. American Int'l Specialty Lines Ins. Co., 200 F. Supp.2d 710, 716 (E.D. Mich. 2002).

The insured, under a claims-made policy, has two very significant no-coverage concerns seriously limiting the insured's claims-made coverage: (i) "Retroactive Exposure" caused by the absence of (or limited) prior-acts claims-made coverage, and (ii) "Tail Exposure" because claims-made policies provide no coverage for post-policy-period claims made against the insured. Attempting to *rectify* the insured's two-fold exposures, claims-made insurers generally offer the insured two endorsement options at an additional premium to the claims-made policy: (i) *Retroactive Premium Endorsement*[9] insuring retroactive ("prior acts") claims made against the insured, and (ii) *Extended Reporting Endorsement*[10] insuring claims made against the insured after the claims-made policy expires at the end of the policy period.

The difference between CGL "occurrence" coverage and "claims made" coverage may be further illustrated by supposing a stove manufacturer switches from one policy to another, that each having a term of one year. Let it be supposed also that the insured has sold a stove, in which a defect causes bodily injury to the buyer, and has thereby incurred a liability, all in Year One. The buyer has presented a claim in Year Two. If the insured has moved from an occurrence-based policy to a claims-made one, it is entitled to protection under both policies. (Possibly an other-insurance clause in one of the policies will make the other *primary* and that one *excess*. Possibly also the claims-made policy will provide no protection unless the insured makes a demand on the issuer within Year Two.)

If, on the other hand, the insured has moved from a claims-made policy to an occurrence-based one, the insured is not entitled to protection under

---

9. The following is an example, in part, of a three year endorsement—standard ISO endorsement form IL 09 19 10 93 Copyright, Insurance Services Office, Inc.:

RETROSPECTIVE PREMIUM ENDORSE-MENT THREE YEAR PLAN—MUL-TIPLE LINES

This endorsement is issued because you chose to have the cost of the insurance rated retrospectively. This endorsement explains the rating plan and how the retrospective premium will be determined.... This endorsement applies in the states listed in the Schedule. It determines the retrospective premium for the insurance provided during the rating plan period by this policy and any policy listed in the Schedule, and the renewals of each. The Rating plan period is the three year period beginning with the effective date of this endorsement. (remainder of form omitted)

10. The following example states only the most pertinent language from the American Home Insurance Company for its Accountants Professional Claims Made Liability Insurance Contract:

Extended Reporting Endorsement

[I]n the event of cancellation or non-renewal of this policy by either the Named Insured or the Company, the Named Insured shall have the right, upon payment of an additional premium of 90% of the total annual premium for this policy within 30 days of such termination, to have issued an endorsement providing a one year extended reporting period for all claims first made against the insured and reported to the Company after the termination of the policy period arising out of any negligent act, error or omission occurring prior to the termination of the policy period and otherwise covered by this policy.

The endorsement includes two important terms: (1) the length of time allowed to extend the reporting period, and (2) the premium charged for the extended coverage. These terms vary from policy to policy. The usual length of time is one, two or three years. Prior to the 1986 ISO standard revision, it was possible to purchase up to six years' extended reporting rights, but thereafter, the maximum extended reporting period typically being offered is three years.

either of the policies. (That result assumes that the Year–Two policy does not contain a retrospective provision.) No claim has been made by the buyer in Year One, and the buyer has suffered no injury in Year Two.

Insurers tend to favor claims-made coverages because they do not have the "long tails" associated with occurrence-based coverages. An issuer of an occurrence-based policy may well have to endure a long period of uncertainty about the extent of its commitments under that policy. The following paragraph is drawn from an opinion more fully represented immediately below. It describes the "core idea behind the move to claims made insurance policies". The idea was

> to *close the gap* between the time when the insurer *prices* a risk and the time when the insurer may incur an obligation to *pay on* that risk. (See Works, *Excusing Nonoccurrence of Insurance Policy Conditions* ..., 5 Conn.Ins.L.J. at p. 516 ["Other things being equal, the insurer's financial people will want to employ a policy trigger that falls later in the sequence than earlier, in order to shorten the time between when a policy obligation is priced and when the extent of the obligation is determined. Statistical models of insurance pools that help inform insurance underwriting and pricing decisions depend in part on the quality of the loss frequency and severity estimations they employ. Consequently, the longer the period for which one must 'develop' immature historical loss data in order to estimate ultimate loss costs for policies written in the past, and the longer into the future one must peer in an effort to trend those estimates of past loss costs in order to make predictions abut future loss costs for new policies, the greater the likelihood for error."].)

On reflection, of course, the idea of closing the pricing gap is unremarkable. Pretty much everybody who has the slightest acquaintance with insurance law knows that the longer the gap between the time the insurer takes the premiums and the time when the insurer pays out on the risk, the more likely the insurer gets burned.

Root v. American Equity Specialty Ins. Co., 30 Cal.Rptr.3d 631, 644 (Cal.App. 2005).

Root's Case

Walter H. Root III, an attorney, received a phone call one Thursday from a law-journal reporter, inquiring about a malpractice suit that had been filed against him, she said, by Farideh Jalali, a former client. Root did not take the call seriously. He was busy, and thought the call might be a prank. In more than twenty years in practice, he had never been sued for malpractice, and he had won for Ms. Jalali a munificent settlement of a claim. On Saturday, Root left for a long holiday weekend. On his return, on Tuesday, he found an article in the law journal describing the suit.

Root held a claims-made policy covering malpractice liability—"Policy One"—for the period when the suit was filed. It expired on midnight of the Sunday of his holiday. Thereafter he had similar coverage under "Policy Two", issued by another insurer. Both insurers declined to defend the client's action. Root's law firm defended him, successfully, and he brought an action against the issuer of Policy One for the cost of that defense.

The trial court entered a summary judgment against Root, assuming the facts to be as stated by him, and stated above. He had failed, within the policy period, to notify the insurer of the suit. The cover page of the policy contained this statement:

> This is a "Claims Made" policy. The coverage afforded by this policy is limited to claims arising from the performance of Professional Services which are first made against the Insured and reported in writing to the Company while the policy is in force.

In what may be called "Reporting Condition a", the insuring agreement reaffirmed the requirement of a written report "while the policy is in force". This requirement created what is called, in the opinion last cited, a *claims-made-and-reported* policy, as opposed to a "pure" claims-made policy.

In addition to Reporting Condition a, the policy required that the insurer be given, in writing and within the policy period, various particulars if "the Insured shall [] become aware of" acts or omissions "with respect to which no Claim has been made but which could reasonably be expected to form the basis of a Claim which might be covered hereby". Call that "Reporting Condition b".

On appeal, the judgment against Root was reversed and the case remanded. (Some of the facts indicated above were based entirely on Root's account of events. That was assumed to be accurate, naturally, given that summary judgment had been sought, and granted, against him.) Of the several rulings by the court, only one is indicated at this point; others are indicated below.

Whether or not any claim had been made against Root within the policy period was the first question addressed by the court. The policy defined the word *claim* as "a demand, including service of suit or institution of arbitration proceedings, for money against an Insured." Root had not been served with process during the policy period. The court concluded that a reasonable insured might well suppose that the filing of a suit against him constituted the making of a "claim" within the policy definition, even though he did not know of the suit.

Either that or the service of process might constitute the making of a claim, the court thought, given the ambiguity of the definition. This thought led the court to speculate that Root might have coverage under both Policy One and Policy Two. On that subject the court wrote as follows:

> [W]hat about the problem that ... there could be a situation in which an insured might have two "claims" against him or her based on just one malpractice suit? (And falling on either side of a policy expiration date, to boot.) The answer is, given the traditional rule that ambiguities in insurance policies are construed according to the reasonable expectations of the insured, it is the insurer, not the insured, who must bear the cost of that ambiguity. If that result seems too

generous to insureds, one has only to contemplate the alternative: The insured could be whipsawed by an ambiguous definition of claim and a parallel requirement of reporting anything which constitutes a reasonable "basis" to believe a claim is being made into having no coverage under policies on either side of a policy period expiration divide. Ambiguities in insurance contracts aren't supposed to work that way.

The court noted that its "two claim" theory might lead to a sharing of loss between the two insurers, one having a claim of contribution against the other.

The court envisaged difficulties that Root might have had in reporting anything of substance to Insurer One before Monday morning. The court observed that he might have sent an e-mail or fax, saying what little he knew, and so might easily have protected himself. "No harm in that", the insurer might say. The court's response was this: "It might very well have harmed [Root] to make such a report. To do so would have been to prejudice his chances of being able to report the claim to his second insurer. By making a report in the policy period of insurer one, most lawyers know that insurer two will pounce on the fact of that report to argue that the claim did not occur in its policy period."

POST–PERIOD CLAIMS

To some extent the coverage of a claims-made policy may extend to claims made outside the policy period, both fore and aft. So it was in the American Equity policy issued to Root. The company agreed to be accountable for a claim made after the end of the policy term if the claim should arise from an act or omission described in Reporting Condition b.[11] More elaborate coverage of post-period claims may be bought in the form of an "Extended Reporting Endorsement". Representative ones apply for a period of 1–3 years, in the event of cancellation or non-renewal of the policy. The claims covered are only those arising out of an act or omission during the policy period. Another provision, also available at a price, is not restricted that way, but extends the time allowed for reporting a claim made during the policy period.

In Root's case the court said: "An extended reporting period endorsement would have given Root a set amount of extra time to report claims . . . In the reported cases, such extended periods have typically been for 60 days." Root said that American Equity—Insurer One—had given him no opportunity to buy that endorsement. As will appear, that fact (if it was a fact) figured in Root's favor. But it is not clear why it should. For one thing, the usual endorsement of that kind does not apply when the policy has simply expired. For another, one cannot tell when the alleged malprac-

---

11. "If the insured strictly complies with the foregoing notice requirements, any Claim that may subsequently be made against the Insured arising out of such act, error or omission shall be deemed for the purposes of this insurance to have been made and reported in writing on the date such notice is received by the Company."

tice occurred, even after reading two extensive opinions about Jalali's claim.

NOTES

(1) *Why the Reporting Requirement?* The opinion in Root's case contains an extensive discussion of the advantages that insurers find in requiring prompt reports of claims. The discussion is surprising both for what it contains and what it does not contain. It does not refer to the advantage of having an opportunity to investigate a claim while the facts are relatively fresh.

The discussion refers to gap-closing as a possible advantage—closing the gap, that is, between the time when an insurer must price its undertaking and the time when it must perform. But gap-closing does not underlie the reporting requirement, the court said. "The basic risk of the late-surfacing claim … has already been addressed by going to claims made coverage."

Having laid aside some other explanations for the notice requirement, the court was able to characterize it as a provision for a "naked forfeiture". As will be seen, that description worked powerfully in Root's favor.

(2) *Policy Limits.* In the main, a lawyer or other professional who experiences heavy malpractice liabilities, in relation to the amount of liability coverage purchased, cannot expect full indemnification if the liabilities are covered ones and if they outrun the policy limit, no matter when the underlying claims are reported. In other words, the purchase of an extended-reporting-period endorsement does not enlarge the policy limit. (But some policies allow for adjustment of the limits, some as required by statute and some not.)

———

Root v. American Equity Specialty Ins. Co.

California Court of Appeal, 2005.
130 Cal.App.4th 926, 30 Cal.Rptr.3d 631.

[The facts assumed in this case—Part II of the opinion—are summarized above. As for Part III–A (*A Claim Was Made*), see p. 306. Part III–B (*State of the Precedent*) is omitted, except for this concluding statement: "We are thus aware of no case, such as the one before us, where the late report was made a *de minimis* time after the expiration of the policy and where the insured had not been given the opportunity to be protected under an extended claim reporting endorsement."]

■ SILLS, P. J.

I. INTRODUCTION

This case involves one of the worst nightmares faced by most every attorney, doctor, accountant or other professional covered by a malpractice insurance policy: the possibility of no malpractice coverage under a "claims made and reported" policy where a claim is made very late in the policy period and the insured learns of the claim under highly ambiguous circumstances, so the claim is not reported until there is confirmation of that claim, which is shortly after the policy has expired.

In such a situation, however, California's traditional common law of contracts bearing on forfeitures and conditions precedent offers a way out for the hapless insured. As our Supreme Court wrote almost 60 years ago, "And where, as in the insurance policies held by O'Morrow [the insured], the condition is express and cannot be avoided by construction, the court may, in a proper case, excuse compliance with it or give equitable relief against its enforcement." (O'Morrow v. Borad (1946) 27 Cal.2d 794, 800 [167 P.2d 483].) As we will now show, the reporting requirement in this case is such a condition that may be equitably excused under the particular circumstances of this case. Accordingly, we reverse the judgment obtained by the malpractice insurer on a summary judgment motion.

However, we emphasize the narrowness of today's decision. We will take great pains to show that by no means do we blanketly apply a blunderbuss "notice-prejudice" rule to this, or any other claims made and reported malpractice policy. (The notice-prejudice rule holds that "[u]nless an insurer can demonstrate actual prejudice from late notice, the insured's failure to provide timely notice will not defeat coverage." (See Croskey *et al.*, Cal. Practice Guide: Insurance Litigation (The Rutter Group 2004) ¶ 3:168, p. 3–377.) [See also pp. 74 ff., above.] In fact, we will devote some space to explaining why the notice-prejudice rule sweeps much too broadly in the context of claims made and reported policies and should not be applied here. (On this point we will thus agree with existing case law.) Even so, there are at least a few times when the established common law of contracts (bearing on when the nonoccurrence of a condition precedent works a forfeiture) may operate to excuse the nonoccurrence of a condition, and this case is one of them.

[III] C. *The Law of Conditions Precedent and Disproportionate Forfeitures*

1. General Considerations

California's common law of contracts has traditionally allowed for the equitable excusal or remediation of nonoccurrence of conditions precedent in contracts when such nonoccurrence works a forfeiture. (See [three cases cited and stated].) There is also a statutory basis for an antiforfeiture rule in section 3275 of the Civil Code: "Whenever, by the terms of an obligation, a party thereto incurs a forfeiture, or a loss in the nature of a forfeiture, by reason of his failure to comply with its provisions, he may be relieved therefrom, upon making full compensation to the other party, except in case of a grossly negligent, willful, or fraudulent breach of duty." ...

The reference in section 3275 to relief conditioned on "making full compensation to the other party" may, at first blush, seem to preclude insurance contracts from condition-precedent-forfeiture analysis. Insurance contracts are, to use the technical term, "aleatory." That is, they are contracts where there is the possibility that one party (the insurer) will never have to make good on its promise. Indeed, both parties actually hope that the one party will never have to make good on its promise. You pay your auto insurance premium hoping that you will never have an accident and the insurer will never have to make good on its promise to indemnify you for it.

This aleatory nature of insurance contracts makes an allowance of "full compensation" impossible when it comes to the *fundamental risk* insured against. It is common knowledge that if you have already had a car accident at a time when your policy has long since expired, you can't simply go back and pay the premiums so that the insurer will be obligated to compensate you for your wrecked car.

But the aleatory nature of insurance contracts does not make compensation an impossibility when it comes to conditions precedent to coverage. We already know this from the great body of case law which (at least outside of claims made and reported policies) has imposed the notice-prejudice rule on insurers.... If notice of a claim is a *condition* of coverage, then it can be excused when it works a forfeiture.

Proof of this point may be found in O'Morrow v. Borad, *supra,* where our Supreme Court made it clear that conditions in insurance policies could be excused under traditional contract forfeiture rules. [The court described the case, which concerned a requirement in an auto policy that the insured cooperate with the insurer in the defense of suits. The court alluded to the *O'Morrow* opinion as follows.] [T]he court ended with the point that even if the usual rules of interpretation could not avoid a forfeiture, a court could still excuse compliance with the condition or give equitable relief against its enforcement: "Forfeitures, however, are not favored; hence a contract, and conditions in a contract, will if possible be construed to avoid forfeiture. [Citations.] This is particularly true of insurance contracts. [Citation.] [¶] And where, as in the insurance policies held by O'Morrow, the condition is express and cannot be avoided by construction, the court may, in a proper case, excuse compliance with it or give equitable relief against its enforcement." (O'Morrow v. Borad at p. 800.)

. . .

2.   A Condition by Any Other Name....

a.   *The Problem*

The central issue in this case, then, is whether the policy period reporting requirement is a condition precedent of coverage that may be equitably excused when it works a forfeiture. The complicating factor is that the reporting requirement here is found in the insuring clause, and therefore at least *looks* as if it is an element of the defining scope of coverage rather than just a mere "condition."

The issue came up in Slater [v. Lawyers' Mutual Ins. Co., 278 Cal.Rptr. 479 (Cal.App. 1991)], where the majority rejected the notice-prejudice rule precisely because of the inclusion of the reporting requirement in the insuring clause. But that point met stiff resistance from the dissenting justice, who argued that there is "no magic about where the reporting requirement is placed within an insurance contract." (See *Slater* at p. 1429 (dis. opn. of Johnson, J.).) Justice Johnson went on to argue that, functionally, it should make no difference where the reporting requirement is placed in the contract because no coverage is still no coverage, whether as the result of the insuring clause, an exclusion, or a condition.

In the case before us we need not and do not go as far as Justice Johnson's dissent might take us. There *are* well-established differences between insuring clauses, exclusions, and conditions that should not be amalgamated into one binary question: coverage yes or no under an "if . . . then" analysis. (See cases collected in American Star Ins. Co. v. Insurance Co. of the West (1991) 232 Cal.App.3d 1320, 1325 [284 Cal.Rptr. 45].)

That said, Justice Johnson certainly had a valid point that *just because* something is mentioned in an insuring clause does not *necessarily* mean that it goes to the scope of basic coverage provided by the insurance policy. . . . As we will now show, the reporting condition in Root's policy here does *not* go to basic coverage but quacks, walks, looks and functions like a condition, not an element of the fundamental risk insured.

b.   *As a Matter of Textual Exegesis*

The first reason to conclude that the policy period reporting requirement is a condition is simple. The policy tells us it is.

[The court dealt here with the fact that the policy referred to notice not only as a condition ("*As a condition precedent* the Insured's right. . . .") but also in the insuring clause. The similarity of the two provisions led the court to conclude that they expressed a single requirement, either as a condition, an element of coverage, or both, and that "condition" was the proper characterization. These conclusions rested largely on a finding of ambiguity in the policy ("practically enigmatic").]

c.   *As a Matter of Commercial Reality*

But even if the policy did not contain the seeds of its own cognitive dissonance . . . , an examination of the commercial reality behind the reporting requirement provides ample proof that it is, fundamentally, a condition.

[Here the court examined (i) the reasons why insurers changed from occurrence-based policies to pure claims-made policies, and (ii) reasons for imposing a timely-notice requirement. Some of the court's remarks on these subjects are reported above.

[In addition, the court described what it regarded as the most important advantage of the notice requirement to insurers: "the administrative convenience of *monitoring* potential payouts. In a word, a reporting requirement gives the insurer administrative 'closure'. . . ."]

. . . Anyone who has ever dealt with insurers and their claims adjusters knows that they tend to put at least a little value on simply being able to close a file. Perhaps more importantly, a policy period reporting requirement facilitates the quicker accumulation of loss history. By the end of the policy period the insurer definitely knows whether X risk generated any claims in Y period, and it knows it quicker (but only slightly quicker) with a claims made and reported policy than it knows it with a pure claims made policy. (However, even this bit of information is of only limited value: While the reporting requirement means that the insurer may know *whether* any claims were filed, it is unlikely to know *how much* it will have to pay out on any late made but timely reported claims.)

. . .

Perhaps the most striking example of insurers charging low premiums to insure against occurrences that would later come back to cost them dearly has been in the area of pollution liability and toxic torts, where claims were made in the 1980's and 1990's against policies which were priced in the 1950's and 1960's. . . .

Professional malpractice insurance underwriting is likewise particularly vulnerable to gaps between the time of pricing and the time of obligation. (See Pacific Employers [Ins. Co. v. Superior Court, 270 Cal.Rptr. 779 (Cal.App., 1990) at p. 784: "Underwriters soon realized, however, that 'occurrence' policies were unrealistic in the context of professional malpractice because the injury and the negligence that caused it were often not discoverable until years after the delictual act or omission.").]

[The court expressed agreement with two earlier cases:] perfectly sound in their resistance to the notice-prejudice rule for claims made and reported policies. Consider the inflexible breadth of the notice-prejudice rule: It can apply to cases involving delays many months, perhaps even years, after the expiration of the policy period, and it puts the burden on the insurer to show prejudice from even long delays in reporting. Application of the rule thus fundamentally rewrites the claims made and reported contract into a pure claims made contract.

But the possible equitable excuse of a condition precedent is much more flexible and nuanced, and does no violence to the claims made and reported nature of the policy.

First of all, it is not a bright-line test. Equities vary with the peculiar facts of each case. Sometimes—indeed most of the time—it will not be equitable to excuse the nonoccurrence of the condition, so it is not excused. Granted, the factually intense nature of the inquiry may make summary judgment more difficult for insurers to obtain in certain cases (like this one), but that is a result that comes with California's common law rule that conditions can be excused if equity requires it.

For example, in the present case, the fact that the insurer did not give the insured the opportunity to buy an extended reporting endorsement which would (if it was anything like the ones in the reported cases) have given him an extra 60 days to report any claims may be of significance. Had Root been given that opportunity, for example, equity might not require excuse of the condition, because its excuse would, in effect, be to give Root the benefit of something that he had the opportunity to buy and passed up. The same might be said if Root had had sufficient time to conduct an investigation as to whether a claim had indeed been made against him, or had delayed reporting the claim beyond the day on which he received confirmation of the claim. But given this record the facts are sufficient to support the equitable excuse of the reporting condition, so summary judgment should not have been granted. In the *O'Morrow* court's phrase, given these facts it would be "most inequitable" to enforce the condition precedent of a report during the policy period.

IV.   DISPOSITION

The judgment is reversed with directions for the trial court to conduct further proceedings not inconsistent with this opinion.

.   .   .

NOTES

(1) *Questions of Drafting and Policy.* Would you suppose that an insurer might surmount the ruling in Root's case by writing either of these terms into its contract?

(a) The requirement of timely notice [stating it] is a condition not subject to equitable excuse or remediation of nonoccurrence.

(b) The requirement ... is not a mere condition limiting the insurer's responsibility, but is an element of coverage.

If either of these terms would otherwise suffice, should it be disregarded on the ground of public policy?

(2) *Compliance Questions.* In a case comparable to Root's case, the insureds became aware of potential claims against them and sent a notice of them by FedEx shortly before midnight of the last day of the policy period. The insurer received the notice at 9:03 the next morning. The policy spoke of *giving* notice within the policy period. Answering certified questions, the court ruled that the insureds had failed of both compliance and substantial compliance with the requirement of notice within the policy period. Catholic Med. Ctr. v. Executive Risk Indem., Inc., 867 A.2d 453 (N.H. 2005).

CHAPTER 6

LIABILITY INSURANCE: THE DEFENSE OBLIGATION

The insurer's obligation to defend an insured against suits is one of the most important obligations imposed by its contract and distinguishes it from most other forms of insurance. Being risk averse, individuals and firms purchase liability insurance to protect against the risk of being sued, as well as the risk of having to pay as a result of a suit.

Unlike an issuer of first party insurance, such as property, life, or health insurance, who makes only a promise to pay (indemnify), a liability insurer makes two promises: to defend the insured and, in the event of a money judgment or settlement, to pay. (The promise to pay judgments or settlements on the insured's behalf is covered in Chapter 7.) These two contract promises are made in the policy's "insuring agreement". Here is an example excerpted from Coverage A of the ISO 2004 Commercial General Liability (CGL) coverage form (used by permission):

1. Insuring Agreement

    a. We will pay those sums that the insured becomes legally obligated to pay as damages because of "bodily injury" or "property damage" to which this insurance applies. We will have the right and duty to defend the insured against any "suit" seeking those damages. However, we will have no duty to defend the insured against any "suit" seeking damages for "bodily injury" or "property damage" to which this insurance does not apply. We may, at our discretion, investigate any "occurrence" and settle any claim or "suit" that may result. But:

        (1) The amount we will pay for damages is limited as described in Section III Limits Of Insurance; and

        (2) Our right and duty to defend ends when we have used up the applicable limit of insurance in the payment of judgments or settlements under Coverages A or B or medical expenses under Coverage C.

Observe that the agreement confers on the insured the *right* to provide a defense as well as a duty to do so, that both the right and the duty are to terminate when an applicable payment limit has been reached, and that it does *not* commit the insurer to make any investigation or to settle any claim.

The determination whether or not the insurer must defend a given suit against its insured has proved often to be difficult. Early in Chapter 5 it has been said that, under the CGL policy form, the defense obligation is limited by reference to the policy coverages, and that an insurer has no obligation to defend unless the charges made against the insured can be understood to include a covered liability. Part A of this chapter refines that statement and includes opinions stating criteria for determining when a defense obligation is triggered.

Parts B and C concern an insurer's decision whether or not, on receiving a demand that it provide a defense for the insured, to accede to the demand. Part B describes some of the risks entailed by acceding to the demand; Part C describes risks entailed by refusing to defend. Part D continues Part B by supposing that the insurer, having incurred expenses in defending the insured, and finding that the expense was needless, hopes to recover it from the insured.

A. Scope of the Duty to Defend

"The duty to defend and the duty to indemnify are distinct and separate duties." King v. Dallas Fire Ins. Co., 85 S.W.3d 185, 186 (Tex. 2002). Perhaps the thing most often said, and with most confidence, about the duty of an insurer of liability to provide the insured with a defense against a suit is that this duty is broader than the duty to indemnify. Good illustrations are cases in which an essential allegation in a complaint against an insured proves to be incorrect. Suppose that a motorist, provided with auto insurance, is sued for having injured a person through negligent driving, and that the claim is unfounded. Perhaps the insured was not negligent, or the claimant has mistaken the car that struck him, or has simply pretended an injury. None of these facts has a bearing on the insurer's duty to provide a defense against the claim. The duty "may apply even in an action where no damages are ultimately awarded." Scottsdale Ins. Co. v. MV Transportation, 115 P.3d 460, 466 (Cal. 2005). If a complaint alleges facts within policy coverage, the insurer is "obligated to defend its insured even if the allegations are groundless, false, or fraudulent." General Agents Ins. Co. of America v. Midwest Sporting Goods Co., 828 N.E.2d 1092, 1098 (Ill. 2005). "[T]he insurer may have a duty to defend ... notwithstanding that at the end of the day [it] is not liable for indemnification." America Online, Inc. v. St. Paul Mercury Ins. Co., 207 F.Supp.2d 459, 466 (E.D.Va. 2002). The duty of an insurer to pay is more constricted, of course, arising only when a claim against the insured has been determined to be well-founded.

A number of courts examining an insurer's duty to provide a defense subscribe to what they call the "eight corners rule". This catchy name was arrived at by adding four and four: the four corners of the complaint and the four corners of the policy. (One court has referred, mysteriously, to the eight corners of a petition.[3]) Alternate names are the "comparison rule"

---

3. Southwest Tank & Treater Mfg. Co. v. Mid–Continent Cas. Co., 243 F.Supp.2d 597 (E.D.Tex. 2003).

and the "complaint allegation rule". See *King* at 186. According to a stringent version of the rule, nothing outside those documents is to be consulted. Other rules, less stringent, are indicated below.

In applying the comparison test, a court must have some idea of what to look for. One possibility is to look, in the complaint, for a claim that is, as to fact and theory, assuredly within the policy statement of coverage. Other, more elusive possibilities are suggested below.

Relaxation of the Comparison Test

"In certain circumstances," it has been said, "extrinsic evidence beyond that contained in the 'eight corners' will be permitted in order to aid in determining whether the insurer has a duty to defend.... A Texas court of appeals summarized the rule on extrinsic evidence as follows:

> Where the insurance company refuses to defend its insured on the ground that the insured is not liable to the claimant, the allegations in the claimant's petition control, and facts extrinsic to those alleged in the petition may not be used to controvert those allegations. But, where the basis for the refusal to defend is that the events giving rise to the suit are outside the coverage of the insurance policy, facts extrinsic to the claimant's petition may be used to determine whether a duty to defend exists. Gonzales v. Am. States Ins. Co. of Tex., 628 S.W.2d 184, 187 (Tex. Civ. App.—Corpus Christi 1982, no writ).

Southwest Tank & Treater Mfg. Co. v. Mid–Continent Cas. Co., 243 F. Supp.2d 597, 602 (E.D. Tex. 2003) (Tex. law).

This position appears to reverse the comparison rule in good part, in favor of insurers. For a similar but more limited reversal see Teachers Ins. Co. v. Schofield, 284 F.Supp.2d 161 (D.Me. 2003), where public policy was said to favor extrinsic evidence that the insured had been convicted of manslaughter.

In California the high court has said: "An insurer must defend its insured against claims that create a *potential* for indemnity under its policy", and that an insurer's duty to defend arises "if any facts stated or fairly inferable in the complaint, *or otherwise known or discovered by the insurer*, suggest a claim potentially covered...." Scottsdale Ins. Co. v. MV Transportation at 466 (emphasis supplied). Compare this statement of New York law: "[E]ven where the complaint does not contain factual allegations establishing a duty to defend, an insurer must provide a defense 'when it has actual knowledge of facts establishing a reasonable possibility of coverage.'" Emerson Enterprises, L.L.C. v. Kenneth Crosby–New York, Inc., 386 F.Supp.2d 151, 159 (W.D.N.Y. 2005).

On reading forward, one should be on the watch for various things to look for in applying the comparison rule, and for signs of relaxation of that rule.

Capital Bank v. Commonwealth Land Title Ins. Co.

Texas Court of Appeals, 1993.
861 S.W.2d 84.

■ Lee Duggan, Jr., Justice

This is an appeal from the entry of a take-nothing judgment following a nonjury trial in a suit arising from an insurer's refusal to defend under a title insurance policy.

In its sole point of error, plaintiff/appellant, Capital Bank ... asserts the trial court erred in granting a take-nothing judgment in favor of defendant/appellee, Commonwealth Land Title Insurance Company and its agent, Commonwealth Title Insurance Company of Houston (Commonwealth), "before the plaintiff had an opportunity to present its evidence and rest."

Capital was a lender/mortgagee and the insured party under a mortgagee's policy of title insurance issued by Commonwealth on February 22, 1983. Commonwealth refused Capital's demand that it defend, under the policy, a tendered lawsuit against Capital. Capital sued Commonwealth, asserting causes of action for breach of contract and breach of Commonwealth's duty of good faith and fair dealing.

The insurer's duty to defend

In ascertaining the scope of an insurer's duty to defend, courts should look to the language of the policy and the allegations in the complaint against the insured. *Fidelity & Guaranty Underwriters v. McManus*, 633 S.W.2d 787, 788 (Tex. 1982); *Feed Store, Inc. v. Reliance Insurance Co.*, 774 S.W.2d 73, 74 (Tex.App.—Houston [1st Dist.] 1989, *writ denied*). As stated in American Reliance Ins. v. Frito–Lay, 788 S.W.2d 152, 153–54 (Tex. App.—Houston [1st Dist.] 1990, *writ denied*):

> Texas courts follow the "Eight Corners" or "Complaint Allegation" rule when determining the duty to defend action. This rule requires the trier of fact to examine only the allegations in the complaint and the insurance policy in determining whether a duty to defend exists. The duty to defend is not affected by facts ascertained before suit, developed in the process of litigation, or by the ultimate outcome of the suit.

788 S.W.2d at 153–54 (citations omitted).

Under this analysis the court cannot consider anything outside (a) the policy and (b) the pleadings. *Feed Store, Inc.*, 774 S.W.2d at 74. The effect of this "eight corners rule" is to minimize uncertainty in assessing a liability insurer's duty, as well as to favor the insured in cases where the merits of the action may be questionable. *Feed Store, Inc.*, 774 S.W.2d at 75.

The policy and the allegations in the adversary proceeding against Capital

In determining that Commonwealth had no duty to defend, the trial court had among Capital's admitted exhibits both (1) the title insurance policy Commonwealth issued to Capital and (2) the adversary pleading containing the allegations against Capital that Commonwealth was called on, under the policy, to defend. The title policy stated in pertinent part that Commonwealth, as insurer:

> will pay to the Insured ... all loss or damage not exceeding the amount stated ... which the Insured ... may sustain or suffer by reason of the failure of, defects in, encumbrances upon, or liens ... against the title of the mortgagors or grantors ... existing at or prior to the date of this policy ... This policy does not insure against loss or damage by reason of defects, liens, encumbrances, adverse claims, or other matters ... (d) attaching or created subsequent to Date of Policy....

Capital's live pleadings alleged that Capital foreclosed on the insured property; that Capital thereafter sold the property to James C. Motley; and that Capital was later sued in an adversary proceeding that arose out of the bankruptcy proceedings of the party Capital had foreclosed on earlier. Capital further pled that Commonwealth provided guidance in the matter but refused to formally accept the defense of the adversary proceedings or pay attorney fees reasonably incurred for defense services.

Under the "eight corners" doctrine, the trial court was restricted to considering only the pleadings and the policy. *Feed Store, Inc.*, 774 S.W.2d at 74. The trial court could determine from the pleadings and the policy that Capital's alleged causes of action against Commonwealth arose as a result of Capital's foreclosure on the insured property. The foreclosure and resulting adversary proceeding occurred after the policy date. The policy expressly excludes coverage for subsequent events. Therefore, Capital's own pleadings and exhibits showed as a matter of law that Commonwealth Title had no duty to defend.

After hearing both parties and receiving all the evidence Capital offered, the trial judge determined that the threshold issue was whether Commonwealth had a duty to defend under the title insurance policy. He instructed both parties to file trial briefs on this issue, recessed, and set the issue for argument. After reviewing the briefs and examining Capital's exhibits in evidence, he found that, as a matter of law, Commonwealth had no duty to defend.

We overrule appellant's point of error. The judgment is affirmed.

■ JUSTICE MICHOL O'CONNOR dissenting.

This is a case where the trial judge, after listening to the lawyers' description of the case, decided he could resolve it without a trial, which he did. We have no procedure in Texas for a trial judge to withdraw a case from the trial docket and decide it without testimony....

NOTES

(1) *Dealing with Doubt.* The opinion in *Capital Bank* leaves one uncertain why the bank's mortgage was alleged, and found, to be vulnerable. Was it because of a

defect in execution? Or because the grant was a transfer voidable in the bankrupt-cy? Improper execution would have occurred before the policy date, of course.

Sometimes the allegations in a complaint require clarification, or more specifi-cation, in order for a court to know whether or not the liability asserted is one within the coverage in question. For that problem one solution is to require that the insurer defend unless it has made an adequate investigation of the facts. The investigation may, of course, reveal that the claim is one not covered. Another solution, more favorable to the insured, is to construe the complaint in a way leading to coverage. (Compare the principle of construing *policies* in a way favorable to the insured.)

As to the former, see Truck Ins. Exchange v. Vanport Homes, Inc., 58 P.3d 276 (Wash. 2002), and Federal Home Loan Mortgage Corp. v. Scottsdale Ins. Co., 316 F.3d 431 (3d Cir. 2003) (New Jersey law). As to the latter, see Porterfield v. Audubon Indem. Co., 856 So.2d 789 (Ala. 2002).

(2) *Different Strokes?* Within ten years of the decision in *Capital Bank*, Texas law on the subject was reviewed twice again, once by the State Supreme Court and again by a federal district court. See King v. Dallas Fire Ins. Co., above, at 187 and *Southwest Tank & Treater Mfg.*, above, at 602. *Question*: Are the analyses in these three cases compatible?

Bucci v. Essex Insurance Company

United States Court of Appeals, 1st Cir., 2005.
393 F.3d 285.

Benjamin Bucci brought an action against the operator of a nightclub in Maine, known as The Industry. He alleged that he had been assaulted while waiting for entry to the club, and that employees of the club had failed to prevent the assault and had failed to come to his assistance. Bucci alleged that he had suffered permanent injuries on being kicked in the head repeatedly by the assailant. His complaint asserted claims for negligence, negligent security, negligent supervision and training, negligent infliction of emotional distress, and conspiracy.[1]

The defendant, "the club" or "The Industry", held CGL coverage provided by Essex Insurance. Essex refused to provide it with a defense. Bucci and the club settled the suit on terms that transferred to him any claim that the club might have against Essex. Bucci brought this action, asserting that Essex had violated its duties both to defend and to indemnify the club.

As to the duty to defend, the trial court granted a summary judgment in favor of Bucci. As to indemnification, the court took evidence and ruled against him. Both parties appealed.

----

1. Bucci alleged that employees of the club sought to protect the assailant from arrest. If so, they must have succeeded, for it seems that the assailant was never identified. Bucci could not supply a description for, he said, the first blow, from behind, rendered him unconscious. Even so, the failure to iden-tify the assailant is puzzling, given Bucci's report that Bucci was waiting in line for admittance to the club, and that club employ-ees knew the assailant.

According to the CGL policy, its coverage did not extend to "any claim, suit, cost or expense arising out of assault and/or battery, or out of any act or omission in connection with the prevention or suppression of such acts, whether caused by or at the instigation or direction of any Insured, Insured's employees, patrons or any other person."

With respect to indemnification, the court said that the case raised "interesting questions" about Maine law. One of these concerned injury, if any, based *both* on the attack and on the club's failure to provide succor to Bucci: Was that injury within the policy exclusion? The insurer contended that it was; but for the attack there would have been no post-attack injuries. This "but for" theory, the court said, was not a frivolous one.

■ LYNCH, CIRCUIT JUDGE.

. . .

. . . The district court determined that the assault/battery exclusion did not exclude claims for bodily injury resulting from conduct occurring after an alleged assault. Because Bucci's complaint in the underlying action included allegations of The Industry's conduct which purportedly caused Bucci injury after the alleged assault, the district court held that Essex did violate its duty to defend The Industry under the insurance policy. The posture of the case at that point was that if there were a duty to indemnify, it had to arise from conduct by The Industry after the assault. The court left for trial the determination of whether Essex violated the separate duty to indemnify and the amount of damages for the violation of the duty to defend.

. . .

[The count conducted a trial on the two issues stated.] The district court found that all of Bucci's injuries resulted from the attacker's actions, and not from later conduct by The Industry. Thus, the district court held that Essex did not violate its duty to indemnify The Industry because the entire stipulated judgment in the underlying state tort action was based on injuries for which coverage was excluded. In addition, the court awarded $7,000 to Bucci (as The Industry's assignee) as damages for Essex's violation of its duty to defend, as well as "reasonable attorney fees" attributable to his claim for Essex's violation of the duty to defend.[2]

. . .

Essex's Violation of the Duty to Defend

Essex contends that the district court erred when it held that Essex violated the duty to defend the underlying action because the complaint contained claims for injuries resulting from The Industry's conduct after the attack. Specifically, the court applied the Maine rule of construction that any ambiguity must be construed against the insurer. The court either

---

2. According to the settlement agreement between Bucci and The Industry, The Industry is entitled to the first $7,000 of any amount that Bucci may recover from Essex to reflect The Industry's payment of $7,000 to Bucci.

found no ambiguity, and/or ruled that assuming the exclusion was ambiguous, it must be read against Essex.

We review the district court's finding that Essex had a duty to defend de novo both because it was resolved on summary judgment and because under Maine law "whether an insurer has an obligation to defend its insured against a complaint is a question of law." Elliott v. Hanover Ins. Co., 711 A.2d 1310, 1312 (Me. 1998).... Further, the question of whether there is an ambiguity in the contract is itself a conclusion of law, reviewed de novo....

Maine has consistently adhered to a pleading comparison test to determine whether there is a duty to defend; that is, Maine resolves the question of "whether there exists a duty to defend ... by comparing the complaint with the terms of the insurance contract." *Elliott* at 1312; see Found. for Blood Research v. St. Paul Marine and Fire Ins. Co., 730 A.2d 175, 177 (Me. 1999) ("It is black letter law in [Maine] that an insurer's duty to defend is determined by comparing the allegations in the underlying complaint with the provisions of the insurance policy."). This is the case even when the undisputed facts show the injury in question was not covered by the policy. *Elliott* at 1312.

Under this comparison test, the insurer has a duty to defend if the underlying complaint discloses a "potential or a possibility" for liability within the policy's coverage. Id. Significantly, "the duty to defend is broader than the duty to indemnify, and an insurer may have to defend before it is clear whether there is a duty to indemnify." Commercial Union Ins. Co. v. Royal Ins. Co., 658 A.2d 1081, 1083 (Me. 1995). Maine requires that insurance policies be "interpreted most strongly against the insurer." Baybutt Constr. Corp. v. Commercial Union Ins. Co., 455 A.2d 914, 921 (Me. 1983), *overruled on other grounds*, Peerless Ins. Co. v. Brennon, 564 A.2d 383 (Me. 1989). "Any ambiguity must be resolved in favor of a duty to defend." Mass. Bay Ins. Co. v. Ferraiolo Constr. Co., 584 A.2d 608, 609 (Me. 1990).

[The court ruled that the assault/battery exclusion did not apply to post-attack injuries. It found authority otherwise "from away", but said: "In interpreting insurance contracts, Maine law does not use the 'but for' test advocated by Essex."]

[The court affirmed the judgment below.]

NOTES

(1) *Joinder of Claims.* If Bucci's allegation of a conspiracy meant that the club and his assailant joined in a plan to assault him, surely that element of his complaint lay outside the policy coverage. That fact would not curtail the insurer's duty to defend, however, if other elements of the complaint lay within the coverage. An insurer's duty to defend arises, it is said, when the complaint alleges facts "*some of which* would, if proved, fall within the risk covered by the policy." *America Online*, p. 315 above (emphasis supplied). "If several theories of recovery are alleged in the underlying complaint against the insured, the insurer's duty to defend arises even if only one of several theories is within the potential coverage of the policy."

General Agents Ins. Co. of Am., Inc. v. Midwest Sporting Goods Co., 828 N.E.2d 1092, 1098 (Ill. 2005). And the duty extends to all the theories alleged. In a case in which that was said, the tail appeared to wag the dog: only one of 27 causes of action asserted was within the coverage. Buss v. Superior Court, 939 P.2d 766 (Cal. 1997).

A suitor may be impelled to make multiple claims in a single action by considerations of efficiency, by the fear of "splitting a cause of action", and by other concerns. One of these, it has been suggested, is a desire to activate an insurer's defense. A possible advantage of doing that is to enhance the possibility of settlement. Another advantage may emerge if the defendant/insured has few financial resources. What might that be? As to joinder strategies see E. Pryor, The Stories We Tell . . ., 75 Tex.L.Rev. 1721 (1997).

Insuring against punitive damages is contrary to public policy in a number of states.[4] But when punitive damages are sought in conjunction with compensatory damages an insurer may well be required to contest an award.

(2) *Case Comparison.* What differences appear between the analyses in *Capital Bank* and in *Bucci*?

(3) *Potentiality.* What is meant by a *potential* liability within a coverage is somewhat variously understood. One scholar understands it to mean that the insurer knows, or can reasonably discover, facts generating a covered liability. R. Jerry II, Understanding Insurance Law 862 (3d ed. 2002). But see *Midwest Sporting Goods Co.* and *America Online*, both at p. 315 above. The opinions in these cases speak of detecting potential liabilities from the facts alleged. An opinion of the California Supreme Court seems to support Dean Jerry's understanding to the extent that he takes account of "extrinsic facts known to the insurer". Going somewhat beyond that, the opinion continues: "that the precise causes of action pled . . . may fall outside policy coverage does not excuse the duty to defend where, under the facts alleged, reasonably inferable, or otherwise known, the complaint could *fairly be amended* to state a covered liability." Scottsdale Ins. Co. v. MV Transportation, 115 P.3d 460, 466 (Cal. 2005) (emphasis supplied).

Question: Should we understand that, in speaking of a "fair" amendment, the California court had in mind fairness to the court? To the defendant? To the defendant's insurer? Or to someone else?

(4) *Cain's Careless Killing.* The parents of Abel, his survivors, bring a wrongful-death action against Cain, alleging that Cain killed Abel with malice aforethought. Is there a possibility that the suitors will get a judgment against Cain based on a finding that Cain killed Abel with a careless blow, intending no harm? If so, and if therefore the action lies within Cain's liability coverage, what has happened to the eight-corners rule?

. . .

The remainder of this chapter addresses these principal questions, among others: What ill effects threaten an insurer if, in a doubtful case, it refuses a demand for a defense? What is an insurer's "reservation of rights" in conjunction with providing an insured with a defense? What ill effects threaten an insurer if it provides for a defense *without* a proper reservation? A question now to be consid-

---

4. See Eric Mills Holmes, 19 Holmes' Appleman on Insurance, Ch. 128 (2d ed. 2001).

ered is different: What ill effects threaten an insurer if, in a doubtful case, it yields to a demand for a defense by the insured?

B. PROVIDING A DEFENSE: THE RISKS

When The Industry was sued by Ben Bucci, and called on Essex Insurance to provide it with a defense, Essex may well have had a reasonable doubt that it was bound to comply. An insurer in that position has to take account of risks that it confronts either way it moves, whether by complying or by rejecting the demand.

This section concerns four risks that an insurer may consider before providing a defense. One is that, if there is bungling by the attorney chosen by the insurer to conduct the defense, the insurer will be charged with vicarious liability. A second is whether the defense attorney, representing the insured, has only one client, the insured, or two clients, the insured and the insurance company. A third risk is the insured's failure to cooperate or assist in the investigation, or settlement or defense of the lawsuit. A fourth is that, unless it acts carefully, the insurer may, by undertaking to defend, bar itself from contending that the claim in question was outside the policy coverage.

Still another risk is this: It may turn out that, by providing the insured with a defense, the insurer has incurred a needless and irretrievable expense. That would be so only if unlike the situation in *Bucci*—it turns out that the insured's coverage does not extend to the claim against it, so that it was not entitled to a defense. That risk is dealt with, not here, but in the concluding section (D) of this chapter.

---

1. Insurer's Vicarious Liability for Defense Counsel's Malpractice

Givens v. Mullikin

Tennessee Supreme Court, 2002.
75 S.W.3d 383.

Givens sued the defendant McElwaney for injuries received in an automobile accident. Allstate Insurance Company ("Allstate") hired Attorney Nichols to represent the insured McElwaney. Sometime after Attorney Nichols substantially completed discovery in the case, Allstate fired Nichols and employed the Richardson Law Firm to represent McElwaney.[1] Thereaf-

---

1. Mr. McElwaney passed away during the course of this litigation, and Mr. Ed Mullikin, as administrator *ad litem* of the estate, was substituted as the party defendant. Any references to Mr. McElwaney, of course, include Mr. Mullikin as the proper party appellant.

ter, the Richardson Law Firm initiated another round of discovery. This new discovery included 237 interrogatories and subparts that sought much of the information the defense already possessed. As a result of this discovery misconduct by the Richardson Law Firm, Givens filed a separate suit against Allstate for the oppressive discovery conduct of defense counsel, the Richardson Law Firm.[a] The principal issue was whether Allstate may be held vicariously liable for defense counsel's alleged tortious conduct.

■ WILLIAM M. BARKER, JUSTICE.

Addressing the claims against Allstate first, the plaintiff asserts that Allstate is liable for the actions of its attorney hired to defend an insured because that attorney acts as a general agent for the insurer. On the other hand, Allstate argues that it cannot be held vicariously liable for the actions of an attorney hired to defend an insured, because such an attorney is properly characterized as an independent contractor, rather than an employee, of the insurance company. We agree that Allstate's characterization of the relationship in this regard is generally the more accurate of the two, but we disagree that an attorney's status as an independent contractor invariably forecloses the possibility that the insurer can be held vicariously liable for the tortious actions of that attorney.

In the typical situation in which an insurer hires an attorney to defend an insured, the relationship of the insurer and its attorney is precisely that of principal to independent contractor. For example, the attorney is engaged in the distinct occupation of practicing law, and this occupation is one in which the attorney possesses special skill and expertise. Moreover, the attorney generally supplies his or her place of work and tools; the attorney is employed and paid only for the cases of individual insureds; and he or she alone, consistent with ethical obligations to ensure competence and diligence in the representation, determines the time to be devoted to each case. Finally, and obviously, the practice of law is not, nor could it be, part of the regular business of an insurer. Cf. Youngblood v. Wall, 815 S.W.2d 512, 517 (Tenn. Ct. App. 1991) (listing similar factors to determine whether an employment relationship enjoys the status of principal-independent contractor).

Moreover, an insurer in Tennessee clearly possesses no right to control the methods or means chosen by an attorney to defend the insured. Cf. Galloway v. Memphis Drum Serv., 822 S.W.2d 584, 586 (Tenn. 1991) (stating that the most important factor to consider in determining whether one is an independent contractor is whether the principal has the right to control or direct the time, place, methods and means by which work is being done). As we stated in In re Youngblood, 895 S.W.2d 322, 328 (Tenn. 1995), the insurer "cannot control the details of the attorney's performance, dictate the strategy or tactics employed, or limit the attorney's professional discretion with regard to the representation [of the insured]." See also Tenn. Bd. of Prof'l Responsibility, Formal Op. 88–F–113 (Aug. 2,

---

a. The new suit, also filed against the insured, is not relevant to our focus on Allstate's vicarious liability. Additionally, Givens alleged other theories of liability against the insured that are not relevant.

1988) (stating that this principle is "a basic and elementary element of the client-attorney relationship"). In addition, we also affirmed without reservation that "any policy, arrangement or device which effectively limits, by design or operation, the attorney's professional judgment on behalf of or loyalty to the client is prohibited by the Code, and, undoubtedly, would not be consistent with public policy." *Youngblood*, 895 S.W.2d at 328. Therefore, because the insurer lacks this important right of control, an attorney hired by an insurer to defend an insured must be considered, at least initially, to enjoy the status of an independent contractor.[3]

However, while the rule is that a principal is not generally liable for the tortious actions of an independent contractor, see, e.g., Hutchison v. Teeter, 687 S.W.2d 286, 287 (Tenn. 1985); Carr by Carr v. Carr, 726 S.W.2d 932, 933 (Tenn.Ct.App. 1986), this rule is subject to many exceptions, and our finding that an attorney in this context should generally be regarded as an independent contractor does not, *ipso facto*, relieve the insurer of all liability from the attorney's acts or omissions. Chief among the some twenty-four exceptions to this general rule listed in the *Restatement (Second) of Torts* is that contained in section 410, which provides that when an independent contractor acts pursuant to the orders or directions of the employer, then the employer "is subject to the same liability ... as though the act or omission were that of the employer himself." Several states have also recognized that when a principal directs or orders an independent contractor to act or fail to act, the principal cannot later assert the agent's status as an independent contractor as a defense to liability.[4]

We are aware of no Tennessee case previously recognizing this principle, but it is certainly consistent with our general common law of agency, which holds that when one directs, orders, or knowingly authorizes another to perform an act, then the principal is liable for the harm proximately caused by those acts. See White v. Revco Disc. Drug Ctrs., Inc., 33 S.W.3d 713, 723 (Tenn. 2000); Kinnard v. Rock City Constr. Co., 286 S.W.2d 352, 354 (1955). Indeed, liability for the directed or authorized acts of an agent may follow irrespective of whether other separate agency relationships also exist. See *White*, 33 S.W.3d at 723 (stating that a principal may be held liable for an agent's tortious act, "even if that act occurs outside of the scope of the agency, if the act was commanded or directed by the principal"). Because a principal's *right* to control an agent, in some cases, is "not necessarily as important as the principal's exercise of *actual* control over the agent," id. (emphasis added), we must recognize that a principal can be held liable for the harm caused by the directed or knowingly authorized

---

3. Indeed, in *Youngblood*, we even characterized an attorney hired to defend an insured as "an independent contractor engaged by the insurer." 895 S.W.2d at 328.

4. See, e.g., Green v. H & R Block, Inc., 735 A.2d 1039, 1051 (Md. 1999) ("We reaffirm the rule that a principal is not liable for any physical injury caused by the negligent conduct of his agent, who is not a servant, during the performance of the principal's business, *unless the act was done in the manner authorized or directed by the principal, or the result was one authorized or intended by the principal*." (emphasis added)); Baldasarre v. Butler, 132 N.J. 278, 625 A.2d 458, 465 (N.J. 1993) (stating that "the principal is [generally] not vicariously liable for the torts of the independent contractor *if the principal did not direct or participate in them*" (emphasis added)).

acts of an agent, even if that agent would otherwise be considered an independent contractor in the absence of any such direction or authorization.

Consequently, although an insurer clearly lacks the *right* to control an attorney retained to defend an insured, we simply cannot ignore the practical reality that the insurer may seek to exercise *actual* control over its retained attorneys in this context.[5] While this practical reality raises significant potential for conflicts of interest, it does not become invidious until the attempted control seeks, either directly or indirectly, to affect the attorney's independent professional judgment, to interfere with the attorney's unqualified duty of loyalty to the insured, or to present "a reasonable possibility of advancing an interest that would differ from that of the insured." See Tenn. Bd. of Prof'l Responsibility, Formal Op. 00–F–145 (Sept. 8, 2000). To be clear, our recognition of the control exercised by insurers in this context does not condone this practice, especially when it works to favor the interests of the insurer over that of the insured; rather, we acknowledge this aspect of the relationship only because it would be imprudent for this Court to hold that attorneys are independent contractors vis-a-vis insurers, but then to ignore the practical realities of that relationship when it causes injury.

Accordingly, we hold that an insurer can be held vicariously liable for the acts or omissions of an attorney hired to represent an insured when those acts or omissions were directed, commanded, or knowingly authorized by the insurer. This having been said, we suspect that cases in which an insurer may be held liable under an agency theory will be rare indeed. We do not hold today that an insurer may be held vicariously liable for the acts or omissions of its hired attorney based merely upon the existence of the employment relationship alone. Nor do we hold that an insurer may be held liable for any acts or omissions resulting solely from the exercise of that attorney's independent professional judgment, and in all cases, a plaintiff must show that the attorney's tortious actions were taken partly at the insurer's direction or with its knowing authorization. Nevertheless, when the insurer does undertake to exercise actual control over the actions of the insured's attorney, then it may be held vicariously liable for any harm to a plaintiff proximately caused thereby.

[The court dismissed the plaintiff's claims of vicarious liability against the insured McElwaney because the complaint did not allege facts showing

5. We expressly recognized this fact in *Youngblood* when we stated that "the insurance company's obligation to defend an action brought by a third person against the insured [often] contemplates that the company will take charge of the defense, including the supervision of the litigation." 895 S.W.2d at 329–30. Moreover, the various aspects of actual control exercised by the insurer over the litigation can usually be seen in the insurance contract itself, which, among other things, typically reserves for the insurer the right to select defense counsel, to guide the litigation of the claim, to control decisions regarding settlement of the claim, and perhaps most importantly, to deny coverage based on the non-cooperation of the insured. See Tenn. Bd. of Prof'l Responsibility, Formal Op. 00–F–145 (Sept. 8, 2000); Formal Op. 99–F–143 (June 14, 1999); see also 44 Am. Jur. 2d *Insurance* § 1393 (1982) (noting how the typical insurance contract gives the insurer control over the action).

that McElwaney directed, commanded, or knowingly authorized the Richardson Firm to engage in its allegedly tortious conduct—an essential element for vicarious liability in this context.]

. . .

[The court held that the complaint in this case stated a claim of vicarious liability against Allstate for abuse of process. However, the plaintiff's remaining claims against Allstate and all of her claims against McElwaney were dismissed.]

NOTES

1. *Imputed Knowledge* v. *Actual Knowledge*. When an attorney retained by the insurer commits malpractice in representing the insured, the question arises whether the insured may hold the insurer vicariously liable. The majority of jurisdictions answer yes—the insurer may be held vicariously liable.[1] However, these jurisdictions are not uniform regarding proof of the insurer's knowledge of defense counsel's malpractice to hold an insurer vicariously liable. Only a few require that the insurer have "actual knowledge" of defense counsel's misconduct. See the above *Givens* opinion and see Delmonte v. State Farm Fire and Cas. Co., 975 P.2d 1159 (Haw. 1999); Rose v. St. Paul Fire & Marine Ins. Co., 599 S.E.2d 673 (W.Va. 2004).

Most jurisdictions do not require that the insurer have actual knowledge but rather impute actual knowledge of defense counsel's misconduct. United Farm Bureau Mut. Ins. Co. v. Groen, 486 N.E.2d 571 (Ind.Ct.App. 1985), for example, explains the position of the imputed-knowledge jurisdictions. In *United Farm Bureau*, the insurer moved for summary judgment on the grounds that it could not be vicariously liable for the actions of the attorney, who was an independent contractor representing the insured. The trial court denied the motion. The insurer filed an interlocutory appeal. The appellate court affirmed the trial court's decision and reasoned as follows:

> An attorney representing a client is not a party to the litigation, he acts on behalf of and in the name of the client. The attorney is the agent of the party employing him, and in court stands in his stead. The attorney has by virtue of the retainer or employment alone, the general implied authority to do on behalf of the client all acts in or out of court necessary or incidental to the prosecution or management of the suit or defense or the accomplishment of the purpose for which he was retained. Indiana courts have held that in the absence of fraud by the attorney the client is bound by the action of his attorney even though the attorney is guilty of gross negligence. The negligence of an attorney is the negligence of his client.
>
> . . . Because of the close identity of an attorney with the client he represents, we hold that neither the absence of a master-servant relationship

---

1. See, e.g., Boyd Bros. Transp. Co. v. Fireman's Fund Ins. Cos., 729 F.2d 1407 (11th Cir. 1984)(Ala. Law); Smoot v. State Farm Mutual Auto. Ins. Co., 299 F.2d 525 (5th Cir. 1962)(Ga. law); Pacific Employers Ins. Co. v. PB Hoidale Co., 789 F.Supp. 1117 (D.Kan. 1992); Hodges v. State Farm Mut. Auto Ins. Co., 488 F.Supp. 1057 (D.S.C. 1980); Continental Ins. Co. v. Bayless and Roberts, Inc., 608 P.2d 281 (Alaska 1980); Lloyd v. State Farm Mut. Auto. Ins. Co., 860 P.2d 1300 (Ariz.App. 1992); Safeco Ins. Co. v. Ellinghouse, 725 P.2d 217, 225 (Mont. 1986); Stumpf v. Continental Cas. Co., 794 P.2d 1228 (Or.App. 1990); Majorowicz v. Allied Mut. Ins. Co., 569 N.W.2d 472 (Wis.App. 1997).

nor the characterization of the attorney as an independent contractor is a bar to liability of the [insurer] for the torts of the attorney acting within the scope of his authority.

United Farm Bureau at 573–74 (internal citations omitted).

(2) *Insurer Not Vicariously Liable.* A minority of jurisdictions have held that an insurer may not be held vicariously liable for the litigation negligence or misconduct of defense counsel.[2] A seminal case, Merritt v. Reserve Ins. Co., 34 Cal.App.3d 858, 110 Cal.Rptr. 511 (Cal.App.1973) explained: "In our view independent counsel retained to conduct litigation in the courts act in the capacity of independent contractors, responsible for the results of their conduct and not subject to the control and direction of their employer over the details and manner of their performance." Id., 110 Cal.Rptr. at 526. However, other courts apply another rationale. Because the defense attorney owes an unqualified loyalty to its sole client the insured, an insurer cannot be vicariously responsible for defense counsel's conduct.

In State Farm Mut. Auto Ins. Co. v. Traver, 980 S.W.2d 625 (Tex. 1998), for example, the court addressed the issue whether an insurer can be vicariously responsible for defense counsel negligence or misconduct:

> A defense attorney, as an independent contractor, has discretion regarding the day-to-day details of conducting the defense, and is not subject to the client's control regarding those details. *See* Restatement, Second, of Agency § 385, cmt. a. While the attorney may not act contrary to the client's wishes, the attorney "is in complete charge of the minutiae of court proceedings and can properly withdraw from the case, subject to the control of the court, if he is not permitted to act as he thinks best." *Id.* Moreover, because the lawyer owes unqualified loyalty to the insured, *see Employers Cas. Co. v. Tilley*, 496 S.W.2d 552, 558 (Tex. 1973), the lawyer must at all times protect the interests of the insured if those interests would be compromised by the insurer's instructions. Under these circumstances, the insurer cannot be vicariously responsible for the lawyer's conduct. *See Ingersoll–Rand Equip. Corp. v. Transportation Ins. Co.*, 963 F.Supp. 452, 454–55 (M.D. Pa. 1997) ("The attorney's ethical obligations to his or her client, the insured, prevent the insurer from exercising the degree of control necessary to justify the imposition of vicarious liability."); . . . *Feliberty v. Damon*, 527 N.E.2d 261, 265 (N.Y. 1988) ("The insurer is precluded from interference with counsel's independent professional judgments in the conduct of the litigation on behalf of its client.") . . . .

Id. at 627 owes unqualified loyalty to the insured. . . ." The Texas Supreme Court has stated:

> Under the policy in question (comprehensive liability) the insurance company's obligation to defend the insurer provides that the attorney to represent the insured is to be selected, employed and paid by the insurance company. Nevertheless, such attorney becomes the attorney of record and the legal representative of the insured, and as such he *owes the insured the same type of unqualified loyalty as if he had been originally employed by the insured.*

---

2. See, e.g., Mirville v. Allstate Indem. Co., 87 F.Supp.2d 1184, 1191 (D. Kan. 2000); Marlin v. State Farm Mut. Auto. Ins. Co., 761 So.2d 380, 381 (Fla.App. 2000); Gibson v. Casto, 504 S.E.2d 705, 708 (Ga.App. 1998); Brocato v. Prairie State Farmers Ins. Ass'n, 520 N.E.2d 1200, 1203 (Ill.App. 1988); Her-bert A. Sullivan, Inc. v. Utica Mut. Ins. Co., 788 N.E.2d 522, 541 (Mass. 2003); Feliberty v. Damon, 527 N.E.2d 261 (N.Y. 1988); Mentor Chiropractic Ctr., Inc. v. State Farm Fire & Cas. Co., 744 N.E.2d 207, 211 (Ohio App. 2000).

Tilley, 496 S.W.2d at 558 (emphasis supplied). That quote segues into the next, about risks to an insurer in providing a defense.

----

2. Conflicts and Defense Counsel's Duty of Loyalty to Whom?

When a lawsuit is filed against an insured, the insurer hires defense counsel to protect its insured's rights and interests thereby creating a tripartite relationship between the insurer, the insured, and appointed defense counsel. At the outset of the representation, if there is no issue regarding coverage, no conflict regarding liability, and the damages demanded are within the policy limits, the insurer and insured have common interests in defending the case. Under these circumstances, the defense attorney retained by the insurer to represent the insured should not be faced with a conflict of interest when defending the insured, and thus there is nothing improper or unethical about representing the interests of both insured and insurer. The great majority of jurisdictions[1] consider the insurer and insured as co-clients of the defense attorney which is described as "dual representation". In sum, the attorney retained by the insurer and appearing for the insured represents both the insured and insurer and owes a duty of loyalty to both.[2]

Thereafter, however, an insurer may face several risks where the defense attorney can not and does not owe a duty of loyalty to the insurer. For example, when the interests of the insured and insurer conflict, defense counsel's duties of dual representation cannot be fulfilled for both the insured and the insurer. A conflict of interest between insurer and insured occurs whenever their common lawyer's representation of one is rendered less effective by reason of the defense lawyer's representation of the other. When a conflict of interest occurs, "the insurer must, unless the insured consents, relinquish all control over the lawyer once insurer and insured turn out to have antagonistic interests." *In re* New Era, Inc., 135 F.3d 1206, 1210 (7th Cir. 1998) (Ill. Law). Conflicts of interest, the defense attorney's loyalty to the insured, and the insured's right to select independent defense counsel are examined later in this chapter, at Part D 1., Control of Defense, commencing at page 348.

----

1. See, e.g., Home Indem. Co. v. Lane Powell Moss & Miller, 43 F.3d 1322 (9th Cir. 1995); The Driggs Corp. v. Pennsylvania Mfgs. Assn. Ins. Co., 3 F.Supp.2d 657 (D.Md. 1998), aff'd, 181 F.3d 87 (4th Cir. 1999). See generally Charles Silver, "Does Insurance Counsel Represent the Company or the Insured?," 72 Tex. L. Rev. 1583 (1994); Ellen S. Pryor & Charles Silver, "Defense Lawyer's Professional Responsibilities: Part I—Excess Exposure Cases," 78 Tex. L. Rev. 599 (2000).

2. The ABA Code of Professional Responsibility promotes a "dual representation" standard. Disciplinary Rule 5–105(C) states that "a lawyer may represent multiple clients if it is obvious that the attorney can adequately represent the interest of each and if each consents to the representation after full disclosure of the possible effect of such representation on the exercise of the attorney's independent professional judgment on behalf of each."

This part examines the insurer's risk of having no representation by defense counsel from the outset, i.e., no dual representation. A significant minority of cases perceive the tripartite relationship as fraught with potential conflict of interests.[3] Consequently, the cases hold that the insured is the *sole* client of the defense attorney from the outset of the defense attorney's representation; see the Texas cases *Travers* and *Tilley*, cited in Note 2 above. Similarly, in Barefield v. DPIC Cos., 600 S.E.2d 256 (W.Va. 2004), the court stated: "In sum, our *Rules of Professional Conduct* compel us to the conclusion that when an insurance company hires a defense attorney to represent an insured in a liability matter, the attorney's ethical obligations are owed to the insured and not to the insurance company that pays for the attorney's services." Id. at 269.

In re the Rules of Professional Conduct

Supreme Court of Montana, 2000.
299 Mont. 321, 2 P.3d 806.

In an original application for declaratory judgment before the state's highest court, petitioner law firms claimed that certain insurer-imposed billing rules and procedures violated Mont. R. Prof. Conduct. The petitioners asserted that insurers' rules potentially limiting or directing the scope and extent of defense counsel's representation of insureds, and requiring defense counsel to disclose detailed descriptions of professional services to third-party auditors without first obtaining the consent of insureds, violated Mont. R. Prof. Conduct.

■ WILLIAM E. HUNT, SR., JUSTICE.

A.   Whether Montana has recognized the dual representation doctrine under the Montana Rules of Professional Conduct.

Petitioners assert that the insured is the sole client of a defense attorney appointed by an insurer to represent an insured pursuant to an insurance policy (hereafter, defense counsel) and that a requirement of prior approval in insurance billing and practice rules impermissibly interferes with a defense counsel's exercise of his independent judgment and his duty of undivided loyalty to his client. Petitioners argue that because the relationship of insurer and insured is permeated with potential conflicts, they cannot be co-clients of defense counsel.

---

3. In Atlanta International Insurance Co. v. Bell, 475 N.W.2d 294 (Mich. 1991), the court stated: "[C]ourts and commentators recognize universally that the tripartite relationship between insured, insurer, and defense counsel contains rife possibility of conflict. The interest of the insured and the insurer frequently differ. Courts have consistently held that the defense attorney's primary duty of loyalty lies with the insured, and not the insurer." Id. at 297. See also Jackson v. Trapier, 42 Misc.2d 139, 247 N.Y.S.2d 315 (Super.Ct. 1964), stating that once defense is undertaken, the defendant is the client and not the insurance carrier, even though the latter may have chosen the counsel and may be paying his fee.

Respondents argue that under Montana law, the rule is that in the absence of a real conflict, the insurer and insured are dual clients of defense counsel. From this fundamental premise, Respondents argue that as a co-client of defense counsel, the insurer may require pre-approval of attorney activities to assure adequate consultation. Respondents argue further that defense counsel must abide by a client's decisions about the objectives of representation and that defense counsel are obliged to consult with a client about the means for the objectives of representation. Respondents also argue that under Montana law, an insurer is vicariously liable for the conduct of defense counsel and that an insurer's control of litigation justifies holding an insurer vicariously liable for the conduct of defense counsel.

We conclude that Respondents have misconstrued our past decisions. This Court has not held that under the Rules of Professional Conduct, an insurer and an insured are co-clients of defense counsel. The Montana decisions chiefly relied upon by Respondents are inapposite because each one concerns situations where the insurer had "absolute" control of the litigation. None of the Montana decisions cited by Respondents addresses whether an insurer is a co-client under the Rules of Professional Conduct.

. . .

B. Whether insurers and insureds are co-clients under Montana's Rules of Professional Conduct.

We turn to the question whether an insurer is a client of defense counsel under the Rules of Professional Conduct. We note that some other courts have concluded that the insurer is not a client of defense counsel. In Atlanta Int. Ins. Co. v. Bell (Mich. 1991), 475 N.W.2d 294, the court addressed whether defense counsel retained by an insurer to defend its insured may be sued by the insurer for professional malpractice. Recognizing the general rule that an attorney will only be held liable for negligence to his client, the court determined that "the relationship between the insurer and the retained defense counsel [is] less than a client-attorney relationship." *Bell*, 475 N.W.2d at 297. The court further determined, however, that although the insurer is not a client of defense counsel, the defense counsel nevertheless "occupies a fiduciary relationship to the insured, as well as to the insurance company." Id. Recognizing further that "the tripartite relationship between insured, insurer, and defense counsel contains rife possibility [sic] of conflict," Id., the court reasoned that "to hold that an attorney-client relationship exists between insurer and defense counsel could indeed work mischief, yet to hold that a mere commercial relationship exists would work obfuscation and injustice." Id.

Nor is Michigan unique in concluding that the insured is the sole client of defense counsel. *See* Jackson v. Trapier (Sup.Ct. 1964), 247 N.Y.S.2d 315, 316 (concluding that once defense undertaken, "defendant is the client and not the insurance carrier even though the latter may have chosen the counsel and may be paying his fee"); Continental Cas. v. Pullman, Comley, et al. (2nd Cir. 1991), 929 F.2d 103, 108 (concluding "it is clear beyond cavil that in the insurance context the attorney owes his allegiance, not to the insurance company that retained him but to the insured defendant''); Point Pleasant Canoe Rental v. Tinicum Tp. (E.D. Pa. 1986), 110 F.R.D. 166, 170 (concluding "when a liability insurer retains a lawyer to defend an insured, the insured is considered the lawyer's client''); First American Carriers v. Kroger Co. (Ark. 1990), 787 S.W.2d 669, 671 (concluding that " 'when a liability insurer retains a lawyer to defend an insured, the insured is the lawyer's client' '').

Respondents argue vigorously that the interests of an insurer and an insured usually coincide and that most litigation is settled within an insured's coverage limits. These arguments gloss over the stark reality that the relationship between an insurer and insured is permeated with potential conflicts. Compare Thomas D. Morgan, *What Insurance Scholars Should Know About Professional Responsibility*, 4 Conn.Ins.L.J. 1, 7–8, 1997 (concluding that designating insurer "a second client ... would routinely create the potential for conflicts of interest''); Kent D. Syverud, *What Professional Responsibility Scholars Should Know About Insurance*, 4 Conn.Ins.L.J. 17, 23–24, 1997 (recognizing "both insurance companies and insureds have important and meaningful stakes in the outcome [of] a lawsuit against the insureds, stakes that include not just the money that the insurance company must pay in defense and settlement, but also the uninsured liabilities of the insured, which include not just any judgment in excess of liability limits, but also the insured's reputation and other non-economic stakes. The history of liability insurance suggests that unbridled control of the defense of litigation by either the insurance company or the insured creates incentives for the party exercising that control to take advantage of the other''). Compare also Restatement (Third) of the Law Governing Lawyers § 215, Comment f(5) (Proposed Final Draft No. 2, 1998) (emphasis added) (recognizing "material divergences of interest might exist between a liability insurer and an insured.... Such occasions for conflict may exist at the outset of the representation *or may be created by events that occur thereafter*''). In cases where an insured's exposure exceeds his insurance coverage, where the insurer provides a defense subject to a reservation of rights, and where an insurer's obligation to indemnify its insured may be excused because of a policy defense, there are potential conflicts of interest.

We reject Respondents' implicit premise that the Rules of Professional Conduct need not apply when the interests of insurers and insureds coincide. The Rules of Professional Conduct have application in all cases involving attorneys and clients. Moreover, whether the interests of insurers and insureds coincide can best be determined with the perfect clarity of hindsight. Before the final resolution of any claim against an insured, there clearly exists the potential for conflicts of interest to arise. Further, we reject the suggestion that the contractual relationship between insurer and insured supersedes or waives defense counsels' obligations under the Rules of Professional Conduct. We decline to recognize a vast exception to the Rules of Professional Conduct that would sanction relationships colored with the appearance of impropriety in order to accommodate the asserted economic exigencies of the insurance market. . . . We hold that under the Rules of Professional Conduct, the insured is the *sole* client of defense counsel.

We caution, however, that this holding should not be construed to mean that defense counsel have a "blank check" to escalate litigation costs nor that defense counsel need not ever consult with insurers. Under Rule 1.5, M.R.Prof.Conduct, for example, an attorney must charge reasonable fees. *See* Rule 1.5, M.R.Prof.Conduct (providing in part that "[a] lawyer's fees shall be reasonable"). Nor, finally, should our holding be taken to signal that defense counsel cannot be held accountable for their work.

. . .

B. Whether the requirement of prior approval violates the Rules of Professional Conduct.

Having concluded that the insured is the sole client of defense counsel, we turn to the fundamental issue whether the requirement of prior approval in billing and practice rules conflicts with defense counsels' duties under the Rules of Professional Conduct. The parties appear to agree that defense counsel may not abide by agreements limiting the scope of representation that interfere with their duties under the Rules of Professional Conduct. . . . We conclude that the requirement of prior approval fundamentally interferes with defense counsels' exercise of their *independent* judgment, as required by Rule 1.8(f), M.R.Prof.Conduct. Further, prior approval creates a substantial appearance of impropriety in its suggestion that it is insurers rather than defense counsel who control the day to day details of a defense.

Montana is not alone in rejecting arrangements that fetter lawyers' undivided duty of loyalty to their clients and their independence of professional judgment in representing their clients. In Petition of Youngblood (Tenn. 1995), 895 S.W.2d 322, the court determined that for inhouse attorney employees of an insurance company to represent insureds was not a *per se* ethical violation. However, the *Youngblood* court emphasized the loyalty that an attorney owes an insured and concluded that

> some of the usual characteristics incident to [the employer-employee] relationship cannot exist between the insurer and the attorney representing an insured. The employer cannot control the details of the attorney's performance, dictate the strategy or tactics employed, or limit the attorney's professional discretion with regard to the representation. Any policy, arrangement or device which effectively limits, by design or operation, the attorney's professional judgment on behalf of or loyalty to the client is prohibited by the Code, and, undoubtedly, would not be consistent with public policy.

Youngblood, 895 S.W.2d at 328. The court went to conclude that "the same loyalty is owed the client whether the attorney is employed and paid by the client, is a salaried employee of the insurer, or is an independent contractor engaged by the insurer." Id.

. . .

Moreover, in American Ins. Ass'n v. Kentucky Bar Ass'n (Ky. 1996), 917 S.W.2d 568, the court affirmed an Advisory ethics opinion that proscribed insurers' use of inhouse attorneys to represent insureds. The court in *Kentucky Bar Ass'n* also affirmed an Advisory ethics opinion concluding that a lawyer may not "enter into a contract with a liability insurer in which the lawyer or his firm agrees to do all of the insurer's defense work for a set fee." *Kentucky Bar Ass'n*, 917 S.W.2d at 569. The court concluded that

> the pressures exerted by the insurer through the set fee interferes [sic] with the exercise of the attorney's independent professional judgment, in contravention of Rule 1.8(f)(2). The set fee arrangement also clashes with Rule 1.7(b) in that it creates a situation whereby the attorney has an interest in the outcome of the action which conflicts with the duties owed to the client: quite simply, in easy cases, counsel will take a financial windfall; in difficult cases, counsel will take a financial loss.

Kentucky Bar Ass'n, 917 S.W.2d at 572. The *Kentucky Bar Ass'n* court stressed that "the *mere appearance of impropriety is just as egregious as any actual or real conflict*. Therefore, [the Advisory opinion] acts as a prophylactic device to eliminate the potential for a conflict of interest or the compromise of an attorney's ethical and professional duties." *Kentucky Bar Ass'n*, 917 S.W.2d at 573 (emphasis added). Recognizing that set fee arrangements are "ripe with potential conflicts," the court concluded that the insurer and insured are "subject to complete divergence at any time. Inherent in all of these potential conflicts is the fear that the entity paying the attorney, the insurer, and not the one to whom the attorney is obligated to defend, the insured, *is controlling the legal representation*." Id. (emphasis added).

We hold that defense counsel in Montana who submit to the requirement of prior approval violate their duties under the Rules of Professional Conduct to exercise their independent judgment and to give their undivided loyalty to insureds.

[The court next considered this question at length: 2. May an attorney licensed to practice law in Montana, or admitted pro hac vice, be required to submit detailed descriptions of professional services to outside persons or entities without first obtaining the informed consent of his or her client and do so without violating client confidentiality?]

We hold that disclosure by defense counsel of detailed descriptions of professional services to third-party auditors without first obtaining the contemporaneous fully informed consent of insureds violates client confidentiality under the Rules of Professional Conduct.

NOTE

ABA's Response. Insurers' billing rules, litigation guidelines and legal auditing by either in-house counsel or third-party firms commenced in the 1990s and grew, in the liability insurance industry, as a thorn in defense counsel's representation of insureds.[1] In response, the ABA Standing Committee on Ethics and Professional Responsibility issued ABA Formal Ethics Op. 01–421 (2001), which in pertinent part states:

> [L]awyers representing insured clients must not permit the client's insurance company to require compliance with litigation management guidelines the lawyer reasonably believes will compromise materially the lawyer's professional judgment or result in his inability to provide competent representation to the insured.

Id. at 1. The opinion also states, in part:

> A lawyer may not disclose the insured's confidential information to a third-party auditor hired by the insurer without the informed consent of the insured, but a lawyer may submit a client's detailed bills that contain confidential information to the client's insurer if the lawyer reasonably believes that disclosure: (1) impliedly is authorized and will advance the interests of the insured in the representation, and (2) will not affect a material interest of the insured adversely.

Id. at 1–2. For an analysis and evaluation of the ABA opinion, see Robert H. Jerry, II, Understanding Insurance Law § 114[5] at 931–34 (3d ed. 2002).

---

3.   Risk of Insured's Noncooperation

The insured's duty to cooperate with and assist the company in defending the liability suit is imposed by language similar to the following: "The insured shall cooperate with the company in the conduct of suits and shall attend hearings and trials and assist in securing and giving evidence and obtaining the attendance of witnesses."

A breach of the cooperation clause by the insured legally relieves the insurer of liability under the policy. *Question*: If the insured's breach of the noncooperation clause relieves the insurer of liability, then how can the insured's noncooperation be a risk to the insurer? Consider the following case.

Cincinnati Ins. Co. v. Irvin

United States District Court, Southern District of Indiana, 1998.
19 F.Supp.2d 906.

Loretta Huff ("Huff"), the driver of one car in a two-car accident, had been given permission by the car's owner to drive the car. The car was

---

1. See, e.g., Susan Randall, "Managed Litigation and the Professional Obligations of Insurance Defense Lawyers," 51 Syr. L. Rev. 1 (2001); Liberty L. Roverts, Note, "Fee Au- dits Cut More Than Fat Out of Bills, Cutting Heart of Insurance Defense," 34 Ind. L. Rev. 179 (2000).

insured by The Cincinnati Insurance Company ("Cincinnati Insurance") under a policy issued to the car's owner Brashear. Huff fled the scene of the collision and was not heard from again. Cincinnati Insurance sought summary judgment on the ground that Huff's flight and disappearance amounted to a breach of the policy's cooperation clause, relieving the insurance company of what would otherwise have been its obligation to defend and indemnify the driver.

■ DAVID F. HAMILTON, JUDGE.

Because Huff had permission to drive Brashear's car, Huff is a "covered person" under the Cincinnati Insurance policy. Cincinnati Insurance's duties to defend her and to indemnify her are subject to conditions of the policy, including the standard cooperation clause, which requires a covered person to cooperate with the investigation and defense of claims. See, *e.g., Peters v. Saulinier*, 222 N.E.2d 871, 874 (Mass. 1967) (permissive driver was subject to cooperation clause); .... Cincinnati Insurance argues that the undisputed facts show that Huff breached her duty to cooperate under the policy.

Indiana law recognizes the validity of cooperation clauses in insurance policies.... Under Indiana law, however, for an insurance company to be relieved of liability based on an insured's breach of its cooperation clause, the insurance company must prove the following elements in addition to the breach itself: (1) that the company used good faith efforts and diligence to obtain the insured's cooperation; (2) that the insured's breach of the cooperation clause was intentional and willful; and (3) that the insured's failure to cooperate prejudiced the company in its defense of the insured. *Smithers v. Mettert*, 513 N.E.2d 660, 662 (Ind. App. 1987); *Newport v. MFA Ins. Co.*, 448 N.E.2d 1223, 1229 (Ind. App. 1983). Defendants concede that Cincinnati Insurance has used good faith efforts and diligence to obtain Huff's cooperation. They argue that Cincinnati Insurance has failed to prove that Huff willfully and intentionally breached the cooperation clause and has failed to prove that Huff's failure to cooperate has caused it any prejudice. The court considers each issue in turn.[3]

Willful and Intentional Breach? Under Indiana law, Cincinnati Insurance clearly bears the burden of proving that Huff's failure to cooperate was willful and intentional. See *Smithers*, 513 N.E.2d at 662 (insurer has the burden of proving the elements of intent, prejudice, and good faith efforts); see also *Miller v. Dilts*, 463 N.E.2d 257, 261 (Ind. 1984) (insurer bears the burden of proving that it suffered actual prejudice before it can avoid liability; *Newport*, 448 N.E.2d at 1229 (insurer has the burden of

---

3. Defendants have also argued that Cincinnati Insurance has waived or is estopped from asserting the lack of cooperation defense because it has not defended Huff in either tort action. The argument is without merit. An insurer, after making an independent determination that it has no duty to defend, must protect its interest by either filing a declaratory judgment action for a judicial determination of its obligations under the policy or hiring independent counsel and defending its insured under a reservation of rights. *Liberty Mut. Ins. Co. v. Metzler*, 586 N.E.2d 897, 902 (Ind. App. 1992). Cincinnati Insurance has preserved its right to assert this defense by filing this declaratory judgment action.

proving that the insured willfully failed to cooperate and that it made good faith attempts to seek the insured's cooperation).

There is no evidence here that Huff even knows about the underlying lawsuits and claims, or that she knows Cincinnati Insurance covered the car she was driving, let alone that she has willfully and intentionally failed to cooperate with the insurer. Using the only fact available to it, however, Cincinnati Insurance argues that this court should find as a matter of law that Huff willfully and intentionally failed to cooperate. The available fact is that Huff fled the scene of the accident. The argument is that her flight constituted a willful expression of her desire to not cooperate with the insurance company. That is too long a stretch to make as a matter of law. There are numerous possible explanations for Huff's flight that have nothing to do with Huff's alleged desire to avoid cooperating with Cincinnati Insurance. Although flight from the scene of an accident is a violation of Indiana law, there is no suggestion that such a violation at the time of an accident is alone sufficient to nullify a driver's insurance coverage.

Moreover, Indiana courts have held that an insured's complete absence from trial is not sufficient to prove that the insured willfully and intentionally failed to cooperate when there is no evidence the insured was even aware of the trial. For instance, in *Smithers*, after several attempts by the insurance company to contact the insured, the insured responded and gave a statement over the telephone regarding the accident at issue. The insured later disappeared without leaving an address. When the injured party later sued the insured, despite the insurance company's attempts to contact him, the insured never responded and did not appear for trial. A default judgment was entered against the insured. The Indiana Court of Appeals held that the evidence failed to show the insured's failure to cooperate was intentional. Because the suit had not been filed until after the insured had disappeared, there was no evidence the insured was even aware of the suit or trial. In that situation, the court held the insured's failure to respond to contacts "does not indicate a refusal to cooperate," and the insurance company was required to show further that the insured had actually been contacted and then refused to respond. *Smithers*, 513 N.E.2d at 663.

The Indiana Court of Appeals reached a similar result in *Newport v. MFA Insurance Co., supra*. In that case, the insured driver killed a boy in an accident. The boy's family filed suit but could not find the driver to make service of process. The family then obtained service of process by publication and obtained a default judgment against the insured. When the family sought to collect from the insurance company, the company argued, among other defenses, that the insured had breached the cooperation clause. The trial court had ruled in favor of the insurance company, but the Court of Appeals reversed and directed entry of judgment in favor of the boy's family. The Court of Appeals found there was no evidence the insurance company had been diligent in securing the cooperation of the insured. In addition, and more to the point here, the Court of Appeals also held that the cooperation clause provided no defense because the evidence did not show that the insured driver "was even aware of the suit and intentionally failed to cooperate." 448 N.E.2d at 1229. Accord, *Continental Cas. Co. v. Burton*, 795 F.2d 1187, 1194 (4th Cir. 1986) (applying Virginia law, where insured lawyer in possession of clients' funds disappeared without explanation before clients filed suit, insurer had no evidence that failure to cooperate in defense of clients' suit was willful; determination of willfulness could be based only on "speculation"); . . . .

In this case, as in *Smithers* and *Newport*, there is still no evidence that Huff is even aware of the claims and lawsuits. In the absence of evidence that Cincinnati Insurance made actual contact with her and asked for her help, and that Huff refused to cooperate, Cincinnati Insurance cannot show a willful and intentional failure to cooperate under *Smithers* and *Newport*. Cincinnati Insurance argues, however, that these cases can be distinguished from this one on the basis that Huff was not the "named" insured on the policy. Cincinnati Insurance argues that where the non-cooperating party is the named insured, the insurance company will have access to more information that would give it a fighting chance to contact the insured, including her name, address, and employer, while it has no such reliable information regarding Huff. The Indiana courts have not addressed this specific problem before, but the distinction argued by Cincinnati Insurance finds no support in the Indiana cases and their reasoning. The lack of reliable identifying information about Huff certainly makes it more difficult for Cincinnati Insurance to find her. Nevertheless, the court fails to see how Cincinnati Insurance's lack of information concerning Huff shows that *Huff's* conduct was willful and intentional. That is the issue under Indiana law, and Indiana law provides no basis for relaxing the burden on the insurer depending on whether the insured is the named insured or a permissive driver. . . . Cincinnati Insurance has not identified cases from other jurisdictions adopting its proposed distinction between named insureds and permissive drivers.

Indiana law makes it plain that where the insurance company fails to make direct contact with the insured, the fact that the insured cannot be found to help the defense is not sufficient to prove the essential element of a willful and intentional failure to cooperate. In such cases, the risks and consequences of the insured's absence fall on the insurance company, regardless of the practical difficulties it may face. See *Smithers*, 513 N.E.2d at 663; *Newport*, 448 N.E.2d at 1229. The same principles apply where the insured is a permissive driver of a covered vehicle rather than the named insured. Cincinnati Insurance is not entitled to summary judgment because it has not shown as a matter of law that Huff has willfully and intentionally breached the cooperation clause.

Prejudice to the Insurer? Indiana law also requires Cincinnati Insurance to demonstrate that the insured's breach of the cooperation clause has caused it material prejudice. *Miller*, 463 N.E.2d at 261 (holding that "an insurance company must show actual prejudice from an insured's noncompliance with the policy's cooperation clause before it can avoid liability under the policy"), relying on *Motorists Mut. Ins. Co. v. Johnson*, 139 Ind. App. 622, 218 N.E.2d 712, 715 (Ind. App. 1966) ("A technical or inconsequential lack of cooperation has often been held insufficient to void the policy and the lack of cooperation to be sufficient must be in some substantial and material respect. Non-cooperation must be material. Prejudice must be shown by insurer."); . . . .

Cincinnati Insurance again relies on Huff's flight from the scene of the accident to prove that it has been materially prejudiced as a matter of law. Cincinnati Insurance argues that it has been prejudiced by Huff's immediate disappearance because it could not obtain Huff's description of the accident and must therefore defend an "empty chair" when liability is contested. Also, it seems likely that Huff's flight from the scene of the accident will not help the defense on issues of liability.

Indiana case law provides limited guidance in determining what constitutes material prejudice in this situation. . . .

An insurer facing the defense of a claim with an absent defendant might reasonably ask how it is supposed to prove that it could have had a better result in a trial if it had been able to locate a key witness whom it never manages to locate. As discussed below, decisions from other jurisdictions offer additional guidance as to when a failure to cooperate might cause prejudice, but they do not necessarily offer much solace to an insurer that never locates the insured and is never able to offer proof of the testimony the insured could have offered if she had appeared for trial. In addition, it is important to keep in mind . . . that the automobile liability insurance policy is not a purely private contract. Such insurance is required by law to protect the interests of innocent third parties injured by the negligence of the insured person. Thus, in the absence of collusion, most courts put the burden of proof, and thus the risk of uncertainty, on the insurer rather than on the person injured by the insured's negligence. See, e.g., *M.F.A. Mut. Ins. Co. v. Cheek*, 363 N.E.2d 809, 813 (Ill. 1977) ("Mindful of the fact that the public is the beneficiary of the automobile policy" and that "the prime objective of the cooperation clause is to prevent collusion," a court requires proof of prejudice resulting from failure to cooperate). . . .

Cases in which the insured actively colludes with and supports the claim of an injured plaintiff present relatively few difficulties, of course, and the most basic purpose of a cooperation clause in a liability insurance policy is to prevent collusion. See, e.g., *Elliott v. Metropolitan Cas. Ins. Co.*, 250 F.2d 680, 684 (10th Cir. 1957) (applying Kansas law, collusion will be deemed prejudicial, while insured's failure to appear for trial must be shown to be prejudicial; because contrary rule "would offer temptation to the insurer to spirit [the insured] beyond the jurisdiction of the court, these cases have sought to prevent such a result by placing the burden upon the insurer to show that its case was adversely affected by his disappearance"). . . .

Where the alleged failure to cooperate is the insured's absence from trial, however, the better reasoned view is that the absence ordinarily cannot be deemed prejudicial as a matter of law:

Although some states hold that absence from trial, in and of itself, is sufficient to substantiate a claim of noncooperation, the majority and better rule appears to be that when the driver of an automobile breaches his insurance contract by failing to appear, the insurer is not prejudiced as a matter of law, by that naked fact alone, and that no presumption to the contrary arises to aid the insurer.

Brooks v. Haggard, 481 P.2d 131, 134 (Colo. App. 1970), citing *Farley v. Farmers Ins. Exchange*, 415 P.2d 680 (Idaho 1966), and *Thrasher v. United States Liability Ins. Co.*, 225 N.E.2d 503 (N.Y. 1967).... [S]ee generally Romualdo P. Eclavea, Annotation, Liability Insurance: Failure or Refusal of Insured to Attend Trial or to Testify as Breach of Co-operation Clause, 9 A.L.R.4th 218 (1981).

Several of these cases illustrate the difficulty in determining whether, as a matter of law, the absence of the insured caused prejudice, especially before the trial in the underlying tort action. In *Farley* the insured had cooperated with his insurer before trial, but he failed to appear for trial, and judgment was rendered against him. When the issue was whether his absence had prejudiced the insurer, the same trial judge who presided over the original trial found that the outcome would have been no different if the insured had appeared. The Idaho Supreme Court affirmed. 415 P.2d at 683–84. Similarly, in *Phillips v. Glens Falls Ins. Co.*, 288 F.Supp. 151 (S.D.W.Va. 1968), the insured failed to appear for trial despite numerous requests for his assistance. After carefully reviewing the transcript of the underlying trial and the unsavory facts that would have been developed if the insured had testified, the district court found the insurer was not prejudiced by the insured's absence: "Indeed, it would appear that his presence at the trial might have influenced the jury to return more substantial verdicts against [the insured]." 288 F. Supp. at 154....

The view that prejudice from the insured's failure to appear for trial ordinarily cannot be determined as a matter of law is the majority view, but it is not universal. See, *e.g., Cameron v. Berger*, 336 Pa. 229, 7 A.2d 293, 295 (Pa. 1938) (insured's voluntary disappearance before trial held prejudicial where she was only witness for defense); ... For a recent review of the subject, see *Darcy v. Hartford Ins. Co.*, 554 N.E.2d 28, 33–34 & n.6 (1990) in which the highest court in Massachusetts overruled its prior doctrine and adopted the majority view that prejudice must be shown even where the insured provides no cooperation to the insurer.

In this court's view, the majority view that the insurer must prove at least a reasonable probability of actual prejudice caused by the insured's failure to appear is in harmony with the more general Indiana holdings that the insurer must prove prejudice, and that prejudice requires proof that the insured's failure to cooperate actually produced a judgment less favorable in the underlying tort action. ... In this case, where Huff has not misled or deceived the insurance company, but has simply disappeared without explanation, Cincinnati Insurance is not entitled to summary judgment on the issue of prejudice. Moreover, the question of prejudice appears impossible to decide before a trial is held in the underlying tort action....

. . .

For the reasons explained above, plaintiff's motion for summary judgment is hereby denied.

PROBLEM

The insured's spouse (a passenger) is injured in an automobile accident and sues the insured, who was driving the car. The insurance company retains defense counsel, who interviews the insured. The insured says, "I wasn't negligent. The accident wasn't my fault." At trial, however, the insured takes the stand and says, "I was negligent. The accident was my fault." Defense counsel then attempts to impeach the insured's testimony by cross-examining the insured, by introducing evidence of prior inconsistent statements, by suggesting that the insured is attempting to maximize the spouse's recovery, by asking whether the insured understands the penalty for perjury, etc.

Questions. Has the insured breached the duty to cooperate? If so, what result should follow? Does cooperation include a duty on the insured to willingly submit to being impeached at trial if the insurer so instructs? Does the insurer-insured liability insurance contract provide a different answer than the law of professional responsibility? If so, which takes precedence?

This problem, in various guises, is discussed in a number of insurance classes, cases and scholarly works. See Charles Silver & Kent Syverud, "The Professional Responsibilities of Insurance Defense Lawyers," 45 Duke L.J. 255, 316–25 (1995); Eric Mills Holmes, "A Conflicts-of-Interest Roadmap for Insurance Defense Counsel: Walking an Ethical Tightrope Without a Net," 26 Willamette L. Rev. 1, 34–38 (1989).

————

4.   Reservation of Rights

This topic falls into two parts: the risk of providing a defense subject to a proper "reservation of rights", and the risk of doing so without having made a proper reservation.

When considering a demand that it provide a defense to an action against its insured, an insurer should take into account the possibility that the demand is unwarranted because the action is not one covered by its policy. How serious that possibility is may figure in the decision how to respond. The more serious it is, the more careful the insurer should be not to foreclose a "no coverage" argument.

Oftentimes, an insurer assumes its insured's defense with coverage questions unanswered or with coverage issues unresolved. Hence, the possibility exists that the insured will contend that by assuming the defense, the insurer is estopped to deny coverage or has waived its right to contest coverage. To foreclose estoppel or waiver arguments, insurers send reservation of rights letters via certified mail. A reservation of rights letter is an insurer's unilateral declaration that it reserves the right to deny coverage notwithstanding its initial decision to defend. One purpose of a reservation-of-rights letter is to facilitate the insured in making intelligent decisions in protecting its own interests re possible coverage denials and conflicts of interest. Consequently, the insurer must specifically reference the policy defenses that may eventually be asserted, and fully and fairly inform the insured of the potential conflict of interest its reservation creates. Reservation of rights letters that are not specific are usually ineffective.

An opinion presented below (*Midwest Sporting Goods*, p. 359) describes a reservation-of-rights letter prepared by an insurer that the court called "Gainsco". The insured had been sued by the City of Chicago. When the insured demanded a defense, Gainsco wrote back that the claim was not one within the policy coverage, specifying some reasons for thinking so. Yet it acceded to the demand. Gainsco's letter concluded:

> Subject to the foregoing, and without waiving any of its rights and defenses, . . . the Company agrees to provide the Insured a defense in the captioned suit. . . .

> Please note that any acts taken by or on behalf of the Company are taken under and pursuant to a full reservation of its rights and defenses under the Policy. Likewise, we will understand that any acts taken by or on behalf of the Insured are taken pursuant to a reservation of rights as well.

The object of these sentences was to preserve to Gainsco the opportunity to disclaim its duty to indemnify the insured in the event that the City prevailed in its action. (The final sentence was significant in that Gainsco's letter entrusted the defense to an attorney selected by the insured. In effect the letter said "We will pay your attorney his expenses and fee, *but* . . . .")

Express assent by an insured to a reservation results in a reservation-of-rights *agreement* (sometimes called a non-waiver agreement). It has been said that agreements of this kind are "in the public interest", serving the interests of insureds. They "furnish temporary protection to the insured even though it may turn out he was not entitled to such protection. Without such an agreement, an insurer would be forced to deny liability in order to protect itself and its defenses." Iowa National Mut. Ins. Co. v. Liberty Mutual Ins. Co., 168 N.W.2d 610, 613 (Wis. 1969). "Where an insurer, without reservation and with actual or presumed knowledge [of noncoverage], assumes the exclusive control of the defense of claims against the insured, it cannot thereafter withdraw and deny liability under the policy on the ground of noncoverage." Safeco Ins. Co. v. Ellinghouse, 725 P.2d 217, 221 (Mont. 1986).

The commitment of a non-reserving insurer just described has been pitched on estoppel. Lawyers are schooled to think, when they hear of an estoppel, of prejudice caused by reliance on some act or declaration by another (a statement of fact, say, or an undertaking). Some courts adhere to this understanding in connection with an insured who asserts an estoppel against an insurer by reason of the insurer's having undertaken to defend the insured. They require a showing of prejudice. Other courts do not. See *Ellinghouse* and Transamerica Ins. Group v. Chubb and Son, Inc., 554 P.2d 1080 (Wash.App. 1976). See generally 2 Eric Mills Holmes, Holmes' Appleman on Insurance § 8.4 (2d ed. 1996).

In *Ellinghouse* the court said: "[P]rejudice to the insured by virtue of the insurer's assumption of the defense [is], in this situation, conclusively presumed ... [T]he loss of the right of the insured to control and manage the case is itself prejudicial." In *Chubb and Son* the court said: "The course cannot be rerun, no amount of evidence will prove what might have occurred if a different route had been taken. By its own actions, [the insurer] irrevocably fixed the course of events concerning the law suit for the first 10 months. Of necessity, this establishes prejudice." Id. at 1083. A lawyer might be excused for thinking "make believe" when an estoppel is established this way.

PROBLEMS

(1) It may happen that an insured defendant has no cash and no credit. In that situation, how would the course be run at all if the insurer were not to provide a defense? (An impecunious claimant can often get representation under a contingent-fee arrangement; but not a defendant.) Should the conclusive presumption of prejudice give way if the only practicable outcome for the insured, on his or her own, is a default judgment?

(2) Notice that in *Ellinghouse* the court spoke of an insurer that "assumes the *exclusive* control of the defense". In *Midwest Sporting Goods*, Gainsco did not do that; it undertook only to pay for its insurer's defense. Would it have been safe, so far as estoppel is concerned, in doing that without reserving its rights?

C. REFUSING TO DEFEND: THE RISKS

Rhodes v. Chicago Insurance Company

United States Court of Appeals, 5th Cir., 1983.
719 F.2d 116.

■ JOHNSON, CIRCUIT JUDGE:

Plaintiff Laura Marie Rhodes appeals from an order of the federal district court granting summary judgment to the defendants. Plaintiff's suit sought payment of damages which had been agreed upon by plaintiff and defendants' insured in a prior state-court proceeding. We reverse and remand.

In 1978, plaintiff Rhodes applied for a modelling position and was interviewed by one John L. Shirley, a personnel and guidance counsellor. Rhodes alleged that, during subsequent counselling, Shirley engaged in sexual misconduct with her, that he hypnotized her without informing her of the risks involved, and that he was otherwise negligent in performing as a personnel and guidance counsellor. The defendants (appellees here), Chicago Insurance Company (Chicago) and Interstate Fire and Casualty

Company (Interstate), were malpractice insurers for Shirley under a group policy. Chicago refused to defend Shirley under Rhodes' original complaint, did not respond to requests for a defense under the first amended original complaint, and tendered a defense to Shirley against the second amended original complaint only under reservation of right. The defense was tendered with reservation of right because the insurers contended that Rhodes' complaint had alleged conduct by Shirley, specifically sexual misconduct, which was not covered by, or was excluded from coverage under, the policy. Shirley refused the tender and pursued his own defense. The suit was settled for $200,000, the policy limit, and the settlement was approved by a Texas state court.... Plaintiff then filed this suit against defendants Chicago and Interstate, seeking payment of the assessed damages. John L. Shirley is not a party to this suit.

Several issues are presented: (1) whether the defendants had a duty to defend Shirley in the initial litigation in the state district court and, if there was a duty to defend, when it arose; (2) whether the duty was breached, and if so, when; and (3) the consequences of the failure to defend as to both the insured and the insurer. All of these issues involve material questions of fact which do not appear to have been resolved by the federal district court.

[The court described the law of Texas about when an insurer's duty to defend arises. Rhodes contended that the insurers owed Shirley a duty of defense by reason of the original complaint. They contended that that duty arose only under the second amended original complaint.]

It is well settled that once an insurer has breached its duty to defend, the insured is free to proceed as he sees fit; he may engage his own counsel and either settle or litigate, at his option. Having forfeited its right to conduct the defense, the insurer is bound by the settlement or judgment. An additional consequence of a breach of the duty to defend is the inability to enforce against the insured any conditions in the policy; the insured is no longer constrained by "no action" or "no voluntary assumption of liability" clauses. A consequence of breach, therefore, is that an insurer who wrongfully fails to defend its insured is liable for any damages assessed against the insured, up to the policy limits,[4] subject only to the condition that any settlement be reasonable. The insured must demonstrate only that, in settling, his conduct conformed to the standard of a prudent uninsured. The insurer may also be liable for attorneys' fees incurred by the insured in order to defend the suit.

If, in the case at bar, the duty to defend arose under the original or first amended original complaint, the duty was clearly breached by the insurer's denial of coverage and failure to defend. The insurer would then be liable for assessed damages[5] and attorneys' fees and would be estopped

---

4. This Court has held that the insurer may be liable even for amounts in excess of the policy limits. *Blakely v. American Employers' Ins. Co.*, 424 F.2d 728, 734 (5 Cir. 1970).

5. The insurer is estopped from denying coverage and must pay all damages assessed, even damages for actions not covered

from alleging failure by the insured to comply with conditions in the policy. The insurer would be bound by the judgment or settlement and would be unable to relitigate issues of fact. The subsequent filing of an amended complaint does not erase the breach or the penalties therefor. "Having thus waived its right to defend the suit, such right was lost forever...." Witt v. Universal Automobile Insurance Co., 116 S.W.2d 1095, 1098 (Tex.Civ. App.—Waco 1938, writ dism'd).

If, however, the duty to defend arose under the second amended original complaint, the question becomes more complex. The insurer offered to defend, but only with a reservation of rights. A reservation of rights is a proper action if the insurer believes, in good faith, that the complaint alleges conduct which may not be covered by the policy.[6] In such a situation, reservation of rights will not be a breach of the duty to defend, but notice of intent to reserve rights must be sufficient to inform the insured of the insurer's position and must be timely. When a reservation of rights is made, however, the insured may properly refuse the tender of defense and pursue his own defense. The insurer remains liable for attorneys' fees incurred by the insured and may not insist on conducting the defense. Refusal of the tender of defense is particularly appropriate where, as here, the insurer's interests conflict with those of the insured. "When the insurer is denying coverage, ... and where coverage, *vel non*, will depend upon the finding of the trier of facts as to certain issues in the main case, ... the insurer is not in a position to defend the insured." Steel Erection Co. v. Travelers Indemnity Co., 392 S.W.2d 713, 716 (Tex.Civ. App.—San Antonio 1965, writ ref'd n.r.e.). The insurer also is barred from enforcing voluntary assumption of liability and no action clauses. Travelers Indemnity Co. v. Equipment Rental Co., 345 S.W.2d 831, 835 (Tex.Civ. App.—Houston 1961, writ ref'd n.r.e.).

If Chicago acted properly in tendering a defense only under the second amended original complaint, *i.e.*, there was no duty to defend under the two prior complaints, there was no breach of its duty to defend. Shirley was then free to refuse the tender and to defend the suit on his own, unrestricted by conditions in the policy. Chicago's duty to pay, however, would then cease to be coextensive with its duty to defend; Chicago would have a duty to pay only to the extent that the damages assessed were predicated on misconduct covered by the policy and upon a showing that the settlement was reasonable and prudent. If Chicago's conduct was proper under the circumstances, it would be inequitable to, in effect, rewrite the policy and force Chicago to insure risks not contemplated by the contract of insurance. Persuasive authority to this effect is found in Garden Sanctuary, Inc. v.

---

by the policy. Ridgway v. Gulf Life Ins. Co., 578 F.2d 1026, 1029 (5th Cir.1978).

6. The insurer's duty to defend the insured may conflict with the insurer's right to raise defenses against the insured. The reservation of rights serves as notice to the insured of the potential conflict of interest; such notice is required by Canon 5 of the Code of Professional Responsibility. Employ-

ers' Casualty Co. v. Tilley, 496 S.W.2d 552, 558 (Tex.1973). Withdrawal or disqualification because of the conflict of interest may prejudice the insured's ability to defend himself. The decision to reserve rights, therefore, must be based on a good-faith determination that the conduct complained of may not be covered by the policy.

Insurance Co. of North America, 292 So.2d 75 (Fla.Dist.Ct.App. 1974). In *Garden Sanctuary*, the court held that, although the insurer had a duty to defend both included and excluded claims, "in so defending ..., the insurance company will not be precluded or estopped from declining to pay that portion of the judgment which is outside the coverage." *Id.* at 78 (footnote omitted). See also Pacific Indemnity Co. v. Acel Delivery Service, Inc., 485 F.2d 1169, 1173 (5th Cir.1973) (Texas law; "It is well settled in Texas that [waiver and estoppel] will not operate to create coverage in an insurance policy where none originally existed."), *cert. denied*, 415 U.S. 921 (1974); Minnesota Mutual Life Insurance Co. v. Morse, 487 S.W.2d 317, 320 (Tex.1972) ("waiver and estoppel cannot enlarge the risks covered by a policy and cannot be used to create a new and different contract with respect to the risk covered and the insurance extended.").

Whether damages are claimed under a settlement or a judgment is of no import here. If the insurer breached its duty to defend, it is bound to pay any damages up to the policy limits assessed against the insured. If the insurer properly reserved its rights and the insured elected to pursue his own defense, the insurer is bound to pay damages which resulted from covered conduct and which were reasonable and prudent, up to the policy limits. In either case, the insured is not constrained by conditions in the policy which limit the insured's ability to settle the claim, and the insurer cannot complain about the insured's conduct of the defense. If the insurer did not breach the duty to defend and damages were assessed only for conduct which was not covered by the policy or the insurer did not have a duty to defend, the insurer has no duty to pay.

On remand, the district court must first determine what the policy covered and then examine the allegations in the complaint in the light of the policy coverage. If, on the basis of the complaint-allegation rule, a duty to defend arose under the original or first amended original complaints, the insurer breached its duty to defend and is liable for all damages assessed.... If the reservation of rights was proper, the damages must be apportioned between covered conduct and uncovered conduct and the reasonableness of the amount of damages determined. In either case, if the amount is excessive under the prudent uninsured standard, remittitur is proper to reduce the damages to an appropriate amount.

The judgment of the district court is reversed and the cause is remanded to the district court for proceedings not inconsistent with this opinion.

NOTES

(1) *Question.* The court's paragraph beginning "It is well settled ..." states a stunning array of consequences, baleful to Chicago Insurance, and advantageous to Shirley (and to Rhodes), that may have resulted from its refusal to provide Shirley with a defense to the original complaint. Which is the worst of these, from the insurer's point of view?

(2) *The Settlement.* The court's only concession is the statement that the Chicago Insurance would not have been accountable for an unreasonably large

settlement. Are there any intimations that the amount of the settlement was unreasonable? Notice that Rhodes settled with Shirley for the amount of the policy limit, and that she did not seek in this action to collect anything from him.

If Shirley had no significant assets, other than those exempt from the claims of creditors, he might have been willing to settle for more than $200,000. And that would have been in Rhodes's interest, would it not? See the court's footnote 4.

(3) *Disclaimer of Coverage.* An insurer who decides to disclaim coverage must give specific and seasonable notice (by custom called a "denial letter"). The denial letter to be valid must fulfill two important requisites: First, the disclaimer must be sufficiently specific for the insured to understand "fully and fairly" the grounds justifying the disclaimer.[1] Second, the disclaimer must be sent as soon as reasonably possible after the insurer learns of the ground(s) for the disclaimer. See, e.g., Whitney v. Continental Ins. Co., 595 F.Supp. 939 (D.Mass. 1984). Prompt notice of the disclaimer is an important requirement. Some states mandate it by statute. New York, for instance, provides:

> If under a liability policy delivered or issued for delivery in this state, an insurer shall disclaim liability or deny coverage for death or bodily injury arising out of a motor vehicle accident or any other type of accident occurring within this state, it shall give written notice as soon as is reasonably possible of such disclaimer of liability or denial of coverage to the insured and the injured person or any other claimant.

N.Y. C.L.S. Ins. § 3420 (2006). Other examples include Cal. Ins. Code § 544; Fla. Stat. Ann. § 627.426, requiring prompt notice of the insurer's disclaimer of coverage. A late disclaimer can have the same effect as not sending a disclaimer.

> Where, as here, the insurer does not communicate its decision to withdraw or explain the basis for its decision but simply denies coverage, it should be precluded from later arguing that coverage under the policy did not exist.

Sauer v. Home Indem. Co., 841 P.2d 176, 180 (Alaska 1992).

Finally, in the disclaimer (denial letter), if an insurer omits ground(s) that the insurer knows or reasonably ought to know, most courts hold that coverage defenses are not waived by the failure to assert the ground(s) in the disclaimer. In Waller v. Truck Ins. Exch., 900 P.2d 619 (Cal. 1995), the court explained:

> [W]aiver is the intentional relinquishment of a known right after knowledge of the facts. The waiver may be either express, based on the words of the waiving party, or implied, based on conduct indicating an intent to relinquish the right. California courts have applied the general rule that waiver requires the insurer to intentionally relinquish its right to deny coverage and that a denial of coverage on one ground does not, absent clear and convincing evidence to suggest otherwise, impliedly waive grounds not stated in the denial.

Id. at 636. See *Ross Jewelers* p. 120 above and Harr v. Allstate Co., p. 126 above.

---

1. See, e.g., Sauer v. Home Indem. Co., 841 P.2d 176 (Alaska 1992); Allstate Ins. Co. v. Keillor, 511 N.W.2d 702 (Mich.App. 1993), *aff'd* 537 N.W.2d 589 (Mich. 1995); Handelsman v. Sea Ins. Co., 647 N.E.2d 1258 (N.Y. 1994).

D.   CONTROL OF DEFENSE; COST OF DEFENDING

1.   Control of Defense

On occasion an insurer, obliged to provide a defense against a suit against the insured, has been required to pay for a defense conducted by an attorney chosen by the insured. This represents a certain disconnect between the duty to defend and the right to do so. The standard case is one in which an attorney chosen by the insurer would face a conflict of interests. An instance was described as follows in Armstrong Cleaners, Inc. v. Erie Insurance Exchange, 364 F.Supp.2d 797 (S.D.Ind. 2005), at 806.

> [A] lawsuit by a person who has been shot and injured by the insured. The victim alleges in Count One that the insured shot him intentionally and in the alternative in Count Two that the insured shot him negligently. Under a typical liability insurance policy, coverage is available for negligent acts but not for intentional acts. The insurer therefore would benefit from either a defense verdict or a finding of intentional wrongdoing. The insured, on the other hand, would benefit from either a defense verdict or a finding of negligence. Absent informed consent of both the insurer and the insured, an attorney trying to represent both the insured and the insurer would face an insurmountable conflict of interest.

This, the court said, was a "classic example in Indiana law". It appears to be a classic case elsewhere as well. A rule of professional conduct, promulgated by the Indiana Supreme Court, forbids the representation of a client if there is a significant risk that it will be "materially limited by the lawyer's responsibilities to another client, a former client or a third person or by a personal interest of the lawyer." Rule 1.7(a)(2).

Litigation analogous to the two-count shooting case is reported in an opinion presented below, Nowacki v. Federated Realty Group. The opinion there recites another well-known instance, Fireman's Fund Ins. Co. v. Waste Management, Inc., 777 F.2d 366 (7th Cir. 1985).

It is prudent for the insurer, in cases like these, to make some provision for a defense, but to reserve its rights as to coverage. The two-count shooting case would be different if the victim were to allege only negligence on the part of the insured. In that case also it might be prudent for the insurer to reserve its rights; it should do so if it wishes to provide a defense, but believes it might avoid paying any judgment by reason, for example, of untimely notice of the shooting. Its interest in the verdict in that case would be aligned with that of the insured, both favoring a finding of no negligence. (Which interest would be the more powerful would depend, of course, on factors such as the lateness of the notice and the wealth of the insured; but they would be aligned.) Sometimes an insured, interested in getting control of the defense, is heard to say that the insurer's reservation of rights generates a conflict of interest. To that argument it suffices to say that it depends on the reason for the reservation. HK Systems v. Admiral Ins. Co., 2005 WL 1563340 (E.D.Wis. 2005). There the court said that the two-count shooting case would present a "real" conflict of interests.

Other cases of divided loyalty, equally real, occur when there are multiple defendants, insured under the same policy, and the defendants have opposing interests.

An insurer's right to conduct a defense on behalf of its insured entails the right to select an attorney to represent the insured. "While some policies may expressly state that the insurer provides a defense 'by counsel of [the insurer's] choice,' . . . the absence of such language does not mean that the insurer has no right to choose the attorney. . . ." *HK Systems* at 2005 WL 1563340 *12. An attorney so designated owes his or her "sole loyalty and duty . . . to the client alone, the client being the insured. . . . No attorney-client relationship exists between an insurance company and the attorney representing the insurance company's insured." Atlanta Internat'l Ins. Co. v. Bell, 448 N.W.2d 804, 805 (Mich.App. 1989). Nevertheless, an insured may reasonably suspect that the loyalty of an attorney designated by the insurer will be deflected by the hope of pinning the "client's" liability, if any, on the ground of a non-covered claim (*e.g.*, an intentional shooting). The books are full of pleas by insured parties that they be permitted to select counsel for their defenses, or that they be consulted about the choice of counsel, or at least that the insurer's selection be made from among "independent counsel".

In *Nowacki*, below, the court ruled that the insured was "free to control its defense and select its own counsel." The opinion treats also the question who is to pay the cost. The insurer, Continental Casualty Insurance Company, thought that if it had to pay it should at least be consulted about the choice. Not so, said the court. These matters are controversial. In *HK Systems* the court declared that, in a case of conflicting interests, an insurer might insist on designating counsel "so long as such counsel is truly independent and the insurer acts in good faith."

NOTE

No New Rights. There is an odd parallelism in the two opinions last cited. In *HK Systems*, the court punctured the insured's pretensions, with respect to certain entitlements respecting defense, by an argument that can be summarized fairly in the phrase "no new rights". No rights, that is, beyond those already established. "[T]he shift of the right to choose counsel appears to be a new substantive right for the insured."[2]

On reading *Nowacki*, one finds the converse argument. There the court recited three ways in which an insurer can "retain its right to challenge coverage while not breaching its duty to defend." Then it accused the insurer of seeking to create a

---

2. The court said, unaccountably, that a federal court hearing a diversity case "should refrain from expanding liability." What it might have said more plausibly is that federal judges should not, whatever the base of their jurisdiction, be inventive about state law.

"fourth alternative . . . in addition to the three established [ones]," and said that the case cited in support "does not create . . . an additional option. . . ."

Nowacki v. Federated Realty Group, Inc.

United States District Court, E.D.Wis., 1999.
36 F.Supp.2d 1099.

Daniel Nowacki and others, who had used the services of Federated Realty ("Federated") as a broker in sales of their properties, brought an action against it, charging various violations of the Real Estate Settlement Practices Act ("RESPA"), 12 U.S.C. §§ 2601–2610. According to the court, the complaint could be characterized as charging "a mixture of intentional and negligent acts". The Continental Casualty Insurance Company ("Continental") intervened. It had issued to Federated a "Real Estate Agents Errors and Omissions Liability Policy".

Continental sought a declaratory judgment that, among other things, it had no duty to provide a defense for Federated, or to indemnify it, that it need not reimburse Federated for attorney fees or costs already incurred, and that if Continental owed a defense to Federated but could not choose defense counsel, Continental could veto Federated's choice of counsel. Continental pointed to a provision of its policy that it would not defend or pay for "any dishonest, fraudulent, criminal or malicious act or omission" by Federated.

There had been some jockeying between Federated and Continental about the defense. At one point—after Federated had hired its own attorney—Continental informed it that Continental would assume Federated's defense, but only on reserving all its rights and defenses under the policy. Federated had responded that it elected to pursue its own defense, not subject to Continental's control, but that Continental would remain liable for all legal fees incurred. To that, Continental said that it would provide Federated with independent counsel, provided counsel was selected by mutual agreement.

Each party moved for summary judgment. The court made rulings, among others, that Continental owed Federated a defense of the action, that it had not violated the duty of defense ("because it properly sought a declaration of its coverage obligations"), and that the court could not resolve the issue of indemnification until further facts were determined.

■ AARON E. GOODSTEIN, U.S. MAGISTRATE JUDGE.

. . .

C. Selection of Counsel

The last issue the parties raise . . . is the degree of autonomy Federated may exercise in selecting its own counsel, and whether Continental is liable for Federated's attorney fees, in light of the fact that Continental is insuring Federated under a reservation of rights. Federated argues that once Continental informed Federated that Continental reserved its right to deny to indemnify Federated for intentional misconduct and criminal and malicious acts, Federated was free to pursue its own defense not subject to Continental's control. According to Federated, Continental must reimburse Federated for attorney fees incurred up to this point in the case and must pay all future attorney fees.

Continental states that it did not breach its duty to defend Federated in this action simply because it is proceeding under a reservation of rights. Therefore, Continental argues, Federated is not entitled to unilaterally select counsel and to have Continental reimburse Federated for its unilaterally selected counsel. Rather, Continental states that it is only obligated to pay the fees of counsel mutually agreeable to itself and Federated.

Continental has complied with the procedure for an insurer to retain its right to challenge coverage, while not breaching its duty to defend the insured, by informing the insured about the insurer's reservation of rights and seeking a declaratory judgment regarding the insured's duty to defend. See Grube v. Daun, 496 N.W.2d 106, 123 (Wis.App. 1992). The discrete issue for resolution here is which party controls the defense? May the insured unilaterally select counsel and seek reimbursement or payment for those attorney fees from the insurer when the insurer reserves its right to deny indemnification, or must the parties mutually select counsel before the insurer is required to pay for the insured's attorney fees?

Federated claims that it is entitled to control its defense and select counsel because there is a conflict of interest for Continental to defend under a reservation of rights. The "conflict," as seen from the discussion of the coverage dispute, is that Continental is not obligated to indemnify Federated for its intentional acts or for multiple damages. In light of this possible result, Federated submits it must have sole control over selection of counsel.

In *Grube*, the Wisconsin Court of Appeals described the procedures by which an insurer can retain its right to challenge coverage while not breaching its duty to defend. First, the insurer and the insured may enter into a nonwaiver agreement whereby the insurer agrees to defend and the insured acknowledges the right of the insurer to contest coverage. Second, the insurer may request a bifurcated trial or declaratory judgment in order to have the coverage issue separately addressed by a court. Third, the insurer may provide the insured notice of its intent to reserve the right to contest coverage. "When a reservation of rights is made, the insured can pursue his own defense not subject to the control of the insurer, but the insurer still would be liable for legal fees incurred." Id. at 123.

Grube is not directly on point with this case because the insurer in *Grube* lost its contractual right to control the insured's defense by inappropriately refusing to defend. Id. at 124. Here, Continental has not refused to defend. However, *Grube*'s statement with respect to the insured selecting its own counsel at the insurer's expense was applied in a case in which the insurer did not breach its duty to defend. In Jacob v. West Bend Mut. Ins. Co., 553 N.W.2d 800 (1996), the Wisconsin Court of Appeals reaffirmed the options available to an insurer when it wants to raise a coverage issue and retain its right to challenge coverage. The court held that the insurer may request a bifurcated trial or declaratory judgment. Alternatively, the insurer may provide the insured notice of the insurer's intent to reserve its coverage rights, which "allows the insured the opportunity to a defense not subject to the control of the insurer although the insurer remains liable for the legal fees incurred." Id. at 805. The court held that the insurer did not breach its duty to defend because it offered a " 'paid for' defense by an attorney of the insured's own choosing." Id. at 805.

In the instant case, Continental chose to provide Federated notice of Continental's intent to reserve its right to contest coverage, which *Grube* and *Jacob* identify as an appropriate method for the insurer to preserve its right to challenge coverage. However, *Grube* and *Jacob* state that a consequence for the insurer who pursues this route is that the insured is allowed to select its own counsel at the insurer's expense. Continental, in effect, seeks to create a fourth alternative for contesting coverage, in addition to the three established in *Grube*. Continental argues, based on Fireman's Fund Ins. Co. v. Waste Management, Inc., 777 F.2d 366 (7th Cir. 1985), that when an insurer notifies the insured of its intent to reserve its right to contest coverage, the insurer is liable for the insured's attorney fees only if the insurer and the insured mutually agree on counsel. However, *Fireman's Fund* does not create or mandate an additional option for the insurer in extension of *Grube* and *Jacob*.

In *Fireman's Fund*, the plaintiffs charged that Waste Management contaminated groundwater through its negligence or intentional acts. Waste Management's insurer, Fireman's Fund, advised Waste Management that it intended to defend Waste Management under a reservation of rights. Meanwhile, Fireman's Fund learned that Waste Management's attorneys might have a conflict of interest because they were related to the plaintiffs. Thus, Fireman's Fund retained its own attorneys, without Waste Management's consent. Waste Management objected to the firm chosen by Fireman's Fund, stating that the firm had a longstanding relationship with the insurer. Fireman's Fund then sought a declaratory judgment in the district court for the Western District of Wisconsin against Waste Management based on an alleged conflict of interest between Waste Management and its law firm. The district court noted that an obvious conflict arose between Fireman's Fund and Waste Management when Fireman's Fund reserved its right to contest coverage because it was in Waste Management's interest to have liability based on negligence, while it was in Fireman's Fund's interest to have liability based on intentional injury. Id. at 368. That is not unlike the situation in this case. The Seventh Circuit affirmed the district's court's opinion that this conflict was not rectified when Fireman's Fund selected counsel for Waste Management without the insured's consent. Id. at 369. Even though the district court found that Fireman's Fund had failed to provide independent counsel, because there were problems with Waste Management's initial selection of counsel, the court found that a fair and equitable method for resolving the conflict of interest between the parties was for the insurer [insured?] to select counsel, subject to the approval and at the expense of the insurer. Id. at

370. The Seventh Circuit affirmed the "mutually agreeable counsel" concept as being an equitable and reasonable way for the parties to end their dispute.

Fireman's Fund is not in conflict with *Grube* because the court only acknowledged the propriety of the insurer and insured agreeing on counsel. See *Fireman's Fund*, 777 F.2d at 369. The Seventh Circuit did not interpret Wisconsin law to *require* the insurer and insured to agree on counsel before the insurer is liable for the insured's legal fees. Moreover, where the determination of coverage is interwoven with the resolution of factual issues, Federated has a heightened interest in selecting its own counsel without input from Continental. Parenthetically, the court notes that other jurisdictions also allow the insured to select its own counsel, at the insurer's expense, when a conflict arises between the insured and the insurer regarding coverage. See San Diego Navy Fed. Credit Union v. Cumis, 208 Cal.Rptr. 494, 497–498 (Cal.Ct.App. 1984) [and three other cases cited].

Under the circumstances of this case, the court concludes that, once Continental tendered its defense to Federated under a reservation of rights, a conflict of interest was created between Federated and Continental. As such, Federated was free to control its defense and select its own counsel. While the parties are also free to mutually agree on counsel, such a procedure is not required. This means that Continental is liable for all attorney fees Federated has incurred and will incur to defend this action. [The court said that Continental was not liable for fees incurred for the defense of another defendant, "Metro", which was also represented by Federated's counsel. Metro was not insured by Continental.] In this regard, Federated will be obligated to apportion the expenses incurred for defending each entity, recognizing that there may be some overlap. The court declines to make any findings or order at this time regarding the amount of attorney fees. The parties are directed to attempt to agree upon Federated's legal fees incurred to date. If the parties are unable to reach an agreement, Federated may file a motion for attorney fees, supported with sufficient documentation, and Continental may respond accordingly.

. . .

NOTES

(1) *Independent Counsel.* When an insured is entitled to be represented by an attorney of its choice, and is, the attorney is sometimes called "*Cumis* counsel" after the style of a well-known California case recognizing the insured's entitlement.[3] The term "independent counsel" is sometimes used to signify an attorney chosen by the insured, as in that case, but it is sometimes used in the broader and more literal sense of an attorney not subservient to the insurer.[4] In *HK Systems* the insurer spared the court the necessity of deciding whether or not an attorney was

3. San Diego Navy Fed. Credit Union v. Cumis Ins. Soc'y, Inc., 208 Cal.Rptr. 494 (Cal. App. 1984). The insured was permitted to have the attorney of its choice as co-counsel.

4. That appears to be the way the term is used in Cal. Civ. Code § 2860. In Federal Ins. Co. v. American Cas. Co. of Reading, Pa., 748 F.Supp. 1223 (W.D.Mich. 1990), the court used the term so as to exclude counsel of the insured's choice.

disqualified as "independent" because his firm had previously represented the insurer. After having designated that attorney, the insurer yielded, permitting the insured to choose defense counsel. But the court cited authority that an insurer might insist on designating counsel "so long as such counsel is truly independent and the insurer acts in good faith."

(2) *The Stakes*. What does an insurer have to fear from having the defense managed by an attorney chosen by the insured? Part of the answer should be clear from the description above (p. 348) of a classic case of conflict. Other parts are suggested by provisions of a California statute enacted after the decision in *Cumis*, Civil Code § 2860. It provides insurers with safeguards against the choice of an inexperienced or incompetent attorney.[5] It places a limit on the insurer's obligation to pay fees to the independent counsel. It also requires counsel to disclose to the insurer information concerning the action, and "to inform and consult with the insurer on all matters relating to the action."[6]

2.   Cost of Defending

Cases in which conflicts of interest figure, and the expense of defending is in issue, can be divided helpfully into two groups, those in which (a) expenses have been incurred by the insured, or are expected to be incurred by someone, or both, and (b) expenses have been incurred by the insurer. A case within group (a) is *Nowacki*, above. In that case, and in others like it, the controversy has developed in this general way: (i) Being notified of a claim or suit against its insured, the insurer discerns what it regards as a conflict of interest. It announces its readiness to provide a defense, but only upon reserving its right to contest its duty to pay if a liability is fastened on the insured and there is a question about the coverage of that liability; (ii) The insured objects to representation on those terms and proceeds to defend itself through counsel of its choice, expecting the insurer to pay the cost; (iii) Whether or not the insurer knew of that expectation, it declines to pay the defense cost. Insurers are reluctant, naturally, to underwrite the expenses of lawyers chosen by others; they are likely to prefer the services of lawyers to whom they give repeat business.

Both in *Nowacki* and in *HK Services*—another "group (a)" case—the courts divined that Wisconsin law required payments by the insurers.

The two following opinions represent "group (b)" cases.

---

5. "When the insured has selected independent counsel to represent him or her, the insurer may exercise its right to require that the counsel selected by the insured possess certain minimum qualifications which may include that the selected counsel have (1) at least five years of civil litigation practice which includes substantial defense experience in the subject at issue in the litigation, and (2) errors and omissions coverage." Subsection (c).

6. "When independent counsel has been selected by the insured, it shall be the duty of that counsel and the insured to disclose to the insurer all information concerning the action except privileged materials relevant to coverage disputes, and timely to inform and consult with the insurer on all matters relating to the action. Any claim of privilege asserted is subject to in camera review in the appropriate law and motion department of the superior court. Any information disclosed by the insured or by independent counsel is not a waiver of the privilege as to any other party." Subdivision (d).

Scottsdale Ins. Co. v. MV Transportation

California Supreme Court, 2005.
115 P.3d 460.

■ BAXTER, JUSTICE

. . .*

In January 2000, Laidlaw filed an action against MV [Transportation] and several of MV's employees who had previously worked for Laidlaw, including MV's new president and chief operating officer (Jon Monson). Laidlaw's complaint . . . alleged causes of action for breach of fiduciary duty, tortious inducement to breach the duty of loyalty and fiduciary duty, intentional interference with contractual relations and with prospective business advantage, misappropriation of trade secrets, and unlawful, unfair, and fraudulent business practices.

. . .

Soon after Laidlaw filed its complaint, MV's legal counsel tendered the defense to its insurer, Scottsdale. Scottsdale asserted that [its] defense obligations were not triggered by the Laidlaw suit. Nonetheless, Scottsdale agreed to provide a defense . . . to MV and the individuals named in the Laidlaw suit under a reservation of certain rights, including the right to seek a declaration of its rights and duties under the policy and "[t]he right to seek reimbursement of defense fees paid toward defending causes of action which raise no potential for coverage, as authorized by the California Supreme Court in *Buss v. Superior Court (Transamerica Ins. Co.)*, 939 P.2d 766 (Cal. 1997)."[a]

[MV and the other defendants settled with Laidlaw, agreeing to grant it various forms of relief.] However, the settlement agreement did not require that MV pay any money to Laidlaw. Attorney fees and costs incurred [by Scottsdale] in defending the Laidlaw suit were approximately $340,000.

[Before the settlement] Scottsdale sued MV (the insurance action), seeking a declaration, *inter alia*, that because its policies afforded no potential coverage of the third party action, it owed no defense, and was therefore entitled to reimbursement of its defense costs.

[The trial court found a potential for coverage. On review, the Court of Appeal disagreed.] Nonetheless, the Court of Appeal concluded that Scottsdale was not entitled to reimbursement. The Court of Appeal reasoned, in

---

* Portions of this opinion are transposed here.

a. "[C]ounsel for Scottsdale informed MV's general counsel that, although Scottsdale did not believe Laidlaw's claims fell within the scope of its policies' 'advertising injury' provisions, Scottsdale would provide a defense subject to various reservations of rights. These included '[t]he right to seek a declaration of [Scottsdale's] rights and duties under its [p]olicies regarding its defense and/or indemnity obligations,' and '[t]he right to seek reimbursement of defense fees paid toward defending causes of action which raise no potential for coverage, as authorized . . . in *Buss, supra.* . . .' Scottsdale thus served notice that it might seek to recover defense fees and costs *already* expended if it were *later* determined that Scottsdale had owed MV no defense."

essence, that its no-potential-coverage determination "extinguished" Scottsdale's defense duty *only from that time forward*. Hence, the Court of Appeal determined, Scottsdale could not "retroactively" recover defense costs expended before its duty was "extinguished."

We disagree. By ruling, as a matter of law, that the third party action never presented any possibility of coverage by Scottsdale's policies, the Court of Appeal established not that the duty to defend was thereupon prospectively "extinguished," but *that it never arose*. Therefore, Scottsdale may recover amounts it expended in defending the insured under its reservation of rights. To the extent the Court of Appeal held otherwise, its judgment must be reversed.

[In Part 1 of the opinion—"General Principles"—the court summarized "familiar principles pertaining to an insurer's duty of defense." This part of the opinion concludes as follows.] If any facts stated or fairly inferable in the complaint, or otherwise known or discovered by the insurer, suggest a claim potentially covered by the policy, the insurer's duty to defend arises and is not extinguished until the insurer negates all facts suggesting potential coverage. On the other hand, if, as a matter of law, neither the complaint nor the known extrinsic facts indicate any basis for potential coverage, the duty to defend does not arise in the first instance.

May a commercial general liability (CGL) insurer obtain reimbursement of its expenses of defending its insured against a third party lawsuit, when it is ultimately determined, as a matter of law, that the policy never afforded any potential for coverage, and that a duty to defend thus never arose? Where, as here, the insurer properly reserved its right to such reimbursement, we conclude that the answer is "yes."

2. Scottsdale's Right to Reimbursement

. . .

As we explained in *Buss, supra*, 939 P.2d 766, the insurer may unilaterally condition its proffer of a defense upon its reservation of a right later to seek reimbursement of costs advanced to defend claims that are not, and never were, potentially covered by the relevant policy. Such an announcement by the insurer permits the insured to decide whether to accept the insurer's terms for providing a defense, or instead to assume and control its own defense. *Id.*, at p. 784, fn. 27.

. . .

Thus, the insurer's duty to defend *arises* whenever the third party complaint and/or the available extrinsic facts suggest, under applicable law, the possibility of covered claims. In such circumstances, if the insured tenders defense of the third party action, the insurer must assume it. The duty to defend then continues until the third party litigation ends, unless the insurer sooner proves, by facts subsequently developed, that the potential for coverage which previously appeared cannot possibly materialize, or no longer exists. The insurer must absorb all costs it expended on behalf of its insured while the duty to defend was in effect—*i.e.*, before the insurer established that the duty had ended. *Montrose* [Chemical Corp. v. Superior Court, 861 P.2d 1153 (Cal. 1993)] at 1156–63. . . .

.   .   .

As *Buss* explained, the duty to defend, and the extent of that duty, are rooted in basic contract principles. The insured pays for, and can reasonably expect, a defense against third party claims that are potentially covered by its policy, but no more. Conversely, the insurer does not bargain to assume the cost of defense of claims that are not even potentially covered. To shift these costs to the insured does not upset the contractual arrangement between the parties. Thus, where the insurer, acting under a reservation of rights, has prophylactically financed the defense of claims as to which it owed no duty of defense, it is entitled to restitution. Otherwise, the insured, who did not bargain for a defense of noncovered claims, would receive a windfall and would be unjustly enriched. *Buss, supra*, 939 P.2d 766, 774–77.

.   .   .

The instant Court of Appeal suggested that an insurer uncertain of its defense obligations might initially assume the defense, then seek to "stop the bleeding" by obtaining a prompt, though prospective, "extinguishment" of its duty to defend. But where, as here, there was never a duty to defend, this limited remedy provides the insured more, and the insurer less, than the parties' bargain contemplated. Moreover, as Scottsdale and its *amici curiae* point out, it also forces the insurer to commence litigation of defense and coverage issues, and to press for early resolution of those issues, while the third party litigation is still pending. However, this is a tactic which, in many cases, the insurer is not allowed to pursue, and in general should be discouraged for policy reasons.

"When an insured calls upon a liability insurer to defend a third party action, the insurer as a general rule may not escape the burden of defense by obtaining a declaratory judgment that it has no duty to defend. Were the rule otherwise, the insured would be forced to defend simultaneously against both the insurer's declaratory relief action and the third party's liability action. Because the duty to defend turns on the potential for coverage, and because coverage frequently turns on factual issues to be litigated in the third party liability action, litigating the duty to defend in the declaratory relief action may prejudice the insured in the liability action. To prevent this form of prejudice, the insurer's action for declaratory relief may be either stayed [citation] or dismissed." *Montrose, supra*, 861 P.2d 1153, 1164. . . .

Indeed, "[i]t is *only* where there is no potential conflict between the trial of the coverage dispute and the underlying action that an insurer can obtain an early trial date and resolution of its claim that coverage does not exist." . . .

The Court of Appeal's analysis contravenes these sound rules and policies. Unlike the Court of Appeal, we decline to require an insurer uncertain about the law relevant to its coverage and defense obligations to engage its insured in a futile "two-front war.". . . .

. . .

Accordingly, we conclude that an insurer under a standard CGL policy, having properly reserved its rights, may advance sums to defend its insured against a third party lawsuit, and may thereafter recoup such costs from the insured if it is determined, as a matter of law, that no duty to defend ever arose because the third party suit never suggested the possibility of a covered claim. Such is the case here. It follows that, insofar as the Court of Appeal denied Scottsdale's right to reimbursement, its judgment should be reversed.

CONCLUSION

Insofar as the Court of Appeal concluded that Scottsdale may not pursue an action for reimbursement of defense costs advanced under a reservation of rights, its judgment is reversed. The judgment of the Court of Appeal is otherwise affirmed.

NOTE

(2) *Mixed Claims, Potential Liability, and Reimbursement.* The California *Montrose-Buss-Scottsdale* rules appear to represent the majority or predominant American view regarding both the insurer's duty to defend mixed (covered and not covered) claims and the insurer's reimbursement for defense costs of claims not potentially covered. In Buss v. Superior Court, 939 P.2d 766 (Cal. 1997), the court applied the potential liability rule to a complaint which asserted many causes of action, of which only one potentially fell within policy coverage. The court ruled that in a "mixed" action, involving claims that are at least potentially covered and claims that are not, an insurer nonetheless has a duty to defend the claim in its entirety. After settling the underlying case, the insured initiated coverage litigation to resolve the reimbursement issue. In *Buss*, the court resolved the reimbursement issue by distinguishing between the mixed "covered and uncovered" claims, as follows:

(1) An insurer may not seek reimbursement for claims that are at least potentially covered. The insured paid premiums and the insurer bargained to bear those costs by defending. As a consequence, "there is no right of reimbursement implied in the policy or implied in law." *Buss*, 939 P.2d at 774–75.

(2) An insurer may seek reimbursement for defense costs as to the claims that are not even potentially covered, if the insurer expressly reserved the right to seek such reimbursement. The insured had not paid premiums to the insurer and the insurer did not bargain to bear those costs in defending "claims are not even potentially covered." Consequently, the insurer has a right to reimbursement implied in law as quasi-contractual. Under the law of restitution, the insured has been "enriched" through the insurer's bearing of unbargained-for defense costs, an enrichment that must be deemed unjust. *Buss*, 939 P.2d at 776–77.

(3) In a "mixed" action, the insurer can obtain reimbursement from the insured those defense costs that can be allocated solely to the claims that are "not even potentially covered." When the insurer seeks reimbursement for defense costs from the insured, the insurer bears the burden of proving by a preponderance of the evidence which specific defense costs it is entitled to recover. *Buss*, 939 P.2d at 779.

(4) The court noted that exceptions would exist if the policy itself provided for reimbursement or if there was a separate contract supported by separate consideration. *Buss*, 939 P.2d at 776.

Buss appears to represent the majority or predominant view in the United States. See, e.g., St. Paul Fire & Marine Ins. Co. v. Compaq Computer Corp., 377 F. Supp. 2d 719 (D. Minn. 2005), applying Texas law and granting St. Paul reimbursement of its defense costs. However, some jurisdictions follow what they label the "minority" view, as in the next case. Although the Illinois Supreme Court gives more details than *Buss* supporting the "majority" rule, the court, in its well reasoned opinion, explains and adopts what it calls the "minority" rule—"refusing to permit an insurer to recover defense costs pursuant to a reservation of rights absent an express provision to that effect in the insurance contract between the parties."

General Agents Ins. Co. of Am. v. Midwest Sporting Goods Co.

Illinois Supreme Court, 2005.
215 Ill.2d 146, 828 N.E.2d 1092.

■ Thomas, Justice

. . .

BACKGROUND

The City of Chicago and Cook County sued Midwest Sporting Goods Company (Midwest) and other defendants for creating a public nuisance by selling guns to inappropriate purchasers. Midwest tendered defense of the suit to General Agents Insurance Company of America (hereinafter Gainsco), its liability carrier. Gainsco denied coverage. [It did so by letter to Midwest's counsel, relying on a number of grounds, including the ground that the suit was not one for damages. The letter concluded as follows.]

> Subject to the foregoing, and without waiving any of its rights and defenses, *including the right to recoup any defense costs paid in the event that it is determined that the Company does not owe the Insured a defense in this matter*, the Company agrees to provide the Insured a defense in the captioned suit. In light of the competing interests between the Company and the Insured in respect of the coverage for this matter, the Company agrees to the Insured's selection and use of your firm as its counsel in this matter. . . .

> Please note that any acts taken by or on behalf of the Company are taken under and pursuant to a full reservation of its rights and defenses under the Policy. Likewise, we will understand that any acts taken by or on behalf of the Insured are taken pursuant to a reservation of rights as well.

Based upon the record in this case, it does not appear that Midwest ever responded to Gainsco's reservation of rights letter. Midwest thereafter accepted Gainsco's payment of defense costs.

... Gainsco filed a declaratory judgment action seeking, *inter alia*, a declaration that it did not owe Midwest a defense in the underlying litigation. [The trial court entered a summary judgment in favor of Gainsco. After Midwest raised several other matters, the trial court ruled for Gainsco and the appeals court affirmed, noting that courts in other jurisdictions had reached a similar result. For example, the court in *Buss v. Superior Court*, 939 P.2d 766 (Cal. 1997), ordered an insured to reimburse its insurer for defense costs paid on claims that were not within the coverage of the insured's policy.... The appellate court relied also on Grinnell Mutual Reinsurance Co. v. Shierk, 996 F.Supp. 836 (S.D.Ill. 1998).]

The appellate court rejected Midwest's argument that the court should not adopt the reasoning of *Buss* and *Grinnell* because those decisions give an insurance company too much leverage. The appellate court stated that if Midwest had refused to accept the funds under Gainsco's conditions, Midwest could have forced Gainsco to either defend without a right of reimbursement or deny a defense and risk losing its policy defense if it was found in breach of the insurance contract. Finally, the appellate court reiterated that the payments made by Gainsco were not made pursuant to Midwest's insurance policy, but rather were an "accommodation pending litigation to determine whether Gainsco owed Midwest, under the insurance contract, a defense." ...

ANALYSIS

. . .

In the instant case, as noted, Gainsco chose both to defend under a reservation of rights and to seek a declaratory judgment that there was no coverage. Gainsco's reservation of rights letter provided that it reserved the right to recoup any defense costs paid in the event it was determined that Gainsco did not owe Midwest a defense. The gravamen of Midwest's argument on appeal is that Gainsco could not reserve the right to recoup defense costs because the insurance contract between the parties does not contain a provision allowing Gainsco the right to recoup defense costs. In turn, the gravamen of Gainsco's response is that there is no contract governing the relationship between the parties because both the circuit and appellate courts have held that the policies issued by Gainsco to Midwest did not apply to the underlying litigation. Accordingly, Gainsco maintains that it had no duty to defend Midwest and thus is entitled to recoup the amounts paid for Midwest's defense.

In support of its argument, Gainsco points to decisions from other jurisdictions where courts have held that an insurer may recover its defense costs if it specifically reserves the right to recoup those costs in the event it is determined that the insurer does not owe the insured a defense. [Gainsco relied on the decisions in Buss v. Superior Court and in *Grinnell*.]

Finally, Gainsco notes that other jurisdictions also have found that an insurer may recover defense costs from its insured where the insurer agrees to provide the insured a defense pursuant to an express reservation of rights, including the right to recoup defense costs, the insured accepts the defense, and a court subsequently finds that the insurer did not owe the insured a defense. [The court referred to decisions in six states favoring insurers. Each of them, the court said, was] based upon a finding that there was a contract implied in fact or law, or a finding that the insured was unjustly enriched when its insurer paid defense costs for claims that were not covered by the insured's policy. . . .

[The court observed that Gainsco would be entitled to reimbursement if the court were to adopt the analysis in these cases.] Our research reveals, however, that other jurisdictions, albeit a minority, have refused to allow an insurer to receive reimbursement of its defense costs even though the underlying claim was not covered by the insurance policy and the insurer had specifically reserved its right to reimbursement.

Upon review, we find the analysis of those decisions refusing to allow reimbursement to be more persuasive and more on point with Illinois case law than the cases cited by Gainsco. [The court quoted from Shoshone First Bank v. Pacific Employers Insurance Co., 2 P.3d 510 (Wyo. 2000), as follows.

> The insurer is not permitted to unilaterally modify and change policy coverage. We agree with the Supreme Court of Hawaii that a reservation of rights letter 'does not relieve the insurer of the costs incurred in defending its insured where the insurer was obligated, in the first instance, to provide such a defense.' First Insurance Co. of Hawaii, Inc. v. State, by Minami, 665 P.2d 648, 654 (Haw. 1983). [The insurer] could have included allocation language in the Policy, but it failed to do so. We look only to the four corners of the policy to determine coverage, and where the policy is unambiguous, extrinsic evidence is not considered. [Citation.] The Policy issued to Shoshone by [the insurer] states a duty to defend, and allocation is not mentioned. In light of the failure of the policy language to provide for allocation, we will not permit the contract to be amended or altered by a reservation of rights letter.

Shoshone First Bank, 2 P.3d at 515–16. . . .]

The court in *Shoshone First Bank* then cited an unpublished [Wyoming opinion] that clearly articulated the problem with allowing an insurer to reserve the right to seek reimbursement of defense costs. That court stated that:

> 15. A reservation of rights letter does not create a contract allowing an insurer to recoup defense costs from its insureds.

> 16. The question as to whether there is a duty to defend an insured is a difficult one, but because that is the business of an insurance carrier, it is the insurance carrier's duty to make that decision. If an insurance carrier believes that no coverage exists, then it should deny its insured a defense at the beginning instead of defending and later attempting to recoup from its insured the costs of defending the underlying action. Where the insurance carrier is uncer-

tain over insurance coverage for the underlying claim, the proper course is for the insurance carrier to tender a defense and seek a declaratory judgment as to coverage under the policy. However, to allow the insurer to force the insured into choosing between seeking a defense under the policy, and run the potential risk of having to pay for this defense if it is subsequently determined that no duty to defend existed, or giving up all meritorious claims that a duty to defend exists, places the insured in the position of making a Hobson's choice. Furthermore, endorsing such conduct is tantamount to allowing the insurer to extract a unilateral amendment to the insurance contract. If this became common practice, the insurance industry might extract coercive arrangements from their insureds, destroying the concept of liability and litigation insurance.

Shoshone First Bank, 2 P.3d at 516.

We agree with the analysis of the court in *Shoshone First Bank*, as well as the [unpublished Wyoming opinion]. As a matter of public policy, we cannot condone an arrangement where an insurer can unilaterally modify its contract, through a reservation of rights, to allow for reimbursement of defense costs in the event a court later finds that the insurer owes no duty to defend. We recognize that courts have found an implied agreement where the insured accepts the insurer's payment of defense costs despite the insurer's reservation of a right to reimbursement of defense costs. However, as stated by the court in [the unpublished opinion] cited by the *Shoshone First Bank* court, recognizing such an implied agreement effectively places the insured in the position of making a Hobson's choice between accepting the insurer's additional conditions on its defense or losing its right to a defense from the insurer.

The United States Court of Appeals for the Third Circuit, applying Pennsylvania law, also has ruled that an insurer cannot recover defense costs even when it defends under a reservation of rights to recover defense costs if it is later determined there is no coverage. *Terra Nova Insurance Co. v. 900 Bar, Inc.*, 887 F.2d 1213 (3d Cir. 1989). The court reasoned that:

A rule permitting such recovery would be inconsistent with the legal principles that induce an insurer's offer to defend under reservation of rights. Faced with uncertainty as to its duty to indemnify, an insurer offers a defense under reservation of rights to avoid the risks that an inept or lackadaisical defense of the underlying action may expose it to if it turns out there is a duty to indemnify. [footnote omitted]. At the same time, the insurer wishes to preserve its right to contest the duty to indemnify if the defense is unsuccessful. Thus, such an offer is made at least as much for the insurer's own benefit as for the insured's. If the insurer could recover defense costs, the insured would be required to pay for the insurer's action in protecting itself against the estoppel to deny coverage that would be implied if it undertook the defense without reservation.

Terra Nova Insurance Co., 887 F.2d at 1219–20.

Again, we find the reasoning of the *Terra Nova* court to be more persuasive than the authorities cited by Gainsco. We agree that when an insurer tenders a defense or pays defense costs pursuant to a reservation of rights, the insurer is protecting itself at least as much as it is protecting its insured. Thus, we cannot say that an insured is unjustly enriched when its insurer tenders a defense in order to protect its own interests, even if it is later determined that the insurer did not owe a defense. . . .

Moreover, as the Supreme Court of Hawaii recognized, "affording an insured a defense under a reservation of rights agreement merely retains any defenses the insurer has under its policy; it does not relieve the insurer of the costs incurred in defending its insured where the insurer was obligated, in the first instance, to provide such a defense." *First Insurance Co. of Hawaii, Inc. v. State of Hawaii*, 665 P.2d 648, 654 (1983). Gainsco's reservation of rights letter could retain only those defenses that Gainsco had under its policy. Gainsco concedes that the insurance policies at issue did not provide for reimbursement of defense costs. Consequently, Gainsco's attempt to expand its reservation of rights to include the right to reimbursement must fail.

. . . Gainsco maintains that because it had no duty to defend, it follows that there is no contract governing the relationship between the parties. The problem with this argument is that Gainsco is attempting to define its duty to defend based upon the outcome of the declaratory judgment action. Although an insurer's duty to indemnify arises only after damages are fixed, the duty to defend arises as soon as damages are sought. . . .

. . . Because Gainsco's obligation to defend continued until the trial court found that Gainsco did not owe Midwest a defense, Gainsco is not entitled to reimbursement of defense costs paid pending the trial court's order in the declaratory judgment action. The fact that the trial court ultimately found that the underlying claims against Midwest were not covered by the Gainsco policies does not entitle Gainsco to reimbursement of its defense costs.

In sum, we acknowledge that a majority of jurisdictions have held that an insurer is entitled to reimbursement of defense costs when (1) the insurer did not have a duty to defend, (2) the insurer timely and expressly reserved its right to recoup defense costs, and (3) the insured either remains silent in the face of the reservation of rights or accepts the insurer's payment of defense costs. We choose, however, to follow the minority rule and refuse to permit an insurer to recover defense costs pursuant to a reservation of rights absent an express provision to that effect in the insurance contract between the parties.

For the foregoing reasons, then, we reverse the decisions of the circuit and appellate courts awarding Gainsco reimbursement of defense costs . . . expended for the defense of Midwest in the underlying litigation.

NOTES

(1) *Questions*. So far as the rulings in *Scottsdale Insurance* and in *General Agents* are opposed, in that one would permit an insurer to recover its defense cost

and the other would not, which is preferable? Does the answer depend substantially on equitable considerations?

(2) *Tactics.* When the holder of a liability coverage demands a defense, and the insurer believes it does not owe one, or doubts that it does, the insurer may make any of several moves, as depicted in *Nowacki*. It may reject the demand. Along with other risks, rejection entails the risk that the insured will mount a less effective defense than the insurer would. (The insured may calculate, and maybe rightly, that it has little to lose.) Other moves do not entail that risk. The insurer may simply accede to the demand. Some risks in doing that are indicated in the Note opening part B above (p. 323). The insurer may accede, but advise the insured that it is reserving its rights, including a right to reimbursement. A risk in doing that is illustrated in *General Agents.*

The insurer may see an advantage in having an issue of coverage resolved before adjudication of the action against the insured. One way is to intervene in that action, if not already a party, and request that the trial be bifurcated, deferring decision on the "underlying" claim. Another way is to institute a separate action for a declaratory judgment about coverage and the duty to defend. Either of these moves may affront the insured, who is embattled on "two fronts" at once. What advantage do they promise to the insurer? Does that advantage outweigh the affront?

For an insurer, perhaps the best of all possible worlds is an agreement with the insured, by which the insurer controls and pays for the defense but will be reimbursed if it can show that it had no duty to defend. As support for the reimbursement obligation some consideration is required. And the insured gives no consideration either by surrendering control of the defense or by promising to cooperate in the defense, for control and cooperation are already entitlements of the insurer. A provision in the New York General Obligations Law, § 5–1103, may make it possible to circumvent the requirement of consideration by amending the policy. But an insurer might be ill-advised to trust in that.

Assume that one of the tactics just described is preferable to the others, all things considered. Possibly the law could be arranged so as to nudge insurers in that direction. This thought suggests the questions *Which is preferable?*, *Why?*, and *How might the "nudging" be done?* Partial answers are suggested in the Note that follows.

(3) *A* vs. *B/UMC.* What has been called an "inherent" dilemma has been ascribed to uninsured motorists' insurance. Envisage a motorist, A, who holds that coverage under a policy issued by the UMC Company, and suffers loss from a collision with B's car. B does not hold liability coverage. A hopes for compensation from A or from UMC or from both. In the negligence action *A vs. B*, UMC seeks to intervene, hoping to establish that B was free of negligence. "The essential problem concerns the issue of whether the questions of contractual and tort liability should be resolved in a single action with a single outcome or in two actions with potentially conflicting outcomes.... The only justification offered in defense of limiting the right of intervention is the insurer's potential conflict of interest.... It is certainly unsettling for the insured [A] when that insurer [UMC] appears in court and presents itself in a thoroughly adversarial posture—indeed even taking up the defense of the other motorist's [B's] position and arguments." Chatterton v. Walker, 938 P.2d 255, 259, 261 (Utah 1997). In any litigated controversy between A and UMC, the court observed, each would have an incentive to engage in maneuvers designed to increase the other's expense, and so to force on the other a favorable

settlement—maneuvers collateral to the "real issue in dispute", the fact and amount of B's liability.

The court ruled that an insurer providing uninsured motorist coverage to an insured involved in an accident may intervene in an action by that motorist against another. To require separate actions, *A vs. B* and *A vs. UMC,* the court said, "merely multiplies the burdens placed on all parties without alleviating the dilemma faced by the insurer and without offering any genuine additional protection to the interests of the insured."

The court suggested measures to minimize the harm that conflicts of interest might threaten to the integrity of the tripartite proceeding. (In doing so, the court had earlier borrowed from a situation of conflicting interests in relation to a liability coverage.) "[T]he trial court can defuse these conflicts by requiring the insurer to furnish independent counsel to represent the insured on the insurer's claims and defenses, or by requiring reimbursement of the insured's reasonable attorney fees for those services."[1]

Compare the tactic which was said, in *Scottsdale Insurance* at p. 357, to be one which "in general should be discouraged for policy reasons."

(4) *Unjust Enrichment.* "[B]ecause there was an express written insurance contract between the parties, Gainsco cannot claim that it is entitled to recover defense costs under a theory of unjust enrichment." This key statement in *General Agents* has a kernel of truth, but is too comprehensive to be wholly convincing. It is true that one who has made an imprudent exchange agreement cannot charge the other party with liability in restitution for the difference in value between the performance of the other party and his own—cannot, that is, in the absence of some disruptive event. The court made an oblique reference to that principle in saying that Gainsco paid the defense costs "pursuant to the insurance policy."

Sometimes, however, the recipient of a contract performance *can* be charged in restitution, by the party who rendered it, and so be made to pay its value. Moreover, that value is sometimes determined by the utility of the performance in advancing the ends of the contract (to adapt words of Cardozo[2]). On that ground an insurer might recover its defense costs even if the defense were unsuccessful.

Possibly there was a disruptive event in *General Agents*, in that Midwest demanded a defense to which it was not entitled. If, however, the insurer adduced that as a reason for reimbursement, it would face the objection that restitution is not available to a "volunteer", one who confers a benefit on another without necessity or other justification. It hardly needs saying that one who confers a benefit under duress is not a volunteer. But insurers are not well situated to assert duress at the hands of their customers, even when subjected to insistent demands. "You should have turned down the demand" is the natural response to any such assertion. *Natural*, yes, but is it a *persuasive* response?

---

1. The passages excerpted from *Chatterson* appear on pp. 259–62. The final one is a quotation from Heisner v. Jones, 169 N.W.2d 606 (Neb. 1969) at 612.

2. See Buccini v. Paterno Construction Company, 170 N.E. 910 (N.Y.1930).

CHAPTER 7

EXCESS LIABILITY OF INSURERS: GOOD AND BAD FAITH, DEPRAVITY AND NEGLIGENCE

Rosina Crisci, the owner of an apartment building, was insured against liability by the Security Insurance Company. A tenant of hers, June DiMare, suffered physical and psychic injuries when a tread gave way under DiMare in a staircase in the building. After judgments were entered against Crisci for those injuries, Security Insurance paid $10,000 to DiMare. That was the upper limit of Crisci's liability coverage. Then Crisci, suing her insurer, won a judgment for $91,000. That amount was the difference between the amount of DiMare's judgments against her ($101,-000) and the policy limit. Crisci's recovery against Security Insurance was one of a type commonly known as "excess liability"—excess of the policy limit, that is. The reasoning on which it was affirmed is presented below, in Crisci v. Security Insurance Company.

Crisci's coverage was third-party insurance. Part A of this chapter concerns the grounds of excess liability imposed on issuers of third-party insurance. Analogous liabilities have been imposed on issuers of first-party insurance—fire insurance, life insurance, health insurance, and the like. For example, an insurer facing a claim for fire loss was said to be obligated to "investigate, negotiate, and attempt to settle the claim in a fair and reasonable manner", and subject to liability in excess of its policy limit for failing to do so. Farmland Mutual Ins. Co. v. Johnson, 36 S.W.3d 368, 375 (2000) (quoting). Part B concerns that and other grounds of excess liability imposed on issuers of first-party insurance. Similar statements of responsibility are commonplace in relation to those insurers; see the Note, *Statutory Standards (Reprise)*, at p. 410 below. But they are not in relation to issuers of third-party insurance.

A. BREACH OF THE DEFENSE OBLIGATION

While Security Insurance was conducting the defense of DiMare's actions against Crisci, it had an opportunity to settle them for $10,000, the policy limit, and later had an even more favorable opportunity to settle. The situation was one, often encountered, in which the interests of the parties were at odds. "[T]he insurer may have an incentive to decline the settlement offer and proceed to trial. The insurer may believe that it can win a verdict in its favor. In contrast, the policyholder may prefer to settle within the policy limits and avoid the risk of trial." Cramer v. Insurance Exchange Agency, 675 N.E.2d 897 (Ill. 1996). In *Crisci* the court spoke of the situation as one of "necessary conflict" between the interests of the insurer and the insured.

The perception of conflict is sharpened by reflecting on relative skills in negotiating. Experience in bargaining with suitors for the settlement of suits, such as insurers accumulate, is not unlike that in bargaining for other goods of uncertain value: it teaches that often the other party's first offer is not the best to hope for. This fact inclines an insurer to reject a suitor's first offer even though it is within the policy limit, whereas the insured may well fear that the first offer will prove to be the final one before the suit produces an outsize plaintiff's judgment, and so prefer that it be accepted. Dean Kent Syverud has acknowledged that for an insurer to decline an offer may produce a result that is harsh on the insured if its fear is realized. But reflection also suggested to him that buyers of insurance may, as a class, benefit from "strategic bargaining" by insurers. "If insurers failed to engage in strategic bargaining—if for example they accepted all demands falling below expected judgments without taking into account expected outcomes of further negotiations—claims costs would rise, and the premiums paid by all insureds would reflect the increase." Syverud, The Duty to Settle, 76 Va.L.Rev. 1113, 1152 (1990).

Notwithstanding the settlement offers made in DiMare vs. Crisci, Mrs. Crisci's insurer proceeded to trial of the action, hoping that it could limit DiMare's recovery to $3,000 at most. The best possible outcome of that action for the insurer was a liability at least $7,000 below its policy limit. The worst outcome was a liability of $10,000, assuming that any recovery by DiMare above that amount would be paid by Crisci, if at all. That was also the worst possible outcome for Crisci. The actual outcome, apart from "excess liability" on Security Insurance, was bad for it ($10,000 owed), and disastrous for Crisci ($91,000 owed). Maybe, when Security was deliberating over settling with DiMare, it should have paid less attention to its hopes and more to Crisci's fears. If so, its excess liability to Crisci has some foundation in fairness.

The doctrine of excess liability, in relation to liability insurance, has been anchored in contract law, notably in the duty of a contracting party to practice good faith and fair dealing in its performance. As long ago as 1882 it was said that the rule of good faith and fair dealing "should enter into and form a part of every insurance contract." Germania Ins. Co. v. Rudwig, 80 Ky. 223, 235. But the passage quoted had more to do with the formation and enforcement of a contract than with its performance, and the case was one about life insurance. The major impetus toward excess liability did not come until well into the 20th century.[1]

---

1. Scholarly literature on "bad faith" is a mountainous mass. A collection of 19 articles and essays citing other scholarly writings is in "Symposium on the law of Bad Faith in Contract and Insurance," 72 Tex.L.Rev. 1203 (1994). For a more detailed historical discussion, see Robert H. Jerry, "The Wrong Side of the Mountain: A Comment on Bad Faith's Unnatural History," 72 Tex.L.Rev. 1317 (1994). See also Stephen S. Ashley, "One Hundred Years of Bad Faith," 15 Bad Faith L. Rpt. 207 (1999) where the noted bad-faith commentator claims that Industrial & Gen. Trust v. Tod, 73 N.E. 7 (N.Y. 1905) is the earliest example of a court invoking an implied covenant of good faith and fair dealing.

The doctrine is sometimes anchored in tort law, and sometimes in the law of agency or, more broadly, in the law of fiduciary relations. It is sometimes attributed to a confluence of contract *and* tort law, as in Comunale v. Traders & General Ins. Co., presented at p. 140 above. "Tortious breach of contract" is the attempt of one court to capture the offenses recognized in *Comunale* and *Crisci*. Richardson v. Employers Liab. Assur. Corp., 102 Cal.Rptr. 547, 552 (Cal.App. 1972). Other combinations are possible. At one time the Kentucky Supreme Court spoke of an insurer's breach of covenant (to act in good faith) as making it a fiduciary, in which capacity it committed a tort. See Federal Kemper Ins. Co. v. Hornback, 711 S.W.2d 844, 845 (1986), referring to Feathers v. State Farm Fire & Cas. Co., 667 S.W.2d 693 (Ky.App. 1983). (But these were cases of first-party coverages, and *Hornback* disapproved the *Feathers* decision.)

These various connections between the doctrine of excess liability and broader legal categories may and may not have important effects on the shape of the doctrine. What effects they have, if any, is considered in the materials that follow. A further possibility is to be considered: the doctrine simply stands alone, not being derived from more general principles.

Development of the Doctrine

Prevalent policy language relating to settlements is this: "We may, at our discretion, investigate any 'occurrence' and settle any claim or 'suit' that may result."[2] If that had been the language of Rosina Crisci's policy, and if DeMare had brought suit against her some fifty years earlier, it might have been said that Security Insurance need not consider any interest other than its own in deciding whether or not to settle with them. For example, given comparable policy language, the New York Court of Appeals was asked, in 1923, to hold an insurer culpable for its failure to enter into a settlement, and answered that the insurer had done "what it had the legal right to do." Auerbach v. Maryland Cas. Co., 140 N.E. 577, 579.

No United States court would be so brusque today; it is established in every state that, on similar facts, an insurer will be liable if it fails to respect the interest of the insured by meeting this or that standard of conduct when presented with an opportunity to settle. Reasonable care is one standard, good faith is another. Five years after it issued the *Auerbach* opinion, the New York court "spoke out clearly on behalf of [the good-faith] standard, ... expressly distinguishing it from the negligence standard." Brown v. United States Fidelity & Guaranty Co., 314 F.2d 675, 678 (2d Cir. 1963). Soon after that the Wisconsin Supreme Court said:

> In express terms the contract imposes no duty at all a breach of which makes the insurer liable to the insured for a failure to settle or

---

2. Insurance Services Office standard form of the CGL policy.

Variations are as follows: "We reserve the right to investigate and settle any claim or lawsuit"; and "The Company shall defend any suit against the insured [but] may make such investigation, negotiation and settlements of any claim or suit as it deems expedient."

compromise a claim. However, *all courts are agreed* that the insurer *does owe to the insured some duty in this respect.*

Hilker v. Western Auto Ins. Co., 235 N.W. 413, 414 (Wis. 1931) (emphasis supplied). One can surmise that the courts' change of attitude was a response to new conditions, in which new liabilities began to emerge in conjunction with motoring and other everyday activities.

Another turning point in the development of excess liability has already been indicated: the 1958 opinion in Comunale v. Traders & General Ins. Co., 328 P.2d 198, 68 A.L.R.2d 883 (Cal.). A précis of the ruling there is as follows:

> It was there reasoned that in every contract, including policies of insurance, there is an implied covenant of good faith and fair dealing that neither party will do anything which will injure the right of the other to receive the benefits of the agreement; that it is common knowledge that one of the usual methods by which an insured receives protection under a liability insurance policy is by settlement of claims without litigation; that the implied obligation of good faith and fair dealing requires the insurer to settle in an appropriate case although the express terms of the policy do not impose the duty; that in determining whether to settle the insurer must give the interests of the insured at least as much consideration as it gives to its own interests; and that when "there is great risk of a recovery beyond the policy limits so that the most reasonable manner of disposing of the claim is a settlement which can be made within those limits, a consideration in good faith of the insured's interest requires the insurer to settle the claim."

This passage is drawn from the opinion in *Crisci*. The *Comunale* opinion is more fully represented at p. 140 above, and that in *Crisci* at p. 371 below.

Responding to Settlement Offers: Standards of Conduct

To say that an insurer must meet this or that standard of conduct when presented with an opportunity to settle, or that "some duty" is owed to the insured, leaves serious questions unanswered. In *Hilker* the Wisconsin court was able to dodge a principal one because it concluded that the insurer had failed to inform itself about the facts of the incident and injury on which the claim against its insured was based. An "inadequate, a careless if not shiftless, investigation", the court said. That being so, the court allowed a jury to charge the insurer with excess liability without setting any high standard of conduct to be observed. The insurer's decision not to settle should be an *honest* one, the court said. If more were to be expected, either reasonable care or good faith, this insurer never made it to the point of testing. "[I]t never at any time was in position to exercise a sound or good-faith judgment...." *Hilker* at 415.

Excess liability might conceivably be imposed on an insurer without regard to either negligence or bad faith, of course. In *Crisci* the court was asked to adopt this rule: "whenever an insurer receives an offer to settle within the policy limits and rejects it, the insurer [has] liability ... for the amount of any final judgment whether or not within the policy limits." (This strict liability rule was advocated by an *amicus curiae*.) The court had much to say in favor of the rule. It is a "simple one to apply". "[I]t will always be in the insured's interest to settle within the policy limits when there is any danger, however slight, of a judgment in excess of those limits. Accordingly ... it may not be unreasonable for an insured ... to believe that a sum of money equal to the limits is available and will be used so as to avoid liability on his part.... Moreover, it is not entirely clear that the proposed rule would place a burden on insurers substantially greater than that ... under existing law.... Finally, and most importantly, there is a more than a small amount of elementary justice in a rule that would require that, in this situation where the insurer's and insured's interests necessarily conflict, the insurer, which may reap the benefits of its determination not to settle, should also suffer the detriments of its decision."

Having said all that, the court refrained from adopting the proposal, for the insurer's liability could be based on other grounds. "We need not [] determine whether there might be some countervailing considerations...." Outside of law journals, the proposal is seldom advocated and has not been adopted in any court of last resort. (The West Virginia court has come closest, saying that proof of a failure to settle that has turned out to be imprudent makes a *prima facie* case of bad faith on the insurer's part. Shamblin v. Nationwide Mut. Ins. Co., 396 S.E.2d 766, 776 (W.Va. 1990).)

Summarizing to this point, one can say first that, when an insurer is engaged in defending its insured and has an opportunity to settle, it must to some extent defer to the interest of the insured; it cannot act in its own interest alone. But second, it does not face strict liability in excess of the policy limit for failing the settle. Excess liability is fastened on the insurer for disregard of the insured's interest at some level lying somewhere between these two extremes. The criterion of wrongful disregard may be negligence in one court, bad faith in another, and still another elsewhere.

As applied, these criteria sometimes blend into one another. How significant, then, are the differences? That is one question to be kept in mind. Another has to do with the sources of the criteria. Contract law and tort law are possible sources mentioned above. A liability for negligence is grounded in the law of torts, whereas one for bad faith in performing a promise is grounded in the law of contracts. If one must choose between these bodies of law, which of them provides the better basis for an insurer's excess liability? The opinion in *Comunale* drew on the law of contracts: "in every contract ... there is an implied covenant of good faith and fair dealing". 328 P.2d at 658. But the court kept one foot on tort law. The California court said later that "an action of the type involved here sounds in both contract and tort".

Both of the propositions just quoted are to be found in the following opinion. A careful reading will disclose why the court was not content with contract law alone as the basis for imposing liability on Security Insurance when it declined to settle with the DiMares for $10,000 or less.

Crisci v. Security Insurance Co.

California Supreme Court, 1967.
66 Cal.2d 425, 426 P.2d 173.

The facts underlying this appeal are indicated above, in part. They include a personal-injury action brought by June DiMare against Rosina Crisci. In that action DiMare alleged that a staircase tread in Crisci's house had broken under her, leaving her hanging 15 feet in the air. That, she said, was the cause of physical injury, a severe psychosis, and medical expenses, for all of which she sought damages of $400,000. DiMare's husband joined her in that action as a plaintiff. As indicated above, they won judgments for $101,000 in total, and were paid $10,000 by Crisci's insurer, Security.

This action was brought against Security not only for the unpaid amount of the DiMare judgment, but also for $25,000 on account of mental suffering inflicted on Crisci. Both amounts were said to be owed because Security had mishandled her defense in the DiMares' action.

■ Peters, Justice.

. . .

Mrs. Crisci had $10,000 of insurance coverage under a general liability policy issued by Security. The policy obligated Security to defend the suit against Mrs. Crisci and the company to make any settlement it deemed expedient.[1] Security hired an experienced lawyer, Mr. Healy, to handle the case. Both he and defendant's claims manager believed that unless evidence was discovered showing that Mrs. DiMare had a prior mental illness, a jury would probably find that the accident precipitated Mrs. DiMare's psychosis. And both men believed that if the jury felt that the fall triggered the psychosis, a verdict of not less than $100,000 would be returned.

An extensive search turned up no evidence that Mrs. DiMare had any prior mental abnormality. As a teenager Mrs. DiMare had been in a Washington mental hospital, but only to have an abortion. Both Mrs. DiMare and Mrs. Crisci found psychiatrists who would testify that the accident caused Mrs. DiMare's illness, and the insurance company knew of this testimony. Among those who felt the psychosis was not related to the accident were the doctors at the state mental hospital where Mrs. DiMare had been committed following the accident. All the psychiatrists agreed, however, that a psychosis could be triggered by a sudden fear of falling to one's death.

The exact chronology of settlement offers is not established by the record. However, by the time the DiMares' attorney reduced his settlement demands to $10,000, Security had doctors prepared to support its position and was only willing to pay $3,000 for Mrs. DiMare's physical injuries. Security was unwilling to pay one cent for the possibility of a plaintiff's

---

1. Mrs. Crisci's own attorney, Mr. Pardini, was consulted by the counsel for the insurance company, but Mr. Pardini did not direct or control either settlement negotiations or the defense of Mrs. DiMare's suit.

verdict on the mental illness issue. This conclusion was based on the assumption that the jury would believe all of the defendant's psychiatric evidence and none of the plaintiff's. Security also rejected a $9,000 settlement demand at a time when Mrs. Crisci offered to pay $2,500 of the settlement.

A jury awarded Mrs. DiMare $100,000 and her husband $1,000. After an [unsuccessful appeal] the insurance company paid $10,000 of this amount, the amount of its policy. The DiMares then sought to collect the balance from Mrs. Crisci. A settlement was arranged by which the DiMares received $22,000, a 40 percent interest in Mrs. Crisci's claim to a particular piece of property, and an assignment of Mrs. Crisci's cause of action against Security. Mrs. Crisci, an immigrant widow of 70, became indigent. She worked as a babysitter, and her grandchildren paid her rent. The change in her financial condition was accompanied by a decline in physical health, hysteria, and suicide attempts. [This action ensued.]

The liability of an insurer in excess of its policy limits for failure to accept a settlement offer within those limits was considered by this court in Comunale v. Traders & General Ins. Co., 328 P.2d 198, 68 A.L.R.2d 883. [Here the court recited the *Comunale* ruling as quoted at p. 369 above.]

In determining whether an insurer has given consideration to the interests of the insured, the test is whether a prudent insurer without policy limits would have accepted the settlement offer. Critz v. Farmers Ins. Group, 41 Cal.Rptr. 401 (Cal.App.) [and four other cases cited].

Several cases, in considering the liability of the insurer, contain language to the effect that bad faith is the equivalent of dishonesty, fraud, and concealment. (See *Critz* [and two other cases cited].) Obviously a showing that the insurer has been guilty of actual dishonesty, fraud, or concealment is relevant to the determination whether it has given consideration to the insured's interest in considering a settlement offer within the policy limits. The language used in the cases, however, should not be understood as meaning that in the absence of evidence establishing actual dishonesty, fraud, or concealment no recovery may be had for a judgment in excess of the policy limits. *Comunale* makes it clear that liability based on an implied covenant exists whenever the insurer refuses to settle in an appropriate case and that liability may exist when the insurer unwarrantedly refuses an offered settlement where the most reasonable manner of disposing of the claim is by accepting the settlement. Liability is imposed not for a bad faith breach of the contract but for failure to meet the duty to accept reasonable settlements, a duty included within the implied covenant of good faith and fair dealing. Moreover, [it is] clear that recovery may be based on unwarranted rejection of a reasonable settlement offer and that the absence of evidence, circumstantial or direct, showing actual dishonesty, fraud, or concealment, is not fatal to the cause of action.

Amicus curiae argues that, whenever an insurer receives an offer to settle within the policy limits and rejects it, the insurer should be liable in every case for the amount of any final judgment whether or not within the policy limits. As we have seen, the duty of the insurer to consider the insured's interest in settlement offers within the policy limits arises from an implied covenant in the contract, and ordinarily contract duties are strictly enforced and not subject to a standard of reasonableness. [The court continued with observations about the proposed rule some of which are quoted on p. 370 above. In addition, the court wrote about it as follows.] (I)t may not be unreasonable for an insured who purchases a policy with limits to believe that a sum of money equal to the limits is available and will be used so as to avoid liability on his part with regard to any covered accident. In view of such expectation an insurer should not be permitted to further its own interests by rejecting opportunities to settle within the policy limits unless it is also willing to absorb losses which may result from its failure to settle.... The size of the judgment recovered in the personal injury action when it exceeds the policy limits, although not conclusive, furnishes an inference that the value of the claim is the equivalent of the amount of the judgment and that acceptance of an offer within those limits was the most reasonable method of dealing with the claim.

... On the basis of these and other considerations, a number of commentators have urged that the insurer should be liable for any resulting judgment where it refuses to settle within the policy limits. [Here the court cited notes in several law reviews.]

We need not, however, here determine whether there might be some countervailing considerations precluding adoption of the proposed rule because, under *Comunale* and the cases following it, the evidence is clearly sufficient to support the determination that Security breached its duty to consider the interests of Mrs. Crisci in proposed settlements. Both Security's attorney and its claims manager agreed that if Mrs. DiMare won an award for her psychosis, that award would be at least $100,000. Security attempts to justify its rejection of a settlement by contending that it believed Mrs. DiMare had no chance of winning on the mental suffering issue. That belief in the circumstances present could be found to be unreasonable. Security was putting blind faith in the power of its psychiatrists to convince the jury when it knew that the accident could have caused the psychosis, that its agents had told it that without evidence of prior mental defects a jury was likely to believe the fall precipitated the psychosis, and that Mrs. DiMare had reputable psychiatrists on her side. Further, the company had been told by a psychiatrist that in a group of 24 psychiatrists, 12 could be found to support each side.

The trial court found that defendant "knew that there was a considerable risk of substantial recovery beyond said policy limits" and that "the defendant did not give as much consideration to the financial interests of its said insured as it gave to its own interests." That is all that was required. The award of $91,000 must therefore be affirmed.

We must next determine the propriety of the award to Mrs. Crisci of $25,000 for her mental suffering. In *Comunale* it was held that an action of the type involved here sounds in both contract and tort and that "where a case sounds both in contract and tort the plaintiff will ordinarily have freedom of election between an action of tort and one of contract.... An exception to this rule is made in suits for personal injury caused by negligence, where the tort character of the action is considered to prevail [citations], but no such exception is applied in cases, like the present one, which relate to financial damage [citations]."[3] Although this rule was applied in *Comunale* with regard to a statute of limitations, the rule is also applicable in determining liability.... Insofar as language in *Critz* v. *Farmers Ins. Group, supra*, 230 Cal.App.2d 788, 799, might be interpreted as providing that the action for wrongful refusal to settle sounds solely in contract, it is disapproved.

Fundamental in our jurisprudence is the principle that for every wrong there is a remedy and that an injured party should be compensated for all damage proximately caused by the wrongdoer. Although we recognize exceptions from these fundamental principles, no departure should be sanctioned unless there is a strong necessity therefor.

The general rule of damages in tort is that the injured party may recover for all detriment caused whether it could have been anticipated or not. Cal.Civ.Code § 3333. In accordance with the general rule, ... mental suffering constitutes an aggravation of damages when it naturally ensues from the act complained of, and in this connection mental suffering includes nervousness, grief, anxiety, worry, shock, humiliation and indignity as well as physical pain.... Such awards are not confined to cases where the mental suffering award was in addition to an award for personal injuries; damages for mental distress have also been awarded in cases where the tortious conduct was an interference with property rights without any personal injuries apart from the mental distress....

We are satisfied that a plaintiff who as a result of a defendant's tortious conduct loses his property and suffers mental distress may recover not only for the pecuniary loss but also for his mental distress.... Recovery of damages for mental suffering in the instant case does not mean that in every case of breach of contract the injured party may recover such damages. Here the breach also constitutes a tort. Moreover, plaintiff did not seek by the contract involved here to obtain a commercial advantage but to protect herself against the risks of accidental losses, including the mental distress which might follow from the losses. Among the considerations in purchasing liability insurance, as insurers are well aware, is the peace of mind and security it will provide in the event of an accidental loss, and recovery of damages for mental suffering has been permitted for breach of contracts which directly concern the comfort, happiness or personal esteem of one of the parties.

---

3. *Comunale* was mainly concerned with the contract aspect of the action. This may be due to the facts that the tort duty is ordinarily based on the insurer's assumption of the defense and of settlement negotiations (see Keeton, *Liability Insurance and Responsibility for Settlement* (1954) 67 Harv.L.Rev. 1136, 1138–1139; Note (1966), 18 Stan.L.Rev. 475), and that in *Comunale* the insurer did not undertake defense or settlement but denied coverage. In any event *Comunale* expressly recognizes that "wrongful refusal to settle has generally been treated as a tort." (50 Cal.2d at p. 663.)

It is not claimed that plaintiff's mental distress was not caused by defendant's refusal to settle or that the damages awarded were excessive in the light of plaintiff's substantial suffering.

The judgment is affirmed.

NOTES

(1) *Winners and Losers.* In the main case Mrs. Crisci was the suitor in name only, it seems. The beneficial claimants were the DiMares, to whom she had assigned her claim against Security. This arrangement is quite usual, according to a comment on the case. Levit, The *Crisci* Case . . . , 1968 Ins.L.J. 12, 13. The *Crisci* opinion leaves open, however, the possibility that Mrs. Crisci was the beneficial claimant as to her mental-suffering. Attempts to assign tort claims were ineffectual at one time, and are still open to some objections. Nothing in the opinion speaks to those objections. They would be serious ones under the law of some other states. See, for example, Electric Ins. Co. v. Nationwide Mut. Ins. Co., 384 F.Supp.2d 1190 (W.D.Tenn. 2005). There the court, quoting from an earlier opinion,* said:

> [A]lthough the *Can Do* Court noted that "contract-based chose[s] in action, except those involving matters purely personal in nature, [are] assignable" and that "tort actions involving injuries to property are also assignable," [it] specifically recognized that, under Tennessee law, "tort actions involving personal injuries and wrongs done to the person, reputation, or feelings of the injured party continue to be unassignable."

On that authority the court dismissed a claim for excess liability based on an assignment.

The assignment made by Mrs. Crisci to the DiMares was supported by Section 954 of the California Civil Code: "A thing in action, arising out of the violation of a right of property, or out of an obligation, may be transferred by the owner." See *Comunale.* How would her assignment stand under Tennessee law?

Persons insured against a liability, as Mrs. Crisci was, are not the only ones who have occasion to complain that an insurer has neglected an opportunity to settle. If the insured holds excess insurance, and neglect of the primary insurer—Insurer A—results in a liability exceeding its policy limit, part or all of that liability will fall on the excess insurer—Insurer B. Hence it may be that Insurer B will complain of mishandling of the defense by Insurer A. A complaint like that was made with success in St. Paul F. & M. Ins. Co. v. United States Fid. & Guar. Co., 375 N.E.2d 733 (N.Y. 1978). In *Electric Insurance* a similar claim failed for want of Tennessee authority that a primary carrier owes any duty to an excess carrier to settle a claim within the policy limit of the former. But the court saw no reason to dismiss a claim by the excess carrier, Electric, based on *subrogation* to the rights of the insured. (In *Crisci* the DiMares could hardly have maintained that they were subrogated to Mrs. Crisci's rights against Security Insurance.)

(2) *Control of the Defense.* Anyone hoping to justify excess liability, whether judge, advocate, or scholar, will want to show that insurers have brought it on themselves through the drafting of liability coverages. Commonplace policy provisions usable for this purpose have been collected in K. Syverud, *The Duty to Settle,* 76 Va.L.Rev. 1113 (1990), at 1118–19:

* Can Do, Inc. v. Manier, Herod, Hollabaugh & Smith, 922 S.W.2d 865 (Tenn. 1996).

Typically, the same part of the liability insurance contract that requires the company to defend the suit also gives the company control over the settlement decision.... Two other clauses ... restrict the insured's control over the settlement process. The cooperation clause permits the insured to pay amounts in settlement, in the absence of the company's consent, only at the insured's own expenses; the no-action clause effectively bars the insured from suing the company for indemnification should she negotiate a settlement without the consent of the insurance company. Together, these provisions allocate control over negotiation and settlement to the insurance company.

The Wisconsin Supreme Court used provisions like these when concluding that an insurer owes "some duty" to the insured with respect to settlements. "This duty is implied as a correlative duty growing out of certain rights and privileges which the contract confers upon the insurer. By the terms of this contract the absolute control of the defense of such actions is turned over to the insurer...." Hilker v. Western Auto. Ins. Co., 235 N.W. 413, 414 (1931). In Comunale v. Traders & General Ins. Co., the court spoke of insurer control in connection with bad-faith refusals to settle: "It is generally held that *since the insurer has reserved control over the litigation and settlement*, it is liable...." Id. at 201 (emphasis supplied). In Haddick v. Valor Insurance, p. 385 below, the court said that the basis for the duty to settle is "the insurer's exclusive control over settlement negotiations and defense of litigation." The New York Court of Appeals has used the fact of control to establish a link between agency law and excess liability: "At the root of the 'bad faith' doctrine is the fact that insurers typically exercise complete control over the settlement and defense of claims against their insureds, and, thus, under established agency principles may fairly be required to act in the insured's best interests." Pavia v. State Farm Mut. Auto. Ins. Co., 626 N.E.2d 24, 26 (1993).

In the *Crisci* opinion nothing is said about the control that Security Insurance exercised over the defense of Mrs. Crisci, and nothing about "established agency principles". Does this mean that the court overlooked an avenue to its decision? It was certainly preoccupied with generalities of tort and contract law, and with the particulars of evidence in the case.

(3) *Fiduciary or Not?* Whether or not a defending insurer can rightly be regarded as an agent of the insured is a disputed matter. See Miller v. Liberty Mut. Ins. Co., 393 F.Supp.2d 399, 407 (S.D.W.Va. 2005):

"When an insurer acts on behalf of the insured in the conduct of the litigation and settlement of claims, it assumes a fiduciary relationship and is obligated to act in good faith. As the champion of the insured, the insurer must consider the insured's interests as paramount rather than its own, and it may not gamble with the insured's funds." Eric Mills Holmes, 22 Holmes' Appleman on Insurance 2d § 137.1[B][3] (2002). As Holmes' treatise on insurance notes, the courts have not uniformly defined the capacity in which an insurer acts when settling an action, with some suggesting that an insurer acts as an independent contractor and others holding that an insurer acts as agent. Id. at § 137.2[K].

Did the court take one position or the other in *Crisci*? If so, which one?

In Farris v. United States Fidelity and Guaranty Co., 587 P.2d 1015 (Ore. 1978), the court declared that an insurer undertakes a fiduciary duty to its insured when it represents the insured as a defendant. But the court distinguished the case before it. The insurer had refused to provide a defense for the insureds. "It did not, in the course of representing plaintiffs, violate its fiduciary duty arising out of sole control of the settlement. It never undertook any fiduciary duty by purporting to act in the interests of the insured." Id. at 1019. Justice Lent, dissenting, cited authority for attaching a fiduciary duty to an insurer's *right* to control a defense, rather than to the *fact* of its control. He wrote: "what the majority has done is simply to pin a label on the insurer to be used when the insurer has been guilty of one kind of bad faith breach of its contract and to deny application of the label in other kinds of bad faith breaches." Id. at 1023, 1026–27.

The issue in *Farris* was liabilities of the insurer for mental suffering and for punitive damages. One advocating those liabilities, as Justice Lent did, might argue either (i) for applying the label "fiduciary" both to ineptitude in defending and to a refusal to defend, or (ii) for detaching the issue of liability from the conception *fiduciary*. Which is the better move?

(4) *Statutory Standards*. Legislation in almost all states has set standards for the conduct of insurers in relation to policy claims. Considerable uniformity has been achieved by the advocacy of the National Association of Commissioners of Insurance. See the Unfair Claims Settlement Practices Act, V NAIC Model Acts.... Section 4(D) of the Act, defining unfair practices, includes this:

> Not attempting in good faith to effectuate prompt, fair and equitable settlement of claims submitted in which liability has become reasonably clear.

The Unfair Claims Settlement Practices Act is more fully examined below, commencing at p. 400.

An Oregon statute, similar in many ways, contains the same language, following the introductory phrase, "No insurer ... shall commit or perform any of the following unfair claim settlement practices". Construing this language, the Oregon high court said in *Farris* that it "does not make clear whether the legislature contemplates only claims filed against an insurance company by its insured, as in the case of collision, fire or theft insurance, or whether it also contemplates the settlement of claims filed against its insureds by third parties, as in the case of liability insurance." Id. at 1017. In another section of the statute, however, the court found reason to believe that both types of claims were contemplated. That section refers to a "substantial increase in the number of lawsuits filed against ... insureds by claimants", as evidence of an insurer's "general business practice" of refusing, without just cause, to settle claims arising under its coverages.

This ruling in *Farris* may not be significant for the Model Act, for although that Act also refers to general business practices it does not refer to lawsuits against insureds. The matter is important because many states have enacted some version of the Model Act, and because in *Farris* the court relied on the Oregon statute to restrict the remedies available to an insured upon a wrongful refusal by its insurer to provide it with a defense. (More information about that ruling appears in n.2 at p. 398 below.)

However, regarding first-party insurance claims, as discussed in "Statutory Awards" at p. 401 below, some jurisdictions hold that their state unfair claims settlement practices statutes provide an implied private cause of action for damages for a violation. See, e.g., Mead v. Burns, 509 A.2d 11 (Conn. 1986); Holmgren v. State Farm Mut. Auto. Ins. Co., 976 F.2d 573 (9th Cir. 1992) (Montana law). In Farmland Mut. Ins. Co. v. Johnson, 36 S.W.3d 368 (Ky. 2000), for instance, the insureds filed a bad-faith failure-to-settle lawsuit under their first-party fire insurance policy and were awarded punitive damages of $2 million for violations of the Kentucky Unfair Claims Settlement Practices Act, Ky. Rev. Stat. § 304.12–230 (1, 4, 6, and 7).

(5) *Weighting the Interests.* In *Comunale* the court said: "The insurer, in deciding whether a claim should be compromised, must take into account the interest of the insured and give it at least as much consideration as it does to its own interest." Id. at 201. Much earlier, in *Hilker*, the Wisconsin court had intimated that an insurer may give paramount consideration to its own interest. Shortly before the decision in *Comunale* the Arizona court had found authority for various tests of the degree of consideration of an insured's interest required of an insurer in order to satisfy its obligation. "The principal difficulty experienced by the courts has been in fixing a test", the court said. Farmers Ins. Exch. v. Henderson, 313 P.2d 404, 406 (Ariz. 1957). It cited *Hilker*, and continued:

> Other jurisdictions have said paramount consideration must be given to protect the insured. A third position is that the insurer must give equal thought to the end that both the insured and the insurer shall be protected. The latter standard was adopted by the trial court and we approve.

Idem. (citations omitted).

Primacy for the interests of insureds seems most appropriate for a court that ascribes the duty to the fiduciary role of insurers. Which of the tests stated above is most compatible with ascribing the duty to an implied covenant of good faith and fair dealing? Is any of them indicated by the test announced in *Crisci*: "whether a prudent insurer without policy limits would have accepted the settlement offer"?

The test of "equal consideration" has an obvious appeal; it draws on the virtue of impartiality. It loses some luster, however, when an attempt is made to apply that test to analogous cases. Let it be supposed that A makes a claim against B for unpaid wages and that B denies they are due. Can it be said that B should pay *something*, on giving equal weight to A's interest in being paid and B's interest in paying nothing?

(6) *Negligence-based Liability.* In two states only, it seems, do the courts refuse to examine an insurer's failure to settle by reference to an obligation of good faith and fair dealing. There, instead, excess liability must be pinned on negligence. See Dumas v. Hartford Accident & Indemnity Co., 56 A.2d 57 (N.H. 1947), and Stowers Furniture Co. v. American Indemnity Co., 15 S.W.2d 544 (Tex.Com.App. 1929). "The duty of an insurer to exercise ordinary care in the settlement of claims to protect its insureds against judgments in excess of policy limits is generically referred to in Texas as the Stowers duty." American Physicians Ins. Exchange v. Garcia, 876 S.W.2d 842, 843 n.2 (Tex. 1994). Although the *Stowers* doctrine is a virtual antique, the Texas Supreme Court has said rather recently that it suffices to protect an insured against the mishandling of a claim by the insurer. "Imposing an additional duty on insurers in handling third-party claims is unnecessary and therefore inappropriate." Maryland Ins. Co. v. Head Indus. Coatings and Servs., Inc., 938 S.W.2d 27, 28 (Tex. 1996).

"Much ink has been spilled in an effort to define and to distinguish the rule of negligence from the rule of bad faith [Citations to "some of the more helpful discussions".] Perhaps the one conclusion upon which almost all authorities agree is that the distinction between negligence and bad faith in these insurance-settlement cases is more difficult to trace than most legal distinctions." Brown v. United States Fidelity & Guaranty Co., 314 F.2d 675, 677 (2d Cir. 1963) (New York law).

Sometimes a gulf is perceived between the standard of care and that of good faith, as applied to a charge of wrongful refusal to settle. That perception is accentuated when "bad faith" is restricted to cases of depravity, as in Centennial Ins. Co. v. Liberty Mut. Ins. Co., 404 N.E.2d 759 (Ohio 1980), at 762. On the other hand, the difference has been dismissed as insignificant. See Bollinger v. Nuss, 449 P.2d 502, 509–10 (Kan. 1969): "The dichotomy ... has tended to dissipate.... [E]ven those courts which reject the negligence test and apply exclusively the test of good faith [] consider the insurer's negligence relevant in determining whether or not the insurer exercised the requisite good faith." (As to negligence as "circumstantial evidence [of] indifference toward an insured's interest," see the opinion that follows.

In a "negligence-only" jurisdiction, would the decision in *Crisci* have come out differently?

———

Johnson v. Tennessee Farmers Mutual Ins. Co.

Tennessee Supreme Court, 2006.
205 S.W.3d 365.

■ Janice M. Holder, Justice.

. . .

I. FACTUAL AND PROCEDURAL BACKGROUND

On October 25, 1994, a collision occurred between a vehicle driven by Robert Steven Johnson ("Johnson") and a vehicle driven by Christopher Moore ("Moore"). Johnson was driving in the left inside lane when a van driven by an unknown motorist ("John Doe") suddenly moved left into his lane of traffic. In an attempt to avoid contact with the van, Johnson swerved left, crossing the median into oncoming traffic and colliding with Moore's vehicle. Moore and Johnson suffered serious injuries. Both Johnson and Moore were insured under separate liability policies issued by Tennessee Farmers Mutual Insurance Company ("Tennessee Farmers"). Both policies had minimum limits of liability coverage ($25,000/$50,000) and equal limits of uninsured motorist coverage.

Moore filed a lawsuit against Johnson.... [Both Moore and Johnson sued the unknown motorist, "Doe", with the apparent object of charging Tennessee Farmers with liability under the uninsured-motorist (UM) coverages of their policies. Tennessee Farmers settled these actions by paying to each suitor his UM-coverage policy limit.] Moore offered to settle his liability claim against Johnson for Johnson's policy limits of $25,000, but Tennessee Farmers refused.

Moore's action against Johnson resulted in a jury verdict in favor of Moore. The jury allocated 50% of the fault to Johnson and 50% to John Doe and awarded damages to Moore in the amount of $387,500. The judgment against Johnson, $193,750, exceeded Johnson's liability coverage of $25,000. Johnson unsuccessfully appealed the verdict. He subsequently filed a lawsuit against Tennessee Farmers alleging that the judgment against him in excess of his liability coverage was the result of Tennessee Farmers' bad faith in failing to adequately investigate and settle his case within the policy limits. Tennessee Farmers moved for a directed verdict, arguing that there was no evidence from which the jury could find that it acted in bad faith in refusing to settle Moore's claim against Johnson. The trial court denied the motion for a directed verdict. The jury determined that Tennessee Farmers acted in bad faith and awarded a judgment against Tennessee Farmers in the amount of $279,430.92 in compensatory damages. The Court of Appeals held that the trial court properly denied Tennessee Farmers' motion for a directed verdict but erred in failing to give four special jury instructions requested by Tennessee Farmers and in improperly commenting upon the evidence. The Court of Appeals reversed the judgment and remanded the case for a new trial. We granted review.

II. ANALYSIS

A. Directed Verdict

In reviewing the trial court's decision to deny a motion for a directed verdict, an appellate court must take the strongest legitimate view of the evidence in favor of the non-moving party, construing all evidence in that party's favor and disregarding all countervailing evidence. Gaston v. Tenn. Farmers Mut. Ins. Co., 120 S.W.3d 815, 819 (Tenn. 2003). A motion for a directed verdict should not be granted unless reasonable minds could reach only one conclusion from the evidence. Id. . . .

"It is well established that an insurer having exclusive control over the investigation and settlement of a claim may be held liable to its insured for an amount in excess of its policy limits if as a result of bad faith it fails to effect a settlement within the policy limits." State Auto. Ins. Co. of Columbus, Ohio v. Rowland, 427 S.W.2d 30, 33 (Tenn. 1968). Bad faith refusal to settle is defined, in part, as an insurer's disregard or demonstrable indifference toward the interests of its insured. . . . This indifference may be proved circumstantially. Bad faith on the part of the insurer can be proved by facts that tend to show "a willingness on the part of the insurer to gamble with the insured's money in an attempt to save its own money or any intentional disregard of the financial interests of the plaintiff in the hope of escaping full liability imposed upon it by its policy." Goings v. Aetna Cas. & Sur. Co., 491 S.W.2d 847, 849 (Tenn.App. 1972). If the claim exceeds the policy limits, then the insurer's conduct is subject to close scrutiny because there is a potential conflict of interest between the insurer and the insured. Tenn. Farmers Mut. Ins. Co. v. Wood, 277 F.2d 21, 35 (6th Cir. 1960).

To discharge its duty to act in good faith, an insurer must exercise ordinary care and diligence in investigating the claim and the extent of damage for which the insured may be held liable. . . . The manner in which the insurer investigates the case "has an important bearing upon the question of bad faith in refusing or failing to settle the claim." [Citation omitted.] Ordinary care and diligence in investigation require the insurer to investigate the claim to such an extent that it can exercise an honest judgment regarding whether the claim should be settled. Perry v. U.S. Fid. & Guar. Co., 359 S.W.2d 1, 6–7 (Tenn.App. 1962). Courts must review the facts that were known to the insurer and its agents and that should have been considered in deciding whether to settle. Id. at 7.

Mere negligence is not sufficient to impose liability for failure to settle.... Moreover, an insurer's mistaken judgment is not bad faith if it was made honestly and followed an investigation performed with ordinary care and diligence. *Perry*, 359 S.W.2d at 7. However, negligence may be considered along with other circumstantial evidence to suggest an indifference toward an insured's interest.... The question of an insurance company's bad faith is for the jury if from all of the evidence it appears that there is a reasonable basis for disagreement among reasonable minds as to the bad faith of the insurance company in the handling of the claim.

The evidence showed that the lanes of traffic at the scene of the accident were twelve feet wide, that the median was four feet wide, and that Johnson's car was five feet wide. According to deposition testimony, John Doe's van came, at most, about halfway, or six feet, into Johnson's lane. A jury, therefore, reasonably could find that Johnson had sufficient room to avoid John Doe's van without crossing the median and colliding with Moore's vehicle. Furthermore, deposition testimony revealed that Johnson may have been traveling in excess of the posted speed limit. Johnson's attorney, George Buxton ("Buxton"), summarized the deposition testimony and sent the summaries to the field claims representative Tennessee Farmers had assigned to investigate the accident, Dennis Hinkle ("Hinkle"). Hinkle, however, admitted that he did not read Buxton's deposition summaries in detail. Hinkle conceded that he was not aware of the lane measurements prior to trial, and he also conceded that had he been aware of all of the facts prior to trial, he would have been concerned that fault would be assessed against Johnson. At the time of depositions, Moore's medical bills totaled $66,412.35. Both Hinkle and Buxton were aware that any percentage of fault allocated to Johnson would result in an award in favor of Moore greatly in excess of Johnson's policy limits given the severity of Moore's injuries. See, e.g., *Rowland*, 427 S.W.2d at 34 (noting that bad faith " 'is most readily inferable when the severity of the plaintiff's injuries is such that any verdict against the insured is likely to be greatly in excess of the policy limits and further when the facts of the case indicate that a defendant's verdict on the issue of liability is doubtful' " (quoting Harris v. Standard Accident & Ins. Co., 191 F.Supp. 538, 540 (S.D.N.Y. 1961)).

Attorney Thomas Scott ("Scott") testified as an expert witness on behalf of Johnson. Scott testified that diligence required re-evaluation of Moore's claim after the depositions. Scott opined that after depositions had been taken, Tennessee Farmers had information that should have put it on notice that there was a significant chance of a judgment in excess of Johnson's liability policy limits. Scott further testified that, in his opinion, Tennessee Farmers failed to adequately evaluate the case, that it should have settled the case, and that its failure to do so was in bad faith. Taking the strongest legitimate view of the evidence in favor of Johnson, the non-moving party, a jury reasonably could conclude that Tennessee Farmers was indifferent to Johnson's financial exposure as evidenced by its failure to fully evaluate all facts and settlement options. Because there was sufficient evidence on which to base the jury's finding that Tennessee

Farmers was guilty of bad faith, the trial court did not err in permitting the jury to decide the issue.

B.   Jury Instructions

The trial court declined to give certain special jury instructions requested by Tennessee Farmers. A trial court should instruct the jury upon every issue of fact and theory of the case that is raised by the pleadings and is supported by the proof.... Reversal of a judgment is appropriate, however, only when the improper denial of a request for a special jury instruction has prejudiced the rights of the requesting party. It is not sufficient that refusal to grant the requested instruction *may* have affected the result; "[i]t must affirmatively appear that it did in fact do so." Otis v. Cambridge Mut. Fire Ins. Co., 850 S.W.2d 439, 446 (Tenn. 1992). Tennessee courts view the jury charge in its entirety and consider the charge as a whole in order to determine whether the trial judge committed prejudicial error. Id. It is not error to deny a requested instruction if its substance is covered in the general charge. Id. at 445.

1.   Special Jury Instruction Request No. 4

The fourth special jury instruction requested by Tennessee Farmers was as follows:

> Mere negligence on the part of an insurance company in failing to settle a claim against its insured is not sufficient to impose liability against the insurance company. Before an insurance company can be held liable for failing to compromise or settle a claim, the refusal to settle within the policy limit must be fraudulent or in bad faith.

... The trial court instructed the jury that

> "[B]ad faith" by the insurance company is, one, failure to investigate a claim to such an extent that it would be in a position to exercise honest judgment as to whether a claim should be settled, or two, failure to fairly consider the facts relative to the accident and a claimant's injuries known to it whether they are the actual facts or not and deciding whether the insured should or should not settle, or three, failure of the insured [sic] with the right to control the litigation and settlement to fairly consider the rights and interest of the insured as compared to the interest of the insurance company.

The trial court further explained that

> ... [I]f the insurer dealt fairly with the insured and acted honestly and according to its best judgment, it is not liable....

Finally, the trial court stated that

> [i]f Tennessee Farmers made an honest judgment and fair investigation of the claim against Robert Johnson and exercised reasonable judgment based upon that investigation, then a mistake in judgment is not bad faith and will not render it liable for failure to settle the claim. There's no duty to settle a claim merely because settlement could have been reached within the policy limits. If a failure to negotiate a settlement is a result of a reasonable business judgment made after

weighing all of the interests, then there is no liability, even if the decision not to settle turns out to be quite wrong.

The trial court's charge is a correct statement of the law....

2.   Special Jury Instruction Request No. 6

The sixth special jury instruction requested by Tennessee Farmers was as follows:

> Bad faith embraces more than bad judgment or negligence and it imports a dishonest purpose, moral obliquity, conscious wrongdoing, breach of a known duty through some ulterior motive or ill will partaking of the nature of fraud, and it embraces an actual intent to mislead or deceive another.

We are aware of no Tennessee cases holding that an insured must prove dishonest purpose [or the three evils specified after that], or an actual intent to mislead or deceive another to obtain a judgment for bad faith refusal to settle. Although this requested instruction properly states that "negligence" and "bad judgment" are not enough to establish bad faith, this instruction was adequately covered in the trial court's jury charge....

[The court considered one other requested instruction about refusal to settle, one "similar to ... Request No. 6 in suggesting that bad faith requires evidence that the insurer acted with dishonesty, ill will, or deceit." The court said, "Tennessee law does not require such proof to prevail in an action for bad faith refusal to settle. The trial court did not err in declining to charge this requested instruction."]

[The court took notice of an erroneous remark by the trial judge about Buxton, Johnson's attorney: "Everybody knew he was representing Tennessee Farmers." The court warned against judicial comments on the evidence: "Judges must be careful...."] The proof, however, clearly and repeatedly demonstrated Buxton's role ... and also Buxton's duty to investigate and report his findings to Tennessee Farmers. The jury charge also correctly stated Buxton's role....

... The jury is presumed to have followed the trial court's instructions.... Therefore, we hold that this comment by the trial court, although error, did not more probably than not affect the judgment or result in prejudice to the judicial process....

III.   CONCLUSION

We agree with the Court of Appeals that Tennessee Farmers' motion for a directed verdict was properly denied. We reverse the Court of Appeals' judgment setting aside the jury verdict and reinstate the jury verdict in favor of Johnson....

NOTES

(1) *"Bad Faith" and Depravity.* The instruction identified in the foregoing opinion as Request No. 6—"Bad faith embraces ..."—is a virtual rescript of a definition of "lack of good faith" to be found in Centennial Ins. Co. v. Liberty Mut. Ins. Co., 404 N.E.2d 759 (Ohio 1980), at 762. Some other courts also have set a high

bar to recoveries for refusals to settle. The New York Court of Appeals ruled that a recovery of punitive damages for bad faith requires "an extraordinary showing of a disingenuous or dishonest failure to carry out a contract." Gordon v. Nationwide Mutual Ins. Co., 285 N.E.2d 849, 854 (N.Y. 1972).

Similar tests of bad faith are applied elsewhere, as shown by cases about first-party coverages. In Pennsylvania, it is said, "In order to recover on a bad faith claim, a plaintiff must show both '(1) that the insurer lacked a reasonable basis for denying benefits; and (2) that the insurer knew or recklessly disregarded its lack of reasonable basis.' " (quoting). Williams v. Hartford Cas. Ins. Co., 83 F.Supp.2d 567, 571 (E.D.Pa. 2000). This combination of "prongs", called respectively *objective* and *subjective*, is a feature also of Wisconsin law. Lewis v. Paul Revere Life Ins. Co., 80 F.Supp.2d 978, 990 (E.D.Wis. 2000).

How does the Tennessee law of bad faith differ from those just quoted? What standard did the court apply in evaluating Tennessee Farmers's refusal to settle? What evidence was there that the insurer violated that standard?

(2) *Two Prudent–Insurer Tests.* According to the *Johnson* opinion, the negligence of an insurer is circumstantial evidence of "indifference toward an insured's interest." So far as one can tell, the standard of care to be applied has to do with the *actual* insurer: Did it act prudently in rejecting a settlement offer? An alternate standard of care has to do with a *hypothetical* insurer. According to the *Crisci* opinion, "the test is whether a prudent insurer *without policy limits* would have accepted the settlement offer."—emphasis supplied. That test has notable scholarly support. See R. Keeton, Liability Insurance and Responsibility for Settlement, 67 Harv.L.Rev. 1136 (1954), and K. Syverud, Duty to Settle, 76 Va.L.Rev. 1113, 1127 n.39 (1990).

Assume that a thoughtful claimant, when deciding on an amount to ask for a settlement, would take account of the test of prudence embodied in applicable law. Would the claimant be likely to ask more, or less, if the test is to be applied to a hypothetical ("without limits") insurer? Is the assumption correct?

What a thoughtful claimant might ask is complicated by the fact that the insured may and may not have assets at risk. It is complicated also by the fact that claimants are often necessitous. It has happened that an insurer was charged with excess liability for having been open-handed: it advanced payments to a claimant and so discouraged the claimant from settling within the policy limit. Bollam v. Fireman's Fund Ins. Co., 709 P.2d 1095 (Ore.App. 1985).

(3) *Probabilities.* The *Johnson* opinion mentions two calculations that should figure in an insurer's decision about a settlement offer: (i) the likelihood of success on the issue of liability, and (ii) the likelihood, if the claimant should succeed on that issue, of a recovery much in excess of the policy limit. See the court's quotation from State Auto. Ins. Co. v. Rowland about doubtful liability and severity of injuries. Those factors are not necessarily independent. In Syverud's *Duty to Settle* he said that juries are commonly asked to compare the amount of a settlement offer and the expected judgment, taking "expected judgment" to mean "the probability of a plaintiff's verdict multiplied by the likely damages should the plaintiff win." Id. at 1124. If the claimant has a thin chance of any recovery at all, the insurer might be allowed to use that fact to offset the possibility of a huge recovery. And a refusal to settle a strong case of liability might be justified by the fact that no recovery could exceed the policy limit by much. Both of these calculations are rosy prospects for insurers. But there is risk for an insurer in making either one. Is the risk

greater in the "weak claim/large damages" calculation or in the "strong claim/small damages" one?

(4) *Competence of Juries.* It must put some strain on a jury to ask it to put itself in the shoes of an insurer, whether an actual one or a hypothetical one, and to multiply what the insurer should have seen, at a time in the past, as the probable recovery by a plaintiff in a different suit, by the then probability of a verdict for that plaintiff. Too much to ask? The kinds of evidence often presented to aid juries in bad-faith cases are wide-ranging. A list of kinds appears in Brown v. United States Fidelity & Guar. Co., 314 F.2d 675 (2d Cir. 1963) (New York law). "By the time the jury retires to deliberate, it has been presented with a thorough description of how attorneys and claims adjustors evaluate the value of a lawsuit." Syverud, *op.cit. supra* at 1126.

————

Haddick, Special Adm'r v. Valor Insurance

Illinois Supreme Court, 2001.
198 Ill.2d 409, 763 N.E.2d 299.

■ JUSTICE GARMAN delivered the opinion of the court:

The issue in this case is at what point in time does an insurance provider's duty to settle arise. Plaintiff, Ella Haddick, as the special administrator of the estate of James Griffith, filed a single-count complaint against defendant, Valor Insurance, alleging that defendant acted in bad faith by failing to settle a claim against its policyholder within the policy limits. [Hereafter in this opinion the editors have inserted, in lieu of *plaintiff* and *defendant* as designations of the parties, the parties' names.] The trial court granted Valor's section 2–615 motion to dismiss the complaint and the appellate court reversed. We consider all well-pleaded facts contained in the allegations of the complaint and the exhibits attached thereto.

BACKGROUND

On May 6, 1996, James Griffith and Larry Woodley, Jr., were involved in a single-car accident, which resulted in Griffith's death. According to the police report, Woodley owned the vehicle and was driving the vehicle at the time of the accident. [At the hospital where Woodley had been taken, he told a police officer that he had been driving. The officer ticketed him for "driving under the influence". A week later Woodley told the officer that he did not remember the accident and did not know who had been driving.]

Woodley had liability coverage through Valor of $20,000 per person. On August 13, 1996, the attorney for the decedent's estate wrote Valor, informing the insurer that the decedent had incurred medical bills totaling $82,544.80 as a result of the accident. After the attorney made a demand for settlement, Valor responded by letter dated August 22, 1996, that it would discuss settlement after it received a copy of the police report. On November 1, 1996, Valor wrote to the attorney acknowledging receipt of the police report and indicating that an investigation was still pending to ascertain the actual driver of the vehicle. According to Valor, Woodley was still unable to recall the accident; therefore, upon completion of the police investigation, Valor would determine its position and a possible resolution of the claim.

On March 7, 1997, Haddick, decedent's mother, was named as the special administrator of his estate. By letter of the same date, she presented to Valor her claim against Woodley for wrongful death. Haddick demanded that Valor settle the claim for the policy limits within 14 days of receipt of the letter, otherwise she would "no longer settle [the] claim within the policy limits." Valor responded that the settlement demand was premature and that it was still investigating to determine who was driving the vehicle. Haddick subsequently extended the settlement deadline to April 7, 1997. When Valor did not offer to settle by the requested date, Haddick informed Valor by letter dated April 9, 1997, that she had filed a wrongful death suit and had "no intention of settling the case at this time."

Approximately one year later, Valor offered to settle the case for the policy limits. Haddick refused this offer. The trial court entered summary judgment in Haddick's favor on the issue of liability and, after trial, entered a judgment in the amount of $150,924.80.

Following the judgment, Woodley assigned all claims against his insurer to Haddick, who then filed the present action. Haddick alleged that Valor acted in bad faith by failing to settle her claim against Woodley within the policy limits. Pursuant to section 2–615 of the Code of Civil Procedure, the trial court dismissed the complaint, finding that Valor had no duty under Illinois law to settle the claim prior to suit being filed and that Haddick could not maintain a bad-faith claim once she withdrew her policy demand.

On review, the appellate court reversed. Citing Cernocky v. Indemnity Insurance Co. of North America, 69 Ill.App.2d 196, 207–08, 216 N.E.2d 198 (1966), the court concluded that the duty to settle is created by the "conception of the insurance contract" because the policyholder relinquishes his right to negotiate settlement on his own behalf when he enters into the contract. "Thus, the same threat exists to the policyholder that the insurer will wrongly refuse to settle within the policy limits and a judgment will be entered against him in excess of the policy whether the third party attempted to negotiate a settlement prior to or after filing suit." 315 Ill.App.3d at 757. Further, noting that many insurance contracts specifically provide for a duty to settle both before and after a suit is filed, the court opined that if it affirmed the trial court's blanket holding, "such a ruling could retroactively limit the duties of an insurer to a policyholder, which were bargained for in the insurance contract." 315 Ill.App.3d at 757. Finally, the court held that Haddick could maintain her cause of action for bad faith even though she revoked her offer to settle within the policy limits.

We granted defendant's petition for leave to appeal and allowed the Illinois Trial Lawyers Association to file an *amicus curiae* brief in support of Haddick.

ANALYSIS

. . .

This court has recognized that an insurance provider has a duty to act in good faith in responding to settlement offers. Cramer v. Insurance Exchange Agency, 174 Ill.2d 513, 526, 675 N.E.2d 897 (1996), citing Krutsinger v. Illinois Casualty Co., 10 Ill.2d 518, 527, 141 N.E.2d 16 (1957). If the insurer breaches this duty, it may be liable for the entire judgment against its insured, including any amount in excess of policy limits. *Cramer*, 174 Ill.2d at 526; Mid–America Bank & Trust Co. v. Commercial Union Insurance Co., 224 Ill.App.3d 1083, 1087, 587 N.E.2d 81 (1992); 14 Couch on Insurance § 203:12 (3d rev. ed. 1999).

An insurer derives the authority to engage in settlement negotiations from the language of the insurance contract. Generally, such language gives the insurer the right to "make such investigation, negotiation, and settlement of any claim or suit as it deems expedient." 14 Couch § 203:7. Therefore, the basis for the duty to settle is the insurer's exclusive control over settlement negotiations and defense of litigation. See *Cernocky*, 69 Ill.App.2d at 207; see also *Cramer*, 174 Ill.2d at 526 (policyholder relinquishes defense of suit); 14 Couch § 203:13 (insurer controls settlement negotiations). This exclusive control, however, necessarily results in a conflict of interest between the insurance provider and its insured. We explained in *Cramer* that:

> "In the typical 'duty to settle' case, the third party has sued the policyholder for an amount in excess of the policy limits but has offered to settle the claim against the policyholder for an amount equal to or less than those policy limits.

> "In this circumstance, the insurer may have an incentive to decline the settlement offer and proceed to trial. The insurer may believe that it can win a verdict in its favor. In contrast, the policyholder may prefer to settle within the policy limits and avoid the risk of trial. The insurer may ignore the policyholder's interest and decline to settle." *Cramer*, 174 Ill. 2d at 525–26.

In such cases, the insurance contract itself does not provide a remedy to the insured faced with a judgment in excess of policy limits; therefore, the law imposes upon the insurer the duty to settle in good faith. See *Cramer*, 174 Ill.2d at 526.

Valor relies upon language from *Cramer*, including the statement that "the 'duty to settle' arises because the policyholder has relinquished defense of the suit to the insurer" (*Cramer*, 174 Ill.2d at 526), to argue that the duty to settle derives from the duty to defend and, thus, does not arise until a lawsuit is filed. Valor also cites *Krutsinger*, 10 Ill.2d at 527, in which we noted that an insurer who undertakes defense of a suit against the policyholder, where the damages sought are in excess of policy limits, cannot arbitrarily refuse a settlement offer within the policy limits. Valor's argument is unpersuasive. In *Cramer*, this court considered whether a plaintiff could pursue a common law fraud action against his insurer arising from the purported cancellation of his insurance policy. *Krutsinger* involved a suit against an insurance company for failure to satisfy judgments against its insured. Neither case stands for the proposition that the duty to settle arises only after the filing of a lawsuit.

Haddick, on the other hand, argues that the duty to settle arises from the "conception of the insurance contract," *i.e.*, from the time the insurer and its insured enter into the policy. We also reject this argument.

When damages sought by a third party against the insured do not exceed policy limits, " 'the question of whether the claim be compromised or settled, or the manner in which it shall be defended, is a matter of no concern to the insured.' " Olympia Fields Country Club v. Bankers Indemnity Insurance Co., 325 Ill.App. 649, 670–71, 60 N.E.2d 896 (1945), quoting Hilker v. Western Automobile Insurance Co., 235 N.W. 413, 414 (1931). In such an instance, the insured is not at risk for personal liability. However, the insured becomes concerned with personal liability once a claim arises in which there is a reasonable probability that the insured will be found liable for an excess judgment. In this instance, the insurer must take the insured's settlement interests into consideration. See *Cernocky*, 69 Ill. App.2d at 206; Adduci v. Vigilant Insurance Co., 98 Ill.App.3d 472, 475, 424 N.E.2d 645 (1981) [and two other cases cited].

For example, in *Adduci*, the First District of the appellate court addressed whether the plaintiffs, assignees of the insured, alleged sufficient facts in their amended complaint to state a cause of action against an insurer for bad faith refusal to settle. The court noted that to state a cause of action for bad faith, the plaintiffs must allege that the duty to settle arose; the insurer breached the duty; and the breach caused injury to the insured. With respect to duty, the court found that the complaint alleged sufficient facts to establish the existence of the insurer's duty in that it alleged that the insurer was aware of the almost certain liability of the insured and that recovery in excess of policy limits was likely. *Adduci*, 98 Ill.App.3d at 476. Although the court in *Adduci* was not faced with the question we address in the case at bar, we find *Adduci* helpful to our analysis.

To survive a motion to dismiss a bad-faith claim, the plaintiff must allege facts sufficient to establish the existence of the duty to settle in good faith. The duty does not arise at the time the parties enter into the insurance contract, nor does it depend on whether or not a lawsuit has been filed. The duty of an insurance provider to settle arises when a claim has been made against the insured and there is a reasonable probability of recovery in excess of policy limits and a reasonable probability of a finding of liability against the insured. Since Illinois law generally does not require an insurance provider to initiate settlement negotiations[1] (*Adduci*, 98 Ill.App.3d at 478 [and two other cases cited]), this duty also does not arise until a third party demands settlement within policy limits.

---

1. There is an exception to this general rule where the probability of an adverse finding on liability is great and the amount of probable damages would greatly exceed policy limits. *Adduci*, 98 Ill.App.3d at 478.

Having established when the duty to settle arises, we turn now to the facts of this case as alleged in Haddick's complaint. Woodley's policy provides that defendant "may make such investigation and settlement of any claim or suit as it deems expedient." At the time of Haddick's March 7, 1997, settlement demand for the policy limits, Valor was aware that decedent's medical bills were in excess of $80,000. This amount clearly exceeded Woodley's $20,000 liability coverage. In addition, defendant possessed the police report, which indicated that Woodley had informed an emergency room doctor that he had been driving the vehicle at the time of the accident. Valor was further aware that Woodley owned the vehicle. Although Woodley subsequently informed a police officer that he could not remember who was driving the vehicle at the time of the accident, we must interpret the facts in the light most favorable to plaintiff. Additionally, in automobile injury cases, proof of ownership raises a presumption that the owner of the vehicle was in control of the vehicle at the time of the accident.... Since Woodley was unable to recall the accident at the time of Haddick's settlement demand, he would have been unable to rebut this presumption.

We conclude that these facts allege a reasonable probability of recovery in excess of policy limits and a reasonable probability of a finding of liability against Woodley. Haddick demanded settlement on March 7, 1997. Therefore, the allegations are sufficient to allege the existence of the duty to settle in good faith on that date.

Finally, the trial court, without explanation, held that Haddick could not maintain her bad-faith claim because she withdrew her demand for settlement within policy limits. We disagree. Once the duty of the insurer to settle arises, the next question is whether the insurer breached that duty. Haddick alleged in her complaint that on March 7, 1997, she demanded that Valor settle her claim for the policy limits of $20,000 within 14 days of receipt of the demand. Valor responded that the demand was premature and that it was still investigating to determine the driver of the vehicle. Haddick extended the time for settlement to April 7, 1997. Valor failed to respond to this extension; consequently, Haddick withdrew her offer and filed suit. Thus, Haddick allowed Valor about one month to settle the claim and approximately 11 months to investigate the accident. Valor did not offer to settle for the policy limits until April 1, 1998, almost one year after Haddick withdrew her settlement demand. We conclude that these facts, along with others alleged in the complaint, are sufficient to allege a breach of the duty to settle in good faith.

... Our decision today affirms the appellate court's holding, but rejects its blanket conclusion that the duty to settle arises from the "conception of the insurance contract." We conclude that an insurance provider's duty to settle arises once a third-party claimant has made a demand for settlement of a claim within policy limits and, at the time of the demand, there is a reasonable probability of recovery in excess of policy limits and a reasonable probability of a finding of liability against its insured. For these reasons we affirm the judgment of the appellate court, which reversed the judgment of the circuit court and remanded the cause for further proceedings.

NOTES

(1) *Triggering the Duty to Settle.* The duty of a liability insurer to indemnify the insured cannot be performed, and so cannot be violated, until a liability has been established against the insured, either by a settlement or by a judgment. Everyone would say, however, that the duty arises from the contract, and no later than the "conception" of the insurance contract. How different is the insurer's duty to act properly about settlement negotiations? It is widely supposed that that duty also inheres in the insurance contract, although it cannot well be performed or violated before a claim, or the prospect of one, is in sight.

In Haddick's case the court ruled that it was possible for Valor Insurance to violate its duty respecting settlement on March 7, 1997, when she offered to settle for $20,000. In August of 1996, we are told, the attorney for the Griffith estate made a demand for settlement. That was on or after Valor heard of medical bills of $82,544.50, but before it had learned of the police report. If the attorney's "demand" named the price of a settlement, was it possible then for Valor to violate its duty? If not, when did it become possible?

(2) *More on Jury Competence.* Near the end of her opinion, Justice Garman issued a caution that the liability of Valor to Haddick for failing to settle, if any, had yet to be decided by the finder of fact. "We express no view with respect to Valor's actions."

Assume that a jury is to be asked to compare Haddick's 1997 settlement offer and the "expected judgment". (See Note 3, p. 384 above, and take *expected judgment* to mean Probability of a verdict for Haddick x Likely damages if she should win.) How easy would the jury find it to make that comparison, based on the facts given in the opinion?

(3) *Insurer's Duty of Initiate Settlement Negotiations.* Generally, the court said, Illinois law "does not require an insurance provider to initiate settlement negotiations." That is consistent with language in the current CGL standard policy form: "We may, at our discretion, ... settle...." Cases in accord and those to the contrary are collected in Anno., 51 A.L.R.5th 701 (1997, updated to Feb. 2007).

One of special interest is American Physicians Ins. Exchange v. Garcia, 876 S.W.2d 842, 51 A.L.R.5th 899 (Tex. 1994). The court said that "the public interest favoring early dispute resolution supports our decision not to shift the burden of making settlement offers ... onto insurers." Id. at 852. The court reached that conclusion by examining the "negotiating incentives" of the parties. In paraphrase, the court's description of those incentives is as follows. ("R" is used here to indicate the insurer, "D" the insured, and "C" the one claiming against D.)

– R may well defer making an offer because it will establish a "floor" amount for settlement. R must reckon, as C knows, on a heightened risk of excess liability if it should thereafter cheapen the offer, or withdraw it.

– An offer made by R well before trial will not be tempting to C if the offer is substantially less than the policy limit because C can expect that R, under the threat of excess liability, will offer more. "Therefore, a claimant will have an incentive to 'play chicken' with the insurer in anticipation that the final offer on the eve of trial will equal either the policy limits or the insurer's reservation price...."

– Even an offer at the policy limit may not tempt C until C has determined that D is unable to pay anything above that limit from assets in hand.

Might it be well, nevertheless, to require that an insurer announce to a claimant that it is open to a settlement offer? Is anything to be lost by that? Anything to be gained? In *Garcia* the court said: "we think claimants are perfectly capable of transmitting suitable settlement demands without assistance from the other side." Id. at 850.

(4) *Reverse Bad Faith*. On occasion an insurer has made a claim against its insured asserting that it was the victim of bad faith on the part of the insured. One instance concerned coverage of the loss of a truck by theft. Tokles & Son, Inc. v. Midwestern Indem. Co., 605 N.E.2d 936 (Ohio 1992). Midwestern asked the court to recognize a reverse-bad-faith claim "whereby an insurer could assert a cause of action against an insured when the insured willfully submits a fraudulent claim and then sues the insurer in tort for the insurer's 'bad faith' in refusing to pay the fraudulent claim."

There is some support for that sort of claim in law journals, but none in an appellate court. One might think that an insured is bound, as insurers are, by the duty of good faith. If bad-faith doctrine is a one-way street, what justification can be given? In *Tokles & Son* the court suggested one: insurers have other means to combat fraudulent claims, one being a refusal to pay. The court hinted at a more general justification: that an insurer is in a dominant position *vis-a-vis* the insured. The insurer is the "holder of the purse strings"; and often the insured "finds himself in dire financial straits after the loss". Id. at 945. Persuasive?

"The strongest argument for recognizing a reverse bad faith cause of action can be made," according to one observer, "where the insured commits fraud when making a claim under a first-party policy." D. Richmond, The Two–Way Street . . . , 28 Loy.U.Chi.L.J. 95, 141 (1996). One can, however, envisage undue stubbornness on the part of a holder of liability coverage which leads to a needless payment by the insurer. Suppose that the coverage is limited by a large deductible, that the insured has been held liable in an amount larger than the deductible amount, and that the insured refused to pay for a settlement at a smaller amount. Would that constitute undue stubbornness if the insured was intent on vindicating its reputation by defeating altogether the claim against it?

B.   First-Party Insurance

Mrs. Edward Santilli was the beneficiary named on a policy of life insurance on the life of her husband. When, after his death, the insurer refused to pay, she brought an action against it for (i) the amount due under the policy and attorney fees, and (ii) compensatory and punitive damages for an alleged bad faith failure to pay her claim. On appeal, the court reversed a summary judgment for the insurer on the first cause of action. As to the second, it ruled that the trial court had not committed reversible error in sustaining a demurrer. Along the way, the court said:

> Plaintiff seeks to have this court recognize a cause of action for tortious breach of an insurer's duty of "good faith and fair dealing" when dealing with its insured. This is a distinct tort which has recently emerged in California and has subsequently found favor in some other

jurisdictions. This tort developed as an outgrowth of the cause of action for an insurer's bad faith refusal to settle within the coverage limits of a liability insurance policy. However, although the two situations are somewhat similar, there is a distinct difference between liability insurance and other types of policies which should not be overlooked. [The court described reasons for imposing on insurers "a high duty of good faith and fair dealing when conducting settlement negotiations on behalf of their insured."] Such considerations are not applicable outside the field of liability insurance. In cases involving the insurer's duty to pay under policies for theft, fire, health, disability or life insurance, the unique relationship which gives rise to the special duty of liability insurers to attempt to settle within their policy limits does not arise. The insured, or his beneficiary, is not subject to the imposition of excess liability, and his rights and responsibilities are limited to those set forth in his contract.

Santilli v. State Farm Life Ins. Co., 562 P.2d 965, 969 (Ore. 1977).

As indicated in the passage quoted, courts in California led the way in the opposite direction. The leading case there is Gruenberg v. Aetna Ins. Co., 510 P.2d 1032 (Cal. 1973), about the duty of insurers to pay under their coverages of fire loss. A sentence drawn from the *Gruenberg* opinion brings the opposition into focus. The court referred to the duty of a liability insurer with respect to settlement offers, as recognized in its earlier decisions in *Comunale* and in *Crisci* (p. 371 above), and said: "These are merely two different aspects of the same duty." Id. at 1037.

Gruenberg established a trend now followed by courts in almost all other states. The trend is represented here by the case that follows, *Grand Sheet Metal*. There the court described *Gruenberg* as follows:

> Gruenberg's cocktail lounge and restaurant were destroyed by fire . . . and shortly thereafter he was arrested by a member of the arson detail. The insurer's adjuster told an arson investigator that Gruenberg was carrying excessive fire insurance on the premises. Charges were dismissed and Gruenberg then agreed to an examination by the insurer, which he had earlier refused because of the pending criminal charges. The insurer denied liability and refused to pay. Gruenberg's suit claimed that the defendants wilfully and maliciously entered into a scheme to deprive him of the benefit of his insurance policies by falsely charging a motive to commit arson and encouraging criminal charges against him. [T]he California Supreme Court found that in every contract of insurance the duty "to act in good faith and fairly in handling the claim of an insured, namely a duty not to withhold unreasonably payments due under a policy" was necessarily implied.

Gruenberg contended that he had suffered a loss of earnings and severe emotional upset by reason of the "outrageous conduct" of his insurers. (Three insurers were among the defendants.) He sought compensatory and punitive damages. The trial court sustained a demurrer filed by the insurers. *Held*: Reversed.

As late as 2004 the California high court was rehearsing its reasoning in *Gruenberg* and its sequels. Jonathan Neil & Assoc., Inc. v. Jones, 94 P.3d 1055 (Cal. 2004). (But see p. 395, Note 1 below.)

Introductory Note to *Grant Sheet Metal*

Although the opinion below does not say so explicitly, evidently the defendant insurer demurred in this case to portions of the complaint by Grand Sheet Metal. Apparently those portions claimed damages "beyond the claimed amount of the policies in question". The opinion does not say what type or types those damages were. It does not say either why the court referred to "policies", the plural. Apart from those omissions, the purport of the opinion seems clear enough.

Grand Sheet Metal Products Co. v. Protection Mutual Ins. Co.

Connecticut Superior Court, 1977.
34 Conn.Supp. 46, 375 A.2d 428.

Superior Court of Connecticut, Fairfield County.

■ Hull, J.

The plaintiff, seeking recovery against its claimed fire insurer and insurance agent, pleads a cause of action against the insurer Protection Mutual Insurance Company, beyond the claimed amount of the policies in question, on the grounds of bad faith and oppressive business conduct. . . .

The plaintiff is asserting a tortious breach of contract based on a tort claim separate from any claim for breach of contract. In so doing, the plaintiff is attempting to import into Connecticut law the theory, if not the exact language, of the landmark California case of Gruenberg v. Aetna Ins. Co., 9 Cal.3d 566, wherein the California Supreme Court held (p. 575): "It is manifest that a common legal principle underlies all of the foregoing decisions; namely, that in every insurance contract there is an implied covenant of good faith and fair dealing. The duty to so act is immanent in the contract whether the company is attending to the claims of third persons against the insured or the claims of the insured itself. Accordingly, when the insurer unreasonably and in bad faith withholds payment of the claim of its insured, it is subject to liability in tort." In so holding, the California court built on its previous position that the failure of an insurer to accept a reasonable settlement within the policy limits, in violation of its duty to consider in good faith the interest of the insured in settlement, would make the insurer liable for the entire judgment against the insured if over the policy limits.

The *Gruenberg* court summed up the application of the good-faith-settlement rule to claims of an insured against an insurer as follows: "Thus in *Comunale* and *Crisci* we made it clear that '[l]iability is imposed [on the insurer] not for a bad faith breach of contract but for failure to meet the duty to accept reasonable settlements, a duty included within the implied covenant of good faith and fair dealing' ... [Crisci v. Security Ins. Co., 66 Cal. 2d 425, 430]. In those two cases, we considered the duty of the insurer to act in good faith and fairly in handling the claims of third persons against the insured, described as a 'duty to accept reasonable settlements'; in the case before us we consider the duty of an insurer to act in good faith and fairly in handling the claim of an insured, namely a duty not to withhold unreasonably payments due under a policy. These are merely two different aspects of the same duty. That responsibility is not the require-ment mandated by the terms of the policy itself—to defend, settle, or pay. It is the obligation, deemed to be imposed by the law, under which the insurer must act fairly and in good faith in discharging its contractual responsibilities. Where in so doing, it fails to deal *fairly and in good faith* with its insured by refusing, without proper cause, to compensate its insured for a loss covered by the policy, such conduct may give rise to a cause of action in tort for breach of an implied covenant of good faith and fair dealing.''

The question raised by the demurrer is whether Connecticut law is or ought to be in conformity with *Gruenberg* and the authority supporting it. Each party admits that there is no Connecticut authority either supporting or opposing such an implied duty of good faith and fair dealing between the insurer and the insured.

Clearly the obligation to accept a good-faith settlement within the policy limits is the law in Connecticut.... The court is faced with the difficult problem of deciding whether it should knock out the type of claim raised in *Gruenberg* because there is no case approving such a cause of action in Connecticut, or, in view of the lack of a clear prohibition against such claims in Connecticut, whether it should consider the matter in the light of developing law and sound public policy. The court will choose the latter course.... Absent some bar, which does not exist here, is it not [] the duty of the trial court to forge new paths if based on convincing legal theory?

The defendant argues, citing the dissent of Roth, J. in Gruenberg v. Aetna Ins. Co., 9 Cal.3d 566, 581, that to make the jump from good faith and fair dealing as regards third parties to such liability for first-party dealings requires a fiduciary relationship. But that is not so if sound logic dictates that the *Gruenberg* obligation is necessarily implicit in every insurance contract. The developing theories in this area often represent an overlapping of contract and tort law with some inevitable confusion. One approach to the problem may be an extension of compensatory and punitive damages in contract actions. This court, however, prefers to follow *Gruen-berg* in focusing on a distinct tort cause of action.

[Here the court described *Gruenberg*, as quoted above.]

The first out-of-state case to rely on *Gruenberg* and its California progenitors is Ledingham v. Blue Cross Plan, 29 Ill.App.3d 339. That case involved a denial of health insurance benefits and, while adopting the *Gruenberg* rationale, it relied heavily on certain strong health insurance precedents in both Illinois and California. A later case, United States

Fidelity & Guaranty Co. v. Peterson, 91 Nev. 617, is of particular cogency in the present case. The insured Peterson sued the insurer to recover consequential damages because of the insurer's bad-faith refusal to pay for damage caused by the insured during construction, which refusal caused the insured to lose his business and his credit. The Nevada Supreme Court adopted *Gruenberg* four square stating (p. 619): "We approve and adopt the rule that allows recovery of consequential damages where there has been a showing of bad faith by the insurer. Where an insurer fails to deal fairly and in good faith with its insured by refusing without proper cause to compensate its insured for a loss covered by the policy such conduct may give rise to a cause of action in tort for breach of an implied covenant of good faith and fair dealing. The duty violated arises not from the terms of the insurance contract but is a duty imposed by law, the violation of which is a tort. Silberg v. California Insurance Company [11 Cal.3d 452] ... (1974); Gruenberg v. Aetna Insurance Company [9 Cal.3d 566] ... (1973); see also concurring opinion Fisher v. Executive Fund Life Ins. Co., 88 Nev. 704 ... (1972). The evidence bearing on the issue of consequential damages was properly admitted."

This court likewise adopts the *Gruenberg* rule.... Suffice it to say that the unequal bargaining power of the parties, the special nature of the insurance business, and the disastrous economic effects that a bad-faith refusal to pay may cause the insured are paramount considerations. And the question of the allowability of punitive damages or damages of any nature beyond the policy limits in the traditional contract action means that fundamental fairness in today's economy requires a separate tort action.

[The court expressed a reservation about the word "oppressive", as frequently used in the complaint.] That language may well confuse the legal issue and would appear to add nothing to the clear mandate of the good-faith-and-fair-dealing rule.

For the reasons stated the demurrer is overruled.

NOTES

(1) *Beyond the Bounds—I*. In *Jonathan Neil*, p. 393 above, the California high court disapproved tort remedies against an insurer for breach of its implied covenant of good faith and fair dealing. The court was careful to circumscribe its ruling to the situation before it, one of alleged over-billing of a premium, and a retroactive premium at that. A reason the court gave is that a billing dispute "does not, by itself, deny the insured the benefits of the insurance policy...." Another is that "traditional tort remedies may be available to the insured who is wrongfully billed a retroactive premium." The policyholders claimed that the over-billing had cost them profits when it forced them to shut down their business. But lost profits could be recovered as *contract* damages, the court observed, if the loss was a natural and direct consequence of breach. And the court mentioned possibilities of recovery by way of torts not peculiar to insurance law: intentional interference with prospective economic advantage, defamation, and malicious prosecution. See 94 P.3d at 1069–70.

In the main case did the court give any reasons for its ruling that do not apply to *Jonathan Neil*?

(2) *Beyond the Bounds—II.* Ridgaway died in a collision allegedly caused by the drunkenness of a driver. His estate and survivors brought an action against insurance agents and brokers, charging them with having failed, as agreed, to arrange liability insurance for a liquor dealer, insurance that would have provided the suitors with enhanced recoveries. The suitors asserted a tortious breach of contract, as exemplified in *Grand Sheet Metal*. Ridgaway v. Cowles & Connell, 2004 WL 2595814 (Conn.Super. 2004). The court struck those parts of the complaint (and all others), saying, "Because the claims asserted . . . do not rest on a direct contract relationship and because the court concludes a third-party beneficiary relationship has not been alleged, these counts do not state claims upon which relief may be granted." Also: "While a duty may run under the common-law tort of bad faith to the insureds, it cannot run to those who cannot bring themselves within the rubric of claiming third-party beneficiary status, pursuant to these allegations."

Apparently the court left open the way for tortious breach of a life-insurance contract to be asserted by a beneficiary who knew nothing of the policy before the death of the CQV. Should that be beyond the bounds?

Silberg's Case and a Question of Custom

Following a work-related injury, Enrique Silberg required a number of hospital treatments and suffered disaster after disaster. He filed a claim for workers' compensation. In addition to workers' comp insurance, he held a Cal Life policy of medical-expense insurance, on which he also filed a claim. The workers' comp carrier deferred paying because it had reason to doubt that Silberg had been acting as an employee at the time of the injury. Cal Life also dragged its feet about paying. The reason was an exclusion in its policy: "This policy does not cover any loss caused by or resulting from injury . . . for which compensation is payable under any Workmen's Compensation Law." Nearly two years after the injury Silberg received a payment from the workers' comp carrier which included about $1,000 for hospital expenses. That left more than $5,000 of those expenses unpaid. The payment was a compromise, not based on any official determination about Silberg's entitlement.

Silberg brought an action against Cal Life, charging it with bad faith and claiming damages for physical and mental distress. A witness for Silberg testified that the prevailing practice of insurers in cases like his was to pay a claim if the workers' comp carrier denied liability, hoping to recoup at least some of the payment from any workers' comp award that might follow. Witnesses for Cal Life testified to the contrary: the custom was to reject a claim or to suspend payment on it until final decision about workers' comp coverage. A jury returned a verdict of $75,000 as compensatory damages for the asserted bad faith of the insurer. The trial judge rejected that award, saying that there was no evidence that, when the insurer issued the policy, it knew or should have known how, in the circumstances, a court would deal with the exclusion.

On appeal, the trial court's grant of a new trial on the issue of compensatory damages was reversed. Silberg v. California Life Ins. Co., 521 P.2d 1103 (Cal. 1974). As to the custom of insurers, the court said that Silberg's claim should prevail even though his evidence failed to establish a custom of being more freehanded than Cal Life was. Part of the court's opinion (Mosk, J.) is as follows.

. . .

[T]he company's policy application declared in large, heavy type, "Protect Yourself Against the Medical Bills That Can Ruin You." Plaintiff's application, filed shortly before the accident, indicated that he had no other hospital or disability insurance. . . . Defendant was aware [when it withheld payment] that plaintiff earned only a modest income and had incurred substantial medical and hospital bills. The company also knew that there was a serious question whether plaintiff would qualify for workmen's compensation benefits, and that the compensation carrier had consistently denied coverage on the ground that plaintiff was not an employee at the time of the accident.

There is no question that if defendant had paid the hospital charges and it was ultimately determined workmen's compensation covered the injury, defendant could have asserted a lien in the workmen's compensation proceeding to recover the payments it had made and it would have been entitled to payment from the proceeds of the award. . . .

No explanation was advanced by defendant as to why it failed to adopt this course in order to vindicate the promise made in the application that the policy was intended to protect the insured against medical bills which could result in financial ruin. Defendant's attitude toward the payment of plaintiff's claim was . . . merely that it was entitled to wait until the pending compensation proceeding was concluded before it paid or denied the claim. The company failed to see a conflict with its express promise to protect against ruinous medical bills.

. . .

Under these circumstances defendant's failure to afford relief to its insured against the very eventuality insured against by the policy amounts to a violation as a matter of law of its duty of good faith and fair dealing implied in every policy. Thus, we conclude the trial court abused its discretion in granting a new trial [as to] compensatory damages.

NOTES

(1) *Questions*. How important was it to the decision that Cal Life began bargaining with Silberg with "**PROTECT YOURSELF** . . ."? How important was it that, when Cal Life withheld payment, Silberg was under financial strain, and that Cal Life knew that?

(2) *Custom*. In Silberg's case the court ruled that deviation by Cal Life from industry custom was not an essential element of his claim. It is a different question whether or not *compliance* with custom is a conclusive answer to a bad-faith claim. Supposing that the jury in Silberg's case had believed Cal Life's evidence about the

custom of insurers in like circumstances, might it have been warranted anyway in awarding damages for bad faith? Indications that it might are found in the *Silberg* opinion and in a New Mexico Uniform Jury Instruction: "[T]he good faith of the insurance company is determined by the reasonableness of its conduct, whether such conduct is customary in the industry or not. Industry [customs] [standards] are evidence of good or bad faith, but they are not conclusive." U.J.I. Civil No. 13–1705.[1]

Objections to Peripheral Damages

It will be convenient to speak of the kinds of damages awarded in Gruenberg v. Aetna Insurance Company—compensation for mental suffering and punitive damages—as "peripheral damages", signifying that they are not traditional remedies for breach of contract. Claims for peripheral damages have met with resistance in other courts. "Courts faced with this problem have traditionally relied upon the established rule of the law of contracts that ordinarily limits damages for the nonperformance of a unilateral or independent obligation to pay a liquidated sum of money to the sum of money itself with interest at the legal rate from the time it was due." A.A.A. Pool Service & Supply, Inc. v. Aetna Cas. & Sur. Co., 395 A.2d 724, 725 (R.I. 1978). Some half-dozen objections to going beyond that are recited in Spencer v. Aetna Life & Casualty Ins. Co., 611 P.2d 149 (Kan. 1980), along with supporting citations. In this connection the court cited three cases more than once. Those citations are given in the footnote.[2]

Some of the objections recited in *Spencer* are simple rebuttals to, and restrictions on, justifications that have been given for peripheral damages. A justification in terms of "adhesion contract" fails, for example, when the contract in question is in a form mandated by statute; so one court has said. *A.A.A. Pool Service* at 726 (standard fire policy). Some courts have rejected the argument that peripheral damages are warranted because the insurance business is "imbued with public interest". Some have rejected the argument that peripheral damages serve to fulfill the peace-of-mind objective of insurance buyers. Also, to the extent that advocates of peripheral-damage awards rely on the success of bad-faith claims against liability insurers, they disregard an important distinction.

Two other objections are less reflexive. First, some would say that peripheral damages are needless for the purpose of compensation, and perhaps also for the purpose of admonition, because more traditional remedies are available and are sufficient. And second:

---

1. This instruction should be given, according to the Court's directions for use, "when the trial court allows evidence of industry custom or standards on the issue of the defendant's bad faith. The appropriate parenthetical is used depending on the nature of the evidence." See also Sloan v. State Farm Mut. Auto. Ins. Co. (N.M. 2004), as appended to Sloan v. State Farm ..., 360 F.3d 1220 (10th Cir. 2004).

2. Lawton v. Great Southwest Fire Ins. Co., 392 A.2d 576 (N.H. 1978); *A.A.A. Pool Service*; Farris v. United States Fidelity and Guaranty Co., 587 P.2d 1015 (Ore. 1978). *Farris* concerned a liability coverage; but the insurer's misstep was not one in the course of defending its insured. Rather, it refused to provide them with a defense. See p. 377 above.

The most widely used argument against recognition of the tort of bad faith is that many states have enacted statutory penalties against companies which fail without good cause to settle claims with their insureds. It is argued these legislative remedies are exclusive, thus eliminating the need for other remedies.

Spencer at 153.

Some of these objections are developed in the Notes that follow. After reading those Notes, make some judgments about the objections: Which are most persuasive? Which are least?

NOTES

(1) *Peace of Mind.* Persons and firms that owe commercial debts, other than insurers, are not usually charged with penalties if they resist payment. (Taxpayers are a large group of debtors charged with penalties for delaying payments. But their obligations are not commercial debts, and the legal mechanism for collecting is in the hands of the taxing authority.) What is exceptional about the payment obligations of insurers? Something of an explanation is expressed by saying that insurance contracts are designed to provide the holders with peace of mind. In the opinion in *Crisci*, p. 371 above, speaking of liability insurance, the court said: "Among the considerations in purchasing [it], as insurers are well aware, is the peace of mind and security it will provide in the event of an accidental loss. . . ."[3] The peace-of-mind factor has been invoked also to support peripheral-damage awards in connection with first-party insurance.

That factor falls short of a full explanation, however, for other entities also lure investors by promising peace of mind. Examples are banks hoping for deposits, and issuers of bills, notes, and bonds, including New York City, and the United States Treasury. Many contracts other than insurance contracts are made for economic and financial peace of mind. So said the court in *Farris*, n.1 above, at 1022. As an answer to that, consider the fact that usually, when a buyer of insurance encounters recalcitrance on the part of the insurer, the buyer will have experienced, recently, another traumatic experience. Unlike banks and other big holders of debt instruments, buyers of insurance are not required to maintain bad-debt reserves.

(2) *Other Remedies Adequate.* For a failure to make a payment when due, a debtor can be charged interest. That is a traditional contract remedy. Moreover, a tort remedy not specific to insurance cases may be available. The *Spencer* court made reference to that, as stated in the Restatement of Torts, Second, § 46:

---

3. In *Crisci*, the court upheld an award for mental distress suffered by the insured Mrs. Crisci, an immigrant widow, whose liability insurer refused to settle within policy limits a third party's tort claim against her. To settle her liability after an excess judgment, Mrs. Crisci paid $22,000 in cash, conveyed a 40–percent interest in a piece of property, and assigned her cause of action against the insurer to the third-party claimant. She was forced to work as a babysitter, and her grandchildren paid her rent. As her financial situation worsened, her physical health declined, and she experienced hysteria and attempted suicide. Although the court upheld a $25,000 award for mental suffering, the court recognized that only "exceptional" circumstances justify an award for emotional damages. Very few third-party insurance cases award damages for mental suffering. See William J. Appel, Annot., "Emotional or Mental Distress as Element of Damages for Liability Insurer's Wrongful Refusal To Settle," 57 A.L.R.4th 801. See generally John H. Bauman, "Emotional Distress Damages and the Tort of Insurance Bad Faith," 46 Drake L. Rev. 717, 746–49 (1998).

"Outrageous Conduct Causing Severe Emotional Distress".[4] That tort, the court said, and the "tort of [an insurer's] bad faith provide remedies for the same wrongs and they are in fact mixed concepts used somewhat interchangeably." Id. at 153.

(3) *Statutory Remedies Exclusive.* Note 4 at p. 377 above refers to the NAIC Model Act, "Unfair Claims Settlement Practices", and a comparable one, and speaks of their bearing on peripheral-damages claims in relation to liability coverages. See again that Note for one of the unfair practices identified in the Act, in § 4(D), "Not attempting in good faith...." According to § 3, for an insurer to conduct itself in that way is, among another shortcomings, an improper claims practice if:

A.   It is committed flagrantly and in conscious disregard of this Act or any rules promulgated hereunder; or

B.   It has been committed with such frequency to indicate a general business practice to engage in that type of conduct.

As for sanctions, § 6 of the Act provides for cease-and-desist and penalty orders, and in an extreme case for suspension or revocation of the insurer's license, any of these to be initiated by the insurance commissioner of the enacting state. (The allowable penalties run from $1,000 to $25,000 per violation, "not to exceed an aggregate penalty of $250,000".)

But as explained in text on the subject of statutory awards, following these Notes, some jurisdictions have held that their state unfair claims settlement practices statutes provide an implied private cause of action for damages for a violation of the statute. See, e.g., Mead v. Burns, 509 A.2d 11 (Conn. 1986).

(4) *Punitive Damages.* Especially vehement objections have been raised against charging insurers with punitive damages for bad faith. An example is a dissenting opinion in a case presented below at p. 408, Curry v. Fireman's Insurance Company. Justices Vance and Cant objected on the ground that for unfair treatment of a policyholder an insured is sufficiently protected by statutes.[5] To that they added a foot-in-the-door argument: "If a breach of contract can be converted into a tort with a veritable Eldorado of punitive damages to be mined, it does not take much imagination to anticipate that in the future every contract breach will be alleged to have been breached in bad faith." Ibid. Is there an answer to that argument?

A number of states have enacted "caps" on the amount of punitive damages that may be awarded. The Supreme Court has found in the Fourteenth Amendment

---

4.   (1) One who by extreme and outrageous conduct intentionally or recklessly causes severe emotional distress to another is subject to liability for such emotional distress, and if bodily harm to the other results from it, for such bodily harm.

(2) Where such conduct is directed at a third person, the actor is subject to liability if he intentionally or recklessly causes severe emotional distress

(a) to a member of such person's immediate family who is present at the time, whether or not such distress results in bodily harm, or

(b) to any other person who is present at the time, if such distress results in bodily harm.

Caveat:

The Institute expresses no opinion as to whether there may not be other circumstances under which the actor may be subject to liability for the intentional or reckless infliction of emotional distress.

5.   "[The] policyholder ... already has two separate avenues to recover damages by bringing suit pursuant to K[entucky].R.S. 304.12–230, the Unfair Claims Settlement Practice Act, and K.R.S. 367.220(1) and 367.170, the Consumer's Protection Act." 784 S.W.2d 176, 178, 179.

a rather loose-fitting one: punitive damages must not be "grossly excessive". BMW of N. Am., Inc. v. Gore, 517 U.S. 559 (1996). The so-called "Gore factors" are (1) the degree or reprehensibility of the defendant's misconduct, (2) the disparity between the harm (or potential harm) suffered by the plaintiff and the punitive damages award, and (3) the difference between the punitive damages awarded and the civil penalties authorized or imposed in comparable cases. Cooper Industries, Inc. v. Leatherman Tool Group, Inc., 532 U.S. 424 (2001). In *Gore* the Court overturned an award of $2 million against a distributor of cars whose misconduct had caused harm to the plaintiff of 0.2% of that. Cf. Motorola Credit Corp. v. Uzan, 413 F.Supp.2d 346 (S.D.N.Y. 2006), fixing a punitive award of $1 billion against some recidivist swindlers who were said to be among the world's richest people.

The high court in Kentucky, along with the Supreme Court and others, has taken note of the danger that a jury will inflate a punitive-damages award because of the wealth of the wrongdoer. No evidence of a defendant's financial condition should be admitted, the court said. See Sand Hill Energy, Inc. v. Smith, 142 S.W.3d 153, 167 (Ky. 2004). In that case the active defendant was the Ford Motor Company. Ford might wish, in light of its vast subsequent losses, that the court had not said that.

(5) *Future Benefits*. A person becoming disabled while holding disability coverage is entitled to periodic payments while the condition lasts. Courts have been vexed with the question what the holder may recover when the insurer wrongfully withholds one or more payments: Is it only the amount withheld, or is it also the amount (discounted to present value) of payments expected to become due in the future? The character of the breach may influence the answer. It is one thing for the insurer to dispute the fact of disability; it is another to renounce the contract.

What, then, of a tort cause of action for breach of the implied covenant of good faith and fair dealing? The California Supreme Court addressed this question in Egan v. Mutual of Omaha Ins. Co., 620 P.2d 141 (Cal. 1979). A jury, it said, "may include in the compensatory damage award future policy benefits that they reasonably conclude, after examination of the policy's provisions and other evidence, the policy holder would have been entitled to receive had the contract been honored by the insurer." Id. at 149 n.7.

Statutory Awards

State insurance laws contain abundant variations on the NAIC Unfair Claim Settlement Act (UCSA), and statutes comparable to it but not modeled on it. The variety is illustrated by the following paragraphs—none of which purports, be it noted, to represent a statute in full.

One which simply presses insurers to make timely payments when due charges them with "damages" of 12% of the amount of loss, and reasonable attorney's fees for delay, "in addition to the amount of the loss".[6] Others attach sanctions to insurer conduct that is more seriously substandard, *e.g.*, vexatious and unreasonable. A Virginia statute ("... failure to pay not made in good faith") serves to double the recovery otherwise available for many claims under auto collision coverages.[7] The statute allows also for attorney's fees and expenses.

---

6. Ark. Code § 23–79–208. Presumably the statute means the *recoverable* amount of the loss, and 12% of that. This reading is reinforced by a provision that the damages and fees are payable even though the insured has demanded something more than the "amount recovered".

7. Va. Code § 8.01–66.1. In theory, but probably not in practice, the statute affects other motor-vehicle coverages as well, so long

An Illinois statute titled "Attorney fees" is about that, and, although the text goes beyond that in terms, it may be about contingent fees in substance. Given vexatious and unreasonable conduct by an insurer, the statute applies in any action presenting an issue about liability on the insurer's policy ("a policy", actually), or the amount payable thereunder. The statute authorizes a court sometimes to add 60% to an allowed loss claim, except that if the insurer has made a settlement offer before the suit a credit may be required for that. (Note "sometimes". The added amount is not to exceed $60,000.)

The Florida legislature has enacted elements of the UCSA, but has modified them in major ways. A remedial section provides, for example, that the remedy there provided does not preempt a "common-law remedy of bad faith", if any exists.[8] The section dispenses in the main with the UCSA requirement that the insurer be shown to have engaged in a "general business practice"; subsection (1)(b). But it requires that showing for an award of punitive damages, under the section, and also that the acts complained of be either "willful, wanton, and malicious" or "in reckless disregard" for the rights of an insured or a life-insurance beneficiary.

Finally, most jurisdictions do not allow a private cause of action for insureds or claimants under their states' unfair claims settlement practices acts. See, *e.g.*, Moradi–Shalal v. Fireman's Fund Ins. Cos., 758 P.2d 58 (Cal. 1988); Hough v. Pacific Ins. Co., 927 P.2d 858 (Haw. 1996). A few state unfair claims settlement practices acts specify that the act does not create or imply a private cause of action. Regarding the Georgia Unfair Claims Settlement Practices Act, O.C.G.A. § 33–6–30 *et seq.*, for example, O.C.G.A. § 33–6–37 (2006) provides: "Nothing contained in this article shall be construed to create or imply a private cause of action for a violation of this article."

Some jurisdictions hold that their state unfair claims settlement practices statutes provide an implied private cause of action for damages for a violation of the statute. See, *e.g.*, Mead v. Burns, 509 A.2d 11 (Conn. 1986); Holmgren v. State Farm Mut. Auto. Ins. Co., 976 F.2d 573 (9th Cir. 1992) (Montana law). In Farmland Mut. Ins. Co. v. Johnson, 36 S.W.3d 368 (Ky. 2000), for instance, the insureds filed a bad-faith failure-to-settle lawsuit under their first-party fire insurance policy and were awarded punitive damages of $2 million for violations of the Kentucky Unfair Claims Settlement Practices Act, Ky. Rev. Stat. § 304.12–230 (1, 4, 6, and 7).

VACILLATION IN KENTUCKY

For some time the law of Kentucky recognized a tort claim available to the holders of a homeowners policy when, having suffered a fire loss, the

---

as the claim is for not more than $3,500. A claim for the theft of a high-mileage car might meet that test.

8. "The civil remedy specified in this section does not preempt any other remedy or cause of action provided for pursuant to any other statute or pursuant to the common law of this state. Any person may obtain a judgment under either the common-law remedy of bad faith or this statutory remedy, but shall not be entitled to a judgment under both remedies. This section shall not be construed to create a common-law cause of action." Fla. Stat. § 624.155(8).

insurer withheld payment without justification. There being no substantial or credible evidence supporting a defense, the insurer "becomes akin to a fiduciary as to the sums that may be owed under the policy." Feathers v. State Farm Fire & Casualty Co., 667 S.W.2d 693, 696 (Ky.App. 1983). The court suggested the possibility of consequential and punitive damages. It relied in part on the California case, Gruenberg v. Aetna Ins. Co.

This position was short-lived. In 1986 the Kentucky Supreme Court said, in a similar case, that *"Feathers* is not, and should not be, the rule in this Commonwealth". Also: "The only fiduciary relationship we recognize attaching to insurance policies is the excess-of-the policy limits cases where good faith is required on the part of the insurance company." Federal Kemper Ins. Co. v. Hornback, 711 S.W.2d 844, 845. From that decision Justice Leibson and two other justices dissented.

The Leibson dissent is set out below. That would be an unusual entry except for the fact that the Kentucky high court reversed course in Curry v. Fireman's Fund Ins. Co., 784 S.W.2d 176 (1989), and said: "Justice Leibson's dissenting opinion in *Federal Kemper* contains an excellent statement of the applicable principles . . . and we incorporate those views in this opinion." Id. at 178.

The entries that follow are (i) the facts in *Federal Kemper*, and the Leibson dissent, and (ii) the facts in *Curry* and the court's opinion.

i.

James and Mabel Hornback won a verdict and judgment for punitive damages against the Federal Kemper Insurance Company for its refusal to pay them for a fire loss. The evidence showed clearly that someone had set the fire. According to the majority opinion in *Federal Kemper*, whether or not the Hornbacks did so was a question for the jury, although there was little evidence that they did. (As will be seen, Justice Leibson disagreed about that.) Federal Kemper appealed, unsuccessfully, and appealed again. As indicated above, the second appeal was successful; the award of punitive damages was reversed, with a direction that the claim be dismissed.

■ Leibson, Justice, dissenting.

With admirable candor, able counsel for the movant/insurer admitted at oral argument that in cases of recent vintage "without exception" every jurisdiction called upon to decide this question has recognized the principle that, given proper circumstances, an insured may pursue a tort claim against his own insurer for bad faith failure to pay first party benefits due and owing under the policy. The question before the court is not whether such a tort claim exists, but rather when will the facts justify an award of punitive damages and, more particularly, does the evidence in the present case justify such an award? . . .

Movant's brief cites us to several cases bearing upon the resolution of an appropriate legal standard for deciding when punitive damages may be recovered in cases such as the present one. In McLaughlin v. Alabama Farm Bureau Mut. Cas., 437 So.2d 86, 90 (Ala. 1983), the court stated: "In short, plaintiff must go beyond a mere showing of nonpayment and prove a bad faith nonpayment, a nonpayment without any reasonable ground for dispute.''

Movant cites Anderson v. Continental Ins. Co., 85 Wis.2d 675, 271 N.W.2d 368 (1978), in which the Wisconsin court stated that an insured must prove three elements in order to prevail against an insurance company for alleged refusal in bad faith to pay the insured's claim: (1) the insurer must be obligated to pay the claim under the terms of the policy; (2) the insurer must lack a reasonable basis in law or fact for denying the claim; and (3) it must be shown that the insurer either knew there was no reasonable basis for denying the claim or acted with reckless disregard for whether such a basis existed. Subsequently, in Davis v. Allstate Ins. Co., 303 N.W.2d 596 (1981), the Wisconsin court amplified this rule, stating an insurer is, however, entitled to challenge a claim and litigate it if the claim is debatable on the law or the facts.

These guidelines as presented by the movant are a fair statement of the law. This amounts to the same standard for imposing punitive damages described by the Kentucky Court of Appeals in Feathers v. State Farm Fire and Casualty Co. *Feathers* stated that the insurance company may be liable for punitive damages where it denies payment after ''the policyholder has substantially complied with the terms and conditions required by the policy, and there is no substantial or credible evidence that the policyholder directly or indirectly set fire to his property for personal gain....'' 667 S.W.2d at 696.

The thrust of the present appeal has not been at the nature of the law, but at the nature of the evidence. The movant points to certain elements of the evidence, and to certain inferences and conclusions based on such elements, which movant maintains mandate a directed verdict on whether there was any ''substantial or credible'' evidence to refuse to pay the claim.

[Justice Leibson said that he found, in the trial court's opinion and order, ''sufficient evidence that the insurer's refusal to pay was arbitrary, unreasonable and in reckless disregard for the insured's rights, i.e., willful and malicious, so as to justify an award of punitive damages''.] The question is whether the trial record, taken as a whole, supports the trial court's conclusions.

... The trial court elected to bifurcate the trial, trying first the insured's claim for breach of the insurance contract. It was only in the second stage that the insured/respondents were called upon to present proof in support of their claim of bad faith and for punitive damages.

In the first stage of the case, trial of the contract claim, the trial court had overruled the insured's motion for a directed verdict and submitted the issue of the insurer's liability to the jury. [Probably, Justice Leibson said, that was error. Disagreeing with the majority, he said that probably the insureds were entitled to a directed verdict. But:] the trial court submitted the case to the jury from an abundance of caution, and said as much on the record.

The movant/insurer insists that if there was a jury issue on the contract claim, it must follow that there was substantial and credible evidence to deny the claim and, therefore, it was entitled to insist on its "day in court" with no penalty. If the *only* evidence presented on the issue of bad faith were the evidence presented before the contract claim was submitted to the jury, this might be true.... However, in the present case the trial was bifurcated. The question as to whether there was a submittable issue regarding bad faith and the right to punitive damages then depended on the state of the evidence at the conclusion of *all* the evidence, which includes part two of the trial, not just part one.

[Justice Leibson recited five points of evidence tending to refute the insurer's suspicion that the insureds had set the fire. They included the following.] (4) that the insureds had been mistakenly identified by the insurance company as the same persons who had been involved in a previous arson at another location; and (5) that the insurance company then turned a deaf ear to overwhelming proof to the contrary showing no involvement with the prior arson.

The holding in *Feathers* was that the insured must prove that there was no "substantial or credible evidence" upon which to deny the claim. This means that the "plaintiff must go beyond a mere showing of nonpayment and prove a bad faith nonpayment, a nonpayment without any reasonable ground for dispute." *McLaughlin* at 437 So.2d 90. But this means there are cases where there may be enough evidence to satisfy the technical requirements for jury submission, but there is other proof which, if believed, proves that this was not a "credible" defense. *Feathers*. We need not decide whether insureds/respondents were entitled to a directed verdict on the contract claim. This point is not at issue on this appeal. However, assuming they were not so entitled, this hypothesis is not dispositive of the bad faith/punitive damages issues in the particular circumstances of this case.

The essence of the question as to whether the dispute is merely contractual or whether there are tortious elements justifying an award of punitive damages depends first on whether there is proof of bad faith and next whether the proof is sufficient for the jury to conclude that there was "conduct that is outrageous, because of the defendant's evil motive or his reckless indifference to the rights of others." Restatement (Second) Torts, Sec. 909(2) (1979), as quoted and applied in Horton v. Union Light, Heat & Power Co., Ky., 690 S.W.2d 382, 388–90 (1985). Then punitive damages are justified. There are recent cases from other jurisdictions involving facts similar to the present, i.e., some evidence of arson or of a substantial financial benefit to the insured, but also other evidence of bad faith in investigating or settling the claim that outweigh it, where punitive damages were awarded. [Alabama and Oklahoma cases cited.]

. . .

Our rule should be that ordinarily, if the evidence presents a factual issue with respect to the validity of the insured's contract claim, this establishes the legitimacy of the insurance company's denial thereof and the tort claim for punitive damages should not be submitted to the jury. But this rule should not be inflexible. It may not be applicable because the trial court decided erroneously that there was sufficient evidence to dispute the contract claim. It may not be applicable because there is other evidence refuting the credibility of the insurer's claim of a defense. Certainly, in present circumstances where the trial court used a bifurcated trial procedure, the evidence must be judged at the conclusion of all the evidence, and not limited to the state of the evidence at the conclusion of the contract phase.

A bifurcated procedure was the proper way to try the present case. This procedure better protected the rights of the insurance company/movant because it kept out of the contract phase evidence which was relevant to the issue of bad faith but unnecessary and possibly prejudicial to the insurance company in the trial of the preliminary question of liability under the insurance contract. But the trial court's decision to utilize this bifurcated procedure . . . should not then become a vehicle that forecloses consideration of the evidence subsequently presented on the issue of bad faith and punitive damages. This case should be judged by the state of the evidence at the conclusion of the whole case. The evidence, taken as a whole, supports the trial court's decision to submit the issue of punitive damages to the jury and the jury's verdict. The trial court's instruction setting out the basis for an award of punitive damages appropriately pointed out the additional findings necessary before making an award of punitive damages.

The majority opinion makes a "shell game" (now you see it, now you don't) out of the fiduciary relationship between the insurance carrier and its insured, a relationship which we have recognized. . . . The Majority Opinion recognizes that a fiduciary relationship exists when the question is should the carrier be required to pay the judgment in excess of the policy limits recovered by a third party against its insured assuming the insurer's refusal to pay was in bad faith. But, we will not recognize the same fiduciary relationship where the bad faith refusal to pay involves a first party claim. Our decision to "overrule" *Feathers* places us in a minority position squarely in conflict with every other state that has considered the matter. What is more, whether we should overrule *Feathers* was a question that was not even presented on this appeal!

The decision of the Court of Appeals, which affirmed the verdict and judgment in the trial court, should be affirmed.

NOTES

(1) *Elements of a Bad-faith Claim.* As Justice Leibson described a bad-faith claim, it rests on these three elements: (i) the insurer's obligation to pay, (ii) its want of a reasonable basis for denying the claim, and (iii) either knowledge by the insurer of that want or reckless disregard on its part whether or not a reasonable basis for denying the claim existed. Justice Leibson failed to mention another fact essential to the claim: it must be the case that the insurer has failed to pay.

As to the first, the claimant must establish, among other things, the existence and validity of the contract, something of the kinds of loss covered, the fact of the loss, and compliance by the claimant with certain conditions in the contract—notice given of the loss, for example. Justice Leibson disagreed with his colleagues about the state of the evidence with respect to a burn by the Hornbacks. He recited some interesting evidence that they had *not* set the fire. Does it seem conclusive? In any event, it is doubtful that the Hornbacks bore the burden of producing evidence to that effect.

One bit of evidence was that the insurer "turned a deaf ear to overwhelming evidence" that the Hornbacks had not been involved in a burn elsewhere. If that was a fact, did it bear on the insurer's obligation to pay? On its basis for denying the claim? On the issue of "reckless disregard"? Or on some combination of those issues?

As to the second element, any serious doubt that the insurer reasonably entertained about, say, the validity of the contract or the fact of loss would bar a bad-faith claim, it seems. Doubt about any of several other subjects would have the same effect, one being the claimant's compliance with a warranty in the policy.

(2) *The Test of Bad Faith*. This, as stated by Justice Leibson, is a test about the insurer's state of mind. (Corporations are often supposed, in law, to have states of mind.) As he put it, element (iii) of a bad-faith claim is either knowledge by the insurer of the want of a reasonable basis for its position or reckless disregard on its part whether or not a reasonable basis for denying the claim existed.[1]

The more usual test is whether or not the position taken by the insurer was fairly debatable. The Kentucky high court has said, speaking some years after it expressed admiration for the Leibson opinion, that "an insurer is ... entitled to challenge a claim and litigate it if the claim is fairly debatable on the law or the facts...." Farmland Mutual Ins. Co. v. Johnson, 36 S.W.3d 368, 375 (2000) (quoting).

While adhering to that proposition, the *Johnson* court went on to say that the existence of jury issues on a policy claim does not preclude a bad-faith claim. "[A]n insurance company still is obligated ... to investigate, negotiate, and attempt to settle the claim in a fair and reasonable manner. In other words, although elements of a claim may be 'fairly debatable,' an insurer must debate the matter fairly." Ibid. So saying, the court undercut the insurer's attempt to justify itself by depicting the claim against it as fairly debatable.

The standard expressed in *Johnson* is objective in a way that Justice Leibson's is not. Which is preferable? At least when liability for punitive damages is in question, one might think that a subjective test is preferable. New Mexico has made that preference clear by amending its pattern jury instruction on the subject of punitive damages based on bad faith. The New Mexico Supreme Court has promulgated a pattern jury instruction, as follows, about punitive damages, for use in connection with both first-party and third-party "bad faith" claims against insurers.

U.J.I. Civ. 13–1718 Punitive damages

If you find that plaintiff should recover compensatory damages for the bad faith actions of the insurance company, and you find that the conduct of the

---

1. This standard has a ring familiar to lawyers; it resembles, for example, the state of mind that is constitutionally required for a claim of libel against a newspaper. See New York Times Co. v. Sullivan, 376 U.S. 254 (1964).

insurance company was in reckless disregard for the interests of the plaintiff,[2] or was based on a dishonest judgment,[3] or was otherwise malicious, willful or wanton,[4] then you may award punitive damages.

Punitive damages are awarded for the limited purposes of punishment and to deter others from the commission of like offenses.

The amount of punitive damages must be based on reason and justice, taking into account all the circumstances, including the nature of the wrong and such aggravating and mitigating circumstances as may be shown. The amount awarded, if any, must be reasonably related to the compensatory damages and injury.

DIRECTIONS FOR USE

. . . The trial court may omit this instruction only in those circumstances in which the plaintiff fails to make a prima facie showing that the insurer's conduct exhibited a culpable mental state.

The court made amendments effective in 2005, adding the definitions in the footnotes and the sentence quoted from the "Directions for use". It did so to "ensure the jury will award punitive damages only in those cases where the insurer's conduct is shown to have manifested a culpable mental state." Sloan v. State Farm Mut. Auto. Ins. Co. (2004), as appended to Sloan v. State Farm . . ., 360 F.3d 1220 (10th Cir. 2003).

ii.

Curry v. Fireman's Fund Ins. Co.

Kentucky Supreme Court, 1989.
784 S.W.2d 176.

Billy & Ethel Curry asked an agent for the Fireman's Insurance Comany to arrange a "full coverage" policy on their store, "Bill & Mae's Jeans". Fireman's issued a policy. Soon after that they lost merchandise in a burglary. Fireman's rejected repeated demands for payment of the loss. The policy it had issued was a standard business owner's policy which did not include theft coverage. In an action brought by the Currys the trial court concluded that the policy should be reformed because the omission of theft coverage was due to a mutual mistake. It directed a verdict in favor of the Currys for the value of the lost merchandise ($13,500), and submitted to the jury questions about consequential and punitive damages. The trial-court judgment included $50,000 for the one, and $15,000 for the other. On a first appeal, the Court of Appeals found no basis for those damages.

2. "Reckless conduct" is the intentional doing of an act with utter indifference to the consequences.

3. "Dishonest judgment" is a failure by the insurer to honestly and fairly balance its own interests and the interests of the insured.

4. "Malicious conduct" is the intentional doing of a wrongful act with knowledge that the act was wrongful. "Willful conduct" is the intentional doing of a wrongful act with knowledge that harm may result. "Wanton conduct" is the doing of an act with utter indifference to or conscious disregard for a person's rights.

■ Lambert, Justice.

. . .

It is unnecessary to engage in a presumptuous analysis of the prior authorities of the courts of Kentucky and other jurisdictions on this issue.... The issue of the bad faith breach of a first party insurance contract has been fully considered by our courts. Although we are reluctant to abandon settled precedent, a majority of this Court is now convinced that our decision in *Federal Kemper* was improvident and should be overruled.

The facts of this case well illustrate the desirability of permitting recovery in tort when an insurance company acts in bad faith in dealing with its own insured. Nothing in *Feathers* suggested that an insurance carrier must pay bogus claims or abandon legitimate defenses. Tort liability was allowed only when "there is no substantial or credible evidence that the policyholder directly or indirectly" caused or contributed to the loss. "The proceeds of the policy may not be withheld unless there is a substantial breach of the contract by the policyholder." *Feathers*, 667 S.W.2d at 696. The essence of a claim for first party bad faith is exposure of the insurance carrier to damages recoverable in tort. Such a claim should not be lightly entertained in view of the contractual nature of the parties' original relationship. Justice Leibson's dissenting opinion in *Federal Kemper* contains an excellent statement of the applicable principles involved herein and we incorporate those views in this opinion....

Our decision in *Federal Kemper* abolished tort liability to a policyholder, regardless of the conduct of the insurance carrier. Such a rule permitted an insurance carrier to deny payment without any justification, attempt unfair compromise by exploiting the policyholder's economic circumstance, and delay payment by litigation with no greater possible detriment than payment of the amount justly owed plus interest.

In this society, first party insurance coverage against a host of risks is recognized as essential. From cradle to grave individuals willingly pay premiums to insurance companies to obtain financial protection against property and personal loss. Without a reasonable means to assure prompt and bargained-for compensation when disaster strikes, the peace of mind bought and paid for is illusory. The rule in *Federal Kemper* is unjust and, despite its recency, should not be perpetuated.

Throughout the history of Anglo–American law, the most important decisions societies have made have been entrusted to duly empaneled and properly instructed juries. Decisions as to human life, liberty and public and private property have been routinely made by jurors and extraordinary confidence has been placed in this decision-making process. We are confident that jurors deciding issues of bad faith will act responsibly and refrain from awarding damages in tort except in those circumstances where such is clearly warranted and then only in appropriate amounts.

For the foregoing reasons, the opinion of the Court of Appeals is reversed and the judgment of the trial court reinstated.

[Chief Justice Stephens filed a concurring opinion, in which Justice Leibson joined. There was a dissent, as indicated above.]

NOTES

(1) *Statutory Standards (Reprise).* Note 4, p. 377 above, refers to the NAIC Model Act on unfair claims settlement practices, and quotes a description there of one of the acts said to constitute unfair practice. Others are

– Failing to adopt and implement reasonable standards for the prompt investigation and settlement of claims arising under [the insurer's] policies; and

– Refusing to pay claims without conducting a reasonable investigation.

Paragraphs C and F of § 4. The Kentucky version of the Model Act includes virtually identical language. See K.R.S. § 304.12–230. When the Kentucky high court said that an insurer was duty bound to "investigate, negotiate, and attempt to settle [a] claim in a fair and reasonable manner", it spoke with reference to that statute. See Farmland Mut. Ins. Co. v. Johnson, 36 S.W.3d 368 (Ky. 2000) discussed in the following Note.

(2) *Statutory Cause of Action.* As explained in Statutory Awards at p. ___, many jurisdictions do not allow a private cause of action for insureds or claimants under their states' unfair claims settlement practices acts; but others do.

In State Farm Mut. Automobile Ins. Co. v. Reeder, 763 S.W.2d 116 (1998), regarding third-party automobile liability insurance, the court held:

> [T]he legislature can enact a law creating a cause of action where none existed at common law. The act in question indicates a definite intention to prohibit unfair claims settlement practices and constitutes the public policy of Kentucky. It is the holding of this Court that private citizens are not specifically excluded by the statute from maintaining a private right of action against an insurer by third party claimants. KRS 446.070 and KRS 304.12–230 read together create a statutory bad faith cause of action.

Id. at 118.

Subsequently, in Farmland Mut. Ins. Co. v. Johnson, Note 1 above, the insureds filed a bad-faith failure-to-settle lawsuit under their first-party fire insurance policy and were awarded punitive damages of $2 million for violations of the Kentucky Unfair Claims Settlement Practices Act, Ky. Rev. Stat. § 304.12–230 (1, 4, 6, and 7). Even though the insured stipulated that the amount of the loss was fairly debatable, the KUCSPA claim was not foreclosed.

EXERCISE

Customer ("C") applied to the same insurer for two policies, first for an auto policy and then for a homeowners policy. There were falsehoods in both applications: first, that C had not been arrested for any offenses other than traffic violations, and second, that he had never been convicted of a crime. The insurer issued both policies, although it knew of a DWI conviction. After C suffered a fire loss at his home the insurer learned of other serious crimes that C had committed, and it refused to pay for that loss. C brought an action in which he claimed punitive damages for a bad-faith refusal to pay. The underwriter who had approved the application for the homeowners policy testified that he would not have done so if the application had been truthful. Should the court submit the punitive-damages claim to the jury? See Conner v. Shelter Mutual Ins. Co., 779 F.2d 335 (6th Cir.), *cert. denied*, 476 U.S. 1117 (1986) (Kentucky law).

Review question: Can the jury make *any* award to C if it believes the underwriter's testimony?

CONCLUDING NOTES

(1) *21st Century Update.* At the turn of the 21st Century, a slight majority (twenty-six states) have adopted the insurance first-party bad faith tort by common-law cases. "Since 1973, at least twenty-five other states [in addition to California] have adopted the new tort, weaving First–Party Bad Faith tightly into the fabric of America's legal system." Dominick C. Capozzola, Note, "First–Party Bad Faith: The Search for a Uniform Standard of Culpability," 52 Hasting L.J. 181, 181–182 (2000). Citing the cases, the New York Supreme Court observed:

> In view of the inadequacy of contract remedies where an insurer purposefully declines or avoids a claim without a reasonable basis for doing so, a majority of states have responded to this need for a more suitable remedy by adopting a tort cause of action applicable to circumstances where an insurer has used bad faith in handling a policyholder's claim

Acquista v. New York Life Ins. Co., 730 N.Y.S.2d 272, 277 (N.Y. App. Div. 2001). Moreover, many states adopt statutory approaches to first-party insurance bad faith, discussed in the next Note. Consequently, by 2004, only a few remaining jurisdictions do not adopt the first-party bad-faith tort in insurance cases. See Steven Plitt, "The Elastic Contours of Attorney–Client Privilege and Waiver in the Context of Insurance Company Bad Faith: There's a Chill in the Air," 34 Seton Hall L. Rev. 513, 517 n.14 (2004).

(2) *State Statutes Update.* Many jurisdictions have statutes empowering courts to award a statutory monetary penalty or attorney fees and costs or both. The amount of penalty that can be awarded varies from state to state. Under some statutes, the penalty is set at a specific percentage of the amount that the court finds is due under the policy. See, e.g., Ark. Code Ann. § 23–79–208 (12% on amount recovered from insurer); Ga. Code Ann. § 33–4–6 (25% of insurer's liability for loss). Others allow liability up to a particular monetary amount. See, e.g., Ill. Rev. Stat. ch. 73, P 767; Mo. Rev. Stat. § 375.420; Tenn. Code Ann. § 56–7–105(a). Some statutes provide for prejudgment interest for breach of insurance contracts specifically; others are more general. See, e.g., Tex. Ins. C. art. 3.62.

Does a state statutory penalty provision preclude a common-law tort cause-of-action for bad faith and the recovery of punitive damages? Maine responds No because the Maine statute, Me. Rev. Stat. Ann. tit. 24–A, § 2436, expressly provides: "5. Nothing in this section prohibits or limits any claim or action for a claim that the claimant has against the insurer." But most state statutes do not specifically address the issue of preempting other causes of action against an insurer. However, if the penalty statute does not require the insurer's conduct to have been vexatious, unreasonable, or in bad faith for the penalty to attach, an insured may file a cause of action for bad faith in addition to recovering the penalties provided by the statute. Only a few courts hold that their state statutes, requiring vexatious, unreasonable, or bad faith conduct by the insurer, are the "exclusive" remedy regarding an insurer's bad-faith conduct in not paying the insured.[1]

---

1. See, e.g., Howell v. Southern Heritage Ins. Co., 448 S.E.2d 275 (Ga.App. 1994) (O.C.G.A. § 33–4–6 are the exclusive remedies); Stump v. Commercial Union, 601

Under many statutes, the penalties will attach only if the insurer's failure or refusal to pay has met a particular standard, such as "vexatious," without reasonable cause, " 'in bad faith,' or 'not in good faith.' " The burden of proof is on the claimant to prove that the insurer's conduct was sufficiently egregious to satisfy the statutory standard of vexatiousness, unreasonableness, or bad faith. See, e.g., Nationwide Mut. Ins. Co. v. St. John, 524 S.E.2d 649 (Va. 2000); United Servs. Auto. Ass'n v. Croft, 175 S.W.3d 457 (Tex.Ct.App. 2005).

However, some state statutes impose a penalty for an insurer's failure to pay without regard to whether the insurer's failure to pay was justified. The presence or absence of the insurer's good faith in not making payments is immaterial—a strict liability approach. See Brokenbaugh v. New Jersey Mfrs. Ins. Co., 386 A.2d 433, 439 (N.J. Super. 1978). See also National Union Fire Ins. Co. v. McDougall, 773 A.2d 388 (Del. 2001).

Finally, Florida courts initially refused to recognize a common-law tort cause of action for a first-party insurer's refusal to pay a claim. See Industrial Fire & Casualty Ins. Co. v. Romer, 432 So.2d 66, 67 (Fla.Ct.App. 1983). However, Florida now has a *statutory* "tort of bad faith" cause of action in first-party cases. See Fla. Stat. § 624.155(1)(b); compare 42 Pa. Cons. Stat. § 8371. As stated above, some jurisdictions hold that their state unfair claims settlement provisions create an implied private cause of action for damages for a violation of the statute. See, e.g., Farmland Mut. Ins. Co. v. Johnson, 36 S.W.3d 368 (Ky. 2000).

The cases adjudicating these various state statutes are collected and discussed in three related annotations.[2]

(3) *California Update.* The California Supreme Court recently reaffirmed its earlier 60s and 70s opinions adopting tortious breach of the implied covenant of good faith and fair dealing in third-party liability insurance (*Crisci*) and in first-party insurance (*Gruenberg, Silberg,* and *Egan*).

" 'Every contract imposes upon each party a duty of good faith and fair dealing in its performance and its enforcement.' ... Because the covenant is a contract term, however, compensation for its breach has almost always been limited to contract rather than tort remedies. As to the scope of the covenant, '[t]he precise nature and extent of the duty imposed by such an implied promise will depend on the contractual purposes.' Initially, the concept of a duty of good faith developed in contract law as 'a kind of "safety valve" to which judges may turn to fill gaps and qualify or limit rights and duties otherwise arising under rules of law and specific contract language.' As a contract concept, breach of the

---

N.E.2d 327 (Ind. 1992). See also Chicago Motor Club v. Robinson, 739 N.E.2d 889 (Ill. App. 2000) (tort claims prohibited by 215 Ill. Comp. Stat. 5/155, but the contract claims were permissible.); Overcast v. Billings Mut. Ins. Co., 11 S.W.3d 62 (Mo. 2000) (Rev. Stat. Mo. § 375.420 preempts only actions based on elements of the insured's contract claim).

2. George L. Blum authored these three annotations: "What Constitutes Bad Faith on Part of Insurer Rendering it Liable for Statutory Penalty Imposed for Bad Faith in Failure to Pay, or Delay in Paying, Insured's Claim—Particular Grounds for Denial of Claim: Risks, Causes, and Extent of Loss, Injury, Disability, or Death," 123 A.L.R.5th 259; "What Constitutes Bad Faith on Part of Insurer Rendering it Liable for Statutory Penalty Imposed for Bad Faith in Failure To Pay, or Delay in Paying, Insured's Claim—Particular Grounds for Denial of Claim: Matters Relating to Policy," 116 A.L.R.5th 247; "What Constitutes Bad Faith on Part of Insurer Rendering It Liable for Statutory Penalty Imposed for Bad Faith in Failure To Pay, or Delay in Paying, Insured's Claim—Particular Conduct of Insurer," 115 A.L.R.5th 589.

duty led to imposition of contract damages determined by the nature of the breach and standard contract principles." . . .

"In the area of insurance contracts the covenant of good faith and fair dealing has taken on a particular significance, in part because of the *special relationship* between the insurer and the insured. 'We [have] held that the insurer, when determining whether to settle a claim, must give at least as much consideration to the welfare of its insured as it gives to its own interests. The governing standard is whether a prudent insurer would have accepted the settlement offer if it alone were to be liable for the entire judgment. The standard is premised on the insurer's obligation to protect the insured's interests in defending the latter against claims by an injured third party.' " . . . A breach of this duty of reasonable settlement gives rise to tort damages. *Crisci v. Security Ins. Co.*, 426 P.2d 173, 177–78 (Cal. 1967).

"The implied covenant imposes obligations not only as to claims by a third party but also as to those by the insured. In both contexts the obligations of the insurer 'are merely two different aspects of the same duty.' . . . For the insurer to fulfill its obligation not to impair the right of the insured to receive the benefits of the [first party insurance] agreement, it again must give at least as much consideration to the latter's interests as it does to its own." *Egan v. Mutual of Omaha Ins. Co.*, 620 P.2d 141, 145 (Cal. 1979). As in the case of failure to properly settle third party claims, " '[w]hen the insurer unreasonably and in bad faith withholds payment of the claim of its insured, it is subject to liability in tort.' " *Id.*

Jonathan Neil & Assoc., Inc. v. Jones, 94 P.3d 1055, 1068 (Cal. 2004). (In this quotation the word "citation" has been omitted systematically.)

———

CHAPTER 8

PROPERTY INSURANCE

A. INSURABLE INTERESTS

A person or firm having no insurable interest in an asset cannot insure it effectively, except for the benefit of one who does. The requirement that there be an insurable interest as to property is dealt with here. It has an analog in the law of insurance on lives. That is dealt with in Chapter 10.

Belton v. Cincinnati Ins. Co.

South Carolina Supreme Court, 2004.
360 S.C. 575, 602 S.E.2d 389.

Circumstances threw a suspicion of arson on Stewart Belton when a commercial building was destroyed by fire, although he testified that he and his family were on vacation when the fire occurred. In fact, Belton was indicted, though not convicted. A "fire analysis" concluded that the fire had been set intentionally. The building had burned about a week after Belton applied to the Cincinnati Company for insurance on it. The company's agent issued a binder on its behalf, creating interim coverage. Ultimately the application was accepted.

Cincinnati rejected Belton's claim on the policy after making an investigation. (It ordered the "fire analysis" in the process.) Belton brought this action. Cincinnati defended on the grounds that he was involved in the intentional burning of the building, and that he had no insurable interest in it. The trial court entered a summary judgment for Cincinnati on the latter ground. On an appeal by Belton, that was reversed by the Court of Appeals. Then Cincinnati appealed.

■ TOAL, CHIEF JUSTICE.

. . .

FACTUAL/PROCEDURAL BACKGROUND

In October 1997, Belton and Charleston attorney Grady Query (Query) entered into a contract entitled "Lease Option to Buy," transferring possession of a commercial building and eleven and a half acres of land to Belton. The contract included (1) a lease provision directing Belton to pay Query monthly payments of $1,200; (2) a purchase provision allocating 80 percent of Belton's monthly payments toward Belton's purchase of the property; (3) a provision establishing that the closing date would occur on or before November 1, 2002; and (4) a provision creating a five percent penalty for late monthly payments. The contract did not provide, however, a provision that Belton would forfeit the equity in the property upon nonpayment of the monthly payments.

Shortly after the contract was signed, Belton fell behind on his payments. In early 1998, Query wrote Belton two letters terminating the agreement and demanding that Belton vacate the premises. When Belton refused to vacate the premises, Query filed a rule to vacate or show cause. In April 1998, Belton declared bankruptcy and received protection from an automatic stay [installed by the Bankruptcy Code], allowing him to remain in possession of the property. [Belton applied for the insurance in August of 1998.]

. . .

[Rulings by the Court of Appeals included this: "[A] party holding an option to purchase has an insurable interest". It remanded the case for findings about (1) whether Belton's option survived Query's attempts to terminate the agreement, and (2) the amount or extent of Belton's insurable interest in the property.]

LAW/ANALYSIS

Standard of Review

The trial court must grant a motion for summary judgment when "the pleadings, depositions, answers to interrogatories, and admissions on file, together with the affidavits, if any, show that there is no genuine issue as to any material fact and that the moving party is entitled to a judgment as a matter of law." Rule 56(c), SCRCP.... When determining whether triable issues of fact exist, all evidence and inferences drawn from the evidence must be viewed in the light most favorable to the non-moving party....

Insurable Interest

Cincinnati argues that the court of appeals erred in finding that a question of fact existed as to whether Belton had an insurable interest in the destroyed property. We agree. Although we do not discount the possibility that an option to purchase land may create an insurable interest, we find that Belton had no insurable interest in the destroyed property because he did not have equity in the property.

Equity and Insurable Interest

The central issue of this case is whether Belton had an insurable interest in the underlying property at the time he contracted for insurance with Cincinnati. Belton argues his option to purchase the property gave him an insurable interest. To accept this argument, we must find that Belton's option survived Query's termination of the agreement.[4]

Nevertheless, regardless of whether Belton's option was enforceable, we hold that Belton did not have an insurable interest in the underlying

---

4. The parties do not dispute that the agreement was terminated upon Belton's default and Query's attempts to have him evicted.

property because he did not have any equity in the underlying property when he contracted for insurance with Cincinnati. Further, we reserve the question of whether an option to purchase real property creates an insurable interest for a later date.

Our holding that a party cannot have an insurable interest in an option to purchase land if that party does not have equity in that land is consistent with our jurisprudence concerning insurable interest. Although, our courts have not used the word "equity", we have certainly equated a party's insurable interest in property with a party's personal stakes in that property. In Benton & Rhodes, Inc., v. Boden, the court of appeals held that "to have an insurable interest in property, one must derive a benefit from its existence or suffer a loss from its destruction." 426 S.E.2d 823, 825 (Ct.App. 1993). The next year, the court of appeals held that an insured may not recover insurance proceeds in excess of his interest in the property. Singletary v. Aetna Cas. & Sur. Co., 447 S.E.2d 869, 870 (Ct.App. 1994). Therefore, our holding that an option cannot create an insurable interest where its holder has no equity in the underlying property is consistent with our prior rulings.

After reviewing the record, it is clear that Belton's equity in the underlying property is *de minimis* at best. It is unclear how many monthly payments, if any, Belton made to Query. But when Query sought relief from the bankruptcy court, he filed a statement indicating that Belton's total arrearage was $7,810. According to the terms of the contract, Belton was to pay a $50 down payment and then $1,200 a month, with 80% of the monthly payment going toward the purchase of the building. Therefore, 80% of the Belton's monthly payments made to Query arguably constitute equity. Nonetheless, Belton has failed to provide any evidence that the equity he accumulated in the property was not diminished and ultimately depleted because of his arrearages.

In addition, as plaintiff, Belton had the burden to set forth specific facts, which included providing evidence that he had equity in the property at the time he contracted for insurance and at the time of loss. The non-moving party may not rest on the mere allegations of his pleading to withstand summary judgment but "must set forth specific facts showing that there is a genuine issue for trial." SCRCP 56(e).... Because Belton has failed to provide such evidence, we hold that summary judgment was proper. We may not draw an inference that Belton had an insurable interest without sufficient evidence to support such a conclusion.

CONCLUSION

We hold that because Belton has failed to show that he had any equity in the destroyed property, he did not have an insurable interest in the property. If Belton had provided evidence that the equity he acquired through monthly payments was in excess of his arrearages, plus interest accrued upon nonpayment, he may have established that he held an insurable interest. Nevertheless, we need not make that determination at this time. [We reverse] and uphold the trial court's order granting summary judgment for Cincinnati....

NOTES

(1) *Time for Testing.* The court ruled against Belton because he had no insurable interest in the property *"when he contracted with Cincinnati"*. Its decision would have been the same, no doubt, if the court had been concerned, instead, about Belton's interest at the time of the fire, or at any time between. "[S]ome jurisdictions require that the insurable interest exist at the time of loss, and a number of other jurisdictions require that an insurable interest must exist both when the contract is created and at the time of loss." Technical Land, Inc. v. Firemen's Ins. Co. of Washington, D.C., 756 A.2d 439, 444 (D.C.App. 2000) (citations omitted). By statute in California, the critical times are "when the insurance takes effect" and the time of loss: Insurance Code § 286 (but an interest "need not exist in the meantime").

As between the time of insuring and the time of loss, which is likely to be the focus of a court concerned about gambling in the guise of insurance? Which is likely to be the focus of a court concerned about incentives to destroy property? What concern would lead a court to require that an insurable interest exist at both times?

The choice between time of insuring and time of loss is momentous in at least one situation, that in which a merchant has bought insurance on its "inventory". Given harm to some or all of the inventory items, it may well be that many or all of those were acquired by the merchant after the policy was issued. A court is likely, in that event, either (i) to test for an insurable interest in the individual items only at the time of loss or (ii) to treat the inventory as a generic entity in which the merchant had an insurable interest at all times. A third possibility, suggested by the California statute, is to say that the insurance "took effect" from time to time, as the merchant acquired new items of inventory. Harm to other assets generically described in the policy (*e.g.* "equipment") is more problematic. Cf. Wilbanks & Wilbanks, Inc. v. Cobb, 601 S.W.2d 601, 603 (Ark.App. 1980)

(2) *Open Questions.* Authorities are divided about whether or not an insurable interest inheres in an option to buy as such. For a collection, see the Court of Appeals opinion, 577 S.E.2d 487 at 490–91. That court was divided. (It concluded that Belton's option had not necessarily expired along with his lease.) Chief Justice Hearn, dissenting, said: "Allowing the holder of an option to purchase insurance prior to his exercise of the option invites the very misbehavior the doctrine of insurable interest endeavors to prevent." Id. at 491, 492. Persuasive?

The high court's opinion leaves open a question about the position of persons and firms who, as many commercial tenants do, occupy premises under extant leases and hold options to purchase. What if there is no value in either the leasehold or the option? (Indexing of the rent, or the option price, or both, as is common, complicates the value of one or both interests.) To invalidate policies held by those tenants would be a shock to many. The cost to a tenant of relocating, even from overpriced premises, might count for something as an expectation of loss. Also, the shock would be cushioned by the fact that many commercial tenants undertake to maintain insurance in force for the benefit of their landlords as well as themselves. That provision in a lease can count as the source of an insurable interest; see the Note after the following case report ("third category").

The Bridge of Lancaster County

In 1882 a privately owned toll road in Pennsylvania had two parts, one on each side of Conestoga creek. Travelers on the road crossed the creek on a covered bridge built and owned by Lancaster County. The road company, New Holland Turnpike, had helped to pay for building the bridge after an earlier one there had been destroyed, and for keeping it in repair. (In the opinion that recites these facts the court said there was no showing why the company did that; but the court added: "It is not difficult to imagine a reason. . . .") The company procured insurance against fire damage to the bridge and, when the bridge burned, made a claim on the policy. The insurer rejected it and the company sued.

The trial court gave this instruction to the jury, among others: "[T]he plaintiff here has shown an insurable interest, although it has no owner-ship in the bridge, legal ownership in the land upon which it was located; but [we hold that the plaintiff has an equitable interest which may be insured.] That is a question of law for the court,—and if the court is wrong in regard to that, of course, the Supreme Court will put us right."

The Pennsylvania Supreme Court did so, reversing a judgment for the company. Farmers' Mut. Ins. Co. v. New Holland Turnpike Road Co., 15 A. 563 (1888). The court said that the insurable-interest question was a novel one, but was "perhaps not difficult of solution." It said that it was quite desirable for the company to have a bridge over which users of its road could travel. "But . . . it was still the fact that the bridge was a public county bridge, free to all travel [and] the property of the county exclusively. Being thus a free, public bridge, there could not possibly be any private estate or ownership in it. The turnpike company could charge no tolls for passing over it. They could exercise no acts of ownership over it. They could not obstruct it nor take it down, even if to rebuild it, without the consent of the county, and perhaps not even with such consent, as it was a part of the public highway." The turnpike company had no insurable interest.

NOTES

(1) *Four Types of Insurable Interests.* In the middle of the 20th century two writers detected some types of insurable interests not recognized in the Bridge case. Attempting to summarize American law, they said: "As seen through the eyes of modern courts the insurable interest concept possesses four main heads. The first and broadest heading embraces property rights, whether legal or equitable. The second and closely allied category includes those types of interests which are reflected in contract rights. The possibility of legal liability as a result of the insured event is the third division, while the fourth is the controversial residuum category of 'factual expectation of damage.' "[1]

Examples of the first category are, in addition to legal title, leaseholds, liens, and the equitable ownership acquired upon contracting to purchase real estate. An example of the second is an option to purchase, assuming that a holder of an option has an insurable interest. (In Belton v. Cincinnati Ins. Co. the court avoided deciding about that, but recognized it as at least a possibility.) An example of the third category, a liability-based interest, is the situation of an insurer of a property,

1. Harnett & Thornton, Insurable Interest in Property, 48 Colum.L.Rev. 1162,
1165 (1948).

which must make a payment if the property should be damaged or destroyed. The insurer may cover that risk by buying a policy of reinsurance.

A case illustrating category four is presented at p. 421 below. There the court espoused what it called the *factual expectation theory*. It said: "Under this theory there is an insurable interest in property if the insured would gain *some economic advantage* by its continued existence or would suffer *some economic detriment* in case of its loss or destruction." What would the decision have been in the Lancaster County bridge case if the court had espoused that theory?

(2) *Extremism, and an Answer.* Much discussion of insurable interests in property aims to answer the question whether or not a factual expectation is a *sufficient* interest—an expectation, that is, of advantage from the preservation of the asset under consideration. Less commonly, the question is whether or not that expectation is a *necessary* component of an insurable interest. Some of the answers recorded go to an extreme. "Not necessary", Lord Eldon said, in Lucena v. Craufurd, 2 Bos. & Pul. 269, 127 Eng.Rptr. 630 (1806). He envisaged a case in which a party has a remainder interest in a ship, so limited that he or she could not expect ever to enjoy its use. "B" is that party. B's interest will vest only if A dies without issue. A has 20 young children; B is 90 years old. That would be a clear interest, Eldon said, even though it be a moral certainty that it is worthless. Justice Lawrence went to the other extreme, saying that insurance is available to protect men against events "which may *in any wise be of disadvantage to them*." (emphasis supplied). That seems to mean that a factual expectation suffices, however remote the expected advantage is. In Eldon's view that would open the way for too many people to insure against damage to a single asset. (As to some structures Eldon was right, was he not? Think of the multitudes who might expect an advantage from the preservation of, say, the Golden Gate Bridge or the Washington Monument.)

The opinion in Belton v. Cincinnati Ins. Co., above, seems to say that a factual expectation of advantage is a necessary component of an insurable interest. The case of the Lancaster County bridge seems to say that is not a sufficient interest. These propositions are compatible in the abstract, are they not? Subscribing to both of them might be a way to avoid going to extremes. Would it be sensible otherwise?

(3) *History.* "The foremost historical justification for the insurable interest requirement was to prohibit wagering contracts in the guise of insurance.[2] Odd as it may strike us today, insurance as an instrument of wagering was a common and accepted practice in mid-eighteenth century England. Beginning then, Parliament passed a series of statutes" tending to suppress the practice. The first of these concerned the writing of marine insurance "interest or no interest". On one view the statute invalidated no-interest policies, theretofore enforceable. So Lord Kenyon

2. *See* Robert E. Keeton and Alan I. Widiss, INSURANCE LAW: A GUIDE TO FUNDAMENTAL PRINCIPLES, LEGAL DOCTRINES, AND COMMERCIAL PRACTICES (Student ed. 1988) at 138.

One moral position is that institutional gambling is a waste of human resources. Judges have been heard to say that their efforts are wasted in enforcing contracts of wager. Objections to wagering are thought in some quarters to be Puritanical, or at least puritanical. But wagers were first declared void in English law by a Restoration Parliament. For a long time statutes on the subject have reflected monetary considerations in

good part. Government-sponsored wagering, now pervasive in the United States, is favored as a source of financial support for government services, notably public education. It produces astonishing proportions of state revenues here and there. Whether or not it taps the right pockets is, however, a serious question. Many people believe that institutional gambling conduces to a maldistribution of wealth. Mixed views obtain also about wagering on sporting events. Bets laid by participants are widely condemned. But betting at tracks has been justified as a means of improving horseflesh.

thought, saying that "at common law a person might have insured without having any interest." Craufurd v. Hunter, 8 T.R. 13, 101 Eng.Rep. 1239 (1798), at 23, 101 Eng.Rptr. at 1245. But in Lucena v. Craufurd, Justice Lawrence expressed doubt about that. He thought that the statute had a lesser effect on prior rulings, both being addressed to the necessity that a claimant make proof of its interest in suing on a marine policy. Prior to the statute there were signs that Kenyon was wrong at least as to fire insurance, marine contracts being distinguished. But the preamble to the statute indicates the view of Parliament that it was making a sea change. It noted that insurance had become "a mischievous kind of gaming," and a justification for the fraudulent destruction of property.

In the United States, certainly, early cases condemned no-interest policies. But, as in England, the subject is now dominated by legislation.

Reasons for the Requirement of an Insurable Interest

One of two reasons is given, generally, as an explanation for the requirement; sometimes they appear in tandem.[3] One is that those who buy insurance against events which do not affect them adversely are engaged in unlawful wagering. The other is that those buyers would have, if their contracts were enforceable, sinister interests in encompassing harm to life, health, or property, as the case might be. An action brought by Debra Delk on a homeowner's policy prompted the court to speak (in an opinion further presented below) about both reasons. It said: "The purpose of the insurable interest requirement must stand at the center of any analysis of the doctrine's application.... Judicial consideration must be given to whether the contract suggests an element of wager on the part of the insured, *i.e.* whether it appears that the insured was betting on the loss of property with which he (or she) had little or no connection. The court must also consider whether recovery by the insured would exceed the loss actually suffered, thereby providing motivation for destroying the property."

In 2005 it was reported that "gambling was so far acceptable in the United States that '48 states [had] legalized some form of gambling.' "[4] The Oklahoma high court regarded the anti-wagering ground of the insurable-interest requirement as somewhat outmoded. The Note that follows is an excerpt from the *Delk* opinion, providing interesting background.

Notwithstanding that court's concern about purposes, it is possible to bypass the reasons for the requirement. One can say simply that the existence of an insurable interest is a defining characteristic of a contract of insurance. (See Chapter 1, p. 3.) It would be possible to draw from that

3. See Welliver, J., dissenting in G. M. Battery & Boat Co. v. L.K.N. Corp., 747 S.W.2d 624 (Mo. 1988), at 628: "This is judicial approval of gambling in the rankest form. In addition, it is a judicial invitation to arson."

4. Not Utah and not Hawaii. Delaware was said to derive some 8% of its revenue from this source. And that was not exceptional, among states of small populations. The proportion in Nevada was exceptional: 42.6%. *The New York Times*, March 31, 2005, Pp. A1, A24.

assertion the inference that an agreement wanting in that characteristic, and otherwise like an insurance contract, is some other kind of enforceable agreement. But that would be a mistake.

Introduction to Delk v. Insurance Company

The court divided its opinion into five parts: two about the occasion for the opinion, and three that expound the law of insurance. At this point parts I–III are presented. Parts IV and V are presented below, under the heading "Measure of Recovery". But the court's catchlines for those parts are included here, so as to indicate the court's rulings in those parts.

The court warned against an "overly technical construction" of the "insurable-interest requirement", one that "frustrates the legitimate expectations of the insured or that permits an insurer to avoid the very risk it intended to insure." The court alluded to the reasons for the requirement, one about wagering and the other about the motivation to destroy property. "The purpose of the ... requirement must stand at the center of any analysis of the doctrine's application." As indicated above, that reflection led the court to espouse the factual expectation theory.

Delk v. Markel American Ins. Co.
Oklahoma Supreme Court, 2003.
81 P.3d 629.

■ OPALA, V.C.J.

The United States District Court for the Western District of Oklahoma (certifying court) certified a question of law.... We have reformulated the question.... We answer the following reformulated question:

> May an insured cotenant who occupies the insured property as her home and who has insured the property for its full value recover (within the policy limits) more than the value of her fractional legal interest in the property?

We answer this reformulated question in the affirmative.

I

THE ANATOMY OF FEDERAL LITIGATION[5]

In April 1998 James Delk executed a warranty deed conveying equal fractional interests in his residence to six of his relatives, including his daughter, Debra Delk (plaintiff or Delk). The other five cotenants named in the deed are plaintiff's adult son, John, his minor children, Julian and Cheyenne Delk, plaintiff's minor son, Tanner Mabry, and plaintiff's adult nephew, Cody Delk. Plaintiff lived in the home with John and his family until it was destroyed by fire in September 2001.

Markel American Insurance Company (defendant) in May 1999 issued to plaintiff as the sole named insured a homeowner's policy covering the

---

5. The material accompanying the federal court's certification order consists of the pleadings, the parties' motions for summary adjudication with attached exhibits, and briefs in support of and in opposition to the motions. The parties submitted additional briefs to this court at our request.

residence. The application did not ask plaintiff about the nature or extent of her legal title. Plaintiff contends that she informed defendant she was taking over as policyholder from her father and that she would be making the premium payments. Plaintiff renewed the policy on a yearly basis at an annual premium of $786. The policy was in force and effect when the house was destroyed by fire. The policy limits for dwelling coverage stand at $104,000.00.[6] The policy at issue is the only property insurance covering the home. Plaintiff alone paid the annual premiums. She and her adult son, John, contend they had an understanding that plaintiff would obtain insurance on the home and that she alone would be entitled to any proceeds recovered in the event of an insured loss.

When the home was destroyed by fire in September 2001, plaintiff made a claim under the policy for the amount of the policy's dwelling coverage limits. Defendant learned while investigating the claim that plaintiff owned only a one-sixth interest in the insured property. Defendant then denied plaintiff's claim as to all but one-sixth of the policy limits on the grounds that her insurable interest—and hence the insurer's indemnification duty—was limited to plaintiff's fractional share of the property's ownership.

Plaintiff then brought this action against defendant in the United States District Court for the Western District of Oklahoma for breach of contract.... Both parties moved for summary judgment. Unable to determine how Oklahoma law would quantify plaintiff's insurable interest in the home, the federal district court judge submitted to this court the certified question of law which we answer today as reformulated.

II
THE NATURE OF THE COURT'S FUNCTION WHEN ANSWERING QUESTIONS FROM A FEDERAL COURT

. . .

Because this case is not before us for decision, we refrain (as we must) from applying the declared state-law responses to the facts in the federal-court litigation, which have been tendered for review by the certifying court either in the form of evidence adduced at trial or by acceptable probative substitutes (so-called "evidentiary materials"). The task of analyzing today's answer for its application to this case is deferred in its entirety to the certifying court.

III
THE PURPOSE OF THE INSURABLE INTEREST REQUIREMENT AND THE GUIDING PRINCIPLE BEHIND ITS IMPLEMENTATION IN OKLAHOMA

An insurance contract is valid and enforceable only to the extent that the insured has an insurable interest in the subject matter of the policy.[11]

---

6. The policy also provides other coverage in the following amounts:

Other Structures Coverage—$10,400.00.
Personal Property Coverage—$41,600.00.

Additional Living Cost and Fair Rental Value—$10,400.00.
Personal Liability—$25,000.00.
Medical Payment to Others—$500.00.

This requirement has long been a part of Oklahoma's common law[12] and also stands today as a statutory prerequisite for the validity of an insurance contract.[13] The pertinent subsection of 36 O.S. 2001 § 3605 states: "No insurance contract on property or of any interest therein or arising therefrom shall be enforceable as to the insurance except for the benefit of persons having an insurable interest in the things insured."[14] The insurance policy at issue in this case also contains a provision limiting defendant's liability to the insurable interest an insured person has in property covered by the policy.[15]

An insurable interest is the relationship or connection a person must have with the subject matter of an insurance policy in order to insure it. The insurable interest doctrine developed over the course of several centuries in response to certain public policy concerns related to insurance. [Here the court followed with the passage quoted in Note 3, p. 419 above.]

The doctrine of insurable interest initially entered American jurisprudence by way of decisional law, but many jurisdictions have over the years enacted insurable interest statutes. While American jurisdictions generally agree on the necessity of an insurable interest, they are divided on what constitutes such an interest. The nature of the interest that qualifies as insurable has changed over time and is gradually broadening.[26] Two competing theories have evolved for measuring the nexus which must be present between the property and its insured for an insurable interest to attach. The literature refers to one of these as the "legal interest" theory[27] and to the other as the "factual expectation" theory.[28]

---

11. Fireman's Fund Ins. Co. v. Cox, 175 P. 493, 493 (Okla.).

12. *Id.*

13. 36 O.S. 2001 § 3605.

14. *See* 36 O.S. 2001 § 3605.A.

15. The policy states in relevant part, "In the event of a loss, we will not pay for more than the insurable interest that an insured person has in the property covered by this policy...."

26. Fagen, ["*Notes on the Development of the Doctrine of Insurable Interest,*" 8 GEO. L.J. 1 (1919)] at 2.

27. While the statutes passed in the eighteenth century required that an "interest" be present, it was left to the judiciary to decide the nature of the connection to the property (or life) which would qualify as an "interest." The legal interest theory requires that the insured's expectation of benefit from the continued existence of the subject of the insurance be based on a legally or equitably cognizable interest in the property. This view has its roots in Lord Eldon's opinion in Lucena v. Craufurd, [2 Bos. & Pul. 269, 127 Eng.Rptr. 630 (1806)], where he reasoned

that "expectation though founded on the highest probability, [is] not interest," *Id.* at 321, 127 Eng.Rptr. at 650, and "if moral certainty be a ground of insurable interest, there are hundreds, perhaps thousands, who would be entitled to insure" the same property. *Id.* at 324, 127 Eng.Rep. at 651. The legal interest theory recognizes as insurable not only the interest of fee holders, but also those of life tenants (Farmers' Mut. Fire & Lightning Ins. Co. v. Crowley, 190 S.W.2d 250 (Mo.1945)); remaindermen, *(Id.)*; reversioners (Convis v. Citizens' Mut. Fire Ins. Co., 86 N. W. 994 (Mich.1901)); lessors (Hale v. Simmons, 139 S.W.2d 696 (Ark. 1940)); lessees (Id.); mortgagees (Allen v. St. Paul Fire & Marine Ins. Co., 208 N.W. 816 (Minn.1926)); pledgees (Dunsmore v. Franklin Fire Ins. Co., 149 A. 163 (Pa. 1930)); and lienholders (Hayward Lumber & Inv. Co v. Lyders, 34 P.2d 805 (Cal.App. 1934)).

28. The factual expectation theory also has its roots in Lucena v. Craufurd, *supra* note [27]. In a separate opinion in that case, Lord Lawrence said, "that insurance is a contract by which one party in consideration of a price paid to him adequate to the risk,

In *Snethen v. Oklahoma State Union of the Farmers Educational and Cooperative Union of America*,[29] we adopted the factual expectation theory of insurable interest.[30] Under this theory there is an insurable interest in property if the insured would gain *some economic advantage* by its continued existence or would suffer *some economic detriment* in case of its loss or destruction.[31] This is also the theory espoused by the provisions of 36 O.S. 2001 § 3605.B., which define insurable interest as: "any actual, lawful, and substantial economic interest in the safety or preservation of the subject of the insurance free from loss, destruction, or pecuniary damage or impairment."[32] *Snethen* held that the word "lawful" as used in § 3605.B. is not synonymous with the word "legal" and does not require the application of the legal interest theory, but is merely used in the sense that the interest was not acquired in violation of the law.[33]

. . .

IV

THE INSURABLE INTEREST OF A COTENANT IN POSSESSION MAY EXCEED THE QUANTUM OF HIS (OR HER) FRACTIONAL LEGAL ESTATE IN THE COTENANCY PROPERTY WHERE THE INSURING COTENANT ACTS AS THE MANAGING AGENT FOR THE JOINT OWNER

. . .

becomes security to the other, that he shall not suffer loss, damage, or prejudice by the happening of the perils specified to certain things which may be exposed to them. If this be the general nature of the contract of insurance, it follows that it is applicable to protect men against uncertain events which may in any wise be of disadvantage to them; not only those persons to whom positive loss may arise by such events, occasioning the deprivation of that which they may possess, but those also who in consequence of such events may be intercepted from the advantage or profit, which but for such events they would acquire according to the ordinary and probable course of things.... To be interested in the preservation of a thing, is to be so circumstanced with respect to it as to have benefit from its existence, prejudice from its destruction." *Id.* at 301–302, 127 Eng.Rptr. at 642–43.

29.   1983 OK 17, 664 P.2d 377.

30.   *Id.* at 380.

31.   [*Ibid.*] . . .

32.   The factual expectation theory has come to enjoy widespread legislative and judicial support. For an enumeration of jurisdictions with a similar or identical definition of insurable interest to that recognized in Oklahoma, *see* Parker [*"Does Lack of an Insurable*

Interest Preclude an Insurance Agent from Taking an Absolute Assignment of His Client's Life Policy," 31 U RICH.L.REV. 71 (1997)] at 109, n. 7. *See also* Harrison v. Fortlage, 161 U.S. 57, 65 (1896), where at the end of the nineteenth century the United States Supreme Court called the factual expectation theory of insurable interest "well settled." It is the preferred theory among legal commentators. *See e.g.* Harnett and Thornton [*Insurable Interest in Property* . . ., 48 COLUM.L.REV. 1162 (1948)] at 1188; 3 G. Couch, CYCLOPEDIA OF INS. LAW § 24.13 (2d ed. 1984); Salzman, [*The Law of Insurable Interest in Property Insurance,* 1966 INS.L.J. 394] at 405; Pinzur, [*Insurable Interest: A Search for Consistency,* 46 INS.COUNSEL J. 109 (1979)] at 111; Note, *"Insurable Interest in Property: An Expanding Concept,"* 44 IOWA L.REV. 513–522 (1958). The factual expectation theory is employed in the definition of insurable interest provided in C. Bennett, DICTIONARY OF INSURANCE 178 (1992) ("the insured must be in a legally recognised relationship with the subject-matter of insurance whereby he benefits by its safety or absence of liability and is prejudiced by its damage or destruction or creation of liability.").

33.   Snethen, *supra* note 29 at 381.

V

A COTENANT IN POSSESSION, BEING LEGALLY LIABLE TO THE OTHER JOINT OWNERS FOR DAMAGE TO OR DESTRUCTION OF THE COMMON PROPERTY, HAS AN INSURABLE INTEREST TO THE EXTENT OF HIS (OR HER) POTENTIAL LEGAL LIABILITY

. . .

CERTIFIED QUESTION ANSWERED

[Justices Hargrave and Kauger concurred in the result. Justice Boudreau concurred in part and dissented in part. Excerpts from his opinion are as follows.]

I agree with the majority that a tenant in common, in possession of the common property, has an insurable interest to the extent of his or her potential legal liability for the loss or destruction of the property. However, I would base this holding on the status based duty of the cotenant in possession to preserve the common property for the benefit of the other cotenants, and not on a duty derived from general negligence principles.[1]

. . .

Insurable interest is defined as "any actual, lawful, and substantial economic interest in the safety or preservation of the subject of the insurance free from loss, destruction or pecuniary damage or impairment." 36 O.S.2001, § 3605(B). Because a cotenant in sole possession of the common property has a legal duty to preserve the common property for the benefit of the other cotenants, she is potentially liable to her cotenants for loss, destruction or impairment of the property. Accordingly, she has an actual, lawful, and substantial economic interest in the safety or preservation of the common property that is the subject of the insurance. This economic interest allows a cotenant in possession of the entire common property to claim an insurable interest in the value of the entire common property.

NOTES

(1) *Policy Terms.* As shown above in the court's footnote 15, Delk's policy contained a provision about her insurable interest, one germane to the question the court addressed. But an insurer may, though its policy does not speak to the subject, contest a claim on the ground that the claimant had no insurable interest. And it may do so even if the policy purports to dispense with the requirement of an insurable interest; public policy overrides the dispensation.

(2) *A Comparable Case.* In Joseph DeWitt's divorce from his wife Betty, he was awarded custody of their only child and she was directed to transfer her interest in

---

1. The insurable interest of a cotenant in possession must be based on the status-based duty to preserve the property for the benefit of the other joint owners, and not on the general duty to exercise ordinary care so as not to injure the person or property of another. The following example illustrates why the difference is important. A lessee under a three-month rental agreement undoubtedly has a duty to exercise ordinary care not to damage the leased premises and is subject to potential liability to the lessor for failure to do so. However, I do not believe the majority would conclude that the lessee has an insurable interest in the leased premised he or she occupies.

the family home to him. (Though they had bought the house together, title was in Betty's name.) Joseph was directed to pay the mortgage debts on the house, although that did not relieve Betty of liability on those debts. She did not make the transfer as ordered. In an opinion reciting these facts the court described the effect of the divorce this way: "Joseph [] held title in equity to the property without deed and plaintiff held legal title in trust for him." DeWitt v. American Family Mutual Ins. Co., 667 S.W.2d 700, 706 (Mo. 1984).

Joseph died less than a year later. Betty reoccupied the house, with the child. She made improvements and procured fire insurance on the house. When the house was destroyed by explosion and fire, the insurer declined to pay. It contended that Betty had no insurable interest. In an action she brought on the policy, the court ruled otherwise. Ibid.

TECHNICAL LAND, INC. v. FIREMEN'S INS. CO. OF WASHINGTON, D.C., 756 A.2d 439 (D.C.App. 2000). Technical Land (TL) was in bankruptcy when a building it occupied suffered water damage due to a burst pipe. TL had only a tenuous hold on the property. It was one of a set of firms acting for William and Judith Moore in their project of turning the property into a motion-picture studio. (It had been a skating rink.) At one time TL had held a deed to the property, but that deed had been invalidated before the damage occurred. Before that, the property had been owned by another of the Moores' firms, 1631 Kalorama Associates. (The property was on Kalorama Road in the District of Columbia.) Associates had entered bankruptcy.

The trustee in that bankruptcy had entered into a "Use Agreement" with a third of the Moores' firms, here called Video. The agreement recognized that the ownership of the property was in dispute, and sought to maximize the use value of the property. Until the dispute was resolved, the property was to be "operated as a motion picture and television production facility." The trustee was to have exclusive control over the property, including authority to sell the building, but the agreement gave Video the right to use all of the space in the building. Video permitted TL to occupy the building, rent-free. That was the situation when the water damage occurred.

In TL's bankruptcy the court directed it to procure insurance on the property. TL complied by buying coverage, including water-damage loss, from Firemen's Insurance. After the water damage, Firemen's canceled the policy and rejected claims on it made by TL. TL sued Firemen's for failure to pay. The trial court ruled in favor of Firemen's after concluding, *inter alia*, that TL did not have an insurable interest in the property.[10] TL appealed.

TL suggested several "factors" that should have led, it said, to a finding of insurable interest. For one example, TL relied on its occupancy

---

10. The trial court also held that Firemen's Insurance did not act in bad faith in not paying the claim and in not completing its coverage inquiry more quickly; Technical Land's appeal is limited to the breach of contract issue.

· · ·

of the property. To that the court answered No: "At most, Technical Land had a 'mere license to occupy' the building by virtue of its association with Video." Other examples: TL had earlier paid taxes on the property and had paid for repairs needed after an earlier incident of water damage.

■ RUIZ, ASSOCIATE JUDGE. [T]he above factors, singly or in conjunction, do not support Technical Land's having an insurable interest in the building. [But TL had more success with an argument that may be called one of "indispensable property". The court's reasoning about that was as follows.]

Technical Land cites *Asmaro v. Jefferson Ins. Co.*, 574 N.E.2d 1118 (Ohio Ct.App. 1989) (per curiam), in support of its claim that these factors do not preclude it from establishing that it had an insurable interest in the property. In *Asmaro*, the Ohio Court of Appeals addressed whether Asmaro, Inc., which owned a business operated in a building destroyed by fire, had an insurable interest in the building.... The court held that Alaa Asmaro, the owner of the building and the sole stockholder of Asmaro, Inc., although he had an insurable interest, could not recover because he was not the named insured on the policy. Asmaro, Inc., the named insured, was held to have an insurable interest, even though it did not have a property interest, on the basis of its economic relationship to the property.... The court concluded that Asmaro, Inc., had an insurable interest in the building because its business was a neighborhood grocery store, dependent on walk-in customers, that would suffer a loss if it were forced to relocate by damage to the building. Thus, the court found an insurable interest based on the fact that the location of the building was integral to the success of the business.

We agree with the *Asmaro* court's reasoning that where economic loss to a tenant is closely tied to the unique traits of a particular property, it can form the basis for an insurable interest. In this case, Technical Land argues that its insurable interest derives from the fact it was created to operate the studio housed in the insured property and derive profits therefrom, and that it could not do so as a result of the water damage to the building.[20] There was evidence presented to the trial court that the studio at 1631 Kalorama Road was unique to the Washington metropolitan area, and that Technical Land suffered economic loss due to its inability to relocate to another site with similar facilities in time to perform its contractual obligations.

. . .

20. Technical Land claims that its business was impaired as a result of water damage to the building and to Techniarts' television production equipment housed in the building. The trial court found that the "Firemen's policy did not insure against lost income or damaged equipment." Technical Land has not appealed that finding of the trial court. We do not understand it to be asserting a claim for lost profits or damaged equipment, however, but for damage to the property, based on its economic, business-related interest in the building. The scope of coverage under the contract of insurance has not been briefed before this court and is not before us.... In this appeal we address only whether the nature of Technical Land's relationship to the insured building constitutes an insurable interest.

As the trial court noted, "there is no question that Technical Land lost income because of its inability to use the property during the time it was damaged." Although we cannot say the trial court erred in not making factual findings concerning the alleged uniqueness of the property in question to Technical Land's business and in finding that Technical Land had no insurable interest in 1631 Kalorama Road based on the precise arguments made to it, we remand the case for the trial court's consideration of the facts in light of the claimed uniqueness of the property and the relationship between Technical Land's loss and the property's unique traits. . . .

NOTES

(1) *Alternate Ground.* Recall that, in TL's bankruptcy, the court had directed it to procure insurance on the property. Possibly that fact brought the case within the principle that one's potential liability for damage to property can constitute an insurable interest. See Note 1, p. 418 above. If so, the court could have taken a more familiar path to its conclusion than the one it took. Was that path open to the court?

(2) *Piercing the Corporate Veil.* The *Asmaro* court is not alone in believing that a stockholder may have an insurable interest because the corporate issuer of the stock has one. "The overwhelming majority of jurisdictions . . . recognize that a stockholder in a corporation has a legal insurable interest in its property in proportion to the amount of his stockholdings." Providence Washington Ins. Co. v. Stanley, 403 F.2d 844, 848–49 (5th Cir. 1968).

PROBLEMS

(1) Ned attended college in the city where his aunt Sarah lived, and made his home with her. She bought a car for Ned's regular use in going to school and to his place of part-time work. After Ned had been graduated and had moved elsewhere, Sarah used the car. It was demolished in a collision. Before being graduated, Ned had bought insurance on the car, covering collision damage. If he and Sarah join in making a claim on the policy, should it fail for want of an insurable interest in Ned? See Universal C.I.T. Corp. v. Foundation Reserve Ins. Co., 450 P.2d 194 (N.M. 1969).

(2) A firm is insured against loss of income due to the destruction (i) of buildings for which it has contracted to provide engineering and janitorial services, and (ii) of buildings "in the same vicinity which attract business to the firm". The firm has suffered losses due to the destruction of a building in each class. It has no other interest in either building. Is the firm barred from recovery of loss due to the destruction of a "contract" building? From recovery of loss due to the destruction of a class 2 building? See Zurich American Ins. Co. v. ABM Industries, Inc., 397 F.3d 158 (2d Cir. 2005). (The insured had contracted to provide services to the public areas of the World Trade Center, and to many areas occupied by tenants.)

Statutes

In about thirty states an insurable interest in property is said by statute to be "any lawful and substantial economic interest in the safety or preservation of property from loss, destruction or pecuniary damage." An Oklahoma statute on the subject of insurable interests is set out in the *Delk* opinion; see p. 423 above. Some others are as follows. The California provisions date from the 19th century. The New York one was first enacted there in 1939, and later in a number of other states. The third statute is a relatively recent enactment, unique to Wisconsin.

California

Necessity

If the insured has no insurable interest, the contract is void.

Definition

Every interest in property, or any relation thereto, or liability in respect thereof, of such a nature that a contemplated peril might directly damnify the insured, is an insurable interest.

Insurable interest in property

An insurable interest in property may consist in:

    1.   An existing interest;

    2.   An inchoate interest founded on an existing interest; or,

    3.   An expectancy, coupled with an existing interest in that out of which the expectancy arises.

Contingency or expectancy

A mere contingent or expectant interest in anything, not founded on an actual right to the thing, nor upon any valid contract for it, is not insurable.

Measure of interest

Except in the case of a property held by the insured as a carrier or depositary, the measure of an insurable interest in property is the extent to which the insured might be damnified by loss or injury thereof.

Carrier or depositary

A carrier or depositary of any kind has an insurable interest in a thing held by him as such, to the extent of its value.

Stipulations as to interest

Every stipulation in a policy of insurance for the payment of loss whether the person insured has or has not any interest in the property insured, or that the policy shall be received as proof of such interest, is void.

– Insurance Code §§ 281–287.

New York

Insurable interest in property No contract or policy of insurance on property made or issued in this state, or made or issued upon any property in this state, shall be enforceable except for the benefit of some person having an insurable interest in the property insured. In this article, "insurable interest" shall include any lawful and substantial economic interest in the safety or preservation of property from loss, destruction or pecuniary damage.

– Ins. Law § 3401.

Wisconsin

Insurable interest and consent.

(1) INSURABLE INTEREST.

No insurer may knowingly issue a policy to a person without an insurable interest in the subject of the insurance.

[*Subsections 2, 3, and 4 concern life, health, and disability insurance policies, and are omitted here.*]

(4) EFFECT OF LACK OF INSURABLE INTEREST OR CONSENT.

No insurance policy is invalid merely because the policyholder lacks insurable interest or because consent has not been given, but a court with appropriate jurisdiction may order the proceeds to be paid to someone other than the person to whom the policy is designated to be payable, who is equitably entitled thereto, or may create a constructive trust in the proceeds or a part thereof, subject to terms and conditions of the policy other than those relating to insurable interest or consent.

– Statutes § 631.07.

B.   ISSUES OF CAUSE AND COVERAGE

Insurance policies abound in the language of causation, language ascribing loss to this or that source. Examples are "perils of the seas" and "loss by fire". This section concerns the effects of expressions like these. The effects depend partly on construing policy language, but only in part.

The matter came into sharp focus in the summer and fall of 2005, when major hurricanes (Katrina, Rita, Wilma) ravaged the Gulf Coast. Aside from lives lost and dislocated, they caused property damage in the billions of dollars. Questions arose almost at once about the extent of insurance claims. Much of the damage could be ascribed to flooding, the subject of a common policy exclusion. A report on the high-stakes insurance litigation that ensued appears below at p. 442.

Materials bearing on the flood-damage exclusion appear in the section on the "doctrine of reasonable expectations" (p. 144 ff.). Others are presented here.

Physical Loss or Damage

Physical loss or damage is a requisite of recovery under an enormous number of property-insurance policies. The three cases briefed here show some effects of that limitation.

(A) *A Case of Mountain Dew*. Pepsico, Inc. and its affiliates ("Pepsico") are producers and vendors of food and drink. The Winterthur International America Insurance Company moved for a partial summary judgment when it was sued by Pepsico. Pepsico claimed that some of its products (*e.g.*, Mountain Dew) became unsaleable through adulteration by contaminated ingredients—not harmful to drink, but off in flavor. Winterthur had insured Pepsico against all risks of "physical loss of or damage to" property in which Pepsico had an interest. Winterthur contended that the "physical damage" had not been shown: what Pepsico alleged was that some of its products were of poor quality at the time of their creation. Winterthur appealed from a denial of its motion. *Held*: Affirmed. "We reject Winterthur's contention that the plaintiffs' products were not 'physically damaged'.... While 'physical damages' are not defined in the policy, we disagree with Winterthur that to prove 'physical damages' the plaintiffs must prove ... that the product has gone from good to bad. It is sufficient under the circumstances of this case ... that the product's function and value have been seriously impaired, such that the product cannot be sold ..." Pepsico, Inc. v. Winterthur Intern'l America Ins. Co., 806 N.Y.S.2d 709 (App.Div. 2005).

(B) *The Stolen Chair Case*. While Peter Patout was in prison, a chair was stolen from his home. So he alleged in an action on a policy of insurance on his home and its contents. Patout alleged further that, after he had learned of the loss, he found the chair in the possession of a furniture restorer and had recovered it through legal proceedings. On motions by Patout and the insurer for summary judgments, Patout contended that his expense in recovering the chair was a covered loss; the insurer contended that it was not. The policy provided that a *covered loss* was "any physical loss to your [home] contents ... caused directly by a peril named below, unless stated otherwise...." Among the perils named were theft and attempted theft. The court granted the motion of the insurer. It said: "The Plaintiff has recovered the chair. There was no physical damage to the chair." Patout v. Vigilant Ins. Co., 2005 WL 2050278 (E.D.La. 2005).

(C) *The Case of the Closed Garage*. Among the many repercussions of the air strikes of 9/11/01, one was a loss of revenue to the Philadelphia Parking Authority, a state agency which operates parking facilities at the Philadelphia International Airport. Twenty minutes after the first strike, the Federal Aviation Administration issued the first of several orders in response, a regional "groundstop". That order effectively closed the Airport. By 11 a.m. the FAA had halted takeoffs and landings at all airports in the United States. The events of the morning led a City agency to close access to the Authority's parking facilities at the Airport.

All this the Authority asserted in an action on a policy insuring it against a loss of income in various circumstances. All of the lost-income clauses required that there be "direct physical loss or damage". One of them, for example, referred to loss due to "the actual interruption of your operations ... when a civil authority prohibits access to your covered property because of *direct physical loss or damage* caused by a covered cause of loss to property" that either was covered or was in its vicinity. There had been direct physical loss to the World Trade Center and to the Pentagon; but neither of these sites was covered or "in the vicinity."

The Authority contended that the phrase italicized above was ambiguous: It might signify both "direct physical loss" and "damage", whether direct or not. Damage there was, the Authority said—its loss of income. But the court granted a motion by the insurer to dismiss the action. It said: "Nowhere in the Complaint does [the Authority] allege that the economic damage for which it seeks recovery actually caused the interruption of [its] business. Instead, it appears the interruption of Plaintiff's business caused Plaintiff's economic damage." Philadelphia Parking Authority v. Federal Ins. Co., 385 F.Supp.2d 280, 287 (S.D.N.Y. 2005).

Two Rules about Causation

This Note introduces two rules about attributing property damage to particular incidents, the "immediate cause" rule and the "efficient proximate cause" rule.* For illustrations, cases about episodes of wet weather and landslides are to be supposed. Some cases in which combinations of those events led to losses are cited below in a Note titled "Earthquakes, Landslides, and Mudslides" (p. 439). In one of them an engineer offered the surmise that "Water is always the catalyst that causes these types of [slope] failures."

You are asked to assume, notwithstanding this evidence, that landslides do occur without regard to water or weather. On that assumption, consider these two cases:

    1. A landslide occurs, unrelated to weather, which blocks the course of a river. The slide backs up water upstream, which enters and damages a home insured against water damage but not against landslide damage.

    2. Heavy rain weakens a cliff, so that it slides and damages a home below. The home is insured against unusual-weather damage, but landslide damage is excluded.

In Case 1 the homeowner's coverage claim might be based on what has been called the *immediate cause* rule. In Case 2 the claim might be based on what has been called the *efficient proximate cause* rule.

---

* As early as the 19th century, the expression "efficient and proximate cause" was in use to determine insurance coverages. See Ermentraut v. Girard Fire & Marine Ins. Co., 65 N.W. 635, 636 (Minn. 1895) ("The question is, was fire the efficient and proximate cause of the loss or damage?"). But the expression was much more commonly used in connection with liabilities in tort and those of carriers of goods.

An English court has expressed the former rule this way: "In an action on a policy, the *causa proxima* is alone considered in ascertaining the cause of loss...." The California Supreme Court has expressed the latter rule this way:

> When a loss is caused by a combination of a covered and specifically excluded risks, the loss is covered if the covered risk was the efficient proximate cause of the loss....

(The English case was quoted in the opinion that follows. The California case is Julian v. Hartford Underwriters Ins. Co., p. 441 below.)

Might it be that the insurer must pay in both cases? See Swischer, Insurance Causation Issues ..., 2 Nev.L.J. 351, 368 (2002): "The better reasoned view [], in order to validate the reasonable expectations of the contracting parties ... would be to permit a court to apply *either* the 'immediate cause' rule *or* the 'efficient' or 'dominant' proximate cause rule according to which rule would provide coverage in a particular insurance contract dispute, especially if there was policy language that was arguably ambiguous." Aside from any supporting precedent, what merit does this view have?

Bird v. St. Paul Fire & Marine Ins. Co.

Court of Appeals of New York, 1918.
224 N.Y. 47, 120 N.E. 86, 13 A.L.R. 875.

■ CARDOZO, JUDGE.

On September 12, 1915, the defendant, a fire and marine insurance company, issued to the plaintiff its policy of insurance covering the body, tackle, apparel and other furniture of the canal boat, the *Henry Bird, Jr.* "Touching the Adventures and perils which the said Company are content to bear and take upon themselves by this Policy, they are of the Sounds, Harbors, Bays, Rivers, Canals and Fires, that shall come to the damage of the said boat, or any part thereof." There was no express exception of damage from explosion.

On the night of July 30, 1916, a fire broke out from some unknown cause beneath some freight cars in the Lehigh Valley Railroad Company's freight yards at Black Tom in the harbor of New York. The cars were loaded with explosives, and after the fire had burned at least thirty minutes, the contents of the cars exploded. This explosion caused another fire, which in turn caused another and much greater explosion of a large quantity of dynamite and other explosives stored in the freight yard. The last explosion caused a concussion of the air, which damaged plaintiff's vessel about one thousand feet distant to the extent of $675. No fire reached the vessel, the damages being solely from the concussion caused by the second explosion. The question is whether the loss is covered by the policy. In a controversy submitted under section 1279 of the Code, these facts stand admitted. The Appellate Division gave judgment for the plaintiff.

There is no doubt that when fire spreads to an insured building and there causes an explosion, the insurer is liable for all the damage (*Wheeler v. Phenix Ins. Co.*, 203 N.Y. 283; *Lynn Gas & Electric Co. v. Meriden Ins. Co.*, 158 Mass. 570; *Scripture v. Mutual Fire Ins. Co.*, 10 Cush. 356; *Waters v. Merchants Louisville Ins. Co.*, 11 Peters, 213, 225). We assume that, in the absence of some exception in the policy, a like liability follows when an explosion caused by fire occurs in neighboring buildings (*Hustace v. Phenix Ins. Co.*, 175 N.Y. 292, 302, 303). But the question here is whether space is a factor in the solution of the problem. The Appellate Division says that it is not; no matter how great the distance, the insurer remains liable. Other courts have held otherwise. The question came before the English Court of Common Pleas in *Everett v. London Assurance Co.* (19 Common Bench N.S., 126). There gunpowder ignited and exploded. The plaintiff's building, half a mile away, was damaged by concussion. The court (Erle, Ch. J., and Willes and Byles, JJ.) gave judgment for the defendant. "Speaking of this injury, no person would say that it was occasioned by fire. It was occasioned by a concussion or disturbance of the air caused by fire elsewhere." A like ruling was made in Louisiana by a divided court (*Caballero v. Home Mut. Ins. Co.*, 15 La.Ann. 217). In Tennessee, the ruling was the same: "Legal conclusions cannot always be safely reached by pressing the processes of logical illation to their ultimate results" (*Hall v. Nat. Fire Ins. Co.*, 115 Tenn. 513, 521).

The problem before us is not one of philosophy (Pollock Torts [10th ed.], p. 37). If it were, there might be no escape from the conclusion of the court below. General definitions of a proximate cause give little aid. Our guide is the reasonable expectation and purpose of the ordinary business man when making an ordinary business contract. It is his intention, expressed or fairly to be inferred, that counts. There are times when the law permits us to go far back in tracing events to causes. The inquiry for us is how far the parties to this contract *intended* us to go. The causes within their contemplation are the only causes that concern us. A recent case in the House of Lords gives the true method of approach (*Leyland Shipping Co. v. Norwich Fire Ins. Society*, 118 Law Times, 120, 125, decided January, 1918, not yet officially reported). Lord Shaw refers in his opinion to the common figure of speech which represents a succession of causes as a chain. He reminds us that the figure, though convenient, is inadequate. "Causation is not a chain, but a net. At each point, influences, forces, events, precedent and simultaneous, meet, and the radiation from each point extends infinitely" (*Leyland Shipping Co. v. Norwich Fire Ins. Society., supra*). From this complex web, the law picks out now this cause and now that one. The same cause producing the same effect may be proximate or remote as the contract of the parties seems to place it in light or shadow. That cause is to be held predominant which they would think of as predominant. A common-sense appraisement of everyday forms of speech and modes of thought must tell us when to stop. It is an act of "judgment as upon a matter of fact" (*Leyland Shipping Co. v. Norwich Fire Ins. Society, supra*).

This view of the problem of causation shows how impossible it is to set aside as immaterial the element of proximity in space. The law solves these problems pragmatically. There is no use in arguing that distance ought not to count, if life and experience tell us that it does. The question is not what men ought to think of as a cause. The question is what they do think of as a cause. We must put ourselves in the place of the average owner whose boat or building is damaged by the concussion of a distant explosion, let us say a mile away. Some glassware in his pantry is thrown down and broken. It would probably never occur to him that within the meaning of his policy of insurance, he had suffered loss by fire. A philosopher or a lawyer might persuade him that he had, but he would not believe it until they told him. He would expect indemnity, of course, if fire reached the thing insured. He would expect indemnity, very likely, if the fire was near at hand, if his boat or his building was within the danger zone of ordinary experience, if damage of some sort, whether from ignition or from the indirect consequences of fire, might fairly be said to be within the range of normal apprehension. But a different case presents itself when the fire is at all times so remote that there is never exposure to its direct perils, and that exposure to its indirect perils comes only through the presence of extraordinary conditions, the release and intervention of tremendous forces of destruction (*Tilton* v. *Hamilton Fire Ins. Co.*, 14 How. Pr. 363, 372, 373). A result which in other conditions might be deemed a mere incident to a fire and, therefore, covered by the policy, has ceased to be an incident, and has become the principal (*Briggs* v. *No. A. & M. Ins. Co.*, 53 N.Y. 446, 449). The distinction is no less real because it involves a difference of degree. In such a case, the damage is twice removed from the initial cause. It is damage by concussion; and concussion is not fire nor the immediate consequence of fire (*Benner* v. *Atl. D. Co.*, 134 N.Y. 156, 161, 162; *Booth* v. *R., W. & O. T. R. R. Co.*, 140 N. Y. 267, 280; *Holland House Co.* v. *Baird*, 169 N.Y. 136). But there is another stage of separation. It is damage by concussion traveling over a distance so remote that exposure to peril is not within the area of ordinary prevision, the range of probable expectation. The average man who speaks of loss by fire does not advert to the consequences of this play of catastrophic forces.

Precedents are not lacking for the recognition of the space element as a factor in causation. This is true even in the law of torts where there is a tendency to go farther back in the search for causes than there is in the law of contracts (Smith, Legal Cause in Actions of Tort, 25 Harvard Law Review, pp. 126, 127, 326). Especially in the law of insurance, the rule is that "you are not to trouble yourself with distant causes" (Willes, J., in *Ionides* v. *Univ. Marine Ins. Co.*, 14 C.B.N.S. 289; *Leyland Shipping Co.* v. *Norwich Fire Ins. Society*, 1917, 1 K.B. 873, 883, 893). "In an action on a policy, the *causa proxima* is alone considered in ascertaining the cause of loss; but in cases of other contracts and in questions of tort the *causa causans* is by no means disregarded" (*Fenton* v. *Thorley & Co.*, 1903 A.C. 443, 454; Smith, *supra*, p. 326). The rule "is based," it is said, "on the intention of the parties" (*Reischer* v. *Borwick*, 1894, 2 Q.B. 550). But even in tort, where responsibility is less dependent on intention, space may break the chain of causes. The wrongdoer who negligently sets fire to a building, is not liable without limit for the spread of the flames. [Here the court referred to other bounds on tort liability.] For our present purposes, it is enough that alike in contract and in tort, contiguity or remoteness in space may determine either the existence or the measure of liability. In doubtful situations a jury must say where the line is to be drawn (*Milwaukee & St. P. R. Co.* v. *Kellogg, supra; Ehrgott* v. *Mayor, etc., of N. Y.*, 96 N. Y. 264, 280, 281).

The case comes, therefore, to this: Fire must reach the thing insured, or come within such proximity to it that damage, direct or indirect, is within the compass of reasonable probability. Then only is it the proximate cause because then only may we suppose that it was within the contemplation of the contract. In last analysis, therefore, it is something in the minds of men, in the will of the contracting parties, and not merely in the physical bond of union between events, which solves, at least for the jurist, this problem of causation. In all this, there is nothing anomalous. Everything in nature is cause and effect by turns. For the physicist, one thing is the cause; for the jurist, another. Even for the jurist, the same cause is alternately proximate and remote as the parties choose to view it. A policy provides that the insurer shall not be liable for damage caused by the explosion of a boiler. The explosion causes a fire. If it were not for the exception in the policy, the fire would be the proximate cause of the loss and the explosion the remote one. By force of the contract, the explosion becomes proximate (*St. John* v. *Am. Mut. F. & M. Ins. Co.*, 11 N.Y. 516; *Ins. Co.* v. *Tweed*, 7 Wall. 44). A collision occurs at sea, and fire supervenes. The fire may be the proximate cause and the collision the remote one for the purpose of an action on the policy. The collision remains proximate for the purpose of suit against the colliding vessel (*N. Y. & B. D. Ex. Co.* v. *Traders' & M. Ins. Co.*, 132 Mass. 377, 382). There is nothing absolute in the legal estimate of causation. Proximity and remoteness are relative and changing concepts.

It may be said that these are vague tests, but so are most distinctions of degree. On the one hand, you have distances so great that as a matter of law the cause becomes remote; on the other, spaces so short that as a matter of law the cause is proximate. The boat moored to the pier is damaged by fire when dynamite about to be loaded from the pier is ignited by a falling match. Fire destroys the city building when the wall of an adjoining building, weakened by the flames, collapses (*Ermentrout* v. *Girard F. & M. Ins. Co.*, 63 Minn. 305; *Russell* v. *German Fire Ins. Co.*, 100 Minn. 528). Between these extremes, there is a borderland where juries must solve the doubt (*Milwaukee & St. Paul R. Co.* v. *Kellogg, supra; Donegan* v. *B. & N. Y. Ry. Co.*, 165 Fed. Rep. 869, 871; *Muller* v. *Globe, etc., Ins. Co.*, 246 Fed. Rep. 759; *Ehrgott* v. *Mayor, etc., of N. Y.*, 96 N. Y. 264, 280, 281; *William France, Fenwick & Co., Ltd.*, v. *North of England P. & I. Assn.*, 1917, 2 K.B. 522).

In this case, the facts are not disputed. The inferences to be drawn from them are not doubtful. The damage was not a loss by fire within the meaning of the policy.

The judgment should be reversed, and judgment ordered for the defendant, with costs in the Appellate Division and in this court.

NOTES

(1) *Of Wind and Groceries.* A windstorm interrupted the power supply at several locations where a grocer stored perishable foods. The foods spoiled, owing to loss of refrigeration there. The sequence of events was, then, storm—loss of power—spoilage. The grocer held several policies of fire insurance on its goods at those locations, with coverage extended to direct loss by windstorm. When the insurers disclaimed liability, the grocer brought an action on the policies. The insurers conceded that the loss of power was the direct result of the storm, but denied that the spoilage was. The court disagreed. Fred Meyer, Inc. v. Central Mutual Ins. Co., 235 F.Supp. 540 (D.Ore. 1964).

Judge Kilkenny had the temerity to doubt the reasoning in *Bird*, although he thought the cases to be distinguishable. He wrote:

> True enough, ... Justice Cardozo[1] refused to recognize the proximate cause rule in *Bird*. The great weight of respectable authority has declined to follow the thinking of that eminent Justice and abandon the "proximate cause" theory. The decisions consider, as suggested by the Justice, the expectation and purpose of the ordinary businessman when making an ordinary business contract. For that matter, I could with all grace and sincerity apply the Cardozo reasoning to the contracts in question. The ordinary businessman when making an ordinary insurance contract would in all probability believe that the language in question would cover this type of loss.... [The insurers'] contention that the food spoilage was a remote and not a direct loss by windstorm is without merit.

Id. at 543–44. Even if *Bird* was not distinguishable, the judge said, he preferred to follow what he called "common sense logic".

The court relied on a decision in a like case: Lipshultz v. General Ins. Co. of America, 96 N.W.2d 880 (Minn. 1959). That opinion does not mention *Bird*. For other authorities see Anno., *What Constitutes "Direct Loss" under Windstorm Insurance Coverage*, 65 A.L.R.3d 1128 (1999).

For another case in which Judge Cardozo eschewed the conception "proximate cause" see Palsgraf v. Long Island R.R. Co., 164 N.E. 564 (1928) (not a case directly about insurance).

(2) *The Case of the Traveling Beans.* A large quantity of pea-beans, grown in Chile and Ethiopia, were fumigated in France before being shipped to a U.S. buyer. On their arrival in Baltimore, an inspector for the Food & Drug Administration found that the fumigant used on some of the beans was not one approved in the United States. The buyer was put to expenses of sorting, reconditioning, and rebagging. It also lost customers and sold the goods at reduced prices. The buyer held "all risk" coverages on the goods; but detention by civil authorities was an excluded cause of loss. In an action by the buyer against its insurer the trial court entered summary judgment for the insurer. On appeal, the buyer contended that the proximate cause of its losses was not the FDA detention, but was the cause of that, the application of an improper fumigant. The court agreed to this extent: "the single cause nearest to the loss in time should not necessarily be found to be the

---

1. *Judge* Cardozo, as he was when on the New York Court of Appeals.

proximate cause." On the other hand, it was leery of using "but for" causation. The court said:

> As this Circuit has noted, "the horrendous niceties of the doctrine of so-called 'proximate cause,' employed in negligence suits, apply in a limited manner only to insurance policies." New York, New Haven & Hartford R. Co. v. Gray, 240 F.2d 460, 465 (2d Cir. 1957). Instead, in such cases we have looked at the reasonable understanding of the parties as to the meaning of their insurance agreements. Cf. Bird v. St. Paul Fire & Marine Insurance Co. ("The question is not what men ought to think of as a cause. The question is what they do think of as a cause.")

The court ruled that the buyer could not recover without establishing what its policies called "physical loss or damage". It remanded for a determination whether or not that was an element of the buyer's claim. So far as the claim was one for its temporary physical loss of the beans, there could be no recovery: "we would rely upon the common sense understanding that [that] was caused by detention." Blaine Richards & Co. v. Marine Indemnity Ins. Co. of America, 635 F.2d 1051 (2d Cir. 1980).

(3) *A Statute.* A North Dakota statute[2] embodies the rule of *Bird*, at least in part:

> *Liability of insurer for loss—Proximate and remote cause.*
>
> An insurer is liable for a loss proximately caused by a peril insured against even though a peril not contemplated by the insurance contract may have been a remote cause of the loss. An insurer is not liable for a loss of which the peril insured against was only a remote cause. The efficient proximate cause doctrine applies only if separate, distinct, and totally unrelated causes contribute to the loss.

In what way does the statute deviate from Cardozo's analysis, if at all?

PROBLEM

Storm-water caused heavy damage to a commercial building. A third of the damage was in electrical switching panels in which holes were blown by an explosion touched off when the water caused a short circuit. Another third was charring of paneling caused by the explosion. The rest was commonplace water damage, having no connection with electricity or electric facilities. The owner was insured against all risks of damage to the building, subject to an exclusion for "electric injury to electrical devices caused by electrical currents artificially generated." The exclusion was, however, qualified as follows: "unless loss or damage from a peril insured ensues and then this policy shall cover for such ensuing loss or damage."

On these facts, how many thirds of the damage are chargeable to the insurer? See Continental Ins. Co. v. Arkwright Mutual Ins. Co., 102 F.3d 30 (1st Cir. 1996).

Loss by "Friendly Fire"

The coverage of "loss by fire" applies only to hostile fires. An article damaged or destroyed in a receptacle by reason of a fire contained there, as intended, is a loss by *friendly* fire, not covered. So the courts have ruled, almost universally.

---

2. N.D. Cent. Code, § 26.1–32–01 (2005).

A friendly fire is defined as being a fire lighted and contained in a usual place for fire, such as a furnace, stove, incinerator, and the like, and used for the purposes of heating, cooking, manufacturing, or other common and usual everyday purposes.

Youse v. Employers Fire Ins. Co., 238 P.2d 472, 476 (Kan. 1951).

The friendly-fire doctrine seems to be out of line with usual practices in construing insurance contracts. It can be considered a constructive exclusion from the coverage of fire losses. What might explain it? Is it that friendly-fire losses are easier to fake than hostile-fire losses are? It has been thought that the doctrine, or one much like it, is necessary in order to foreclose recovery when, say, a cake is incinerated in an oven. That it does. But claims of that sort can readily be foreclosed by a modest deductible. More notable applications of the doctrine concern jewelry and manuscripts that are shoveled accidently into stoves.

PROBLEMS

(1) A blaze occurred in tissues on a homeowner's kitchen counter. Frightened, she swept the mass of tissues into an oven, forgetting that she had laid a valuable silver spoon in them. There the spoon is destroyed. Is her loss the result of a hostile fire?

(2) A homeowner, intent on applying linseed oil to a table, set a pan of oil to warm on his kitchen stove. He was distracted by the arrival of firefighters at the home of a neighbor, where flames had escaped the furnace. Being enlisted to help the firefighters, for some time he was absent from his own home and was not mindful of the pan of oil. On returning, he found that smoke from the boiling oil had coated the interiors of several rooms, and all their contents, with soot. For the expense of cleaning and painting, the homeowner makes a claim against his insurer for loss by fire. Must the claim be paid?

Earthquakes, Landslides, and Mudslides

Earthquakes, landslides, and mudslides are instances of what insurers commonly refer to as "earth movement". They are threats to many properties in some states, especially western states. A policy insuring against another peril is likely not only to segregate loss due to earth movement—one coincident with that other peril, perhaps—but also to exclude loss from that other peril if earth movement should contribute to the loss. Provisions narrowing coverages in that way have sometimes been condemned as contrary to public policy. An example of these provisions, abbreviated, is this:

> We do not insure against loss caused directly or indirectly by [earth movement, as defined]. Such loss is excluded regardless of any other cause or event contributing concurrently or in any sequence to the loss. . . .

If that provision were to appear in a fire-insurance policy, it would be significant in situations depicted in these ways (among others):

> (i) Earthquake -> **fire** -> loss;
>
> (ii) **Rainstorm** -> mudslide -> loss.

In these diagrams the insured peril is identified by bolding. In the first of these situations the earth movement is supposed to have caused ("contributed to") the loss via a more immediate (nonconcurrent) cause. It is otherwise in the second.

California courts have encountered situations more or less like these over many decades. One case concerned a claim on a fire policy that the claimant's clubhouse had been destroyed in the San Francisco conflagration of 1906. The insurer's answer did not say that, as is widely supposed, an earthquake caused the conflagration; rather, it said that earthquake had ruptured water mains and so had prevented firefighters from dousing the fire. That answer was not good enough, the court thought. It did not bring into play the policy exclusion of loss "caused directly or indirectly by [] earthquake", a phrase encompassing loss caused (directly or indirectly) by earthquake alone. See Pacific Union Club v. Commercial Union Assurance Co., 107 P. 728, 730 (Cal.App. 1910). The policy exclusion quoted and indented above can be seen as a reaction against rulings like that. (Again: "regardless of any other cause ... concurrently or in any sequence....")

Question: Might Cardozo have said that, on the facts alleged in *Pacific Union*, the earthquake was too remote a cause of the loss to count?

Landslide and mudslide cases tend to be converse to *Pacific Union*, as indicated above. In Washington State, it seems, public policy requires a recovery in a case like (ii) above. There the high court has said:

> Where a peril specifically insured against sets other causes in motion which, in an unbroken sequence and connection between the act and final loss, produce the result for which recovery is sought, the insured peril is regarded as the proximate cause of the entire loss.

Safeco Ins. Co. of America v. Hirschmann, 760 P.2d 969, 972 (1988). The Alaska Supreme Court has distanced itself from that view. "We can discern no sound policy reason for preventing the enforcement of the [] exclusion to which the parties in this case agreed." State Farm Fire & Cas. Co. v. Bongen, 925 P.2d 1042, 1045 (1996).

The present position in California rests on this statute, section 530 of the Insurance Code:

> An insurer is liable for a loss of which a peril insured against was the proximate cause, although a peril not contemplated by the contract may have been a remote cause of the loss; but he is not liable for a loss of which the peril insured against was only a remote cause.

As the California Supreme Court has construed this statute, it embodies the doctrine of *efficient proximate cause*. Pursuant to the efficient proximate cause doctrine, "When a loss is caused by a combination of a covered and specifically excluded risks, the loss is covered if the covered risk was the efficient proximate cause of the loss," but "the loss is not covered if the covered risk was only a remote cause of the loss, or the excluded risk was the efficient proximate, or predominate[sic] cause." Julian v. Hartford Underwriters Ins. Co., 110 P.3d 903, 904 (2005) (quoting).

Julian was a case of rain-induced landslide. (Also, the landslide toppled a tree onto the claimant's home.) The insurer conceded that its policy insured against a loss having weather conditions as the cause, and no other contributing cause. But the policy excluded loss by landslide, and it excluded also loss caused by weather conditions that "contribute in any way" to an excluded cause or event. The court sustained a summary judgment against the claimant. It held that "the weather conditions clause excludes the peril of rain inducing a landslide and that as applied here the clause does not violate section 530 or the efficient proximate cause doctrine."

The court was divided, however, about a hypothetical case in which a loss is attributable 99% to weather conditions and 1% to earth movement. That would raise troubling questions, the court said, about consistency of the policy with the efficient proximate cause doctrine. Not so, according to a concurring opinion. "I believe," Justice Brown wrote, "[that] the majority's approach leaves the door open for courts to step in and rewrite insurance contracts, in derogation of the parties' reasonable expectations as set forth in the contracts."

NOTE

Unnatural Causes. Excavation was negligently done at a Chicago building site, causing damage to neighboring structures; so it was alleged in an action against a builder by owners of those structures. Whether or not the builder was entitled to a defense of that action, under a liability coverage, was an issue in Nautilus Ins. Co. v. Vuk Builders, Inc., 406 F.Supp.2d 899 (N.D.Ill. 2005).

The policy defined "subsidence" as earth movement, and excluded property damage resulting from or contributed to by the subsidence of land. Attempting to evade the exclusion, the builder contended that because the term "earth movement" was ambiguous, it should be confined to incidents having natural causes. Among other precedents, the court considered Mattis v. State Farm Fire & Cas. Co., 454 N.E.2d 1156 (Ill.App.Ct.1983), in which the court said (quoting) that "[t]he majority of the courts which have considered this particular exclusion have found it to be ambiguous and have applied the doctrine of *ejusdem generis* to limit the definition of 'earth movement' to causes of the same class as earthquake and landslide." (The builder's policy gave landslide as one instance of earth movement.)

Mattis did not concern a liability coverage, however; rather, it concerned a property coverage. In *Vuk Builders* the insurer contended that it would be nonsense to exclude only naturally caused events from a liability coverage, for those events entail no liability. The court saw some appeal in that argument, but called it superficial, and envisaged some counterexamples. "For example, the owner of a house built on a hill could be liable for damages if a landslide caused his home to collapse onto his neighbor's property."

The court accepted the builder's narrowing reading of the exclusion. The insurer had sought a declaratory judgment that it need not provide the builder with a defense. The court granted a motion by the builder to dismiss the action.[3]

---

3. Actually, Vuk Builders was only one of several defendants in the negligence action and in the declaratory-judgment action. Movants other than Vuk Builders also prevailed in the latter.

In the Wake of Hurricanes

"Since Hurricane Katrina struck, [] insurance companies have paid $5.3 billion for damage to more than 330,000 homes in Mississippi and $10.3 billion for nearly a million homes in Louisiana."[4] This Note sketches what is publicly known about the subject, with respect to homeowners insurance, late in the first quarter of 2007. Following that is a report on resistance made by some insurers to claims, made by some homeowners, to what the insurers depicted as "flood" losses.

Questions arose almost at once about the extent of insurance claims. Much of the damage could be ascribed to flooding, and much to high winds. Among the homeowners affected, those in the best position were holders of insurance written—by private insurers—pursuant to the National Flood Insurance Act. These were the minority: some 8% in the county embracing Biloxi, according to federal data. Many others faced a water-damage exclusion, as follows, in their homeowner's policies.

Property Exclusions (Section I)

1. We do not cover loss to any property resulting directly or indirectly from any of the following. Such a loss is excluded even if another peril or event contributed concurrently or in any sequence to cause the loss.

> . . .

> b) Water or damage caused by water-borne material. Loss resulting from water or water-borne material damage described below is not covered even if other perils contributed, directly or indirectly to cause the loss. Water and water-borne material damage means:

> > (1) flood, surface water, waves, tidal waves, overflow of a body of water, spray from these, whether or not driven by wind.[5]

The form from which this exclusion is taken contains also a windstorm-damage exclusion. That exclusion is much more limited, however, applying to certain structures, for example, with a "roof-like" metal covering.

How apply the "flood exclusion" when it is unclear whether a collapse is due to flooding or to wind? How apply it when a collapse is traceable to

---

4. *The New York Times*, Jan. 24, 2007, pp. C1, C8. Other circumstances described below are drawn largely from that and earlier reports in the *Times*. See also the issues of March 16 (C1) and March 20 (C4), 2007.

5. The list beginning "flood" is substantially identical to one in "Section 1 EX-CLUSIONS" of the ISO Homeowners 2 Broad Form (#HO 00 02 04 91), generally insuring against "physical loss caused by . . .

1. Fire or lightning.

2. Windstorm or hail."

high water driven onshore by wind (the "storm surge")? And what of damage produced by the waters of Lake Pontchartrain, pouring through broken levees in New Orleans? These were among the questions facing homeowners, adjusters, and the courts.

By mid-September the attorney general of Mississippi, Jim Hood, was asking for a restraining order by which insurers would be prevented from— among other things—denying coverage by reason of flood exclusions. According to a news report,[6] he accused them of "selling confusing policies that fell short of homeowners' reasonable expectations of coverage." The same report quoted an insurance executive as saying: "In essence, the attorney general is challenging the validity of contracts in Mississippi." Private actions were in prospect; one plaintiffs' attorney said that he planned to sue for flood damage on behalf of hundreds of homeowner-clients.

Early in 2007 Mr. Hood was placing before a grand jury evidence that might have led to the indictment of the nation's largest insurer, State Farm, for misconduct in the adjustment of hurricane damage. Meanwhile, State Farm had settled with many thousands of homeowners. Hundreds of those homeowners brought actions challenging the settlements.

On January 23 a more comprehensive settlement was announced. It concerns Mississippi properties only. Persons having influence on the terms included Judge L.T. Senter, Jr., of the Southern District of Mississippi (with whom most of the individual suits were lodged), and Richard F. Scruggs, the attorney mentioned above. Also State officials: Mr. Hood and George Dale, the Mississippi commissioner of insurance. (Initially, it is reported, Dale and Hood expressed reservations. "Both officials said they wanted to make sure that homeowners got the best possible deal. Mr. Dale, though, said it was also important that any agreement not be overly burdensome for the insurance companies." Ibid.)

State Farm said that it will reopen earlier settlements, will make assured payments to 1,640 claimants—not less than $80 million to a minor fraction of those. Most of those, and tens of thousands of others, are to be permitted to reopen their claims. State Farm committed at least $50 million to those projected cases, and may be required to disburse as much as twelve times that amount, according to estimates. The settlement is expected to be a prototype for settlements with other insurers.

Mr. Hood's civil action, and the criminal investigation, will be terminated. Crafting the sentences about the latter was said to have been the "final sticking point". (One can imagine a worry about the appearance of having used a grand jury to reinforce civil claims.)

State Farm had earlier decided to write no new business on homes in Florida. Homeowners there and elsewhere, as far north as New England,

6. "Mississippi Sues Insurers . . .", *The Times*, Sept. 16, 2005, p. C4.

found that either their coverages with various insurers would not be renewed or their premiums would be sharply increased, in the hurricanes' wake.

· · ·

"Flood" Exclusions

One opinion on this subject concerned a set of five claims by New Orleans homeowners who, they alleged, suffered losses due to a break in a wall of the infamous 17th Street Canal, causing water to enter the streets and their homes. The claimants contested the application of water-damage exclusions in their policies. They contended also that the exclusions were "unconscionable and void".[7]

All of the policies concerned provided that they did not insure against loss caused by "water damage", defined essentially as above.[8] The insurers moved to dismiss the actions. These motions were the first in a "daunting line of litigation", the court said, adding that the potential impact of its decisions "might be considered overwhelming." In re Katrina Canal Breaches Consolidated Litigation, 466 F.Supp.2d 729 (E.D.La. 2006) (Nov. 27). Judge Duval expressed regret that he could not certify the issues to the Louisiana Supreme Court.

The court denied most of the insurers' motions. One of its major assertions was to characterize the homeowner-policy coverages as "all risk". Judge Duval made a critical ruling when he found that the word "flood" could be understood reasonably as an inundation caused by a natural event, such as rain or tide, only. He did so partly by reason of his independent search of dictionary definitions ("numerous meanings"), and partly because of "the plethora of *insurance* case law where the issue of causation is at play with respect to the application of a water damage exclusion".

Much of the opinion is commentary on the Colorado case Kane v. Royal Ins. Co., 768 P.2d 678, 681 (1989). There the court took the word *flood* to comprise a rise in the Fall River when Lawn Lake "overtopped" its dam. Distinguishable, the court said, from the collapse of the walls of the 17th Street Canal, "when faced with conditions they were allegedly designed to withstand." But Judge Duval plainly preferred the dissenting position in *Kane*. He cited cases taking the word *flood* in a narrower sense. In some of those cases the courts gave color to the word by reference to its association with others not caused by artifice—"waves", for example, and "tidal water".

---

7. In the opinion cited here that contention was not considered.

8. The term "tidal water" being used, however, instead of "tidal waves".

The policy issued by State Farm differed in an important respect from the others. As to the language quoted here, however, it differed only in that the last comma was replaced by the word "all". The State–Farm policy was not an "ISO policy".

The court relied also on an earth-movement case, Fayad v. Clarendon Nat'l Ins. Co., 899 So.2d 1082 (Fla. 2005), saying that the Florida court had "noted the practical differences for the insurer between losses caused by natural occurrences as opposed to man-made occurrences. The insurer would have the right to subrogation against the tort-feasor in the event that the loss was caused by a man-made event, rather than a natural occurrence. This factor from an underwriting standpoint supports the proposition that the insurer was excluding a loss for which it had no recourse."

One of the insurers, State Farm, was more successful than the others, owing to a difference in its policy language. (See n.8 above.) We do not insure, State Farm wrote, for *inter alia*, flood loss *regardless of . . . the cause of the excluded event . . .* [or] whether the event . . . arises from natural or external forces. . . . (emphasis by the court) "Such language is clear to the Court and as such, the Court must find that the State Farm policy as written excludes coverage for all flooding." The court's appreciation of that language worked to the disadvantage of the other insurers; "some insurers made efforts to be clear in their intentions", it said.

NOTES

(1) *Federal Jurisdiction?* Many actions against insurers growing out of Katrina and Rita have included claims against selling agents, charged with misconduct with relation to flood insurance. Agents have been charged with having advised, improvidently, that a customer did not need flood insurance or needed less than a customer held, with having failed to advise the purchase of flood insurance or to advise that a higher limit be bought, and with having failed, as promised, to procure it, or to increase the amount of it. In a number of cases insurers have rushed to the defense of their agents. That might have been expected; but one motive lies beneath the surface. The insurers seem to have a strong preference for litigation in a federal court, as contrasted with a Louisiana or Mississippi court. Given a large claim by a Mississippi citizen, say, removal from a state court would ordinarily satisfy that preference for a major insurer, not being a "citizen" of Mississippi. But it does not when a plausible claim is made, under state law, against another defendant who is, like the plaintiff, a citizen of Mississippi. (There is not, then, *complete* diversity.) Federal judges have had to deal with several contentions by out-of-state insurers that the joinder of a local agent was a flimsy stratagem to prevent removal.[9]

A test case is one in which a local agent is charged with having promised to procure insurance for the plaintiff under the National Flood Insurance Act, and having failed to do so. If that claim were one based on federal law, it would present a "federal question", and so would open the way to removal notwithstanding the common citizenship of the plaintiff and the defendant agent. Courts have had repeated occasions to observe that a claim like that rests on state law. (Mississippi law opens an agent to liability for negligence in handling a customer's account.) The courts have contrasted a claim arising out of faulty administration of a flood policy,

---

9. "This Court has issued extensive opinions on the full range of legal issues regarding motions to remand in Hurricane Katrina insurance litigation." Jo Ellen In- vestments, L.L.C. v. Lafayette Ins. Co., 2006 WL 3627675 (E.D.La. 2006). In Mississippi, many like matters have come before Judge L.T. Senter, Jr., of the Southern District.

or of fault in adjusting a claim under a flood policy, to which federal-question jurisdiction extends. By and large, then, diversity jurisdiction has failed often to give major insurers the access they want to the United States courts for the Eastern District of Louisiana or for the Southern District of Mississippi.

(2) *"Good Neighbor"*. In what is said to have been the first of the "Katrina lawsuits" to be tried before a jury, the defendant was the State Farm Fire & Cas. Company. It had removed the action from a state court to the Southern District of Mississippi. Norman and Genevieve Broussard charged State Farm with bad faith in having rejected their claim, one based on the destruction of their home by a tornado. State Farm contended that the loss was excluded from its coverage as the result of a storm surge. "The Broussards claimed that State Farm's 'Like a good neighbor, State Farm is there' advertisement [was] a fraudulent misrepresentation", or that the ad gave rise to a fiduciary relation violated when their claim was rejected. Judge Senter rejected arguments made by State Farm about the burden of proof and directed a verdict for the Broussards in the amount of the policy limit. He then submitted a claim for punitive damages to the jury. It awarded $2.5 million. Mealey's Litigation Report: Catastrophic Loss, Vol. 2, Issue #4 (2007).

C.   LOSSES INSURED: KINDS AND MEASURES

At the outset this section continues the topic *insurable interest*, here in relation to the measure of a claimant's recovery. Thereafter it concerns a limitation on insurers' liabilities expressed in the policy term "direct physical loss", contrasting that kind of loss with other kinds of insurable losses. The section deals also with policy expressions that indicate how to determine the amount of an insured loss ("actual cash value", for example).

In general, the efforts of insurers illustrated in this section are to deny or to curtail claims even though the insurers have issued policies that are enforceable and that cover the events on which the claims rest, and even though the claimants have suffered losses. A claim might be curtailed because the claimant had less than full ownership of the property insured. A claim might be curtailed or denied because the policy limits the kinds of loss payable. And a claim might be curtailed because the claimant relies on an over-generous measure of loss.

Related grounds for denying or curtailing a claim are policy provisions that set dollar limits on amounts payable. These provisions go by the familiar names *policy limit*, *deductible*, and *co-pay*. These limitations are not considered here because they are not at all singular to property insurance.

Delk v. Markel American Ins. Co.

The facts supposed in this case, and some of the court's rulings, appear above at p. 421.

IV. THE INSURABLE INTEREST OF A COTENANT IN POSSESSION MAY EXCEED THE QUANTUM OF HIS (OR HER) FRACTIONAL LEGAL ESTATE IN THE COTENANCY PROPERTY WHERE THE INSURING COTENANT ACTS AS THE MANAGING AGENT FOR THE JOINT OWNER[34]

Defendant invokes the oft-repeated statement that a cotenant's insurable interest is limited to his (or her) interest in the property.[35] While we agree with this as a general proposition, we note that it is an abstraction that begs the question of what qualifies as an interest. Defendant argues that the intent of the general proposition is to limit a cotenant's interest to the quantum of his (or her) legal title. We grant that under some circumstances a cotenant's insurable interest may properly be so limited, but we regard Oklahoma's factual expectation approach to insurable interest as authorizing under proper circumstances recovery by a cotenant of more than the cotenant's fractional interest in the insured property.

Tenancy in common is a joint interest in property.[36] Its only essential element is a unity of the right of possession.[37] While each tenant in common has a separate and distinct title which is held independently of the other cotenants,[38] each stands to the other in a relation of mutual trust and confidence.[39] One tenant in common may not act or claim "in derogation of"[40] the interest of the other joint owners.[41] This means that a cotenant is not allowed to lessen or diminish the value or effect of the other cotenant's right, title, interest or status in the land.[42]

34. [The insurer argued that, owing to a supposed lacuna in the evidence, the court should not consider the possibility of Delk's insurable interest as a managing agent. The record was not explicit about an agreement on her part about procuring insurance, except with respect to son John.

[The court rejected the argument. It relied partly on John's presumed authority to act for his children, partly on evidence suggestive of an agency, and partly on the court's role as a provider of various "scenarios" in which an insurable interest might and might not be ascribed to Delk.]

35. *See e.g.* 3 COUCH ON INSURANCE 3d, § 42:45 (1997), which states: "A tenant in common has an insurable interest to the extent of his or her interest in the property ... When a part owner insures his or her individual interest, he or she need not specify the nature of his or her interest, but it is essential that he or she not insure for more than his or her interest...."

36. De Mik v. Cargill, 485 P.2d 229, 233 (Okla.1971).

37. Matthews v. Matthews, 961 P.2d 831, 834 (Okla.1998). The common law concept of unity of possession means that each

cotenant is entitled to occupy every part of the co-owned property regardless of the quantum of the occupier's fractional interest, subject only to the other cotenants' equal right of possession.

38. *Id*.

39. Rex Oil Refining, Inc. v. Shirvan, 443 P.2d 82, 87 (Okla. 1967).

40. The term "derogation" is "ordinarily used to indicate an avoidance of; the abrogation of; *or the lessening in value of, a right or other legal relationship or status."* JOHN M. CARTWRIGHT, GLOSSARY OF REAL ESTATE LAW 270 (1972) (emphasis supplied). For an in-depth discussion of the term, see Sharon v. Sharon, 16 P. 345, 370 (Cal. 1888) (Thornton, J., dissenting) (stating that "derogation is ... the act of taking away or destroying the value or effect of anything, or of limiting its extent, or of restraining its operation; ...").

41. *Rex Oil Refining, supra* note 39 at 87 (cotenants stand to each other in a relation of mutual trust and confidence; neither will be permitted to act in hostility to the other in reference to the joint estate)....

42. *Matthews, supra* note 37 at 835.

While none of these attributes of cotenancy places an affirmative duty on one cotenant to insure the common property for the benefit of the other joint owners, cotenants clearly have a mutual and reciprocal interest in the safety and preservation of the common property. This is especially true where the cotenants are all family members and the common property is the residence of some or all of them. Each has a reciprocal expectation of economic advantage from the home's continuing existence and its availability as a residence for the others. When the residence is destroyed, the occupants lose more than their individual fractional legal interests in the property. Before the home's destruction, they all have a place to live. Afterwards, they are homeless and must go to the expense of securing another home.

In such a case it would not be unusual for one of the resident cotenants to be given the responsibility of maintaining and protecting the property for the benefit of the other co-owning family members. A cotenant who has assumed or who has been given such general managerial authority over the property is free to exercise that authority by taking any measure which a reasonably prudent person in that position would take to protect the property, including purchasing insurance for the benefit of all joint owners.[43] A tenant in common who manages family-owned property which serves as the residence of all or some of the family clearly has a substantial economic interest in the continued existence of the property both as an individual and as the representative of the family.

Whether Delk was in fact authorized by the other cotenants as their agent to secure fire coverage for the co-owned premises is a question of fact for resolution by the certifying court.[44] We would only note here that the realities of a cotenancy relationship in which the cotenants are all family members, some or all of whom occupy the premises as their home, suggest that something less than a formal agreement would suffice to establish the requisite agreement or understanding.[45]

---

43.   Gray v. Holman, 909 P.2d 776, 779–80 (Okla. 1995) (recognizing that a mother with no legal estate in her son's property might nevertheless, acting as her son's agent, insure the son's property in her own name but on her son's behalf).

44.   Agency has been defined as "a contract by which one person, with greater or less discretionary powers, undertakes to represent another in certain business relations." FRANCIS WHARTON, A COMMENTARY ON THE LAW OF AGENCY AND AGENTS § 1 at 1(1876). See also RESTATEMENT OF THE LAW (SECOND) OF AGENCY § 1, which defines agency as "the fiduciary relation which results from the manifestation of consent by one person to another that the other shall act on his behalf and subject to his control, and consent by the other so to act." For a history of common-law agency, see B.S. MARKESINIS and R.J.C. MUNDAY, AN OUTLINE OF THE LAW OF AGENCY pp. 1–225 (Butterworths 1992).

45.   The certification order points out that three of the six cotenants in this case are minors. Minors have statutory limitations on their capacity to enter into insurance contracts and they are barred by statute from appointing agents. See the provisions of 36 O.S. 2001 § 3606 (insurance contracts by minors) and 15 O.S. 2001 § 17 (appointment of agents by minors), respectively. No person in Oklahoma, including a parent, has control over the property of a child unless appointed by the court. Yet parents are the natural guardians of their children. As their children's natural guardians, parents ordinarily have the minimal right to their custody, control, and care. It is their duty to support and educate their children. 10 O.S. 2001 § 4. They are liable to third persons for necessities furnished their children when they ne-

The provisions of 36 O.S. 2001 § 3605.C. state, "The measure of an insurable interest in property is the extent to which the insured *might be damnified* by loss, injury, or impairment thereof." The statutory formulation is simply another way of saying that the insured may recover the amount which will indemnify him (or her) for the loss suffered. Indemnification is measured by the extent to which the insured has been economically impacted by the happening of the insured event. Assuming the existence of the requisite agency relationship between plaintiff and her co-owners, anything less than a recovery in the amount of the value of the property (up to the policy limits) will not constitute full indemnity for the loss.

It might be objected that allowing a fractional interest holder to recover the full value of the fee interests under an insurance contract implicates the public policy concerns underlying the insurable interest requirement. In response we would underscore that the insuring cotenant acts as an agent for the other co-owners in acquiring insurance on the premises and any recovery is held in trust by the insuring cotenant for the benefit of the other joint owners. An agent is a fiduciary with respect to any matter in the scope of the agency relationship.[46] An agent receiving money belonging to the principal holds the money in trust for the principal's benefit.[47] Should the insuring cotenant fail to account to the other joint owners for their share of the proceeds, an action to impress the funds with a constructive trust would be available.[48] The insuring cotenant can have no motivation for wagering on the property's loss and cannot profit by its destruction where the insurer is required to pay the coverage limits, but each cotenant is legally entitled to only his share of the proceeds.[49]

---

glect to provide the children with necessities. 10 O.S. 2001 § 13. The right of parents to the care, custody, companionship and management of their child is a fundamental right protected by the federal and state constitutions. The relationship is in the nature of a trust, subject to control and regulation by the state. Implicit in a parent's duty to care for a child is the means to carry out that duty, including the authority to take reasonable measures to protect the child's property interests. This may include obtaining insurance on property the child owns. When the parent and child are cotenants and the parent insures his (or her) own interest in the co-owned premises or authorizes another cotenant to procure insurance to protect the parent's interest in the property, the parent may also agree on behalf of the child that any insurance obtained protect the child's interest as well. Whether the parent has done so is a question of fact. [Case citations in this footnote omitted.]

46. RESTATEMENT OF THE LAW (SECOND) OF AGENCY § 13.

47. A fiduciary stands in the status of trustee in relation to his (or her) principal. Panama Processes, S.A. v. Cities Service Co., 796 P.2d 276, 290 (Okla. 1990).

48. An implied trust or constructive trust arises by operation of law. It is imposed against an individual when the individual obtains a legal right to property through fraudulent, abusive means or through a method which violates equity and good conscience. Matter of Estate of Ingram, 874 P.2d 1282, 1287 (Okla. 1994). A constructive trust is one of equity's most powerful fraud-rectifying devices. The primary reason for imposing a constructive trust is to avoid unjust enrichment. Easterling v. Ferris, 651 P.2d 677, 680 (Okla. 1982).

49. The certification order states that plaintiff's adult son, John, not only agreed with plaintiff that she would procure the insurance on the property but also that she alone would collect the proceeds in the event of an insured loss. Whether such an agreement is contrary to public policy and whether it can bind the interests of the minor cotenants even if valid between the adults are issues not presented by, nor fairly comprised in, the question certified to us, which addresses only the relative rights of the insurer and the insured.

The ordinary person purchasing insurance cannot be expected to understand a term of art such as insurable interest in a policy of insurance. All the insured knows is that he (or she) has paid money to secure protection for the insured property and in case it is destroyed the insurer will cover the loss. The policy of insurance in this case states that it covers "your [the insured's] dwelling." On the eleventh page of the policy, fifth among a list of fifteen conditions is the insurable interest limitation. The insurer never asked the insured about her legal interest in the insured property. The policy limits and the premium paid by this insured clearly demonstrate her intent that more than her bare legal interest be insured. An insurer cannot lead an unsophisticated insured into believing that protection of the family home has been procured and then after the occurrence of the insured event deny full coverage.[50]

Finally, it is immaterial to the risk assumed by the insurer whether this plaintiff was acting as the agent of the joint owners or whether she was the property's sole owner. The insurer believed it was entering into a contract of indemnity for the full value of the home up to the coverage limits. Its obligations are not increased by the actual status of the legal title to the insured premises. The risk it assumed is the risk it incurred.[51]

V. A COTENANT IN POSSESSION, BEING LEGALLY LIABLE TO THE OTHER JOINT OWNERS FOR DAMAGE TO OR DESTRUCTION OF THE COMMON PROPERTY, HAS AN INSURABLE INTEREST TO THE EXTENT OF HIS (OR HER) POTENTIAL LEGAL LIABILITY

Plaintiff also urges us to instruct the certifying court that she has an insurable interest in the whole dwelling by virtue of her use and occupancy of it as her residence. We need not decide whether bare possession would suffice to permit a cotenant in possession of a dwelling to insure it for its full value. This is so because we recognize the traditional common-law rule that whenever one person is by circumstances placed in such a position with regard to another, that, if he (or she) did not use ordinary care and skill in his (or her) own conduct, he (or she) would cause danger of injury to the person or property of the other, a duty arises to use ordinary care and skill to avoid such danger.[52] A cotenant who occupies and uses the common property falls within this rule. He (or she) is obligated to use ordinary care in the use of the common property and stands liable to the other joint tenants for damage to or destruction of the property. A cotenant in possession may hence become subject to pecuniary loss in tort if the dwelling is damaged or destroyed. This legal liability provides an insurable interest for purposes of property insurance.[53]

---

50. *See* Collins v. Quincy Mutual Fire Ins. Co., 256 S.E.2d 718, 721 (N.C. 1979); [Convis v. Citizens' Mut. Fire Ins. Co., 86 N.W. 994 (Mich. 1901)] at 622–23.

51. *Collins, supra.*

52. Iglehart v. Board of County Comm'rs of Rogers County, 60 P.3d 497, 502 (Okla. 2002); Heaven v. Pender, 11 Q.B.D. 503, 509, 1883 WL 19069.

53. [Keeton & Widiss, INSURANCE LAW: A GUIDE TO FUNDAMENTAL PRINCIPLES, LEGAL DOCTRINES, AND COMMERCIAL PRACTICES (Student ed. 1988)] at 111.

The separate writing of the justice who partially concurs in today's pronouncement suggests that our answer to the certified question establishes as a matter of law that a cotenant in possession has an insurable interest in the common property by virtue of the cotenancy relationship. This is a misstatement of our holding, which rests on the potential liability of a cotenant in possession to the other cotenants for damage to or destruction of the common property and not on a status-based duty to insure the common property for the benefit of the other joint owners.[54]

The objection could be raised that a cotenant who could recover all the insurance proceeds upon a total loss of the common property might be tempted to destroy the property and then either keep the proceeds or use them to rebuild, excluding the former cotenants from ownership of the new premises. Cotenancy principles preclude this result. Just as the acquisition of an adverse title inures to the benefit of other joint owners,[55] so, too, must the recovery of insurance proceeds. The insuring cotenant in possession must account to the other joint owners for their share of the insurance proceeds and a suit to impress a constructive trust on the proceeds would be available to the other cotenants if the insuring cotenant fails to make the required accounting.

. . .

Language of Loss-measurement

"Actual cash value" and the cost of repair or replacement are the principal determinants of recoveries for losses insured against in fire policies. The opinion that follows construes the expression quoted as it appeared in this policy phrase:

> . . . to the extent of the actual cash value of the property at the time of the loss, but not exceeding the amount which it would cost to repair or replace the property with material of like kind and quality. . . .

The opinion relies on the leading case, McAnarney's case in New York. The New York Standard Fire Policy provides for coverage

TO THE LESSER AMOUNT OF EITHER:

1) THE ACTUAL CASH VALUE OF THE PROPERTY AT THE TIME OF THE LOSS, OR

2) THE AMOUNT WHICH IT WOULD COST TO REPAIR OR REPLACE THE PROPERTY WITH MATERIAL OF LIKE KIND AND QUALITY WITHIN A REASONABLE TIME AFTER SUCH LOSS. . . .

---

54. None of the cases cited in the separate writing *holds* that the duty of a cotenant in possession to preserve the common property includes an affirmative duty to insure. [Here the court reviewed those cases.]

55. *See* cases cited *supra* note 41.

N.Y. Ins. L. § 3404(e) at 1. "Actual cash value" is commonly abbreviated to "ACV".

For a structure of substantial age the cost of repair or replacement is usually greater than ACV. In general, homeowners are offered coverage to the extent (within policy limits) of that cost rather than ACV, which would be less expensive. Many insurance-company forms, it is said, permit a buyer to choose between ACV and replacement-cost recovery. A form developed by the Insurance Services Office permits an insured, having chosen ACV recovery, to switch upon providing notice within 180 days of the loss.

NOTE

Replacement Cost and the World Trade Center Towers. Among the many claim-adjustment problems generated by the destruction of the towers, one concerned a policy underwritten by SR International ("Swiss Re"). Some parties affected found it desirable to claim ACV recovery. See SR International Business Ins. Co. v. World Trade Center Properties, LLC, 381 F.Supp.2d 250 (S.D.N.Y. 2005). The claimants there were holders of 99–year leases on the towers, and were known as the Silverstein Parties. They were insured for more than $3.5 billion per occurrence. Of that amount, about a quarter was underwritten by Swiss Re.

In litigation about the claimants' loss the parties agreed that the replacement cost exceeded ACV. The policy permitted the claimants to recover that cost. That, the court said, was "as would be expected with a 'pro-insured' form drafted by insurance brokers".

Soon after the disaster the claimants brought an action (actually a counterclaim in a declaratory-judgment action) against Swiss Re for at least a partial payment calculated by reference to ACV. The claimants moved for a summary judgment on that demand. Before claiming ACV, Larry Silverstein had announced his intention to rebuild the lost commercial space at the World Trade Center site. Presumably, however, that plan was thwarted by long running controversies and negotiations attending reconstruction at "ground zero".

Swiss Re resisted the motion by reference to a provision in its policy requiring it to pay ACV "in the event" that the insured elected not to rebuild, a provision operating, the court said, as a condition precedent. To that, the claimants objected by reference to the standard fire policy which, by statute, would replace any term less favorable to the insured. Denying the motion, the court said:

> The standard policy does not require an ACV payment up front or give the insured a right to elect between ACV and replacement cost recovery, regardless of whether the insured decides to rebuild.... [The actual policy] provision is more favorable to the Silverstein Parties.... Under the standard policy, ACV would be the most the Silverstein Parties could recover. Alternatively, the Silverstein Parties still can recover ACV if they elect not to rebuild. Put another way, they can choose to receive more insurance than is guaranteed under the statutory policy by electing to rebuild, or receive the same amount of insurance guaranteed under the statutory policy by electing not to rebuild.

Id. at 258.

PROBLEM

In Delk v. Insurance Company, above, the court suggested that Debra Delk may have been entrusted by her co-tenants, family members all, with managerial responsibility for the home that she and others occupied, a property in which all the co-tenants had rights of occupancy. Suppose that she was. Suppose also that the insurance she bought limited recovery to ACV, although it would have been prudent of her to buy replacement cost insurance. (That cost, say, was substantially greater than ACV, and the additional expense would have been reasonable.) Should Delk be accountable to her co-tenants for having neglected their interests by under-insuring? Recall this observation by the court: "An agent is a fiduciary with respect to any matter in the scope of the agency relationship."

The *Delk* opinion says only that the amount claimed against the insurer was the policy limit. Possibly, then, Ms. Delk *did* hold replacement-cost insurance, only not enough. That too might mean that she neglected the interests of her co-tenants.

If she was accountable to them for either reason, it does not follow that a similar charge can be laid against one who has made an ordinary commercial commitment to maintain insurance, in an unspecified amount, for the benefit of another. But perhaps it should?

Elberon Bathing v. Ambassador Insurance Co.

Supreme Court of New Jersey, 1978.
77 N.J. 1, 389 A.2d 439.

■ CONFORD, P. J. A. D. (temporarily assigned).

The principal question on this appeal concerns the valuation methods to be used in ascertaining the "actual cash value" of a partial loss under the Standard Form Fire Insurance Policy, N.J.S.A. 17:36–5.15 *et seq*. We are also required to determine whether failure to apply the appropriate standard is sufficient cause to set aside an appraisal award. The appeal arises in the context of a judgment in the Law Division in favor of the insured plaintiffs in the amount of $52,000 for excess coverage based on a $77,000 appraisement minus $25,000 primary coverage (on another policy) for a loss due to fire. The Appellate Division affirmed in an unreported opinion.

Defendant, Ambassador Insurance Company, issued a fire insurance policy to plaintiffs, Elberon Bathing Co., Inc. and Elberon Bathing Club, to indemnify them against loss by fire to club facilities and contents situated in Long Branch. The $125,000 policy represented excess coverage over a $25,000 primary policy issued plaintiffs by Great Southwest Fire Insurance Company.

On January 8, 1975, while the policy was in effect, plaintiffs' bathing club was damaged by fire to an amount "greatly in excess of $25,000." Great Southwest promptly paid Elberon the $25,000. However, plaintiffs and defendant were unable to adjust plaintiffs' covered loss under the excess policy. Pursuant to the terms of the policy and an "agreement for submission to appraisers," plaintiffs and defendant each appointed an appraiser. The appraisers were, in turn, to select a disinterested umpire. However, they were unable to reach agreement thereon. Plaintiffs then filed a complaint and an order to show cause requesting the court to appoint an umpire pursuant to the terms of the policy.[1] The court appointed an umpire.

Shortly thereafter the appraisers and umpire went to inspect the insured premises which had already been repaired. According to affidavits of the umpire and defendant's appraiser, the umpire and plaintiffs' appraiser believed that their role was merely to determine the replacement cost of the damaged property. The umpire and plaintiffs' appraiser determined the actual cash value of the entire property to be $180,000 and the amount of fire loss to the property to total $77,000. This consisted of $8,500 for damage to personal property and $68,500 for pure replacement cost of the realty destroyed. Defendant's appraiser refused to sign the award.

Plaintiffs sought entry of judgment on the appraisement. Defendant answered, denying the finality of the award on the basis of its contention that the umpire had not heard all the evidence nor considered all matters submitted to him. . . . Defendant demanded that the award be vacated, and requested a jury trial. . . .

The trial judge heard oral argument and reviewed the pleadings and affidavits. He stated that the appraisers could properly determine that replacement cost was the appropriate measure of the actual loss recoverable under the policy. He also found that there was no manifest mistake justifying setting aside the award. After deduction for the primary insurance coverage judgment was entered for plaintiff for $52,000. The Appellate Division, agreeing with the trial judge that under the appropriate narrow standard of review "the facts in the case do not dictate a basis for vacating the award . . .," affirmed. We granted certification.

I

Defendant argues that an award based on replacement cost without deduction for depreciation contravenes the measure of recovery provided for in the policy, that being "actual cash value." We agree.

N.J.S.A. 17:36–5.15 *et seq.* regulates the subject of fire insurance. As required by N.J.S.A. 17:36–5.19, the policy before us insured Elberon ". . . to the extent of the actual cash value of the property at the time of the loss, but not exceeding the amount which it would cost to repair or replace the property with material of like kind and quality. . . ." This appeal calls for a determination of the meaning of "actual cash value." That phrase is also found in the appraisal provision of the Standard Form Policy which conforms to the statute.

In case the insured and this Company shall fail to agree as to the actual cash value or the amount of loss, then, on the written demand of either, each shall select a competent and disinterested appraiser and notify the other of the appraiser selected within twenty days of such demand. The appraisers shall first select a competent and disinterested umpire; and failing for fifteen days to agree upon such umpire, then,

---

1. The complaint requested appointment of an umpire "in accordance with the provisions of N.J.S.A. 2A:24–5," the Arbitration and Award Act. The appropriate statute governing the appointment of the umpire under a fire policy is N.J.S.A. 17:36–5.20.

on request of the insured or this Company, such umpire shall be selected by a judge of a court of record in the State in which the property covered is located. *The appraisers shall then appraise the loss, stating separately actual cash value and loss to each item*; and, failing to agree, shall submit their differences, only, to the umpire. An award in writing, so itemized, of any two when filed with this Company shall *determine the amount of actual cash value and loss....* (emphasis added) N.J.S.A. 17:36–5.20

The appraisal award here under review purported to follow the stated procedure.

A review of the record indicates that the appraisal was based on replacement cost without consideration of the element of depreciation. Plaintiffs argue that straight replacement cost is a permissible standard. We reject this contention. A standard of replacement without depreciation is inconsistent with the intent and the language of the statute which, as noted above, provides for insurance to the extent of the actual cash value of the property at the time of loss but not to exceed the amount it would cost to repair or replace the property with material of like kind and quality. Repair or replacement costs constitutes an upper limit on, not the absolute measure of, the insurer's liability. See Riegel & Miller, Fire Insurance from Insurance Principles and Practices, 360 (3d ed. 1947). To equate "actual cash value" with replacement cost alone would render the limiting phrase meaningless. If actual cash value is less than replacement cost in a particular case the former controls.

Rejection of pure replacement cost is further consonant with the legislative provision permitting insurers to provide for extended coverage to include replacement cost under an extended coverage endorsement. N.J.S.A. 17:36–5.22 provides that under such an endorsement the insurer may agree "to reimburse and indemnify the insured for the difference between the actual value of the insured property at the time any loss or damage occurs and the amount actually expended to repair, rebuild or replace with new materials of like size, kind and quality...." Such an endorsement specifically precludes deduction for depreciation. See Ruter v. Northwestern Fire and Marine Ins. Co., 72 N.J.Super. 467, 471–473, 178 A.2d 640 (App.Div.), *certif. den.* 181 A.2d 12 (1962). It seems clear that if a specific provision is required to reimburse for pure replacement cost then the basic policy should not be so construed.

Finally, allowing pure replacement cost would violate the principle of indemnity by providing a windfall to the insured:

To allow the insured to recover the original value of real estate that has depreciated, ... would be for the insurance company to pay for losses that were not caused by fire. Such prodigality would simply furnish an incentive for the destruction of property, because more could be recovered as insurance than the undamaged property was worth. Even under present conditions it is found that business depressions, which reduce the values of buildings and stocks of goods, are sometimes accompanied by large increases in the fire losses. Such conditions furnish an incentive for a fire. Riegel & Miller, *supra*, at 358–359.

See Bonbright & Katz, "Valuation of Property to Measure Fire Insurance Losses," 29 Colum.L.Rev. 857, 878–879 (1929).

[The court discounted cases, cited by the plaintiffs, from Pennsylvania and Wisconsin. The court considered them to be either inapposite, inconclusive, or incorrect.]

We thus conclude that an appraisal based on replacement cost without consideration of depreciation does not measure "actual cash value" under our statute and is therefore improper.

This appeal constitutes an appropriate vehicle for stating the principles which should guide appraisers in determining "actual cash value." The matter of correct standards has been widely litigated elsewhere.[2] Case law reflects three general categories for measuring "actual cash value": (1) market value, (2) replacement cost less depreciation, and (3) the "broad evidence" rule. See Note, "Valuation and Measure of Recovery Under Fire Insurance Policies," 49 Colum.L.Rev. 818, 820–823 (1949); Cozen, [Measure and Proof of Loss to Buildings and Structures Under Standard Fire Insurance Policies—the Alternatives and Practical Approaches], 12 Forum [647] at 648–658; Hinkle, "The Meaning of 'Actual Cash Value,'" 1967 Ins.L.J. 711. See generally Annot., 61 A.L.R.2d 711 (1958).

Market value is generally defined as the price a willing buyer would pay a willing seller, at a fair and *bona fide* sale by private contract, neither being under any compulsion.... But there is a problem in that a building ordinarily has no recognized market value independent of the parcel of property in entirety, land and building together. See Note, *op. cit.*, *supra*, 49 Colum.L.Rev. at 820, where it is observed that the majority of courts have rejected market value as the sole criterion or standard of "actual cash value" although they have allowed the fact-finder to consider it as a factor in computing the actual cash value of a building.[3] It is common practice for a valuation expert to develop a residual market value for a structure by deducting from the market value of the whole parcel the appraised market value of the land. In case of a partial loss, the market value approach looks to determination of the difference between the respective market values of the structure before and after the fire. Note, *op. cit.*, *supra*, 49 Colum.L.Rev. at 825–826.

Replacement cost less depreciation has the advantage of relative definiteness. It is also easily ascertained. However, it is inflexible, and this characteristic often results in excessive recovery. Many structures today have a high replacement value because of the inflated cost of building materials even though their true commercial value—represented by rent-

---

2. Every state has some statutorily prescribed fire insurance policy. Most states, like New Jersey, follow the New York Standard form. *Riegel & Miller, supra*, at 351–352.

3. California follows the market value rule. Jefferson Insurance Co. of N. Y. v. Superior Court, 475 P.2d 880 (Cal.1970), as does Maine. Forer v. Quincy Mutual Fire Ins. Co., 295 A.2d 247 (Maine 1972).

als, prospective profits, usefulness to the present owner, location and age—is considerably less. *Id.* at 821. See Harper v. Penn Mut. Fire Ins. Co., 199 F.Supp. 663, 664–665 (E.D.Va.1966).

The problem of excessive recovery under the replacement cost less depreciation rule together with the occasional uncertainty of market value prompted development of what is now the most widely accepted rule, generally denominated as the "broad evidence rule." That rule was well explained by the New York Court of Appeals in McAnarney v. Newark Fire Insurance Co., 159 N.E. 902 (N.Y. 1928).

In *McAnarney* the insured built a brewery just before Prohibition. The brewery burned down shortly thereafter (arson was not proven). The insured claimed replacement cost minus depreciation, which because of impending Prohibition was more than the building was worth. The insurer was willing to allow market value, which, for the same reason, was probably less than the building would ordinarily have been worth. The Court of Appeals rejected both of these fixed standards of recovery and held that:

> Where insured buildings have been destroyed, the trier of fact may, and should, call to its aid, in order to effectuate complete indemnity, every fact and circumstance which would logically tend to the formation of a correct estimate of the loss. It may consider original cost and cost of reproduction; the opinions upon value given by qualified witnesses; the declarations against interest which may have been made by the assured; the gainful uses to which the buildings might have been put; as well as any other fact reasonably tending to throw light upon the subject. 159 N.E. at 905.

McAnarney was intended to assure application of the principle of indemnity (*i. e.*, to make the measure of recovery for fire insurance losses correspond to the actual pecuniary loss sustained by the insured). *Id.* at 904–905. See Bonbright & Katz, *op. cit.*, *supra*, 29 Colum.L.Rev. at 899. Under-valuation denies the insured the indemnification due him under the policy. Over-valuation tempts the insured to cause the very loss covered, or at least, to provide inadequate safeguards against the loss. *Id.* at 863.

The commentators generally view the broad evidence rule with approval. See *id.* at 898–899 (a flexible test which can be modified in such a way as to accord more nearly with the principle of indemnity); Cozen, *op. cit.*, *supra*, 12 Forum at 657 (sacrificing an easily applied standard for a far more equitable result). It has been adopted in numerous jurisdictions.[4]

. . .

We find the rationale of the broad evidence rule to be compelling. It requires the fact-finder to consider all evidence an expert would consider relevant to an evaluation, and particularly both fair market value and replacement cost less depreciation. If the appraiser finds it appropriate under the particular circumstances he may, after weighing both factors,

---

4. *E.g.*, [22 cases cited].

settle on either alone. . . . Normally, replacement cost minus depreciation can be significant evidence of value but it is not necessarily conclusive. . . . Thus under the broad evidence rule the two stated criteria do not bind the fact-finder but instead become guidelines, along with other relevant evidence. No evidence is *per se* exclusive of other evidence; any evidence may be used jointly or alternatively according to the circumstances and the property to be evaluated. . . .

The broad evidence rule is consistent with the narrow standard of judicial review generally accorded to appraisal awards. . . . The wider the range of evidence considered by the fact-finder, the more reasonable it is for a court to accept his conclusions. A result reached under the broad evidence rule is more likely to be reliable than one based on either of the other standards alone. If the appraiser gives reasonable consideration to all relevant evidence, his award should ordinarily stand.

We thus hold that the proper standard for evaluating "actual cash value" under the New Jersey Standard Form Policy is the broad evidence rule.[5]

II[a]

We turn to the question whether the failure of the appraisers to deduct depreciation from replacement cost constitutes sufficient cause to set aside the award.

Initially, the trial-judge and Appellate Division were correct in approaching the matter of review of the appraisal award from a narrow perspective. It is not in the public interest to encourage litigation over procedures which were designed to resolve disputes without litigation. Thus every reasonable intendment and presumption comes to the support of such awards.

An appraiser, however, can make no legal determinations. The instant appraisers awarded pure replacement cost under a contract and statute which allowed for recovery only to the extent of the "actual cash value." As indicated in Point I above, to the extent that replacement cost is or may be a proper criterion of actual cash value, there must normally be a deduction for depreciation lest the insured receive more than indemnity for his loss. In failing to make such a deduction, the appraisers violated the terms of the policy and committed a mistake of law.

There is an alternative justification for setting aside the award. During discussions among the appraisers as to the amount of loss, Thomas, defendant's appraiser, attempted to ascertain such factors as the actual

---

5. We perceive no reason for distinguishing between the standard of evaluation for a total loss and that for a partial loss. N.J.S.A. 17:36–5.19 makes no such distinction; it specifies but one measure of recovery, "actual cash value." Any such distinction may lead to anomalous results. See Note, *supra*, 49 Colum.L.Rev. at 826, n. 60 (insured might recover more for a partial loss than a total loss). It is realized, however, that where an appraisal is made after a partial loss there may be difficult proof problems in arriving at the putative market value of the portion of the structure destroyed as distinguished from the entirety.

a. Case citations in this and the ensuing parts are omitted.

cost to Elberon of effecting the repairs, the actual extent of repairs made, the age of the building, depreciation, the use to which the building had been put and the condition of the building prior to the fire. However, the umpire and the other appraiser refused to attempt to elicit or consider such information.

We have held above that "actual cash value" is to be ascertained by consideration of all relevant evidence. The courts of California and New York have vacated appraisals where the appraisers failed to comply with the applicable standard for ascertaining loss.

We consequently conclude that the refusal of these appraisers even to consider such factors as those listed above constituted legal misconduct and of itself justifies vacation of the award.[6] Compare N.J.S.A. 2A:24–8(c), which provides that where arbitrators refuse to hear evidence pertinent and material to the controversy, the court shall vacate the award.

III

Defendant raises the question whether the trial court was required to proceed in this matter under and pursuant to the Arbitration Act, N.J.S.A. 2A:24–1 *et seq.* It asserts that if the act was applicable, the award should be vacated because the procedures followed by the appraisers did not conform thereto. We have concluded that the Arbitration Act is not applicable.

A comparison of appraisal and arbitration will be helpful. The purposes of both are the same: to submit disputes to third parties and effect their speedy and efficient resolution without recourse to the courts. To assure minimum judicial intervention, the scope of judicial review of both types of recourse is narrow.

The distinctions are significant. An agreement for arbitration ordinarily encompasses the disposition of the entire controversy between the parties, and judgment may be entered upon the award, whereas an appraisal establishes only the amount of loss and not liability. Arbitration is conducted as a quasi-judicial proceeding, with hearings, notice of hearings, oaths of arbitrators and oaths of witnesses. Appraisers act on their own skill and knowledge, need not be sworn and need hold no formal hearings so long as both sides are given an opportunity to state their positions. Note, "Arbitration or Appraisement?," 8 Syracuse L.Rev. 205, 206 (1957).

The instant policy provision clearly called for an appraisal. That the procedures mandated by the Arbitration Act, see, *e.g.*, N.J.S.A. 2A:24–6, were not followed and that there was no finding with respect to liability tends to indicate that the fact-finders purported to conduct an appraisal. This was entirely proper.

Nothing in the Arbitration Act requires that fire insurance appraisals comply with that statute. Indeed, the word "appraisal" is not found in the

---

6. In some cases a refusal to consider relevant evidence, while improper, might not in itself be cause to set aside an award if the result reached appeared reasonable. Here, however, exclusion of depreciation while applying replacement cost new prevents the result from being reasonable.

act. The intention to change a long-established rule or principle is not to be imputed to the Legislature in the absence of a clear manifestation thereof.

Furthermore, since application of the broad evidence rule to appraisals will promote the interchange of information between the appraisers and the parties, one may expect enhancement of the fairness of the procedure without burdening the appraisal with the formalities of arbitration (*e.g.*, oaths, notice of hearings, etc.).

Finally, since arbitrators are entrusted with the broader obligation to determine liability as well as the amount of the award, it is reasonable to require broader procedural safeguards in arbitration. The subject-matter responsibility of appraisers being less, the procedural safeguards attending an appraisal may be lower. However, the Court must consider any erroneous exercise of jurisdiction by an appraiser.

[The insurer had disclaimed liability altogether, charging Elberon with fraud in submitting a claim which it knew to be substantially in excess of the cost of repair. The policy followed the statutory form in providing for avoidance if the insured should practice fraud or willful concealment or misrepresentation, before or after the loss, of any material fact or circumstance concerning the insurance. The high court ruled, in part IV, that the trial court had erred in failing to make an "independent finding" as to the insurer's liability.]

V

If the judge on the remand finds liability on the part of defendant, he shall direct the appraisal procedure to be instituted anew with instructions that the new appraisers make their evaluation of loss based on consideration of all relevant evidence, pursuant to the principles outlined above. If the judge sustains the defense of fraud, willful misrepresentation or concealment, he shall enter judgment for defendant.

The judgment is reversed and the cause is remanded to the Law Division for further proceedings conforming to this opinion.

NOTES

(1) *The Burned Brewery Case.* In the *McAnarney* case, described at p. 457, the claimant had bought the property for $8,000 the year before the fire. He claimed the amount insured, $42,750, asserting the buildings to be worth $60,000. In the trial, the court had refused to let the jury hear evidence, offered by the insurer, that the claimant had informed the board of tax assessors that the property had no value except for the production of malt, and that the owners would accept $15,000 for the property. The court also excluded evidence that the property had been advertised for $12,000 and that the best offer was $6,000.

If in that case an appraisal had been made under the policy, and the appraisers (hearing all the evidence offered) had concluded that the loss was $15,000, would a court accept that as conclusive? See Schnitzer v. South Carolina Insurance, 661 P.2d 550 (Ore.App. 1983).

If the only evidence offered was that the buildings would cost $60,000 to replace, would it support an appraisers' award of the amount claimed? A jury verdict of that amount? See Incardona v. Home Indemnity Co., 400 N.Y.S.2d 944 (App.Div. 1977).

(2) *Real or Nominal Loss*? The owner of a building informs his insurer that the property has been listed with brokers for sale for some time, without result, and that he intends to demolish the building. Eleven days later the building is destroyed by fire. Has the owner suffered any insured loss? For the answer Yes, see Garcy Corp. v. Home Insurance Co., 496 F.2d 479 (7th Cir. 1974). The evidence did not show that the building had been "irrevocably abandoned" to the wrecking crew. But, the court said, its review of similar cases produced "an amazing array of analyses."

According to an Iowa case, building damage ought to entail an insurance recovery even though it entails no immediate out-of-pocket monetary loss to the policyholder, or actual reduction in his net worth.[1] The court said: "It is common knowledge in this state that many existing and useful farm buildings do not enhance the market value of the farm upon which they are located. It is likewise common knowledge the market value of some city business area real estate might be undiminished after loss of functional structures still in use." Kintzel v. Wheatland Mutual Insurance Association, 203 N.W.2d 799, 810–11, 65 A.L.R.3d 1110 (Iowa 1973). *Question*: Are these observations at variance with the *McAnarney* case?

(3) *Indexing Homeowners' Policies.* Inflation of home prices and building costs, either during the life of a policy or over a period covered by successive policies, is one major cause of "risk retention" that can be unwelcome to both parties to a homeowners policy. Insurers have dealt with that through more or less automatic accretions in the face amounts of homeowners policies. (This feature is marketed as "inflation guard coverage".) Some policies compensate for that with a graduating deductible.

(4) *Appraisals.* "A number of basic distinctions" between appraisal under a fire policy and a statutory arbitration are pointed out in Matter of Delmar Box Co., 127 N.E.2d 808 (N.Y. 1955).[2] That decision is, however, heavily criticized in the valuable article by Sturges & Sturges, Appraisals of Loss and Damage Under Insurance Policies, 11 Miami L.Q. 1, 323 (1956).

PROBLEMS

You represent a client in making claims, based on a single policy, for two different types of loss. The policy provides for appraisal as described in *Elberon Bathing*. You must decide whether or not to demand an appraisal.

(a) As to the Type–A loss, the insurer concedes coverage, but disputes the client's assessment of the amount. As to the Type–B loss, on any reckoning a much larger one, the insurer denies coverage. You believe that, with or without an appraisal, the client has about an even chance of winning the coverage dispute. According to applicable law, if you demand an appraisal the award will be a conclusive determination of the coverage issue. That is, if the award includes the Type–B loss the insurer cannot further question the coverage you assert; if it does

---

1. This was said, however, in connection with post-loss compensation to an insured party from a source other than insurance.

2. See also Happy Hank Auction Co. v. American Eagle Fire Insurance Co., 136

N.E.2d 842 (N.Y. 1956); Annot., 69 A.L.R.2d 1296 (1960); 25 A.L.R.3d 680 (1969). An appraisal was sustained in Lakewood Manufacturing Co. v. Home Insurance Co. of New York, 422 F.2d 796 (6th Cir.1970).

not, you cannot further assert coverage. Would you demand an appraisal—or advise your client to do so?

(b) Suppose now that the insurer has denied coverage for both types of loss. Would you demand an appraisal?

Note that the rule of law supposed in the Problems assigns more weight to an appraisers' award than the rule described in *Elberon Bathing*. The "Problems" statement is derived from opinions about Florida law; see Three Palms Pointe, Inc. v. State Farm Fire & Cas. Co., 362 F.3d 1317 (11th Cir. 2004).

––––––––

Valued Policies

Valuation by Statute

A hurricane that struck the home of Zennon Mierzwa, in Fort Lauderdale, may have been a financial blessing to him. From different insurers Mierzwa had bought windstorm-damage and flood-damage insurance on the house. The hurricane inflicted both wind and flood damage, the wind damage being the somewhat greater part. From the windstorm insurer Mierzwa was entitled to the policy limit, $281,000. The amount of his flood insurance is not reported. Assuming, however, the amount of $219,000, the hurricane may have put him in a position to recover half a million dollars for damage that could have been repaired for less than $128,000.

Mierzwa's loss was actually greater than the cost of repair; it was the value of his house. Official calculations showed that, at most, the house was worth some $245,000. It was not, that is, worth twice the cost of repair. It followed, under City ordinances, that the home had to be demolished. It was a constructive total loss. Even so, the hurricane put Mierzwa "in the money."

The key to his good fortune was a valued-policy law (VPL). The following excerpt shows a deletion ("if any") and an addition (in italics) subsequently made.

> In the event of the total loss of any building ..., located in this state and insured by any insurer as to a covered peril ... the insurer's liability, under the policy for such total loss, *if caused by a covered peril*, shall be in the amount of money for which such property was so insured as specified in the policy ...—Fla. Stat. § 627.702(1).

The court applied this statute in an action by Mierzwa against his windstorm insurer. Mierzwa v. Florida Windstorm Underwriting Ass'n, 877 So.2d 774 (Fla.App. 2004). "The VPL is part of every real property casualty insurance policy written on property in Florida," the court said.

Presumably the statute was part also of Mierzwa's flood-insurance policy. The court did not, however, actually rule that he could recover the policy limit in both policies. Rather, it dealt with this contention by the windstorm insurer: because its policy disclaimed liability for flood damage, it was accountable for only a fraction—though a major one—of the total damage. The court ruled otherwise, saying that "if the insurance carrier has *any* liability at all to the owner for a building damaged by a covered peril and deemed a total loss, that liability is for the face amount of the policy". Id. at 775–76. The ruling evoked sharp responses. One attorney called the case a "Category Five". J. Garaffa, Florida's "Valued Policy" Law ..., 79 Fla. Bar J. 1 (2005). He and other doubters began to construct hypothetical cases of a covered peril contributing, although only in a trivial way, along with a peril not covered, to a total loss. See Chauvin v. State Farm Fire & Cas. Co., 450 F.Supp.2d 660, 666 (E.D.La. 2006) (20 shingles lost to wind); Garaffa, Letter, 80 Fla. Bar J. 4 (2006) (one shingle). According to the opinion of the majority in Mierzwa's case, they had no occasion to consider situations so extreme. In *Chauvin*, Judge Vance expressed regret that she could not press the Louisiana VPL into service for hurricane victims; but she declined to construe it so as to yield absurd consequences. She declined also to follow the lead of *Mierzwa*, a decision repudiated on its home ground by the amendment, as noted above, of Florida's VPL.[1]

Valued-policy statutes exist in about half the states. The pioneer was the Wisconsin statute. In general, the statutes apply only to real-property losses. Most of them are confined to cases of total loss, but some apply explicitly to cases of partial loss also. The Florida statute is set out above. The footnote here sets out the Ohio and Wisconsin statutes.[2] Unlike those, the Missouri statute applies to losses of both real and personal property, and to partial losses. It allows for depreciation.[3]

As to the objects of valued-policy statutes, the Minnesota high court has referred to a book by Professor Patterson. His book, the court said, "attributes the passage of valued policy statutes to the indifference of insurance agents to the amount of insurance which their customers needed; to the fact that agents received larger commissions by selling the insured needless protection; and to the fact that the honest insured paid unneces-

---

1. The Louisiana VPL, R.S. § 22:695, opens "Under any fire insurance policy...." This framed a question of interest in *Chauvin*: Does the statute apply to a case of loss by a peril that is not fire but is covered in a "fire policy"? The court preferred not to choose between conflicting authorities.

2. Ohio Rev. Code § 3929.25. *Extent of liability under policy*

A person, company, or association insuring any building or structure against loss or damage by fire or lightning shall have such building or structure examined by his or its agent, and a full description thereof made, and its insurable value fixed, by such agent. In the absence of any change increasing the risk without the consent of the insurers, and in the absence of intentional fraud on the part of the insured, in the case of total loss the whole amount mentioned in the policy or renewal, upon which the insurer received a premium, shall be paid. However, if the poli-

cy of insurance requires actual repair or replacement of the building or structure to be completed in order for the policyholder to be paid the cost of such repair or replacement, without deduction for depreciation or obsolescence, up to the limits of the policy, then the amount to be paid shall be as prescribed by the policy.

The cellar and foundation walls shall not be considered a part of such building or structure in settling losses, despite any contrary provisions in the application or policy.

Wis. Stat. § 632.05(2). TOTAL LOSS.

Whenever any policy insures real property that is owned and occupied by the insured primarily as a dwelling and the property is wholly destroyed, without criminal fault on the part of the insured or the insureds assigns, the amount of the loss shall be taken conclusively to be the policy limits of the policy insuring the property.

3. Mo.Rev.Stat. § 379.140.

sary premiums and the dishonest insured was tempted to commit arson. But even so, according to Patterson, the insurance companies found it more economical to pay excessive claims than to make an appraisal of every property insured. Thus, the purpose of valued policy statutes is twofold: (1) To prevent overinsurance by requiring prior valuation; and (2) to avoid litigation by prescribing definite standards of recovery in case of total loss." Nathan v. St. Paul Mut. Ins. Co., 68 N.W.2d 385, 388 (1955) (citations omitted). The court's reference was to *Essentials of Insurance Law*, § 32, p. 118. For an explanation of the statutes with a farm-belt beat, see the argument for the plaintiff in error in Milwaukee Mechanics' Ins. Co. v. Russell, 62 N.E. 338 (Ohio 1901).

Valuation by Contract

A policy may be a valued one, not by statute as in Mierzwa's case, but by agreement expressed in the policy. If neither a statute nor an agreement makes it so, it is an *open* policy, in which the policy limit is just that, and not also a minimum recovery. In Milwaukee Mechanics' Ins. Co. v. Russell, above, counsel for the insurer explained how buying insured, unvalued, is like buying wrapping-paper (though it doesn't keep as well). He made this argument:

> [The court should] consider the contract of insurance, the terms of which provide that the limit of the liability of the insurer shall be the amount of the policy and that the losses shall be paid according to what they actually are, up to this limit. That the insured has contracted for a greater amount of indemnity than he needs is no reason why any loss he has suffered should be magnified up to the limit of the insurer's obligation to indemnify him. If I buy more of an article than I can use I am the loser of so much as goes to waste on my hands.

(The insurer in *Russell* sought to replace the property destroyed rather than to pay the amount of the loss; it relied on a policy provision permitting that. But that provision was repugnant to an applicable valued-policy statute, according to the court.)

A valuation term in an insurance contract has been said to be only an instance of stipulated damages. The phrase "valued at" is the usual form for stipulating damages in an insurance contract.[4] Marine insurance supplies the prototype of valued policies. "A valued policy is a policy which specifies the agreed value of the subject-matter insured," according to the British Marine Insurance Act.[5] "Subject to the provisions of this Act, and in the absence of fraud, the value fixed by the policy is, as between the insurer and assured, conclusive of the insurable value of the subject intended to be insured, whether the loss be total or partial."[6] Among the subjects commonly insured under a valuation clause are jewelry, works of art, vessels, and cargo. As to each, why might it be so?

4. See St. Paul Fire & Marine Ins. Co. v. Pure Oil Co., 63 F.2d 771 (2d Cir. 1933).

5. Section 27(2).

6. Section 27(3).

NOTES

(1) *Overstatements of Value.* A misrepresentation made in presenting a claim—a post-loss misrepresentation—may have the effect of defeating the claim. Insurers have reason for concern about claimants who, in presenting claims, overstate the value of assets destroyed or lost. In principle, this concern is less warranted in relation to valued policies than it is in relation to open policies. Given a total loss under a valued policy, a claimant may well have no incentive to inflate the value of the asset. And if the claimant does misrepresent its value by overstatement, the misrepresentation may well be immaterial: nothing turns on what the asset was worth. In Heady v. Farmers Mutual Ins. Co., 349 N.W.2d 366 (Neb. 1984), the insurer had offered evidence that Heady had overstated the value of a house he owned after it was destroyed by fire. The court concluded that, in light of the State's valued-policy statute, the evidence was inadmissible. Concealment in presenting a claim is likely to have as much effect, or as little, as misrepresentation.

A misrepresentation made in applying for a policy—a pre-loss misrepresentation—may avoid the policy; see p. 187 ff. above. Consider an overstatement of asset value at that juncture. If the policy is an open one, what would motivate the applicant to overstate an asset value? And if he did, how would the falsehood be material? If, instead, a knowing overstatement of value is made in applying for a valued policy, these questions may be easy to answer.

Heady's case is instructive on these points as well. The court found divided authority about whether or not evidence of a pre-loss overstatement of value is admissible. It decided that the valued-policy statute overrode a defense based on that. But the insurer sought to prove that Heady had burned the house deliberately. Hence, the court said, a pre-loss overstatement of value, if made by Heady, could be considered for the limited purpose of showing that he had an incentive to commit arson.

Glance again at the British Marine Insurance Act, as quoted above, and note the qualifier, "in the absence of fraud". If that qualifier had appeared in the Nebraska statute, could the *Heady* court have said that the statute overrode the defense of fraud by Heady in stating, pre-loss, the value of his house?

(2) *More on Misrepresentation.* Long ago the U.S. Supreme Court gave thought to an extravagant value innocently placed by the owner of a brig when buying a valued policy on it. Although the Court made no decision about that, the Court said that "an underwriter cannot reasonably ask to be relieved beyond the excess complained of." Hodgson v. Marine Ins. Co. of Alexandria, 9 U.S. 100 (1809). Moreover, in pleading defenses, the insurer had failed to aver that any supposed misrepresentation was "material to the risk of the voyage". Is there a fallacy in either of these observations?

Perhaps the Court would have taken a different view of materiality if the insured had *understated* the value of the brig. According to her owner, the brig had been seized by British vessels, sailed to Jamaica, and sold. The risk of that might have been enhanced, it seems, by the prize-worthiness of the brig, unsuspected by the insurer.[7]

Of course one can give on *opinion* of great value, honestly held, without making a misrepresentation at all. Owners of a number of daubs have thought, mistakenly, that Rembrandt was the painter.

---

7. Amazingly, this policy claim came before the Supreme Court two more times. The insurer, though tenacious, was ultimately defeated.

PROBLEM

The owner of a painting procured valued insurance on it in the amount of £20,000, having had it appraised by an expert. Before the appraisal, the owner had bought the painting for £25 and had labeled it "Raphael". He did not disclose this history to the insurer when buying the policy. Is the policy voidable for concealment? See Jowitt, Some Were Spies 120–28 (1954) (English case; compromised).

Required Upgrades

Escalation in the cost of repair and replacement of structures may occur from one or more of these causes: inflation, more stringent building codes, and lost stability or grade of the site.

Owing to explicit exclusions, a replacement-cost coverage may fail to compensate the insured for site work required for rebuilding. That was the case in Fire Insurance Exchange v. Superior Court, 10 Cal.Rptr.3d 617 (Cal.App. 2004). This was the exclusion applied there: "We do not cover any costs required to replace, rebuild, stabilize or otherwise restore the land." The court distinguished cases of "dwelling" coverage in which "the covered peril (earth movement) was a continuing one, so that the insurer's obligation with regard to resulting damage to the residence would continue so long as the underlying soil remained unstable, and the cost of stabilizing the land far exceeded policy limits." Id. at 623.

As for revised building codes, conflict has arisen over provisions like this:

> We do not insure for loss either consisting of, or caused directly or indirectly by: ... Enforcement of any ordinance or law regulating construction, repair or demolition of a building or other structure, unless endorsed to this policy.

Fire Insurance Exchange cites holdings that language like this excludes unambiguously increased costs made necessary by changed building codes. But it also cites contrary holdings. These include Bering Strait School Dist. v. RLI Ins., 873 P.2d 1292 (Alaska 1994), where the court said:

> "As we read this provision, it ... merely states that if the loss itself is caused by an ordinance or law, there is no coverage.... However, when the cost of repairing or replacing a building that had been damaged by fire is increased by the requirements of an ordinance or a law, [the insurance company] is not relieved of that cost."

Id. at 1296, quoting Garnett v. Transamerica Ins. Services, 800 P.2d 656 (Idaho 1990).

The California statute setting forth the terms of the standard fire policy, Insurance Code § 2071(a), includes this provision:

> [Insurer] does insure [insured] ... to the extent of the actual cash value of the property at the time of loss, but not exceeding the amount which it would cost to repair or replace the property with

material of like kind and quality within a reasonable time after the loss, without allowance for any increased cost of repair or reconstruction by reason of any ordinance or law regulating construction or repair....

Under this provision, it seems, revised building codes do not augment the insurer's liability. See McCorkle v. State Farm Ins. Co., 270 Cal.Rptr. 492 (Cal.App. 1990). There, considering comparable language, the court ruled that the insurer was not required to pay for a new cement garage floor to replace a destroyed wood floor, even though a new building code required cement. Liability is not augmented, naturally, simply by a preference the insured may have developed for a design or materials superior to those lost or damaged.

D.   THIRD PARTIES: RIGHTS AND LIABILITIES
Subrogation

When a party has paid a debt for which both it and another party are accountable, and, as between the two of them, the other is the one primarily chargeable, the "other's" claim can be resuscitated and vested in the payor. That is a partial statement of a remedy known as *subrogation*. (For a more compendious statement, see the sentence from the Restatement of Restitution quoted in the footnote.[8] That sentence refers to the payor as the *plaintiff*, to the "other" party as the *defendant*, and to the payee as the "obligee or lien-holder".) Insurers often find themselves in the position of a payor entitled to be subrogated to rights of a person insured— or think that they do. Others commonly entitled to rights by subrogation are sureties. Indeed, a firm that takes payments systematically for "going surety" may well be called an insurer.

The foregoing paragraph describes *equitable* subrogation. There is another kind: *conventional*. It rests on an agreement between an obligor and the holder of a different obligation that if the obligor is required to satisfy its obligation, and does, it will succeed to the rights of the obligee.

A common instance of subrogation in favor of an insurer concerns one that has provided insurance for the holder of a security interest against damage to or destruction of the collateral. Say that the collateral is a home, on which a bank holds a mortgage, and that the bank has bought insurance on its interest in the home. Upon the destruction of the home, the insurer may well have to pay the bank enough to satisfy the mortgage. That being done, and nothing more, the owner of the home would be unjustly enriched at the insurer's expense. So as to remedy that, the insurer can, as the Restatement says, "maintain a proceeding in equity to revive [the mort-

---

8.   "A court of equity may give restitution to the plaintiff and prevent the unjust enrichment of the defendant, where the plaintiff's property has been used in discharging an obligation owed by the defendant or a lien upon the property of the defendant, by creating in the plaintiff rights similar to those which the obligee or lien-holder had before the obligation or lien was discharged."—Comment *a* to § 162.

gage]" for the benefit of the insurer. *Ibid*. In that situation it can usually be expected that the insurer is entitled also to conventional subrogation, for the policy would be likely to provide that the insurer would succeed to the bank's rights upon full satisfaction of the mortgage debt. (Partial satisfaction is another matter, both from the standpoint of contracting parties and from that of equity.) Given full payment of that debt, probably the bank would anyway grant succession to its claim by assigning it to the insurer.

Subrogation works also for the benefit of insurers who provide collision coverage on cars. Upon paying for repairs, they get rights via subrogation against motorists whose bad driving caused damage to the policyholders' cars. A case of that kind differs from the mortgage case, of course, in that the target of the subrogation claim is an alleged tortfeasor. The insurer of a homeowner might also acquire, by subrogation, a claim against a tortfeasor—one who torched the home, for example. And a contract "car" claim would be the subject of subrogation if the interest insured were a security interest in the car.

Two kinds of subrogation have been mentioned. There is a third, *statutory* subrogation, of special relevance here. An example is this New Jersey statute:

> Every fire insurance policy shall contain certain standard provisions [in these words]:
>
> . . .
>
> *Subrogation*. This Company may require from the insured an assignment of all right of recovery against any party for loss to the extent that payment therefor is made by this Company.

N.J.S.A. 17:36–5.20.

The remainder of this section features cases in which subrogation for insurers has met serious resistance. Part 1 illustrates antipathy to subrogation as such. Part 2, much longer, presents claims by third parties to insurance benefits which, if successful, foreclose claims against them by way of subrogation because "there is no subrogation against an insured".

1. Subrogation Suppressed

The Penns Grove (New Jersey) Water Company resisted subrogation with some success in Weinberg v. Dinger, 524 A.2d 366 (N.J. 1987). The court's principal decision was to overturn the immunity that suppliers of water to the public had enjoyed, against claims for fire losses attributed to faulty maintenance of their systems. The strongest argument in support of the immunity was, the court said, that liability was needless "because most property owners are already insured against fire loss." The court decided to retain a remnant of the former rule, however: No claims arising in favor of insurers, by way of subrogation, are to be allowed.

The arguments and opinions include interesting points about water rates and insurance rates. One argument was that liability insurance for water companies, if available at all, would be expensive due to the extreme risk, and this cost will be passed on to water consumers. This form of compulsory insurance through water rates, it is argued, is inefficient because water rates do not vary with fire hazard.

Id. at 375.

Justice Garibaldi dissented, believing that the immunity should be preserved. She made the point that the cost of insuring property varies not only with the estimated risk but also with property values. Not so the cost of water to an owner: "An owner of a home worth $100,000 pays the same uniform water rate as the owner of commercial property worth $1,000,000." She saw analogies to taxes: insurance premiums to progressive ones, and water rates to regressive ones. In her view, to impose liability on a water company was not only inefficient, but also unfair. "I believe it is fairer to allocate the risk of protecting the more valuable property to those who own the property." Id. at 381, 386.

NOTES

(1) *"Subrogation is an equitable doctrine."* This observation was a premise of the decision in Weinberg v. Dinger to distinguish between claims by insurers and claims by uninsured property owners. The court quoted as follows from its earlier decision in A. & B. Auto Stores v. Newark, 279 A.2d 693 (N.J.1971).

> When, as here, an insurance carrier which has satisfied a loss it was paid to cover, seeks to recoup by asserting a claim its insured has against another with respect to that loss, the final question must be whether justice would be furthered by that course. Id. at 703.

Is justice served by the rules announced in *Weinberg*?

(2) *Legislation.* There are statutory anti-subrogation rules, as well as judicial ones. An example is Section 2A:48–1 of the New Jersey Statutes:

> *Liability of municipality or county; amount recoverable; persons covered by insurance*
>
> When, by reason of a mob or riot, any property, real or personal, is destroyed or injured, [either a county or a municipality] shall be liable to the person whose property was so destroyed or injured for the damages sustained thereby, ... in an amount not to exceed $10,000 for the aggregate of damage done to all such property ... at each separate location within a municipality; provided, however, that *no person, and no subrogee of such person, having insurance coverage in whole or in part for the said destruction or injury, shall have a cause of action against such municipality or county....*

It seems, from the language italicized here, that this statute goes beyond suppressing subrogation, and bars actions by persons holding insurance in an amount less than $10,000, and less than the amount of loss.

2. Third-party Entitlements

This part presents authority for each of these propositions about property-insurance contracts: (i) A contract can be made for the benefit of a third party, someone other than the insurance buyer, in the strong sense that an interest of that party is insured. (ii) It can be designed so as to confer on the third party a better entitlement than that of the buyer. (iii) A contract can be written so as to insure only interests of the buyer, but to impose a duty on the insurer, when settling a claim with the buyer, to take account of a payment right that a third party has against the buyer. This is a third-party-benefit contract in a weaker sense than that first indicated.

It is helpful to have in mind, at the outset, illustrations of these three propositions. Take first the case of an art gallery which exhibits for sale, along with works that it owns, the works of Famous Artist that are owned by the painter. The gallery is, in other words, a consignee of valuable and fragile goods. It may be necessary for the gallery to provide insurance on the consigned paintings, for the benefit of F.A., else she will entrust her paintings to a competing gallery. That may be accomplished with a policy identifying the property insured as "works of art exhibited by you, both your own and those of others." Given damage to one of F.A.'s paintings by a covered peril, she has her own claim against the insurer. That claim cannot be compromised by a settlement between the gallery and the insurer. F.A. may not be content with an agreement by the gallery that it will compensate her for damage to her paintings while consigned to it. Sometimes a policy refers to property held "in trust or on commission" to indicate that it is a third-party beneficiary contract in the strong sense.

Turning now to the third proposition, one can imagine a bank loan secured by a property that the borrower owns. The bank's mortgage, or other security interest, might describe the collateral as a painting, a car, or a home. On making a loan so secured, a prudent banker may well require that the borrower have in place insurance against destruction of the collateral. Even so, the banker may fear that the loan will not be paid if the collateral is "turned into money" by an insurance payment to the borrower. The borrower might decamp with the insurance proceeds. Or might enter bankruptcy, causing the proceeds to be distributed ratably among all the creditors. The bank may be able to protect itself against the bankruptcy risk by writing the security interest so as to include any insurance proceeds as part of the collateral, along with the primary asset. Insurance law makes possible a different, and in some ways superior, precaution: let the policy name the bank as a *loss payee*. Language commonly used has the form "Loss payable to Alpha Bank as its interest may appear." From this it follows that the insurer, upon receiving a viable claim of loss, should apply the proceeds first to pay the outstanding balance of the bank's loan, and only then make a payment to the borrower. If it should fail in that, a probable consequence is that the insurer must make double payment of at least some of the loss. It is much as if the borrower had made an assignment to the bank, in advance, of a share in the insurance proceeds, notifying the insurer of the assignment. (A security agreement that covers a car and any proceeds of insurance on it is in fact an assignment in advance.)

Bankers taking security interests in homes and other structures commonly insist on further protection. That is, they require that their own interests in the collateral be insured, not only those of the borrowers. An agreement for a secured loan is likely to require the borrower to show that the lender is named as a person insured, even though the borrower applies for, and pays for, the policy. Prudent bankers and prudent painters have some things in common. A difference is that probably Famous Artist would not expect to be identified by name in the gallery's policy, whereas Alpha Bank would.

Home-mortgage bankers go farther; they take account of the possibility that a home owner's policy may prove to be unenforceable—unenforceable, say, because of fraud on the insurer or because of breach of warranty. According to proposition (ii) above, this risk can be controlled by a policy term known as the *standard mortgagee clause*. One version begins this way:

> Loss or damage, if any, under this policy, shall be payable to [name and address of mortgagee] ... as interest may appear, and this insurance, as to the interest of the mortgagee only therein, shall not be invalidated by any act or neglect of the mortgagor or owner of the within described property....

The phrase "any act or neglect" encompasses many kinds of misconduct. It includes, for example, a willful burn of the property by its owner. Given that, the insurer must anyway satisfy the mortgage debt. (The clause goes on to say that once the insurer has paid the mortgagee it can recover from a wrongdoing owner by way of subrogation to the mortgage.)

This part illustrates also a fourth proposition: In some situations a property-insurance contract is regularly treated as a third-party-benefit contract in the strong sense of proposition (i) above even though, when made, it was not intended for the benefit of anyone other than the buyer. The standard example concerns a contract for the sale of real property on which the vendor holds insurance. The purchaser who does not buy insurance for itself, immediately upon making the purchase contract, is at considerable risk. That risk is greatly moderated, however, by the willingness of courts to confer on the purchaser the benefit of the vendor's insurance. See, for example, Vogel v. Northern Assurance Co., p. 483 below.

B. N. Exton & Co. v. Home Fire & Marine Ins. Co.

New York Court of Appeals, 1928.
249 N.Y. 258, 164 N.E. 43, 61 A.L.R. 718.

■ CRANE, JUDGE.

In October of 1922, Miller, Tompkins & Co. ordered nineteen rolls of paper from the Brown Company. The former company was a domestic corporation, manufacturing paper bags and sacks; the latter a foreign corporation manufacturing paper. The rolls of paper were delivered at 485–487 Washington Street, Manhattan Borough, New York City, the purchaser's place of business. The paper was rejected as not of the quality ordered and by agreement the purchase was canceled. Brown Company, however, requested Miller, Tompkins & Co. to hold the merchandise in its place of business for further instructions. The paper remained in the premises of Miller, Tompkins & Co. until it was destroyed by fire on January 13, 1923.

The defendants had insured Miller, Tompkins & Co. against loss by fire, the policies covering "on stock, materials and supplies, including labor performed thereon in all stages, including packages and labels, contained in said premises No. 485–487 Washington Street, New York City, the property of the assured or held in trust or on commission, or sold but not delivered or held on joint account with others and also the property of others for which the assured may be or agree to become liable in case of loss or damage by fire."

The insured had not agreed to become liable for the property of the Brown Company in case of loss or damage by fire, and was not liable for any negligence in causing the fire.

Miller, Tompkins & Co. refused to include any claim for such merchandise belonging to the Brown Company in its proof of loss.

The property of Miller, Tompkins & Co. was also damaged and destroyed to the amount of $55,049.69, the total amount of the insurance under the policies issued by the defendants being $61,000. There was insurance sufficient to cover all losses.

With notice of the claims and the loss of the Brown Company, the defendants settled with Miller, Tompkins & Co., but failed and refused to pay the loss of the Brown Company, denying all and any liability to it under the policies. The defense is that the policies covered only the property of Miller, Tompkins & Co. and not that which it held as bailee. The Brown Company, on the other hand, claims that under the "trust and commission" clause, so called, the policies covered its nineteen rolls of paper which the Miller, Tompkins Co. was holding in its place of business.

The plaintiff in this action is an assignee of the Brown Company's claim. [The court below had entered a judgment for the plaintiff.]

We are of the opinion that the policies in this case covered the Brown Company's paper. It was property "held in trust" by the Miller, Tompkins Co. for the Brown Company, within the meaning which has been given to these words in the insurance business and insurance law.

"The words 'in trust' may, with entire propriety, be applied to any case of bailment, where goods belonging to one person are entrusted to the custody or care of another, and for which the bailee is responsible to the owner." (Stillwell v. Staples, 19 N.Y. 401.)

"The phrases describing property 'as held in trust,' or 'on commission,' and kindred terms, in a policy to an agent, factor or the like, have been held as giving to the owner of the property a right to take the place of the insured, to adopt the contract, and to enforce it in his own name or that of his agent." (Waring v. Indemnity Fire Ins. Co., 45 N.Y. 606, p. 610, p. 612.

See, also, ... Home Insurance Co. v. Baltimore Warehouse Co., 93 U.S. 527, where it was said that the phrase "held in trust" is to be understood in its mercantile sense.)

. . .

The Brown Company's paper was, therefore, covered by the defendant's policies. Yet it will do the company little good unless this action can be maintained. Miller, Tompkins Co. refused to include the loss in its proof of claim; it settled for the damage to its own property, leaving out the Brown Company, and of course refused to maintain any action on the policies in behalf of the latter company. Its position was and is that the policies did not cover the Brown Company's damage. The insurance companies took a like position and settled with the Miller, Tompkins Co., knowing of the Brown Company's loss and claim. Unless this action lies, the Brown Company and its assignee are without remedy. Such lapses the law seeks to avoid.

What would be the procedure if an insured included in his proof of loss the damage suffered to his bailor's property and was willing to undertake its collection, we are not called upon to decide upon the facts here presented.

The judgment should be affirmed, with costs.

NOTES

(1) "*... sold but not delivered*". This phrase, in the Miller, Tompkins policy, would have application to bags and sacks of its manufacture which it had identified to a contract with a customer—*e.g.*, had marked with the customer's name and address—but had held in its warehouse awaiting shipment, if ownership had passed to the customer. The law of goods sales (UCC Article 2) would determine what items met this description, if any. If any did, they would be the subject of insurance in favor of the customer.

In a paragraph omitted above the court referred to a parallel drawn by another court between the phrases "in trust or on commission" and "for whom it may concern". The court seems to have thought that the parallel was damaging to the plaintiff's claim. How might that be? The "sold" phrase, the "in trust" phrase, and the "for whom" phrase produce multiple overlaps, do they not? Should that fact be held against a policyholder?

(3) *Question.* How would one expect the several claims to be adjusted, in the main case, if the amount of insurance that Miller, Tompkins had bought was *not* sufficient to cover all losses to its own goods, those held "in trust or on commission", and those otherwise insured?

Introduction to *Tower Air*

This case stands at an intersection between insurance law and the law of security interests as stated in Article 9 of the Uniform Commercial Code. Much of the court's discussion of Article 9, as enacted in Arizona, is obsolescent because the legislature there has enacted the Article as now revised. What is presented here is chiefly the court's observations about the unrevised Article and about insurance law. (The court said: "We take no position on what the result might be under the revised UCC....")

Stanziale v. Finova Capital Corp. (In re Tower Air, Inc.)

United States Court of Appeals, 3d Cir., 2005.
397 F.3d 191.

On a number occasions FINOVA Capital Corporation financed purchases by Tower Air, Inc. In 1996 FINOVA advanced $21 million for the purchase of a Boeing 747 airframe and four engines. For this advance FINOVA took a security interest in the goods, their replacements and accessories, "and all ... insurance proceeds ... in respect of such aircraft and engines." This and other similar agreements provided for cross-collateralization; that is they made properties earlier financed by FINOVA collateral for this loan, and the goods securing this loan collateral for earlier ones. Hence the latter stood security, along with a large part of Tower's assets, for all that it owed FINOVA.

One of the engines suffered in-flight damage in 1997. Tower spent nearly $2 million repairing that damage.

In 2000 Tower entered first rehabilitation, and then liquidation, bankruptcy. Charles Stanziale, Jr. was appointed trustee of the bankruptcy estate. FINOVA was a creditor, it said, to the extent of $56 million. During the bankruptcy this debt was reduced by the surrender to FINOVA of some of its collateral, including the repaired engine. FINOVA remained unpaid, it said, in the amount of some $20 million.

Stanziale discovered that Tower had held an accident-insurance policy on the engine, and made claim under it. The insurers agreed to pay more than $950,000 into the estate. (There was a $1 million deductible.) When Stanziale sought approval in the bankruptcy court for this settlement, FINOVA objected that it was entitled to the proceeds. The court agreed. Stanziale appealed, and, losing, appealed again. He argued that FINOVA's security interest did not extend to the insurance money because it was not "proceeds" properly understood, and that awarding it to FINOVA would constitute a double recovery forbidden by the Uniform Commercial Code (UCC).

In part III(A) of the opinion the court rejected the first of these arguments, relying on a Code provision defining "proceeds": section 9–306. In part III(B) the court dealt with Official Comment 3 to that section, where it is said: "The secured party may claim both proceeds and collateral, but may of course have only one satisfaction." The court said:

> We acknowledge that there is significant intuitive appeal to the notion that a creditor should not be able to recover both his collateral and the proceeds thereof. Such a situation bears a resemblance to a double recovery.

The part of the opinion next presented is under the court's heading "IV. The Contractual Provisions".

■ Becker, Circuit Judge.

. . .

B.   The Standard Mortgage Policy Language

It is well settled, in non-UCC (mainly real property) contexts, that certain mortgagees can claim insurance proceeds on their collateral, even when they suffer no loss. See, *e.g.*, Savarese v. Ohio Farmers' Ins. Co., 182 N.E. 665, 668 (N.Y. 1932). The cases that so hold depend on the nature of the insurance clause involved.

The Bankruptcy Court cited one representative example, Grange Mut. Cas. Co. v. Central Trust Co., N.A., 774 S.W.2d 838, 840 (Ky.App. 1989), in which a mortgagee bank sued an insurer who refused to pay out on a fire insurance policy because the mortgagor had, at his own expense, repaired the mortgaged property. The Kentucky court stated:

> The right of the mortgagee under a standard mortgage [insurance] clause is not dependent upon his sustaining loss. That is, the mortgagee under such a clause acquires a right to the insurance proceeds even though he suffers no actual loss, as when the building was restored to its former condition by the mortgagor.

Id. This language applies to mortgagee payees, but not to loss payees.

The difference between mortgagee and loss payees has been spelled out by an Arizona court. A loss payee is "a mere appointee to receive the proceeds to the extent of his interest." Granite State Ins. Co. v. Employers Mut. Ins. Co., 609 P.2d 90, 92 (Ariz.App. 1980) (quoting 5A J. Appleman, Insurance Law and Practice § 3335). In loss-payee cases "the policy [is] subject to any act or omission of the insured which might void, terminate, or adversely affect the coverage; and if the policy is not collectible by the insured, the appointee, likewise, cannot recover thereunder." Id. (quoting Appleman, *supra*, § 3335). On the other hand, "in contradistinction with a basic loss payee whose rights are totally derivative, a mortgagee payee has an independent agreement with the insurer." Id. The mortgagee payee is treated "just as if [he or she] had applied for the insurance entirely independently of the mortgagor." Id. at 93 (quoting Appleman, *supra*, § 3401).

The choice of which category the payee falls under depends on the language of the insurance clause: a "standard" or "union" clause creates a mortgagee payee, while a "simple" clause creates a loss payee. *See* 4 Lee R. Russ *et al.*, Couch on Insurance §§ 65:8, 9, 32 (3d ed. 1984) (hereinafter Couch). The main difference is that the loss payee "is subject to such defenses as the insurer may have against the mortgagor, while the [mortgagee payee] is not." Id. § 65:9.

It seems clear that FINOVA is a mortgagee payee. The insurance certificate issued to FINOVA provides that "with respect to the interest of the Certificate Holder, the insurance afforded shall not be invalidated by any act or neglect of the Named Insured,'' which creates a mortgagee-payee interest. The certificate also does not specifically state that FINOVA may receive proceeds only to the extent of its interest, which is a normal element of the "simple" (loss payee) clause, *see* 4 Couch § 65:9.

Because FINOVA is a mortgagee payee, it can, by analogy to non-UCC insurance law, recover the proceeds to the extent of its debt, even though Tower repaired the damage to its collateral:

> A mortgagee may recover policy proceeds under a standard mortgage clause, even though, because of a restoration of the property by the mortgagor, the mortgagee has suffered no actual loss.... As a corollary of the view that restoration does not defeat the right of the mortgagee to recover, it is held that *the fact that the mortgagor has repaired the damage does not entitle him or her to recover the proceeds of the insurance.*

4 Couch § 65:62 (emphasis added). The mortgagee's "loss is measured in terms of the value of the debt, not the actual economic loss to the mortgagee." Id. § 65:36.[14]

The Trustee argues that that it was "erroneous and improper" for the Bankruptcy Court to rely on non-UCC, non-bankruptcy mortgage cases. We are not persuaded. We agree that, if relevant UCC precedents clearly established that Tower has a right to the proceeds, reliance on contrary non-UCC law would be misplaced. Where, however, there are no UCC cases directly on point ... and what cases there are suggest that FINOVA can recover the proceeds ... we think it is reasonable to look to analogous non-UCC law to strengthen our conclusion that this recovery accords with basic fairness and the common law.[15]

---

14. On the other hand, the mortgagee's right to retain insurance proceeds "is limited by the mortgagee's duty, under § 4.7(b), to permit use of the funds for restoration of the loss or damage to the real estate." Restatement (Third) of Property: Mortgages § 4.7, cmt. d (2004); see also id. § 4.7(b); 12 Couch § 178:58. This provides little guidance in cases where the mortgagor has *already* restored (and then liquidated) the property—or in cases, such as this one, where a contractual clause specifically gives the mortgagee the discretion of how to apply proceeds. [Paragraph 5.4(a) of the security agreement gave FINOVA the right to approve any use of any insurance proceeds by Tower, and allowed FINOVA the right to, "in its sole discretion, apply such [proceeds] to the satisfaction of the Obligations." The court said, in a passage omitted above: "It is undisputed that Tower repaired the engine without either filing an insurance claim or asking for FINOVA's approval.... Tower's decision to repair the engine, rather than file an insurance claim and get FINOVA's approval on the use of the proceeds, deprived FINOVA of the benefit of ¶ 5.4(a)."] Had Tower followed the requirements of [that paragraph], and demanded that FINOVA allow it to use the insurance funds to repair the engine, the Restatement's approach might apply. In the case at bar, it does not.

15. Similarly, we see no reason to ignore the line of cases exemplified by *Savarese, supra,* merely because they occurred outside of bankruptcy. As we have already determined that the insurance payments are proceeds of collateral for UCC purposes ..., FINOVA can recover them under § 552 of the Bankruptcy Code unless such recovery would constitute a double satisfaction. We look to insurance law, and the *Savarese* cases, to determine whether FINOVA has a non-bankruptcy right to receive the proceeds without regard to Tower's repairs. Because FINOVA does have such a right to those proceeds, despite Tower's repairs, there is less reason to think that the proceeds constitute an unfair double satisfaction.

In sum, FINOVA's contractual right of approval over Tower's use of the insurance proceeds, and its mortgagee payee rights in the insurance contracts, further support its claim to treat the insurance proceeds as part of its security. Because this accords with our UCC conclusion in Part III, we conclude that FINOVA is entitled to recover the insurance proceeds under the UCC and the Bankruptcy Code.

V.   The Equity Exception

The Trustee also argues that, even if his claim fails as a legal matter, the Bankruptcy Court abused its discretion in refusing to grant him equitable relief under 11 U.S.C. § 552(b), which allows a court to modify security interests as a matter of equity.[16]

[The court gave reasons to reject this argument, all omitted here except the following.]

[A]ll of the repairs were made long before the bankruptcy petition was filed.[17] While the pre-petition repairs to the engine did increase the value of FINOVA's collateral, Tower's apparent negligence seems to have caused the destruction of other FINOVA collateral, and left FINOVA greatly undersecured. Thus, FINOVA's recovery here hardly constitutes a windfall. Instead, FINOVA will simply recover what it is due as a secured creditor with a valid security interest in the insurance proceeds. The Trustee has advanced no reason for us to conclude that this result is inequitable.

[In an earlier part of the opinion, about "The Meaning of 'One Satisfaction'", the court said that a difficult case would arise if, together, the value of the original collateral and the amount of proceeds exceeded the value of the original collateral, but fell short of the amount owing. "In that case, may the creditor recover the collateral and proceeds (limited only by the amount of its debt), or is it limited to the value of its original collateral? This is a vexing question, and one that does not seem to have been directly decided." The court declined to decide it.]

VI.   Conclusion

We hold that the Bankruptcy Court was correct in awarding the insurance proceeds to FINOVA, and did not abuse its discretion in refusing to invoke the equitable exception. We will therefore affirm the order of the District Court.

NOTE

Revised UCC. In a passage omitted above the court observed that UCC Article 9, as revised, defines *proceeds* so as to include, "to the extent of the value of

---

16. The Bankruptcy Code provides that prepetition security interests extend to postpetition "proceeds, product, offspring, or profits" of prepetition collateral, "to the extent provided by such security agreement and by applicable nonbankruptcy law, *except to the extent that the court, after notice and a hearing and based on the equities of the case, orders otherwise.*" 11 U.S.C. § 552(b)(1) (emphasis added)....

17. From this fact, the Bankruptcy Court drew the conclusion that the insurance proceeds would not otherwise have been part of Tower's estate, and thus available to pay its general unsecured creditors. We find this conclusion inexplicable; the insurance proceeds are simply a pool of money, and if they were not reserved to FINOVA, then they would seem to be assets of the estate and available to pay general creditors.

collateral and to the extent payable to the debtor or the secured party, insurance payable by reason of the loss or nonconformity of, defects or infringement of rights in, or damage to the collateral."

This provision, the court said, "might allow the creditor to recover only the original value of his collateral.... While [the new] language is not perfectly clear, it would seem to limit recovery to the value of the original collateral; insurance payments beyond that value would, it seems, not constitute 'proceeds.' But, of course, the revised UCC was not in effect at any time relevant to this case...."

If that is what the revisers of Article 9 intended, how could they explain that the result in *Tower Air* was unfair to other creditors holding unsecured claims?

Introduction to Brownell v. Board of Education

Much of the story that follows is one of revulsion against outcomes like the one in this case. But the decision has not been impeached in New York, and its premises are broadly accepted.

Subject to some qualifications, the making of a contract for the sale of improved real estate shifts from the vendor to the purchaser the risk of casualty to the improvements. This is a doctrine long established in the law. It is identified with the expression "equitable conversion". It is grounded in the remedy specific performance, which is granted routinely upon breach by the vendor or by the purchaser. The doctrine has some support in the maxim that equity regards that as done which ought in good conscience to be done. See Gilles v. Sprout, 196 N.W.2d 612 (Minn. 1972). The thought is that, in equity, ownership passes to the purchaser when the sale agreement becomes effective, although the parties have deferred executing the deed or other document of transfer—have put off "closing", that is. From the moment of contracting forward, then, the purchaser bears the risk of fortuitous damage to the property. If misconduct by the vendor causes the loss, of course it does not fall on the purchaser. That is one qualification on the doctrine. Another is that the parties may, by contract, allocate the risks as they choose. Other qualifications reflect moves made by legislatures and courts to limit the doctrine.

A move on the legislative front is the Uniform Vendor–Purchaser Risk Act, adopted in several states.[1] Section 1 of the Act, "Risk of Loss", refers to contracts "made in this State for the purchase and sale of realty". They are to be "interpreted", the section says, as including an agreement— unless the contract expressly provides otherwise—specified in clauses (a) and (b). One or the other clause applies when all or a material part of the realty ("subject matter") has been destroyed, without fault of the vendor, or has been taken by eminent domain. Clause (a) applies to highly executory contracts: when neither the legal title nor the possession of the subject matter has been transferred. Clause (b) applies when *either* has been transferred. (And so, it would seem, when both have been.) In the former

---

1. In 2006 in thirteen states, including California, Illinois, Michigan, and North Carolina.

case, "the vendor cannot enforce the contract, and the purchaser is entitled to recover any portion of the price that he has paid". In the latter case, "the purchaser is not [] relieved from a duty to pay the price, nor is he entitled to recover any portion thereof that he has paid." Without the aid of legislation, at least one court has reached a similar position.[2]

Nearly three decades after *Brownell* was decided, the Uniform Vendor and Purchaser Risk Act became effective in New York. If it had been enacted before the deal between Brownell and the Board, the statutory "agreement" would not have entered into their contract, for they included an explicit agreement much like that of clause (1)(a) of the Uniform Act.

One reason to restrict the doctrine of equitable conversion is the surprise and dismay it may occasion when, although the vendor holds insurance against a loss, the casualty risk resides with the purchaser, who does not. A number of courts have responded to that situation by conferring on the purchaser the benefit of the vendor's insurance, or some of it. In Brownell's case, he was the purchaser, asking the court to do likewise. As will be seen the court refused, saying: "The benefit of the vendor's policy belonged to the vendor...." The opinion hints that earlier rulings to the contrary were signs of sentimentality.

Brownell v. Board of Education

Court of Appeals of New York, 1925.
239 N.Y. 369, 146 N.E. 630, 37 A.L.R. 1319.

■ POUND, J.

The parties seek a declaratory judgment.... Prior to September 10, 1923, the defendant board of education owned and was in possession of premises on Lake avenue in the city of Saratoga Springs, on which were situated a high school building and two other small structures of comparatively little value. The building had become unsuitable or inadequate for use as a high school, and before the date specified defendant had purchased other property and was erecting thereon a new high school building. On September 10, 1923, plaintiff and defendant entered into a written contract whereby plaintiff agreed to purchase and defendant to sell the Lake avenue premises for $30,000, of which $3,000 was paid upon the execution of the contract. The balance was to be paid upon the completion of the new high school building, estimated to be about September 1, 1924, at which time a deed to the Lake avenue property and possession thereof were to be given to plaintiff. The contract provided that the premises were to be delivered "in as good condition as they now are, natural wear excepted;" that defendant was to pay taxes and assessments during the period of its occupancy and until the delivery of the deed; and that in case either party failed to perform, the party so failing should pay to the other the sum of

---

2. Anderson v. Yaworski, 181 A. 205, 101 A.L.R. 1232 (Conn. 1935). See also Potwin v. Tucker, 259 A.2d 781 (Vt. 1969).

$3,000, which was agreed upon as liquidated damages for such failure. The contract was silent as to insurance. However, at the time of the contract and for a considerable period prior thereto defendant carried insurance on the premises and the contents thereof in substantial amounts, including $28,000 upon the high school building. This insurance was payable to defendant in the event of loss. No change in the form of the insurance was made at any time. It was continued after the contract was executed. Plaintiff did not secure other insurance. On October 26, 1923, while the premises were still in defendant's exclusive possession, a fire occurred without fault of either party which totally destroyed the roofs and interior of the high school building and practically destroyed its outer walls. Defendant by reason thereof was compelled to vacate the building, and no repairs have been made upon it. The building was considered by defendant and the insurance companies as a total loss, and defendant has received from the insurers and still retains the full sum of $28,000 insurance carried thereon. This is exclusive of other amounts of insurance received by it for loss on the building's contents.

On this state of facts plaintiff asks that the contract of September 10, 1923, be specifically performed by defendant, by a conveyance of the title to the real estate and by application of the insurance money upon the purchase price. Defendant declines to do this, but offers to return to plaintiff the $3,000 with interest paid by him upon the execution of the contract.

The courts below have held that defendant continued to hold the insurance money in place of the destroyed building in trust for plaintiff. With this conclusion we are not in accord. The benefit of the vendor's policy belonged to the vendor, and the vendee had no claim on the insurance money. Such is the weight of English and American authority resting on Rayner v. Preston (1881) (18 Ch.Div. 1).*

The English rule has been changed by act of Parliament (1922) (12 & 13 Geo. V, c. 16, sec. 105), so as to provide that the vendee may claim the insurance money received by the vendor, subject, however, to any stipulation to the contrary. The question is unsettled in this court. When the risk of loss falls on an uninsured vendee . . . , the rule in Rayner v. Preston has given some dissatisfaction. In some jurisdictions the courts have sought to follow the general and manifestly unsound reasoning of Lord Justice James in his dissenting opinion to the effect that the policy is for the benefit of all persons interested in the property. Professor Vance in the note in the Yale Law Journal (34 Yale L.J. 87), suggests that in the business world the insurance runs with the land and that the courts should give effect to that understanding. Other jurisdictions have sought so to extend the rule that the vendee becomes the beneficial owner of the land for certain purposes . . . as to include the insurance money. In Millville Aerie v. Weatherby (1913) (82 N.J.Eq. 455, 88 A. 847) the court says: "As purchaser under a

* See Woodruff's Cases on Insurance, 2d ed. p. 223; "Risk of Loss in Equity between the Date of Contract to Sell Real Estate and Transfer of Title," by Professor Vannemore, 8 Minn.L.Rev. 127; also, note on the decision below, 34 Yale L.J. 87.

valid contract of purchase vendee became the equitable owner of the property; in equity the property is regarded as belonging to him, the vendor retaining the legal title simply as trustee and as security for the unpaid purchase money. By reason of this equitable relation of the parties to a contract of sale of land, it has been determined by the great weight of American authority that money accruing on a policy of insurance, where the loss has occurred subsequent to the execution of the contract, will in equity inure to the benefit of the vendee; the vendor still retaining his character as trustee, and the insurance money in his hands representing the property that has been destroyed."

These reasons may savor of layman's ideas of equity, but they are not law. The majority of the court in Rayner v. Preston were sound in principle. Insurance is a mere personal contract to pay a sum of money by way of indemnity to protect the interest of the insured.... In common parlance the buildings are insured but every one who stops to consider the nature of the insurance contract understands that they are not. Both in the forum and the market place it is known that the insurance runs to the individual insured and not with the land. The vendor has a beneficial interest to protect, *i.e.*, his own. The vendee has an insurable interest and may protect himself. The trustee as such has no insurable interest and can only act for the *cestui que trust*. Plaintiff may not have the insurance money collected by defendant. It is not a part of the *res* bargained for and no trust relation exists in regard to it.

Plaintiff asks that if the relief he seeks cannot be granted, the rights of the parties be stated. In this regard the parties have by the terms of their contract taken themselves out of the old rule of Paine v. Meller (6 Ves.Jr. 349) ..., which places the loss on the vendee when the buildings are destroyed before the transfer is made. The vendor contracted to deliver the premises "in as good condition as they now are" and the parties agreed that in case of failure to perform the defaulting party should pay the sum of $3,000 as liquidated damages. The loss must, therefore, be borne by the defendant, except as it has protected itself from such loss by insurance. By reason of the accidental destruction of a substantial part of the premises, it can neither perform nor compel performance.... The purchaser may seek to rescind the contract or take the position that it is at an end for impossibility of performance and recover back the $3,000 he has paid on the purchase price, or he may stand on the contract under the terms of which he paid the $3,000 and claim the stipulated damages. He is not in a position to do both. The measure of defendant's liability in either case is the sum of $3,000.

The judgments below should be reversed and a declaratory judgment granted in accordance with opinion....

NOTES

(1) *Other Views.* The court's view of the fire insurance contract as "personal" is entrenched in history.[1] Yet what it referred to disdainfully as "layman's ideas of equity" prevails as the law in probably the majority of American courts. Many cases

support the view that the proceeds of the vendor's insurance are payable to him "in trust" for the benefit of the purchaser. For a thorough discussion of the authorities concerning a vendor's insurance in relation to land sales, see G. Palmer, Law of Restitution, Vol. 4, § 23.2 (1978).

(2) *Equities*. Perhaps Brownell was in a weak position to claim the benefit of the Board's insurance. Even a sympathetic court might call it unbecoming of him to claim surprise and dismay on finding that insurance is "a mere personal contract". He had, after all, bargained with the Board for it to deliver the premises to him "in as good condition as they [were], natural wear excepted".

Some decisions suggest that equity, like law, can be at odds with sympathies. In Acree v. Hanover Ins. Co., 561 F.2d 216 (10th Cir. 1977), the purchasers of a home obtained the benefit of insurance on it that the vendor had bought, even though they chose not to take advantage of a provision in the sale contract that they could withdraw in the event of appreciable damage. See also Estes v. Thurman, 192 S.W.3d 429 (Ky.App. 2005). According to the opinion there, a vendor held proceeds of a policy she had bought—part of them—in trust for purchasers of her insured property even though they had failed to comply with a provision in the sale contract requiring them to procure and pay for insurance on the vendor's interest.

(3) *New York Law— Continued.* A subsequent opinion in New York may mark a retreat from the court's view as expressed in *Brownell*, although the court sought to distinguish *Brownell*. See Raplee v. Piper, 143 N.E.2d 919, 64 A.L.R.2d 1397 (1957). The critical distinction was this, it seems: The sale contract required that the purchaser pay premiums on the policy issued to the vendor, and he did. (Also, the purchaser was in possession at the time of the loss.) The court ruled, in an action by the purchaser for specific performance, that he was entitled to credit for the insurance proceeds against the unpaid part of the purchase price. Even so, three of the judges dissented, believing that the decision undercut the *Brownell* decision.

A question remaining is whether the court would permit enrichment of a vendor through receipt *both* of his insurance proceeds *and* the full contract price. Professor George Palmer concluded that the issue is in doubt in New York; see Law of Restitution, Note 1 above, at Vol. 4, p. 348n. He argued that the vendor would be unjustly enriched.

(4) *Insurer's Liability*. In 1939 this statute took effect in New York, now section 3204 of the Insurance Law:

> *Executory contract not a change in interest, title or possession.* The making of a contract to sell or to exchange real property shall not constitute a change in the interest, title or possession, within the meaning of the applicable provisions of any contract of fire insurance, including any contract supplemental thereto, covering property located in this state.

The Court of Appeals has not said that this statute overturned its decision in *Brownell*. It could be understood as being addressed to one or both of two other problems, each concerning the effect of an executory land-sale contract on the vendor's insurance. Does the contract exonerate the insurer altogether? If not, does it restrict the insurer's liability? Neither of those questions arose in *Brownell*.

---

1. See Lynch v. Dalzell, 4 Brown's Parliamentary Cases 431, 2 Eng.Rep. 292 (1729). In Brown's report, no opinion of the court is given; but Park, Insurance 452 (3d ed.) gives an opinion by Lord Chancellor King.

To the first of those questions the Court of Appeals had answered "No" long before it decided *Brownell*. Browning v. Home Ins. Co., 71 N.Y. 508 (1877). To the second question, other New York courts have answered "No". See Johnson v. New York Mutual Underwriters Ins. Co., 582 N.Y.S.2d 871 (App.Div. 1992).[2]

The statute might be read to ratify the result in *Browning* and to do little more. But it has been read to concern also the amount of a vendor's insurance recovery. *Ibid.*

Courts taking the view that a purchaser is entitled to benefit from the vendor's insurance have drawn the conclusion that the insurer's liability is not diminished by the making of a sale contract. First National Bank of Highland Park v. Boston Ins. Co., 160 N.E.2d 802 (Ill. 1959) (action by insured seller, represented by purchaser's attorney: "the contract price did not conclusively determine the value of the vendor's interest"). See also cases cited in Martin v. Coleman, 2001 WL 673701 (Tenn.App. 2001), including Parker v. Tennessee Farmers Mutual Ins. Co., 1988 WL 138923 (Tenn.App. 1988). The policy in question in *Parker* contained this term: "We will not pay more than the insurable interest an insured person has in the covered property at the time of loss." But that seems to have had no effect.

Vogel v. Northern Assurance Co.

United States Court of Appeals, Third Circuit, 1955.
219 F.2d 409.

■ GOODRICH, CIRCUIT JUDGE.

This is an appeal from a decision in an insurance case. With a stipulated loss of $12,000 the plaintiff finds himself in the happy possession of a judgment against two insurance companies which aggregates $15,000. The insurance companies, quite naturally, appeal.

The whole question is one of Pennsylvania law. The property insured against fire was located in Pennsylvania; the insurance policies were written and delivered in Pennsylvania. Our sole problem is to determine as best we can the Pennsylvania law which governs this situation.

The undisputed facts present a question with all the tantalizing niceties of the type which examiners pose to law students. Indeed, the problem of the case can be posed in the form of a hypothetical examination question. Here it is:

> S, a seller of real property, (in the actual case a man named Shank) agrees to sell the land to V, the vendee, for $15,000. (The vendee's real name in this case is Vogel, so the initials fit happily.) S then takes out fire insurance on the property in the amount of $6,000; V does likewise but in the amount of $9,000. Before S conveys the property to V a fire occurs, damaging the house on the land to the extent of $12,000. V goes ahead and completes his part of the purchase

---

2. In Rosenbloom v. Maryland Ins. Co., 15 N.Y.S.2d 304 (App.Div. 1939), the court said, referring to the statute, that the rule prevailed in New York prior to its enactment. For that, however, the court cited *Browning*. *Browning* concerned this provision in a poli-cy: "if the property be sold or transferred, or any change take place in title or possession, then and in every such case the policy shall be void." The court ruled that an executory contract of sale did not bring this provision into play.

agreement and receives a deed from S. Following this, S assigns to V all of his rights against the insurance company under the policy. V then sues both S's insurer (Northern Assurance Company Ltd.) and his own insurer (Mount Joy Mutual Insurance Company).[1] Was the district court correct in giving judgment against each company even though the total recovery exceeds the stipulated loss by $3,000?[2]

We start the analysis with the well-settled rule in Pennsylvania, derived from English law, that when a contract to sell land is made the equitable ownership passes forthwith to the buyer. The seller's "title" which he retains until final conveyance is but a "security title" and the risk of loss or advantage of gain is borne by the buyer. . . .

The seller with this security title may take out fire insurance to protect his interest. The Pennsylvania decisions say unequivocally that as between the seller and the insurance company the seller is the owner of the property. Insurance Co. v. Updegraff; Dubin Paper Co. v. Insurance Co. of North America. See also Reed v. Lukens and Heidisch v. Globe & Republic Ins. Co. of America.[a] Of course, upon the performance of the contract of sale, the seller no longer has an insurable interest. Grevemeyer v. Southern Mutual Fire Ins. Co., 62 Pa. 340 (1869); Light v. Countrymen's Mutual Fire Ins. Co. of Lebanon County, 32 A. 439 (Pa. 1895). The Pennsylvania cases demonstrate very clearly, however, that a seller of real estate, having taken out fire insurance, can collect from the insurance company under the policy for a loss occurring prior to the date of settlement. The reason assigned is that the rights and liabilities of the parties to the insurance contract become fixed when the loss occurs. It is not valid argument, according to these authorities, that the seller has suffered no loss because the vendee has later completed the contract of sale and paid the seller. *Updegraff*, *Reed*, *Dubin Paper*. Compare also *Heidisch*.

So far, so good. Is the insurance money thus collected by the seller his own to do with as he pleases? May he use it to buy himself a new car, give it to a favorite grandchild or otherwise dispose of it as people do who have some extra money? In this particular case S, instead of collecting the

---

1. The action was originally begun in the Court of Common Pleas of Delaware County, Pennsylvania. Northern, a foreign corporation, removed the case to the United States District Court for the Eastern District of Pennsylvania. The removal took with it the litigation against Mount Joy. See 28 U.S.C. § 1441(c) (1952).

2. The hypothetical statement oversimplifies the fact situation just a little. The actual chronological order of events in this case was as follows: Prior to August 29, 1950, the property was owned by one Riddle who had entered into an agreement of sale with Shank. On August 29, 1950, Shank entered into an agreement of sale with Vogel. On October 3, 1950, Shank received a deed to the property from Riddle. It was not until Octo-

ber 16, 1950, that Shank made his insurance contract with Northern Assurance Co. The next day, October 17, 1950, Vogel entered into the insurance contract with Mount Joy Mutual Insurance Co. The fire occurred eleven days later, on October 28, 1950, which was prior to the date of settlement. On November 24, 1950, Vogel received the deed to the property after paying Shank the full purchase price. On December 1, 1950, Shank assigned all his "right, title, interest, right of action and claim" that he had against Northern to Vogel.

a. The citations for these four cases are, respectively, 21 Pa. 513 (1853); 63 A.2d 85, 8 A.L.R.2d 1393 (1949); 44 Pa. 200 (1863); and 84 A.2d 566, 29 A.L.R.2d 884 (1951).

money, assigned his rights against the insurance company to V. The district judge indicates that he thinks that S was under no obligation to do this. See Vogel v. Northern Assur. Co., 114 F.Supp. 591 (E.D.Pa. 1953). If that were so and this insurance money, or the claim to it belonged to S free and clear, then his gift of the insurance proceeds to V, or to anybody else, would certainly be none of the insurance company's business. It would simply be a case where a man is allowed to do what he pleases with his own.

We think the district court was mistaken on this point because under Pennsylvania law the seller becomes the trustee of the property and rights incident thereto and holds them in trust for the vendee. *Updegraff*; *Reed*; Hill v. Cumberland Valley Mutual Protection Co., 59 Pa. 474 (1868); Parcell v. Grosser, 1 A. 909 (1885). The most recent case in Pennsylvania which involved this point directly is *Dubin Paper*. In the *Dubin* case the loss occurred prior to the date of settlement of the contract of sale. The vendee having performed his contract, the seller upon receiving checks from his insurance companies to cover the fire loss returned them to the insurance companies. Then the vendee brought an action in equity against the insurance companies and the seller to compel the insurance companies to pay the proceeds to the seller and to have the court declare that the seller hold the proceeds as trustee for the plaintiff. The problem was discussed at length by Chief Justice Maxey. The conclusion was that the action was well brought and that the plaintiff was entitled to the relief for which he prayed.

This decision clearly shows that the insurance money which S collects from the insurance company after he has been paid by the vendee is not his to keep or spend but in equity belongs to the vendee. As we read the *Dubin* and earlier Pennsylvania cases no other conclusion is possible. So, in this particular instance, when V had complied with the terms of the contract of sale, the proceeds due on the insurance which S had taken out was something to which V was equitably entitled. That means that in this case V (Vogel) may clearly maintain his action against the insurance company which was the insurer on S's contract.

Northern makes two arguments with considerable plausibility. One is that the insurance which S takes out covers only the security title which he has. If he gets his money from the vendee he suffers no loss and should not be allowed to recover anything against the insurance company. Northern also argues that it is entitled to subrogation to the insured's right to the extent that the insured has a claim over and above the amount of his loss. Both of these arguments are pretty good. But in this case the federal court is bound to apply state law as best it can. The state law has been settled, and firmly settled, against Northern's arguments by the series of decisions which we have already cited above.

Then we pass to the claim of V against his insurer. This insurance policy was taken out by V himself in the amount of $12,000, but contains a three-fourths value clause.[b] There is no doubt that a vendee who has made

b.   As to this see Mowbray & Blanchard, Insurance (4th ed. 1955) 109: "The *three-* *fourths value clause* limits the liability of the insurer to three-fourths of the value of the

a contract of sale to buy land can himself take out insurance. Imperial Fire Ins. Co. of London v. Dunham, 12 A. 668 (1888); Millville Mut. Fire Ins. Co. v. Wilgus, 88 Pa. 107 (1878). This is only common sense; if the vendee bears the risk of loss he certainly has a risk which he can insure against. What is there, then, to prevent V from recovering against the insurance company for the loss which it is agreed took place?

Mount Joy argues that it is excused from paying because there was in the policy a place for the noting of other insurance and the insured gave Mount Joy no information on this. Therefore, it says, this provision being one to guard against fraud in over insurance, it does not have to pay anything. As pointed out by the district judge, however, these policies were taken out on different interests. S took out a policy to protect his interest as seller; V took out a policy to protect his interest as an equitable owner. The settled interpretation of the "other insurance" clause is that the other insurance must be "on the same interest and subject, and against the same risk." 3 Richards on Insurance 1667 (5th ed., Freedman, 1952). The district court was correct in holding the other insurance clause inapplicable.

Furthermore, it is to be pointed out that what S assigned to V was not an insurance policy. He assigned to V his claim against the insurance company for a loss which had already taken place and which left him with a claim against the insurance company. *Reed.* See also Imperial Fire Ins. Co. of London v. Dunham, 12 A. 668 (1888), at 673; 3 Richards on Insurance 1635. And under the Pennsylvania cases which we have set out above that claim was for the face of the policy, not for the protection of S's security title.

This brings us out to an affirmance of a judgment for $15,000, $3,000 more than the loss. This, it is true, seems incongruous in view of the often stated generalization that fire insurance is indemnity insurance. Vance on Insurance § 14 (3d ed., 1951); 1 Richards on Insurance 3. The incongruity, if there is one, reaches clear back to 1853 in the settled rule in Pennsylvania that the seller can recover fully against the insurance company for a loss occurring between the time of the agreement and final settlement even though the buyer has taken title according to the terms of the contract. We have no doubt that the ingenuity of insurance counsel will draft a provision whereby total recovery can be limited to actual loss if that is an object to be desired. And if this Court has failed in its examination of Pennsylvania law on the subject, it will be compelled to take the course over.

The judgment of the district court will be affirmed.

NOTES

(1) *Grade: A-.* Apparently—to continue the court's pass-fail figure—it had to take the course over. In the following year the Pennsylvania Supreme Court ruled,

insured property, or if there is other insurance, to its pro-rata share of three-fourths of the value. Limitation of the permissible amount of insurance is a part of the clause. The *three-fourth loss clause* goes further and limits the insurer's liability to its pro-rata share of three-fourths of any loss." The object of each is "to require the insured to have an interest in preserving his property from loss." Was this object attained?

on roughly comparable facts, that the insurers for a transferor and a transferee should share the loss "in the proportion of the amounts of their respective policies". That would mean, given the dollar amounts in *Vogel*, a payment by S's insurer of 40% (6/15ths) of the loss, and one by V's insurer of the remainder. For the transferee to recover an amount greater than his loss was a result, the court said, that "the law will not permit." Insurance Company of North America v. Alberstadt, 119 A.2d 83 (1956).

No examination paper is perfect.

(2) *A Texas Retort*. The *Vogel* opinion goes beyond saying that the making of a sale contract does not diminish the vendor's insurance recovery. The court said: "It is not valid argument . . . that the seller has suffered no loss because the vendee has later . . . paid the seller." For an opposing view see Paramount Fire Ins. Co. v. Aetna Cas. & Sur. Co., 353 S.W.2d 841 (Tex. 1962). In that case the court said that it had found only two cases in which the "constructive trust theory" was applied in favor of a purchaser provided with its own insurance. One was *Vogel*; the other was *Alberstadt*. Those decisions depended, the court said, on a rule stated this way in *Vogel*: "the rights and liabilities of the parties to the insurance contract become fixed when the loss occurs." The Texas court rejected that rule. For other decisions based on the rule see New Hampshire Insurance Co. v. Vetter, 326 N.W.2d 723 (S.D.1982).

(3) *Liability of Vendor's Insurer*. In Brownell v. Board, the Board's insurers paid it, apparently without demur, almost ten times the amount in which it was liable to Brownell. In contrast, the Northern Assurance Company balked at paying anything to its insured, Shank, on finding that he had been paid all he asked for his property. As to the force of that objection in New York, see Note 4, p. 482 above.

Question: What result in *Vogel* if Shank, not getting any more money from Vogel after the fire, had not made the assignment and had simply sued his own insurer ("Shank v. Northern Assurance")? For a case resembling that, see New Hampshire Insurance Co. v. Vetter, 326 N.W.2d 723 (S.D. 1982).

(4) *The Constructive Trust*. It is an instance of constructive trust that "the insurance money which S collects from the insurance company . . . is not his to keep." The *Dubin Paper* case, cited in *Vogel*, is thought to be the first in which a purchaser succeeded in enforcing collection of the loss claim by bringing an action against the insurer. In Gilles v. Sprout, 196 N.W.2d 612 (Minn. 1972), a purchaser sought specific performance of his land-sale contract by suing to have the seller's fire insurance proceeds applied in satisfaction of the balance due on the contract. The court took note of Brownell's case but chose not to follow its reasoning: "there is no manifest disruption of the law if the equitable result is favored, especially if the vendee is required to reimburse the vendor for his cost of maintaining the insurance during the vendee's possession and the insurance proceeds are credited to the unpaid purchase price only to the extent of the market value of the dwelling immediately before the loss."

Although the constructive trust theory has found favor in many American courts,[1] some strong-minded ones have resisted it. But even those doing so are

---

1. Professor Vance advocated the majority view persuasively; see Vance, Insurance 778–81 (3d ed. 1951). For a quasi-contractual analysis, see Campbell, Non–Consensual Suretyship, 45 Yale L.J. 69, 100 (1935).

Professor Palmer protested against the trust language, and related expressions, in the main case. The true principle, he believed, is that unjust enrichment of the vendor should be prevented. On that principle, if the proceeds under the vendor's policy exceed

adept at finding reasons to give the purchaser the benefit of the seller's insurance, in special circumstances.[2]

Strict adherence to the view that insurance is "personal to the insured" might mean that (a) upon payment by an insurer to a vendor, it is entitled by subrogation to the unpaid purchase price, and (b) a post-loss settlement between vendor and purchaser releases the insurer by impairing the right of subrogation. But courts espousing the constructive trust can comfortably reject each of these propositions—and they have done so.[3]

(5) *Variant Case.* Suppose the fire that prompted the dispute in *Vogel* had not occurred until after the date of settlement, when S gave V a deed to the property. And suppose that V had given S a purchase-money mortgage in lieu of full payment of the purchase price. In that case an expectable result is this: Northern pays S (not more than the amount of the unpaid price) and asserts S's rights to enforce the mortgage, by way of subrogation, against V. Mount Joy pays V. Is this resolution wholly satisfactory?

Cf. Mann v. Glens Falls Ins. Co., 541 F.2d 819, 821 (9th Cir. 1976) ("Despite some criticism, the widely accepted rule is that the mortgagor is not entitled to insurance protection under a mortgagee-only type insurance policy.").

(6) *Other Insurance.* The point made by the court in the paragraph beginning "Mount Joy" is rejected by some courts. Hence it may happen that a vendor finds his claim on his own policy curtailed by the fact that the purchaser has procured insurance. The barebones situation is this: Hanover Company insures S; Windsor Company insures V. Each policy provides that, in the event of a loss insured by "other insurance," the issuer of that policy will pay only a pro-rata portion of the loss. Upon a loss so insured, some courts will evidently not require aggregate payments exceeding the amount of loss.

Suppose that the amount insured in each policy is $50,000 and that the loss is $10,000. Hanover refuses to pay anything. Windsor pays V $10,000 and V assigns to Windsor whatever rights he may have against Hanover. In the suit, Windsor v. Hanover, three possibilities of outcome are obvious: (a) no recovery, (b) judgment for $5,000, and (c) judgment for $10,000. If the court accepts the reading of the other-insurance clause as made in *Vogel*, the outcome might be (c). Otherwise, Windsor will presumably recover no more than $5,000. For cases so indicating, see Insurance Co. of North America v. Nicholas, 533 S.W.2d 204 (Ark. 1976) (a sale-and-resale case); Root v. Hamilton Mutual Insurance Co., 323 N.W.2d 298 (Mich.

---

the contract price—as has happened—the vendor may retain the excess. But the point has rarely arisen, and Palmer conceded that the talk of constructive trust is commonplace. See 4 G. Palmer, Law of Restitution, § 23.2 (1978).

2. The following set of cases make for especially interesting comparisons:

(a) Twin City Fire Insurance Co. v. Walter B. Hannah, Inc., 444 S.W.2d 131 (Ky. 1969);

(b) Raplee v. Piper, Note 3, p. 482 above;

(c) Northwestern Mutual Insurance Co. v. Jackson Vibrators, Inc., 402 F.2d 37 (6th Cir. 1968); and

(d) Wilson v. Fireman's Insurance Co. of Newark, New Jersey, 403 Mich. 339, 269 N.W.2d 170 (1978).

None of these cases avowedly favors a buyer as such with a restitutionary claim on the seller's insurance, but they tend in that direction. In each case the sale contract contained some provision with reference to insurance on the property.

3. (a) Alabama Farm Bureau Mutual Insurance Service, Inc. v. Nixon, 105 So.2d 643 (Ala. 1958); (b) Milwaukee Mechanics Insurance Co. v. Maples, 66 So.2d 159 (Ala. App. 1953).

App. 1981); St. Paul Fire & Marine Insurance Co. v. Allstate Insurance Co., 543 P.2d 147 (Ariz.App. 1975) ("Windsor's" policy payable to "S" as his interest might appear).

(7) *The Prepaid Premium.* Suppose that S refuses to assign his rights against Northern to V unless V pays both the full purchase price and the amount S has paid as a premium for the period following the sale contract. Has V any choice but to pay? Conceivably the courts might imply a term in every contract to buy improved property by which the purchaser must reimburse the seller for prepaid premiums, unless the insurance is cancelled.[4] Would that be wise? If sellers have a right to premium-reimbursement in the event of loss, it is hard to see why it should be otherwise in the absence of loss.

It is usually possible, without expense, to have a purchaser's name added to the vendor's policies, so that both are named insureds, and the proceeds of loss are payable to them "as their interests may appear." When this arrangement is made, the purchaser commonly assumes some responsibility for premiums. Sometimes he does so, of course, without change in the insuring terms.

PROBLEMS

(1) S agrees to sell improved property to V for $15,000. S holds fire insurance for $6,000 on the improvements; V fails to insure. An insured loss occurs. The insurer pays $5,000 to S as its part of a settlement with S. On the date set for closing of the sale, V tenders $9,000 to S, demanding in return a conveyance of the damaged property. S demands $10,000. V objects (and later proves) that S could have collected $6,000 from the insurer if S had been more aggressive in the adjustment negotiations. The applicable law is as stated in *Vogel*. Which of the demands is rightful? Would the problem be affected by changing the facts so that V had obtained insurance of $9,000 on the property for himself?

See Patrick & Wilkins Co. v. Reliance Insurance Co., 456 A.2d 1348 (Pa. 1983). The holding in that case, it is said, "may signal a shift away from applying the trust theory without regard to insurance principles in cases where there are multiple policies." Bixby, the Vendor–Vendee Problem . . ., 19 The Forum 112, 124 (1983).

(2) A contract for the sale of A's home to B required that A keep it insured against fire through the year 2006, and required B to have it insured thereafter, each in the amount of $125,000. The home was destroyed by fire in the spring of 2007, before any transfer had occurred under the contract. A still had the required insurance, and more: her policy was for $150,000. B had bought no insurance on the property. A has collected the policy limit.

Opinions differ about the credit A should give B against the purchase price. A thinks it should be $125,000; B thinks $150,000. C, who is A's brother, thinks it should be zero. Who has it right? See Berlier v. George, 607 P.2d 1152 (1980).

(3) To alter the facts of problem (2), let it be supposed that B went into possession of the property on March 1, 2007. Suppose also that B is entitled to a credit. Authorities cited in n.4 above suggest reducing the credit by some part of the premium charged to A. The offset might be a pro-rata part of the premium

---

4. See Alabama Farm Bureau Mutual Insurance Service, Inc. v. Nixon, 105 So.2d 643 (Ala. 1958). [This holding has been limited; see McGuire v. Wilson, 372 So.2d 1297 (Ala. 1979).]

Compare Barrett v. Dark Tobacco Growers' Co-operative Association, 3 S.W.2d 634 (Ky. 1928); Millville, Aerie, No. 1836, F. O. E. v. Weatherby, 82 N.J.Eq. 455, 88 A. 847 (1913).

representing the period following either January 1 or March 1. Which is the better choice?

Loss-payee and Standard-mortgagee Clauses

Assets of almost all types stand as security for debts. The volume of secured debt is enormous. Both the debtors and the creditors face risks of damage to and destruction of tangible assets securing payments (and, in cases of intangible assets, risks of other kinds of impairment). For creditors these risks are especially troublesome because a loss to a debtor may well thrust it into insolvency. One way of controlling these risks is monitoring for safety. Both a debtor and a creditor have incentives to practice that. But courts have recognized an inefficiency in duplicate monitoring. Michelin Tires (Canada) Ltd. v. First Nat'l Bank of Boston, 666 F.2d 673, 679–80 (1st Cir. 1981).

Insuring is another way for a debtor and a secured creditor to control their risks. Inefficiency also attends duplicate insurances. It can be moderated by insuring, in a single policy, both the interest of the debtor and that of the secured party. Parties to security agreements—mortgages and the like—practice that on a large scale. Banks and other vocational lenders commonly include, when extending secured credit, provisions in their credit agreements requiring the debtor to procure and maintain insurance on the assets backing up the credit (the "collateral").

Compliance with that requirement would not, in itself, give a creditor complete protection. In the event of a loss, a claim by the debtor, and payment in full by the insurer to the debtor, the creditor might find its position changed as follows: The collateral is totally destroyed; the debtor's cash position is enhanced to the value of the collateral; the debtor is insolvent; and (unlike the lost collateral) the cash infusion is subject to pro-rata distribution among the debtor's creditors. In other words, the creditor has lost its priority as a *secured* creditor.

Against that eventuality, two precautions are practiced. One is to write the security agreement so as to include in the description of collateral, along with the back-up asset, any insurance proceeds resulting from its damage or destruction. The other precaution is a loss-payee clause in the insurance policy. In the opinion that follows, that is referred to as a "clause making the mortgagee a payee". In practical effect, a loss-payee clause requires that, upon paying for a loss to a debtor, the insurer issue a check payable jointly to the debtor and the creditor. That check cannot be collected without the indorsement of both.

Even so, a debtor might comply with the letter of the creditor's requirement by procuring a property coverage that includes a "loss-payee" clause, yet violate its spirit by some infraction of the insurance contract, making it unenforceable. Infractions that come to mind are misrepresentation, breach of warranty, and willful destruction of the property. Moved long ago by this consideration, creditors and insurers have developed what is known as the "standard mortgagee clause". An example of that clause is reproduced in footnote 1 below, and a discussion of it in the opinion that follows.

Polar Manufacturing Co. v. Integrity Mutual Ins. Co.

Wisconsin Supreme Court, 1959.
7 Wis.2d 443, 96 N.W.2d 822.

An action by Polar Manufacturing on a policy issued to it by Integrity Mutual resulted in a judgment for the claimant, based on a jury verdict. The opinion suggests that the subject of the insurance was a structure owned by Polar, but does not indicate what happened to it. Fire damage may be supposed.

On this appeal the insurer won a reversal and remand. The trial judge had instructed the jury incorrectly about a misrepresentation in the application for the policy. A Wisconsin statute made a misrepresentation innocuous unless it was "made with intent to deceive, or unless the matter misrepresented ... increased the risk or contributed to the loss." Apparently the jury was asked about falsity and intent to deceive. "The trial court interpreted the statute to mean that any inaccurate statement in the application must be false and made with intent to deceive in order to avoid the policy." But the appellate court rejected this understanding of the statute, emphasizing the word *or* in it. "Further inquiry should have been made as to whether or not the inaccurate statement increased the risk to the defendant company. The jury should have been instructed to answer the last question regardless of its answer to the first."

Another claimant in the action, relying on the same policy, was the Fidelity Savings Bank, which held a mortgage on the damaged property.

■ BROADFOOT, JUSTICE.

. . .

The bank contends that the judgment should be affirmed to the extent of its mortgage interest in the insured property regardless of how the other questions are determined. This raises the question of the effect of a standard mortgage clause attached to a standard fire insurance policy. [The opinion does not quote that clause. One later used in Wisconsin is set out in Estate of Ensz v. Brown Insurance Agency, Inc., 223 N.W.2d 903 (Wis. 1974), at 908, and in the footnote.[1]] Our attention is called to three

1. "Standard Mortgage Clause (Without Contribution and With Waiver of Mortgagee's Liability for Premium or Assessments)

"Loss or damage, if any, under this policy, shall be payable to Security Savings & Loan Ass'n 2701 W. National Ave., Milwaukee, Wis. or its assigns, mortgagee, as interest may appear, and this insurance, as to the interest of the mortgagee only therein, shall not be invalidated by any act or neglect of the mortgagor or owner of the within described property, nor by any foreclosure or other proceedings or notice of sale relating to the property, nor by any change in the title or ownership of the property, nor by the occupation of the premises for purposes more hazardous than are permitted by this policy; provided that in case the mortgagor or owner shall neglect to pay any premium or assess-

opinions by this court touching on the subject. In Prudential Ins. Co. of America v. Paris Mut. Fire Ins. Co., 250 N.W. 851 (Wis. 1933), the court was confronted with a situation where the owner of the insured property changed the use of the premises to one that increased the risk to the insurance company. So far as the mortgagee's interest is concerned, the court merely stated:

> We are not here concerned whether installation ... of the still voided the policy as to the owner, as the terms of the mortgage clause of the rider expressly provide that acts of the owner or occupation of the premises for more hazardous purposes shall not invalidate the insurance of the mortgagee.

Id. at 853.

In State Bank of Chilton v. Citizens Mut. Fire Ins. Co., 252 N.W. 164 (Wis. 1934), the issue was the right of the insurance company under a clause in the policy to repair or rebuild a building damaged or destroyed by fire. The mortgagee felt that it was not bound by that provision in the policy. This court held that it was bound by the provisions of the policy since it was a form of policy prescribed by statute. However, the court made the following statement with reference to mortgagees:

> ... One having a mortgagee interest in property may protect that interest in one of three ways: (1) Under a simple loss payable or option mortgage clause, the mortgagee may be simply an appointee of the insurance fund; (2) by virtue of the standard mortgage clause, often referred to as the subrogation clause such as the one attached to the policy in this case; (3) by a policy procured by and issued to the mortgagee....

Id. at 165.

In Bank of Cashton v. La Crosse County Scandavian Town Mut. Ins. Co., 216 Wis. 513, 257 N.W. 451, judgment was entered in favor of the mortgagee for the amount of fire loss even though the owner of the property had increased the risk to the insurance company by the operation of an illicit still. The mortgage clause thereon was a so-called uniform mutual insurance mortgage clause which differed in some respects from the standard mortgage clause.

ment due under this policy, the mortgagee may on demand pay the same, but in no event shall such mortgagee be legally liable therefor; the benefit of the provisions of any law to the contrary being expressly waived by the insuror.

" ...

"Whenever this Company shall pay the mortgagee any sum for loss or damage under this policy, and shall claim that, as to the mortgagor or owner, no liability therefor existed, this Company shall, to the extent of such payment, be thereupon legally subrogated to all the rights of the party to whom such payment shall be made, under all securities held as collateral to the mortgage debt, or may at its option, pay to the mortgagee the whole principal due or to grow due on the mortgage, with interest accrued thereon to the date of such payment, and shall thereupon receive a full assignment and transfer of the mortgage and of all such other securities; but no subrogation shall impair the right of the mortgagee to recover the full amount of its claim."

In an annotation in 124 A.L.R. 1034 it is stated that a majority of the courts in this country hold that the standard mortgage clause making the mortgagee a payee and stipulating that the insurance shall not be invalidated by the mortgagor's acts or neglect constitutes an independent contract between the mortgagee and the insurer. Consideration therefor is found in the requirements of duties to be performed by the mortgagee under the terms of the mortgage clause, such as notifying the company of any change of ownership or occupancy or increase of hazard which shall come to the knowledge of the mortgagee, and the promise of the mortgagee to pay premiums for increased hazards and to pay premiums upon demand in case of default in payment thereof by the mortgagor.

[The court found the conception "independent contract" also in two legal encyclopedias.]

In none of the three Wisconsin cases referred to above has this court stated directly that the mortgage clause constitutes a separate independent contract. However, language in the opinions in those cases indicates that this court considered the standard mortgage clause to be such an independent contract.

We do not think it would be proper procedure to affirm the judgment as to the mortgagee's interest since a new trial must be held as to the liability of the insurance company to the plaintiff [Polar?]. However, when judgment is entered following the new trial the bank will be entitled to recover from the defendant the amount of its mortgage with interest, unless it should develop that the bank had failed to comply with any of its obligations under the mortgage clause. In the event that the new trial results in a determination of no liability by the defendant to Polar, the judgment shall provide for subrogation of the mortgagee's rights to the defendant as provided in the mortgage clause.

Judgment reversed and cause remanded for further proceedings in accordance with this opinion.

NOTES

(1) *Surprise!* Scenic Airlines, Inc., having obtained an aircraft by lease from one Bell, procured hull insurance on it, along with others, as required by the lease. Thereafter it terminated the lease and returned the plane to Bell. It also had the plane removed from the policy. Bell leased the plane to another party, who loaned it to still another. Later the plane was lost to all these parties through seizure by the United States. That occurred in Puerto Rico, where the plane was apparently being used for drug trafficking.

When an action was brought on the policy, the insurer appeared to have several defenses. According to notes made by the trial judge, "No one was paying any premiums.... [T]he plane was not hangered [sic] in the Continental United States.... And that was one of the requirements in the insurance policy. The airplane ... was not being flown by approved pilots. We don't know who was flying it. And, therefore, the insurance company could not have evaluated the risks for the purposes of pricing the policy. There was no meeting of the minds."

But the plaintiff was a bank which held a security interest in the plane (given to it by Bell), and which was named as payee in an endorsement containing a standard mortgagee clause. No one had told the bank, before the loss, that the plane had been deleted from the policy. As to that, the endorsement provided: "In the event this Policy or this endorsement is cancelled by the Company thirty (30) days prior notice shall be sent to the said Lienholder named herein."

On an appeal in the case the court sustained the bank's claim on all the points suggested above. Union Planters National Bank v. American Home Assurance Co., 2002 WL 1308344 (Tenn.App. 2002). As to the thirty-day notice provision, the insurer contended that it applied only to a wholesale cancellation affecting all the aircraft—more than twenty—that the policy and endorsement covered. That reading was unreasonable, the court said.

(2) *Changing Ways*. A good while ago it was said that the distinction between a simple loss-payee clause and a standard mortgagee clause had declined. In recent times "mortgagees are almost universally insured under standard mortgage clauses, not loss payable clauses." Lev, Mortgagees and Insurers: The Legal Nuts and Bolts of Their Relationship, No. 662 Ins.L.J. 168, 169–170 (1978).

(3) *The* Vision *Case*. An insurer named Midwest Family Mutual (MFM) issued a business owner's policy to Mufti Hospitality Group, covering not only personal property belonging to Mufti but also business personal property in Mufti's care, custody, or control, owned by others but located at a motel owned by Mufti. Computer equipment that Mufti had obtained by lease from Vision Financial Group was within that description. Vision was named in the policy as loss payee. The equipment was stolen. When MFM refused to pay it, Vision brought an action in which it was given summary judgment.

On appeal, the court reversed and directed that judgment be entered for MFM. It ruled that two "exclusions" were applicable, one to do with dishonesty and one with false pretenses. (Mufti's president had stolen the equipment.) A recovery for Vision was barred, the court said, by each of the two exclusions.

The court wrote as follows about the loss-payee provision: "Vision Financial argues that the policy exclusions are not applicable to [it] because it is a loss payee. This assertion is belied by the policy's loss payable provision. [It] provides that the loss payee generally will not be denied coverage due to the acts of the insured; however, 'all terms of the [policy] will then apply directly to the Loss Payee.' Wisconsin courts interpret similar clauses in mortgage contracts, known as standard mortgage clauses, as creating a separate contract between the loss payee and the insurer. See Estate of Ensz v. Brown Ins. Agency, Inc., 223 N.W.2d 903, 909–10 (Wis. 1974). Both parties concede that the loss payable clause in the instant contract is akin to a standard mortgage clause and it too creates a separate contract between the loss payee and the insurer. Thus, a separate agreement exists between Vision Financial and Midwest that makes all the terms of the policy, including the policy exclusions, applicable to Vision Financial." Vision Financial Group, Inc. v. Midwest Family Mutual Ins. Co., 355 F.3d 640, 642 (7th Cir. 2004).

(4) *The Separate-contract Conception*. In Ideal Financial Services, Inc. v. Zichelle, 750 N.E.2d 508 (Mass.App. 2001), at 514, this conception was put even more strongly than in the main case: "There are two contracts of insurance here...." But one can think of the conception as a false quantity, needless in the main case and doubly so in the *Vision* case (Note 3).

Courts that find a separate contract in the standard mortgagee clause do so in order to make use of the principle that a defense that would be available to a party (insurer) when sued on one contract does not serve as an excuse for that party when it is sued on another, even though the parties to the two contracts are the same. That is true enough. It is hard to say, however, that a single document expresses two contracts, at least when the parties assented to all its terms at one stroke. The result in the main case could have been achieved, it seems, by calling the policy a third-party-beneficiary contract—the Fidelity Savings Bank being the third party. A two-party contract can install a third party as the beneficiary of a promise in that contract and create in that party rights superior to those of the promisee. Needless, therefore, to invoke the separate-contract conception.

In the *Vision* case, because neither Mufti nor the loss payee could collect on the policy, the notion of separate contracts seems quite beside the point.

(5) *Fires and Foreclosures*. Say that a loss by fire is a "Stage One" loss if it occurs before the foreclosure of a mortgage, whether or not the debtor is in default. A Stage Two loss is one occurring after a foreclosure sale, in which the mortgagee has been the successful bidder; and a Stage Three loss is one occurring after the mortgagee has taken title by deed.

The New York standard mortgagee clause contains language protective of financiers at all three stages. The statutory clause in Massachusetts is somewhat idiosyncratic in that it does not. Massachusetts law was considered, in relation to a "Stage Three" fire in *Zichelle* (Note 4), Ideal Financial being the financier. There the insurer made this argument:

> [B]y virtue of Ideal's own acts of foreclosing and taking ownership of the property by foreclosure deed, it was not a mortgagee at the time of the fire. [A]t the time of the fire, Ideal's insurable interest was not that of "mortgagee," but that of "owner" and Ideal was not insured in that capacity.

The court sustained that argument.

The opinion canvasses precedents around the country. It quotes from a contrasting case concerning the New York standard clause, as follows:

> The policy language protecting the mortgagee despite foreclosure or other proceedings or notice of sale relating to the property and despite change of title or ownership necessarily implies that the interest of the entity identified as the mortgagee continues regardless of whether the entity's status as mortgagee changes. . . . The result of such proceedings is an enlargement or increase of the mortgagee's interest . . . .

Federal Natl. Mort. Assn. v. Hanover Ins. Co., 255 S.E.2d 685, 686 (Ga. 1979). The opinion in that case explains also why a "mortgagee" who fails to notify the insurer of the foreclosure does not violate a policy provision requiring notice of a change of ownership: "Buying the property in after sale under power in the deed is not a 'change of ownership'. . . ." The notification provision would be triggered, it seems, if someone other than the financier were the winning bidder at the sale.

CHAPTER 9

Automobile Insurance

A. Liability Insurance

A case of a bicyclist run into by a careless motorist, a hypothetical one, appears here as the focus of a preview of this chapter.

While his car was being repaired, David borrowed the car of his friend Arthur to drive himself to school and back. While at school David and a classmate, Jon, decided to visit a bar for a beer before returning home. David drove Jon as a passenger to a bar. Leaving, David drove toward Jon's home. The two engaged in some horseplay which distracted David's attention from a stoplight. Running through "red", David struck a bicyclist, causing bodily injury. Both David and Jon are liable to the victim for negligence. As between them, their shares of the liability are determined by local tort law. It appears, however, that their assets, taken together, are not sufficient to compensate the cyclist, and would not be even if none of their assets was exempt from execution under the local law of creditor's rights.

The cyclist is an exemplar of the huge class of persons suffering road injuries each year. Concern about compensating them properly is well-nigh universal in nations where motoring has become a major facet of life.[1] In the United States that concern has activated, in various ways, motorists, insurers, legislatures, and courts. For example, one legislative step in that direction that might apply to the cyclist's case is to fix liability for the injury on Arthur, as well as on David and Jon, as the owner of the carelessly driven car. An example is this provision of the California Vehicle Code Section 17150, Liability of Private Owners:

> Every owner of a motor vehicle is liable and responsible for death or injury to person or property resulting from a negligent or wrongful act or omission in the operation of the motor vehicle, in the business of the owner or otherwise, by any person using or operating the same with the permission, express or implied, of the owner.

Of course, aside from doubt about the scope of the permission given by Arthur to David, that measure does not of itself assure the cyclist of proper compensation. Further measures have installed various insuring arrangements. The following are possible ones in the case supposed.

---

1. The predominance of automobile insurance among the various third-party liability coverages as well first-party coverages, such as uninsured motorist and no fault coverages, justifies giving it special attention. Likewise, with 40,000 persons killed and 3 million injured yearly in auto accidents, and over $150 billion spent yearly on a variety of auto insurance policies, the subject merits thoughtful consideration.

a.   Arthur holds a liability coverage under a policy he has been required by a state "compulsory motor vehicle liability insurance statute" to buy as a condition of registering his car.[2]

b.   David holds a similar coverage. His coverage extends to a liability he incurs while driving another person's car—"Drive Other Cars" coverage that is called DOC for short. It was David's choice to buy DOC coverage.

c.   Very possibly David is also insured against his liability under Arthur's auto policy. That coverage may be provided by a term of the policy known as the "omnibus clause". The omnibus clause is mandated by statute as a feature of Arthur's policy. The coverage extends to persons using Arthur's car, as David certainly was,[3] although they are not identified by name in the policy. But commonly it does so only if the use was one permitted by the named insured (Arthur). The case of the cyclist presents the obvious question whether or not the excursion to the bar was a permitted use. As will be seen, courts have expressed their concern for compensation of road injuries by expansive readings of omnibus clauses.

d.   Possibly the passenger Jon is also insured against his liability under Arthur's policy by virtue of the omnibus clause. As with David, one needs to know about the scope of the permitted use of the car. Two further questions arise in this connection, however. One is whether or not Jon was a permitted user at all, for Arthur had no reason to expect that anyone other than David would be using his car. And there is the more fundamental question whether or not Jon made any "use" of the car, considering that he was only a passenger (albeit a boisterous one).

If one or more of the foregoing possibilities were realized in the cyclist's case, and the injury was minor, they would assure full compensation for the victim. If both Arthur's insurer and David's insurer can be called to account, there will be a question about allocating the loss as between the two.

If the cyclist suffered a serious and permanent injury, full compensation would not be assured even if all the foregoing possibilities were realized, for the aggregate amount of liability coverages under all accessible policies might not equal the assessment of harm. The liability coverages demanded of motorists by statute vary in amount from state to state; $25,000 is a fair average (doubled in the case of multiple victims of the same incident). Moreover, it is more than conceivable that Arthur, or

---

2. Unlike ordinary liability insurance, compulsory motor vehicle liability insurance does not protect the owner or operator *alone* but also provides compensation to persons injured by the automobile being driven. Massachusetts was the first state to make automobile-liability insurance compulsory, effective in 1927. New York and North Carolina followed in the 50's. For about a generation after that, no other state followed. Now with the exception of New Hampshire, Tennessee, and Wisconsin, all states and the District of Columbia have "compulsory motor vehicle liability insurance statutes" requiring every person who registers a motor vehicle in the state to purchase liability insurance at least in a specified amount and also requires certain mandatory terms in the auto insurance policy's omnibus clause.

3. The typical omnibus clause defines any person (e.g., David), using the named insured's covered auto with permission, as an additional insured, typically called an "omnibus insured".

David, or both of them, flouted the law by failing to provide themselves with the coverages demanded of them. A substantial fraction of motorists on the road are either "uninsured" or "underinsured". Legislatures have addressed problems of shortfall in the following ways, among others.

e.   Buyers of automobile insurance are encouraged, as a rule, and sometimes required, to provide themselves with insurance against harm they may suffer at the hands of an uninsured motorist. "Uninsured motorist coverage", or UMC, is not liability insurance.

f.   Buyers are encouraged, as a rule, and sometimes required, to provide themselves with "underinsured motorist coverage", or UIMC.

g.   In some states and for some situations, governmental insurance pays the amount of a judgment that cannot be otherwise collected. A commonplace name for one of these arrangements is "unsatisfied judgment fund".

Neither UMC nor UIMC would be of help to an injured cyclist unless he or she happened to hold, or otherwise have the benefit of, auto insurance. These are instances of first-party insurance. Particulars are provided below in Part B. That part includes a treatment of "stacking" problems, a set of problems that arise from concurrent coverages of one loss. One subset concerns the possibility of multiple recoveries; another concerns the source of recovery when the claimant must be content with a single recovery.

On changing the facts (but still supposing that the cyclist had access to an auto policy), one finds still another possibility of compensation via insurance. Almost certainly personal-injury protection, known also as no-fault insurance, would be provided by that policy. If so the cyclist could recover to some extent even if the injury were found to be his or her own fault, or no one's. Part B below provides some particulars of that coverage also.

Part C, concluding this chapter, concerns first-party automobile coverages that are purchased voluntarily by most motorists, *collision* coverage and *comprehensive* coverage. These apply to property losses, the one caused chiefly by impacts of vehicles on one another and on fixed objects, and the other by a miscellany of mishaps, including fire, theft, and "impact with a missile, falling object, bird or animal". The owner of a car damaged by the negligence of any driver might be compensated through liability coverage available to that driver. This possibility is augmented by DOC coverage and by omnibus coverage. It may be augmented also by UMC or UIMC coverage. Often both an owner's collision coverage and a driver's liability coverage call for payment by an insurer, especially when the damage exceeds the deductible in the first-party coverage. Usually, as between the two insurers, the one providing liability coverage is the one primarily accountable, for upon compensating the owner the issuer of collision coverage is subrogated to the owner's claim against the driver.

Any step designed to provide proper compensation for road-injuries imposes cost on some group other than the persons injured. Any mandate requiring that motorists be provided with insurance, or setting a minimum on the extent of their coverage, imposes a cost on them, on their insurers, or on both. Hence steps to that end—especially mandates about insuring—have been and are subjects of intense political maneuvering. "Paternalism" is a rallying cry for those opposing mandatory first-party coverage. (Some of these, however, favor controlling the cost of coverages that protect them against ruinous liabilities.) For those who favor imposing the full cost of motoring on motorists, "efficiency" is a rallying cry. (Some of these, however, also favor medical-expense insurance provided at the expense of taxpayers.) Many insurance buyers favor imposing more of the cost of insuring on insurers. Most people who consider themselves good drivers favor imposing heavier costs of insuring on bad drivers. And so on.

1.   Compulsory Coverages

It is unlawful throughout the United States for the owner of a car or truck to operate it on a public way, or to permit someone else to do so, without having in place an arrangement insuring to some extent against various liabilities that may arise from road injuries caused by a fault in maintaining the vehicle or in operating it. Compulsory insurance statutes so provide. A vehicle of a class described in one of these statutes cannot be registered without showing evidence of the arrangement. (An alternate arrangement in the form of a cash deposit or surety's bond is usually permitted. But relatively few individuals can, and even fewer do, use one of these arrangements.) Outrage against motoring on public ways without having liability insurance in place is such that criminal sanctions are attached. Also, the voters of California have classified uninsured motorists along with convicted felons, as persons who are deprived of civil remedies for some wrongs inflicted on them. See Horwich v. Superior Court, 980 P.2d 927 (Cal.App. 1999). Among judges charged with administering civil remedies, that sanction seems not to be a favorite.

The dominant legislative object is to assure some degree of compensation to victims of road injuries caused by faulty motoring. That much is certain. The statutes may stem partly from a desire to protect motorists from financially ruinous liabilities. But that is uncertain. The matter is put to a test when a coverage, mandated by statute, is written so as to exclude a motorist's liability of a kind that does not arouse much sympathy, if any, for the motorist. If the statute is held to override that exclusion, one can infer that compensation for victims was at least the dominant, and perhaps the only, legislative object. The opinion that follows illustrates an encounter between an exclusion of that kind and a compulsory auto-insurance statute. According to the facts assumed, the unsympathetic motorist was Jeffry Hiatt. It will be seen that the exclusion in question appeared in a policy issued, not to him, but to an acquaintance who gave him a lift, Kimberly Fricke. That complication does not invalidate the test, because the statute concerned required that Fricke's policy provide coverage for Hiatt equivalent to hers. (The part of the opinion so ruling is represented on p. 520 below.)

Speros v. Fricke

Utah Supreme Court, 2004.
98 P.3d 28.

A Jeep Wrangler owned and operated by Kimberly Fricke veered into oncoming traffic and collided with a Honda Civic owned and operated by Ted Speros, injuring him and damaging his car. Hiatt was a passenger in the Jeep. Speros held auto insurance issued by the West American Insurance. West American compensated him for the damage to his Honda, and for the expense of renting a substitute car. Then it sought to recover these outlays by bringing an action based on subrogation to Speros's claim.[1] West American sought to recover not only from Fricke and Hiatt, but also from the Nationwide Mutual Insurance Company, which had insured Fricke against liabilities as a motorist. No negligence could be ascribed to her, the trial court ruled. West American persisted, contending that Hiatt had been at fault, and that his liability was covered by the Nationwide policy.

Nationwide denied that its coverage extended to Hiatt. Whether it did or not depended on statutory and policy provisions about making use of another person's car with that person's permission. The Utah Supreme Court concluded that, for this purpose, Hiatt had been using Fricke's Jeep with her permission at the time of the collision, and was therefore insured against liability under the Nationwide policy. (On this subject see further p. 504 below.)

Another objection to West American's claim was an *intentional acts* exclusion in the Nationwide policy: "... does not cover property damage or bodily injury caused intentionally by or at the direction of an insured". Events leading up to the collision gave some color to a charge of intended harm on the part of Hiatt. The collision occurred in the early hours of a morning, after Fricke and Hiatt had been together at a nightclub. She was driving him home. He asked her to stop on the way at her home, and take him in. She declined. An argument ensued. Soon after Fricke drove her Jeep past her home, Hiatt grabbed the steering wheel without giving warning. Thereupon the Jeep veered into oncoming traffic, striking Speros's Honda.

The trial court entered a judgment against Hiatt upon his default. It entered a summary judgment in favor of Nationwide. On an appeal by West American the court determined, as indicated above, that Hiatt was a person insured under the Nationwide policy. It turned then to the intentional acts exclusion.

■ PARRISH, JUSTICE.

. . .

... Nationwide argues that Hiatt's actions in grabbing and turning the steering wheel were intended to cause injury or damage and therefore were

---

1. West American had made payments to Speros also for bodily injury, under his personal-injury protection, and it sought to recover that outlay as well. That effort failed because of a statutory provision that reimbursement of those payments could be sought only in arbitration.

not covered. West American contends that Nationwide's intentional acts exclusion runs afoul of Utah's statutorily mandated coverage requirement. See Utah Code Ann. § 31A–22–303(1)(a)(ii)(A) (2003). We agree with West American.

The Utah legislature has enacted a comprehensive statutory scheme mandating minimum liability coverage for motor vehicles. See id. §§ 31A–22–303 to–304. This legislative enactment reflects a public policy requiring vehicle owners to carry a minimum level of liability coverage to protect innocent victims of automobile accidents. In the case of an owner's liability policy, the statute requires that the policy insure the person named in the policy and any permissive users "against loss from the liability imposed by law for damages arising out of the ownership, maintenance, or use of these motor vehicles within the United States and Canada ... in [dollar] amounts not less than the minimum limits specified." Id. § 31A–22–303(1)(a)(ii).

The statute recognizes no distinction between liability arising out of negligent acts and liability arising out of intentional acts; it simply requires coverage for all liabilities imposed by law. Because the law imposes liability for damages caused negligently and intentionally, we conclude that the statute requires coverage of liability arising out of intentional, as well as negligent, acts.[6]

Our conclusion is buttressed by the fact that the statutory scheme expressly contemplates some exclusions from coverage,[7] but does not authorize exclusions from coverage for the intentional acts of otherwise covered persons. In light of the clear statutory language mandating coverage "against loss from the liability imposed by law for damages arising out of the ownership, maintenance, or use" of a motor vehicle and the public policy requiring minimum coverage to protect innocent victims of automobile accidents, the legislature's failure to authorize such intentional acts exclusions is dispositive. Accordingly, we hold that the intentional acts exclusion is unenforceable against accident victims up to the minimum liability limits prescribed by the statute.[8]

---

6. Other courts have reached the same conclusion when analyzing similar statutory language. See, e.g., [ten cases cited]. But see [four cases cited].

7. For example, the statute recognizes the validity of limitations applicable to motor vehicle businesses, and provides that policies need not insure any liability arising under workers' compensation laws or resulting from damage to property owned by the insured. The statutory scheme also expressly provides that an insurer may exclude from coverage other residents of an insured's household who have obtained their own liability insurance. [Statutory citations omitted from this footnote.]

8. Our holding does not render intentional acts exclusions to automobile liability policies entirely invalid. Contracting parties are free to limit coverage in excess of the statutory minimum requirements. See State Farm Mut. Auto Ins. Co. v. Mastbaum, 748 P.2d 1042, 1044 (Utah 1987) (holding a "household" or "family" exclusion valid and enforceable as to amounts and benefits provided by an automobile policy in excess of statutorily mandated amounts); Allstate Ins. Co. v. United States Fid. & Guar. Co., 619 P.2d 329, 333 (Utah 1980) (upholding the validity of a named driver exclusion for coverage in excess of the minimum statutory coverage requirements). Moreover, although an insurer cannot enforce such an exclusion to deny compensation to an innocent victim of an automobile accident, an insurer may rely on the exclusion to seek reimbursement from

Our holding with respect to the limited validity of the intentional acts exclusion is consistent with our holdings regarding the validity of other exclusions in the arena of automobile liability coverage. [The court cited a decision about the exclusion of a named driver, and one about the exclusion of liability for bodily injury to members of the insured's household. The reasoning in the latter case applied equally, the court said, to the intentional acts exclusion.][9]

At the time of the accident and throughout the duration of this action, the statute required a minimum coverage of $25,000 for liability for bodily injury to or death of one person arising out of the use of a motor vehicle in any one accident and $15,000 for liability for property damage in any one accident. Utah Code Ann. § 31A–22–304 (2003). West American has requested reimbursement of a property damage payment to its insured of $11,514.65, along with rental car expenses of $499.70. Because the amounts at issue in this case fall within the statutory minimums, the intentional acts exclusion does not excuse Nationwide from any obligation it may have to reimburse West American for the payments it made to Speros.

NOTES

(1) *An Inference Reconsidered*. In a paragraph preceding the *Speros* opinion it was suggested that one can infer from the decision that compensation for victims was at least the dominant, and perhaps the only, object of the Utah legislature in making auto liability insurance compulsory. The opinion contains, in footnote 8, a further indication that the object was *not* to protect from financial ruin motorists who incur liabilities by the intentional infliction of harm; see the sentence beginning "Moreover . . .". On the other hand, that sentence may undercut the inference suggested earlier, as applied to the much more numerous class of motorists incurring liability for simple negligence.

The *Speros* opinion can be regarded as a case of opposition between two public policies, one favoring compensation for road injuries, and the other favoring sanctions against wrongdoing that is intended to, and does, inflict harm. If those two policies came into conflict on the facts of the case, obviously the latter gave

the insured who committed the intentional act giving rise to liability. . . .

9. Nationwide asserts that the intentional acts exclusion differs from those invalidated in our prior cases because it is contrary to public policy to provide insurance coverage for intentional acts. We have upheld the validity of an intentional acts exclusion in the context of a homeowner's policy. Utah Farm Bureau Ins. Co. v. Crook, 1999 UT 47, P16, 980 P.2d 685. That case, however, is clearly distinguishable inasmuch as there is no statutory scheme requiring minimum liability coverage for homeowners. . . . Here, we find the exclusionary provision contrary to the statutory scheme requiring minimum liability coverage for the benefit of victims of automobile accidents. . . .

The principle that one should not be permitted to insure against his own intentional wrongdoing applies to voluntary insurance, not compulsory insurance. Where the Legislature makes coverage compulsory, instead of leaving it to the voluntary market, it has already balanced the public interest in prohibiting insurance for intentionally harmful acts against the public interest in compensating the victims of at fault motorists. By making coverage compulsory, it chooses to weigh the latter interest more heavily than the former. Once the Legislature has made that choice, there is no room for the courts to impose a different judgment based upon their own notions of public policy.

S. C. Farm Bureau Mut. Ins. Co. v. Mumford, 382 S.E.2d 11, 14. (S.C.Ct.App. 1989).

way. Another case in which the court downplayed that policy is Ambassador Ins. Co. v. Montes, 388 A.2d 603 (N.J. 1978). But the notion of reimbursement, advanced by the Utah court in its n. 8, goes far to reconcile the two public policies.

(2) *Other Exclusions*. Face-offs have occurred between compulsory auto-liability insurance statutes and coverage exclusions other than "intentional acts" exclusions. The opinion in *Speros* refers to earlier cases in which the court had denounced a "named insured" exclusion and a "household" exclusion.

The "named driver" exclusion excludes coverage of a high-risk driver, e.g., one who has suffered a DUI conviction or the suspension of a driver's license. Some state compulsory motor vehicle liability statutes expressly authorize the "named driver" exclusion. See, e.g., St. Paul Fire and Marine Insurance Co. v. Smith, 787 N.E.2d 852 (Ill.App. 2003). The court held that an exclusion for a named driver does not contravene Illinois public policy and is a statutorily created exception to the mandatory insurance law. The St. Paul policy listed William Smith's parents as the insureds and drivers under the policy. St. Paul removed William from their policy six months before William became involved in the accident in question. It did so because of his prior driving offenses. St. Paul had also required William's parents to sign an exclusion for any accidents or losses incurred while the car was driven by William.

The "household" exclusion provides that no liability coverage exists for "any obligation . . . for bodily injury to the insured or any member of the family of the insured residing in the same household of the insured." Concerned about the risk of familial collusion in trumping up a judgment for an injured family member, auto insurers use the exclusion to remove the insurer's liability coverage when one family member's negligence causes injury to another family member. Concern about collusion is the basis also for intrafamily immunities. Both interspousal immunity and parent-child immunity have been repealed or considerably limited in nearly all states. In most jurisdictions a tension between household exclusions and the compulsion to insure against liability has been resolved against the exclusions.[1] For a collection of cases about the tension, see Anno., 52 A.L.R.4th 18.

(3) *Fixing the Jeep*. What of the damage done to Fricke's car? If, as seems likely, both Nationwide and Hiatt were liable to her for the cost of repairing it, and Nationwide had paid for its repair, must Hiatt reimburse it? See Universal Underwriters Group v. Heibel, 901 A.2d 398 (N.J.App. 2006). Referring to New Jersey statutes, that court said: "while the law imposes an obligation on the owner of a registered vehicle to maintain liability insurance that covers a permissive user's damages to a third party, no such requirement exists with respect to collision insurance [*i.e.*, damage to the owner's vehicle]." Id. at 405. (A deductible in Fricke's collision coverage would in any event complicate a reimbursement claim.)

----

1. Some state have devised ingenious compromises, either regarding tort liability or regarding an exclusion. For example, in Arkansas, parental immunity survives, but only when it does not serve the interest of a liability insurer. See Fields v. Southern Farm Bureau Cas. Ins. Co., 87 S.W.3d 224, 231 (Ark. 2002). And in some states household exclusions have been invalidated only to the extent of the dollar amounts of insurance required to carried. See Hartline v. Hartline, 39 P.3d 765 (Okla. 2001); Liberty Mutual Fire Ins. Co. v. Sanford, 879 S.W.2d 9 (Tex. 1994).

2. The Omnibus Clause and Compulsory Motor Vehicle Liability Insurance Statutes

Historically, "permission" was the key term in an omnibus clause. For decades prior to the 1990s, the omnibus clause defined the additional insured as any person using the insured auto "with the permission of the named insured". (Similar language has been used sometimes.) In an Allstate Auto Policy,[2] for example, the omnibus clause appears as (1)(c) in the following term:

Persons Insured

(1) While using *your* insured auto

     (a) *You*,

     (b) Any *resident* relative, and

     (c) Any other person using it with *your* permission.

In the 1980s, states enacted "property and liability policy simplification" statutes to establish language and format standards meant to make policies easier to read.[3] New "plain language" auto policies, *inter alia*, were issued. The rub is that the plain-language policies omitted, in the omnibus clause, well-established, often-litigated language such as "with the permission of the named insured". For example, the plain-language ISO Personal Auto Policy ("PAP") provides omnibus coverage without express reference to anyone's permission; see line B–2 in the following excerpt.

PART A LIABILITY COVERAGE

INSURING AGREEMENT

     A.   [omitted]

     B.   "Insured" as used in this Part means:

         1.   [omitted]

         2.   Any person using "your covered auto".

The question arises: Does a court construe that and comparable language without regard for the familiar "permission" requirement and the countless cases construing it? An answer draws on state compulsory motor vehicle liability insurance statutes.

Almost every state has a statute that mandates an omnibus clause. The mandated term refers to a person's use of a vehicle "with permission", or contains similar language. The Hawaii statute is an example:

---

2. The policy was construed in Travelers Indem. Co. v. Erie Ins. Exchange, 510 F.Supp. 261, 262 (W.D. Pa. 1981). For a similar omnibus clause see Curtis v. State Farm Mut. Auto. Ins. Co., 591 F.2d 572 (10th Cir. 1979) (Wyoming law).

3. See generally Eric Mills Holmes, Vol. 1 Holmes' Appleman on Insurance 2d § 4.3 Anti–Jargon, Easy-to-Read Legislation (1996).

An Owner's Policy of Liability Insurance

(1) [omitted]

(2) Shall insure the person named therein and any other person, as insured, using any such motor vehicle ... *with the express or implied permission of the named insured*, against loss from the liability imposed by law for damages arising out of the ownership, maintenance, or use of the motor vehicle[.] (emphasis supplied)

Hawaii Revised Statutes § 287–25(2). If an owner's auto policy does not include the language emphasized, it will be "read into the policy in issue." AIG Hawai'i Ins. Co. v. Vincente, 891 P.2d 1041, 1043 (Haw. 1995). In sum, if modern plain-language auto insurance polices omit the mandated terms in the omnibus clause, courts will enforce the state compulsory statutes by inserting them. [4]

---

3.   Omnibus Insureds and Permission to Use a Vehicle

Permission to use a vehicle is the subject of a mass of case opinions. This section covers the contours of that permission. Note that the omnibus clause permits a practice contrary to the usual insurance procedure. Usually, the insurer selects the risks it desires to cover and rejects those it believes are undesirable . Under the omnibus clause, the named insured selects the risk to be covered by granting a person permission to use the covered vehicle.

French v. Hernandez

New Jersey Supreme Court, 2005.
184 N.J. 144, 875 A.2d 943.

The Harleysville Insurance Company of New Jersey (Harleysville) issued a policy to John Decker, who owned a pickup truck and used it in his landscaping business. The policy afforded liability coverage to him and to "[a]nyone else while using with [his] permission a covered 'auto' [he] own[ed]...." The pickup was a "covered 'auto'" within this expression.

Enrique Hernandez was a short-term seasonal employee of Decker's. He was a teenager, not licensed to drive. Sometimes Decker permitted him to drive the pickup, but only on private property when at work and only under Decker's direct supervision. Only Decker drove it on a public road. But Hernandez did so one Sunday evening, and thereby caused injury to Linda French, another motorist. Driving while intoxicated, he crossed a center line and struck French's vehicle head-on. She brought an action

---

4. The Utah state statute, like Hawaii's and virtually all other state statutes, requires that a vehicle owner's policy insure "any ... person using any named motor vehicle with the express or implied permission of the named insured." Utah Code Ann. § 31A–22–303(1)(a)(ii)(A).   Similarly, Virginia Code § 38.2–2204 requires that an automobile insurance policy provide coverage for a person who is "using" a motor vehicle "with the expressed or implied consent of the named insured." See Hartford Fire Ins. Co. v. Davis, 436 S.E.2d 429, 431 (Va. 1993).

against him and Decker, adding Harleysville as a defendant with the permission of the trial court. The question arose whether or not Hernandez's use of the pickup, at the time of the injury, was with Decker's permission. Hernandez had told an investigating police officer that he did not have Decker's permission; and Decker testified that he never gave Hernandez permission to take the pickup on a non-workday onto the public roads for an excursion.

The trial court ruled that the Harleysville policy afforded liability coverage to Hernandez at the time of the injury, applying the so-called *initial permission* rule. Earlier, the high court of New Jersey, declaring applicable law, had described that rule as follows: "As long as the initial use of the vehicle is with the consent, express or implied, of the insured, any subsequent changes in the character or scope of the use ... do not require the additional specific consent of the insured." (Consider this rule in relation to the use of Arthur's car by David, in the hypothetical case at p. 446 above.)

Another party in the case was the New Jersey Manufacturers Insurance Company (NJM), which provided uninsured motorist coverage to French. It intervened to protect its interests. If Hernandez did not qualify as an insured under the Harleysville policy, he was an uninsured motorist, and it would follow that NJM would have to indemnify French up to the limit of her UMC.

The trial court entered a judgment against Hernandez for nearly $600,000. (As to liability, he had defaulted.) The court dismissed Decker as a defendant, finding no evidence that Hernandez had been acting in the scope of his employment at the time of the injury. The court entered summary judgments against Harleysville, in favor of French and NJM. Harleysville appealed. The Appellate Division disapproved the application of the "initial permission" rule. But it affirmed. It relied on the doctrine of implied permission to show that Hernandez was a permitted user of the pickup at the time of French's injury. French v. Hernandez, 850 A.2d 585 (2004).

The State's high court granted Harleysville's petition for certification.

■ ALVIN, JUSTICE.

   . . .[1]

The Appellate Division properly posed the question that we must decide: whether Hernandez was a permissive user of his employer's pickup truck on the evening of the accident. Specifically, we must determine whether Decker gave Hernandez either express or implied permission to enter his business's garage and take the truck for a drive on a weekend evening when Hernandez was not working.

---

1. A number of citations are omitted from the opinion as presented here, without notation of ellipses—notably repetitious unof- ficial citations without references to cited pages.

We first look to the scope of insurance coverage, which is defined in the omnibus clause of the Harleysville policy, as required by *N.J.S.A.* 39:6B–1.[3] ... Under the policy, Harleysville must provide coverage if Decker gave either express or implied permission to Hernandez to operate the truck.

Historically, we have given "an expansive view of the omnibus clause" because of the strong public interest in ensuring coverage to the insured and compensation to the victims of automobile accidents. State Farm Mut. Auto. Ins. Co. v. Zurich Am. Ins. Co., 62 N.J. 155, 179–80, 299 A.2d 704 (1973) (Weintraub, C.J., concurring in part). Indeed, one of the principal purposes of requiring automobile owners to maintain liability insurance coverage is "to assure that persons who cause automobile accidents are able to answer financially to their innocent victims." Matits v. Nationwide Mut. Ins. Co., 33 N.J. 488, 496, 166 A.2d 345 (1960).... With those policy goals in mind, our courts have liberally construed automobile insurance policies, resolving all doubts in favor of coverage. That does not mean, however, that an insurance policy can be stretched beyond all reason to fit a set of facts that fall beyond the reach of the omnibus clause.

... We agree with the Appellate Division that applying the initial-permission rule to the few times Hernandez parked the truck in a private lot would not allow us to conclude that Hernandez had permission to drive the truck on the night of the accident. In *Matits*, *supra* we set forth the contours of the initial-permission rule and held

> that if a person is given permission to use a motor vehicle in the first instance, any subsequent use short of theft or the like while it remains in his possession, though not within the contemplation of the parties, is a permissive use within the terms of a standard omnibus clause in an automobile liability insurance policy.

[33 N.J. at 496–97.]

The rule provides that "[a]s long as the initial use of the vehicle is with the consent, express or implied, of the insured, any subsequent changes in the character or scope of the use ... do not require the additional specific consent of the insured." Verriest v. INA Underwriters Ins. Co., 142 N.J. 401, 413, 662 A.2d 967 (1995) (per curiam) (internal quotations omitted). Simply put, once an owner gives his vehicle's keys to another person for a drive, the courts ordinarily will find coverage, even if the driver deviates from the expected scope of use of the vehicle, unless the driver's later conduct amounts to a theft or the like of the vehicle.

The initial-permission rule was adopted because it " 'best effectuate[d] the legislative policy of providing certain and maximum coverage.' " *Verriest*, *supra*, 142 N.J. at 412 (quoting *Matits*, *supra*, 33 N.J. at 496). We were

---

3. *N.J.S.A.* 39:6B–1(a) provides:

Every owner or registered owner of a motor vehicle registered or principally garaged in this State shall maintain motor vehicle liability insurance coverage, under provisions approved by the Commissioner of Banking and Insurance, insuring against loss resulting from liability imposed by law for bodily injury, death and property damage sustained by any person arising out of the ownership, maintenance, *operation or use* of a motor vehicle.... [(Emphasis added).]

concerned that adopting a narrower rule would "render coverage uncertain in many cases, foster litigation as to the existence or extent of any alleged deviations, and ultimately inhibit achievement of the legislative goal." *Matits, supra*, 33 N.J. at 496.

However, as noted by the Appellate Division, one of the essential components of the initial-permission rule is "continuous possession of the vehicle" by the user following the grant of permission. While supervised, Hernandez had parked his employer's truck several times on private property. It was not until weeks later, on a non-workday, that he entered the Decker Landscaping garage, took the truck without express permission, and crashed it into plaintiff's vehicle. In other words, Hernandez did not remain in continuous possession of the truck from the time of his initial limited use until the day of the accident.

Like the Appellate Division, we conclude that "[t]his case does not fall within the usual paradigm of the initial permission rule because of the break in" possession after the original limited authorization. In particular, we agree with the panel that "earlier uses by Hernandez do not constitute initial permission" for the later use of the vehicle. This Court has never extended the initial-permission rule to a case in which the user or his delegate did not remain in continuous possession of the vehicle. *See, e.g.,* [six cases cited].

That the initial-permission rule does not apply to Hernandez's early instances of parking the truck does not end our inquiry into whether plaintiff may recover under the Harleysville policy. As the Appellate Division recognized, we still must decide whether Decker gave Hernandez implied permission to use the pickup truck on the night of the accident. Accordingly, we turn to the doctrine of implied permission.

Implied permission has been defined as "actual permission circumstantially proven." *State Farm, supra*, 62 N.J. at 167–68 (internal quotations omitted). It may arise from "a course of conduct or relationship between the parties in which there is mutual acquiescence or lack of objection signifying consent." *Id.* at 167 (internal quotations omitted). Implied permission customarily is proven by circumstantial evidence and requires the fact-finder to consider the surrounding circumstances in deciding whether the use of a vehicle was not contrary to the intent of its owner. *Id.* at 168. As mentioned, the relationship between the owner and user will be important. Not surprisingly, a finding of implied permission may be more likely when the vehicle's operator is a friend or employee of the owner. *See id.* at 179–80 (Weintraub, C.J., concurring in part) ("Weight must be given to the relationship of the parties and to the probabilities which that relationship would normally generate."). Equally significant will be a pattern of permitted use of the vehicle, which may give rise to an inference that the owner gave his consent to use on a subsequent occasion. Ultimately, the resolution of the issue will be fact-sensitive and depend on the totality of the circumstances. In analyzing whether Hernandez had implied permission to drive the truck, we give plaintiff the benefit of our canon of "liberal construction of [automobile] liability insurance [policies] to effect the broadest range of protection" to those who travel on and across roadways. *Id.* at 168.

[The court found significant parallels between this case and one in which a boy of twelve or thirteen had driven his father's car, a number of times, under his parents' direct supervision, in the family driveway and at an airfield, and many months later, although told not to drive on public roads, had secretly taken friends on drives there. On one of those drives he crashed the car. The ruling was that the boy's permitted uses of the car were so remote from that event that his use of it on the day of the crash could not be regarded reasonably as being related to the permission he had been granted. Nicholas v. Sugar Lo Co., 471 A.2d 44 (N.J.App. 1983), *certif. denied*, 475 A.2d 582 (N.J. 1984). In *Nicholas* the court said:

> We do not suggest . . . that subsequent permission to use a vehicle could not be inferred from the granting of initial permission at different times. Thus it might well be reasonable to hold from a course of dealings between parties that the continuous granting of permission to use a vehicle implied permission to use it without express consent on another occasion.

The court said, in *French*, that it subscribed to that observation.]

The Appellate Division found the present case to be "close." We find that although the panel properly charted the law, the facts do not justify the conclusion that it reached. Even viewing, as we must, the evidence in the light most favorable to plaintiff, and liberally construing the Harleysville policy in favor of coverage, we cannot conclude that Hernandez had either express or implied permission to drive Decker's vehicle.

. . . Nothing in the record remotely suggests that Hernandez had implied permission to enter the Decker Landscaping garage on a Sunday, take the keys to the truck, and then operate it on public roads. We note that had Hernandez been given either express or implied permission to drive the truck that Sunday, then his use of the truck, "short of theft or the like[,] while it remain[ed] in his possession" would have provided the basis for coverage under the initial-permission rule. *Matits*, *supra*, 33 N.J. at 496–97.

In viewing the totality of the circumstances, including both Decker's and Hernandez's assertions, we hold that no reasonable trier of fact could conclude that Hernandez had implied permission to drive the truck on the night of the accident. It is the absence of any evidence to support plaintiff's claim that compels us to reach this result. We, therefore, find that summary judgment should have been entered in favor of Harleysville and against plaintiff and NJM.

. . .

NOTES

(1) *Three Judicial Rules.* A considerable volume of judicial opinions regarding judicial construction of omnibus clauses has resulted in three different rules.

Near the polar extreme of the foregoing decision is a "strict" or "conversion" rule that withholds coverage from a driver who has had permission to make some use of a vehicle but who has departed in any way from the permitted use. That rule has few adherents now. The Utah Supreme Court has argued against it with a *reductio ad absurdum*: "[T]he typical automobile owner does not authorize permissive users to exceed the speed limits, run red lights, drive recklessly, or engage in any negligent or ill-advised actions. [A] person driving someone else's automobile with permission, but without permission to act negligently, would find himself without liability coverage." Speros v. Fricke, 98 P.3d 28, 35 (2004). That thought can be extended readily into one about public policy supporting the compensation of road-injury victims.

At the other extreme is the "liberal" or "initial permission" rule: if permission to use the automobile was initially given, recovery may be had regardless of the manner in which the automobile was thereafter used. As long as the named insured grants permission to any person to drive the insured vehicle, that driver (primary permittee) and all other drivers in the sequence of permission (secondary, tortiary ...) are authorized to grant permission to other permittees to use the vehicle notwithstanding any limitations made by the named insured in the initial permission. Decisions like that in French v. Hernandez are also subject to caricature. Some of them are said to exemplify a "hell or high water" rule.[1] No matter how explicitly limited a grant of permission is, the grantee is insured while making any use whatever of the vehicle concerned. Decisions like those have won adherents in recent years on the ground that it is good public policy to ensure motor vehicle liability insurance coverage to the insured, thereby protecting persons injured in automobile accidents against uninsured motorists.

An intermediate rule is the "minor deviation" rule: a minor deviation from the scope of the initial permission does not end coverage, but a major deviation does.[2] Is the intermediate rule open to serious objection in that its application turns on a vague distinction? If you were a juror, would you be comfortable in determining the difference between a minor and a major deviation?

Which of the three approaches do you prefer? Why? In the Appendix is the Sample Personal Automobile Policy (PAP). Part A. Exclusion (8) in the PAP appears to take a different approach from the foregoing three rules. How would you explain the PAP approach?[3]

1. The modern trend is to adopt the "liberal" or "initial permission" rule. See Commercial Union Ins. Co. v. Johnson, 745 S.W.2d 589 (Ark. 1988) (citing authorities that adopt and reject the rule); Raitz v. State Farm Mut. Auto. Ins. Co., 960 P.2d 1179, 1183 (Colo. 1998); Founders Ins. Co. v. Contreras, 842 N.E.2d 177 (Ill.App. 2005); Valdetero v. Commercial Union Ins. Co., 782 So.2d 1210 (La.App. 2001). Nebraska probably comes the closest to this so-called "hell or high water" rule. Hull v. Allstate Ins. Co., 187 N.W.2d 650 (Neb. 1971).

2. See, e.g., Grinnell Select Ins. Co. v. Continental Western Ins. Co., 639 N.W.2d 31, 34–36 (Iowa 2002); O'Neill v. Long, 54 P.3d 109 (Okl. 2002); Old Amer. County Mut. Fire Ins. Co. v. Renfrow, 130 S.W.3d 70 (Tex. 2004).

3. The plain language PAP defines the word *insured* to include "any person using your 'covered auto.'" That unqualified language would include a thief or other person driving without permission. Hence, the policy in Exclusion (8) states that "[w]e do not provide Liability Coverage for any person ... using a vehicle without a reasonable belief that that person is entitled to do so." Non-plain language policies defined the insured to include "any other person using such automobile, provided the actual use thereof is with the permission of the named insured." The change of the qualification from definition (i.e., from coverage provisions) to the exclusions might shift the burden of proof.

(2) *Secondary Permittee.* The owner of a vehicle may authorize anyone to entrust its use to a third person, and so may extend liability coverage to that person. Often, however, coverage is claimed for a third person (C) whose use was authorized by a primary permittee (B), but not contemplated by the owner (A). The cases are legion; for a collection running to 165 pages, see Anno., 21 A.L.R.4th 1146. Aside from the terms of A's entrustment to B, the variables include these: (i) whether or not C's use of the vehicle was of the type permitted for B; (ii) whether or not C's use was explicitly permitted by B; and (iii) whether or not B was in the vehicle at the critical time.

(3) *Wishes of the Named Insured.* Irrespective of permission, it is usual for a liability coverage to extend to "any resident relative" of the named insured. That provision reflects the presumed wishes of the named insured with respect to the persons insured. It does not suggest that the wishes of the named insured count for anything if declared after a mishap has occurred. *Post hoc,* an owner insured by name may be heard to say either "I wish I had designated her as a person insured", or "I wish he had asked for my permission to use my car as he did". There is authority that the first of these wishes cannot count, even if the policy purports to grant it. Capital Insurance & Surety Co. v. Globe Indemnity Co., 382 F.2d 623 (9th Cir. 1967). The named insured was the Philco Corporation. Its policy permitted it to nominate an employee for coverage upon the making of a claim against the employee. Contrary to public policy, the court decided, in that it conferred an arbitrary power on Philco.

As for the second wish, the signals are mixed. In a case concerning a secondary permittee, the court detected a "legal gap" between an entrustment by the named insured and an entrustment by the primary permittee. The named insured sought to ratify the latter. The court ruled that the gap could not be bridged that way. Johnson v. State Farm Mut. Auto. Ins. Co., 194 F.2d 785 (8th Cir. 1952). But see Fireman's Fund Ins. Co. v. Brandt, 217 F.Supp. 893 (D.N.H. 1962). Chief Justice Weintraub of New Jersey once wrote: "Since the named insured's authority to extend the coverage is unlimited, the restriction upon it should sensibly be construed to exclude *only those whom the named insured would not want to benefit.*" But that was written in a dissent. Baesler v. Globe Indemnity Co., 162 A.2d 854, 859 (1960).

(4) *Step-down Clauses.* Automobile liability policies have provisions fixing a "limit of liability" to a stated dollar amount in case of injury to one or more persons. Additionally, some automobile liability policies provide coverage at a certain monetary level for the named insured and other persons, such as family members and relatives, but limit the monetary amount of coverage afforded to other ordinary permissive users, including renters of an automobile or business customers. These provisions are commonly known as "step-down" clauses.

In one policy having that feature the maximum payout for bodily injury to a single person injured by a permittee was only half the amount otherwise provided: $25,000 vs. $50,000. The lower amount was keyed to the coverage required by the applicable financial-responsibility statute. (In the event of ample other insurance for the permittee, the payout was to be zero.) The court ruled that the step-down provision was invalid for failure to meet a statutory disclosure requirement; it should have appeared on a separate page. Mid–Century Ins. Co. v. Lyon, 562 N.W.2d 888 (S.D. 1997). *Accord*: Haynes v. Farmers Ins. Exchange, 89 P.3d 381 (Cal. 2004). But see Farmers Ins. Co. v. Pierrousakos, 255 F.3d 639 (8th Cir. 2001) (Missouri law). Other step-down clauses have been struck because, as in *Lyon,* they did not state both policy limits as dollar amounts. See Cullum v. Farmers Ins.

Exch., 857 P.2d 922 (Utah 1993). But there is contrary authority. See Marjorie A. Caner, Anno. "Validity and Operation of "Step–Down" Provision of Automobile Liability Policy Reducing Coverage for Permissive Users," 29 A.L.R.5th 469.

Should step-down clauses be struck down, however prominently displayed?

EXERCISES

In each of the following problems the vehicle concerned is a "covered 'auto' " in the sense of a liability coverage held by a person or firm identified in italics. That person or firm is the named insured; no one else is. The vehicle is owned by that person. The coverage extends to anyone using the vehicle with the permission of that person. "The insurer" is the issuer of that coverage.

(1) Roustabout customarily used *Company's* truck to drive home from work. That was in accord with a Company policy, for it enabled employees like Roustabout to report early to sites where they were assigned to work on Company's oil rigs. One evening Roustabout made a detour of some forty miles, taking a friend to a bar. Early on the following morning, on the return trip, Roustabout drove the truck off the road, injuring the friend. Roustabout was not sober. The friend has made a negligence claim against him. Was Roustabout a person insured at the time of the injury? See Old Am. County Mut. Fire Ins. Co. v. Renfrow, 130 S.W.3d 70 (Tex. 2004).

(2) *Father* asked Son to drive Mother to her place of work. Leaving her there, Son drove to the home of a friend named Leo. The two set out for the home of a friend to both, Leo at the wheel. Father had not instructed Son against letting others use the car, but they had an understanding that it was to be driven by family members only. Leo's bad driving led to a collision, an injury to a pedestrian, and a judgment against him. Must the insurer respond to that judgment? See Liberty Mut. Ins. Co. v. Maryland Auto. Ins. Fund, 841 A.2d 46 (Md.App. 2004).

(3) Nelson found a car, unattended, with the keys in it. The car belonged to *Daniel*. Nelson drove it away, carrying his date as a passenger. On these facts alone, one would suppose that Nelson was a thief, and not a person insured. But other circumstances raise a question about that. It appears that Nelson and Daniel were classmates at a small college in Hanover, New Hampshire, where it was the practice of students to lend their cars to one another. The two were acquainted, and were at the same party at the time of the drive, but were not otherwise connected. The occasion for the drive was that Nelson had loaned his own car to a friend, also a classmate, who needed it to run an errand in Hanover. The hour had grown late and Nelson had grown worried about his friend and his car. Taking Daniel's car seemed to be the quickest way to provide help as might be needed. Daniel was to testify later that, if Nelson had explained that purpose and had asked for permission to use Daniel's car, he would have acceded readily.

Nelson's date suffered an injury in a collision between Daniel's car and another during the drive. She has brought an action against Nelson, charging him with negligence in driving Daniel's car. Must the insurer provide him with a defense? See Fireman's Fund Ins. Co. v. Brandt, cited in Note 3, p. 511 above.

Car-rental Firms

Car-rental firms have sought to minimize their liabilities and those of their insurers by the terms of rental contracts. Litigated examples have appeared in the contracts of Alamo Rent–A-Car, Budget Rent–A–Car, and Discount Rent-a-Car. The Alamo contract promised liability coverage for a customer, but sought to make that coverage simply a backup for any other coverage available to the customer. That attempt failed, owing to a statutory mandate about vehicle-liability insurance, and Alamo was required to defend a customer against claims of bodily injury and property damage. Bowers v. Alamo Rent–A–Car, Inc., 965 P.2d 1274 (Hawaii 1998).

The Budget contract—not dissimilar from many others—provided that its car should not "under any circumstances" be operated by a person other than the customer and certain specified "authorized drivers". A comparable restriction was relied on by the insurer of the Philco Corporation as a limitation on the group of persons enjoying its liability coverage; see Capital Insurance & Surety Co. v. Globe Indemnity Co., Note 3, p. 511 above. In New York and elsewhere that attempt has been condemned. In Motor Vehicle Accident Indemnification Corp. v. Continental Nat'l Am. Group Co., 319 N.E.2d 182 (N.Y. 1974), concerning an insurer seeking to impose the rental company's restrictions, the court stated:

> A slight deviation from such a restrictive lease could render an injured victim devoid of adequate protection, which is contrary to the legislative intent envisaged by section 388 of the Vehicle and Traffic Law. . . .
> To put it another way, these considerations of sound public policy will prevent the evasion of the liability of one leasing cars for profit (and, in turn, his insurer) via the attempted device of restrictions on or conditions of use which run counter to the recognized realities and, in a measure, disguise the transaction.

Id. at 184–85. In accord: Metropolitan Prop. & Cas. Ins. Co. v. Hertz Corp., 981 P.2d 1091 (Colo. 1999) (en banc).

The Hertz Corporation exhibited a certain bravado by advertising that its rental fees bought "proper liability insurance, meeting the highest standards". Customers could not readily judge of that, for the policy terms were not available to them. One term that might have unsettled a customer was a provision excluding any liability of an authorized driver to a passenger. What should a court say to an insurer invoking that exclusion? What should it say about the ad, when a customer charges Hertz with false advertising? See Hertz Corp. v. Cox, 430 F.2d 1365 (5th Cir. 1970) (Georgia law).

Finally, car rental firms are exposed to liabilities incurred by their customers under state "owner's liability" statutes. An example appears on p. 496 above. Moreover, some jurisdictions have specific auto rental company statutes that fix liabilities on rental car companies particularly unless they have made an arrangement for liability insurance, or a substitute, and have certified that fact. *E.g.*, Wis. Stat. § 344.51, *Financial Responsibility for Domestic Rented or Leased Vehicles.*

————

4.   Liability "Arising Out of the Use" of a Motor Vehicle

Peagler v. USAA Ins. Co.

South Carolina Supreme Court, 2006.
368 S.C. 153, 628 S.E.2d 475.

Kathy Thompson died as a result of the mishandling of a shotgun by her husband. On the day before he and the couple's teenage son had taken the gun on an expedition in preparation for the upcoming hunting season. Returning, they had left it, loaded, in the rear seat of their pickup truck. On the following day Mr. Thompson was removing it while Mrs. Thompson was belted into the driver's seat. In the process, the gun was accidentally discharged, causing her death.

The Thompsons held coverage against liabilities arising from the ownership, maintenance, or use of the pickup. The representative of Mrs. Thompson's estate brought an action against the insurer, USAA, seeking a declaratory judgment that the coverage extended to Mr. Thompson's liability, if any. When the case reached the United States Court of Appeals for the Fourth Circuit, that court certified this question to the South Carolina Supreme Court:

> Did Decedent's fatal injury arise out of the "ownership, maintenance, or use" of a motor vehicle pursuant to S.C. Code Ann. § 38–77–140 (2002), such that the vehicle's insurance policy provides coverage for the accidental discharge of a shotgun which occurred during the unloading of firearms from a stationary, occupied vehicle which had been used for hunting purposes the previous day?

■ BURNETT, JUSTICE.

. . .

[Because] the policy in this case is silent on the issue [it] must be resolved based on statutes which mandate coverage for damages arising out of the "ownership, use, or maintenance" of a motor vehicle, and cases arising under those statutes which establish a method of resolving the issue. *Cf.* Hogan v. Home Ins. Co., 194 S.E.2d 890 (S.C. 1973) (statute controls when provision in automobile policy excluding coverage conflicts with statute).

. . . South Carolina Code Ann. § 38–77–140 (2002) provides that "[n]o automobile insurance policy may be issued or delivered in this State to the owner of a motor vehicle or may be issued or delivered by an insurer licensed in this State upon any motor vehicle then principally garaged or principally used in this State, unless it contains a provision insuring the persons defined as insured against loss from the liability imposed by law for damages arising out of the ownership, maintenance, or use of these motor vehicles...." ...

We enunciated a three-part test in [State Farm Fire & Cas. Co. v. Aytes, 503 S.E.2d 744 (S.C. 1998)] to determine whether an injury arises out of the "ownership, maintenance, or use" of a motor vehicle. The party seeking coverage must show (1) a causal connection exists between the vehicle and the injury, (2) no act of independent significance breaks the causal link between the vehicle and the injury, and (3) the vehicle was being used for transportation purposes at the time of the injury. To date, this issue has been addressed by our appellate courts primarily in the context of various types of assault involving intentional conduct by an assailant; it has not been addressed in the context of an accident involving unintentional conduct, with one exception.[3]

In analyzing whether an injury arose out of the ownership, maintenance, or use of a vehicle, "no distinction is made as to whether the injury resulted from a negligent, reckless, or intentional act." ... The three-part test in *Aytes* applies regardless of whether the injury occurred as a result of an intentional assault or an accident. The focus is on the extent of the role, if any, the vehicle played in causing the injuries or damage, or whether a particular activity is a covered use as required by statute or a policy provision....

The determination of whether coverage exists in this case rises or falls on the analysis of the first *Aytes* factor. A causal connection between the vehicle and the injury must exist in order for an injury to be covered by an automobile insurance policy. In this context, we have held that causal connection means: (a) the vehicle was an "active accessory" to the injury; (b) the vehicle was something less than the proximate cause but more than the mere site of the injury; and (c) the injury was foreseeably identifiable with the normal use of the vehicle. State Farm Mut. Auto. Ins. Co. v. Bookert, 523 S.E.2d 181, 182 (1999) (citing *Aytes*). "The required causal connection does not exist when the only connection between an injury and the insured vehicle's use is the fact that the injured person was an occupant of the vehicle when the shooting occurred." *Aytes*, 503 S.E.2d at 746.

[I]n *Aytes*, an assailant used a car to transport the victim to a location with the expressed intent of killing the victim. The assailant got out of the car, took from the victim a handgun she had retrieved from the car's glove compartment and shot at the victim as she sat in the car, injuring her. We held, in part, the assault was not covered by the insurance policy because

---

3.   ... The one exception is Canal Ins. Co. v. Ins. Co. of North America, 431 S.E.2d 577 (S.C. 1993). In that case, a truck-mounted crane tipped over and damaged a building. [W]e held the accident was not covered by the liability policy on the truck crane because it was not being used for transportation purposes at the time of the injury.

the parked car was not an "active accessory" in the shooting; it was merely the site of the injury. *Aytes*, 503 S.E.2d at 746.

Our appellate courts have found no causal connection between the vehicle and the injury in similar assault cases. See [among six cases cited] Carraway v. Smith, 467 S.E.2d 120 (S.C.App. 1995) (no causal connection between vehicle and injury where driver of car was injured when bullet fired by bystander on sidewalk shattered his windshield; any causal link was broken by assailant exiting vehicle in front of motorist and conversing on sidewalk with another person for several minutes before shooting occurred).

There is a distinction between the above cases and those in which coverage exists because the vehicle was actively used to perpetrate an assault or injury on another person. See [Home Ins. Co. v. Towe, 441 S.E.2d 825 (S.C. 1994)] (finding causal connection between vehicle and injury where victim, who was driving an oncoming tractor, suffered injuries when the steering wheel of his tractor was struck by a bottle thrown by passenger in passing car; car was an active accessory that gave rise to the injury). . . .

We have considered, but decline to follow, precedent in which other courts have found that insurance coverage exists for accidental injuries or deaths which occur during the loading and unloading of a firearm from a vehicle, despite the lack of a policy provision which addressed whether the loading or unloading of a vehicle was a covered use. . . .

We decline to depart from or modify the *Aytes* analysis in this accidental weapon discharge case. The injury was foreseeably identifiable with the normal use of the pickup truck. Many vehicles in South Carolina, and certainly many pickup trucks, are used for hunting purposes. Using a vehicle to transport firearms to and from hunting grounds is not an abnormal or unanticipated use of a vehicle. However, Plaintiff has not demonstrated the truck was an active accessory to the injury. The truck was not actively used or involved in causing the injury; it was merely the site of the injury. As stated in *Aytes*, "[t]he required causal connection does not exist when the only connection between an injury and the insured vehicle's use is the fact that the injured person was an occupant of the vehicle when the shooting occurred." *Aytes*, 503 S.E.2d at 746. Plaintiff has failed to show, under the facts as stipulated, that a causal connection exists between the pickup truck and the accidental shooting of Decedent.

Our resolution of the causal connection factor makes it unnecessary to analyze the remaining *Aytes* factors, *i.e.,* whether an act of independent significance broke the causal link between the vehicle and the injury, and whether the vehicle was being used for transportation purposes at the time of the injury. . . .

We answer "no" to the question certified by the Court of Appeals. . . .

■ WALLER, J., dissenting. [Justice Pleicones concurred in this dissent.]

. . . In my opinion, the unloading of the firearms from the vehicle, in preparation for transportation of the children to school, with the motor running, provides a sufficient causal connection to warrant coverage. See Taliaferro v. Progressive Specialty Ins. Co., 821 So.2d 976, 979–80 (Ala. 2001) (because the principal use of an automobile is transportation—being dependent upon the operations of loading and unloading—the act of removing a rifle was an inherent use of a pickup truck for purposes of insurance coverage); Kohl v. Union Ins. Co., 731 P.2d 134 (Colo. 1986) (where accident occurred as truck owner lifted rifle out of the jeep's gun rack in preparation to unload rifle and store it for journey home, owner's actions were intimately related to his use of the vehicle as transportation for himself and his rifle); Allstate Ins. Co. v. Truck Ins. Exchange, 216 N.W.2d 205 (Wis. 1974) (loading and unloading of guns from van constitutes "use" of the vehicle in spite of the absence of any specific "loading and unloading" clause from the policy).

Other courts have reached similar conclusions in cases of accidental weapon discharges. See [in addition to two other cases cited,] Shinabarger v. Citizens Mut. Ins. Co., 282 N.W.2d 301, 306 (Mich.App. 1979) (in cases involving accidental discharge of firearms, courts generally have been more liberal in finding a causal connection between use of the vehicle and injury when accident occurs during the loading or unloading process than when accident simply occurs in or near the vehicle, but not during loading).

Further, I would hold that no act of independent significance broke the causal link between the vehicle and the injury. There was no intervening cause wholly disassociated from, independent of, or remote from the use of the truck in this case. On the contrary, the injury here occurred due to the insured's foreseeable use of unloading his vehicle of the shotguns loaded in the back. . . .

Lastly, I would find the pickup truck was being used for transportation purposes when the injury occurred. Kathy Thompson and her children were sitting in the car, ready to leave home and go to work and school. They were preparing to drive away, and the engine was running. As the District Court in this case noted, under "USAA's theory coverage conceivably would not extend to injuries sustained under any factual scenario where a vehicle is parked only momentarily or, far worse, where injuries are sustained while a vehicle is stationary at an intersection during the course of travel." Peagler v. USAA Ins. Co., 325 F.Supp.2d 620, 627 (D.S.C. 2004). Clearly, the vehicle here was being used for transportation.

I would hold that the "ownership, maintenance, or use" of a vehicle includes the loading and unloading of firearms after the vehicle has been used for hunting purposes, a use which is foreseeably identifiable with normal use of the vehicle. Accordingly, I would conclude insurance coverage exists in this case.

. . .

NOTES

(1) *Local Color.* Justice Burnett observed that many vehicles are used for hunting purposes in South Carolina. Notice that Justice Waller, dissenting, relied

on decisions on comparable facts in Alabama and Colorado. Can it be that hunters on wheels are more exceptional in those states? And if so, how can it matter?

(2) *Guns, Bombs, and Dogs.* The causal connection between an injury and a vehicle, or its use, has been tested repeatedly. Some "gun cases", in which a marksman shot from within a vehicle, are reviewed in Sigmund v. Progressive Northern Ins. Co., 374 F.Supp.2d 33 (D.D.C. 2005). That was a "bomb case": a car being wired, it exploded when the claimant turned the key. The connection was incidental, the court ruled. It cited a case in which a marksman used a car to get where he wished to take a shot, another case of an incidental connection.

The cases are said to be divided about dogs that bite people in cars. One view is that "something about the vehicle itself or attachments to the vehicle", must have provoked the dog. See Farmers Union Co-op. Ins. Co. v. Allied Property, 569 N.W.2d 436, 440 (Neb. 1997).

(3) *Two Conceptions of "Use".* It is said that, under the law of at least one state, if something exiguous to a vehicle is the "but-for" cause of an injury, the injury cannot be said to arise from a use of the vehicle. AXA Re Property & Cas. Ins. Co. v. Day, 162 Fed.Appx. 316 (5th Cir. 2006) (Mississippi law). In that case the monoxide-poisoning death of a guest sleeping in a trailer resulted from a defect in the ventilation of a generator that was occasionally attached to the trailer so as to heat it. Is the decision in *Peagler* consistent with the rule stated?

Some Mississippi decisions are far less stringent than the one just described. See Johnson v. United States Fid. & Guar. Ins. Co., 726 So.2d 167 (1998), where the court said that it had elected to interpret the term *use* "very broadly". The claim there was made on behalf of a boy who was struck by a motorist while walking toward a school bus. The motorist had disregarded the sign "Stop" on the bus. The court said that the boy was using the bus when struck, although he was 141 feet away from it. The difference, as noted in *AXA Re*, is that the boy's claim was based on a uninsured-motorist (UM) coverage, not on a liability coverage as in *AXA Re*. As to the former, and not the latter, the Mississippi court has taken the word *use* in a broad sense. (Some cases cited in the foregoing Note are also uninsured-motorist-coverage cases.)

(4) *Passenger and Use of a Motor Vehicle.* "On the one hand, the term 'use' encompasses an active role such as operating a vehicle. On the other hand, it could refer to a more passive role, such as that of a passenger employing a vehicle for transportation." Padgett v. Georgia Farm Bureau Mut. Ins. Co., 625 S.E.2d 76, 78 (Ga.App. 2005). For a court so saying, the choice is predictable. The Georgia court applied what it called a *strict* construction—strictly against the insurer as the drafter of the policy. In a comparable case a court applied what it called a *liberal* construction—liberally for a claimant. Earth Tech, Inc. v. United States Fire Ins. Co., 407 F.Supp.2d 763 (E.D.Va. 2006) .

The Georgia case is a curious one. It is one of many in which insurers have contended that one does not "use" a car by being driven around in it. A number of those cases concerned unusually aggressive passengers. An example, presented above, is *Speros v. Fricke* (p. 500). Both in that case and in *Padgett* the courts purported to decide that passengers are users of cars in which they ride. But either of these decisions could have been based on a narrower ground. As will be seen, the law of South Carolina differentiates between passengers as such and aggressive ones. It requires the showing of a causal connection between vehicle and injury. "The required causal connection does not exist when the only connection between an injury and the insured vehicle's use is the fact that the injured person was an occupant of the vehicle when the [injury] occurred.'' State Farm Fire & Cas. Co. v. Aytes, 503 S.E.2d 744, 746 (S.C. 1998). Certainly the wheel-grabbing in *Speros* was something more of a link between the presence of the passenger and the injury than that.

In *Padgett*, the Georgia case, the link was more attenuated. Oddly, the fact that Phillip Padgett was in the insured vehicle when it collided with another had nothing to do with the tort attributed to him. The supposed tort was negligence in entrusting the vehicle to its driver at the time. (Oddly, again, both driver and passenger were employees of the owner, who was the driver's father.) Why the court felt called upon to declare Padgett a user-as-passenger is unclear. Whether or not he was a user at all is another question. Should the court have declared that he was, whether or not he was in the vehicle?

Earth Tech, cited above, presented the question whether or not the giving of directions by a ''flagman'' to the driver of a tractor-trailer amounted to a use of the rig by the flagman. Yes, the court said, under Virginia law, while acknowledging conflict in the precedents. ''[T]he terms 'use' and 'using' in the omnibus clause should be broadly construed. . . .'' Id. at 771. What, then, of a passenger who says to a driver, ''All clear on the right'', when it's not? If giving bad directions to a driver from outside a vehicle constitutes a use of the vehicle, does it follow that the negligent selection of a driver does?

(5) *Drive-By Shooting.* In recent years, drive-by shootings have become an increasingly common part of the American experience. In your opinion, is shooting from a moving vehicle to kill a pedestrian caused by the use of a motor vehicle? See Charles W. Benton, Anno., ''Automobile insurance coverage for drive-by shootings and other incidents involving the intentional discharge of firearms from moving motor vehicles,'' 41 A.L.R.5th 91.

PROBLEM

Ice on a road caused an SUV to flip over. A passing motorist stopped and got out of her car to give aid. An oncoming motorist saw her and tried to stop, but slid into her, causing her bodily injury. The right of the good Samaritan to insurance compensation depends upon whether or not her injury arose from the use of the SUV. Her injury would not have occurred but for the fact that it flipped over. What arguments can be made for and against compensating her? See Progressive Cas. Ins. Co. v. Farm Bureau Mut. Ins. Co., 53 P.3d 740 (Colo.App. 2002). Compare the schoolboy's case in Note 3 above.

Direct Actions

Issuers of liability insurance are inclined to believe that they need protection against the sympathies, antipathies, and vagaries of juries. They attempt to secure that protection by deploying a condition proscribing an action against them by anyone other than an insured until a liability of the insured has been established. A representative ''no action'' clause contains this provision:

> No action shall lie against the company unless, as a condition precedent thereto, . . . the amount of the insured's obligation to pay shall have been finally determined either by judgment against the insured after actual trial or by written agreement of the insured, the claimant and the company.

The insurer's liability is *not* contingent, be it noted, on satisfaction of the liability by the insured; and the provision goes on to say that the insured's *inability* to pay does not relieve the insurer of its obligations.

Statutes in some states override no-action clauses; they are said to authorize "direct actions". Notable examples are La.R.S. 22:655 and Wis. Stats. § 632.24. By virtue of one of these statutes, to take an example, a victim of an insured's negligence need not first get a judgment against the tortfeasor and then use a collection process to enforce it against the insurer; the two proceedings can be telescoped, it has been said.

A side effect of direct actions would be greatly to enlarge the diversity dockets of the federal courts, except that Congress has acted to forestall that: see 28 U.S.C. § 1332(c)(1). What that statute means by "direct action" has been actively litigated. See Exantus v. Metropolitan Prop. & Cas. Ins. Co., 2007 WL 703610 (D.Conn. 2007) ("Every court that has addressed this question has concluded that [an action] by an insured against his own insurer, is not a 'direct action' under section 1332(c)."

B. NO-FAULT INSURANCE; UNINSURED-MOTORIST AND UNDERINSURED-MOTORIST COVERAGES

Much has been done to compensate victims of road injuries by combining tort liability and liability insurance. Liabilities in tort have been extended by various doctrines of vicarious liability, and liability insurance has been extended by mandating coverages. These measures fall well short of achieving compensation for all victims, much less full compensation for all. For one thing, many road injuries do not entail any liability. For another, many people flout the law by taking to the roads without being provided with the amount of liability coverage required of them, and many without being provided with any of that coverage. The materials that follow concern measures designed to reduce the number and amounts of uncompensated road injuries by deploying first-party insurance. In good part these measures are dictated by statute. The measures to be described are of two main types: personal-injury-protection, or "no-fault" insurance, and the pair of coverages known as uninsured-motorist insurance and underinsured-motorist insurance.

1. Personal Injury Protection (PIP)

Rather than imposing tort liability on those who negligently cause auto-related injuries, "pure" no-fault legislation directed that victims shoulder their own injury costs by purchasing insurance. A pure auto no-fault plan would provide first-party benefits to injured parties for economic losses, without regard to fault, and would eliminate the insured's right to a tort recovery for any losses. But no such plan exists because no jurisdiction has adopted a plan that eliminates tort actions for all loss.[1] Current auto

---

1. The Michigan statute, Mich. Comp. Laws §§ 3101–500.3179, is the closest to a "pure" PIP plan because it has the most restrictive threshold requirement that effectively limits most tort recovery and allows the most liberal PIP benefits.

no-fault statutes have two prongs: the mandatory purchase of no-fault (PIP) insurance directly protecting victims, and the abolition of tort liability.

These two prongs resulted in two types of state auto PIP (no-fault) plans: Modified PIP Plans and Add-on PIP Plans.[2] Under a modified PIP plan, first-party benefits are paid regardless of fault and some restrictions are placed on the claimant's ability to commence a tort action. To restrict tort liability, modified plans employ different thresholds—either the injury (or "verbal") threshold[3] or the monetary (or "dollar") threshold.[4] Only claimants whose injuries exceed the threshold may file a tort suit. An example of statutes instituting modified plans is Section 5102 of the New York Insurance Law.

Add-on plans provide first-party PIP coverage for medical expenses and wage losses in addition to third-party liability insurance coverage. An add-on plan preserves the tort system and does not bar the claimant from suing in tort other than, in some jurisdictions, a preclusion from obtaining the same damages twice. An example of a statute instituting add-on plans is Chapter 231, § 6D of the Massachusetts General Laws.

Allen v. State Farm Mut. Auto. Ins. Co.

Michigan Court of Appeals, 2005.
268 Mich.App. 342, 708 N.W.2d 131.

Ben Strother and Heidi Allen had been "live-in companions" for nine years. They had two children together. He provided all the household income, and she was responsible for many household tasks, including paying bills. Strother had lost his driver's license owing to alcohol-related offenses. He nevertheless took her car for a drive, without her permission. Being injured on the drive, he brought an action on the PIP coverage in Allen's policy. (In point of fact, the court referred to Allen as the plaintiff, in her capacity as conservator of Strother's estate.) The trial court ruled that Strother was not qualified for recovery under the applicable "no fault" law, that of Michigan. This appeal followed.

The Court of Appeals said that Strother was "clearly" not qualified under the statutory phrase, "the person named in the policy, the person's

---

2. See generally Eric Mills Holmes, Holmes' Appleman on Insurance 2d, Ch. 154 Basic Features of No–Fault Plans (2004) (with Eileen Swarbrick).

3. The verbal or injury threshold classifies the types of injuries permitting a tort action for non-economic loss. Typically, tort actions may be commenced for "serious injuries," such as death, disfigurement or scarring, dismemberment, fractures, loss of fetus, disability, permanent injury, and loss of sight

or hearing. The claimant suffering a less serious injury is compensated only for economic loss and is barred from commencing an action for non-economic loss.

4. The monetary threshold specifies the dollar amount of medical expenses sustained in a motor vehicle accident that a claimant must incur as a condition precedent to filing a tort action for non-economic loss. See, e.g., Estate of Wallace v. Fisher, 567 So.2d 505 (Fla.App. 1990).

spouse, and a relative of either domiciled in the same household". The court turned its attention then to the possibility that Strother was qualified as "a person suffering accidental bodily injury arising from a motor vehicle accident while an occupant of a motor vehicle". The court concluded, however, that Strother was in any event barred from recovery by the following statutory provision, section 500.3113(a) of the Michigan Compiled Laws:

> A person is not entitled to be paid personal protection insurance benefits for accidental bodily injury if at the time of the accident . . .:
>
> (a) The person was using a motor vehicle . . . which he or she had taken unlawfully, unless the person reasonably believed that he or she was entitled to take and use the vehicle.

The court considered several precedents about unlawful takings. The court described the "leading case" as one in which some members of the court "created a judicial exception to the statutory bar for 'joyriding' family members, generally, teenagers taking their parents' vehicles without permission." These justices—three of seven sitting—"believed that because joyriding was such a common occurrence in families, benefits should not be denied in that situation, because that was not what the Legislature presumably intended." That case was Priesman v. Meridian Mut. Ins. Co., 490 N.W.2d 314 (Mich. 1992). Justice Boyle concurred in the result only. Three justices, led by Griffin, dissented.

■ BANDSTRA, J.

. . .

This Court, in Butterworth Hosp. v. Farm Bureau Ins. Co., 225 Mich.App. 244, 248–249; 570 N.W.2d 304 (1997), recognized that *Priesman* was not binding precedent, but, nonetheless, felt compelled to follow its reasoning. This Court held that when a vehicle is taken by a family member, benefits will only be denied under MCL 500.3113(a) if there was an actual intent to steal the vehicle. The majority declined to accept the concurring judge's position that the exception for joyriding offenses should extend beyond family members. Similarly, this Court specifically declined to extend the joyriding exception to individuals who are not family members in Mester v. State Farm Mut. Ins. Co., 235 Mich.App. 84, 88; 596 N.W.2d 205 (1999). There is no evidence to suggest that Strother ever intended to permanently deprive Allen of her vehicle, and his conduct could be termed "joyriding" as the exception has been discussed following *Priesman*. However, Strother is not a "family member" entitled to the joyriding exception. Neither party contends that Strother and Allen are legally or biologically related in any way. Accordingly, pursuant to *Butterworth* and *Mester* the joyriding exception does not apply, and Strother is precluded from recovering PIP benefits under MCL 500.3113(a).

. . .

We affirm.

■ KELLY, J., concurring.

. . .

... I do not believe there is any authority that permits this Court to limit the application of MCL 500.3113(a) only to car thefts, given the clear terms adopted by the Legislature.... As noted in *Priesman, supra* at 66–67, the Legislature refused to follow the language of the Uniform Motor Vehicle Accident Reparations Act, a model act that excluded coverage for "converters" of vehicles. The Legislature instead chose a term, "taken unlawfully," that encompasses crimes other than larceny or stealing of a motor vehicle. "The Legislature is presumed to have intended the meaning it has plainly expressed, and if the expressed language is clear, judicial construction is not permitted and the statute must be enforced as written." Robertson v. DaimlerChrysler Corp., 641 N.W.2d 567 (Mich. 2002). Courts may not rewrite the plain language of the statute and substitute their own policy decisions for those already made by the Legislature....

■ BORRELLO, P.J., dissenting.

[T]he controlling issue in this case is whether Strother and Allen are "family members" within the meaning of the exception to MCL 500.3113(a). In contrast to the majority's holding in this case, I would conclude that they are family members. This Court has previously recognized that "the reality of the nature of families existing in today's society" precludes restricting the definition of "family" to "include only persons related by consanguinity." Youngblood v. DEC Properties, 204 Mich.App. 581, 583; 516 N.W.2d 119 (1994). Rather, "the relevance of 'family' does not pertain to blood or lineage, but rather to members of a household...." Id. ...[1]

QUESTIONS

(1) In the court's prior *Butterworth* decision, the claimant was an adult son of the named insured, not living with him, who had taken his father's car in the face of an express refusal of permission. What other interesting cases of familial and non-familial joyriding might Michigan courts have reason to expect? Some answers may be suggested by this passage in the opinion that is said to have invented the joyriding exception: "Legislators generally are also parents and sometimes grandparents. Some may have had experience with children, grandchildren, nephews, nieces, and children of friends who have used a family vehicle without permission. Some may have themselves driven a family vehicle without permission." *Priesman* at 318.

(2) In *Allen*, should it matter that, as was the fact, Strother had no license to drive? If he had been on an errand of mercy—to buy medicine for a sick child, say—should that matter?

---

1. In response to the majority's contention that my view would expand coverage to "unrelated adults," I would respond that perhaps the majority should consider a more expansive definition of what constitutes a "family member" to more accurately reflect the myriad types of families that actually exist in society today. The majority seems content to narrowly define the term "family member" by judicial edict in a manner that comports with its social values, with no consideration or recognition of the fact that families are created by more than blood....

Bronson Methodist Hospital v. Forshee, 198 Mich.App. 617, 499 N.W.2d 423 (1993). Stanley Pefley loaned his car to his son Thomas. Early on the following morning the car sailed for about fifty feet through the air, after an evening of carousing by Thomas and some friends, two arrests, an attempt at a third arrest, and a high-speed chase. The occupants at that time were friends Mark and William. Thomas had been placed in a police cruiser after the second arrest. ("During the second stop, a deputy confiscated two cases of beer and a billy club and arrested Thomas Pefley for violating his probation by carrying a concealed weapon.") An arresting officer had asked William to take custody of the Pefley car, and from the cruiser Thomas yelled to William, "Take the car home." Instead of that, William drove a fourth friend home and, with Mark, picked up another case of beer. William and Mark were later to disagree about which of them was driving at the time of the chase. William said that, because he was uncomfortable using a manual shift, he had turned the wheel over to Mark at some point. That, and testimony by a police officer, was to persuade a trial court that Mark was the driver.

Judy Forshee, Mark's mother, brought an action against two insurers, seeking to recover part of the heavy medical expenses she had incurred for Mark's benefit. (Both he and William had been critically injured in the crash.) One defendant was her auto insurer, the Michigan Mutual Insurance Company; the other, State Farm Mutual Auto, had insured the Pefley car. Contesting liability, the insurers—chiefly Michigan Mutual—contended that Mark was not qualified for PIP benefits because he had taken the car unlawfully. The trial court agreed with that. But that ruling was disapproved on appeal. (The Hospital had brought an action for the cost of its services to Mark.)

The court said that Mark's use of the Pefley car was with the consent of its owner (Stanley), inasmuch as Stanley had entrusted it to his son Thomas, who in turn entrusted it to William, who entrusted it to Mark. "Given this unbroken chain of permissive use, we cannot say that Forshee's taking of the automobile was unlawful." The court was not affected by the fact that Mark was not a licensed driver. The statutory exclusion relates, the court said, not to the unlawful *use* of a car, but to its unlawful *taking*.

■ SAWYER, J.

. . .

Michigan Mutual also argues that Forshee is precluded from recovery of benefits under [the Michigan no-fault statute] because his injuries were so recklessly sustained as to be intentional within the meaning of that statute. The cited statute does, in fact, exclude from personal protection insurance benefits injuries that are suffered intentionally. Michigan Mutual argues that Forshee's conduct was so reckless as to constitute wanton or reckless conduct that rises to the level of being intentional conduct or constituting an intentional injury. Thus, fleeing and eluding would also be exempted from the no-fault act under this portion of . . . the no-fault act. We disagree.

As this Court explained [elsewhere], the intentional injury exclusion . . . requires that the injury be intended, not that an intentional act gave rise to an injury. In the case at bar, although Forshee did act intentionally in fleeing and eluding the police, there is no indication that he intended to be injured as a result. . . . Indeed, the evidence indicated that Forshee braked the car [and] that the car was unable to stop completely because of the excessive speed. Thus, it would certainly appear that Forshee attempted to avoid the accident, rather than create one.

NOTES

(1) *Consent*. The court relied heavily on a decision about the Michigan owner's liability statute, Cowan v. Strecker, 229 N.W.2d 302 (Mich. 1975). In *Cowan* a borrower of a car had permitted her son to use it despite the owner's instruction not to let anyone else drive it. The court ruled that the owner was accountable under an owner's liability statute for harm done by the son's faulty driving, having "consented" to his use of the car. The purpose of the statute is, the court said, "to place the risk of damage or injury on the person who has ultimate control of the vehicle, *i.e.*, the owner. . . ." That purpose would be frustrated, it said, if the word *consent* were not broadly construed. In the *Forshee* case the court said: "Of course, the statute involved here is not concerned with placing the liability of[on?] the proper party, but, rather, to preclude the receipt of personal protection insurance benefits by someone who has unlawfully taken an automobile. . . . Nevertheless, we believe that the broad definition of 'consent' employed . . . in the owner liability context is of equal applicability here."

(2) *Primary Coverage*. Having decided that Mark was entitled to PIP benefits, the court had to decide which of two insurers was primarily accountable: his mother's insurer, Michigan Mutual, or State Farm Mutual as the insurer of the Pefley car. According to the statute, that depended on the question whether or not, at the time of Mark's injury, he was domiciled with his mother. Because the evidence on that point was in conflict, the court approved the finding of the trial court that he was. Hence the primary carrier was Michigan Mutual.

(3) *Cop Car Users*. Earlier Michigan precedents, cited in *Forshee*, suggest the interesting possibility that, if Mark was not qualified for PIP benefits as a user of the Pefley car, he was qualified as a user of the police vehicle chasing him. But in each of those cases it was concluded that "there was not a sufficient nexus between the police cruiser and the accident to establish that the injury incurred was linked to a motor vehicle."

Suppose that the police car in which Thomas Pefley was driven away from the scene of his arrest had suffered a collision in which he was injured. Should it be said that he was making use of that car at the time?

---

2. Uninsured Motorists (UM) and Underinsured Motorists (UIM) Coverages

These are first-party coverages made available in one form or another by force of statute in all but a few states. Insurers must offer them, that is, to buyers of auto insurance. Some statutes simply require that the coverages be included. Otherwise, a buyer may decline the coverages by rejecting the insurer's offer explicitly. Failing that, the coverages are installed by law. In all but two states UM coverage must be either provided or offered. Insurers cannot expect to circumvent these requirements through policy drafting. Statutes that either require or encourage the purchase of UIM coverage usually appear as adjuncts to, and are coordinated with, those concerning UM coverage. One cannot recover, for a single injury, under both coverages.

An example of the basic insuring agreement in UM coverage is this: "We will pay compensatory damage which an 'insured' is legally entitled to recover from the owner or operator of an 'uninsured motor vehicle'...."

Statutes instituting UM and UIM coverages reflect the fact, indicated above, that many motorists fail to provide themselves with liability coverage, or with the amount of it that is dictated by law; *delinquent* motorists these may be called. Taken together, the two coverages insure, in at least an amount specified by statute, for the ravages of road injuries, such as medical expenses and lost wages. A measure of property-damage coverage is required by some recent statutes. The amounts of coverage contemplated by a legislature are typically those it has specified as amounts of *liability* insurance to be provided as a condition of motoring.

Let it be supposed, for example, that the owner-operator of a car has run down a pedestrian, carelessly, and owes $40,000 to the pedestrian for medical expenses and lost income. The motorist held insurance against that liability to the limit of $15,000. That amount should have been $25,000, a per-person amount appearing in a statute mandating the coverage. Very possibly, then, the pedestrian can recover $10,000 under a UIM coverage. If the motorist had not been provided with any liability coverage, the pedestrian might well recover $25,000 under UM coverage. The pedestrian might hold only UM coverage, of course, and might not hold either one. If he or she lived and walked in Manhattan, where most residents do not own cars, and many who do carry no auto insurance, probably neither coverage would have been offered, even, to the pedestrian.

There are variations from state to state in the amounts of expected first-party coverage. In West Virginia, for example, where coverage is mandated, the mandated amounts are the limits of the *buyer*'s liability coverage; and beyond that, the buyer must be offered coverage of $100,000 per person. In New York and several other states, in contrast, a maximum is set on the amount of UIM coverage that may be purchased. This oddity reflects the somewhat vengeful view that a person unwilling to protect his prospective victims via liability coverage beyond, say, $25,000 ought not to enjoy benefits beyond that when he is himself a motorist's victim.

The benefits of UM and UIM coverages are accessible chiefly to persons who have claims against delinquent and identified motorists. The benefits required by statute do not exceed the proved amount of an established claim. On occasion benefits are accessible also to a person who would have a claim except that the delinquent motorist is protected by an immunity (*e.g.*, an immunity associated with a PIP statute). And on occasion benefits are accessible to one who has a claim against a motorist who, whether "delinquent" or not, cannot be identified. Controversies attend these occasions, as will be seen.

The references above to "delinquent motorists" must be understood to refer to fault in arranging for liability insurance, not to fault in motoring, although someone's fault in motoring is the usual predicate for a claim on which UM and UIM benefits are contingent. Moreover, the term "delinquent motorist" misstates somewhat the focus of the statutes. The statutory focus is "uninsured vehicle", a defined term. The point is made in the insuring agreement quoted above.

The point was a decisive one when Beth Throesch brought an action on her UM coverage—the one quoted. She had suffered a serious road injury which she attributed, convincingly, to the negligence of a truck driver. The trial court awarded her a judgment even though it had no way of knowing whether or not the truck was an "uninsured motor vehicle". The court relied on a statute under which the truck driver was presumed to have been uninsured. (The presumption attached because the driver had failed to file, following the accident, a certificate that he or she held liability coverage as required by applicable law.) On appeal, the judgment for Throesch was reversed. It could be affirmed only on a showing that the *truck* was uninsured. The statutory presumption enabled Throesch to show only that the *driver* was. (Another part of the opinion is presented next.)

Beyond its literal sense. the term *uninsured motor vehicle* comprises a vehicle that is insured, but in an amount less than that required. Under some statutes, curiously, the term comprises a vehicle for which the required amount of liability coverage is in place. The vehicle may be considered "uninsured" if the issuer of that coverage is insolvent, or if it has simply disclaimed accountability. By and large, however, *uninsured motor vehicle* signifies one as to which some motorist should have arranged liability coverage, or should have arranged greater coverage, and did not. Hence, "delinquent".

NOTE

"Vehicle". Sometimes it is a question what counts as a *vehicle*, as the word is used in a statute or policy about UM or UIM coverage. A motorcycle is not necessarily a statutory "vehicle". On the other hand, a moped was a policy "vehicle", although not a statutory one, according to Hill v. State Farm Mut. Auto. Ins. Co., 375 S.E.2d 727 (Va. 1989). A policy restriction on the word may fail because the restriction does not appear in a relevant statute.

————

Throesch v. United States Fidelity & Gaur. Co.

United States Court of Appeals, 8th Cir., 2001.
255 F.3d 551.

■ WOLLMAN, CHIEF JUDGE.

United States Fidelity and Guaranty Company (USF&G) appeals from the district court's entry of judgment entitling Beth R. Throesch to coverage under her vehicle's automobile insurance policy; Throesch cross-appeals. We reverse in part and affirm in part. [Part of the court's reasoning is described next.]

I.

The facts of this case are undisputed. On April 26, 1997, while driving south on Highway 67 near Pocahontas, Arkansas, Throesch swerved off the road and onto the shoulder. She subsequently lost control of the vehicle, which overturned, causing her serious injuries. According to Throesch and two eyewitnesses, Throesch swerved to successfully avoid colliding with a truck coming from the opposite direction that had crossed the center line of traffic and entered her lane. The truck's driver did not stop, and Throesch was unable to identify him or locate him or the truck.

In relevant part, Throesch's insurance policy issued by USF&G provides:

PART C—UNINSURED MOTORISTS COVERAGE

. . .

We will pay compensatory damages which an "insured" is legally entitled to recover from the owner or operator of an "uninsured motor vehicle" . . .

. . .

"Uninsured motor vehicle" means a land motor vehicle or trailer of any type:

   1. To which no bodily injury liability bond or policy applies at the time of the accident.

. . .

   3. Which is a hit-and-run vehicle whose operator or owner cannot be identified and which hits:

   a. You or any "family member";

   b. A vehicle which you or any "family member" are "occupying"; or

   c. "Your covered auto".

Throesch seeks coverage under provisions 1 and/or 3, which provide different definitions for the "uninsured motor vehicle" involved in the accident.

USF&G denied Throesch's request for coverage under provision 3 because the truck did not hit her or her vehicle, and determined that because Throesch had not shown that the truck was uninsured, her injuries were not covered under provision 1.

The district court granted summary judgment to USF&G on the hit-and-run policy provision, concluding that, in this case, it required physical contact between the vehicles as a condition of coverage. [But the court entered judgment for Throesch, believing that she had shown the truck to be an "uninsured motor vehicle" by adducing a statutory presumption.] USF&G appeals from the court's judgment and ruling on the statutory presumption, and Throesch cross-appeals the court's grant of summary judgment on the hit-and-run provision.

II.

[In subpart A of the opinion, the court dealt with the statutory presumption and with provision 1 of the definition of "uninsured motor vehicle". The court concluded that the trial court had erred when it concluded that Throesch could recover under provision 1. The opinion contains the following observations on that subject.]

We agree with USF&G that the plain language of the statute does not create a presumption that the truck was uninsured. By its own terms, the section's presumption applies only to motorists, not vehicles. . . .

Under Arkansas law, the distinction between an uninsured motorist and the vehicle he was driving is critical. . . . For uninsured vehicles, the claimant must specifically demonstrate that the vehicle is uninsured, not just the driver. . . . Therefore, assuming arguendo that section 27–19–503 creates a statutory presumption that the motorist was uninsured, it does not aid Throesch's claim because it contains no mention of uninsured vehicles.

Because Throesch's attempts to locate either the driver or the truck have been unsuccessful, she has no evidence to show that the truck was uninsured. Her claim, therefore, cannot succeed.

B. Hit-and-Run Provision

Noting that the Arkansas Supreme Court has upheld against public policy challenges a hit-and-run provision that provided coverage only for injuries "arising out of physical contact," the district court held that Throesch was required to establish that the on-coming truck made physical contact with her vehicle as a condition of coverage under her policy.

We agree with the district court that the language of the hit-and-run provision is unambiguous and that it requires that the uninsured vehicle be one "which hits," that is, physically contacts the insured or another vehicle. . . . The cases cited by Throesch indicate that hit-and-run policy provisions may encompass "miss-and-run" situations, but they reach that conclusion through either an interpretation of the term "hit-and-run" in clauses that lack the additional requirement of "which hits" and thus do not apply in the present case, or through the voiding of a physical contact requirement through the interpretation of state public policy and state statutes. See, *e.g.,* Clark v. Regent Ins. Co., 270 N.W.2d 26, 27–31 (S.D. 1978) (discussing various approaches; voiding contact provision on statutory grounds).

Throesch accordingly turns to public policy arguments. She contends that a clause like the one in this case, which does not provide coverage for a "near hit" even when supported by eyewitness accounts, is unconscionable under Arkansas public policy and does not further the clause's purported purpose of preventing fraud. As the district court observed, although the Arkansas Supreme Court has not addressed this specific argument, it has concluded that a hit-and-run provision that requires physical contact is valid and does not violate public policy. See Ward v. Consolidated Underwriters, 535 S.W.2d 830, 832 (Ark. 1976). We agree with the district court that given this precedent the Arkansas courts are unlikely to find the provision to be unconscionable or contrary to the public policy of the state. The physical contact requirement of the hit-and-run provision of Throesch's policy is thus enforceable, and her claim under this provision also fails.

... [T]he judgment is affirmed in part and reversed in part, and the case is remanded to the district court with instructions to enter judgment in favor of USF&G.

NOTES

(1) *Other Views.* Statutes in a number of states deal with problems of "hit & run". They do so variously. These are some illustrations:

> In Texas, the required policy provisions relating to UM coverage include one that, given an unknown owner or operator of a vehicle that causes bodily injury or property damage, for the insured to recover, "actual physical contact must have occurred between the motor vehicle owned or operated by the unknown person and the person or property of the insured." Insurance Code § 1952.104(3).

> In California the comparable statute speaks to the subject in a more limited way. Speaking of bodily injury, it defines "uninsured motor vehicle" so as to include an automobile *used without the owner's permission* if the injury has arisen out of physical contact between that automobile and either the insured or an automobile that the insured is occupying. Insurance Code § 11580.2(b).

> In Kansas UM and UIM coverages extend to injuries at the hands of hit-and-run drivers, but a policy may limit the coverage, or exclude the case "when there is no evidence of physical contact with the uninsured motor vehicle and when there is no reliable competent evidence to prove the facts of the accident from a disinterested witness not making claim under the policy".

Would the decision in *Throesch* have been different under any of these statutes? It would have been, presumably, under an Arizona statute requiring, in the circumstances, that the insured provide "corroboration that the unidentified motor vehicle caused the accident", and defines *corroboration* so as to include "any ... evidence that strengthens and adds weight or credibility to the insured's representation of the accident." (What, though, of a claim by the insured's estate, the insured having been killed and so being unable to make any representation of the accident?) The rule in West Virginia, judicially developed, is similar. Hamric v. Doe, 499 S.E.2d 619 (W.Va. 1997).

(2) *Hits and Misses in Wisconsin.* The Wisconsin Supreme Court has had an ongoing struggle with a statute requiring UM coverage in which *uninsured motor vehicle* is defined so as to include an "unidentified motor vehicle involved in a hit-and-run accident". In an early encounter the court considered dictionary definitions of "hit-and-run", and concluded that the expression consists plainly of two ele-

ments: "a 'hit' or striking, and a 'run', or fleeing from the scene of an accident." Hayne v. Progressive Northern Ins. Co., 339 N.W.2d 588, 590 (1983). Later the court had to deal with a case in which a vanishing vehicle had knocked another into the path of the insured's car, and with some "flying object" cases. (In one of these a slab of ice, falling from the top of a vehicle, had struck the claimant's car; in another the claimant's car had been struck by a detached part of a truck's chassis.) Still later the court was to say that it had steadily adhered to the *Hayne* decision; and it adhered to it again. Progressive Northern Ins. Co. v. Romanshek, 697 N.W.2d 417 (2005).

Chief Justice Abrahamson dissented, as she had in *Hayne*. Her thought was, in part, that the statutory term "hit and run" was not limited to "strike and flee". She also thought that, even if it was, the statutory *inclusion* of strike-and-flee did not operate to *exclude* miss-and-flee.

———

Stacking of Coverages

Problems that come under the heading "stacking" are described and illustrated here in relation to uninsured-motorist (UM) coverage. They are far from unique to that coverage, and occur in relation also to underinsured-motorist coverage, to liability coverages, and to property coverages. The field of UM coverage exhibits a wide array of the problems and a number of the solutions have analogs in relation to other fields.

Earl and Marion Taft held a policy, issued by the Allstate Insurance Company, which covered both of the two cars they owned. The policy provided uninsured-motorist coverage with respect to each car in the amount of $10,000. Their daughter was killed at the hands of an uninsured motorist, one Cerwonka. The Tafts brought an action against him and against Allstate. Allstate made motions, after a jury had heard the evidence, which raised a question about the maximum amount of its liability. These amounts were considered: $10k (favored by Allstate), $33k (favored by the jury), and $20k (favored by the trial justice).

On appeal, the Supreme Court of Rhode Island stated the issue this way: "whether [the Tafts] should be permitted to 'stack' the uninsured-motorist coverage provided for each of the two automobiles". The court's reasoning and conclusion are presented below.

The court said that the fact situations in "stacking" cases tend to be similar. That is demonstrably incorrect. Not more than two sentences away, the court described one major dissimilarity: "Intra-policy stacking is the aggregation of the limits of liability for uninsured-motorist coverage on each car covered in one policy, whereas inter-policy stacking involves he aggregation of coverage under more than one policy." As indicated above, the Tafts' case concerned the former. A question of inter-policy stacking might have arisen if they had bought UM coverage in two policies, each covering one of their cars. The difference is important; in a number of states stacking would be permitted in that case, and not in a case like the Tafts'. On the other hand, statutes in about a third of the states preclude inter-policy stacking.

Another distinction has given rise to names that sound, respectively, tautological and oxymoronic: *vertical* stacking and *horizontal* stacking. This distinction rests on the fact that persons protected by UM coverage are protected in differing capacities. One may be protected as a named insured, or a relation of a named insured ("Class I"), and another as an occupant of a covered vehicle ("Class II"). Given more than one policy, a single person may be protected in two or more capacities. For example, a person protected as a named insured in one policy may be protected also as an occupant of a car covered by another. If a man so protected were to claim benefits under each of the policies as if the other did not exist, benefits exceeding in total the policy limit in one of the policies, he would be aiming at "vertical" stacking. In contrast, the Tafts aimed at "horizontal" stacking, for they qualified as Class–I claimants. That fact is important because in some states stacking is permitted in favor of Class–I claimants, and not in favor of Class–II claimants.

No stacking of any kind warrants recoveries that exceed, in total, the amount of the loss. And no question of stacking arises unless that amount exceeds the limit of liability for some one of the coverages concerned.

Insurers have sought to curtail stacking by deploying policy terms. Two examples are given in Note 3, p. 536 below. Attempts like these have sometimes been defeated on the ground that they violate a statute mandating UM coverage. They have usually succeeded in the absence of a mandate of coverage, although there is contrary authority resting on a state's public policy. Stacking of one kind or another is precluded by some statutes. But one statute of that kind was held to be constitutionally infirm. Hardy v. Progressive Specialty Ins. Co., 67 P.3d 892 (Mont. 2003).

The opinion in *Taft* reads like a search for a reason to allow stacking. It leaves to the imagination reasons to *disallow* stacking. Aside from antistacking policy terms, what might lead a legislature or court to do so?

Taft v. Cerwonka

Rhode Island Supreme Court, 1981.
433 A.2d 215, 23 A.L.R.4th 1.

■ MURRAY, JUSTICE.

The plaintiffs, Earl W. Taft and his wife, Marian F. Taft, brought this civil action to recover for the alleged wrongful death of their daughter, Beverly A. Taft (Beverly), alleging that the negligence of the defendant Eric A. Cerwonka (Cerwonka) in operating a motor vehicle was the proximate cause of their daughter's death. Because the defendant Cerwonka, and the defendant Richard A. Miller (Miller), the owner of the vehicle, were uninsured at the time of the fatal mishap, the plaintiffs also filed a complaint against their insurer, Allstate Insurance Company (Allstate) under the uninsured-motorist provisions of their policy. Prior to trial, the two suits were consolidated. . . .

Prior to trial, plaintiffs moved for partial summary judgment on the issue of whether they would be able to "stack" the uninsured-motorist coverage provided for each automobile on the one policy underwritten by defendant Allstate. Such motion was granted by a justice of the Superior Court. The matter then proceeded to trial in the Superior Court. After all parties had rested, defendant Allstate moved for a directed verdict, stating "that if there is a verdict for the plaintiff, and I see no reason why at this juncture that the verdict for the plaintiff should not be entered, that the jury be instructed and directed that the verdict should be the minimum verdict of five thousand dollars. . . ." The trial justice denied this motion and then gave his instructions to the jury, which returned a verdict in favor of plaintiffs in the sum of $33,000. Subsequently, Allstate moved for a new trial on the issue of damages, and it also moved the court to enter judgment against it in the amount of $10,000, the amount it contended was the limit of its liability under the policy issued to plaintiffs. The trial justice's denial of these motions and his entry of judgment in the amount of $20,000 (the aggregate limits of Allstate's liability) against defendant Allstate forms the basis of its present appeal.

In passing upon defendant's contention, we are called upon to determine an issue of first impression in this jurisdiction. That issue is whether plaintiffs should be permitted to "stack" the uninsured-motorist coverage provided for each of the two automobiles insured by Allstate.

Because the fact situations in "stacking" cases tend to be similar and because the Rhode Island uninsured-motorist statute is typical of those in other jurisdictions, decisions of other courts that have confronted this issue merit analysis here. In those jurisdictions where intra-policy stacking has been allowed,[3] courts have advanced one or more of three general theories in support of their decisions. *See* Comment, *Intra-Policy Stacking of Uninsured Motorist and Medical Payments Coverage: To Be or Not To Be*, 22 S.D. L. Rev. 349 (1977). One theory advanced is the theory that the applicable provisions of the insurance contract are ambiguous and that such ambiguities are to be resolved against the insurer. For example, in *Jeffries v. Stewart*, 159 Ind. App. 701, 309 N.E.2d 448 (1974), the Supreme Court [sic] of Indiana found an ambiguity in that the separability clause and the limits-of-liability clause conflicted with each other. The court resolved the ambiguity in favor of the insured and allowed him to stack the limits of liability. *See Id.* at 709, 309 N.E.2d at 453.

Another theory cited in support of stacking is that the particular jurisdiction's uninsured-motorist statute requires such a result. Representative of this class of cases is *Tucker v. Government Employees Insurance Co.*, 288 So.2d 238 (Fla. 1974). In that case, the Supreme Court of Florida held that their uninsured-motorist statute, Fla. Stat. Ann. § 627.727 (West 1977) "does not disclose any statutory basis for a 'stacking' exclusion in a policy combining auto liability coverage for two or more automobiles of the

---

3. Intra-policy stacking is the aggregation of the limits of liability for uninsured-motorist coverage of each car covered in one policy, whereas inter-policy stacking involves the aggregation of coverage under more than one policy.

named insured with uninsured motorist coverage included." *Id.* at 241.[4] Another court in *Holloway v. Nationwide Mutual Insurance Co.*, 376 So.2d 690 (Ala. 1979), held that the jurisdiction's uninsured-motorist statute *mandated* stacking for the primary insured.

A final theory is the double-premiums theory, under which courts have held that the payment of separate premiums for uninsured-motorist coverage for each vehicle covered by the policy entitles the insured to stack the limits of liability for each insured vehicle of the policy. A recent case espousing this view is *Kemp v. Allstate Insurance Co.*, 601 P.2d 20 (Mont. 1979).

In the jurisdictions where intra-policy stacking has not been allowed, courts have attempted to discredit each of the above theories. In *Grimes v. Concord General Mutual Insurance Co.*, 422 A.2d 1312 (N.H. 1980), the Supreme Court of New Hampshire discarded the double-premium theory, stating:

> "Neither can we agree, with confidence that the plaintiff is paying an extra premium without receiving something in return. When an insured owns two vehicles that are constantly available for use, not only by him, but by members of his family and others, the risk that someone operating one of those vehicles will be involved in an accident with an uninsured motorist is obviously greater than if only one vehicle were available for use. Consequently, an insurance carrier's exposure to that risk may be enhanced. Other courts have recognized that the second premium paid on the second car does afford some extra protection that otherwise would not exist." [Citations omitted.] *Id.* at 1315.

The court went on to hold that their uninsured-motorist statute did not require intra-policy stacking.[5]

. . .

It is not disputed that plaintiffs paid two separate premiums for uninsured-motorist coverage; nevertheless, Allstate contends that to allow stacking is to render a "tortured" construction of the policy and of our uninsured-motorist statute. To give credence to Allstate's contentions, however, would defeat the reasonable expectations of a policyholder.

> "It is reasonable to expect the same coverage where comparable premium dollars are paid to insure the same two cars, for convenience, under a single policy. A combination coverage should not be the predicate for an exclusion of coverage. Such a result would allow a simple change in form to defeat the insured's reasonable expectation, as well as the substance of law." [Citation omitted.] *Allstate Insurance Co. v. Maglish*, 586 P.2d 313, 315 (Nev. 1978).

4. We note here that the legislature in the State of Florida has since passed anti-stacking legislation. *See* Fla. Stat. Ann. § 627.4132 (West 1977).

5. See N.H. Rev. Stat. Ann. § 268:15–a.

Indeed if plaintiffs had insured their automobiles under two separate policies and had paid uninsured-motorist premiums for each car, they would be entitled to $20,000 in uninsured-motorist coverage from Allstate. Under these circumstances we find persuasive the statement of dissenting Justice Douglas of the Supreme Court of New Hampshire in *Grimes v. Concord General Mutual Insurance Co.*, 422 A.2d at 1317, that

> "it is an anomaly that if the same two premiums were paid to two *different* companies, we would permit *inter*-policy stacking of 'as many uninsured motorist policies as are applicable to him, up to his total damages,' *Courtemanche v. Lumbermens Mut. Cas. Co.*, 118 N.H. 168, 173, 385 A.2d 105, 108 (1978), but because the two different coverages were both purchased from the same insurer, we do not." (Emphasis in original.)

Other cases have reflected the same view. . . .

We hold therefore that under the circumstances of this case where plaintiffs have paid two separate premiums providing each vehicle with uninsured-motorist coverage, they are entitled to recover under the uninsured-motorist provisions of the policy sums found legally recoverable up to the aggregate sum of the motor vehicles so insured. *Accord, Kemp v. Allstate Insurance Co.*, 601 P.2d 20, 24 (Mont. 1979). We are careful to limit our holding on this issue to cases factually similar to the one at bar, for we foresee and rue the day when our reasoning may be twisted to achieve an absurd result. For example, what is the result to be if a plaintiff was injured while riding in an automobile which was insured as only one of a fleet of cars?[a] We defer decision on this and related issues until a case with the appropriate factual setting presents itself for review.[7]

.   .   .

Accordingly, the defendant's appeal is denied and dismissed. The judgment appealed from is affirmed, and the case is remanded to the Superior Court.

NOTES

(1) *Question*. Does the court's reasoning make a blend of the intra-and inter-stacking problems.?

(2) *Ambiguity Illustrated; and an Antidote*. The court cited an Indiana case as an example of the "ambiguity theory": Jeffries v. Stewart, 309 N.E.2d 448 (Ind.App. 1974). The policy providing Jon Jeffries with UM coverage applied to three Ford vehicles. He made a claim for $30,000 under that coverage, although if the policy had covered only one vehicle his recovery would have been limited to $10,000. His

a. See Janet Boeth Jones, Annot., "Combining or 'stacking' uninsured motorist coverages provided in fleet policy," 25 A.L.R.4th 896 (2006).

7. In these circumstances even in those jurisdictions where intra-policy stacking for two or three vehicles is allowed, courts have uniformly denied such an extension of the stacking theory. *See, e.g. Holloway v. Nationwide Mutual Insurance Co.*, 376 So. 2d 690 (Ala. 1979); *Ohio Casualty Insurance Co. v. Stanfield*, 581 S.W.2d 555 (Ky. 1979); *Linderer v. Royal Globe Insurance Co.*, 597 S.W.2d 656 (Mo. App. 1980); *Continental Casualty Co. v. Darch*, 620 P.2d 1005 (Wash.App. 1980).

claim was sustained by reason, in part, of a separability clause in the policy: "When two or more automobiles are insured hereunder, the terms of this policy shall apply separately to each...." The court detected a conflict between that term and the otherwise-applicable limit of liability. The court relied also on what might be called a "triple-premiums" theory.

Additional language has been developed as an antidote to decisions like *Jeffries*. Titled "Limits of Liability", it begins "Regardless of the number of ... vehicles to which this policy applies...." Language like this has been held effective in Rhode Island, as elsewhere. Hoder v. United Servs. Auto. Ass'n, 637 A.2d 357 (1994).

(3) *"Other-insurance" Clauses*. The additional language quoted in the foregoing Note is addressed to (as the jargon goes) intra-policy stacking, both vertical and horizontal. Upon reading the two following other-insurance clauses set out here, in standard forms, consider what types of stacking they address.

a. *An "excess" clause*: With respect to bodily injury to an insured while occupying an automobile not owned by the named insured, the insurance under Uninsured Motorist shall apply only as excess insurance over any other similar insurance available to such insured and applicable to such automobile as primary insurance, and this insurance shall then apply only in the amount by which the limit of liability for this coverage exceeds the applicable limit of liability of such other insurance.

b. *A "pro-rata" clause*: Subject to the foregoing paragraph if the insured has other similar insurance available to him against a loss covered by this coverage, then the damages shall be deemed not to exceed the higher of the applicable limits of liability of this insurance and such other insurance, and the company shall not be liable under this coverage for a greater proportion of the applicable limit of liability of this coverage than such limit bears to the sum of the applicable limits of liability of this insurance and such other insurance.

Excess and pro-rata clauses commonly appear in combination, and are generally effective.

(4) *Pricing*. Ideally, perhaps, the presence of an other-insurance clause in an individual policy would affect its price. It does not. On the other hand, the addition of a vehicle to one already covered by a policy does not double the price of UM coverage; there is a discount for each addition. What bearing do these facts have on the "double premiums" theory?

(5) *"Escape" Clauses*. The term "escape clause" is "generally defined as a clause providing that there shall be no coverage where there is other valid and collectible insurance," Automobile Underwriters, Inc. v. Fireman's Fund Ins. Cos., 874 F.2d 188, 191 (3d Cir. 1989). It appears that Pennsylvania courts discountenance escape clauses "because they find 'it unacceptable for an insurance company to provide no coverage under a policy for which it received premiums.' " Ibid. Excess and pro-rata clauses are not so disfavored. A clause in a Fireman's Fund policy, issued to a car-repair firm, was characterized as an escape clause in the case cited (applying Pennsylvania law), because the clause excepted from its liability coverage customers of the firm while driving "loaners". So it was, even though the clause went on to confer excess coverage on a customer so far as needed to comply with a compulsory coverage statute. Compare clause (a) in Note 3 above. Does it provide for "escape"?

———

C. Vehicles As Insured Assets: Collision and Comprehensive Coverages

Typical insuring agreements about loss of and damage to vehicles open with one of these sentences (emphasis supplied):

We will pay for loss to an insured car caused by collision with another object or vehicle, or by upset.

We will pay for loss to an insured car *not* caused by collision [continuing as above].

Manifestly the latter, expressing "comprehensive" coverage, is designed to abut the former, expressing "collision" coverage. That purpose is further manifested in this sentence expressing collision coverage: "Under this coverage, we will not pay for loss covered under your comprehensive coverage." Another sentence, expressing comprehensive coverage, expands that coverage, and so curtails collision coverage: "Under this coverage, we will consider certain kinds of loss *not* to be caused by collision or upset. These are: breakage of glass, loss caused by fire, theft or larceny, ... loss inflicted by impact with a missile, falling object, bird or animal [and a number of other kinds of loss]."

Damage caused by an ordinary collision may be within comprehensive coverage, owing to a general understanding that collision loss is not *excluded* from that coverage, and that collision is rather an *excepted cause*. That understanding leads to the usual sort of problem when there are concurrent causes of loss, collision being only one. It can be imagined readily, for example, that a theft of a car is a cause contributing to its collision with another vehicle (perhaps a patrol car). In that event, whether or not the impact damage is within comprehensive coverage is an obvious question, especially pressing if the owner holds only that coverage. There would be coverage if the loss were ascribed to the theft as the efficient cause. The insurer might be expected to emphasize the language quoted above, "loss ... not caused by collision"; and the owner might be expected to emphasize the language "certain kinds ... theft". The principle of construction *contra proferentem* would support the claimant; and courts have allowed similar claims. That principle can be pushed too far, however. So it was when a claimant invoked a reference to impact with an animal in support of his claim for damage caused by a drunken pedestrian who had run into his car. McKay v. State Farm Mut. Auto. Ins. Co., 933 F.Supp. 635 (S.D.Tex. 1995).

One solution to a problem of concurrent causes is to apportion the loss as between the causes. That leads to a difference in result in the following cases of comprehensive coverage: (i) a fire in combustibles on board causes a driver to crash his car, and (ii) a crash damages a car and causes a fire which damages it further. The authorities indicate a recovery of the aggregate loss in case (i), but a recovery of only the fire damage in case (ii).

Stigma Damage

It is a well attested fact that, of two used vehicles offered for sale, identical except that one is known to have suffered significant damage, the other one will fetch the higher price, no matter how successfully the first has been repaired. That fact has led to reported litigation in most states about the amount payable by an insurer for vehicle damage. It is said that while the discount may be small in single instances, two large insurers have calculated that charging all such discounts to them would cost them more than $200 million in one state alone. T. Farrish, "Diminished Value" in Automobile Insurance ..., 12 Conn.Ins.L.J. 39, 40–51 (2005/06). According to Mr. Farrish: "The terms of the policy unambiguously entitled the insured to limit its liability to the cost of physical repairs, and the insured cannot credibly claim that this limitation frustrates any of her reasonable expectations." Id. at 75. The rulings overall are about evenly divided. But among a dozen states in which appellate courts have addressed the issue in this century, the rulings in ten favored insurers. One of those rulings is reported as follows.

Allgood v. Meridian Security Ins. Co.

Indiana Supreme Court, 2005.
836 N.E.2d 243.

Meridian Security Insurance responded to a claim made by Cynthia Allgood under collision coverage that she held. It refused to pay her for any diminution in value of her car attributable solely to its having suffered damage in a "crash". She brought a class action for damages and for a declaration that the coverage required payment for that diminution. The trial court dismissed Allgood's complaint, ruling that the diminution was not a payable "loss". On a first appeal the court (Hoffman, J.) disagreed and reversed. Thereafter the case was transferred to this court.

■ BOEHM, JUSTICE.

. . .

Liability for Diminution in Value

Allgood argues that Meridian's agreement to indemnify her for her loss was an agreement to make her whole. Otherwise stated, she contends that unless a repair will restore the fair market value of the vehicle to its pre-crash level, Meridian is obligated to pay for the decline in market value after the repair to fully indemnify her loss.

Allgood is correct that under common law tort doctrines, the measure of damages recoverable from a tortfeasor is generally adequate compensation for the loss sustained. She is also correct that under Indiana law that measure of damages includes diminution in value. But tort doctrines are not relevant here.... Because Allgood's contention presents an issue of interpretation of the policy, it presents a question of law....

Allgood's automobile policy provides the following "Coverage for Damage to [an Insured's] Auto":

> "We will pay for direct and accidental loss to 'your covered auto' or any 'non-owned auto,' including their equipment, minus any applicable deductible shown in the Declarations."

Allgood argues that this "Coverage" agreement by Meridian to pay for "direct and accidental loss" to her vehicle unambiguously includes compensation for diminution in value her car suffered when it was damaged even though it was repaired. Alternatively, she contends that she is entitled to reimbursement for her "loss," and points out that "loss" is not defined in the policy and the common dictionary definitions of the term are not helpful. She cites a variety of decisions from other jurisdictions interpreting policies similar or identical to hers. These decisions are divided as to whether coverage for "loss" includes diminution of value, so she argues the term is ambiguous and therefore must be construed in her favor.

Meridian responds that the policy includes a "Limit of Liability" provision, which reads:

> A.   Our limit of liability for loss will be the lesser of the:
>
> 1.   Actual cash value of the stolen or damaged property; or
>
> 2.   Amount necessary to repair or replace the property with other property of like kind and quality.
>
> B.   An adjustment for depreciation and physical condition will be made in determining actual cash value in the event of a total loss.
>
> C.   If a repair or replacement results in better than like kind or quality, we will not pay for the amount of the betterment.

Meridian argues that this provision is unambiguous and eliminates any claim for compensation for diminution in value.

The usual principles of policy construction apply here. . . .

Meridian contends that whatever "loss" means, the Limit of Liability provision gives it the choice to pay the insured either the actual cash value of the vehicle or the costs associated with repairing or replacing the vehicle with "property of like kind and quality." For a vehicle that is a total wreck, the replacement may be less than cost of repair. In this case, Meridian chose to repair Allgood's vehicle. Allgood does not dispute that her vehicle was adequately restored to its pre-accident level of performance and function. Allgood argues that Meridian could have written the contract to exclude coverage for diminution in value. She contends that without any explicit mention of diminished value the Limit of Liability is ambiguous. Thus, even if the Limit of Liability applies, she urges that the policy must be construed in her favor.

． ． ．

We agree with Judge Hoffman that the "Limit of Liability" is unambiguous and bars Allgood's claim for diminished value. Meridian has promised to repair the vehicle or to replace it with property of like kind and quality, but there is no promise to restore the value of the vehicle. Merriam Webster's Collegiate Dictionary 991 (10th ed. 1993), defines "repair" as "to restore by replacing a part or putting together what is torn or broken; to restore to a sound or healthy state." By this definition, and the common understanding of the term, repair means to restore something to its former condition, not necessarily to its former value. See [six cases cited].

We believe this contract makes clear that "like kind and quality" refers to "replace," not "repair" which encompasses the notion of restoring property to its former condition. Only to the extent parts are replaced does a "repair" entail "property of like kind or quality." To say one would repair an item with goods of like kind or quality is simply not correct English. An item of property (or a part of that item) is "replaced" with other property, but it is "repaired" with tools and labor. We therefore conclude that "like kind and quality" unambiguously refers only to replacement, not to repairs, and the verb "restore" appears nowhere in the policy. Similarly, ordinary English usage rebuts Allgood's claim that the policy's promise to provide the "amount necessary to repair or replace the property with other property of like kind and quality" includes an amount for diminution of value. Diminution in value can be compensated, but it cannot be "repaired" or "replaced." Given v. Commerce Ins. Co., 796 N.E.2d 1275, 1280 (Mass. 2003) ("damage caused by stigma, a form of damage that, by definition, defies remedy by way of 'repair' or 'replacement' ").

Finally, if the policy provided for compensation for diminution in value in addition to repair and replacement, the quoted language in the Limit of Liability provision would be meaningless. The policy provides that the insurer may choose to pay either the actual cash value of the vehicle or the amount necessary to repair, not some combination of the two. If the latter were the case, as the Supreme Court of Texas explained, "The insurer's obligation to compensate the loss would be cumulative—repair or replace *and* pay diminished value—in effect insuring the vehicles 'actual cash value' in every instance and undermining the insurer's right under the policy to choose a course of action." American Mfrs. Mut. Ins. Co. v. Schaefer, 124 S.W.3d 157, 159 (Tex. 2003) (emphasis in original); see also . . . Lupo v. Shelter Mut. Ins. Co., 70 S.W.3d 16 (Mo.App. 2002) at 23 ("To hold Shelter [Ins. Co.] liable for the automobile's diminished value would make it an insurer of the automobile's cash value in all instances and would render meaningless its expressed right under the 'limits of liability' provision to elect to repair or replace rather than to pay the actual cash value of the automobile at the time of the loss.").

We note that some jurisdictions have reached the opposite conclusion as to similar policy provisions.[2] [That fact, the court said, did not compel it to find an ambiguity in the policy.] We think the meaning of the contractu-

---

2. See, e.g., MFA Ins. Co. v. Citizens Nat'l Bank, 545 S.W.2d 70, 71 (Ark. 1976); Hyden v. Farmers Ins. Exch., 20 P.3d 1222, 1225 (Colo. Ct. App. 2000); State Farm Mut. Auto. Ins. Co. v. Mabry, 556 S.E.2d 114, 120–21 (Ga. 2001). Venable v. Import Volkswagen, Inc., 519 P.2d 667, 673 (Kan. 1974).

al terms at issue in Meridian's automobile policy is clear and we therefore find no ambiguity.

The trial court's grant of Meridian's motion to dismiss and its denial of Allgood's motion for partial summary judgment are affirmed.

Avery v. State Farm Mutual Automobile Ins. Co.

Illinois Supreme Court, 2005.
216 Ill.2d 100, 835 N.E.2d 801, *cert. denied*, 126 S.Ct. 1470 (2006).

Prompted by Michael Avery and others, the circuit (trial) court certified a large class of claimants—nearly nationwide—in an action against the insurer, "State Farm". One complaint was that it had broken its contracts with the claimants to make repairs, or to pay for repairs, of damage to their vehicles. Another was that State Farm had violated the Illinois Consumer Fraud Act. "Non–OEM crash parts" figured strongly in the case. It seems that some parts of a car can, when damaged, be replaced with items from a source other than the maker of those parts—with, that is, items not produced by the "original equipment manufacturer" (hence, "non-OEM"). Often these items, procured in the so-called *aftermarket*, are less expensive than OEM parts. Crash parts include grilles, hoods, doors, tailgates, and (if not chrome) bumpers. What State Farm had done was use non-OEM parts in making repairs and in calculating the cost of repairs. It was held liable for more than $1.186 billion. On a first review the judgment was reduced by $30 million. State Farm appealed.

■ CHIEF JUSTICE MCMORROW delivered the opinion of the court:

[The court ruled that, because the class members were in differing situations, the circuit court should not have certified the class. It ruled also that the judgment could not be sustained with reference to any subclass. More than one possible subclass had to be considered, for State Farm's undertakings to the claimants had taken different forms. One was "to restore ... vehicles to their pre-loss condition using parts of *like kind and quality*." A second spoke of parts "sufficient to restore the vehicle to its pre-loss condition", and continued: "You agree with us that *such parts may include* either parts furnished by the vehicle's manufacturer or *parts from other sources* including non-original equipment manufacturers." (Emphasis by the editors.) The court ruled that the holders of these two insuring agreements did not belong in the same class, as plaintiffs, and showed a nice sense of understatement in doing so: "In our view, these two policy forms are *not* the same." The court mentioned also another variation, describing it in a passage set out here in the footnote.*

---

* The putative class also includes State Farm insureds with policies that contain *neither* the "like kind and quality" *nor* the "pre-loss condition" promise. State Farm's Massachusetts policies, for example, simply promise to pay "the actual cash value" of "parts at the time of the collision." The same is true of most of State Farm's "assigned risk" policies, which are used in the "residual market" of high-risk consumers that insurers are re-

[The court ruled that State Farm's use of non-OEM crash parts could not amount to a breach of a policy containing the "you agree" language, or of a policy in the form described in the footnote. Then it proceeded to consider the phrase "parts of like kind and quality", appearing in policies in the first form mentioned above. A class of plaintiffs holding policies in that form could not be certified, the court ruled, owing to a gap in the record. Having said that, the court went on to say, nevertheless, that State Farm had not broken its "like kind and quality" promises. Of the court's lengthy opinion, what appears next is only a part of its explanation of that conclusion.]

. . . Plaintiffs' contention throughout this case has been that the non-OEM parts that were at issue were categorically inferior to their OEM counterparts. . . .

In our view, there are several difficulties with this theory. . . . If the purpose of State Farm's promise "to repair or replace the property or part with *like kind and quality*" (emphasis added) were to require the specification of OEM parts, then there is no reason why the indirect phrasing "like kind and quality" would have been used. The provision could simply have promised that OEM parts would be specified. Implicit in the phrase "like kind and quality" is the likeness or similarity of *one thing* to *another*. Common sense indicates that an item that is of "like kind and quality" to another is not that very item, but rather is something of "like kind and quality" to it.

Also contradicting the position that "like kind and quality" means OEM parts is the contract language *accompanying* the "like kind and quality" promise. In the "like kind and quality" provision as set forth above, the sentence immediately following the "like kind and quality" promise states: "If the repair or replacement results in *better than like kind and quality* [emphasis added], *you* must pay for the amount of the betterment [emphasis in original]. . . ." This policy language . . . presumes a standard of quality that is "better than like kind and quality." However, under plaintiffs' reasoning, there is nothing better than "like kind and quality."

. . . According to plaintiffs, *all* the non-OEM parts at issue in this case are categorically inferior to OEM parts. This means, of necessity, that OEM parts represent the highest possible standard of quality. In addition, according to plaintiffs, because non-OEM parts are categorically inferior to OEM parts, the "like kind and quality" promise can only be met by specifying OEM parts. Thus, because OEM parts are the best possible parts, and because the "like kind and quality" promise means OEM parts, plaintiffs also necessarily take the position that the term "like kind and quality" refers to the highest possible standard of quality.

quired to cover. Just as with the Massachusetts policies, the majority of the "assigned risk" policies contain neither the "like kind and quality" nor the "pre-loss condition" language. Instead, the "assigned risk" policies promise to pay an "amount necessary to repair or replace the property."

But this reasoning cannot be correct. State Farm's policy cannot be referring to OEM parts when it uses the term "like kind and quality" because the policy itself says that there is a standard of quality which is *better* than "like kind and quality" parts. Plaintiffs are clearly incorrect in equating "like kind and quality" with OEM parts.

.   .   .

State Farm maintains that "pre-loss condition" is what defines "like kind and quality," rather than the other way around. For State Farm it is irrelevant whether non-OEM parts are of like kind and quality to OEM parts. The determinative issue is whether the parts specified are sufficient to restore the vehicle to its preloss condition, *i.e.*, the condition of the vehicle shortly before the accident. Under this definition of "like kind and quality," the specification of non-OEM parts would not necessarily breach the "like kind and quality" promise.

We agree with State Farm. . . . We therefore conclude that the specification of non-OEM parts would not necessarily constitute a breach of the "like kind and quality" promise. Thus, we cannot affirm the jury's breach of contract verdict with respect to a subclass consisting of policyholders insured under this provision.

[Justice Freeman dissented in part. He began his lengthy opinion as follows: "I agree with my colleagues with respect to some, but not all, of the issues raised in this appeal. Apart from my disagreement on these legal matters, I am troubled by the tone and tenor of today's opinion."]

NOTES

(1) *The Saddest Words* . . . A hasty reader might suppose that the plaintiffs could not have fared worse. At least in principle, however, the unnamed plaintiffs holding the "like kind and quality" promise might have. If that subclass of plaintiffs had been certifiable, their claims would have been foreclosed by the court's construction of that promise. Their claims were not foreclosed by a decision on the issue of certification. The court denied certification of the subclass because the record did not contain a policy in the "like kind and quality" form that was held by any of the *named* plaintiffs. A class cannot be certified, the court said, unless one of the named plaintiffs has a cause of action.

(2) *State Farm's Friends.* Four *amicus* briefs were filed on behalf of the plaintiffs, including two by associations of trial lawyers. But those filed on behalf of State Farm were more numerous, and included these *amici*: the United States and Illinois Chambers of Commerce, the General Motors Corporation, three state departments of insurance, the National Conference of Insurance Legislators, and the National Association of Insurance Commissioners. Given support like that, State Farm might have hoped to win back in the Illinois legislature any ground it lost in the courts.

(3) *Consumer Fraud.* The circuit court had entered judgments against State Farm based on violations of the Illinois Consumer Fraud Act, 815 ILCS 505/1 *et seq.* As to that the plaintiffs' claim, as refined, depended chiefly on references to "quality replacement parts" in newspaper and magazine articles attributed to State Farm, and in estimates and brochures provided to persons making damage claims. The high court reversed those judgments. The reversal resulted in part from a

provision of the Act that it does not apply to practices permitted by another Illinois statute. The decisive statute was Section 155.29 of the Illinois Insurance Code. One purpose of that section is "to regulate the use of aftermarket crash parts by requiring disclosure when any use of an aftermarket non-original equipment manufacturer's crash part is proposed". It appeared that State Farm had made the required disclosure in estimates it had provided to its customers.

Does it follow, from the statutory requirement of disclosure about non-OEM crash parts, and State Farm's compliance with it, that State Farm could not have broken a promise expressing collision coverage?

———

CHAPTER 10

LIFE INSURANCE

A. INSURABLE INTERESTS; CONSENT TO BE INSURED

This part states first a number of general rules on these subjects, and describes a number of exceptions to them. Throughout the chapter, a person whose life is insured is sometimes indicated as the CQV, the acronym for *cestui que vie* (one who lives); that shorthand is convenient and is in common use.

Five rules having general acceptance are as follows; others are stated below. With each of the five a brief statutory text appears, one that expresses that rule or supports it in a general way.

(A) *A person may effect insurance on his or her own life for the benefit of anyone.*

> Any person of lawful age may on his own initiative procure or effect a contract of insurance upon his own person for the benefit of any person, firm, association or corporation.[1]

(B) *A contract of insurance on a person's life is not enforceable unless, at or before the time of contracting, that person has consented to its making.*

> [N]o contract of insurance upon the person ... shall be made or effectuated [subject to two stated exceptions] unless at or before the making of such contract the person insured, being of lawful age or competent to contract therefor, applies for or consents in writing to the making of the contract...."[2]

(C) *An entity—person or firm—can effect insurance on the life of a different person only if it has an insurable interest in the life of that person.*

> If the insured has no insurable interest, the contract is void.[3]

(D) *To have an insurable interest in a life is to have an interest in the continuance of that life. One has an insurable interest in the life of anyone (i) to whom he or she is nearly related by blood or marriage, and (ii) on whom he or she is financially dependent.*

> [In this section] The term, "insurable interest" means:

---

1. New York Ins. Law § 3205(b)(1).

2. New York Ins. Law § 3205(c), concerning individual policies of life insurance.

3. Cal. Ins.Code § 280.

(a) in the case of persons closely related by blood or by law, a substantial interest engendered by love and affection;

(b) in the case of other persons, a lawful and substantial economic interest in the continued life, health or bodily safety of the person insured, as distinguished from an interest which would arise only by, or would be enhanced in value by, the death, disablement or injury of the insured.[4]

(E) *A valid policy is not avoided by the cessation of an insurable interest, unless so provided by the policy.*

No person shall procure or cause to be procured ... any contract of insurance upon the person of another unless the benefits under such contract are payable to the person insured or his personal representatives, or to a person having, at the time when such contract is made, an insurable interest in the person insured.[5]

Versions of rules (C) and (D) appear in the opinion presented next.

Grigsby v. Russell

United States Supreme Court, 1911.
222 U.S. 149, 32 S.Ct. 58, 56 L.Ed. 133.

■ MR. JUSTICE HOLMES delivered the opinion of the court.

This is a bill of interpleader brought by an insurance company to determine whether a policy of insurance issued to John C. Burchard, now deceased, upon his life, shall be paid to his administrators or to an assignee, the company having turned the amount into court. The material facts are that after he had paid two premiums and a third was overdue, Burchard, being in want and needing money for a surgical operation, asked Dr. Grigsby to buy the policy and sold it to him in consideration of one hundred dollars and Grigsby's undertaking to pay the premiums due or to become due; and that Grigsby had no interest in the life of the assured. The Circuit Court of Appeals in deference to some intimations of this court held the assignment valid only to the extent of the money actually given for it and the premiums subsequently paid. 168 Fed. Rep. 577. [In that opinion the court said that the validity of the assignment depended on whether or not it was "contrary to principles of public policy."]

Of course the ground suggested for denying the validity of an assignment to a person having no interest in the life insured is the public policy that refuses to allow insurance to be taken out by such persons in the first place. A contract of insurance upon a life in which the insured has no interest is a pure wager that gives the insured a sinister counter interest in having the life come to an end. And although that counter interest always exists, as early was emphasized for England in the famous case of Wainewright (Janus Weathercock), the chance that in some cases it may prove a

---

4. New York Ins. Code § 3205(a)(1).   **5.** New York Ins. Code § 3205(b)(2).

sufficient motive for crime is greatly enhanced if the whole world of the unscrupulous are free to bet on what life they choose. The very meaning of an insurable interest is an interest in having the life continue and so one that is opposed to crime. And, what perhaps is more important, the existence of such an interest makes a roughly selected class of persons who by their general relations with the person whose life is insured are less likely than criminals at large to attempt to compass his death.

But when the question arises upon an assignment it is assumed that the objection to the insurance as a wager is out of the case. In the present instance the policy was perfectly good. There was a faint suggestion in argument that it had become void by the failure of Burchard to pay the third premium *ad diem*, and that when Grigsby paid he was making a new contract. But a condition in a policy that it shall be void if premiums are not paid when due, means only that it shall be voidable at the option of the company. Knickerbocker Life Insurance Company v. Norton, 96 U.S. 234; Oakes v. Manufacturers' Fire & Marine Ins. Co., 135 Massachusetts, 248. The company waived the breach, if there was one, and the original contract with Burchard remained on foot. No question as to the character of that contract is before us. It has been performed and the money is in court. But this being so, not only does the objection to wagers disappear, but also the principle of public policy referred to, at least in its most convincing form. The danger that might arise from a general license to all to insure whom they like does not exist. Obviously it is a very different thing from granting such a general license, to allow the holder of a valid insurance upon his own life to transfer it to one whom he, the party most concerned, is not afraid to trust. The law has no universal cynic fear of the temptation opened by a pecuniary benefit accruing upon a death. It shows no prejudice against remainders after life estates, even by the rule in Shelley's Case.[a] Indeed, the ground of the objection to life insurance without interest in the earlier English cases was not the temptation to murder but the fact that such wagers came to be regarded as a mischievous kind of gaming. St. 14 George III, c. 48.

On the other hand, life insurance has become in our days one of the best recognized forms of investment and self-compelled saving. So far as reasonable safety permits, it is desirable to give to life policies the ordinary characteristics of property. This is recognized by the [onetime] Bankruptcy Law, § 70, which provides that unless the cash surrender value of a policy like the one before us is secured to the trustee within thirty days after it has been stated the policy shall pass to the trustee as assets. Of course the trustee may have no interest in the bankrupt's life. To deny the right to sell except to persons having such an interest is to diminish appreciably the value of the contract in the owner's hands. The collateral difficulty that arose from regarding life insurance as a contract of indemnity only, Godsall

---

a. "Rule ... A principle of the common law that where the ancestor takes a freehold, and by the same conveyance, deed, or devise, it is limited, either mediately or immediately, to his heirs, the word 'heirs' is a word of limitation, not of purchase, and he is thereby vested with the fee simple title. Abolished or modified by various state statutes." The Law Dictionary, © 2002 Anderson Publishing Co.

v. Boldero, 9 East, 72, long has disappeared. Phoenix Mutual Life Ins. Co. v. Bailey, 13 Wall. 616. And cases in which a person having an interest lends himself to one without any as a cloak to what is in its inception a wager have no similarity to those where an honest contract is sold in good faith.

Coming to the authorities in this court, it is true that there are intimations in favor of the result come to by the Circuit Court of Appeals. But the case in which the strongest of them occur was one of the type just referred to, the policy having been taken out for the purpose of allowing a stranger association to pay the premiums and receive the greater part of the benefit, and having been assigned to it at once. Warnock v. Davis, 104 U.S. 775. [What Justice Holmes called an "intimation" was this statement in *Warnock* (p. 778): "The assignment of a policy to a party not having an insurable interest is as objectionable as the taking out of a policy in his name."] On the other hand it has been decided that a valid policy is not avoided by the cessation of the insurable interest, even as against the insurer, unless so provided by the policy itself. Connecticut Mutual Life Ins. Co. v. Schaefer, 94 U.S. 457. And expressions more or less in favor of the doctrine that we adopt are to be found also in [two cases cited]. It is enough to say that while the court below might hesitate to decide against the language of Warnock v. Davis, there has been no decision that precludes us from exercising our own judgment upon this much debated point. It is at least satisfactory to learn from the decision below that in Tennessee, where this assignment was made, although there has been much division of opinion, the Supreme Court of that State came to the conclusion that we adopt, in an unreported case, Lewis v. Edwards, December 14, 1903. The law in England and the preponderance of decisions in our state courts are on the same side.

Some reference was made to a clause in the policy that "any claim against the company arising under any assignment of the policy shall be subject to proof of interest." But it rightly was assumed below that if there was no rule of law to that effect and the company saw fit to pay, the clause did not diminish the rights of Grigsby as against the administrators of Burchard's estate.

Decree reversed.

NOTES

(1) *The* Erie *Earthquake*. "At least satisfactory", Justice Holmes said, to learn that the Court's view was aligned with that of the Tennessee Supreme Court. In the Sixth Circuit the court had said that the question was "obviously one to be determined by the general law". It was under no obligation, the court said, to follow the decisions of the Tennessee Supreme Court, citing Section 34 of the Judiciary Act of 1789 and Swift v. Tyson, 16 Pet. 1 (1842). That ceased to be the case in 1938, upon the decision in Erie R. Co. v. Tompkins, 304 U.S. 64. Hence, if the same situation were to recur today, a federal court (including the Supreme Court) would have to defer to the view of the Tennessee court—assuming that the state where the case arose would apply Tennessee law to the issue. Holmes's wry phrase, "at

least satisfactory", may be taken as a hint that the *Erie* earthquake was in the offing.

Before *Grigsby* reached the Supreme Court, the author of the opinion below, Judge Lurton, had become Justice Lurton of that Court. He took no part in the decision there.

It is at least amusing to notice that, ten years after the decision in *Erie*, the Supreme Court of Tennessee relied on Holmes's perception of Tennessee law to support an assignment to a woman having no insurable interest in the life of the CQV. Hammers v. Prudential Life Ins. Co., 216 S.W.2d 703 (1948). Despite what Holmes said, in point of fact Judge Lurton had not examined Tennessee law on the point. But see the following Note.

(2) *Choice of Law.* Owing to *Erie*, questions about what state's law applies is more important than it was before. On that subject Judge Lurton pointed out the following facts. Burchard was a resident of Tennessee, and applied for the policy there. The insurer was the Penn Mutual Life Insurance Company, of Philadelphia. The contract was concluded there. It provided that Pennsylvania was the "place of contract". For that reason, the court said, it would be construed according to Pennsylvania law. "But the contract of assignment ... was made in Tennessee...." Hence, the court said, curiously, its validity was to be determined by Tennessee law. Holmes may have seen *Erie* on the horizon; but *Lurton*?

(3) *Hazards to Life.* "Obviously", Holmes said, it is one thing to license everyone to insure against anyone's death, and "quite a different thing ... to allow the holder of a valid insurance upon his own life to transfer it to one whom he, the party most concerned, is not afraid to trust." Compare this observation: "The want of insurable interest is just as absolute where it has ceased as where it never existed, and the inducement to destroy the life insured, for gain, is just as strong in the one case as in the other." Cheeves v. Anders, 28 S.W. 274, 276 (Tex. 1894).[1] Consistent? Well, of course the cessation of an insurable interest is, with some frequency, associated with acrimony; often that is the case in the dissolution of a marriage or a partnership.

PROBLEM

At the end of the 4th paragraph of the *Grigsby* opinion, Holmes mentioned cases in which a person having an insurable interest "lends himself [to a person having none] as a cloak to ... a wager". If you were advising persons like these, how would you suggest that they set up the subterfuge? See Warnock v. Davis; McRae v. Warmack, 135 S.W. 807 (Ark. 1911); Bromley's Adm'r v. Washington Life Ins. Co., 92 S.W. 17 (Ky. 1906).

Creditors' Rights

One further rule about insurable interests, and an exception to another, relate in particular to insurance bought by a creditor on the life of a debtor.

1. *Cheeves* is not current Texas law. A provision of Subchapter B of the Texas Insurance Code is at odds with *Cheeves*. With respect to the life of "an individual who is insured" under a policy, § 1103.053 vests, as a general rule, an insurable interest in an entity to which the policy is transferred or assigned "in accordance with this subchapter". The subchapter permits a policy, or an interest in it, to be assigned by an "individual of legal age who is insured under [the policy]" only in writing, but with few other restrictions. Section 1103.055. The subchapter applies to policies issued by legal reserve and mutual assessment life-insurance companies.

Rule (F). *A creditor has an insurable interest in the life of a person indebted to the creditor.*

Rule (G). *The issuer of a life policy that is enforceable and has matured must pay the amount of the stated death benefit to a beneficiary even if it can be shown that the extent of the beneficiary's interest in the life of the CQV is a lesser and measurable amount.* For example, if a man has bought insurance on his life, payable to his wife, it is not open to the insurer to limit its liability by showing that, absent the insurance, the loss caused to his widow by his death is only a tenth of the face amount of the policy, or indeed that she gained by his death.

Exception: A creditor who, in that capacity, buys insurance on the life of a debtor is limited by the law of some states to recovery of an amount keyed to the amount of debt outstanding when the debtor dies. This restriction is illustrated by a case in which the CQV was a motorcyclist.

The Danger of Motorcycling

In July of 1986 Kevin Breton, driving his motorcycle, collided with a car and later died of his injuries. He had bought the motorcycle in June from Manuel Jimenez, his employer, with whose family he lived. The sale price was $5,500, payable in installments. The two men had discussed the dangers of motorcycling. (In this they were prescient. A contributing cause of the collision may have been the want of a brake on the front wheel of the cycle.) They discussed also how Jimenez would be paid if Breton were to be injured or killed. The upshot was that they arranged insurance on Breton's life, in favor of Jimenez, in the amount of $160,000, and "double indemnity" in the event of accidental death. Jimenez paid the first premium.

The insurer (actually a successor firm) refused to pay the full benefits of the policy, and paid less than $6,000. That, it said, was the extent of Jimenez's insurable interest in Breton's life. The major part of that was the amount of the unpaid purchase price of the motorcycle. A minor part was the amount of the first premium, $101.34. Jimenez brought an action against the insurer for breach of contract. The trial court entered judgment for Jimenez in the amount of $320,000, less what the insurer had paid. On appeal, *held*: Reversed. The extent of Jimenez's insurable interest was, the court said, the amount of the debt, plus the refund of the initial premium, plus interest on those two amounts, set at 7%—just what the insurer had paid. Jimenez v. Protective Life Ins. Co., 10 Cal.Rptr.2d 326 (Cal.App. 1992).

The trial court had received worrisome evidence about the circumstances in which the policy was bought. The insurer's agent made this statement:

> Jimenez & Breton walked into office and wanted to buy insurance, that is Jimenez wanted to purchase insurance on Breton with Jimenez as beneficiary. I told them that I could not do that as Jimenez had no insurable interest in Breton. It came up in subsequent conversation that Breton owed Jimenez money. I told them that the loan gave

Jimenez the insurable interest, so I quoted 100,000 life, the amount that was requested. The rate was less than $100 per quarter, and Jimenez wanted to pay that amount, so they settled on 160,000 making the quarterly payment close to $100. I wrote it up, I had not known either of these two people before this, they had just walked in to my office. The amount of the debt was never discussed. I never did determine why they came in to the office for the insurance in the first place.

The home office had required a second application, and had raised a question about Jimenez's insurable interest.

NOTE

The Danger of Being a CQV. It behooves an insurer to make inquiry, before issuing a policy of life insurance, about the applicant's interest in the life of the proposed CQV. A reason is indicated by Wren v. New York Life Ins. Co., 59 F.R.D. 484 (N.D.Ga. 1973). The suitor, Judith Wren, had bought insurance on the life of Roger Wren, identifying herself as his former wife. The policy named her as the primary beneficiary, and Roger's ex-mother-in-law as the contingent beneficiary. When, after Roger died, Judith brought an action on the policy, his widow, Elizabeth intervened. She sought to recover in tort against New York Life, alleging that Judith had killed Roger.

Insurance murders have been alleged, or found, in a distressing number of reported cases. They afford considerable support for the tort of facilitating homicide by negligence in the issuance of insurance. On that subject see p. 581 below.

————

Creditors as Buyers of Insurance (The Calculating Creditor)

Jimenez's case represents a rejection of "Rule (G)"—what might be called the *all-or-nothing* rule. Jimenez could have recovered nothing if he had had no insurable interest in Breton's life. A long-enduring debate attends the application of the all-or-nothing rule to cases like *Jimenez*. The debate was especially intense late in the 19th century, as is shown here by opposing decisions on the subject.

The cost to a creditor of insuring a debtor's life is a factor in the debate. A person thinking of buying insurance on the life of a debtor, for the purpose of assuring payment, would have to take that cost into account—the *expected* cost, that is. On consulting a mortality table for the "life expectancy" of a 25–year–old debtor, the creditor might find it prudent to insure for much more than the debt owed. The creditor might well wish to insure to an amount including, in addition to that amount, the interest on it, as promised, for some years to come, the sum of the periodic premiums for those years, and some amount of interest on the latter amount.

In a 19th-century case in the Pennsylvania Supreme Court, Chief Justice Paxson did a calculation like that, after the fact. The debtor, Andrew Bleistine, was a man of 42; insurance on his life had been assigned to his creditors, traders named Reinoehl and Meily. Using a mortality table,

Paxson concluded that the cost of insuring to the amount of the debt only would have left the traders with a loss if the debtor should live to the age 59, and a major one if the debtor should live, as was to be expected, to 68. The court's conclusion was that a creditor should be permitted to recover the full death benefit on a policy unless it is greatly disproportionate to the amount owed. Ulrich v. Reinoehl, 22 A. 862 (Pa. 1891) (policy for $3,000 securing debt of $110.02).

Not long after that, Presiding Justice Lumpkin, of Georgia, speaking for his court, called this reasoning fallacious ("With the utmost respect...."). "The man of forty-two is no more apt to live out his expectancy of twenty-six years than the man of seventy-five is to live out his expectancy of seven years. Life-insurance premiums are fixed relatively to the different ages and expectancies of the persons insured.... Some live longer and others shorter periods, but the company looks to the average, and on the average basis it must take in more than it pays out, or else ultimately fail. Clearly, therefore, in every instance of life-insurance there is a chance for the insured, or the person paying the premiums, to pay in more than the policy will bring back; and as a consequence, there can, under the doctrine announced in Pennsylvania, be no such thing as a wagering policy. The test that the amount of a policy taken out to secure a debt must not be out of proportion to the amount of the debt with added premiums and interest thereon will not stand scrutiny, for every one carrying the burden of keeping up a life policy may, whether a debt be thereby secured or not, suffer loss by paying out more than is finally received on the policy. In the case of a man who insured his life for the benefit of his wife and paid out in premiums more than the insurance company paid to her after his death, the loss would be the difference between the sum of the premiums with interest and the proceeds of the policy."

The court proceeded to state two hypothetical cases of insuring by a creditor, one to secure a small debt ($10), and the other to secure one of $25,000. The court calculated the creditor's losses, making certain assumptions. (One is that "the debtor (whether young or old) lived out his expectancy and died leaving no assets but the insurance money".) The conclusion was that the creditor's loss in the latter case would be greater than in the former by $24,990, plus interest. "There would be no difference in principle between the two cases. It is therefore to be regretted that the Pennsylvania court, while declaring that there should be 'a fixed rule' for determining when a creditor was, and when he was not, obtaining an 'excess of insurance,' did not succeed in evolving a more satisfactory one." Exchange Bank of Macon v. Loh, 31 S.E. 459, 463 (Ga. 1898).

The Georgia court's first premise was that "effecting insurance for the purpose of securing an indebtedness is a contract of indemnity, and nothing else." It concluded that a creditor's insurable interest in a debtor's life cannot exceed the amount of the secured indebtedness. The court allowed for a comprehensive understanding of *indebtedness*. But it said: "A creditor can not, however, rightfully appropriate the proceeds of a policy held by him as a collateral security to the repayment to himself of sums voluntarily paid by him for premiums for which the debtor was in no way liable and which could not lawfully be made a demand against his estate or its assets." The opinion bristles with rhetorical questions.[2]

Policy as Collateral for Debt

A necessitous owner of a life policy may well find it appealing to *borrow* on the policy, rather than to sell it as Burchard did in Grigsby v. Russell. An "ordinary" policy accumulates a substantial cash surrender value after a number of premiums have been paid, and insurers make much of that value available to policyholders in the form of policy loans, usually at a modest rate. (Analytically, a policy "loan" is a kind of advance payment of the death benefit.) Alternately, a policyholder may find a financier willing to take an assignment as security for a loan. The financier is not burdened with the necessity of making a public filing with respect to the transfer under Article 9 ("Secured Transactions") of the Uniform Commercial Code.[3]

Financing on a life policy may lead to a dispute, of course. So it did when a policyholder named Rison borrowed against a policy of term insurance on his life. He did so in buying merchandise on credit from T.W. Wilkerson & Co., apparently to start a business. After Rison died, a dispute arose over the death benefit between his wife and children on one hand and the Wilkerson firm on the other. For a time before Rison's death, the firm had paid the premiums. Mary Rison brought an action to recover from the firm, to which the proceeds had been paid. Each party claimed the entire amount.[4] Both positions were wrong, the court ruled. As to the firm: "the transfer was only made to secure the debt of the defendants, and they can retain no more of the fund than is sufficient [to pay the debt and] to reimburse the amount paid by them in annual premiums...." Rison v. T.W. Wilkerson & Co., 35 Tenn. 565, 570 (1856). The initial transaction was far different from one in which a creditor buys insurance for itself on the life of a debtor. That is so even though the Wilkerson firm seems to have prompted Rison to buy his policy, and even though the two kinds of transaction were conflated in the *Ulrich* and *Loh* opinions. The cap on collections imposed by the Tennessee court on the Wilkerson firm was entirely warranted, assuming that the court was right in saying that the transfer was made only to secure Rison's debt.

2. "Whenever a creditor undertakes to stipulate for more than the amount of his just demands, what distinguishes the transaction from a wagering contract, pure and simple, having for its object speculative gain? If he can lawfully take one dollar more than the amount of his debt, why can he not take any number of dollars within the limits of the policy? Where, and upon what principle, is the line to be drawn?"

3. Section 9–109(d):

This article does not apply to:

. . .

(8) a transfer of an interest in or an assignment of a claim under a policy of insurance, other than an assignment by or to a health-care provider of a health-care-insurance receivable and any subsequent assignment of the right to payment....

4. But it is reported that, for himself, as a partner, Wilkerson made a donation of his share to Rison's family.

Question: It is not obvious that the Wilkerson firm should have been reimbursed for the premiums it paid. Consider these possibilities about the assignment agreement: (i) Rison promised Wilkerson that he would keep the policy in force by paying the premiums as they came due; (ii) Wilkerson promised Rison that it would pay future premiums; and (iii) Nothing was said about paying those premiums. Which of these arrangements would best explain Wilkerson's entitlement to reimbursement for premiums it had paid?

(To speak again of *Grigsby v. Russell*: Why Burchard *sold* his policy to Dr. Grigsby, rather than using it as collateral, is not evident. The dates suggest that the then value of the policy was small: Burchard had bought it hardly more than two years before he sold it.)

NOTE

Exemption Laws. Life-insurance values are a popular subject of legislation exempting a debtor's assets from collection processes otherwise available to his or her creditors. See, for example, the sweeping sets of exemptions stated in the New York Insurance Law, § 3212 ("proceeds and avails"). These and like exemptions go beyond any reason, other than to stimulate purchases of insurance.

In Mrs. Rison's suit she relied on an exemption statute reading, in part: "[A]ny husband may effect a life insurance on his own life, and the same shall in all cases enure to the benefit of his widow and heirs ... without being in any manner subject to the debts of said husband...." As the court read the statute, it preferred a widow over a creditor only when her husband had not given security for the debt by assigning the policy to the creditor. "This method is often resorted to, as in this case, by men in slender circumstances, whose ability to pay is supposed to depend upon their personal exertions, and it cannot be supposed that the legislature intended to deprive poor men of this mode of obtaining credit, and thereby getting into business, and making a living for themselves and families." *Rison* at 569–70.

The New York exemption statute cited above is in general accord; according to subdivision (e)(1), "Every assignment or change of beneficiary or other transfer is valid, except in cases of transfer with actual intent to hinder, delay or defraud creditors, as defined by [Debtor–Creditor Law Art. 10]."

Statutes

Snippets of California and New York statutes on the subjects of consent and insurable interests appear above at pp. 545–46. Other parts of those statutes are as follows.

. . .

California

Section 10110. Insurable interest

Every person has an insurable interest in the life and health of:

(a) Himself.

(b) Any person on whom he depends wholly or in part for education or support.

(c) Any person under a legal obligation to him for the payment of money or respecting property or services, of which death or illness might delay or prevent the performance.

(d) Any person upon whose life any estate or interest vested in him depends.

New York

Section 3205. Insurable interest in the person; consent required; exceptions

(a) In this section:

(1) The term, "insurable interest" means:

[See pp. 545–46 above, "Rule (D)".]

(2) The term "contract of insurance upon the person" includes any policy of life insurance and any policy of accident and health insurance.

(3) The term "person insured" means the natural person, or persons, whose life, health or bodily safety is insured.

(b)

(1) Any person of lawful age may on his own initiative procure or effect a contract of insurance upon his own person for the benefit of any person, firm, association or corporation. Nothing herein shall be deemed to prohibit the immediate transfer or assignment of a contract so procured or effectuated.

(2) *[Prohibition on the procurement of a contract of insurance upon the person of another unless benefits properly payable; see p. 545 above, "Rule (E)".]*

(3) *[Authorization for certain charitable, educational, and religious corporations to procure, notwithstanding (1) and (2), a contract on a person's life, in which the corporation is the beneficiary]*

(4) If the beneficiary, assignee or other payee under any contract made in violation of this subsection receives from the insurer any benefits thereunder accruing upon the death, disablement or injury of the person insured, the person insured or his executor or administrator may maintain an action to recover such benefits from the person receiving them.

(c) *[Written consent, when required]*

. . .

NOTES

(1) *Naked Public Policy.* Judges have sometimes made remarks dismissive of rules about what constitute insurable interests. They draw, that is, directly on public policy, unmediated by the categories that figure in those rules, "family member", "creditor", "key employee", and the like. Remarks like these appear in some South Carolina opinions. In one of them a man had bought a small policy on the life of his mother. The State's high court made an orthodox remark in saying

that a son has an insurable interest in the life of his mother "from the mere fact of such relationship." To that it added, however, a statement that the court could not conceive, given the facts alleged, "that a policy of insurance taken out by a son on the life of his mother in the sum of $200 would expose her to dangers of any kind." Holloman v. Life Ins. Co. of Virginia, 7 S.E.2d 169, 171 (S.C. 1940). The suggestion is that the enforceability of the policy depended on the particulars of the case rather than on the category—parent/child—that figures in rules about insurable interests. (The court could have explained its decision, probably, without referring at all to the law of insurable interests.) A like opinion is that in Dixon v. Western Union Assurance Co., 164 S.E.2d 214 (S.C. 1968). There also the court affirmed the parent-child category; but it also observed that youthful U.S. military men in overseas service are not much endangered by having insurance placed on their lives by their parents at home. See also the opinion of Circuit Judge Eppes, set out in Ramey v. Carolina Life Ins. Co., 135 S.E.2d 362 (1964): "As a general rule, a wife has an insurable interest in the life of her husband.... This, however, is not invariably so."

The South Carolina legislature has not pronounced for or against the usual categories of insurable interests.

(2) *Qualified Complainants.* The Pioneer Foundry Company, which employed Jack Secor, bought insurance on his life and, upon his death, collected the proceeds: $50,000. Some time before his death Secor had ceased to work for the company. His widow and the administratrix of his estate, Florence Secor, brought an action against the company in which she sought to impose a constructive trust on the proceeds. The action failed. Secor v. Pioneer Foundry Co., 173 N.W.2d 780 (Mich. App. 1969). The court said that even if the insurer could have resisted paying, on the ground that Pioneer had no insurable interest in Secor's life at the time of his death, his widow was not qualified to raise that point.

The court went beyond the issue before it, saying that no one other than the issuer of a life policy can object that the beneficiary lacked an insurable interest. Id. at 612. Although the proposition was said to be well supported, it is plainly an over-generalization. It is contradicted, for example, by the case presented next. Legislation to the contrary is subdivision (b)(4) of the New York statute quoted just above.

The *Secor* court was unwilling to say that the insurer could have resisted paying anyone, owing to the change in circumstances between the issuance of the policy and Jack Secor's death. In that connection it quoted as follows from Grigsby v. Russell, above: "life insurance has become in our days one of the best recognized forms of investment and self-compelled saving. So far as reasonable safety permits, it is desirable to give to life policies the ordinary characteristics of property." See "Rule (E)", p. 546 above. The court left open the possibility—not an attractive one—that the insurer was at liberty to pay either Pioneer Foundry or Jack Secor's estate.

(3) *Secor and the Statutes.* To repeat a quotation (p. 545 above) of a California statute: "If the insured has no insurable interest, the contract is void." Compare that with the New York statute after that quotation: "No person ...", and especially with the phrase there "at the time when such contract is made". The "when made" phrase has an obvious bearing on the facts of Secor v. Pioneer Foundry. Is the California statute at odds with that, so as to prevent the enforcement of the policy on Jack Secor's life?

Introduction to *Mayo v. Wal–Mart Stores*

This case turned in part on statutes that have been amended and recodified. The opinion is representative, however, of widespread views concerning insurable interests. A current statute on the subject is Section 1131.703 of the Texas Insurance Code, set out in the footnote.[1]

Sims [*et al.* (including Mayo[2])] v. Wal–Mart Stores, Inc.[3]

United States Court of Appeals, 5th Cir., 2004.
354 F.3d 400.

■ E. GRADY JOLLY, CIRCUIT JUDGE:

Wal–Mart Stores, Inc. ("Wal–Mart") took out life insurance on its employees and made itself the beneficiary. This interlocutory appeal arises from a grant of partial summary judgment involving a dispute over death benefits from one of these company-owned life insurance ("COLI") policies. Douglas Sims' estate sued Wal–Mart on the ground that the COLI policy taken out in Sims' name violated the Texas insurable interest doctrine....

I

In 1993, Wal–Mart established a trust[a] to serve as the legal holder of life insurance policies insuring the lives of its employees and naming itself as beneficiary.... Wal–Mart acted in pursuit of tax benefits related to the deductibility of premium payments, and was only one of many similarly situated companies which took this course of action. After Congress and the IRS eliminated the tax advantages of Wal–Mart's COLI program, Wal–Mart unwound the otherwise unprofitable program, surrendering the last of its policies by 2000.

Wal–Mart's COLI policies insured the lives of all employees (also called "associates") with service time sufficient for enrollment in the Wal–Mart Associates' Health and Welfare Plan, unless those associates elected not to participate in a special death benefit program that Wal–Mart introduced in conjunction with the COLI program. Fewer than one percent of the 350,000 eligible employees opted out of the program, which was discontinued by early 1998. Wal–Mart's COLI program was intended to be "mortality neutral," such that the death benefits paid to Wal–Mart upon its associ-

---

1. *Insurance for Liabilities Related to Fringe Benefits*

(a) Notwithstanding any other law, an employer may insure the lives of the employer's officers, directors, employees, and retired employees under Section 1131.064 to and in an amount necessary to provide funds to offset liabilities related to fringe benefits.

(b) An employer shall submit evidence of the purpose of the policy to the commissioner.

(c) A policy issued for the purpose described by this section does not reduce any other life insurance benefits offered or provided by the employer.

2. The official style of the case is *Mayo v. Wal–Mart Stores, Inc.*

3. Other defendants were the Hartford Life Ins. Co., Wal–Mart Stores Inc. Corporation Grantor Trust, and Wachovia Bank of Georgis, N.A.

a. The trustee was Wachovia Bank.

ates' deaths would fund employee benefit plans and death expenses, or otherwise be repaid to the insurer as self-correcting "cost of insurance" adjustments.

Douglas Sims was a Wal–Mart associate from May 1987 until his death on December 1, 1998, and was insured under a COLI policy from December 21, 1993 until his death (though the special death benefit program had been discontinued prior to Sims' death). On June 28, 2001, after his estate discovered the existence of this policy, it sued Wal–Mart [in the district court for the Southern District of Texas], alleging a violation of the Texas insurable interest doctrine. The estate sought, in relevant part, a declaratory judgment of its rights under Sims' COLI policy, the imposition of a constructive trust on the policy benefits, and disgorgement of the money Wal–Mart unjustly received at some point in 1999.

[The sequence of certain significant dates was, then: Wal–Mart discontinued its COLI program early in 1998; Sims died on Dec. 1, 1998; Wal–Mart received the proceeds of the policy on Sims's life at some time in 1999; and it "unwound" its insuring program, surrendering all its policies by 2000.

[Wal–Mart moved for summary judgment. The district court denied this motion. Sims moved for partial summary judgment, seeking a declaration that Wal–Mart lacked an insurable interest in his life. Wal–Mart made a cross-motion for summary judgment on this issue alone. The district court granted Sims's motion. But Wal–Mart obtained leave to appeal the interlocutory orders, presenting the three issues stated in the paragraph that follows.]

II

This court reviews grants or denials of summary judgment de novo, applying the same legal standards as the district court.... The issues we will address are: 1) the choice of which state's law to apply; 2) an analysis of the Texas insurable interest doctrine as it applies to this case; and 3) the applicable statute of limitations. We take these up in order.

A

[The court decided that the trial judge was right in applying Texas law, rather than that of Georgia as favored by Wal–Mart. (The instrument establishing the trust called for the application of Georgia law. But that was of no moment, the court said, in that Sims was not a party to that instrument.) Guided by the law of the forum state, Texas, the court consulted several provisions of the Restatement, Second, of Conflict of Laws. These included Section 6—"the starting point for analysis", which "lists several general factors to be used by courts in making choice of law determinations...." One factor is the relevant policies of the forum.[b]] The

---

b. The full list, as found in § 6(2), is this:

    a) the needs of the interstate and international systems;

b) the relevant policies of the forum;

c) the relevant policies of other interested states and the relative interests of

district court thoroughly and conscientiously analyzed each § 6 factor as it applies to this case. We have little to add ..., only emphasizing that Sims' claim centers on an alleged violation of the Texas insurable interest doctrine (as it has evolved via common law and legislative guidance), and that Texas' [sic] interest in seeing its policy correctly applied far overwhelms any other consideration.

[So far as they might apply, the court thought, other Restatement provisions supported a reference to Texas law. Among the facts so indicating were these: "The parties 'reside' in Texas (Wal–Mart by place of business) and the employment relationship was also wholly in Texas."[c] The court gave weight to the "principle" of § 192, which speaks to the validity of life-insurance contracts. It did so even though the section applies in terms only to policies applied for, and issued to, *the insured*. The section points courts, in general, to the law of the domicile of that person. Sims did not take out the policy, of course. The court said: "We fail to see how the fact that Wal–Mart took it out militates against this principle."]

B

We now apply Texas' insurable interest doctrine. Wal–Mart contends that, even if Texas law applies, the district court erred in determining that its COLI policy violated the Texas insurable interest doctrine. The district court concluded that the policy was void because Wal–Mart lacks a sufficient financial interest in the lives of its rank-and-file employees.

For this diversity action, and because the Texas Supreme Court has not ruled on the insurable interest doctrine in the light of a half-century's legislative amendments, the district court was required to make an Erie-guess as to how that court would apply substantive state law. Erie R.R. Co. v. Tompkins, 304 U.S. 64 (1938); Transcontinental Gas Pipe Line Corp. v. Transportation Ins. Co., 953 F.2d 985, 988 (5th Cir.1992) ("It is the duty of the federal court to determine as best it can, what the highest court of the state would decide.").

[Wal–Mart moved for certification of that question to the Texas Supreme Court. This court said that the question was "not so complex or opaque as to justify certification." The court said that it would review the district court's "Erie-guess" *de novo*.]

Texas requires a person insuring the life of another to have an insurable interest in the insured person's life. Empire Life Ins. Co. of America v. Moody, 584 S.W.2d 855, 859 (Tex.1979); Drane v. Jefferson

---

those states in the determination of the particular issue;

d) the protection of justified expectations;

e) the basic policies underlying the particular field of law;

f) certainty, predictability, and uniformity of result; and

g) ease in determination and application of the law to be applied.

c. As for § 188, the court observed that it did not help much. It calls for an inquiry "directed at unearthing and upholding contracting parties' intent as to the governing law." That seemed inapposite to the court, given that Sims was not a party to the insurance contract, and that there was no dispute about the contractual undertakings.

Standard Life Ins. Co., 161 S.W.2d 1057, 1058–59 (Tex.1942). The state's common law insurable interest doctrine deems that "it is against the public policy of the State of Texas to allow anyone who has no insurable interest to be the owner of a policy of insurance upon the life of a human being." Griffin v. McCoach, 123 F.2d 550, 551 (5th Cir.1941). Consequently, insurance policies procured by those lacking a sufficient interest in the life of the insured are unenforceable. Going back to 1942, Texas courts have recognized three categories of individuals having an adequate interest: 1) close relatives; 2) creditors; and 3) those having an expectation of financial gain from the insured's continued life. *Drane*, 161 S.W.2d at 1058–59; Tamez v. Certain Underwriters at Lloyd's, London, 999 S.W.2d 12, 17–18 (Tex.App. 1998); Stillwagoner v. Travelers Ins. Co., 979 S.W.2d 354, 361 (Tex.App. 1998).

Wal–Mart argues that it has a reasonable expectation of pecuniary benefit in the continued lives of its employees sufficient to bring it within the last of the three categories described in *Drane*. Texas courts have held, however, that the state of employment alone does not give an employer an insurable interest. See, *e.g.*, *Stillwagoner*, 979 S.W.2d at 361 ("The mere existence of an employer/employee relationship is never sufficient to give the employer an insurable interest in the life of the employee.").

Wal–Mart contends that, in addition to the bare employer/employee relationship, it possesses an expectation of financial gain from the continued lives of its employees by virtue of the costs associated with the death of an employee, such as productivity losses, hiring and training a replacement, and payment of death benefits. These are costs that are associated with the loss of *any* employee, however, and, as Texas precedent clearly indicates, employers lack an insurable interest in ordinary employees. *E.g.*, id. at 362. Indeed, Texas courts have recently rejected similar arguments based on the costs flowing from an employee's death.[d] And, as Sims ripostes, Wal–Mart does not claim that Sims was of any special importance to the company, much less that Wal–Mart's "success or failure was dependent upon [the insured employee]." *Stillwagoner*, 979 S.W.2d at 362–63.

Given that courts will uphold the insurable interest doctrine in the absence of contrary legislation, Wal–Mart argues that just such legislative pronouncements have expanded the definition of insurable interest after *Drane*. A review of this legislation shows, however, that while the Texas Legislature has crafted certain addenda to the insurable interest doctrine, none of these modifications are relevant to the present case.

[The court referred to an enactment that allows a business to be named as the beneficiary in a policy insuring the lives of its officers, stockholders, and partners. It referred also to an enactment by which

d. [Court's n. 4] See *Tamez*, 999 S.W.2d at 18–19 ("An employer does not have a pecuniary interest in the continued life of its employee, unless that employee is crucial to the operation of the business."); *Stillwagoner*, 979 S.W.2d at 361–62 ("Even in the absence of evidence we may assume that [decedent's] death forced some readjustments which normally accompany the death of an employee. But an insurable interest does not result from the cessation of ordinary service.").

adults can consent in writing to another party's application for, or the purchase of, insurance on his or her life.]

Finally, in 1989, the Legislature enacted a provision that, under certain circumstances, allows an employer to obtain insurance on the lives of its employees to provide funds to offset fringe-benefit-related liabilities.[e] The COLI policy at issue does not meet the requirements of the 1989 statute, however, and Wal–Mart does not contend that it does (Wal–Mart merely cites the statute as an example of the Legislature's action in this area). Thus, to the extent that this provision expanded insurable interests, it did so in a way that does not affect the disposition of this case.

None of these legislative enactments—which were thoroughly briefed by the parties and analyzed by the district court—apply [sic] to the facts of this case, and we have found no other ones that do. . . .

. . .

It is clear that *Drane* and its progeny have held fast to the common law insurable interest doctrine, and the Texas Legislature's enactments altering that well-established doctrine have been slow and careful. While the statutory provisions analyzed *supra* demonstrate an ever-broadening approach to insurable interests, there is no indication that the Texas Supreme Court would create other exceptions without explicit statutory authorization. And, as the district court concisely put it, it is not the role of federal courts sitting in diversity to ignore longstanding and consistently applied Texas legal authorities. We decline to either contradict state court precedent or expand upon the express language of legislative enactments.

We therefore reject Wal–Mart's challenge to the Texas insurable interest doctrine, and find that its COLI policy on the life of Douglas Sims violated Texas law.[f] The district court's ruling on this issue is *Affirmed*.

C

Now that we have found that Sims has presented a valid claim under Texas law as properly applied, we must look at whether such a claim is barred by the relevant statute of limitations.

[The court concluded that the district court did not err in withholding summary judgment for Wal–Mart on this issue. Some particulars are stated in the footnote.[g]]

---

e. Effective June 1, 2003, the relevant provision became Tex. Ins. Code § 1131.703 (Vernon 2003) [See fn.1 above.]

f. [Court's n. 10] In such a case, once the named beneficiary (the one lacking an insurable interest) is paid, Texas law applies the equitable remedy of constructive trust to enable recovery by the wronged party. *De-Leon*, 259 F.3d at 350–51; Cheeves v. Anders, 28 S.W. 274, 275–76 (Tex.1894); *Tamez*, 999 S.W.2d at 15–16 and n.1; *Stillwagoner*, 979 S.W.2d at 360. In this manner—and if there is no procedural bar such as the statute of

limitations discussed *infra*—the lawful beneficiary, Sims, recovers the proceeds unlawfully procured by Wal–Mart.

g. The district court had mistakenly applied a four-year period of limitations. In so ruling, the court reasoned that Sims had stated a single "underlying cause of action", although it was one that could be stated in two ways: "Sims claims that Wal–Mart engaged in either unjust enrichment or conversion stemming from the insurable interest violation. However labeled, that cause of ac-

III

For the foregoing reasons, Wal–Mart's motion to certify to the Texas Supreme Court is *Denied*, the rulings of the district court are *Affirmed*, and this case is *Remanded* for proceedings not inconsistent with this opinion.

Motion to certify denied; Affirmed and remanded.

B.   Rights of Beneficiaries and Assignees

Simonds v. Simonds

New York Court of Appeals, 1978.
45 N.Y.2d 233, 380 N.E.2d 189.

When Frederick Simonds died he was survived by his former wife, Mary, and Reva, his second wife. After his divorce from Mary, three policies of insurance on his life had been issued, including two providing for death benefits of more than $50,000 payable, and paid, to Reva. Mary brought an action against Reva, asking that a constructive trust be imposed, to the extent of $7,000, on those policy proceeds.

When Frederick and Mary were divorced the decree incorporated a separation agreement between them. It recited that policies on his life were in effect, in the sum of $21,000. It required Frederick to keep them in force. "Husband further agrees that the Wife [Mary] shall be the beneficiary of said policies in an amount not less than $7,000...." Apparently these policies were canceled, or permitted to lapse. "It does not appear from the record why, how, or when this happened...." Frederick's estate was insolvent.

The trial court imposed a constructive trust on the proceeds in the hands of Reva. That decision was affirmed on a first appeal, and Reva appealed again.

■ BREITEL, CHIEF JUSTICE.

.   .   .

There is no question that decedent breached his obligation to maintain life insurance with his first wife as beneficiary. Consequently, the first wife would of course be entitled to maintain an action for breach against the estate. The estate's insolvency, however, would make such an action fruitless. Thus, the controversy revolves around plaintiff's right, in equity, to recover $7,000 of the insurance proceeds.

[The court discussed the origins of equity jurisdiction, and its "principles of right, justice, and morality".]

---

tion was subject to a two-year period of limitations."

In order to invoke this period, however, Wal–Mart should have produced evidence that it had received the policy proceeds more than two years before the action was brought. And this it had not done. "In short, Wal–Mart has failed to carry its burden of proof."

It is agreed that the purpose of the constructive trust is prevention of unjust enrichment. . . .

Unjust enrichment, however, does not require the performance of any wrongful act by the one enriched. . . . Innocent parties may frequently be unjustly enriched. What is required, generally, is that a party hold property "under such circumstances that in equity and good conscience he ought not to retain it" (Miller v. Schloss, 218 N.Y. 400, 407. . . .). A bona fide purchaser of property upon which a constructive trust would otherwise be imposed takes free of the constructive trust, but a gratuitous donee, however innocent, does not. . . .

[Mary had made a claim against a daughter of Frederick and Reva, based on her receipt of the proceeds of a third policy. The trial court had dismissed that claim and Mary did not appeal. Her failure to appeal did not, this court said, limit her remedy against Reva. It surmised that Reva might have a right to contribution against her daughter.]

The unjust enrichment in this case is manifest. . . . Had the husband kept his promise, the beneficiaries would have collected $7,000 less in proceeds. To that extent, the beneficiaries have been unjustly enriched, and the proceeds should be subjected to a constructive trust.

Whatever the legal rights between insurer and insured, the separation agreement vested in the first wife an equitable interest in the insurance policies then in force. An agreement for sufficient consideration, including a separation agreement, to maintain a claimant as a beneficiary of a life insurance policy vests in the claimant an equitable interest in the policies designated. . . . This interest is superior to that of a named beneficiary who has given no consideration, notwithstanding policy provisions permitting the insured to change the designated beneficiary freely.

This is not to say that an insurance company may not rely on the insured's designation of a beneficiary. None of this opinion bears on the rights or responsibilities of the insurer in law or in equity.

Obviously, the policies now at issue are not the same polices in existence at the time of the separation agreement. But it has been held that mere substitution of policies, or even substitution of insurance companies, does not defeat the equitable interest of one who has given sufficient consideration for a promise to be maintained as beneficiary under an insurance policy. . . . The persistence of the promisee's equitable interest is all the more evident where the agreement expressly provides for a change in policies, and in effect provides further that the promisee's right shall attach to the new policies.

For a certainty, the first wife's equitable interest would be easier to trace if the new policies were quid pro quo replacements for the original policies. The record does not reveal whether this was so. But inability to trace plaintiff's equitable rights precisely should not require that they not be recognized, much as in the instance of damages difficult to prove. . . . The separation agreement provides nexus between plaintiff's rights and the later acquired policies. The later policies were expressly contemplated by the parties, and it was agreed that plaintiff would have an interest in them. No reason in equity appears for denying plaintiff that interest, so long as no one who has given value for the policies or otherwise suffered a detriment is involved. The second wife's innocence does not offset the wrong by the now deceased husband.

The conclusion is an application of the general rule that equity regards as done that which should have been done.... Thus, if an insured, upon lapse or cancellation of insurance, followed by replacement with new insurance, has a contractual obligation to designate a particular person as beneficiary, equity will consider the obligee as a beneficiary.

In this case, then, the first wife's interest in the original policies extended as well to the later acquired policies. The husband, upon lapse or cancellation of the earlier policies, had by virtue of the separation agreement an obligation to name her as beneficiary on the later policies, an obligation enforceable in equity despite the husband's failure to comply with the terms of the separation agreement. Due to the husband's failure to do what he should have done, the first wife acquired not only a right at law to sue his estate for breach of contract, a right now worthless, but also an equitable right in the policies, a right which, upon the husband's death, attached to the proceeds....

And, since the first wife was entitled to $7,000 of the insurance proceeds at the time of the husband's death, she is no less entitled because the proceeds have already been converted by being paid, erroneously, to the named beneficiaries.... Her remedy is imposition of a constructive trust.

In the words of Judge Cardozo, "[a] constructive trust is the formula through which the conscience of equity finds expression. When property has been acquired in such circumstances that the holder of the legal title may not in good conscience retain the beneficial interest, equity converts him into a trustee" (Beatty v. Guggenheim Exploration Co., 225 N.Y. 380, 386)....

. . .

The issues in this case should not generate significant controversy. The action is in equity, and the equities are clear. True, some courts have decided the issues differently.... Those cases, however, rely heavily on formalisms and too little on basic equitable principles, long established in Anglo–American law and in this State and especially relevant when family transactions are involved. "A court of equity in decreeing a constructive trust is bound by no unyielding formula. The equity of the transaction must shape the measure of relief" (Beatty v. Guggenheim Exploration Co., 225 N.Y. 380, 389 [Cardozo, J.], *supra*).

Accordingly, the order of the Appellate Division should be affirmed, with costs.

NOTES

(1) *Four Factors*. In a part of the opinion omitted above, Judge Breitel found, in Sharp v. Kosmalski, 351 N.E.2d 721 (N.Y. 1976), a list of four factors conducive

to the relief sought. He said that constructive trusts need not be cabined by those factors, but nevertheless tested Mary Simonds's claim against them. "It so happens ... that the four factors ... are perceptible in this case: a promise, a transfer in reliance on the promise, the fiduciary relation between decedent and his first wife, and the 'unjust enrichment' of the second wife. Because decedent and plaintiff were husband and wife, there is a duty of fairness in financial matters extending even past the contemplated separation of the spouses ... Thus, at the time of the separation agreement decedent and plaintiff remained in a confidential or fiduciary relationship."

Which of the factors is the hardest to perceive in the facts of *Simonds*?

(2) *Drafting a Separation Agreement*. What lesson on this subject can be gathered from the *Simonds* opinion? The court said that the agreement between Frederick and Mary provided the nexus between her rights and the later acquired policies, meaning apparently that a term in that agreement referred to policies he might procure thereafter. Was that an essential feature of Mary's claim?

(3) *Other Facts*. Suppose that Reva Simonds had loaned to Frederick the money with which he paid the premiums on the policies naming her as the beneficiary. Suppose that she had *given* him the money. On either of those suppositions, should the proceeds have been charged with a constructive trust?

———

Wells v. John Hancock Mutual Life Ins. Co.

California Court of Appeal, 2d Appellate Dist., 1978.
85 Cal.App.3d 66, 149 Cal.Rptr. 171.

■ Kaus, P.J.

Plaintiff, Ruth Wells, appeals from judgment in favor of defendant John Hancock Mutual Life Insurance Company (John Hancock) after John Hancock's demurrer to her first amended complaint was sustained with leave to amend, but she failed to do so.

Facts

The various causes of action which plaintiff has attempted to allege against John Hancock, arise out of these basic facts:

One Robert S. Parker, who died on March 11, 1975, had been plaintiff's accountant and financial adviser for over 20 years. Between May 1, 1973, and August 1, 1974, plaintiff loaned Parker a total of $31,000.[1] On September 1, 1974—one month after the last loan had been made to him— Parker assigned to plaintiff as security for these loans a life insurance policy which John Hancock had issued to him on January 20, 1972. The policy in question was a 10–year decreasing term policy, which at no time had any surrender or nonforfeiture value. The initial sum insured was

---

1. The loans were evidenced by three promissory notes. The first, in the amount of $15,000, was executed on May 1, 1973, and payable on May 1, 1976; the second in the amount of $6,000, was executed on December 6, 1973, and repayable in installments; the third note in the sum of $10,000 was dated August 1, 1974, and payable in full on August 1, 1977.

$100,000. At the time of the assignment to plaintiff it was $85,900. At the time of issue, Parker had been 46 years old.

The assignment was executed on a printed form furnished by John Hancock. It recites the amount of the loan which the policy purportedly secures—$31,000. A duplicate of the assignment was filed at John Hancock's home office on October 3, 1974. On that date John Hancock in fact acknowledged receipt of the assignment as follows: "The John Hancock Mutual Life Insurance Company, without assuming any responsibility for the validity or the sufficiency of the foregoing assignment, has, on this date, filed a duplicate thereof at its Home Office." This acknowledgment is itself part of John Hancock's printed form.[2]

On May 22, 1974, however, Parker had assigned the same policy to First Los Angeles Bank to secure a loan of $35,000. This assignment had also been filed with John Hancock's home office on June 14, 1974, but John Hancock at no time advised plaintiff of its existence.

Another blemish of the assignment was that at the time John Hancock received and acknowledged the assignment, the policy did not really exist— it had in fact lapsed for nonpayment of premiums and the passage of the grace period.[3] John Hancock at no time advised plaintiff of the fact that the policy had lapsed.

The First Amended Complaint

The first amended complaint contains [four] causes of action ... which concern John Hancock.... The second cause of action, labeled *Fraud and Deceit*, alleges that John Hancock fraudulently represented to plaintiff that there had been no prior assignment of the policy and that it was in full force and effect and that John Hancock made these misrepresentations intending to defraud plaintiff in various respects.[4] Had plaintiff been advised of the true condition of the policy she would have taken necessary action to obtain other, more adequate, security for the ... three notes. In addition, John Hancock's nondisclosure of the lapse of the policy prevented plaintiff from attempting to revive it by paying the overdue premiums and submitting proof of insurability.[5]

---

2. Right below the John Hancock signature line appears a six-part notice, the first part of which reads as follows: "The company furnishes this form of assignment for the convenience of the parties, and it assumes no responsibility for its sufficiency or validity."

3. The policy could, however, have been reinstated on evidence of insurability satisfactory to John Hancock and payment of overdue premiums with interest.

4. "... with the intent to defraud and deceive plaintiff, to lull her into an unwarranted sense of security, to induce her not to pay premiums due or require Robert S. Parker to submit evidence of insurability, to induce her to forbear making an investigation into Robert S. Parker's financial condition or to otherwise take any action calculated to obtain other, more adequate, security for the aforementioned three notes."

5. See footnote 3, *ante*. Plaintiff does not allege that proof of Parker's insurability could have been furnished. We note again that Parker died only six months later; we are not told, however, whether his death was accidental or the result of an illness which made him uninsurable in October 1974. One can, of course, speculate that his proven ability to borrow large sums of money on a term policy suggests that he did not look well.

The third cause of action, labeled *Negligence*, omits the allegations of intentional fraud and pleads more benignly that John Hancock negligently failed to inform plaintiff that there had been a prior assignment and that the policy had lapsed.

Plaintiff's fourth cause of action repeats the gist of the second and third counts and adds the conclusion that by reason of the pleaded facts John Hancock is estopped to claim that the subject policy was not in full force and effect at the time of Parker's death.

The fifth cause of action seeks declaratory relief.... It adds no relevant allegations, but does contain the intriguing news that on January 20, 1975, Parker had once more assigned the policy to one Phyllis Bracker as security for a loan of $15,000.

Discussion

[Nobody connected with the litigation, the court said, took seriously Wells's allegations of fraud with intent to deceive.] In truth, plaintiff has always made it clear that in spite of the liberal use of pejoratives in her pleadings, her grievance is not any hard-core lie by John Hancock, but its failure to advise her, in connection with its acknowledgment of having received a copy of the assignment, that the policy had lapsed and that there had been a previous assignment to another creditor of Parker.

What it boils down to is simply this: When a life insurance company is advised that a policy issued by it has been assigned as security for a loan and acknowledges in writing that it has received a duplicate of such assignment, is it under a duty to inform the assignee that it has been advised of other assignments of the same policy, that the policy has lapsed for nonpayment of premiums, or both?

The Previous Assignment: Plaintiff gives us neither authority nor persuasive reason for holding that John Hancock was under any obligation to advise her of the previous assignment of which it had notice.[6] John Hancock had no way of knowing whether the debt secured by that assignment had been paid off in whole or in part or whether the Los Angeles Bank had accepted different security for the loan due to it. John Hancock's books are not like the records of a county recorder, where satisfaction of mortgages and reconveyances of deeds of trust are recorded. To advise plaintiff that Parker had made a previous loan on the strength of the policy could have been an officious betrayal of confidential information, serving possibly no useful purpose.

In brief, we are satisfied that John Hancock was under no duty to reveal previous assignments known to it.

The Lapse of the Policy. The fact that at the time John Hancock acknowledged receiving a copy of the assignment the policy had actually lapsed, presents an entirely different problem. Unlike a previous assign-

---

6. It so happens that under the facts of this case the previous assignment was the least of plaintiff's worries. As noted, the sum insured at the time of Parker's death was $85,900 and the previous assignment secured a loan of $35,000, leaving plenty to satisfy plaintiff's three notes.

ment—which may or may not be still in effect as far as the insurer knows— the fact that a policy has lapsed and that, therefore, the insurer is under no legal obligation if the insured dies, is, of course, a fact of which the insurer must be fully aware.

The simple question to be decided by us is, therefore, whether under all of the circumstances John Hancock was under a duty to advise plaintiff that the policy which she had accepted as security for a $31,000 loan was, in fact, worthless?

Several considerations are relevant to a correct answer:

First: this is not a case of a former obligor who has casually learned that a former obligee has purported to assign the extinguished obligation for value and who would have to go out of his way to tell the assignee that he has bought the Brooklyn Bridge. Since John Hancock was returning the duplicate assignment form to plaintiff anyway—precisely as was contemplated by its own procedures—it would not even have had to buy an extra stamp to advise plaintiff that the assignment was worthless.

Second: John Hancock is not entirely a disinterested third party in connection with assignments of the policies it sells. Life insurance companies conduct business of a quasi-public nature. (Barrera v. State Farm Mut. Automobile Ins. Co. (1969) 71 Cal.2d 659, 673, 456 P.2d 674.) The life insurance industry as a whole and—according to the allegations of the complaint—John Hancock in particular, have quite properly emphasized the role of life insurance policies as convenient security devices. In order to regularize assignment procedures with respect to its own policies and to keep itself advised, John Hancock has devised a useful form on which such assignments for security purposes can be made and which does double-duty as a means of notifying John Hancock of the assignment and, in turn, of notifying the parties that John Hancock has been so notified. By thus involving itself in the transaction, John Hancock acts in part in its own interest: it not only promotes the efficiency of life insurance policies as a security device, but also keeps itself informed concerning the changing interests of owners and creditors of owners in the policies which it has issued.[7]

Third and most vitally: As between the creditor who accepts a life insurance policy as security for a debt and the life insurance company itself, knowledge concerning the legal status of the policy is peculiarly that of the insurer. A long unbroken line of California decisions recognizes that such disparity of knowledge may result in an imperative of disclosure. [Four cases and a treatise cited.][8] We think the present situation easily falls within the principle of these decisions.

---

7. The policy provides: "The Company will not be on notice of any assignment unless it is in writing, nor until a duplicate of the original assignment has been filed at the Home Office of the Company. The Company assumes no responsibility for the validity or sufficiency of any assignment."

8. The rule is stated in the Restatement Second of Torts in section 551 as follows: (1) One who fails to disclose to another a fact that he knows may justifiably induce the other to act or refrain from acting in a business transaction is subject to the same

In sum, since the processing of assignments of policies was part of John Hancock's regular business, since its involvement served a business purpose of its own and, finally, since it was fully aware of a vital fact—the lapse of the policy—unknown to the plaintiff, we hold that it was under a duty to disclose that fact.[9]

[The insurer based an argument on two disclaimers in its acknowledgment of receipt of the assignment: one quoted in n.2 above, and the other quoted just before the footnote reference. The argument had no merit, the court said. The disclaimers might relate to the *assignment*, but neither had anything to do with the validity or sufficiency of the policy itself.]

To support its claim that it had no duty to notify plaintiff of the lapse of the policy, John Hancock relies on a series of cases which stand for the proposition that the insurer is under no obligation to notify an assignee that premiums are coming due and that the policy is about to lapse.... The validity and good sense of these authorities need not be questioned. They are, however, not in point. Plaintiff does not contend that she would have been entitled to continuous nudges from John Hancock concerning matters that had to be done in order to keep the policy alive. All that she claims is that if the company is notified in writing that the insured has purported to assign the policy and the company acknowledges that it has received such notification and knows that the policy has, in fact, lapsed, it should advise the assignee of that fact. We think that simple fairness demands nothing less.

If we are correct so far, and John Hancock was under an obligation to advise plaintiff what it knew for a fact—that the policy had lapsed—our holding really swallows up plaintiff's purported cause of action for negligence: there is no point in asking whether John Hancock was negligent in failing to inform plaintiff about the true status of Parker's policy when it was under a positive obligation to do so.

Estoppel: In plaintiff's fourth cause of action she claims that by reason of all of the facts previously pleaded, John Hancock is estopped to claim that the subject policy was not in full force and effect at the time of Robert S. Parker's death. If that pleading was intended as nothing but another way of asserting that John Hancock should have revealed that the policy had lapsed, it presumably does no harm. If, as seems more likely, the claim

---

liability to the other as though he had represented the nonexistence of the matter that he has failed to disclose, if, but only if, he is under a duty to the other to exercise reasonable care to disclose the matter in question. (2) One party to a business transaction is under a duty to exercise reasonable care to disclose to the other before the transaction is consummated, ... (e) facts basic to the transaction, if he knows that the other is about to enter into it under a mistake as to them, and that the other, because of the relationship between them, the customs of the trade or other objective circumstances, would reasonably expect a disclosure of those facts.

9. Actually a layman may think that it would have been so natural for John Hancock to note that the assignment of which it was notified and which it formally acknowledged was, in fact, worthless, that a jury might reasonably infer that the failure to do so amounted to more than mere nondisclosure: that it was an implied representation that the policy was valid. We need not and do not go that far in our holding. We merely cite the reasonableness of such a conclusion in support of what we do hold: that there was a duty to speak.

of estoppel is intended to dispense with the proof of damages, some remarks are in order.

All that we have held so far is that John Hancock should have informed plaintiff that the policy had lapsed. Although plaintiff sanguinely pleads that, had she been so informed, she would have taken necessary action to obtain other, more adequate security, the general impression one gets from the few facts pleaded in the complaint is that no such security would have been available, that Parker was barely one step ahead of his creditors and that John Hancock's failure to inform plaintiff that her security was worthless probably caused no damage. If, on the other hand, it were the law that John Hancock is estopped to claim that the policy was not in full force and effect, plaintiff would find herself in a creditor's paradise: there would be $85,900 in insurance, plenty to satisfy her and all the other assignees who have surfaced so far. Yet, at least as far as this plaintiff is concerned, an estoppel to deny full coverage would be an undeserved windfall: it should be recalled that plaintiff had parted with her $31,000 long before there were any communications from John Hancock. By no stretch of the facts, therefore, can she claim that whatever John Hancock did or did not do caused her to relinquish $31,000. Her loss is measured by the other, more adequate, security she was led not to demand and obtain. The burden of proving the exact amount of such loss cannot be swept under the rug by a glib slogan: that John Hancock is estopped to deny full coverage.

The judgment is reversed.

NOTES

(1) *Nudging an Assignee.* In a footnote omitted above the court referred to its statement that an insurer is under no obligation to notify an assignee that premiums are coming due and that the policy is about to lapse. The footnote cites an addition to the State's Insurance Code, changing this "apparently general" rule of law. Section 10173.2 obligates an insurer to give the assignee not less than ten days notice before 'the final lapse of the policy, . . .' It permits the insurer to charge $2.50 for each such notice.

Meanwhile, a sister court concluded that the *Wells* court got it wrong about an assignee's right to notification of a prospective lapse. Kostler v. Life Insurance Company of California, 159 Cal.Rptr. 794 (Cal.App. 1979). Somewhat ironically, the *Kostler* court appealed to the reasoning of *Wells* (quasi-public nature of the life insurance business) to justify departing from the supposed rule that an insurer is under no duty to nudge an assignee. "We find the reasoning of *Wells* as compelling [to that end] as it was to find a duty on the part of the insurer to notify the assignee that the assigned policy has already lapsed." Id. at 798.

The court also ascribed the supposed rule to courts less demanding of insurers than those of California. What reason is there to be less demanding in this respect?

(2) *Beneficiaries.* Ordinarily, "the insured may permit his or her policy to lapse and no one may complain." See 4 L. Russ & T. Segalla, Couch on Insurance 3d § 58.22, at 58–29 (1997). The authorities cited in the foregoing Note do not entitle an ordinary beneficiary to notification of a lapse in prospect. See and compare the *Gonsalves* case described below under the heading "An Ex-wife's Complaint".

(3) *Speculations on Health*. In footnote 5 to the *Wells* opinion the court offered the speculation that Parker "did not look well" at times in 1974 when he was borrowing "large sums of money on a term policy". Possibly, that is, Wells or the First Los Angeles Bank was prepared to venture a good deal on the possibility of Parker's early death. The thought is reminiscent of a practice said to prevail in 18th-century England. News of the illness of a celebrity prompted idlers, it was said, to effect insurance on the patient's life, sometimes paying heavy premiums. When sufferers, "casting an eye over a newspaper ... saw that their lives had been [so insured], they despaired of all hopes; and thus their dissolution was hastened." Wright & Fayle, History of Lloyd's 93–94 (1928), quoting from T. Mortimer, The Mystery and Iniquity of Stock Jobbing (13th ed. 1781).

PROBLEMS

Suppose that, although Parker's policy had not lapsed at the time of his assignment to Wells, John Hancock had learned that he had made, with intent to deceive, a material misrepresentation in applying for the policy, on which John Hancock had justifiably relied. Would it have been obliged to notify Wells of that fact? Suppose rather that John Hancock had not known of deceit by Parker, but had begun to suspect it. Notification required in that case?

Assume that the answer to both of the foregoing questions is Yes. Would the answer change if it also appeared that John Hancock had continued to accept premium payments after, in the one case, having learned of the deceit or, in the other, having entertained a suspicion of it?

————

An Ex-wife's Complaint

This Note is drawn from an unpublished opinion about California law: Gonsalves v. Sunset Life Ins. Co., 215 F.3d 1333 (9th Cir. 2000). After reading about the case, you should refer again to the decision in *Ulrich v. Reinoehl*, as described in the Note, *Creditors' Rights*, at p. 549 above, and consider this question: Is it possible to subscribe to the decision in *Ulrich* and also to that in *Gonsalves*?

Linda Gonsalves was a party to various agreements with one Gygax, including a marital settlement. One agreement, referring to policies of insurance on Gygax's life, was called a "Change of Beneficiary Agreement". A Property Settlement Agreement granted to Gonsalves an interest in the policies securing certain obligations of Gygax to her by designating her as beneficiary "in an amount equivalent to the outstanding balances" of those obligations. Gonsalves complained later that, before his death, Gygax had caused one of the policies to lapse for the nonpayment of premiums. Her complaint was against the issuer of the policy—Sunset Life: she should have been notified of the lapse and permitted to pay the premiums herself.

The amount recoverable, if any, was a subject of comment by the court. "Gonsalves's status as an irrevocable beneficiary," it said, "extends only so far as the Marital Settlement Agreement and the Property Settlement Agreement allow. The [latter designates] her as beneficiary of [the] policies 'in an amount equivalent to the outstanding balances' of those obligations.

Therefore, Gonsalves's entitlement to proceeds of the Sunset policy depends on (and is limited by) the balance on the loans secured unless the fact that she was not given notice of lapse—and that the estate can make no competing claim—makes a difference."

An "ordinary" beneficiary may not complain, the court said, of a policy lapse. But Gonzalez has "secured a different position for herself", and was in a position to complain. "This makes her more like an assignee than a beneficiary, because an assignee is entitled to notice under California law.... However, an assignee's loss on account of a lapse that the insurer should have disclosed (but did not) is measured by the assignee's actual damages, not the face value of the policy....

"The same is true if Gonsalves were deemed a creditor-beneficiary of Gygax, for a creditor-beneficiary's insurable interest in a life insurance policy is also limited to the amount of the secured debt (here, the outstanding balance on the enumerated debts at the time of Gygax's death pursuant to the Property Settlement Agreement), plus the amount of premiums paid by the creditor-beneficiary to maintain the policy in force, plus interest....

"Either way, Gonsalves's loss must be measured by and limited to the amount of the debt for which the policy was security. If Gonsalves had been given notice of lapse as she should have been, had paid the premiums, and the policy had remained in force, she would be entitled to recover no more than the outstanding balance on the debts pursuant to the Marital Settlement Agreement and the Property Settlement Agreement (together with a refund of the premium and interest) because both her status as a beneficiary and the extent of her vested equitable interest in Gygax's policy stem from those Agreements. Her position now—whether as a creditor beneficiary or an assignee of a lapsed policy—is no different and gives her no greater rights than she would otherwise have had."

C.   BINDING RECEIPTS

A helpful introduction to this subject is a passage from the opinion in Service v. Pyramid Life Ins. Co., 440 P.2d 944 (Kan. 1968), at p. 956, as follows:

"It is the practice of many life insurance companies to state in their applications that the contract of insurance shall not take effect until the application has been approved by the company, the first premium paid by the applicant, and the policy delivered. Where this is the situation a period intervenes between the signing of the application by the applicant and the delivery of the policy. During this period no money has been advanced to the insurance company, and no insurance is in effect. This interval, of a few days to several weeks, depending upon the time consumed in investigation and physical examination of the applicant, in passing upon his application at the home office, and in the traveling of the application and policy to and from the home office, is undesirable from the point of view of the insurer as well as the applicant. The disadvantage to the applicant consists in the fact he is not covered by insurance during this period, while the disadvantage to the insurer consists in the fact that during this period the applicant possesses the power to revoke the offer made in his application. This disadvantage is a real one as far as the insurer is concerned, because the applicant may decide to exercise his power, either because he chooses not to carry any insurance at all, or because he chooses to purchase it from a rival company. In that event the company suffers to lose what it has expended for the investigation and medical examination of the applicant, aside from the loss of business itself.

"To alleviate this situation insurance companies have seized upon the idea of issuing binding receipts to the applicant upon the payment of the first premium. These binding receipts, or conditional receipts, as they are sometimes called, usually contain a provision to the effect that the insurance shall be considered as in force from the date of the receipt, or the date of the medical examination, provided the application is approved and accepted at the home office of the insurer.

. . .

"The issuance of these binding receipts effectively does away with the disadvantage threatening the insurer. The applicant to whom the binding receipt is issued feels contractually obligated to perform, and it serves to give the insurer the use of premium money at the earliest date possible. It further offers a selling point of which no agent fails to make the utmost in his talks with prospective customers."

The Kansas court made use of this passage in its opinion in the case that follows—sharply edited here.

National Inspection and Repair, Inc. v. Valley Forge Life Ins. Co.

Kansas Supreme Court, 2002.
274 Kan. 825, 56 P.3d 807.

■ ALLEGRUCCI, J.:

The central issue in this case is whether there was temporary insurance coverage on the life of William Thomas Gaines at the time of his death. Gaines died within the temporary coverage period set by the conditional premium receipt. When National Inspection and Repair, Inc., (NIR) demanded payment of $500,000 in life insurance on Gaines, Valley Forge Life Insurance Company and Continental Assurance Company (collectively known as CNA) denied coverage.

[Gaines had filled out an application, directed to CNA, for insurance on his life on September 18, 1998. He named as the beneficiary National Inspection and Repair (NIR), his employer. At the same time Straub issued to NIR, "in return" for a payment described below, a "Conditional Premium Receipt". It read as follows, in part:

The insurance under the policy for which application is made shall be effective on date of this receipt or the date of completion of the medical examination (if, and when required by the Company), whichever is the later date, if in the opinion of the authorized Officers of the Company at its Home Office in Webster Groves, Missouri, the Proposed Insured is insurable and acceptable for insurance under the rules and practices on the plan of insurance.

The receipt stated four dates on which "Any coverage which takes effect through this Receipt [might] terminate". That coverage *will* terminate, the receipt said "on the EARLIEST" of the four dates, one of them being "A. Ninety (90) days after the date of this Receipt." Some other terms of the receipt are set out in the footnote.[1]

[The application contained this question:

In the past 90 days, has any person proposed for insurance been admitted to a hospital or other medical facility, been advised to be admitted, contemplated surgery, or had surgery performed or recommended?

To that question Gaines answered by checking a "Yes" box. He added an explanation referring to a motorcycle accident and hospital treatment for a broken ankle, and saying "all healed." Beneath that and another question the application form contained this statement: "If either question in this section is answered 'Yes' or left blank, a premium payment cannot be accepted with this application and any conditional receipt is void."

[Straub "accepted" the application. He had been an advisor to NIR, and had suggested to its president the purchase of "key man" insurance on Gaines's life. Once the president had chosen CNA as the preferred issuer, Straub sought status with CNA as the solicitor, in order to earn a commission on the sale of the insurance. Along with the application, he accepted a check from NIR the amount of which included a three-month premium of $441.84 for insurance on Gaines's life. (It included also the amount of a premium for a comparable policy on the life of a fellow employee.) "Technically", he should not have done so, according to the trial court, because of Gaines's answer to the question about hospitalization.

[Findings by the trial court included these:] Straub did not disclose that this insurance was contingent in any way and in fact stated that upon the acceptance of the check the company would be covered and if the individuals died the next day that the insurance would be in effect. Defendant CNA does not dispute that the statement may have been made

---

1. IMPORTANT: This receipt does NOT automatically create interim insurance coverage. NO INSURANCE IS EVER IN FORCE under this receipt until after ALL of its conditions are met.

. . .

EFFECTIVE DATE OF CONDITIONAL COVERAGE

If all the Conditions in Section I are COMPLETELY satisfied, then insurance coverage will begin on the LATER of the following dates:

A.   The Underwriting Date, or

B.   The Policy Date, if any, requested in the application.

but denies it was valid or that Straub had authority to make it or that it would give rise to a temporary insurance contract.

[On the following day Straub forwarded the application to a firm—Financial Brokerage, Inc. (FBI)—that processed applications on behalf of CNA, and then went to China for a month. FBI acknowledged receipt of the application by letter of September 24. CNA cashed the check on October 2. On October 9 and again on October 29, FBI sent to Straub "status updates". They read, respectively, as follows:

> We may consider $234,500 as maximum for key man insurance [owing to Gaines's salary]. Please verify if the applicant was diagnosed with schizophrenia in August of 98? Thank you for your business."

> I have given the underwriter the medical information regarding schizophrenia and we will continue to underwrite this case. I will contact you as soon as I have a decision. Thank you.

Gaines died, unexpectedly, on November 15.

[Beginning late in December, NIR began attempted to collect $500,000 from CNA on account of Gaines's death. In a letter dated January 8, 1999, CNA attempted to refund to NIR the entire amount of NIR's September check. The letter stated that "any coverage that may have been provided under our Conditional Premium Receipt no longer applies." NIR refused to cash the refund check.]

NIR sued CNA and Eugene Straub. Against CNA, NIR alleged breach of contract and, in the alternative, negligence. Against Straub, it alleged negligence or misrepresentation and acting without authority in failing to procure the insurance. CNA filed a cross-claim against Straub for improperly accepting the application and initial premium for Gaines. On cross-motions, the district court granted summary judgment in favor of NIR and against CNA. The district court dismissed CNA's cross-claim against Straub. CNA appealed.]

[The court analyzed a number of precedents with respect to CNA's liability. Its decision turned chiefly, however, on this part of a Kansas statute:

> (a) When an application for an individual life insurance policy and an initial premium therefor has been received by an insurance company or agent acting on behalf of such company, the coverage for which application is made shall, subject to the limitations in subsection (b), be deemed to be temporarily in effect until the insurance company or agent has, in the event of an adverse underwriting decision, as defined in K.S.A. 40–2,111 and amendments thereto, notified in writing the applicant of such adverse underwriting decision and returned any unearned premium in accordance with K.S.A. 40–2,112 and amendments thereto.

Subsection (b) states certain ways in which an insurer may limit, exclude, or void the coverage so provided; for the court's observation about it see the footnote.[2]]

The general rule of K.S.A. 40–451(a) is that, when an insurance company receives an application and an initial premium, coverage is deemed to be temporarily in effect.... Hence, the general statutory provision is to be read into the conditional premium receipt for Gaines' premium. The terms of the receipt, in particular the bold disclaimer—"This receipt does NOT automatically create interim insurance coverage. NO INSURANCE IS EVER IN FORCE under this receipt until after ALL of its conditions are met."—conflict with the statutory provision. As the federal district court observed [in Stauffer v. Jackson Nat. Life Ins. Co., 75 F.Supp.2d 1271 (D.Kan. 1999)], at the very least, the application of the statutory provisions to the interim receipt creates an ambiguity. Where there is an ambiguity, the construction most favorable to the insured must prevail. Brumley v. Lee, 265 Kan. 810, 812, 963 P.2d 1224 (1998).

Also conflicting with the statute is the receipt provision that would delay the effective date of conditional coverage beyond the statutory provision for coverage upon the insurer's receipt of the application and initial premium. The statutory provision prevails here, too.

Financial Brokerage, Inc.'s notice to ... September 29, 1998, that premium money could not be accepted with Gaines' application apparently was on account of Gaines' affirmative answer to [the application question about hospitalization].... Beneath [that and another question] is this statement: "If either question in this section is answered 'Yes' or left blank, a premium payment cannot be accepted with this application and any conditional receipt is void."

CNA contends that Gaines' affirmative answer ... renders the conditional premium receipt *void* and that the entry of summary judgment must be reversed because it was made on the basis that the receipt was merely *voidable*. According to CNA, the significance of the void receipt is that it, unlike a voidable writing, cannot be acquiesced in or validated or ratified by any subsequent conduct of the parties. We note that based on Gaines' explanation of his answer ..., more than 90 days had passed since his accident. Thus, on its face, yes was an incorrect answer. Nonetheless, K.S.A. 40–451 controls once an application and initial premium have been received for an individual life insurance policy. In this case, despite Gaines' affirmative answer, his application and premium were accepted.

[A complication arose from the facts that Straub had designated one Bammes to act for him during Straub's visit to China, and that the NIR check included premiums for a second policy. When FBI reported to Bammes about the "maximum for key man insurance" on Gaines, on or about September 29, he had told FBI to apply the whole amount of the check to the second application, and to reapply $441.84 to Gaines's file if a

---

2. [N]one of the exceptional circumstances identified in 40–451(b) seems to apply. Subsection (b)(1) excludes coverage in the event of suicide, (b)(2) voids coverage if the applicant makes a material misrepresentation, and (b)(4) voids coverage if a check or draft for the premium payment is not honored. There is no question that none of these applies.

policy was issued on his life. Bammes passed the communication along to Straub, but not to NIR.]

CNA retained the premium and was in possession of it at the time of Gaines' death. . . . It was not until January 8, 1999, that CNA wrote to NIR that it did not intend to insure Gaines. . . .

With regard to the insurer's receipt of an initial premium, CNA takes a stab at arguing that it never received an initial premium for Gaines because the premium eventually was applied to [the second] application. In this regard, the district court found that on September 18, 1998, the agent took the applications of Burkhead and Gaines along with a check for the amount of the combined Burkhead/Gaines initial premiums. The statute provides that coverage for Gaines is deemed to be temporarily in effect upon that transaction. K.S.A. 40–451(a). There is no merit to the argument that it should be deemed never to have received an initial premium for Gaines.

. . .

Kansas statutes provide that the coverage will be deemed to remain in effect until the applicant has been notified of an adverse underwriting decision in writing accompanied by the return of the unearned premium. K.S.A. 40–451(a); K.S.A. 40–2,112(d)(1). In this case, Gaines never was notified in writing of an adverse underwriting decision and NIR was not notified in writing until after Gaines' death. Thus, coverage is deemed to have remained in effect until after Gaines' death.

. . .

Finally, at oral argument, counsel for the appellant argued that the maximum amount of coverage under the premium receipt was $234,500. The basis for that argument was the notice given to Bammes that . . . the maximum coverage may be only $234,500. The fallacy in appellant's argument is its failure to comply with K.S.A. 40–451. It gave no written notice to NIR limiting the amount of coverage under the premium receipt, nor did it return the unearned premium resulting from the reduction in coverage. Accordingly, at the time of Gaines' death, the amount of coverage provided in the premium receipt was $500,000.

The district court did not err in granting summary judgment to NIR.

NOTE

A World Away. A troublesome case about the inception of coverage is cited above in Note 1, p. 555 above: Dixon v. Western Union Assurance Co., 164 S.E.2d 214 (S.C. 1968). It concerned policy terms mailed by an insurer to a couple, with a solicitation that they apply for those terms, and so insure the life of their absent son. The young man had died on the day the application was mailed, and before it was. Notwithstanding that, an order enforcing the policy was entered by Circuit Judge Spruill. The South Carolina Supreme Court agreed with the *result.* Quotations to follow are from the Spruill opinion. To begin with one near the end:

While he can find no authority for the position, the writer knows of no reason in law or public policy why a policy of life insurance could not be antedated to cover a risk which may already have occurred to a life, where both parties are in ignorance of such loss and are acting in good faith to cover the risk from a time prior to actual issuance of the policy.

Id. at 220. The judge found an analogy in the law of marine insurance; "lost or not lost" is the expressive language in marine policies.

The judge was put to some trouble finding language which "antedated" the coverage. He found some help in papers naming, as the "in force" date, the postmark date on the envelope in which the claimants enclosed their application. As opposed to a postmark *time*, the court reasoned, a postmark *date* begins well before daybreak.

Further perplexity developed from what the judge called a proviso in the policy, limiting the insurer's liability to the return of any premiums paid. The policy was not to take effect "unless such premium is received at the home office of the company while the insured is alive and in sound health". If that condition existed, and was not excused, the claim on the policy had to fail, for the premium had not even been mailed during the son's life. The court ruled that the condition did not exist, and was anyway excused. Mysteriously, he said that "this alleged condition precedent . . . is not set out in any of the written instruments." Perhaps he meant "not set out in any papers *other than the policy*." Those papers included a presidential sales pitch, enclosing the proposed policy and what was in effect an application (called "Ownership Certificate") to be filled out and mailed back, with a premium. Language in the cover letter, in the application, and in an "In Force Certificate"—the subject of a third mailing—persuaded the judge that the insurer was "not in a position" to assert the supposed condition. "The law of waiver and estoppel should be sufficient to sustain this position." The third of those papers asserted: "This certificate confirms the In Force Date of your policy, which is the postmarked date of the original application."

The policy contained this statement: "This Instrument . . . and the In Force Certificate shall constitute the entire contract of insurance between the parties hereto."

Questions: (a) If the insurer could have prevented an adverse result by some simple change in its documentation, what change comes to mind? Would it have been well advised to make more than one change?

(b) Consider a rule that would have required Western Union, and any other insurer in the same market, to cover a death occurring within a stated period *before* an applicant mails a first-premium check, on condition that no word of the death has reached the applicant by that time. What might be said for that rule?

D. INSURANCE MURDERS

The two topics under this heading are first, the disqualification, as recipients of life-insurance proceeds, of murderous persons, and second, the possibility of a tort claim against an insurer for having put a life at risk by insuring it.

1.   Diverting Gains from Felons

"It would be a reproach to the jurisprudence of the country, if one could recover insurance money payable on the death of a party whose life he had feloniously taken. As well might he recover insurance money upon a building that he had willfully fired." New York Mut. Life Ins. Co. v. Armstrong, 117 U.S. 591, 600 (1886) (Field, J.). It would be a reproach also if, in like circumstances, assets were to pass from the decedent to the felon by will or by intestate succession. Riggs v. Palmer, 22 N.E. 188 (N.Y. 1889) (youngster poisoned his grandfather in order to make a will operative). A large majority of state legislatures have sought to forestall the latter result by enacting so-called "slayer statutes".[1] Some of the statutes address the matter of life insurance; others do not.

Slayer Statutes

The following is a conspectus of rules about the disposition of life-insurance proceeds in cases in which a beneficiary has killed the CQV. It is provided by the opinion in an Ohio case, Ahmed v. Ahmed, 817 N.E.2d 424 (Ohio App. 2004) (all citations omitted).

. . .

As of 1993, forty-four states and the District of Columbia had enacted slayer statutes, four states had a general common law rule prohibiting a killer from benefiting from his crimes, one had a common law rule barring a beneficiary who kills an insured from recovering from a life insurance policy, and the law in the one remaining state is unclear.

First, the states differ over the nature of the killing that disqualifies the beneficiary. Every statute disqualifies beneficiaries that have committed the equivalent of either murder or aggravated murder, but some include offenses like voluntary manslaughter, or causing suicide while others do not. And many states disqualify a beneficiary who has "feloniously and intentionally" killed the insured without defining what they mean by felonious and intentional killings.

Second, states require varying burdens of proof upon the person seeking to disqualify the killer as a beneficiary. For instance, in the absence of a conviction some states will disqualify a beneficiary if the trial court determines by a preponderance of the evidence "that the person would be found criminally accountable for the felonious and intentional killing of the decedent." In contrast, other states require that the killing be proven by clear and convincing evidence. Ohio disqualifies the beneficiary only after he is convicted of or pleads guilty to one of the stated violations. Still other states only disqualify a beneficiary who has been convicted after all the beneficiary's appellate rights "have been exhausted."

---

1.   For a compendium see Cook v. Grierson, 845 A.2d 1231, 1233 n.3 (Md. 2004).

Further complicating the matter is that some states, like Ohio, believe that a slayer statute only supplements, rather than supercedes [sic], common law, while others come to the contrary conclusion. According to others, a criminal conviction does not conclusively prove that a beneficiary is prohibited from recovering life insurance proceeds, some going so far as to bar evidence of such a conviction. In contrast, Ohio only bars a beneficiary from recovering *after* a criminal conviction.

NOTES

(1) *California, Round I.* In Beck v. West Coast Life Ins. Co., 241 P.2d 544 (Cal. 1952), Justice Traynor considered three ways to allot the proceeds of a policy on the life of a woman (W) whose husband (H) had killed her. One possible taker was her estate; another was a friend (F) who was nominated in the policy as the taker if W should outlive H. Ordinarily impossible, the court said, to determine which would have taken but for the murder. Mortality tables might indicate whether H or F was the more likely to outlive the other. But the decision favored F, irrespective of that.

Actually, mortality tables do not break out the experiences of murderers, separating them from the general population.

Decades later, the California legislature confirmed the *Beck* ruling by enacting Probate Code § 252 ("... payable as though the killer had predeceased the decedent"). That section is part of a series that includes the State's slayer statute.

(2) *California, Round II.* Richard bought insurance on his life, payable primarily to his wife Teresa. After the couple were separated, he killed her and within hours killed himself. One claimant to the policy proceeds was the contingent beneficiary, Richard's mother, Margaret. Another was Teresa's estate. The trial court awarded the bulk of the proceeds to Margaret. The administratrix of the estate appealed. The appellate judges agreed on reversal, but disagreed about the amount owed to Teresa's estate. The majority ruled that the estate should get about 86%; the dissenter would have made it 100%. (The disagreement rested on a difference of opinion about the relevance of California's community-property laws.) Estate of Selio, 2005 WL 1168415 (2005).

The estate's victory rested on the theory that "allowing Margaret, as Richard's choice of alternative beneficiary, to obtain proceeds from the Policy, would give effect to the murderer's intent and provide him with a motive to kill Teresa." (The majority calculated that Richard could have enriched his mother by killing his wife only to the extent of his separate interest in the policy.)

Probate Code § 252, cited in Note 1, does not capture this case, one that is unusual both on its facts and as a construction of section 253. The latter applies to cases in which a person feloniously and intentionally kills another, and which are not provided for in another nearby section. In such a case, the section says, "any acquisition of property, interest, or benefit by the killer as a result of the killing of the decedent shall be treated in accordance with the principles of this part."

Curious, is it not, that the California legislature, while ratifying the decision in *Beck*, expressed a "principle" that disfavors a contingent beneficiary?

Ahmed's Case

In *Ahmed*, the policy in question had been bought by Lubiana Ahmed on her own life. She had designated Nawaz Ahmed as the primary beneficiary, and Ibtisam, her son by Nawaz, as the contingent beneficiary. After that, the couple had a second son, Ahsan. Nawaz murdered Lubaina (and was sentenced to death).

The insurer paid half of the death benefit to Ibtisam as the contingent beneficiary. It withheld the other half because Ahsan claimed it. His claim, a somewhat convoluted one, was that the policy proceeds, otherwise payable to Nawaz, should be held in constructive trust equally for him and his brother.

The court concluded that the proceeds should be paid into Lubiana's estate. (That did not resolve the dispute, for the court did not know how her estate should be distributed.) Ohio law would favor Ibtisam's claim, the court said. The proceeds were to be distributed, by statute, as if Nawaz had died before Lubiana. But federal law overrode Ohio law in this case, the court thought. The reason was that the policy had been provided by her employer, a health-services firm, as a fringe benefit. (She was a physician.) Therefore the issue was governed by the Employees' Retirement Income Security Act (ERISA).

The preemption applied in *Ahmed* is debatable. It depends on an understanding of the opinion in Egelhoff v. Egelhoff, 532 U.S. 141 (2001). "In *Egelhoff*, the [Court] held that ERISA pre empts a statute that automatically revoked any designation of a spouse as a beneficiary of a nonprobate asset upon divorce to the extent that the statute applies to ERISA plans. It recognized that its decision might affect whether slayer statutes are pre-empted by ERISA, but it refused to answer that question at that time.... The cases that have addressed the issue after *Egelhoff* have carefully sidestepped the question." *Ahmed* at 429–30. The *Ahmed* court was moved by an ideal expressed in *Egelhoff*: that there be nationally uniform administration of employee-benefit plans. The Supreme Court had said (quoting) that "Requiring ERISA administrators to master the relevant laws of 50 States and to contend with litigation would undermine the congressional goal of 'minimizing the administrative and financial burdens' on plan administrators—burdens ultimately borne by the beneficiaries." Id. at 149–150.

2. The Tort of Insuring

Between them, it seems, insurers and would-be killers have threatened a number of lives. "[W]e believe," one court has said, "it is reasonably foreseeable that a policy taken out on someone's life without his knowledge or consent could lead to injury or death at the hands of the person who procured the policy". Bajwa v. Metropolitan Life Ins. Co., a case presented below. Another court has said that the life of a person is placed in a position of extreme danger when it is insured in favor of someone having no insurable interest in it.[1] This Note concerns the liability of an insurer to a person injured by an attempt on that person's life, or to a survivor of a murder victim. In some of the instances mentioned here—summary-judg-

[1] Liberty National Life Insurance Co. v. Weldon, 100 So.2d 696 (Ala. 1957).

ment cases—the "facts" are those asserted by the claimant, but not established.

In what has been called the leading case,[2] the claimant was a man who survived his wife's attempt to poison him. He charged an insurer with negligence in issuing to her a policy on his life without his consent. Another "poisoning" case was brought by the father of a girl who was killed by her aunt-in-law. *Weldon*, n.1 above (three policies; aggregate amount, $6,500). In another case the claimants were the heirs of a man whose former wife had insured his life, and had killed him.[3] In *Bajwa*, so far as the opinion indicates, the applicant was not even acquainted with the CQV.[4]

Assuming that an insurer might be liable for the claimant's harm in any circumstances, these are possible rules of liability:

    A.   It is liable if it had actual notice of a plot by the beneficiary to murder the insured; otherwise not.

    B.   It is liable if it issued a policy with knowledge that the applicant lacked an insurable interest in the life of the CQV, and that the CQV had not consented to the issuance of the policy; otherwise not.

    C.   It is liable if it carelessly failed to learn either (i) that the applicant lacked an insurable interest in the life of the CQV, or (ii) that the CQV had not consented to the issuance of the policy.

Some variations on these rules can be supposed readily. What is the superior rule?

Rule (C) has support in the cases, according to the *Bajwa* opinion.[5] One court observed, however, that "[t]he negligent issuance of a life insurance policy is unlikely to lead to an attempt on the insured's life."[6] You may well take this observation more seriously than the court did.

2. Ramey v. Carolina Life Ins. Co., 135 S.E.2d 362 (S.C. 1964).

3. As to murder within a business partnership, see Bacon v. Federal Kemper Life Assur. Co., 512 N.E.2d 941 (Mass. 1987).

4. See also Vereen v. Liberty Life Insurance Co., 412 S.E.2d 425 (S.C.App. 1991).

5. "[C]ourts ... have recognized a cause of action for negligent issuance or continuation of a life insurance policy in three situations: (1) where the beneficiary who procured the insurance lacks an insurable interest; (2) where there is a lack of knowledge and consent to the policy by the insured; and (3) where the insurer has actual notice of a plot by the beneficiary to murder the insured." Bajwa v. Metropolitan Life Ins. Co., 804 N.E.2d 519 (Ill. 2004) (citations omitted).

In *Ramey*, n.2 above, the insurer did not escape liability by reason of the fact that the would-be murderer had an insurable interest in the life of the CQV (her husband). In *Bajwa*, the court concluded that "an insurance company owes a duty of due care to advise a proposed insured of a life insurance policy taken out on his life." It approved the statement by the court below that "an insurer may not, with impunity, provide coverage on someone's life without undertaking reasonable precautions to ascertain whether the insured is aware of and has consented to the issuance of the policy." The court cited Holloman v. Life Insurance Co. of Virginia, 7 S.E.2d 169 (S.C. 1940), for the proposition that "the authorities are generally to the effect that, except in the case of an infant, a policy of life insurance taken out without the knowledge and consent of the insured is not enforceable."

6. Williams v. John Hancock Mutual Life Ins. Co., 718 S.W.2d 611, 613 (Mo.Ct. App. 1986).

Bajwa v. Metropolitan Life Ins. Co.

Illinois Supreme Court, 2004.
208 Ill.2d 414, 804 N.E.2d 519.

■ JUSTICE THOMAS delivered the opinion of the court:

Plaintiff, Khalid J. Bajwa, as administrator of the estate of Muhammad Cheema, filed an action under the Wrongful Death Act (740 ILCS 180/1 *et seq.* (West 1998)), alleging that the negligent issuance of a life insurance policy by defendant, Metropolitan Life Insurance Company (Met Life), proximately caused the murder of Muhammad Cheema (decedent or A. Cheema) by the beneficiary of the policy. Met Life filed a motion to dismiss.... The circuit court of Cook County granted the motion. The appellate court reversed and remanded the cause for further proceedings.... We granted Met Life's petition for leave to appeal ..., to consider an issue of first impression in Illinois: whether a cause of action for negligent issuance of a life insurance policy should be recognized, where there are a number of anomalies in the application process and plaintiff alleges that the insurer should have known that the supposed insured did not know of the policy and did not give his consent to it, thereby proximately causing the death of the insured.

BACKGROUND

The plaintiff's fourth amended complaint and the attached exhibits reveal that in December 1992, Muhammad U. Cheema (U. Cheema) met with Met Life account representative Imtiaz Sheik to fill out an insurance policy on the life of A. Cheema. U. Cheema falsely represented himself as the son of A. Cheema and provided some personal information necessary to fill out part A of the application. U. Cheema designated himself as the beneficiary and arranged for the policy premiums to be deducted from his own bank account. U. Cheema then told the agent that he would take the application to his "father" to obtain his signature. This was a violation of Met Life's standard procedural rules, requiring that the agent meet personally with the proposed insured to witness the signature on the application and to propound certain questions to the proposed insured. Nevertheless, Sheik agreed to this deviation from procedure, and U. Cheema returned the application with it signed "A. Cheema." Agent Sheikh then signed part A of the application, under the heading "Witness," indicating that he had personally witnessed the proposed insured sign the application. When the policy was contested following the decedent's death, Sheikh admitted that he had not witnessed the proposed insured's signature.

For part B of Met Life's application process, the proposed insured was required to submit to a medical examination conducted by a paramedical examiner hired by Met Life. The medical exam resulted in a number of discrepancies between part A and part B of the application.... [These discrepancies related to mailing address, social security number, and medical history. For example, part B indicated previous surgery, whereas part A indicated none. The person given a medical examination and the decedent were of different heights and weights.]

Prior to the issuance of the policy, a Met Life underwriter noticed a number of additional irregularities in the application that required further investigation. In that regard, he questioned why U. Cheema, rather than A. Cheema's wife, was the policy beneficiary, and why the beneficiary was paying the premiums rather than the insured, and finally, he questioned why the policy was for $200,000 when A. Cheema's income, according to Met Life's guidelines, did not qualify him for that large of a policy amount. Despite these discrepancies, the underwriter decided the application was acceptable and issued the policy on January 18, 1993.

After the policy was issued, someone identifying himself as "Muhammad Cheema" called Met Life on five different occasions, purporting to be the insured and asking questions about possible coverage in the event of the insured's death. Met Life found these calls "strange enough" to send the case to the Consulting Services area, where the file was "noted." Nine days after the last of those calls was made to Met Life, the real A. Cheema was stabbed and beaten to death in his apartment. According to plaintiff, U. Cheema murdered the decedent in order to collect the life insurance benefits from the policy provided by Met Life.

Plaintiff filed a [complaint] alleging that Met Life negligently issued an insurance policy on the life of the decedent. Count IV of that complaint alleged that Met Life was negligent in the following ways: (1) issued a life insurance policy on the life of the decedent without investigating the veracity of the information on the insurance application and personally meeting with the insured; (2) issued a policy in favor of a beneficiary who did not possess an insurable interest on the life of the insured; (3) relied upon misrepresentations of its agent in underwriting the policy; (4) failed to warn decedent of the suspicious phone calls; and (5) provided motivation for the murder. Count V alleged gross negligence for the same acts. Count VI alleged negligent supervision of agent Sheik. The trial court granted Met Life's 2–615 motion to dismiss these counts of the complaint.[1]

The appellate court reversed, finding that plaintiff could maintain a cause of action for negligent issuance of an insurance policy. In so doing, it looked to cases from other jurisdictions that have considered the matter and found that courts in those states have recognized the validity of such claims on three different grounds: (1) where the insurer should have known that the person who procured and owned the policy, and who was named as beneficiary, had no insurable interest in the life of the insured; (2) where the insurer had knowledge that the insured was unaware of and did not consent to the policy; and (3) where the insurer had actual knowledge of the beneficiary's intent to murder the insured and failed to take action.

---

1. Plaintiff's fourth amended complaint contained seven counts. Counts I through III involved allegations of negligence against other defendants.... Count VII alleged that Met Life had "actual knowledge" of the following: the person who took the paramedical exam was an imposter; U. Cheema was not the son of the decedent; and U. Cheema procured the policy with the intent to murder the decedent and collect the policy benefits. The circuit court granted summary judgment in favor of Met Life on count VII, and the appellate court affirmed. Plaintiff does not argue the propriety of this ruling before this court.

As to the insurable interest ground, the appellate court noted that "while it has long been the established law of Illinois that the purchaser of an insurance policy must have an insurable interest in the insured's life [citation], it has also long been held that 'one may insure his own life for the benefit of another having no insurable interest therein [citation].' " 333 Ill.App.3d at 568. The court then found that plaintiff's pleadings were insufficient because they failed to make this distinction—plaintiff did not allege that Met Life issued an insurance policy on the life of the decedent *to* an individual who did not possess an insurable interest, but, rather, that Met Life allowed the policy owner to designate a beneficiary who did not possess an insurable interest. Accordingly, the court concluded that plaintiff's allegations as they relate to an insurable interest were insufficient to state a cause of action.

With respect to the second ground of possible recovery, however, the appellate court found that Met Life had a duty to ascertain, prior to the issuance of a policy on the life of another, whether the individual named as the insured is aware of and has consented to the procurement of the policy. The court found that the various irregularities in the application process, combined with the suspicious phone calls, were sufficient to put the insurer on notice that an investigation was warranted. The court then rejected the notion that actual knowledge was necessary to establish liability on the part of the insured.

ANALYSIS

... A section 2–615 motion to dismiss challenges the legal sufficiency of the complaint.... In reviewing a section 2–615 dismissal, a reviewing court must decide whether the allegations, when construed in the light most favorable to the plaintiff, are sufficient to establish a cause of action upon which relief may be granted.... A cause of action should be dismissed only if it is clearly apparent from the pleadings that no set of facts can be proven which will entitle the plaintiff to recovery....

To recover in a negligence action, a plaintiff must allege facts from which a court will find a duty of care owed by the defendant to the plaintiff, a breach of that duty, and an injury proximately caused by the breach.... The existence of a duty depends on whether the plaintiff and the defendant stood in such a relationship to each other that the law will impose upon the defendant an obligation of reasonable conduct for the benefit of the plaintiff.... Whether a duty of care exists is a question of law to be determined by the court.... However, the question of whether defendant breached its duty and whether the breach was the proximate cause of the plaintiff's injuries are factual matters for the jury to decide....

As the appellate court correctly noted, courts in other jurisdictions have recognized a cause of action for negligent issuance or continuation of a life insurance policy in three situations: (1) where the beneficiary who procured the insurance lacks an insurable interest (Liberty National Life Insurance Co. v. Weldon, 100 So.2d 696 (Ala. 1957)); (2) where there is a lack of knowledge and consent to the policy by the insured (Ramey v. Carolina Life Insurance Co., 135 S.E.2d 362 (S.C. 1964) ...); and (3) where the insurer has actual notice of a plot by the beneficiary to murder the insured.... Because plaintiff does not challenge the appellate court's ruling that the allegations of [the] complaint failed to state a cause of action under the first and third grounds noted above, we will limit our analysis to the second ground—whether plaintiff stated a cause of action based on the decedent's lack of knowledge and consent to the policy.

The leading case on point is *Ramey*.... In *Ramey*, the wife procured the policy on the life of her husband without his consent, forged his signature on the application, and named herself beneficiary. After surviving his wife's attempt to murder him by poisoning, the husband brought an action against the insurer for the personal injuries he sustained, contending that issuance of the policy proximately caused his wife to poison him with the hope of collecting the proceeds of the policy. The insurer knew that the husband was unaware of the policy and that the signature was a forgery. The court noted that generally a wife has an insurable interest, but nevertheless concluded that even with an insurable interest, insurance taken out on the life of another, without consent, is against public policy.... The *Ramey* court concluded by holding that "an insurance company has a duty to use reasonable care not to issue a policy of life insurance in favor of a beneficiary ... without the knowledge or consent of the insured, and this would especially be true, where as here, the company knew or had reason to know that such was the situation." *Ramey*, 135 S.E.2d at 366.

In reaching its holding, *Ramey* relied upon *Weldon*. There, an aunt obtained life insurance on her two-year-old niece and then poisoned the child to death. The father of the child filed suit against the insurer, alleging that the company "knew or should have known" that the aunt had no insurable interest, and the company failed to exercise reasonable diligence to ascertain whether an insurable interest existed.... In finding that a duty existed, the Alabama Supreme Court noted that the rule against issuing policies on the life of a person without his knowledge and consent is designed to protect human life. It stated that an insured is placed in a position of extreme danger where a policy of insurance is issued in favor of a beneficiary with no insurable interest. Given that such policies are unreasonably dangerous because of the risk of murder, the court held that "it would be an anomaly to hold that insurance companies have no duty to use reasonable care not to create a situation which may prove to be a stimulus for murder." *Weldon*, 100 So.2d at 708.

[The court reviewed several other decisions.]

The foregoing cases provide ample and persuasive authority for concluding that an insurance company owes a duty of due care to advise a proposed insured of a life insurance policy taken out on his life. We believe that the appellate court correctly concluded that "an insurer may not, with impunity, provide coverage on someone's life without undertaking reasonable precautions to ascertain whether the insured is aware of and has consented to the issuance of the policy." 333 Ill.App.3d at 578.

Our conclusion is supported by consideration of the traditional factors that are relevant to a court's imposition of a duty. To determine whether a duty exists under certain circumstances, a court must consider the following factors: (1) the reasonable foreseeability of the injury; (2) the likelihood of the injury; (3) the magnitude of guarding against the injury; (4) the consequences of placing that burden on the defendant.... The question of the existence of a duty turns largely on public policy considerations....

Here, we believe that it is reasonably foreseeable that a policy taken out on someone's life without his knowledge or consent could lead to injury or death at the hands of the person who procured the policy, and that there is a sufficient likelihood of injury. As the *Ramey* court noted, it is well recognized that "a policy of insurance taken out on the life of another without his knowledge or consent is void and against public policy in that it might be a fruitful source of crime." *Ramey*, 135 S.E.2d at 365. The rule against issuing these kinds of policies is designed to protect human life, and policies issued in violation of the rule are not considered " 'dangerous because they are illegal[, but] they are illegal because they are dangerous.' " *Ramey*, 135 S.E.2d at 366, quoting *Weldon*, 100 So.2d at 708.

The remaining factors of the duty analysis also favor placing a burden of due care on the insurance company under the circumstances of the present case. Such a burden would be a modest one compared to the potential for serious injury. When faced with various anomalies in the application process, an insurance company may be able to satisfy its duty of due care by simply refusing to issue the policy, or by postponing the decision to issue the policy and requiring more documentation from the proposed insured, or by undertaking some minimal background investigation. In some cases, the insurer may be able to meet its burden of care by following its own internal procedures, which are presumably designed to detect fraud in the application process. In reaching our conclusion that a duty of care existed in the present case, we make no determination as to whether Met Life's conduct amounted to a breach of that duty.

Met Life argues that the appellate court adopted the wrong standard of care when it concluded that Met Life had a duty to take reasonable precautions to determine whether the insured was aware of the policy. Met Life maintains that a plaintiff should not be able to state a cause of action for negligent underwriting unless he alleges that there is "actual knowledge" on the part of the insurance company that the policy application was somehow fraudulent. It claims that none of the cases cited by the appellate court support a "should have known" standard. Met Life asserts that in all of the cases relied upon by the appellate court, including *Ramey*, the insurance companies possessed actual knowledge either that the application was fraudulent or that the insured's life was in jeopardy.

. . .

Met Life's assertion that actual knowledge is required must be rejected. It misconstrues the holding of *Ramey*....

As the appellate court correctly noted,

> "Whether based upon actual knowledge or whether the insurer is held to a reasonable duty of inquiry, its liability would still be predicated · upon a negligence theory.... [T]he insurer [has not] provided any basis that would permit this court to limit the liability of the insurer to willful negligence alone. Such actual knowledge would merely heighten

the element of foreseeability, which could then be considered by the fact finder. To draw the line at actual knowledge rather than what the insurer reasonably should have known would be an arbitrary compartmentalization, legislative in nature." 333 Ill.App.3d at 579.

[The court rehearsed the plaintiff's allegations of fact.] Viewing all of these facts cumulatively and in the light most favorable to plaintiff, we believe that plaintiff has alleged sufficient facts so as to survive a motion to dismiss the complaint for failure to state a cause of action under section 2–615 of the Code.

[Met Life argued that a plaintiff's exhibit about the medical examination prevented the assumption that A. Cheema knew about the policy. The court denied that, saying that the exhibit indicated only the examiner's belief that *someone he believed to be named A. Cheema*" appeared for the exam. Met Life argued also that it had satisfied its duty because, as it offered to show, the person examined had produced a state-issued ID card for A. Cheema. The court answered that the complaint did not put in issue the supposed identification. Also, it said, whether or not reliance on the supposed ID card would trump various anomalies known to Met Life was a "quintessential question of fact".

[The trial court had dismissed a part of the complaint which charged Met Life with negligence because the beneficiary had no insurable interest. The plaintiff appealed from that ruling. As to that, the court pointed out an obvious difficulty he faced: How allege that U. Cheema lacked an insurable interest, absent evidence who A. Cheema was? This part of the opinion turned into a discussion of the plaintiff's request to amend his complaint.]

CONCLUSION

For the foregoing reasons, we conclude that plaintiff's fourth amended complaint sufficiently alleges a cause of action for negligent issuance of a life insurance policy based on the proposed insured's lack of knowledge and consent to the policy. We further conclude that on remand, plaintiff may amend his pleadings to properly plead a cause of action based on a lack of an insurable interest. Accordingly, we affirm the judgment of the appellate court as modified.

QUESTIONS

(1) After all this, one still does not know whether or not, under Illinois law, an insurer can make itself accountable for a person's death by insuring that person's life in favor of someone having no interest in it. Why did the court pass over that question? Was it because (according to Bajwa's complaint) Met Life allowed U.C. to designate himself as the beneficiary of a policy on A.C.'s life, and because U.C. was permitted to do that whether or not he had an insurable interest?

(2) Suppose that A.C. had known all about U.C.'s plan to obtain the policy, including the supposed plan to deceive Met Life about his identity, but had not imagined any threat to his life. Suppose, that is, that A.C. had consented to the issuance of the policy to a person having no insurable interest in his life. Should Met Life be accountable for A.C.'s death if it let itself be deceived too readily?

———

APPENDICES: Policy forms

Standard Fire Policy

Note: If the expression "standard fire policy" were understood to signify a text used universally, and without variation, under that title, there would not be a standard fire policy. There is, however, a text used generally, and with little variation, under that title, both in statutes and in contracts—so much so that experienced readers can say, on looking at a text, "That is (or is a part, or a version, of) the *standard fire policy*."

What follows is an approximation, derived from two sources. The source of the "FIRST PAGE" is Section 3404(e) of the New York Insurance Law. The source of the remainder is Section 176:36:–5:20 of the New Jersey statutes. Editorial changes can be discerned in each part. For example, in the penultimate paragraph (*Suit*), the period "two years" is the product of an amendment to the New York statute. The comparable period in the New Jersey statute is twelve months. That and other legislative history is given in Port Auth. v. Affiliated FM Ins. Co., 2000 U.S. Dist. LEXIS 20274 (D.N.J. 2000), as follows:

> In 1943, the New York state legislature passed a standard form for the insurance of property against loss caused by fire and other perils. N.Y. Ins. Law § 3404(e)(formerly § 168).... This form is commonly referred to as the "Standard Fire Policy" or the "165–line policy," because the format of this policy included 165 numbered lines ..... From July 1, 1943 to September 1, 1975, the New York Standard Fire Policy included [a] one year suit limitation period.... "Effective September 1, 1975, however, 'twelve months' was changed to 'two years' by statutory amendment." N.Y. Ins. Law § 3404(e). [*Footnote*: New Jersey, on the other hand, has retained the twelve month suit limitation period ... to the present day.]

Except for the first six of the "165 lines", the editors have omitted line numbering, and indeed have run lines together. The first six lines (*Concealment, fraud*) are set up as in the statute as an example.

The New York statute cited above contains this Proviso: "[T]he commissioner [*sic*] may approve for use within the State a form of policy which does not correspond to the standard fire insurance policy as provided by this section if the coverage with respect to the peril of fire provided in such approved form is, when viewed in its entirety, substantially equivalent to or more favorable to the insured than that contained in the standard fire insurance policy established by this section."

. . .

The statute continues: "The form of the standard fire insurance policy of the state of New York (with permission to substitute for the word "company" a more accurate descriptive term for the type of insurer) shall be as follows:"

FIRST PAGE ...

No. [___]

[Space for insertion of name of company or companies issuing the policy and other matter permitted to be stated at the head of the policy.]

[Space for listing amounts of insurance, rates and premiums for the basic coverages insured under the standard form of policy and for additional coverages or perils insured under endorsements attached.]

In Consideration of the Provisions and Stipulations herein or added hereto and of ... **Dollars Premium**

this Company, from ___ at noon, Standard Time, to ___.

does insure ___ and legal representatives TO THE LESSER AMOUNT OF EITHER:

1) THE ACTUAL CASH VALUE OF THE PROPERTY AT THE TIME OF THE LOSS, OR

2) THE AMOUNT WHICH IT WOULD COST TO REPAIR OR RE-PLACE THE PROPERTY WITH MATERIAL OF LIKE KIND AND QUAL-ITY WITHIN A REASONABLE TIME AFTER SUCH LOSS, WITHOUT ALLOWANCE FOR ANY INCREASED COST OF REPAIR OR RECON-STRUCTION BY REASON OF ANY ORDINANCE OR LAW REGULAT-ING CONSTRUCTION OR REPAIR, AND WITHOUT COMPENSATION FOR LOSS RESULTING FROM INTERRUPTION OF BUSINESS OR MANUFACTURE, OR

3) TO AN AMOUNT NOT EXCEEDING [___] DOLLARS, BUT IN ANY EVENT FOR NO MORE THAN THE INTEREST OF THE IN-SURED, AGAINST ALL DIRECT LOSS BY FIRE, LIGHTNING AND BY REMOVAL FROM PREMISES ENDANGERED BY THE PERILS IN-SURED AGAINST IN THIS POLICY, EXCEPT AS HEREINAFTER PRO-VIDED, to the property described hereinafter while located or contained as described in this policy, or pro rata for five days at each proper place to which any of the property shall necessarily be removed for preservation from the perils insured against in this policy, but not elsewhere.

Assignment of this policy shall not be valid except with the written consent of this Company.

This policy is made and accepted subject to the foregoing provisions and stipulations and those hereinafter stated, which are hereby made a part of this policy, together with such other provisions, stipulations and agreements as may be added hereto, as provided in this policy.

In Witness Whereof, this Company has executed and attested these presents; but this policy shall not be valid unless countersigned by the duly authorized Agent of this Company at. . . .

Secretary.   President.

AGENT Countersignature and Date _____, 2____.

1 *Concealment,*   This entire policy shall be void if, whether
2 *fraud.*   before or after a loss, the insured has
3   wilfully concealed or misrepresented any
4 material fact or circumstance concerning this insurance or the
5 subject thereof, or the interest of the insured therein, or in case
6 of any fraud or false swearing by the insured relating thereto.

Uninsurable and excepted property. This policy shall not cover accounts, bills, and currency, deeds, evidences of debt, money or securities; nor, unless specifically named hereon in writing, bullion or manuscripts.

Perils not included. This Company shall not be liable for loss by fire or other perils insured against in this policy caused, directly or indirectly, by: (a) enemy attack by armed forces, including action taken by military, naval or air forces in resisting an actual or an immediately impending enemy attack; (b) invasion; (c) insurrection; (d) rebellion; (e) revolution; (f) civil war; (g) usurped power; (h) order of any civil authority except acts of destruction at the time of and for the purpose of preventing the spread of fire, provided that such fire did not originate from any of the perils excluded by this policy; (1) neglect of the insured to use all reasonable means to save and preserve the property at and after a loss, or when the property is endangered by fire in neighboring premises; (j) nor shall this Company be liable for loss by theft.

Other Insurance. Other insurance may be prohibited or the amount of insurance may be limited by endorsement attached hereto.

Conditions suspending or restricting Insurance. Unless otherwise provided in writing added hereto this Company shall not be liable for loss occurring

> (a) while the hazard is increased by any means within the control or knowledge of the insured; or
>
> (b) while a described building, whether intended for occupancy by owner or tenant, is vacant or unoccupied beyond a period of sixty consecutive days; or
>
> (c) as a result of explosion or riot, unless fire ensue, and in that event for loss by fire only.

Other perils or subjects. Any other peril to be insured against or subject of insurance to be covered in this policy shall be by endorsement in writing hereon or added hereto.

Added provisions. The extent of the application of insurance under this policy and of the contribution to be made by this Company in case of loss, and any other provision or agreement not inconsistent with the provisions of this policy, may be provided for in writing added hereto, but no provision may be waived except such as by the terms of this policy is subject to change.

Waiver provisions. No permission affecting this insurance shall exist, or waiver of any provision be valid, unless granted herein or expressed in writing added hereto. No provision, stipulation or forfeiture shall be held to be waived by any requirement or proceeding on the part of this Company relating to appraisal or to any examination provided for herein.

Cancellation of policy. This policy shall be cancelled at any time at the request of the insured, in which case this Company shall, upon demand and surrender of this policy, refund the excess of paid premium above the customary short rates for the expired time. This policy may be cancelled at any time by this Company by giving to the insured a five days' written notice of cancellation with or without tender of the excess of paid premium above the pro rata premium for the expired time, which excess, if not tendered, shall be refunded on demand. Notice of cancellation shall state that said excess premium (if not tendered) will be refunded on demand.

Mortgagee interests and obligations. If loss hereunder is made pay-able, in whole or in part, to a designated mortgagee not named herein as the insured, such interest in this policy may be cancelled by giving to such mortgagee a ten days' written notice of cancellation.

If the insured fails to render proof of loss such mortgagee, upon notice, shall render proof of loss in the form herein specified within sixty (60) days thereafter and shall be subject to the pro visions hereof relating to appraisal and time of payment and of bringing suit. If this Company shall claim that no liability existed as to the mortgagor or owner, it shall, to the extent of payment of loss to the mortgagee, be subrogated to all the mortgagee's rights of recovery, but without impairing mortgagee's right to sue; or it may pay off the mortgage debt and require an assignment thereof and of the mortgage. Other provisions relating to the interests and obligations of such mortgagee may be added hereto by agreement in writing.

Pro rata liability. This Company shall not be liable for a greater proportion of any loss than the amount hereby insured shall bear to the whole insurance covering the property against the peril involved, whether collectible or not.

Requirements in case loss occurs. The insured shall give immediate written notice to this Company of any loss, protect the property from further damage, forthwith separate the damaged and undamaged personal property, put it in the best possible order, furnish a complete inventory of the destroyed, damaged and undamaged property, showing in detail quantities, costs, actual cash value and amount of loss claimed; and within sixty days after the loss, unless such time is extended in writing by this Company, the insured shall render to this Company a proof of loss, signed and sworn to by the insured, stating the knowledge and belief of the insured as to the following: the time and origin of the loss, the interest of the insured and of all others in the property, the actual cash value of each item thereof and the amount of loss thereto, all encumbrances thereon, all other contracts of insurance, whether valid or not, covering any of said property, any changes in the title use, occupation, location, possession or exposures of said property since the issuing of this policy, by whom and for what purpose any building herein described and the several parts thereof were occupied at the time of loss and whether or not it then stood on leased ground, and shall furnish a copy of all the descriptions and schedules in all policies and, if required, verified plans and specifications of any building, fixtures or machinery destroyed or damaged. The insured, as often as may be reasonably required, shall exhibit to any person designated by this Company all that remains of any property herein described, and submit to examinations under oath by any person named by this Company, and subscribe the same; and, as often as may be reasonably required, shall produce for examination all books of account, bills, invoices and other vouchers, or certified copies thereof if originals be lost, at such reasonable time and place as may be designated by this Company or its representative, and shall permit extracts and copies thereof to be made.

Appraisal. In case the insured and this Company shall fail to agree as to the actual cash value or the amount of loss, then, on the written demand of either, each shall select a competent and disinterested appraiser and notify the other of the appraiser selected within twenty days of such demand. The appraisers shall first select a competent and disinterested umpire; and failing for fifteen days to agree upon such umpire, then, on request of the insured or this Company, such umpire shall be selected by a judge of a court of record in the state in which the property covered is located. The appraisers shall then appraise the loss, stating separately actual cash value and loss to each item, and, failing to agree, shall submit their differences, only, to the umpire. An award in writing, so itemized, of any two when filed with this Company shall determine the amount of actual cash value and loss. Each appraiser shall be paid by the party selecting him and the expenses of appraisal and the umpire shall be paid by the parties equally.

Company's options. It shall be optional with this Company to take all, or any part, of the property at the agreed or appraised value, and also to repair, rebuild or replace the property destroyed or damaged with other of like kind and quality within a reasonable time, on giving notice of its intention so to do within thirty days after the receipt of the proof of loss herein required.

Abandonment. There can be no abandonment to this Company of any property.

When loss payable. The amount of loss for which this Company may be liable shall be payable thirty days after proof of loss, as herein provided, is received by this Company and ascertainment of the loss is made either by agreement between the insured and this Company expressed in writing or by the filing with this Company of an award as herein provided.

Suit. No suit or action on this policy for the recovery of any claim shall be sustainable in any court of law or equity unless all the requirements of this policy shall have been complied with, and unless commenced within two years next after inception of the loss.

Subrogation. This Company may require from the insured an assignment of all right of recovery against any party for loss to the extent that payment therefor is made by this Company.

HOMEOWNERS 3—SPECIAL FORM

AGREEMENT

We will provide the insurance described in this policy in return for the premium and compliance with all applicable provisions of this policy.

DEFINITIONS

A. In this policy, "you" and "your" refer to the "named insured" shown in the Declarations and the spouse if a resident of the same household. "We", "us" and "our" refer to the Company providing this insurance.

B. In addition, certain words and phrases are defined as follows:

1. "Aircraft Liability", "Hovercraft Liability", "Motor Vehicle Liability" and "Watercraft Liability", subject to the provisions in b. below, mean the following:

   a. Liability for "bodily injury" or "property damage" arising out of the:

      (1) Ownership of such vehicle or craft by an "insured";

      (2) Maintenance, occupancy, operation, use, loading or unloading of such vehicle or craft by any person;

      (3) Entrustment of such vehicle or craft by an "insured" to any person;

      (4) Failure to supervise or negligent supervision of any person involving such vehicle or craft by an "insured"; or

      (5) Vicarious liability, whether or not imposed by law, for the actions of a child or minor involving such vehicle or craft.

   b. For the purpose of this definition:

      (a) [*Omitted: definitions of "Aircraft", "Hovercraft", and "Watercraft".*]

      (4) Motor vehicle means a "motor vehicle" as defined in 7. below.

2. "Bodily injury" means bodily harm, sickness or disease, including required care, loss of services and death that results.

3. "Business" means:

   a. A trade, profession or occupation engaged in on a full-time, part-time or occasional basis; or

   b. [*subject to exceptions, certain activities for which an "insured" has received little or no compensation*].

4. "Employee" means an employee of an "insured", or an employee leased to an "insured" by a labor leasing firm under an agreement between an "insured" and the labor leasing firm, whose duties are other than those performed by a "residence employee".

5. "Insured" means:

   a. You and residents of your household who are:

      (1) Your relatives; or

      (2) Other persons under the age of 21 and in the care of any person named above;

b. A student enrolled in school full time, as defined by the school, who was a resident of your household before moving out to attend school, provided the student is under the age of:

(1) 24 and your relative; or

(2) 21 and in your care or the care of a person described in a.(1) above; or

c. Under Section II:

(1) With respect to animals or watercraft to which this policy applies, [*certain persons and organizations legally responsible for them*].

(2) With respect to a "motor vehicle" to which this policy applies:

(a) Persons while engaged in your employ or that of any person included in a. or b. above; or

(b) Other persons using the vehicle on an "insured location" with your consent.

Under both Sections I and II, when the word an immediately precedes the word "insured", the words an "insured" together mean one or more "insureds".

6. "Insured location" means:

a. The "residence premises";

b. The part of other premises, other structures and grounds used by you as a residence; and

(1) Which is shown in the Declarations; or

(2) Which is acquired by you during the policy period for your use as a residence;

c. Any premises used by you in connection with a premises described in a. and b. above;

d. Any part of a premises:

(1) Not owned by an "insured"; and

(2) Where an "insured" is temporarily residing;

e. Vacant land, other than farm land, owned by or rented to an "insured";

f. Land owned by or rented to an "insured" on which a one, two, three or four family dwelling is being built as a residence for an "insured";

g. Individual or family cemetery plots or burial vaults of an "insured"; or

h. Any part of a premises occasionally rented to an "insured" for other than "business" use.

7. "Motor vehicle" means:

a. A self-propelled land or amphibious vehicle; or

b. Any trailer or semitrailer which is being carried on, towed by or hitched for towing by a vehicle described in a. above.

8. "Occurrence" means an accident, including continuous or repeated exposure to substantially the same general harmful conditions, which results, during the policy period, in:

a. "Bodily injury"; or

b. "Property damage".

9. "Property damage" means physical injury to, destruction of, or loss of use of tangible property.

10. "Residence employee" means:

   a. An employee of an "insured", [*and certain persons leased to an "insured", including one whose duties are domestic services at the "residence premises"*].

11. "Residence premises" means:

   a. The one family dwelling where you reside;

   b. The two, three or four family dwelling where you reside in at least one of the family units; or

   c. That part of any other building where you reside;

   and which is shown as the "residence premises" in the Declarations.

   "Residence premises" also includes other structures and grounds at that location.

DEDUCTIBLE

Unless otherwise noted in this policy, the following deductible provision applies:

Subject to the policy limits that apply, we will pay only that part of the total of all loss payable under Section I that exceeds the deductible amount shown in the Declarations.

SECTION I—PROPERTY COVERAGES

A. Coverage A—Dwelling

1. We cover:

   a. The dwelling on the "residence premises" shown in the Declarations, including structures attached to the dwelling; and

   b. Materials and supplies located on or next to the "residence premises" used to construct, alter or repair the dwelling or other structures on the "residence premises".

2. We do not cover land, including land on which the dwelling is located.

B. Coverage B—Other Structures

1. We cover other structures on the "residence premises" set apart from the dwelling by clear space. This includes structures connected to the dwelling by only a fence, utility line, or similar connection.

2. We do not cover:

   a. Land, including land on which the other structures are located;

   b. Other structures rented or held for rental to any person not a tenant of the dwelling, unless used solely as a private garage;

   c. Other structures from which any "business" is conducted; or

   d. Other structures used to store "business" property. However, we do cover a structure that contains "business" property solely owned by an "insured" or a tenant of the dwelling provided that "business" property does not include gaseous or liquid fuel, other than fuel in a permanently installed fuel tank of a vehicle or craft parked or stored in the structure.

3. The limit of liability for this coverage will not be more than 10% of the limit of liability that

applies to Coverage A. Use of this coverage does not reduce the Coverage A limit of liability.

C. Coverage C—Personal Property

1. Covered Property

We cover personal property owned or used by an "insured" while it is anywhere in the world. After a loss and at your request, we will cover personal property owned by:

    a. Others while the property is on the part of the "residence premises" occupied by an "insured"; or

    b. A guest or a "residence employee", while the property is in any residence occupied by an "insured".

2. Limit for Property At Other Residences

Our limit of liability for personal property usually located at an "insured's" residence, other than the "residence premises", is 10% of the limit of liability for Coverage C or $1,000, whichever is greater. However, this limitation does not apply to personal property:

    a. Moved from the "residence premises" because it is being repaired, renovated or rebuilt and is not fit to live in or store property in; or

    b. In a newly acquired principal residence for 30 days from the time you begin to move the property there.

3. Special Limits of Liability

The special limit for each category shown below is the total limit for each loss for all property in that category. These special limits do not increase the Coverage C limit of liability.

[*The entries that follow state dollar amounts for eleven categories, ranging from $200 to $2,500. Many of the items included are readily tradeable* (e.g., money). *Entry f is "$1,500 for loss by theft of jewelry, watches, furs, precious and semiprecious stones". Only two other entries mention a particular cause of loss. Liability is limited for the loss of a manuscript existing on computer software; and the limit "includes the cost to research, replace or restore the information from the lost or damaged material."*]

4. Property Not Covered

We do not cover:

    a. Articles separately described and specifically insured, regardless of the limit for which they are insured, in this or other insurance.

    b. Animals, birds or fish;

    c. "Motor vehicles".

    (1) This includes:

        (a) Their accessories, equipment and parts; or

        (b) Electronic apparatus and accessories designed to be operated solely by power from the electrical system of the "motor vehicle". Accessories include antennas, tapes, wires, records, discs or other media that can be used with any apparatus described above.

The exclusion of property described in (a) and (b) above applies only while such property is in or upon the "motor vehicle".

(2) We do cover "motor vehicles" not required to be registered for use on public roads or property which are:

(a) Used solely to service an "insured's" residence; or

(b) Designed to assist the handicapped;

d. Aircraft meaning any contrivance used or designed for flight including any parts whether or not attached to the aircraft.

We do cover model or hobby aircraft not used or designed to carry people or cargo;

e. Hovercraft and parts. Hovercraft means a self-propelled motorized ground-effect vehicle and includes, but is not limited to, flarecraft and air cushion vehicles;

f. Property of roomers, boarders and other tenants, except property of roomers and boarders related to an "insured";

g. Property in an apartment regularly rented or held for rental to others by an "insured", except as provided in E.10. Landlord's Furnishings under Section I—Property Coverages;

h. Property rented or held for rental to others off the "residence premises";

i. "Business" data, including such data stored in:

(1) Books of account, drawings or other paper records; or

(2) Computers and related equipment.

We do cover the cost of blank recording or storage media, and of prerecorded computer programs available on the retail market;

j. Credit cards, electronic fund transfer cards or access devices used solely for deposit, withdrawal or transfer of funds except as provided in E.6. Credit Card, Electronic Fund Transfer Card Or Access Device, Forgery And Counterfeit Money under Section I—Property Coverages; or

k. Water or steam.

Coverage D—Loss of Use

The limit of liability for Coverage D is the total limit for the coverages in 1. Additional Living Expense, 2. Fair Rental Value and 3. Civil Authority Prohibits Use below.

1. Additional Living Expense

If a loss covered under Section I makes that part of the "residence premises" where you reside not fit to live in, we cover any necessary increase in living expenses incurred by you so that your household can maintain its normal standard of living.

Payment will be for the shortest time required to repair or replace the damage or, if you permanently relocate, the shortest time required for your household to settle elsewhere.

2. Fair Rental Value

If a loss covered under Section I makes that part of the "residence premises" rented to others or held for rental by you not fit to live in, we cover the fair rental value of such premises less any expenses that do not continue while it is not fit to live in.

Payment will be for the shortest time required to repair or replace such premises.

3. Civil Authority Prohibits Use

If a civil authority prohibits you from use of the "residence premises" as a result of direct damage to neighboring premises by a Peril Insured Against, we cover the loss as provided in 1. Additional Living Expense and 2. Fair Rental Value above for no more than two weeks.

4. Loss or Expense Not Covered

We do not cover loss or expense due to cancellation of a lease or agreement.

The periods of time under 1. Additional Living Expense, 2. Fair Rental Value and 3. Civil Authority Prohibits Use above are not limited by expiration of this policy.

E. Additional Coverages

1. Debris Removal

[*"We will pay your reasonable expense", in specified circumstances, for the removal of debris of covered property; also for the removal of trees from the "residence premises". In the latter case $500 is the most that is payable for the removal of a single tree, and $1,000 for any loss. "This coverage is additional insurance."*]

2. Reasonable Repairs

a. We will pay the reasonable cost incurred by you for the necessary measures taken solely to protect covered property that is damaged by a Peril Insured Against from further damage.

b. If the measures taken involve repair to other damaged property, we will only pay if that property is covered under this policy and the damage is caused by a Peril Insured Against. This coverage does not:

(1) Increase the limit of liability that applies to the covered property; or

(2) Relieve you of your duties, in case of a loss to covered property, described in B.4. under Section I — Conditions.

3. Trees, Shrubs and Other Plants

We cover trees, shrubs, plants or lawns on the "residence premises", for loss caused by the following Perils Insured Against:

[*Among the perils listed are fire, vandalism, and theft. Modest limits of liability are stated. "This coverage is additional insurance."*]

[*Entries 4 and 5 relate to fire-department services charges, as limited, and to loss "from any cause" to covered property "while being removed from a premises endangered by a Peril Insured Against".*]

6. Credit Card, Electronic Fund Transfer Card or Access Device, Forgery and Counterfeit Money

a. We will pay up to $500 for:

(1) The legal obligation of an "insured" to pay because of the theft or unauthorized use of credit cards issued to or registered in an "insured's" name;

(2) Loss resulting from theft or unauthorized use of an electronic fund transfer card or

access device used for deposit, withdrawal or transfer of funds, issued to or registered in an "insured's" name;

(3) Loss to an "insured" caused by forgery or alteration of any check or negotiable instrument; and

(4) Loss to an "insured" through acceptance in good faith of counterfeit United States or Canadian paper currency.

All loss resulting from a series of acts committed by any one person or in which any one person is concerned or implicated is considered to be one loss.

This coverage is additional insurance. No deductible applies to this coverage.

b. We do not cover:

(1) Use of a credit card, electronic fund transfer card or access device:

(a) By a resident of your household;

(b) By a person who has been entrusted with either type of card or access device; or

(c) If an "insured" has not complied with all terms and conditions under which the cards are issued or the devices accessed; or

(2) Loss arising out of "business" use or dishonesty of an "insured".

c. If the coverage in a. above applies, the following defense provisions also apply:

[*Here follow a few sentences comparable to those found in liability-insurance forms.*]

7. Loss Assessment

[*Entry 7 provides for paying, with in limits, non-governmental assessments, typified by those of condo associations, on account of loss to communal property. The loss must be one caused by one of the Coverage–A perils other than earthquake and volcanic eruption).*]

This coverage is additional insurance.

Collapse

With respect to this Additional Coverage:

(1) Collapse means an abrupt falling down or caving in of a building or any part of a building with the result that the building or part of the building cannot be occupied for its current intended purpose.

(2) A building or any part of a building that is in danger of falling down or caving in is not considered to be in a state of collapse.

(3) A part of a building that is standing is not considered to be in a state of collapse even if it has separated from another part of the building.

(4) A building or any part of a building that is standing is not considered to be in a state of collapse even if it shows evidence of

cracking, bulging, sagging, bending, leaning, settling, shrinkage or expansion.

b. We insure for direct physical loss to covered property involving collapse of a building or any part of a building if the collapse was caused by one or more of the following:

(1) The Perils Insured Against named under Coverage C;

(2) Decay that is hidden from view, unless the presence of such decay is known to an "insured" prior to collapse;

(3) Insect or vermin damage that is hidden from view, unless the presence of such damage is known to an "insured" prior to collapse;

(4) Weight of contents, equipment, animals or people;

(5) Weight of rain which collects on a roof; or

(6) Use of defective material or methods in construction, remodeling or renovation if the collapse occurs during the course of the construction, remodeling or renovation.

c. Loss to an awning, fence, patio, deck, pavement, swimming pool, underground pipe, flue, drain, cesspool, septic tank, foundation, retaining wall, bulkhead, pier, wharf or dock is not included under b.(2) through (6) above, unless

the loss is a direct result of the collapse of a building or any part of a building.

d. This coverage does not increase the limit of liability that applies to the damaged covered property.

9. Glass or Safety Glazing Material

[*Coverage is extended to, among other things, the breakage of windows in a covered building, and to losses to covered property caused "solely by fragments, but not—aside from the latter—to loss suffered by covered property "because [the window] has been broken".*]

10. Landlord's Furnishings

We will pay up to $2,500 for your appliances, carpeting and other household furnishings, in each apartment on the "residence premises" regularly rented or held for rental to others by an "insured", for loss caused by a Peril Insured Against in Coverage C, other than Theft.

This limit is the most we will pay in any one loss regardless of the number of appliances, carpeting or other household furnishings involved in the loss.

This coverage does not increase the limit of liability applying to the damaged property.

11. Ordinance or Law

a. You may use up to 10% of the limit of liability that applies to Coverage A for the increased costs you incur due to the enforcement of any ordinance or law which requires or regulates:

(1) The construction, demolition, remodeling, renovation or repair of

that part of a covered building or other structure damaged by a Peril Insured Against;

(2) The demolition and reconstruction of the undamaged part of a covered building or other structure, when that building or other structure must be totally demolished because of damage by a Peril Insured Against to another part of that covered building or other structure; or

(3) The remodeling, removal or replacement of the portion of the undamaged part of a covered building or other structure necessary to complete the remodeling, repair or replacement of that part of the covered building or other structure damaged by a Peril Insured Against.

b. You may use all or part of this ordinance or law coverage to pay for the increased costs you incur to remove debris resulting from the construction, demolition, remodeling, renovation, repair or replacement of property as stated in a. above.

c. We do not cover:

(1) The loss in value to any covered building or other structure due to the requirements of any ordinance or law; or

(2) The costs to comply with any ordinance or

law which requires any "insured" or others to test for, monitor, clean up, remove, contain, treat, detoxify or neutralize, or in any way respond to, or assess the effects of, pollutants in or on any covered building or other structure.

Pollutants means any solid, liquid, gaseous or thermal irritant or contaminant, including smoke, vapor, soot, fumes, acids, alkalis, chemicals and waste. Waste includes materials to be recycled, reconditioned or reclaimed.

This coverage is additional insurance.

12. Grave Markers

We will pay up to $5,000 for grave markers, including mausoleums, on or away from the "residence premises" for loss caused by a Peril Insured Against under Coverage C.

This coverage does not increase the limits of liability that apply to the damaged covered property.

SECTION I—PERILS INSURED AGAINST

A. Coverage A—Dwelling and Coverage B—Other Structures

1. We insure against risk of direct physical loss to property described in Coverages A and B.

2. We do not insure, however, for loss:

a. Excluded under Section I—Exclusions;

b. Involving collapse, except as provided in E.8. Collapse under Section I—Property Coverages; or

c. Caused by:

(1) Freezing of a plumbing, heating, air conditioning or automatic fire protective sprinkler system or of a household appliance, or by discharge, leakage or overflow from within the system or appliance caused by freezing. This provision does not apply if you have used reasonable care to:

(a) Maintain heat in the building; or

(b) Shut off the water supply and drain all systems and appliances of water.

However, if the building is protected by an automatic fire protective sprinkler system, you must use reasonable care to continue the water supply and maintain heat in the building for coverage to apply.

For purposes of this provision a plumbing system or household appliance does not include a sump, sump pump or related equipment or a roof drain, gutter, downspout or similar fixtures or equipment;

(2) Freezing, thawing, pressure or weight of water or ice, whether driven by wind or not, to a:

(a) Fence, pavement, patio or swimming pool;

(b) Footing, foundation, bulkhead, wall, or any other structure or device that supports all or part of a building, or other structure;

(c) Retaining wall or bulkhead that does not support all or part of a building or other structure; or

(d) Pier, wharf or dock;

(3) Theft in or to a dwelling under construction, or of materials and supplies for use in the construction until the dwelling is finished and occupied;

(4) Vandalism and malicious mischief, and any ensuing loss caused by any intentional and wrongful act committed in the course of the vandalism or malicious mischief, if the dwelling has been vacant for more than 60 consecutive days immediately before the loss. A dwelling being constructed is not considered vacant;

(5) Mold, fungus or wet rot. However, we do insure for loss caused by mold, fungus or wet rot that is hidden within the walls or ceilings or beneath the floors or above the ceilings of a structure if such loss results from the accidental discharge or overflow of water or steam from within:

(a) A plumbing, heating, air conditioning or automatic

fire protective sprinkler system, or a household appliance, on the "residence premises"; or

(b) A storm drain, or water, steam or sewer pipes, off the "residence premises".

For purposes of this provision, a plumbing system or household appliance does not include a sump, sump pump or related equipment or a roof drain, gutter, downspout or similar fixtures or equipment; or

(6) Any of the following:

(a) Wear and tear, marring, deterioration;

(b) Mechanical breakdown, latent defect, inherent vice, or any quality in property that causes it to damage or destroy itself;

(c) Smog, rust or other corrosion, or dry rot;

(d) Smoke from agricultural smudging or industrial operations;

(e) Discharge, dispersal, seepage, migration, release or escape of pollutants unless the discharge, dispersal, seepage, migration, release or escape is itself caused by a Peril Insured Against named under Coverage C.

Pollutants means any solid, liquid, gaseous or thermal irritant or contaminant, including smoke, vapor, soot, fumes, acids, alkalis, chemicals and waste. Waste includes materials to be recycled, reconditioned or reclaimed;

(f) Settling, shrinking, bulging or expansion, including resultant cracking, of bulkheads, pavements, patios, footings, foundations, walls, floors, roofs or ceilings;

(g) Birds, vermin, rodents, or insects; or

(h) Animals owned or kept by an "insured".

Exception to c.(6)

[*An "accidental discharge or overflow of water or steam" from a drain or pipe may produce a covered loss to property covered under Coverage A or Coverage B, whether the apparatus is on or off the "residence premises". Overflow from a household appliance on the premises may produce a covered loss. (Sump pumps, gutters, and downspouts don't count as household appliances for this purpose.) "We do not cover loss to the system or appliance from which this water or steam escaped."*]

B. Coverage C—Personal Property

We insure for direct physical loss to the property described in Coverage

C caused by any of the following perils unless the loss is excluded in Section I—Exclusions.

1. Fire or Lightning

2. Windstorm or Hail

     This peril includes loss to watercraft of all types and their trailers, furnishings, equipment, and outboard engines or motors, only while inside a fully enclosed building.

     This peril does not include loss to the property contained in a building caused by rain, snow, sleet, sand or dust unless the direct force of wind or hail damages the building causing an opening in a roof or wall and the rain, snow, sleet, sand or dust enters through this opening.

3. Explosion

4. Riot or Civil Commotion

5. Aircraft

This peril includes self-propelled missiles and spacecraft.

6. Vehicles

7. Smoke

This peril means sudden and accidental damage from smoke, including the emission or puffback of smoke, soot, fumes or vapors from a boiler, furnace or related equipment.

This peril does not include loss caused by smoke from agricultural smudging or industrial operations.

8. Vandalism or Malicious Mischief

9. Theft

     a. This peril includes attempted theft and loss of property from a known place when it is likely that the property has been stolen.

     b. This peril does not include loss caused by theft:

          (1) Committed by an "insured";

[*Nor does it include loss by theft that occurs at all locations. For example, it does not include loss by theft occurring off the "residence premises" if the property is at another residence owned by, rented to, or occupied by an "insured". A qualification on that restriction applies to case of temporary quarters. Another applies to dormitory life. "Property of an "insured" who is a student is covered while at the residence the student occupies to attend school as long as the student has been there at any time during the 60 days immediately before the loss."*]

10. Falling Objects

This peril does not include loss to property contained in a building unless the roof or an outside wall of the building is first damaged by a falling object. Damage to the falling object itself is not included.

11. Weight of Ice, Snow or Sleet

This peril means weight of ice, snow or sleet which causes damage to property contained in a building.

12. Accidental Discharge or Overflow of Water or Steam

     a. This peril means accidental discharge or overflow of water or steam from within a plumbing, heating, air conditioning or automatic fire protective sprinkler system or from within a household appliance.

     b. This peril does not include loss:

(1) To the system or appliance from which the water or steam escaped;

(2) Caused by or resulting from freezing except as provided in Peril Insured Against 14. Freezing;

(3) On the "residence premises" caused by accidental discharge or overflow which occurs off the "residence premises"; or

(4) Caused by mold, fungus or wet rot unless hidden within the walls or ceilings or beneath the floors or above the ceilings of a structure.

c. In this peril, a plumbing system or household appliance does not include a sump, sump pump or related equipment or a roof drain, gutter, downspout or similar fixtures or equipment.

d. Section I—Exclusion A.3. Water Damage, Paragraphs b. and c. that apply to surface water and water below the surface of the ground do not apply to loss by water covered under this peril.

13. Sudden and Accidental Tearing Apart, Cracking, Burning or Bulging

This peril means sudden and accidental tearing apart, cracking, burning or bulging of a steam or hot water heating system, an air conditioning or automatic fire protective sprinkler system, or an appliance for heating water.

We do not cover loss caused by or resulting from freezing under this peril.

14. Freezing

a. This peril means freezing of a plumbing, heating, air conditioning or automatic fire protective sprinkler system or of a household appliance but only if you have used reasonable care to:

(1) Maintain heat in the building; or

(2) Shut off the water supply and drain all systems and appliances of water.

However, if the building is protected by an automatic fire protective sprinkler system, you must use reasonable care to continue the water supply and maintain heat in the building for coverage to apply.

b. In this peril, a plumbing system or household appliance does not include a sump, sump pump or related equipment or a roof drain, gutter, downspout or similar fixtures or equipment.

15. Sudden and Accidental Damage From Artificially Generated Electrical Current

This peril does not include loss to tubes, transistors, electronic components or circuitry that are a part of appliances, fixtures, computers, home entertainment units or other types of electronic apparatus.

16. Volcanic Eruption

This peril does not include loss caused by earthquake, land shock waves or tremors.

SECTION I—EXCLUSIONS

A. We do not insure for loss caused directly or indirectly by any of the following. Such loss is excluded regardless of any other cause or event contributing concurrently or in any sequence to the loss. These exclusions apply whether or not the loss event results in widespread damage or affects a substantial area.

1. Ordinance or Law

    Ordinance or Law means any ordinance or law:

    a. Requiring or regulating the construction, demolition, remodeling, renovation or repair of property, including removal of any resulting debris. This Exclusion A.1.a. does not apply to the amount of coverage that may be provided for in E.11. Ordinance Or Law under Section I—Property Coverages;

    b. The requirements of which result in a loss in value to property; or

    c. Requiring any insured's or others to test for, monitor, clean up, remove, contain, treat, detoxify or neutralize, or in any way respond to, or assess the effects of, pollutants.

    Pollutants means any solid, liquid, gaseous or thermal irritant or contaminant, including smoke, vapor, soot, fumes, acids, alkalis, chemicals and waste. Waste includes materials to be recycled, reconditioned or reclaimed.

    This Exclusion A.1. applies whether or not the property has been physically damaged.

2. Earth Movement

    Earth Movement means:

    a. Earthquake, including land shock waves or tremors before, during or after a volcanic eruption;

    b. Landslide, mudslide or mudflow;

    c. Subsidence or sinkhole; or

    d. Any other earth movement including earth sinking, rising or shifting;

    caused by or resulting from human or animal forces or any act of nature unless direct loss by fire or explosion ensues and then we will pay only for the ensuing loss.

    This Exclusion A.2. does not apply to loss by theft.

3. Water Damage

    Water Damage means:

    a. Flood, surface water, waves, tidal water, overflow of a body of water, or spray from any of these, whether or not driven by wind;

    b. Water or water-borne material which backs up through sewers or drains or which overflows or is discharged from a sump, sump pump or related equipment; or

    c. Water or water-borne material below the surface of the ground, including water which exerts pressure on or seeps or leaks through a building, sidewalk, driveway, foundation, swimming pool or other structure;

    caused by or resulting from human or animal forces or any act of nature.

Direct loss by fire, explosion or theft resulting from water damage is covered.

4.   Power Failure

Power Failure means the failure of power or other utility service if the failure takes place off the "residence premises". But if the failure results in a loss, from a Peril Insured Against on the "residence premises", we will pay for the loss caused by that peril.

5.   Neglect

Neglect means neglect of an "insured" to use all reasonable means to save and preserve property at and after the time of a loss.

[*Exclusions 6 and 7, with respect to war and nuclear hazard, respectively, are omitted here.*]

8.   Intentional Loss

Intentional Loss means any loss arising out of any act an "insured" commits or conspires to commit with the intent to cause a loss.

In the event of such loss, no "insured" is entitled to coverage, even "insured" who did not commit or conspire to commit the act causing the loss.

9.   Governmental Action

Governmental Action means the destruction, confiscation or seizure of property described in Coverage A, B or C by order of any governmental or public authority.

This exclusion does not apply to such acts ordered by any governmental or public authority that are taken at the time of a fire to prevent its spread, if the loss caused by fire would be covered under this policy.

B.   We do not insure for loss to property described in Coverages A and B caused by any of the following.

However, any ensuing loss to property described in Coverages A and B not precluded by any other provision in this policy is covered.

1.   Weather conditions. However, this exclusion only applies if weather conditions contribute in any way with a cause or event excluded in A. above to produce the loss.

2.   Acts or decisions, including the failure to act or decide, of any person, group, organization or governmental body.

3.   Faulty, inadequate or defective:

a.   Planning, zoning, development, surveying, siting;

b.   Design, specifications, workmanship, repair, construction, renovation, remodeling, grading, compaction;

c.   Materials used in repair, construction, renovation or remodeling; or

d.   Maintenance;

of part or all of any property whether on or off the "residence premises".

SECTION I—CONDITIONS

A.   Insurable Interest and Limit of Liability

Even if more than one person has an insurable interest in the property covered, we will not be liable in any one loss:

1.   To an "insured" for more than the amount of such "insured's" interest at the time of loss; or

2.   For more than the applicable limit of liability.

B.   Duties After Loss

In case of a loss to covered property, we have no duty to provide coverage under this policy if the failure to comply with the following duties is prejudicial to us. These duties must be performed either by you, an "insured" seeking coverage, or a representative of either:

1. Give prompt notice to us or our agent;

2. Notify the police in case of loss by theft;

3. Notify the credit card or electronic fund transfer card or access device company in case of loss as provided for in E.6. Credit Card, Electronic Fund Transfer Card Or Access Device, Forgery And Counterfeit Money under Section I—Property Coverages;

4. Protect the property from further damage. If repairs to the property are required, you must:

    a. Make reasonable and necessary repairs to protect the property; and

    b. Keep an accurate record of repair expenses;

5. Cooperate with us in the investigation of a claim;

6. Prepare an inventory of damaged personal property showing the quantity, description, actual cash value and amount of loss. Attach all bills, receipts and related documents that justify the figures in the inventory;

7. As often as we reasonably require:

    a. Show the damaged property;

    b. Provide us with records and documents we request and permit us to make copies; and

    c. Submit to examination under oath, while not in the presence of another "insured", and sign the same;

8. Send to us, within 60 days after our request, your signed, sworn proof of loss which sets forth, to the best of your knowledge and belief:

    a. The time and cause of loss;

    b. The interests of all "insureds" and all others in the property involved and all liens on the property;

    c. Other insurance which may cover the loss;

    d. Changes in title or occupancy of the property during the term of the policy;

    e. Specifications of damaged buildings and detailed repair estimates;

    f. The inventory of damaged personal property described in 6. above;

    g. Receipts for additional living expenses incurred and records that support the fair rental value loss; and

    h. Evidence or affidavit that supports a claim under E.6. Credit Card, Electronic Fund Transfer Card Or Access Device, Forgery And Counterfeit Money under Section I—Property Coverages, stating the amount and cause of loss.

C. Loss Settlement

In this Condition C., the terms "cost to repair or replace" and "replacement cost" do not include the increased costs incurred to comply with the enforcement of any ordinance or law, except to the extent that coverage for these increased costs is provided in E.11. Ordinance Or Law under Section I—Property

Coverages. Covered property losses are settled as follows:

1. Property of the following types:

    a. Personal property;

    b. Awnings, carpeting, household appliances, outdoor antennas and outdoor equipment, whether or not attached to buildings;

    c. Structures that are not buildings; and

    d. Grave markers, including mausoleums;

    at actual cash value at the time of loss but not more than the amount required to repair or replace.

2. Buildings covered under Coverage A or B at replacement cost without deduction for depreciation, subject to the following:

    a. If, at the time of loss, the amount of insurance in this policy on the damaged building is 80% or more of the full replacement cost of the building immediately before the loss, we will pay the cost to repair or replace, after application of any deductible and without deduction for depreciation, but not more than the least of the following amounts:

        (1) The limit of liability under this policy that applies to the building;

        (2) The replacement cost of that part of the building damaged with material of like kind and quality and for like use; or

        (3) The necessary amount actually spent to repair or replace the damaged building.

    If the building is rebuilt at a new premises, the cost described in (2) above is limited to the cost which would have been incurred if the building had been built at the original premises.

    b. If, at the time of loss, the amount of insurance in this policy on the damaged building is less than 80% of the full replacement cost of the building immediately before the loss, we will pay the greater of the following amounts, but not more than the limit of liability under this policy that applies to the building:

        (1) The actual cash value of that part of the building damaged; or

        (2) That proportion of the cost to repair or replace, after application of any deductible and without deduction for depreciation, that part of the building damaged, which the total amount of insurance in this policy on the damaged building bears to 80% of the replacement cost of the building.

    c. To determine the amount of insurance required to equal 80% of the full replacement cost of the building immediately before the loss, do not include the value of:

        (1) Excavations, footings, foundations, piers, or any other structures or devices that support all or part of the building, which are below the

undersurface of the lowest basement floor;

(2) Those supports described in (1) above which are below the surface of the ground inside the foundation walls, if there is no basement; and

(3) Underground flues, pipes, wiring and drains.

d. We will pay no more than the actual cash value of the damage until actual repair or replacement is complete. Once actual repair or replacement is complete, we will settle the loss as noted in 2.a. and b. above.

However, if the cost to repair or replace the damage is both:

(1) Less than 5% of the amount of insurance in this policy on the building; and

(2) Less than $2,500;

we will settle the loss as noted in 2.a. and b. above whether or not actual repair or replacement is complete.

e. You may disregard the replacement cost loss settlement provisions and make claim under this policy for loss to buildings on an actual cash value basis. You may then make claim for any additional liability according to the provisions of this Condition C. Loss Settlement, provided you notify us of your intent to do so within 180 days after the date of loss.

D. Loss to a Pair or Set

In case of loss to a pair or set we may elect to:

1. Repair or replace any part to restore the pair or set to its value before the loss; or

2. Pay the difference between actual cash value of the property before and after the loss.

E. Appraisal

If you and we fail to agree on the amount of loss, either may demand an appraisal of the loss. *[The remainder of this provision describes the mechanics and effect of appraisals. It resembles the paragraph "Appraisal" in the Standard Fire Policy (Appendix A).]*

F. Other Insurance and Service Agreement

If a loss covered by this policy is also covered by:

1. Other insurance, we will pay only the proportion of the loss that the limit of liability that applies under this policy bears to the total amount of insurance covering the loss; or

2. A service agreement, this insurance is excess over any amounts payable under any such agreement. Service agreement means a service plan, property restoration plan, home warranty or other similar service warranty agreement, even if it is characterized as insurance.

G. Suit Against Us

No action can be brought against us unless there has been full compliance with all of the terms under Section I of this policy and the action is started within two years after the date of loss.

H. Our Option

If we give you written notice within 30 days after we receive your signed, sworn proof of loss, we may repair or replace any part of the damaged property with material or property of like kind and quality.

I. Loss Payment

We will adjust all losses with you. We will pay you unless some other person is named in the policy or is legally entitled to receive payment. Loss will be payable 60 days after we receive your proof of loss and:

1. Reach an agreement with you;

2. There is an entry of a final judgment; or

3. There is a filing of an appraisal award with us.

J. Abandonment of Property

We need not accept any property abandoned by an ''insured''.

K. Mortgage Clause

1. If a mortgagee is named in this policy, any loss payable under Coverage A or B will be paid to the mortgagee and you, as interests appear. If more than one mortgagee is named, the order of payment will be the same as the order of precedence of the mortgages.

2. If we deny your claim, that denial will not apply to a valid claim of the mortgagee, if the mortgagee:

    a. Notifies us of any change in ownership, occupancy or substantial change in risk of which the mortgagee is aware;

    b. Pays any premium due under this policy on demand if you have neglected to pay the premium; and

    c. Submits a signed, sworn statement of loss within 60 days after receiving notice from us of your failure to do

so. Paragraphs E. Appraisal, G. Suit Against Us and I. Loss Payment under Section I—Conditions also apply to the mortgagee.

3. If we decide to cancel or not to renew this policy, the mortgagee will be notified at least 10 days before the date cancellation or nonrenewal takes effect.

4. If we pay the mortgagee for any loss and deny payment to you:

    a. We are subrogated to all the rights of the mortgagee granted under the mortgage on the property; or

    b. At our option, we may pay to the mortgagee the whole principal on the mortgage plus any accrued interest. In this event, we will receive a full assignment and transfer of the mortgage and all securities held as collateral to the mortgage debt.

5. Subrogation will not impair the right of the mortgagee to recover the full amount of the mortgagee's claim.

L. No Benefit to Bailee

We will not recognize any assignment or grant any coverage that benefits a person or organization holding, storing or moving property for a fee regardless of any other provision of this policy.

M. Nuclear Hazard Clause

[*The clause limits coverage of losses caused by the nuclear hazard (as defined). A loss so caused is not to be considered ''loss caused by fire''; but direct loss by fire resulting from the nuclear hazard is covered.*]

N. Recovered Property

If you or we recover any property for which we have made payment under this policy, you or we will notify the other of the recovery. At your option, the property will be returned to or retained by you or it will become our property. If the recovered property is returned to or retained by you, the loss payment will be adjusted based on the amount you received for the recovered property.

O. Volcanic Eruption Period

One or more volcanic eruptions that occur within a 72 hour period will be considered as one volcanic eruption.

P. Policy Period

This policy applies only to loss which occurs during the policy period.

Q. Concealment or Fraud

We provide coverage to no "insureds" under this policy if, whether before or after a loss, an "insured" has:

1. Intentionally concealed or misrepresented any material fact or circumstance;

2. Engaged in fraudulent conduct; or

3. Made false statements;

relating to this insurance.

R. Loss Payable Clause

If the Declarations show a loss payee for certain listed insured personal property, the definition of "insured" is changed to include that loss payee with respect to that property.

If we decide to cancel or not renew this policy, that loss payee will be notified in writing.

SECTION II—LIABILITY COVERAGES

A. Coverage E—Personal Liability

If a claim is made or a suit is brought against an "insured" for damages because of "bodily injury" or "property damage" caused by an "occurrence" to which this coverage applies, we will:

1. Pay up to our limit of liability for the damages for which an "insured" is legally liable. Damages include prejudgment interest awarded against an "insured"; and

2. Provide a defense at our expense by counsel of our choice, even if the suit is groundless, false or fraudulent. We may investigate and settle any claim or suit that we decide is appropriate. Our duty to settle or defend ends when our limit of liability for the "occurrence" has been exhausted by payment of a judgment or settlement.

B. Coverage F—Medical Payments to Others

We will pay the necessary medical expenses that are incurred or medically ascertained within three years from the date of an accident causing "bodily injury". Medical expenses means reasonable charges for medical, surgical, x-ray, dental, ambulance, hospital, professional nursing, prosthetic devices and funeral services. This coverage does not apply to you or regular residents of your household except "residence employees". As to others, this coverage applies only:

1. To a person on the "insured location" with the permission of an "insured"; or

2. To a person off the "insured location", if the "bodily injury":

a. Arises out of a condition on the "insured location" or the ways immediately adjoining;

b. Is caused by the activities of an "insured";

c. Is caused by a "residence employee" in the course of the "residence employee's" employment by an "insured"; or

d. Is caused by an animal owned by or in the care of an "insured".

SECTION II—EXCLUSIONS

A. "Motor Vehicle Liability"

[*in many commonplace situations of road injury. The detailed prescriptions on this subject include one about vehicles being operated in an organized race, one about those being used to carry persons or cargo for a charge, and one about motorized golf carts.*]

B. "Watercraft Liability"

[*The provisions on this subject are comparable to those about "Motor Vehicle Liability". They feature, however, references to small sailing vessels and to engines of 25 and 50 horsepower.*]

C. "Aircraft Liability"

This policy does not cover "aircraft liability".

D. "Hovercraft Liability"

This policy does not cover "hovercraft liability".

E. Coverage E—Personal Liability and Coverage F—Medical Payments to Others

Coverages E and F do not apply to the following:

1. Expected or Intended Injury

"Bodily injury" or "property damage" which is expected or intended by an "insured" even if the resulting "bodily injury" or "property damage":

a. Is of a different kind, quality or degree than initially expected or intended; or

b. Is sustained by a different person, entity, real or personal property, than initially expected or intended.

However, this Exclusion E.1. does not apply to "bodily injury" resulting from the use of reasonable force by an "insured" to protect persons or property;

2. "Business"

a. "Bodily injury" or "property damage" arising out of or in connection with a "business" conducted from an "insured location" or engaged in by an "insured", whether or not the "business" is owned or operated by an "insured" or employs an "insured".

[*This provision continues by specifying situations to which the exclusion does and does not apply. It does not necessarily apply because, for example, an insured uses part of the insured location as a home office.*]

3. Professional Services

"Bodily injury" or "property damage" arising out of the rendering of or failure to render professional services;

4. "Insured's" Premises Not An "Insured Location"

"Bodily injury" or "property damage" arising out of a premises:

a. Owned by an "insured";

b. Rented to an "insured"; or

c. Rented to others by an "insured";

that is not an "insured location";

5. War

[*Omitted.*]

6. Communicable Disease

"Bodily injury" or "property damage" which arises out of the transmission of a communicable disease by an "insured";

7. Sexual Molestation, Corporal Punishment or Physical or Mental Abuse

"Bodily injury" or "property damage" arising out of sexual molestation, corporal punishment or physical or mental abuse; or

8. Controlled Substance

"Bodily injury" or "property damage" arising out of the use, sale, manufacture, delivery, transfer or possession by any person of a Controlled Substance as defined by the Federal Food and Drug Law at 21 U.S.C.A. Sections 811 and 812. Controlled Substances include but are not limited to cocaine, LSD, marijuana and all narcotic drugs. However, this exclusion does not apply to the legitimate use of prescription drugs by a person following the orders of a licensed physician.

Exclusions A. "Motor Vehicle Liability", B. "Watercraft Liability", C. "Aircraft Liability", D. "Hovercraft Liability" and E. "Insured's" Premises Not An "Insured Location" do not apply to "bodily injury" to a "residence employee" arising out of and in the course of the "residence employee's" employment by an "insured".

F. Coverage E—Personal Liability

Coverage E does not apply to:

1. Liability:

a. For any loss assessment charged against you as a member of an association, corporation or community of property owners, except as provided in D. Loss Assessment under Section II—Additional Coverages;

b. Under any contract or agreement entered into by an "insured". However, this exclusion does not apply to written contracts:

(1) That directly relate to the ownership, maintenance or use of an "insured location"; or

(2) Where the liability of others is assumed by you prior to an "occurrence";

unless excluded in a. above or elsewhere in this policy;

2. "Property damage" to property owned by an "insured". This includes costs or expenses incurred by an "insured" or others to repair, replace, enhance, restore or maintain such property to prevent injury to a person or damage to property of others, whether on or away from an "insured location";

3. "Property damage" to property rented to, occupied or used by or in the care of an "insured". This exclusion does not apply to "property damage" caused by fire, smoke or explosion;

4. "Bodily injury" to any person eligible to receive any benefits voluntarily provided or required to be provided by an "insured" under any:

a. Workers' compensation law;

b. Non-occupational disability law; or

c. Occupational disease law;

5. "Bodily injury" or "property damage" for which an "insured" under this policy:

a. Is also an insured under a nuclear energy liability policy issued by the:

(1) Nuclear Energy Liability Insurance Association;

(2) Mutual Atomic Energy Liability Underwriters;

(3) Nuclear Insurance Association of Canada;

or any of their successors; or

b. Would be an insured under such a policy but for the exhaustion of its limit of liability; or

6. "Bodily injury" to you or an "insured" as defined under Definitions 5.a. or b.

This exclusion also applies to any claim made or suit brought against you or an "insured":

a. To repay; or

b. Share damages with;

another person who may be obligated to pay damages because of "bodily injury" to an "insured".

G. Coverage F—Medical Payments to Others

Coverage F does not apply to [*certain instances of "bodily injury", including injury to a person who is or should be provided with workers' compensation benefits.*]

SECTION II—ADDITIONAL COVERAGES

We cover the following in addition to the limits of liability:

A. Claim Expenses

We pay:

1. Expenses we incur and costs taxed against an "insured" in any suit we defend;

[*Three other entries are omitted here. One relates to earnings lost by an "insured" for assisting, as requested, in the investigation or defense of a claim; another relates to interest on a judgment.*]

B. First Aid Expenses

We will pay expenses for first aid to others incurred by an "insured" for "bodily injury" covered under this policy. We will not pay for first aid to an "insured".

C. Damage to Property of Others

1. We will pay, at replacement cost, up to $1,000 per "occurrence" for "property damage" to property of others caused by an "insured".

[*Subparagraph 2 states a number of qualifications. Some of these are about damage arising out of the ownership or use of certain motor vehicles, or arising out of a "business" engaged in by an "insured", and about damages caused intentionally by an "insured" of 13 years or older.*]

D. Loss Assessment

[*This provision is cognate to the "Additional Coverage" (# 7) extended in connection with "SECTION II—LIABILITY COVERAGES." It applies, however, to assessments made (i) "as a result of 'bodily injury' or 'property damage' not excluded from coverage under Section II—Exclusions", and sometimes (ii) as a result of liability for an act of a director, officer or trustee in his capacity as such.*]

SECTION II—CONDITIONS

A. Limit of Liability

Our total liability under Coverage E for all damages resulting from any one "occurrence" will not be more than the Coverage E limit of liability shown in the Declarations. This limit is the same regardless of the number of "insureds", claims made or persons injured. All "bodily injury" and "property damage" resulting from any one accident or from continuous or repeated exposure to substantially the same general harmful conditions shall be considered to be the result of one "occurrence".

Our total liability under Coverage F for all medical expense payable for "bodily injury" to one person as the result of one accident will not be more than the Coverage F limit of liability shown in the Declarations.

B. Severability of Insurance

This insurance applies separately to each "insured". This condition will not increase our limit of liability for any one "occurrence".

C. Duties After "Occurrence"

In case of an "occurrence" you or another "insured" will perform the following duties that apply. We have no duty to provide coverage under this policy if your failure to comply with the following duties is prejudicial to us. You will help us by seeing that these duties are performed:

1. Give written notice to us or our agent as soon as is practical, which sets forth:

   a. The identity of the policy and the "named insured" shown in the Declarations;

   b. Reasonably available information on the time, place and circumstances of the "occurrence"; and

   c. Names and addresses of any claimants and witnesses;

2. Cooperate with us in the investigation, settlement or defense of any claim or suit;

3. Promptly forward to us every notice, demand, summons or other process relating to the "occurrence";

4. At our request, help us:

   a. To make settlement;

   b. To enforce any right of contribution or indemnity against any person or organization who may be liable to an "insured";

   c. With the conduct of suits and attend hearings and trials; and

   d. To secure and give evidence and obtain the attendance of witnesses;

5. With respect to C. Damage To Property Of Others under Section II—Additional Coverages, submit to us within 60 days after the loss, a sworn statement of loss and show the damaged property, if in an "insured's" control;

6. No "insured" shall, except at such "insured's" own cost, voluntarily make payment, assume obligation or incur expense other than for first aid to others at the time of the "bodily injury".

D. Duties of An Injured Person—Coverage F—Medical Payments to Others

   [*The responsibilities indicated have to do with making proof of claim and procuring medical information. The latter may entail submitting to examinations by "a doctor of our choice . . . as often as we reasonably require."*]

E. Payment of Claim—Coverage F—Medical Payments to Others

Payment under this coverage is not an admission of liability by an "insured" or us.

F. Suit Against Us

1. No action can be brought against us unless there has been full compliance with all of the terms under this Section II.

2. No one will have the right to join us as a party to any action against an "insured".

3. Also, no action with respect to Coverage E can be brought against us until the obligation of such "insured" has been determined by final judgment or agreement signed by us.

G. Bankruptcy of An "Insured"

Bankruptcy or insolvency of an "insured" will not relieve us of our obligations under this policy.

H. Other Insurance

This insurance is excess over other valid and collectible insurance except insurance written specifically to cover as excess over the limits of liability that apply in this policy.

I. Policy Period

This policy applies only to "bodily injury" or "property damage" which occurs during the policy period.

J. Concealment or Fraud

We do not provide coverage to an "insured" who, whether before or after a loss, has:

1. Intentionally concealed or misrepresented any material fact or circumstance;

2. Engaged in fraudulent conduct; or

3. Made false statements;

relating to this insurance.

SECTIONS I AND II—CONDITIONS

A. Liberalization Clause

If we make a change which broadens coverage under this edition of our policy without additional premium charge, that change will automatically apply to your insurance as of the date we implement the change in your state, provided that this implementation date falls within 60 days prior to or during the policy period stated in the Declarations.

This Liberalization Clause does not apply to changes implemented with a general program revision that includes both broadenings and restrictions in coverage, whether that general program revision is implemented through introduction of:

1. A subsequent edition of this policy; or

2. An amendatory endorsement.

B. Waiver or Change of Policy Provisions

A waiver or change of a provision of this policy must be in writing by us to be valid. Our request for an appraisal or examination will not waive any of our rights.

C. Cancellation

[*This provision states when and how the policy may be cancelled by "you" (easy), and when and how "we" may cancel. The latter is somewhat restricted. If the policy was written for a year or less, and has been in effect for as much as 60 days, the issuer may cancel for only a couple of obvious reasons ("you have not paid the premium"; material misrepresentation) and for one not obvious: "the risk has changed substantially since the policy was issued".*

[*There are provisions for advance notification, and about premium refunds.*]

D. Nonrenewal

We may elect not to renew this policy. We may do so by delivering to you, or mailing to you at your mailing address shown in the Declarations, written notice at least 30 days before the expiration date of this policy. Proof of mailing will be sufficient proof of notice.

E. Assignment

Assignment of this policy will not be valid unless we give our written consent.

F. Subrogation

An "insured" may waive in writing before a loss all rights of recovery against any person. If not waived, we may require an assignment of rights of recovery for a loss to the extent that payment is made by us.

If an assignment is sought, an "insured" must sign and deliver all related papers and cooperate with us.

Subrogation does not apply to Coverage F or Paragraph C. Damage to Property of Others under Section II—Additional Coverages.

G. Death

If any person named in the Declarations or the spouse, if a resident of the same household, dies, the following apply:

1. We insure the legal representative of the deceased but only with respect to the premises and property of the deceased covered under the policy at the time of death; and

2. "Insured" includes

    a. An "insured" who is a member of your household at the time of your death, but only while a resident of the "residence premises"; and

    b. With respect to your property, the person having proper temporary custody of the property until appointment and qualification of a legal representative.

COMMERCIAL GENERAL LIABILITY (CGL) COVERAGE

Various provisions in this policy restrict coverage. Read the entire policy carefully to determine rights, duties and what is and is not covered.

Throughout this policy the words "you" and "your" refer to the Named Insured shown in the Declarations, and any other person or organization qualifying as a Named Insured under this policy. The words "we", "us" and "our" refer to the company providing this insurance.

The word "insured" means any person or organization qualifying as such under Section II—Who Is An Insured.

Other words and phrases that appear in quotation marks have special meaning. Refer to Section V—Definitions.

SECTION I—COVERAGES

COVERAGE A BODILY INJURY AND PROPERTY DAMAGE LIABILITY

1. Insuring Agreement

    a. We will pay those sums that the insured becomes legally obligated to pay as damages because of "bodily injury" or "property damage" to which this insurance applies. We will have the right and duty to defend the insured against any "suit" seeking those damages. However, we will have no duty to defend the insured against any "suit" seeking damages for "bodily injury" or "property damage" to which this insurance does not apply. We may, at our discretion, investigate any "occurrence" and settle any claim or "suit" that may result. But:

        (1) The amount we will pay for damages is limited as de-

scribed in Section III—Limits of Insurance; and

        (2) Our right and duty to defend ends when we have used up the applicable limit of insurance in the payment of judgments or settlements under Coverages A or B or medical expenses under Coverage C.

    No other obligation or liability to pay sums or perform acts or services is covered unless explicitly provided for under Supplementary Payments—Coverages A and B.

    b. This insurance applies to "bodily injury" and "property damage" only if:

        (1) The "bodily injury" or "property damage" is caused by an "occurrence" that takes place in the "coverage territory";

        (2) The "bodily injury" or "property damage" occurs during the policy period; and

[*In this bracketed description, the word entity is used to refer to one within either of two categories. These categories are referred to repeatedly in subparagraphs b(3), c, and d: an insured listed elsewhere, and an "'employee' authorized by you to give or receive notice of an 'occurrence' or claim". Each of the three provisions concerns knowledge by an entity that an instance of "bodily injury" or "property damage" has occurred.*

According to (b)(3), the insurance does not apply to an instance of in-

jury or damage if, prior to the policy period, an entity knew that it had occurred ("in whole or in part"). Subparagraph d states a set of junctures at the earliest of which injury or damage "will be deemed to have been known to have occurred". One of these is the moment when an entity "(3) Becomes aware by any other means that 'bodily injury' or 'property damage' has occurred or has begun to occur."

Subparagraphs b(3) and c speak further to a "continuation, change or resumption" of an instance of injury or damage: "CCorR", for short. First, given knowledge, pre-policy-period, that precludes coverage of an injury or damage, any CCorR is "deemed to have been known prior to the policy period." On the other hand, subparagraph c provides that CCorR after the end of the policy period is included within an injury or damage that occurs within the policy period, unless there was pre-policy-period knowledge, by an entity, of the injury or damage.]

e. Damages because of "bodily injury" include damages claimed by any person or organization for care, loss of services or death resulting at any time from the "bodily injury".

2. Exclusions

This insurance does not apply to:

a. Expected or Intended Injury

"Bodily injury" or "property damage" expected or intended from the standpoint of the insured. This exclusion does not apply to "bodily injury" resulting from the use of reasonable force to protect persons or property.

b. Contractual Liability

"Bodily injury" or "property damage" for which the insured is obligated to pay damages by reason of the assumption of liability in a contract or agreement.

[This exclusion is made inapplicable to liability for damages specified in two clauses. One concerns liability that the insured would have in the absence of the contract or agreement. The other concerns certain liabilities assumed in an "insured contract". As to these, in some circumstances, defense costs are "deemed to be damages because of 'bodily injury' or 'property damage'". "Insured contract" is defined in paragraph 9 of Section V (Definitions). The expression includes six specified arrangements. One of them is, within limits, a "[part of a] contract or agreement pertaining to your business ... under which you assume the tort liability of another party to pay for 'bodily injury' or 'property damage' to a third person or organization.

c. Liquor Liability

"Bodily injury" or "property damage" for which any insured may be held liable by reason of:

(1) Causing or contributing to the intoxication of any person;

(2) The furnishing of alcoholic beverages to a person under the legal drinking age or under the influence of alcohol; or

(3) Any statute, ordinance or regulation relating to the sale, gift, distribution or use of alcoholic beverages.

This exclusion applies only if you are in the business of manufacturing, distributing, selling, serving or furnishing alcoholic beverages.

d. Workers' Compensation and Similar Laws

Any obligation of the insured under a workers' compensation, disability benefits or unemployment compensation law or any similar law.

e.   Employer's Liability

"Bodily injury" to:

(1) An "employee" of the insured arising out of and in the course of:

     (a) Employment by the insured; or

     (b) Performing duties related to the conduct of the insured's business; or

(2) The spouse, child, parent, brother or sister of that "employee" as a consequence of Paragraph (1) above.

This exclusion applies:

(1) Whether the insured may be liable as an employer or in any other capacity; and

(2) To any obligation to share damages with or repay someone else who must pay damages because of the injury.

This exclusion does not apply to liability assumed by the insured under an "insured contract".

f.   Pollution

(1) "Bodily injury" or "property damage" arising out of the actual, alleged or threatened discharge, dispersal, seepage, migration, release or escape of "pollutants":

     (a) At or from any premises, site or location which is or was at any time owned or occupied by, or rented or loaned to, any insured. However-

er, this subparagraph does not apply to:

(i) "Bodily injury" if sustained within a building and caused by smoke, fumes, vapor or soot from equipment used to heat that building;

(ii) "Bodily injury" or "property damage" for which you may be held liable, if you are a contractor and the owner or lessee of such premises, site or location has been added to your policy as an additional insured with respect to your ongoing operations performed for that additional insured at that premises, site or location and such premises, site or location is not and never was owned or occupied by, or rented or loaned to, any insured, other than that additional insured; or

(iii) "Bodily injury" or "property damage" arising out of heat, smoke or fumes from a "hostile fire";

(b) At or from any premises, site or location which is or was at any time used by or for any insured or others for the handling, storage, disposal, processing or treatment of waste;

(c) Which are or were at any time transported, handled, stored, treated, disposed of, or processed as waste by or for:

(i) Any insured; or

(ii) Any person or organization for whom you may be legally responsible; or

(d) At or from any premises, site or location on which any insured or any contractors or subcontractors working directly or indirectly on any insured's behalf are performing operations if the "pollutants" are brought on or to the premises, site or location in connection with such operations by such insured, contractor or subcontractor. However, this subparagraph does not apply to:

(i) [*An example of "property damage" included here is that arising out of the unintended escape of oil from its container in the engine of a bulldozer.*]

(ii) "Bodily injury" or "property damage" sustained within a building and caused by the release of gases, fumes or vapors from materials

brought into that building in connection with operations being performed by you or on your behalf by a contractor or subcontractor; or

(iii) "Bodily injury" or "property damage" arising out of heat, smoke or fumes from a "hostile fire".

(e) At or from any premises, site or location on which any insured or any contractors or subcontractors working directly or indirectly on any insured's behalf are performing operations if the operations are to test for, monitor, clean up, remove, contain, treat, detoxify or neutralize, or in any way respond to, or assess the effects of, "pollutants".

(2) Any loss, cost or expense arising out of any:

(a) Request, demand, order or statutory or regulatory requirement that any insured or others test for, monitor, clean up, remove, contain, treat, detoxify or neutralize, or in any way respond to, or assess the effects of, "pollutants"; or

(b) Claim or "suit" by or on behalf of a governmental authority for damages because of testing for, monitoring, cleaning up, removing, containing, treating, detoxifying or neutralizing, or in any way responding to, or assessing the effects of, "pollutants".

However, this paragraph does not apply to liability for damages because of "property damage" that the insured would have in the absence of such request, demand, order or statutory or regulatory requirement, or such claim or "suit" by or on behalf of a governmental authority.

g.   Aircraft, Auto or Watercraft

"Bodily injury" or "property damage" arising out of the ownership, maintenance, use or entrustment to others of any aircraft, "auto" or watercraft owned or operated by or rented or loaned to any insured. Use includes operation and "loading or unloading".

[*In some instances, the exclusion is made to apply "even if the claims against any insured allege negligence or other wrongdoing in the supervision, hiring, employment, training or monitoring of others by that insured".*]

[*The exclusion does not apply in some specified instances; e.g., parking an "auto" of unknown ownership on "premises you own or rent".*]

[*Exclusions h ("Mobile equipment"), h ("War"), and j ("Damage To Property") are omitted here. Instances of the latter are damage to property "you own, rent, or occupy" (qualified as to short-term rentals), to property loaned to you, and to personal property "in the care, custody or control of the insured". (Sidetrack agreements are a special case.)*]

k.   Damage to Your Product

"Property damage" to "your product" arising out of it or any part of it.

l.   Damage to Your Work

"Property damage" to "your work" arising out of it or any part of it and included in the "products completed operations hazard".

This exclusion does not apply if the damaged work or the work out of which the damage arises was performed on your behalf by a subcontractor.

m.   Damage to Impaired Property or Property Not Physically Injured

"Property damage" to "impaired property" or property that has not been physically injured, arising out of:

(1) A defect, deficiency, inadequacy or dangerous condition in "your product" or "your work"; or

(2) A delay or failure by you or anyone acting on your behalf to perform a contract or agreement in accordance with its terms.

This exclusion does not apply to the loss of use of other property arising out of sudden and accidental physical injury to "your product" or "your work" after it has been put to its intended use.

n.   Recall of Products, Work or Impaired Property

Damages claimed for any loss, cost or expense incurred by you or others for the loss of use, withdrawal, recall, inspection, repair, replacement, adjustment, removal or disposal of:

(1) "Your product";

(2) "Your work"; or

(3) "Impaired property";

if such product, work, or property is withdrawn or recalled from the market or from use by any person or organization because of a known or suspected defect, deficiency, inadequacy or dangerous condition in it.

o. Personal and Advertising Injury

"Bodily injury" arising out of "personal and advertising injury".

Exclusions c. through n. do not apply to damage by fire to premises while rented to you or temporarily occupied by you with permission of the owner. A separate limit of insurance applies to this coverage as described in Section III—Limits of Insurance.

COVERAGE B PERSONAL AND ADVERTISING INJURY LIABILITY

1. Insuring Agreement

    a. We will pay those sums that the insured becomes legally obligated to pay as damages because of "personal and advertising injury" to which this insurance applies. We will have the right and duty to defend the insured against any "suit" seeking those damages. However, we will have no duty to defend the insured against any "suit" seeking damages for "personal and advertising injury" to which this insurance does not apply. We may, at our discretion, investigate any offense and settle any claim or "suit" that may result. But:

        (1) The amount we will pay for damages is limited as described in Section III—Limits Of Insurance; and

        (2) Our right and duty to defend end when we have used up the applicable limit of insurance in the payment

of judgments or settlements under Coverages A or B or medical expenses under Coverage C.

No other obligation or liability to pay sums or perform acts or services is covered unless explicitly provided for under Supplementary Payments—Coverages A and B.

b. This insurance applies to "personal and advertising injury" caused by an offense arising out of your business but only if the offense was committed in the "coverage territory" during the policy period.

2. Exclusions

This insurance does not apply to:

a. Knowing Violation of Rights of Another

"Personal and advertising injury" caused by or at the direction of the insured with the knowledge that the act would violate the rights of another and would inflict "personal and advertising injury".

b. Material Published With Knowledge of Falsity

"Personal and advertising injury" arising out of oral or written publication of material, if done by or at the direction of the insured with knowledge of its falsity.

c. Material Published Prior to Policy Period

"Personal and advertising injury" arising out of oral or written publication of material whose first publication took place before the beginning of the policy period.

d. Criminal Acts

"Personal and advertising injury" arising out of a criminal act committed by or at the direction of the insured.

e. Contractual Liability

"Personal and advertising injury" for which the insured has assumed liability in a contract or agreement. This exclusion does not apply to liability for damages that the insured would have in the absence of the contract or agreement.

f. Breach of Contract

"Personal and advertising injury" arising out of a breach of contract, except an implied contract to use another's advertising idea in your "advertisement".

g. Quality or Performance of Goods—Failure to Conform to Statements

"Personal and advertising injury" arising out of the failure of goods, products or services to conform with any statement of quality or performance made in your "advertisement".

h. Wrong Description of Prices

"Personal and advertising injury" arising out of the wrong description of the price of goods, products or services stated in your "advertisement".

i. Infringement of Copyright, Patent, Trademark or Trade Secret

"Personal and advertising injury" arising out of the infringement of copyright, patent, trademark, trade secret or other intellectual property rights.

However, this exclusion does not apply to infringement, in your "advertisement", of copyright, trade dress or slogan.

j. Insureds in Media and Internet Type Businesses

"Personal and advertising injury" committed by an insured whose business is:

(1) Advertising, broadcasting, publishing or telecasting;

(2) Designing or determining content of web-sites for others; or

(3) An Internet search, access, content or service provider.

However, this exclusion does not apply to Paragraphs 14.a., b. and c. of "personal and advertising injury" under the Definitions Section.

For the purposes of this exclusion, the placing of frames, borders or links, or advertising, for you or others anywhere on the Internet, is not by itself considered the business of advertising, broadcasting, publishing or telecasting.

k. Electronic Chatrooms or Bulletin Boards

"Personal and advertising injury" arising out of an electronic chatroom or bulletin board the insured hosts, owns, or over which the insured exercises control.

l. Unauthorized Use of Another's Name or Product

"Personal and advertising injury" arising out of the unauthorized use of another's name or product in your e-mail address, domain name or metatag, or any other similar tactics to mislead another's potential customers.

m. Pollution

"Personal and advertising injury" arising out of the actual, alleged or threatened discharge, dispersal, seepage, migration, release or escape of "pollutants" at any time.

n. Pollution–Related

Any loss, cost or expense arising out of any:

(1) Request, demand or order that any insured or others test for, monitor, clean up, remove, contain, treat, detoxify or neutralize, or in

any way respond to, or assess the effects of, "pollutants"; or

(2) Claim or suit by or on behalf of a governmental authority for damages because of testing for, monitoring, cleaning up, removing, containing, treating, detoxifying or neutralizing, or in any way responding to, or assessing the effects of, "pollutants".

COVERAGE C MEDICAL PAYMENTS

[*The insuring agreement under this heading promises payments, regardless of fault, of certain medical expenses "for 'bodily injury' caused by an accident". A description of the expenses concerned begins with first aid, and concludes with funeral services. The coverage is restricted to accidents on premises "you own or rent" or on adjoining ways, and to those attributable to "your operations". It is constrained also by other factors of time and place, and by some conditions and exclusions not noticed here.*]

[*The paragraph headed 'Exclusions" begins, "We will not pay expenses for 'bodily injury'...." Among the paragraphs that follow, one is, "Excluded under Coverage A." Other notable ones leave out, in most instances, injuries to an insured and those to persons in the service of an insured.*]

SUPPLEMENTARY PAYMENTS— COVERAGES A AND B

[*Two paragraphs, omitted here. The first enumerates sums that "We will pay", without reduction of the limits of insurance, "with respect to any claim we investigate or settle, or any 'suit' against an insured we defend". One entry is "All expenses we*

incur"; another is "All costs taxed against the insured in the 'suit'." Others relate to prejudgment interest, and to interest on a judgment.

[*Paragraph 2 is primarily an undertaking to defend an indemnitee of the insured in certain circumstances.*]

SECTION II—WHO IS AN INSURED

1. If you are designated in the Declarations as:

   a. An individual, you and your spouse are insureds, but only with respect to the conduct of a business of which you are the sole owner.

   b. A partnership or joint venture, you are an insured. Your members, your partners, and their spouses are also insureds, but only with respect to the conduct of your business.

   c. A limited liability company, you are an insured. Your members are also insureds, but only with respect to the conduct of your business. Your managers are insureds, but only with respect to their duties as your managers.

   d. An organization other than a partnership, joint venture or limited liability company, you are an insured. Your "executive officers" and directors are insureds, but only with respect to their duties as your officers or directors. Your stockholders are also insureds, but only with respect to their liability as stockholders.

   e. A trust, you are an insured. Your trustees are also insureds, but only with respect to their duties as trustees.

2. [*Paragraph 2 identifies various others as "also an insured". An impor-*

tant group (2a) is "your 'employ-ees' " (excepting certain "executive officers" and managers), "but only for acts within the scope of their employment by you or while perform-ing duties related to the conduct of your business." The inclusion of these workers, and others, is quali-fied, however: "none ... are in-sureds" for certain species of injury or damage. Not for bodily injury, for example, "To you (or, in a common case) to a co-'employee' ". And not for property damage to property "Owned, occupied or used by ... you...."

[Some entities qualify as also in-sured "if you die".

[According to paragraph 3, one who is driving "mobile equipment"—e.g., a bulldozer—on a public road may well be also insured if the equipment is "registered in your name" and the driving is with your permission". But the inclusion of these persons is subject to qualifi-cations similar to those that apply to workers under 2a. The significance of this inclusion is sharply limited by the definition of mobile equip-ment (Section V, paragraph 12). The definition excludes most buses and trucks, they being "maintained pri-marily for purposes other than the transportation of persons or cargo."]

[Paragraph 4 extends temporary coverage, within limits, to certain organizations that "you [may] newly acquire or form".]

SECTION III—LIMITS OF INSUR-ANCE

[This section states a set of highly articulated rules setting limits. One that is specialized is the "Products–Completed Operations Aggregate Limit", applicable to certain dam-ages under Coverage A. These dam-ages are the subject of an exception in the rule stating a "General Ag-gregate Limit": ... the most we will pay for the sum of:

a. Medical expenses under Coverage C;

b. Damages under Coverage A (except the damages last re-ferred to); and

c. Damages under Coverage B.

[The section states four other limit-ing rules, including an "Each Oc-currence Limit". It states also the periods to which the limits apply.]

SECTION IV—COMMERCIAL GEN-ERAL LIABILITY CONDITIONS

1. Bankruptcy

Bankruptcy or insolvency of the in-sured or of the insured's estate will not relieve us of our obligations un-der this Coverage Part.

2. Duties in the Event of Occurrence, Offense, Claim or Suit

a. You must see to it that we are notified as soon as practicable of an "occurrence" or an offense which may result in a claim. To the extent possible, notice should include:

(1) How, when and where the "occurrence" or offense took place;

(2) The names and addresses of any injured persons and witnesses; and

(3) The nature and location of any injury or damage aris-ing out of the "occurrence" or offense.

b. If a claim is made or "suit" is brought against any insured, you must:

(1) Immediately record the spe-cifics of the claim or "suit" and the date received; and

(2) Notify us as soon as practi-cable.

You must see to it that we receive written notice of the claim or "suit" as soon as practicable.

c. You and any other involved insured must:

(1) Immediately send us copies of any demands, notices, summonses or legal papers received in connection with the claim or "suit";

(2) Authorize us to obtain records and other information;

(3) Cooperate with us in the investigation or settlement of the claim or defense against the "suit"; and

(4) Assist us, upon our request, in the enforcement of any right against any person or organization which may be liable to the insured because of injury or damage to which this insurance may also apply.

d. No insured will, except at that insured's own cost, voluntarily make a payment, assume any obligation, or incur any expense, other than for first aid, without our consent.

3. Legal Action Against Us

No person or organization has a right under this Coverage Part:

a. To join us as a party or otherwise bring us into a "suit" asking for damages from an insured; or

b. To sue us on this Coverage Part unless all of its terms have been fully complied with.

A person or organization may sue us to recover on an agreed settlement or on a final judgment against an insured; but we will not be liable for damages that are not payable under the terms of this Coverage Part or that are in excess of the applicable limit of insurance. An agreed settlement means a settlement and release of liability signed by us, the insured and the claimant or the claimant's legal representative.

4. Other Insurance

If other valid and collectible insurance is available to the insured for a loss we cover under Coverages A or B of this Coverage Part, our obligations are limited as follows:

a. Primary Insurance

This insurance is primary except when b. below applies. If this insurance is primary, our obligations are not affected unless any of the other insurance is also primary. Then, we will share with all that other insurance by the method described in c. below.

b. Excess Insurance

This insurance is excess over:

[(i) certain other "primary insurance available to you", and,

(ii) (listing various "other insurance" coverages,) any of that other insurance, "whether primary, excess, contingent or on any other basis".]

When this insurance is excess, we will have no duty under Coverages A or B to defend the insured against any "suit" if any other insurer has a duty to defend the insured against that "suit". If no other insurer defends, we will undertake to do so, but we will be entitled to the insured's rights against all those other insurers.

When this insurance is excess over other insurance, we will pay only our share of the amount of the loss, if any, that exceeds the sum of:

(1) The total amount that all such other insurance would

pay for the loss in the absence of this insurance; and

(2) The total of all deductible and self-insured amounts under all that other insurance.

We will share the remaining loss, if any, with any other insurance that is not described in this Excess Insurance provision and was not bought specifically to apply in excess of the Limits of Insurance shown in the Declarations of this Coverage Part.

c. Method of Sharing

If all of the other insurance permits contribution by equal shares, we will follow this method also. Under this approach each insurer contributes equal amounts until it has paid its applicable limit of insurance or none of the loss remains, whichever comes first.

If any of the other insurance does not permit contribution by equal shares, we will contribute by limits. Under this method, each insurer's share is based on the ratio of its applicable limit of insurance to the total applicable limits of insurance of all insurers.

5. Premium Audit

a. We will compute all premiums for this Coverage Part in accordance with our rules and rates.

[*Adjustments of premiums are provided for, the rule making reference to premiums of these types: "advance", "earned", "audit", and "retrospective".*]

6. Representations

By accepting this policy, you agree:

a. The statements in the Declarations are accurate and complete;

b. Those statements are based upon representations you made to us; and

c. We have issued this policy in reliance upon your representations.

7. Separation of Insureds

Except with respect to the Limits of Insurance, and any rights or duties specifically assigned in this Coverage Part to the first Named Insured, this insurance applies:

a. As if each Named Insured were the only Named Insured; and

b. Separately to each insured against whom claim is made or "suit" is brought.

8. Transfer of Rights of Recovery Against Others to Us

If the insured has rights to recover all or part of any payment we have made under this Coverage Part, those rights are transferred to us. The insured must do nothing after loss to impair them. At our request, the insured will bring "suit" or transfer those rights to us and help us enforce them.

9. When We Do Not Renew

If we decide not to renew this Coverage Part, we will mail or deliver to the first Named Insured shown in the Declarations written notice of the nonrenewal not less than 30 days before the expiration date.

If notice is mailed, proof of mailing will be sufficient proof of notice.

SECTION V—DEFINITIONS

1. [*Definitions omitted here are for these terms*: 6. Executive officer; 8. Impaired property; 9. Insured contract; 10. Leased worker; 12. Mobile equipment; 19. Temporary worker; *and* 20. Volunteer worker.] "Advertisement" means a notice that is broadcast or published to the gener-

al public or specific market segments about your goods, products or services for the purpose of attracting customers or supporters. For the purposes of this definition:

a. Notices that are published include material placed on the Internet or on similar electronic means of communication; and

b. Regarding web-sites, only that part of a web-site that is about your goods, products or services for the purposes of attracting customers or supporters is considered an advertisement.

2. "Auto" means a land motor vehicle, trailer or semitrailer designed for travel on public roads, including any attached machinery or equipment. But "auto" does not include "mobile equipment".

3. "Bodily injury" means bodily injury, sickness or disease sustained by a person, including death resulting from any of these at any time.

4. "Coverage territory" means:

   [*The "Coverage territory" extends to the world in certain cases, including some in which the injury or damage arises out of "Personal and advertising injury" offenses that take place through the internet or similar electronic means of communication".*]

5. "Employee" includes a "leased worker". "Employee" does not include a "temporary worker".

7. "Hostile fire" means one which becomes uncontrollable or breaks out from where it was intended to be.

11. "Loading or unloading" means the handling of property:

a. After it is moved from the place where it is accepted for movement into or onto an aircraft, watercraft or "auto";

b. While it is in or on an aircraft, watercraft or "auto"; or

c. While it is being moved from an aircraft, watercraft or "auto" to the place where it is finally delivered;

but "loading or unloading" does not include the movement of property by means of a mechanical device, other than a hand truck, that is not attached to the aircraft, watercraft or "auto".

13. "Occurrence" means an accident, including continuous or repeated exposure to substantially the same general harmful conditions.

14. "Personal and advertising injury" means injury, including consequential "bodily injury", arising out of one or more of the following offenses:

a. False arrest, detention or imprisonment;

b. Malicious prosecution;

c. The wrongful eviction from, wrongful entry into, or invasion of the right of private occupancy of a room, dwelling or premises that a person occupies, committed by or on behalf of its owner, landlord or lessor;

d. Oral or written publication, in any manner, of material that slanders or libels a person or organization or disparages a person's or organization's goods, products or services;

e. Oral or written publication, in any manner, of material that violates a person's right of privacy;

f. The use of another's advertising idea in your "advertisement"; or

g. Infringing upon another's copyright, trade dress or slogan in your "advertisement".

15. "Pollutants" mean any solid, liquid, gaseous or thermal irritant or contaminant, including smoke, vapor, soot, fumes, acids, alkalis, chemicals and waste. Waste includes materials to be recycled, reconditioned or reclaimed.

16. "Products-completed operations hazard":

   a. Includes all "bodily injury" and "property damage" occurring away from premises you own or rent and arising out of "your product" or "your work" except:

      (1) Products that are still in your physical possession; or

      (2) Work that has not yet been completed or abandoned. However, "your work" will be deemed completed at the earliest of the following times:

         (a) When all of the work called for in your contract has been completed.

         (b) When all of the work to be done at the job site has been completed if your contract calls for work at more than one job site.

         (c) When that part of the work done at a job site has been put to its intended use by any person or organization other than another contractor or subcontractor working on the same project.

      Work that may need service, maintenance, correction, repair or replacement, but which is otherwise complete, will be treated as completed.

   b. Does not include "bodily injury" or "property damage" arising out of:

      (1) The transportation of property, unless the injury or damage arises out of a condition in or on a vehicle not owned or operated by you, and that condition was created by the "loading or unloading" of that vehicle by any insured;

      (2) The existence of tools, uninstalled equipment or abandoned or unused materials; or

      (3) Products or operations for which the classification, listed in the Declarations or in a policy schedule, states that products-completed operations are subject to the General Aggregate Limit.

17. "Property damage" means:

   a. Physical injury to tangible property, including all resulting loss of use of that property. All such loss of use shall be deemed to occur at the time of the physical injury that caused it; or

   b. Loss of use of tangible property that is not physically injured. All such loss of use shall be deemed to occur at the time of the "occurrence" that caused it.

For the purposes of this insurance, electronic data is not tangible property.

As used in this definition, electronic data means information, facts or programs stored as or on, created or used on, or transmitted to or from computer software, including systems and applications software, hard or floppy disks, CD–ROMS, tapes, drives, cells, data processing devices or any other media which are used with electronically controlled equipment.

18. "Suit" means a civil proceeding in which damages because of "bodily injury", "property damage" or "personal and advertising injury" to which this insurance applies are alleged. "Suit" includes:

a. An arbitration proceeding in which such damages are claimed and to which the insured must submit or does submit with our consent; or

b. Any other alternative dispute resolution proceeding in which such damages are claimed and to which the insured submits with our consent.

21. "Your product":

a. Means:

(1) Any goods or products, other than real property, manufactured, sold, handled, distributed or disposed of by:

(a) You;

b) Others trading under your name; or

(c) A person or organization whose business or assets you have acquired; and

(2) Containers (other than vehicles), materials, parts or equipment furnished in

connection with such goods or products.

b. Includes

(1) Warranties or representations made at any time with respect to the fitness, quality, durability, performance or use of "your product"; and

(2) The providing of or failure to provide warnings or instructions.

c. Does not include vending machines or other property rented to or located for the use of others but not sold.

22. "Your work":

a. Means:

(1) Work or operations performed by you or on your behalf; and

(2) Materials, parts or equipment furnished in connection with such work or operations.

b. Includes

(1) Warranties or representations made at any time with respect to the fitness, quality, durability, performance or use of "your work", and

(2) The providing of or failure to provide warnings or instructions.

APPENDIX D

PERSONAL AUTO POLICY

AGREEMENT

In return for payment of the premium and subject to all the terms of this policy, we agree with you as follows:

DEFINITIONS

A. Throughout this policy, "you" and "your" refer to:

   1. The "named insured" shown in the Declarations; and

   2. The spouse if a resident of the same household.

   [*A sentence omitted here concerns continuation, for a time, of coverage for a spouse who has ceased to be a resident of the same household.*]

B. "We", "us" and "our" refer to the Company providing this insurance.

C. For purposes of this policy, a private passenger type auto, pickup or van shall be deemed to be owned by a person if leased:

   1. Under a written agreement to that person; and

   2. For a continuous period of at least 6 months.

   Other words and phrases are defined. They are in quotation marks when used.

D. "Bodily injury" means bodily harm, sickness or disease, including death that results.

E. "Business" includes trade, profession or occupation.

F. "Family member" means a person related to you by blood, marriage or adoption who is a resident of your household. This includes a ward or foster child.

G. "Occupying" means in, upon, getting in, on, out or off.

H. "Property damage" means physical injury to, destruction of or loss of use of tangible property.

I. "Trailer" means a vehicle designed to be pulled by a:

   1. Private passenger auto; or

   2. Pickup or van.

   It also means a farm wagon or farm implement while towed by a vehicle listed in 1. or 2. above.

J. "Your covered auto" means:

   1. Any vehicle shown in the Declarations.

   2. A "newly acquired auto".

   3. Any "trailer" you own.

   4. Any auto or "trailer" you do not own while used as a temporary substitute for any other vehicle described in this definition which is out of normal use because of its:

      a. Breakdown;

      b. Repair;

      c. Servicing;

      d. Loss; or

      e. Destruction.

      This Provision (J.4.) does not apply to Coverage For Damage To Your Auto.

K. "Newly acquired auto":

   [*There follow a definition of "newly acquired auto", and provisions about the extent and duration of coverage with respect to a newly defined auto.*]

636

PART A—LIABILITY COVERAGE

INSURING AGREEMENT

A. We will pay damages for "bodily injury" or "property damage" for which any "insured" becomes legally responsible because of an auto accident. Damages include prejudgment interest awarded against the "insured". We will settle or defend, as we consider appropriate, any claim or suit asking for these damages. In addition to our limit of liability, we will pay all defense costs we incur. Our duty to settle or defend ends when our limit of liability for this coverage has been exhausted by payment of judgments or settlements. We have no duty to defend any suit or settle any claim for "bodily injury" or "property damage" not covered under this policy.

B. "Insured" as used in this Part means:

1. You or any "family member" for the ownership, maintenance or use of any auto or "trailer".

2. Any person using "your covered auto".

3. For "your covered auto", any person or organization but only with respect to legal responsibility for acts or omissions of a person for whom coverage is afforded under this Part.

4. For any auto or "trailer", other than "your covered auto", any other person or organization but only with respect to legal responsibility for acts or omissions of you or any "family member" for whom coverage is afforded under this Part. This Provision (B.4.) applies only if the person or organization does not own or hire the auto or "trailer".

SUPPLEMENTARY PAYMENTS

In addition to our limit of liability, we will pay on behalf of an "insured":

> [*certain charges, including something for loss of earnings because of attendance at a trial "at our request".*]

EXCLUSIONS

A. We do not provide Liability Coverage for any "insured":

1. Who intentionally causes "bodily injury" or "property damage".

2. For "property damage" to property owned or being transported by that "insured".

3. For "property damage" to property:

   a. Rented to;

   b. Used by; or

   c. In the care of;

   that "insured".

   This Exclusion (A.3.) does not apply to "property damage" to a residence or private garage.

4. For "bodily injury" to an employee of that "insured" during the course of employment. This Exclusion (A.4.) does not apply to "bodily injury" to a domestic employee unless workers' compensation benefits are required or available for that domestic employee.

5. For that "insured's" liability arising out of the ownership or operation of a vehicle while it is being used as a public or livery conveyance. This Exclusion (A.5.) does not apply to a share-the-expense car pool.

6. While employed or otherwise engaged in the "business" of:

   a. Selling;

   b. Repairing;

   c. Servicing;

   d. Storing; or

   e. Parking;

vehicles designed for use mainly on public highways. This includes road testing and delivery. This Exclusion (A.6.) does not apply to the ownership, maintenance or use of "your covered auto" by:

   a. You;

   b. Any "family member"; or

   c. Any partner, agent or employee of you or any "family member".

7. Maintaining or using any vehicle while that "insured" is employed or otherwise engaged in any "business" (other than farming or ranching) not described in Exclusion A.6.

This Exclusion (A.7.) does not apply to the maintenance or use of a:

   a. Private passenger auto;

   b. Pickup or van; or

   c. "Trailer" used with a vehicle described in a. or b. above.

8. Using a vehicle without a reasonable belief that that "insured" is entitled to do so. This Exclusion (A.8.) does not apply to a "family member" using "your covered auto" which is owned by you.

9. [*This provision refers to bodily injury and property damages for which "that 'insured'" is an insured under a "nuclear energy liability policy", as defined, or would be so insured but for a limit of liability in that policy.*]

B. We do not provide Liability Coverage for the ownership, maintenance or use of:

1. Any vehicle which:

   a. Has fewer than four wheels; or

   b. Is designed mainly for use off public roads.

   This Exclusion (B.1.) does not apply:

   a. While such vehicle is being used by an "insured" in a medical emergency;

   b. To any "trailer"; or

   c. To any non-owned golf cart.

2. Any vehicle, other than "your covered auto", which is:

   a. Owned by you; or

   b. Furnished or available for your regular use.

3. Any vehicle, other than "your covered auto", which is:

   a. Owned by any "family member"; or

   b. Furnished or available for the regular use of any "family member".

However, this Exclusion (B.3.) does not apply to you while you are maintaining or "occupying" any vehicle which is:

   a. Owned by a "family member"; or

   b. Furnished or available for the regular use of a "family member".

4. Any vehicle, located inside a facility designed for racing, for the purpose of:

   a. Competing in; or

   b. Practicing or preparing for;

any prearranged or organized racing or speed contest.

LIMIT OF LIABILITY

A. The limit of liability shown in the Declarations for each person for Bodily Injury Liability is our maximum limit of liability for all damages, including damages for care, loss of services or death, arising out of "bodily injury" sustained by any one person in any one auto accident. Subject to this limit for each person, the limit of liability shown in the Declarations for each accident for Bodily Injury Liability is our maximum limit of liability for all damages for "bodily injury" resulting from any one auto accident.

The limit of liability shown in the Declarations for each accident for Property Damage Liability is our maximum limit of liability for all "property damage" resulting from any one auto accident.

This is the most we will pay regardless of the number of:

1. "Insureds";

2. Claims made;

3. Vehicles or premiums shown in the Declarations; or

4. Vehicles involved in the auto accident.

B. No one will be entitled to receive duplicate payments for the same elements of loss under this coverage and:

1. Part B or Part C of this policy; or

2. Any Underinsured Motorists Coverage provided by this policy.

OUT OF STATE COVERAGE

If an auto accident to which this policy applies occurs in any state or province other than the one in which "your covered auto" is principally garaged, we will interpret your policy for that accident as follows:

A. If the state or province has:

1. A financial responsibility or similar law specifying limits of liability for "bodily injury" or "property damage" higher than the limit shown in the Declarations, your policy will provide the higher specified limit.

2. A compulsory insurance or similar law requiring a nonresident to maintain insurance whenever the nonresident uses a vehicle in that state or province, your policy will provide at least the required minimum amounts and types of coverage.

B. No one will be entitled to duplicate payments for the same elements of loss.

FINANCIAL RESPONSIBILITY

When this policy is certified as future proof of financial responsibility, this policy shall comply with the law to the extent required.

OTHER INSURANCE

If there is other applicable liability insurance we will pay only our share of the loss. Our share is the proportion that our limit of liability bears to the total of all applicable limits. However, any insurance we provide for a vehicle you do not own shall be excess over any other collectible insurance.

PART B–MEDICAL PAYMENTS COVERAGE

[The primary undertaking here is to pay "reasonable expenses incurred for necessary medical and funeral services because of 'bodily injury' sustained by an insured, and caused by accident." Provisions under the headings "EXCLUSIONS", "LIMIT OF LIABILITY", and "OTHER INSURANCE"

coordinate the benefits with those provided or available as workers' compensation, under other coverages of this policy, and under other auto medical payments insurance.]

PART C—UNINSURED MOTORISTS COVERAGE

INSURING AGREEMENT

A. We will pay compensatory damages which an "insured" is legally entitled to recover from the owner or operator of an "uninsured motor vehicle" because of "bodily injury":

1. Sustained by an "insured"; and

2. Caused by an accident.

The owner's or operator's liability for these damages must arise out of the ownership, maintenance or use of the "uninsured motor vehicle".

Any judgment for damages arising out of a suit brought without our written consent is not binding on us.

B. "Insured" as used in this Part means:

1. You or any "family member".

2. Any other person "occupying" "your covered auto".

3. Any person for damages that person is entitled to recover because of "bodily injury" to which this coverage applies sustained by a person described in 1. or 2. above.

C. "Uninsured motor vehicle" means a land motor vehicle or trailer of any type:

1. To which no bodily injury liability bond or policy applies at the time of the accident.

2. To which a bodily injury liability bond or policy applies at the time of the accident. In this case its limit for bodily injury liability must be less than the minimum limit for bodily injury liability specified by the finan-

cial responsibility law of the state in which "your covered auto" is principally garaged.

3. Which is a hit-and-run vehicle whose operator or owner cannot be identified and which hits:

a. You or any "family member";

b. A vehicle which you or any "family member" are "occupying"; or

c. "Your covered auto".

4. To which a bodily injury liability bond or policy applies at the time of the accident but the bonding or insuring company:

a. Denies coverage; or

b. Is or becomes insolvent.

However, "uninsured motor vehicle" does not include any vehicle or equipment:

1. Owned by or furnished or available for the regular use of you or any "family member".

2. Owned or operated by a self-insurer under any applicable motor vehicle law, except a self-insurer which is or becomes insolvent.

3. Owned by any governmental unit or agency.

4. Operated on rails or crawler treads.

5. Designed mainly for use off public roads while not on public roads.

6. While located for use as a residence or premises.

EXCLUSIONS

A. We do not provide Uninsured Motorists Coverage for "bodily injury" sustained:

1. By an "insured" while "occupying", or when struck by, any motor vehicle owned by that "insured" which is not insured for this coverage under this policy. This includes a trailer of any type used with that vehicle.

2. By any "family member" while "occupying", or when struck by, any motor vehicle you own which is insured for this coverage on a primary basis under any other policy.

B. We do not provide Uninsured Motorists Coverage for "bodily injury" sustained by any "insured":

1. If that "insured" or the legal representative settles the "bodily injury" claim without our consent.

2. While "occupying" "your covered auto" when it is being used as a public or livery conveyance. This Exclusion (B.2.) does not apply to a share-the-expense car pool.

3. Using a vehicle without a reasonable belief that that "insured" is entitled to do so. This Exclusion (B.3.) does not apply to a "family member" using "your covered auto" which is owned by you.

C. This coverage shall not apply directly or indirectly to benefit any insurer or self-insurer under any of the following or similar law:

1. Workers' compensation law; or

2. Disability benefits law.

D. We do not provide Uninsured Motorists Coverage for punitive or exemplary damages.

LIMIT OF LIABILITY

A. The limit of liability shown in the Declarations for each person for Uninsured Motorists Coverage is our maximum limit of liability for all damages, including damages for care, loss of services or death, arising out of "bodily injury" sustained by any one person in any one accident. Subject to this limit for each person, the limit of liability shown in the Declarations for each accident for Uninsured Motorists Coverage is our maximum limit of liability for all damages for "bodily injury" resulting from any one accident.

This is the most we will pay regardless of the number of:

1. "Insureds";

2. Claims made;

3. Vehicles or premiums shown in the Declarations; or

4. Vehicles involved in the accident.

B. No one will be entitled to receive duplicate payments for the same elements of loss under this coverage and:

1. Part A. or Part B. of this policy; or

2. Any Underinsured Motorists Coverage provided by this policy.

C. We will not make a duplicate payment under this coverage for any element of loss for which payment has been made by or on behalf of persons or organizations who may be legally responsible.

D. We will not pay for any element of loss if a person is entitled to receive payment for the same element of loss under any of the following or similar law:

1. Workers' compensation law; or

2. Disability benefits law.

OTHER INSURANCE

If there is other applicable insurance available under one or more policies or provisions of coverage that is similar to the insurance provided under this Part of the policy:

1. Any recovery for damages under all such policies or provisions of coverage may equal but not exceed the highest applicable limit for any one vehicle under any insurance providing coverage on either a primary or excess basis.

2. Any insurance we provide with respect to a vehicle you do not own shall be excess over any collectible insurance providing such coverage on a primary basis.

3. If the coverage under this policy is provided:

   a. On a primary basis, we will pay only our share of the loss that must be paid under insurance providing coverage on a primary basis. Our share is the proportion that our limit of liability bears to the total of all applicable limits of liability for coverage provided on a primary basis.

   b. On an excess basis, we will pay only our share of the loss that must be paid under insurance providing coverage on an excess basis. Our share is the proportion that our limit of liability bears to the total of all applicable limits of liability for coverage provided on an excess basis.

ARBITRATION

A. If we and an "insured" do not agree:

   1. Whether that "insured" is legally entitled to recover damages; or

   2. As to the amount of damages which are recoverable by that "insured";

from the owner or operator of an "uninsured motor vehicle", then the matter may be arbitrated. However, disputes concerning coverage under this Part may not be arbitrated.

Both parties must agree to arbitration. [*The remainder of this provision describes the mechanics and effect of arbitrations.*]

PART D—COVERAGE FOR DAMAGE TO YOUR AUTO

INSURING AGREEMENT

A. We will pay for direct and accidental loss to "your covered auto" or any "non-owned auto", including their equipment, minus any applicable deductible shown in the Declarations. If loss to more than one "your covered auto" or "non-owned auto" results from the same "collision", only the highest applicable deductible will apply. We will pay for loss to "your covered auto" caused by:

1. Other than "collision" only if the Declarations indicate that Other Than Collision Coverage is provided for that auto.

2. "Collision" only if the Declarations indicate that Collision Coverage is provided for that auto.

If there is a loss to a "non-owned auto", we will provide the broadest coverage applicable to any "your covered auto" shown in the Declarations.

B. "Collision" means the upset of "your covered auto" or a "non-owned auto" or their impact with another vehicle or object.

Loss caused by the following is considered other than "collision":

1. Missiles or falling objects;

2. Fire;

3. Theft or larceny;

4. Explosion or earthquake;

5. Windstorm;

6. Hail, water or flood;

7. Malicious mischief or vandalism;

8. Riot or civil commotion;

9. Contact with bird or animal; or

10. Breakage of glass.

If breakage of glass is caused by a "collision", you may elect to have it considered a loss caused by "collision".

C. "Non-owned auto" means:

1. Any private passenger auto, pickup, van or "trailer" not owned by or furnished or available for the regular use of you or any "family member" while in the custody of or being operated by you or any "family member"; or

2. Any auto or "trailer" you do not own while used as a temporary substitute for "your covered auto" which is out of normal use because of its:

   a. Breakdown;

   b. Repair;

   c. Servicing;

   d. Loss; or

   e. Destruction.

TRANSPORTATION EXPENSES

A. In addition, we will pay, without application of a deductible, up to a maximum of $600 for:

1. Temporary transportation expenses not exceeding $20 per day incurred by you in the event of a loss to "your covered auto". We will pay for such expenses if the loss is caused by:

   a. Other than "collision" only if the Declarations indicate that Other Than Collision Coverage is provided for that auto.

   b. "Collision" only if the Declarations indicate that Collision Coverage is provided for that auto.

2. Expenses for which you become legally responsible in the event of loss to a "non-owned auto". We will pay for such expenses if the loss is caused by:

   a. Other than "collision" only if the Declarations indicate that Other Than Collision Coverage is provided for any "your covered auto".

   b. "Collision" only if the Declarations indicate that Collision Coverage is provided for any "your covered auto".

However, the most we will pay for any expenses for loss of use is $20 per day.

B. If the loss is caused by:

1. A total theft of "your covered auto" or a "nonowned auto", we will pay only expenses incurred during the period:

   a. Beginning 48 hours after the theft; and

   b. Ending when "your covered auto" or the "non-owned

auto'' is returned to use or we pay for its loss.

2. Other than theft of a ''your covered auto'' or a ''non-owned auto'', we will pay only expenses beginning when the auto is withdrawn from use for more than 24 hours.

C. Our payment will be limited to that period of time reasonably required to repair or replace the ''your covered auto'' or the ''non-owned auto''.

EXCLUSIONS

We will not pay for:

1. Loss to ''your covered auto'' or any ''non-owned auto'' which occurs while it is being used as a public or livery conveyance. This Exclusion (1.) does not apply to a share-the-expense car pool.

2. Damage due and confined to:

   a. Wear and tear;

   b. Freezing;

   c. Mechanical or electrical breakdown or failure; or

   d. Road damage to tires.

   This Exclusion (2.) does not apply if the damage results from the total theft of ''your covered auto'' or any ''non-owned auto''.

3. Loss due to or as a consequence of:

   a. Radioactive contamination;

   b. Discharge of any nuclear weapon (even if accidental);

   c. War (declared or undeclared);

   d. Civil war;

   e. Insurrection; or

   f. Rebellion or revolution.

[Entries 4–6 are about losses to various types of electronic equipment and accessories thereto (e.g., certain tape decks), and loss to media used with that equipment.]

7. A total loss to ''your covered auto'' or any ''nonowned auto'' due to destruction or confiscation by governmental or civil authorities.

This Exclusion (7.) does not apply to the interests of Loss Payees in ''your covered auto''.

8. Loss to:

   a. A ''trailer'', camper body, or motor home, which is not shown in the Declarations; or

   b. Facilities or equipment used with such ''trailer'', camper body or motor home. Facilities or equipment include but are not limited to:

      (1) Cooking, dining, plumbing or refrigeration facilities;

      (2) Awnings or cabanas; or

      (3) Any other facilities or equipment used with a ''trailer'', camper body, or motor home.

   This Exclusion (8) does not apply to a:

   a. ''Trailer'', and its facilities or equipment, which you do not own; or

   b. ''Trailer'', camper body, or the facilities or equipment in or attached to the ''trailer'' or camper body, which you:

      (1) Acquire during the policy period; and

(2) Ask us to insure within 14 days after you become the owner.

9. Loss to any "non-owned auto" when used by you or any "family member" without a reasonable belief that you or that "family member" are entitled to do so.

10. Loss to equipment designed or used for the detection or location of radar or laser.

11. Loss to any custom furnishings or equipment in or upon any pickup or van. Custom furnishings or equipment include but are not limited to:

a. Special carpeting or insulation;

b. Furniture or bars;

c. Height-extending roofs; or

d. Custom murals, paintings or other decals or graphics.

This Exclusion (11.) does not apply to a cap, cover or bedliner in or upon any "your covered auto" which is a pickup.

12. Loss to any "non-owned auto" being maintained or used by any person while employed or otherwise engaged in the "business" of:

a. Selling;

b. Repairing;

c. Servicing;

d. Storing; or

e. Parking;

vehicles designed for use on public highways. This includes road testing and delivery.

13. Loss to "your covered auto" or any "non-owned auto", located inside a facility designed for racing, for the purpose of:

a. Competing in; or

b. Practicing or preparing for;

any prearranged or organized racing or speed contest.

14. Loss to, or loss of use of, a "non-owned auto" rented by:

a. You; or

b. Any "family member";

if a rental vehicle company is precluded from recovering such loss or loss of use, from you or that "family member", pursuant to the provisions of any applicable rental agreement or state law.

LIMIT OF LIABILITY

A. Our limit of liability for loss will be the lesser of the:

1. Actual cash value of the stolen or damaged property; or

2. Amount necessary to repair or replace the property with other property of like kind and quality.

However, the most we will pay for loss to:

1. Any "non-owned auto" which is a trailer is $500.

2. Equipment designed solely for the reproduction of sound, including any accessories used with such equipment, which is installed in locations not used by the auto manufacturer for installation of such equipment or accessories, is $1,000.

B. An adjustment for depreciation and physical condition will be made in determining actual cash value in the event of a total loss.

C. If a repair or replacement results in better than like kind or quality, we will not pay for the amount of the betterment.

PAYMENT OF LOSS

We may pay for loss in money or repair or replace the damaged or stolen property. We may, at our expense, return any stolen property to:

1. You; or
2. The address shown in this policy.

If we return stolen property we will pay for any damage resulting from the theft. We may keep all or part of the property at an agreed or appraised value.

If we pay for loss in money, our payment will include the applicable sales tax for the damaged or stolen property.

NO BENEFIT TO BAILEE

This insurance shall not directly or indirectly benefit any carrier or other bailee for hire.

OTHER SOURCES OF RECOVERY

If other sources of recovery also cover the loss, we will pay only our share of the loss. Our share is the proportion

that our limit of liability bears to the total of all applicable limits. However, any insurance we provide with respect to a "non-owned auto" shall be excess over any other collectible source of recovery including, but not limited to:

1. Any coverage provided by the owner of the "non-owned auto";
2. Any other applicable physical damage insurance;
3. Any other source of recovery applicable to the loss.

APPRAISAL

A. If we and you do not agree on the amount of loss, either may demand an appraisal of the loss. [*The remainder of this provision describes the mechanics and effect of arbitrations.*]

B. We do not waive any of our rights under this policy by agreeing to an appraisal.

PART E—DUTIES AFTER AN ACCIDENT OR LOSS

We have no duty to provide coverage under this policy unless there has been full compliance with the following duties.

A. We must be notified promptly of how, when and where the accident or loss happened. Notice should also include the names and addresses of any injured persons and of any witnesses.

B. A person seeking any coverage must:

1. Cooperate with us in the investigation, settlement or defense of any claim or suit.
2. Promptly send us copies of any notices or legal papers received in connection with the accident or loss.
3. Submit, as often as we reasonably require:

a. To physical exams by physicians we select. We will pay for these exams.
b. To examination under oath and subscribe the same.

4. Authorize us to obtain:

a. Medical reports; and
b. Other pertinent records.

5. Submit a proof of loss when required by us.

C. A person seeking Uninsured Motorists Coverage must also:

1. Promptly notify the police if a hit-and-run driver is involved.
2. Promptly send us copies of the legal papers if a suit is brought.

D. A person seeking Coverage For Damage To Your Auto must also:

© ISO Properties, Inc., 2000

1. Take reasonable steps after loss to protect "your covered auto" or any "non-owned auto" and their equipment from further loss. We will pay reasonable expenses incurred to do this.

2. Promptly notify the police if "your covered auto" or any "non-owned auto" is stolen.

3. Permit us to inspect and appraise the damaged property before its repair or disposal.

PART F—GENERAL PROVISIONS

BANKRUPTCY

Bankruptcy or insolvency of the "insured" shall not relieve us of any obligations under this policy.

CHANGES

A. This policy contains all the agreements between you and us. Its terms may not be changed or waived except by endorsement issued by us.

[Entry B relates to changes to the information used to develop the policy premium: "we may adjust your premium." An example is "The place of principal garaging of insured vehicles". Entry C concerns the insurer's change broadening coverage without additional premium charge. One rule stated concerns "subsequent edition of your policy". Given that event, sometimes the broadening will "automatically apply to your policy as of the date we implement the change in your state"; and sometimes not.]

FRAUD

We do not provide coverage for any "insured" who has made fraudulent statements or engaged in fraudulent conduct in connection with any accident or loss for which coverage is sought under this policy.

LEGAL ACTION AGAINST US

A. No legal action may be brought against us until there has been full compliance with all the terms of this policy. In addition, under Part A, no legal action may be brought against us until:

1. We agree in writing that the "insured" has an obligation to pay; or

2. The amount of that obligation has been finally determined by judgment after trial.

B. No person or organization has any right under this policy to bring us into any action to determine the liability of an "insured".

OUR RIGHT TO RECOVER PAYMENT

A. If we make a payment under this policy and the person to or for whom payment was made has a right to recover damages from another, we shall be subrogated to that right. That person shall do:

1. Whatever is necessary to enable us to exercise our rights; and

2. Nothing after loss to prejudice them.

However, our rights in this Paragraph (A.) do not apply under Part D, against any person using "your covered auto" with a reasonable belief that that person is entitled to do so.

B. If we make a payment under this policy and the person to or for whom payment is made recovers damages from another, that person shall:

1. Hold in trust for us the proceeds of the recovery; and

2. Reimburse us to the extent of our payment.

POLICY PERIOD AND TERRITORY

A. This policy applies only to accidents and losses which occur:

1. During the policy period as shown in the Declarations; and

2. Within the policy territory.

B. The policy territory is:

1. The United States of America, its territories or possessions;

2. Puerto Rico; or

3. Canada.

This policy also applies to loss to, or accidents involving, "your covered auto" while being transported between their ports.

TERMINATION

A. Cancellation

This policy may be cancelled during the policy period as follows:

1. The named insured shown in the Declarations may cancel by:

   a. Returning the policy to us; or

   b. Giving us advance written notice of the date cancellation is to take effect.

2. We may cancel by mailing to the named insured shown in the Declarations at the address shown in this policy:

   a. At least 10 days notice:

      (1) If cancellation is for nonpayment of premium; or

      (2) If notice is mailed during the first 60 days this policy is in effect and this is not a renewal or continuation policy; or

   b. At least 20 days notice in all other cases.

3. After this policy is in effect for 60 days, or if this is a renewal or continuation policy, we will cancel only:

   a. For nonpayment of premium; or

   b. If your driver's license or that of:

      (1) Any driver who lives with you; or

      (2) Any driver who customarily uses "your covered auto";

   has been suspended or revoked. This must have occurred:

      (1) During the policy period; or

      (2) Since the last anniversary of the original effective date if the policy period is other than 1 year; or

   c. If the policy was obtained through material misrepresentation.

B. Nonrenewal

If we decide not to renew or continue this policy, we will mail notice to the named insured shown in the Declarations at the address shown in this policy. Notice will be mailed at least 20 days before the end of the policy period. Subject to this notice requirement, if the policy period is:

[*depending on one or another time period, "we will have the right not to renew or continue this policy" at specified times.*]

C. Automatic Termination

If we offer to renew or continue and you or your representative do not accept, this policy will automatically terminate at the end of the current policy period. Failure to pay the required renewal or continuation premium when due shall mean that you have not accepted our offer.

If you obtain other insurance on "your covered auto", any similar insurance provided by this policy will terminate as to that auto on the effective date of the other insurance.

D. Other Termination Provisions

1. We may deliver any notice instead of mailing it. Proof of mailing of any notice shall be sufficient proof of notice.

2. If this policy is cancelled, you may be entitled to a premium refund. If so, we will send you the refund. The premium refund, if any, will be computed according to our manuals. However, making or offering to make the refund is not a condition of cancellation.

3. The effective date of cancellation stated in the notice shall become the end of the policy period.

TRANSFER OF YOUR INTEREST IN THIS POLICY

A. Your rights and duties under this policy may not be assigned without our written consent. However, if a named insured shown in the Declarations dies, coverage will be provided for:

[*Entries omitted here relate, within limits, to the surviving spouse, and to the legal representative of the deceased person.*]

B. Coverage will only be provided until the end of the policy period.

TWO OR MORE AUTO POLICIES

If this policy and any other auto insurance policy issued to you by us apply to the same accident, the maximum limit of our liability under all the policies shall not exceed the highest applicable limit of liability under any one policy.

LIFE POLICY (TERM)

Note: This appendix presents a specimen policy, with minor changes in format. It does not include the cover sheet (with index), or the table of contents. Moreover, as indicated in footnotes added by the editors, it does not contain other accompanying tables. Those tables are indicated by the policy text to be parts of the "Policy Specifications", which, in turn, are said to be components of the contract; see the paragraph headed "Entire Contract", below. (Another component—the application—is omitted also.) Hence, while the appendix represents a *policy* nearly in full, it falls well short of the full *contract*.

Centered lines of dots indicate page breaks.

THE INSURANCE COMPANY

[Address and Telephone Number]

TWENTY DAY RIGHT TO EXAMINE POLICY

We want you to be satisfied with the policy you have purchased. We urge you to examine it closely. If for any reason, you are not satisfied, you may return the policy to us or to any of our agents within twenty days after you received it. We will cancel it and refund all of the premium you paid.

We will pay the Death Benefit to your Beneficiary upon receipt at our Home Office of due proof, as provided by this policy, that your death occurred while this policy was in force. We will require surrender of this policy in the course of any settlement.

Executed at our Home Office in ___.

Secretary   President

Level Term Life Insurance to Expiry Date Policy

Convertible to the Policy Anniversary Stated on the Policy
Specifications Page
Premiums Payable to Expiry Date
Nonparticipating

INSURED: JOHN DOE

POLICY NUMBER: XXX

. . . . .

POLICY SPECIFICATIONS

BENEFIT	AMOUNT OF BENEFIT	DURATION OF PREMIUM PAYMENTS	INITIAL PREMIUM PER STATED INTERVAL	YEAR OF MATURITY OR EXPIRY
LEVEL TERM TO EXPIRY DATE	$100,000	64 YEARS(1)	142	2069(2)

GUARANTEED TERM PERIOD   [20] YEARS
EXCHANGE DATE   [02/   ]
CONVERSION DATE   02/0   2040(3)]
                                    [N/A(3)]
REINSTATEMENT INTEREST RATE   6% PER YEAR
MINIMUM SETTLEMENT OPTION INTEREST RATE   .0%

(1) PREMIUMS ARE PAYABLE FOR THE PERIOD WHILE THE IN-
SURED IS LIVING, FROM THE POLICY DATE FOR THE NUMBER
OF POLICY YEARS STATED.

(2) BENEFIT WILL MATURE OR EXPIRE ON THE POLICY ANNIVER-
SARY IN THE YEAR SHOWN.

[(3) CONVERSION DATE IS THE POLICY ANNIVERSARY NEXT FOL-
LOWING YOUR 70th BIRTHDAY.]

[(3) CONVERSION IS NOT AVAILABLE TO INSUREDS 70 OR OLDER
AT THE TIME THE POLICY IS ISSUED.]

POLICY NUMBER   XX   DATE OF ISSUE   02/01/2005
INSURED   JOHN DOE POLICY DATE   02/01/2005
GENDER   MALE   EXPIRY DATE   02/01/2069
AGE   35

AMOUNT OF BENEFIT $100,000.

LEVEL TERM TO EXPIRY DATE
                  ANNUAL PREMIUM INTERVALS
                  FIRST INTERVAL PREMIUM TOTAL   142.00

BENEFICIARY AS STATED IN THE ATTACHED APPLICATION UN-
LESS SUBSEQUENTLY CHANGED
STANDARD PREMIUM CLASS—SELECT

. . . . .

DEFINITIONS

In this policy, the insured will be referred to as "you" or "your" and
The Life Insurance Company as "us," "we," or "our."

Expiry Date

means the date on which insurance terminates because of expiration of a Term Period. It is shown in the Policy Specifications.

Death Benefit

means the Amount of Benefit stated in the Policy Specifications unless otherwise provided in this policy.

In Writing

means in a written form satisfactory to us and received at our Home Office.

Policy

means the legal contract between you a

Policy Anniversary

means an anniversary of the Policy Date. Policy years and policy months are measured from the Policy Date.

Policy Date

means the date that the policy becomes effective. It is shown in the Policy Specifications. Premium due dates, policy months, years and anniversaries are measured from this date.

PREMIUM PAYMENTS

General

All premiums are payable in advance as shown in the Policy Specifications either:

1. At our Home Office; or

2. To our authorized agent in exchange for a receipt signed by our President or Secretary and countersigned by the agent.

The first premium is due on the Policy Date. Each premium after the first is due at the end of the period for which the preceding premium was paid.

Amount of Premium

The initial premium payable under this policy is as shown in the Policy Specifications. The initial premium will not be increased above that shown.

At the end of the Guaranteed Term Period as shown in the Policy Specifications, we may change the premium level as shown in the Policy Specifications to an amount not greater than the Maximum Premium stated in the Table of Maximum Annual Premiums.[1]

---

1. The Table—not reproduced here—gives a dollar amount for each age of "John Doe", by years, from 35 (his age at the date of issue) to 98. Given a "Guaranteed Term

Any change in premium will be at our sole discretion and apply to all policies in the same class in which the policy is issued. We will give written notice to you at your last known address of any change of premium before the Policy Anniversary after which the change of premium becomes effective. Any change in premiums will not change any values or benefits listed in the Policy Specifications.

If we change the level of premium for any policy year, we will use your original issue age, premium class, and the duration of the policy to determine any premium payable for any subsequent year.

Grace Period

We will allow a grace period of 31 days after the due date of payment of each premium after the first. This policy will continue in force during the grace period. If you die during the grace period, the unpaid premium will be deducted from the Death Benefit. If a premium is not paid by the end of its grace period, this policy will terminate.

Payment Frequency

You may change the frequence of premium payments, provided:

1. You notify us in Writing before the end of the grace period;

2. The premium satisfies our minimum amount rules; and

3. The frequency requested is currently available.

If you elect to pay premiums other than annually, the total amount of the premiums you pay each year will be greater than the annual premium. The Policy Specifications show each available frequency and the additional cost for frequencies other than annual for the first year.[2] The premiums for subsequent years will be equally affected.

Reinstatement

This policy may be reinstated at any time within five years after the due date of the first unpaid premium, provided:

1. Evidence of insurability satisfactory to us is furnished;

2. Past due premiums with interest at the rate as stated in the Policy Specifications are paid; and

3. A written application for reinstatement is submitted to us.

Period" of 20 years, the amounts stand at $142 from age 35 through 54. Thereafter the amounts rise sharply: at attained age 55, $1,239; and at attained age 95, $54,917.

2. A table—not reproduced here—shows that, for example, quarterly premiums would amount to $37.63.

When this policy is reinstated, a new two-year contestable period will apply with respect to material misrepresentations made in the application for reinstatement.

POLICY CONTROL

Ownership

You are the owner of this policy unless:

1. Another person is designated as owner in the application; or

2. A new owner has been designated as provided in the Change of Owner provision.

Change of Owner

The owner may designate a new owner by notifying us in Writing while you are alive. When we receive written notice, the change will be effective on the date the notice was signed. Change is subject to any payment or action we may have taken before receiving the notice.

Assignment

The owner may assign this policy. Until we are notified in Writing, no assignment will be effective against us. We are not responsible for the validity of any assignment. The rights of the owner and beneficiary will be subject to the rights of any assignee.

BENEFICIARY

Your beneficiary is as stated in the application unless a new beneficiary has been designated as provided below.

Change of Beneficiary

The owner may change the beneficiary by notifying us in Writing while you are alive. When we receive written notice, the change will be effective on the date the notice was signed. Change is subject to any payment or actions we may have taken before receiving the notice.

No Named Beneficiary

If no named beneficiary survives you, then, unless this policy provides otherwise:

1. The owner will be the beneficiary; or

2. If you are the owner, your estate will be the beneficiary.

THE CONTRACT

Entire Contract

The entire contract consists of this policy, the application, the Policy Specifications, and any attached papers that we call riders, amendments or endorsements. A copy of the application is attached at issue. This contract is made in consideration of the application and the payment of premiums. We will not use any statement to void this policy or to defend against a claim under it, unless that statement is contained in the attached written application. All statements in the application will, in the absence of fraud, be deemed representations and not warranties.

Modifications

The only way this contract may be modified is by a written agreement signed by our President or Secretary.

Nonparticipation

This policy is nonparticipating. it does not share in our surplus earnings. You will, therefore, receive no dividends under it.

Misstatement of Age or Gender

If your age or gender is misstated, we will adjust any benefit under this policy. The adjusted benefits will be those the premium paid would have purchased at your correct age and gender, based on our rates in effect when this policy was issued.

Suicide

If, within two years from the date of issue, you die by suicide, while sane or insane, the amount payable will be limited to the sum of the premiums paid.

Incontestability

We cannot contest this policy after it has been in force, during your lifetime, for two years from its date of issue, except for:

1. Nonpayment of premiums; or

2. Any rider providing disability or accidental death benefits.

CONVERSION PRIVILEGE

General

While this policy is in force you may surrender it for a new policy on your life, provided:

1. You request conversion, in Writing;

2. Your request is received prior to the Conversion Date shown in the Policy Specification; and

3. You are not totally disabled as defined in any rider of this policy providing waiver of premium.

Evidence of insurability will not be required under this conversion privilege.

Conversion Policy

Your new policy may be on any eligible flexible premium life, level premium life or endowment plan issued by us on the date of conversion other than term insurance or one issued on a select underwriting basis, provided:

1. The new plan provides level Death Benefits;

2. The Amount of Benefit is not greater than the Amount of Benefit of this policy on the date of conversion; and

3. The Amount of Benefit is not less than the minimum required by us for the plan selected.

The new policy will contain riders providing waiver of premium and accidental death benefit, provided:

1. Such riders are in force on this policy on the date of conversion; and

2. We regularly issue such riders to individuals the same age as your age last birthday on the date of conversion.

The period of time used in the suicide and incontestability provisions of any new policy to which this policy is converted will run from the date of issue of this policy. Your mortality classification will be the same as this policy.

The Policy Date will be the date of conversion. Premiums will be based on current rates for your age last birthday.

EXCHANGE PROVISION

This policy may be exchanged for a new Level Term to Expiry Date Policy provided:

1. This policy was not issued as a result of an exchange;

2. This policy is in force and premiums are paid to the Exchange Date;

3. The exchange is requested in Writing 90 days prior to the Exchange Date as shown in the Policy Specifications;

4. Evidence of insurability satisfactory to us if furnished; and

5. The Amount of Benefit on the new policy is not greater than the Amount of Benefit of this policy.

Premiums for the new policy will be based on the table of premiums in effect on the Exchange Date for your attained age and rate class on the Exchange Date.

The new policy will become effective when:

1. We approve issuance of the new policy; and

2. We receive the first premium on the new policy.

Coverage under this policy terminates when coverage under the new policy begins.

Rider benefits included with this policy will be included with the new policy subject to our rules then in effect.

SETTLEMENT PROVISIONS

General

The proceeds payable at death may be paid in one sum. They may also be paid under one or more of the settlement options provided:

1. The total payment due is at least $5,000; and

2. Each income payment provided by the option is at least $50.

Election

The payee may elect an option by notifying us in Writing. No settlement option will be available except with our consent if:

1. The policy is assigned; or

2. The payee is a corporation, association, partnership, trustee, or estate.

The payee may change the election of an option by notifying us in Writing on or before the settlement date. The change will be effective on the date the notice is signed. The change is subject to any payment or actions we may have taken before receiving the notice.

If no election is in effect on the settlement date, the payee may make an election at that time.

Settlement Options

Option 1—Income for Fixed Period:

We will pay no less than the income elected from Table A.[3] Payments will be guaranteed for the number of years chosen, not to exceed 30 years.

Option 2—Life Income With Payments Guaranteed For Ten Years:

We will pay no less than the income determined from Table B. Payments will be made while the payee is alive. Payment will be guaranteed to ten years. If the payee dies before payments have been made for the ten-year period, the value of the remaining guaranteed payments will be paid as a final payment and will be determined using no less than the minimum settlement option interest rate shown in the Policy Specifications.

3. Table A—not reproduced here—show that, for example, the choice of a fixed income for ten years would yield a monthly income of $8.75.

Table B, referred to under "Option 2", contains entries such as these: Age 50: Men, $2.96 / Women, $2.73.

Option 3—Income of Fixed Amount:

We will make equal payments of the amount chosen. These payments will be made until the amount left under this Option, with interest, is exhausted. The rate of interest will not be less than the minimum settlement option interest rate shown in the Policy Specifications. The final payment will be for the balance only.

Option 4—Current Purchase Option:

If the payee is a natural person, the payee may elect, in his own right, to receive an income equal to 102% of the income provided by our corresponding single premium immediate annuity rates for the amount of the proceeds applies. The payee may elect this option by making application, in Writing, within 31 days of the settlement date.

INDEX

†